THE PRACTICE OF SOCIAL RESEARCH

Second Edition

Earl R. Babbie

University of Hawaii

Wadsworth Publishing Company, Inc.   Belmont, California

DEDICATION

Georg von Bekesy
1899–1972

Werner Erhard

Practicing Social Research, 2nd Ed., by Earl R. Babbie
and Robert E. Huitt, guided activities to accompany
The Practice of Social Research, 2nd Ed., is available
from your bookstore.

Sociology Editor: Stephen Rutter
Production Editor: Greg Hubit Bookworks
Designer: Nancy Benedict
Copy Editor: Carolyn Geiger

Printed in the United States of America
3 4 5 6 7 8 9 10—83 82 81 80

Library of Congress Cataloging in Publication Data

Babbie, Earl R
  The practice of social research.

  Bibliography: p.
  Includes index.
  1. Social science research. 2. Social sciences—
Methodology. I. Title

H62.B2 1979   300′.7′2   78-21513
ISBN 0-534-00630-2

CONTENTS IN BRIEF

CONTENTS IN DETAIL

CHAPTER 2
SOCIAL AND SCIENTIFIC INQUIRY   33

CHAPTER 5
CONCEPTUALIZATION AND MEASUREMENT   115

CHAPTER 6
OPERATIONALIZATION 137

CHAPTER 7
THE LOGIC OF SAMPLING 159

PART THREE
MODES OF OBSERVATION   202

CHAPTER 8
FIELD RESEARCH   205

CHAPTER 9
CONTENT ANALYSIS AND THE ANALYSIS OF EXISTING DATA   233

PART FOUR
ANALYSIS OF DATA   354

CHAPTER 13
QUANTIFYING DATA   357

PREFACE

The purpose of this book is to introduce you to the *logic* and the *skills* of social scientific research. First, I want to give you all the fundamentals you need to *do* social research on your own. The acid test of the book in that regard will come when you set out to do an empirical research project, find that the situations facing you do not exactly match anything dealt with in the book, and discover that you are able to create compromises that represent the best bridge between your situation and the fundamental logic of scientific inquiry.

Secondly, I want to train you as a responsible *consumer* of social scientific research. You will be bombarded with the findings of this kind of research for the rest of your life. To evaluate it effectively, you must be familiar with the accepted techniques for research and know the logic that makes them acceptable. With this knowledge, you'll be able to assess the importance and implications of the research findings presented to you by others.

There is a big gap between the world of research in the abstract and the world of actually conducting a social scientific experiment. On one side, things are perfectly neat, logical, and "scientific." On the other side, chaos reigns. Subjects don't show up for experiments, interviewers make mistakes and lose questionnaires, people lie and misunderstand, and no findings are as clear and conclusive as we'd like.

It was my desire to bridge this gap—to create a teaching method that would deal effectively with both worlds—that led me to write my first textbook, *Survey Research Methods*. Published in 1973, *SRM* dealt with a specialized area of social research, but we soon found teachers asking for a similar approach in a more general research methods text. In response to this suggestion, I wrote the first edition of this book, *The Practice of Social Research*. The book was published in 1975, and we were delighted to find that both students and faculty found it useful.

Between 1975 and now, my own teaching methods have changed as I have experimented with new techniques in my own classes and have learned other techniques from faculty members around the country. At the 1977 meetings of the American Sociological Association in Chicago, methods instructors met at a workshop to discuss common problems in teaching and solutions we had discovered. It was an unusually moving experience, as we quickly dropped conventional pretenses and shared our problems and concerns freely. I think we all came away from the workshop with an experience of being engaged in a common enterprise—teaching social research methods—even though we were geographically separated in our individual pursuits of it.

This experience and my own growth as a methods instructor suggested that it was time to revise *The Practice of Social Research*. Even though the first edition has been popular and widely used, the sense of excitement and growth in the field led Wadsworth and me to produce the best methods book we were capable of, even if it ended up looking more like a new book than a second edition of an established text. As a result, this second edition is about half new.

The overall organization of the book remains much the same. A major change throughout is that in rewriting I have included many more examples of real research projects, both pure and applied. I have found these concrete examples to be extremely useful in my own teaching, and other instructors have had the same experience.

In writing *Survey Research Methods* and the first edition of this book, I was troubled by the English language convention of using masculine pronouns whenever gender was unspecified (e.g., "The researcher, when he . . ."). I complained that someone should do something about that. Between 1975 and now, it occurred to me that textbook authors are the ones responsible for doing something, and I think you'll find this book free of inadvertent sexism.

I have also made some structural changes in this edition.

1. I have given the topics of research ethics and political issues greater prominence in this edition because I wanted to reflect their importance in the real world of social research.

2. I have treated conceptualization and operationalization separately here. In my own teaching, I have found that these topics need extensive explanation, and giving them the coverage they deserve makes the later discussions of data analysis a lot clearer.

3. I have expanded the discussion of reliability and validity in Part 2.

4. I have considerably shortened the discussion on sampling designs and have moved that topic into Chapter 7 instead of treating it in a separate chapter. Several of my colleagues suggested that the discussion of this topic in the first edition was more complex than necessary in an introductory methods course.

5. I have added a discussion on analysis of existing data to Chapter 9.

6. At the same time, I have added a chapter on evaluation research. It is now clear that this form of social research is going to continue growing in importance in the years to come, and you should be familiar with it.

7. One further addition in the area of data analysis really excites me. Two of my graduate students—Jim Dannemiller and Gary Sakihara—have prepared an appendix for this edition that presents SPSS (Statistical Package for the Social Sciences), a widely used package of computer programs for the analysis of social science data. If SPSS is available to you, I think you'll find the appendix extremely useful. It is written from a user's standpoint and parallels the topics and examples in the text.

To conclude, I want you to know how excited I am to share this book with you. Social science research is a fascinating field, peopled by lively and engaging human beings. I have tried to convey this feeling in *The Practice of Social Research*.

ACKNOWLEDGMENTS

It would be impossible to acknowledge adequately all the people who have been influential in forming this book. My earlier methods text, *Survey Research Methods*, was dedicated to Samuel Stouffer, Paul Lazarsfeld, and Charles Glock. I would like to state again the acknowledgment of my debt to them.

Several colleagues were acknowledged for their comments during the writing of the first edition of this book, and I would like to repeat my thanks to them here. Though revised, the present book still reflects their contributions. Many other colleagues were of assistance in the revision of the book. I particularly want to thank Stephen J. Cutler, Oberlin College; Michael J. Chernoff, Georgia State University; Sr. Kristen Wenzel, College of New Rochelle; Mark Evers, Duke University; David C. Eaton, Illinois State University; Theodore C. Wagenaar, Miami University; Steven D. McLaughlin, Utah State University; Thomas Dimieri, Wellesley College; and David Nasatir, California State University, Dominguez Hills.

The book, both in its present form and in its first edition, is also very much a product of my relationship with Steve Rutter, now executive editor in charge of social sciences and humanities at Wadsworth Publishing Company. Steve is truly a master at his craft, and working with him has been one of the special joys of creating this book. The book's publication has also been greatly assisted by the efforts and skills of the following three people at Wadsworth: Barbara Cuttle, administrative assistant; Jerry Holloway, production services manager; and Bill Ralph, manufacturing manager. My genuine thanks also go to Greg Hubit of Bookworks for his support during the production of the book.

In this edition, I am especially grateful for the SPSS appendix prepared by Gary Sakihara and Jim Dannemiller. Jessie Ohta and Jan Tanahara not only gave clerical assistance on the book but, more important, created a supportive environment within which I could work.

My wife, Sheila, has contributed to this book in more ways than can be stated. Her insight and support take me always to the horizon of my purpose and allow me to look beyond it.

Finally, I would like to dedicate this book on social research to two people who are not regarded as social scientists. The first is Georg von Bekesy, a distinguished physiologist whom I met about four years before his death in 1972. Professor von

Bekesy was that rare Renaissance man: a person interested in and insightful about everything, winner of the 1961 Nobel Prize in Medicine-Physiology, possessor of a dozen or so doctorates and fluent in as many languages, an expert in fine art, the gentlest of people, and the *compleat* scientist.

Despite our short acquaintance, Professor von Bekesy gave me a feeling for science that has affected my own research and the contents and spirit of this book. He provided a model of the scientist intent on using science to improve the quality of life on the planet and contribute to the lives of others.

The second dedication is to Werner Erhard, founder of the *est* training. Werner is not a scientist in the customary meaning of that term, yet he has had a profound influence on this book. My experience of the *est* training greatly enhanced the clarity and enthusiasm I was able to bring to my writing and to the science I was writing about. My continued association with Werner during the years that separate the first and second editions of the book has brought still another dimension to my writing. Like von Bekesy, Werner offers a model of service to others as a way of being more than just a passenger on Spaceship Earth. He has inspired me to view my teaching and textbook writing in the context of service to others and making a difference in the world.

In this same spirit, I offer this book to you: to support you in learning the skills and logic of social research, to share the challenge and the excitement of it with you, and to encourage you to use what you learn to make your own contribution to the quality of life on the planet.

PROLOGUE

THE IMPORTANCE OF SOCIAL RESEARCH

In many ways, the twentieth century hasn't been one of our better periods. Except for the relatively carefree twenties, we've moved from World War I to the Great Depression to World War II to the Cold War and its threat of thermonuclear holocaust to Vietnam and on to the current concerns over the environmental destruction of our planet. Many sage observers have written about the insecurity and malaise of people who grew up during portions of this century. One of my most trying moments in recent years came as I was driving my son—then five years old—home from preschool when he asked: "Daddy, what's the 'energy crisis'?" I had to fight back tears as I tried to answer.

A case could be made that these are not the best of times. At the same time, this period in history has seen countless individual efforts and social movements aimed at making the world work. Much of the commitment to creating humane social affairs has arisen on college campuses, and perhaps you find that commitment in yourself.

As you look at the flow of events in the world around you, if you want to make a significant contribution to the lives of future generations, you have a broad range of choices available to you. Environmental problems are many and varied. Prejudice and discrimination are with us still, and there are several different targets for you to focus your attention on. Or consider the fact that some fifteen million people die each year as a consequence of starvation. There is, in short, no end of the ways in which you could demonstrate to yourself that your life matters, that you make a difference.

Given all the things you could choose from—things that really *matter*—why should you spend your time learning social research methods? I want to address that question at the start, since I'm going to suggest that you devote some of your time and attention to learning about such things as social theory, sampling, interviewing, experiments, computers, and so forth—things that can seem pretty distant from solving the world's pressing problems. The point I'll make in the following few pages is that social science is not only relevant to the kinds of major problems I've just listed, but it holds *the* answers to them.

Many of the *big* problems we've faced and still face in this century have been the result of technology. The threat of nuclear war is an example. Not unreasonably, therefore, we have tended to look to technology and the technologists for solutions to those problems. Unfortunately, every technological solution so far has turned out to be a new problem. At the beginning of this century, for example, many people worried about the danger of horse manure piling up continually higher and higher in city streets. That problem was averted, through technology, with the invention of the automobile. Now, no one worries about manure in the streets; instead we worry about a new and deadlier kind of pollutant in the air we breathe.

Similarly, we have attempted to avoid nuclear attack by building better bombs and missiles of our own—so that no enemy would dare attack. But that hasn't worked either. Since our potential enemies operate on the same reasoning that we do, they too have built ever bigger and more powerful weapons. There is no technological end in sight for the escalating nuclear weapons race.

The simple fact is that technology alone will never save us. It will never make the world work. You and I are the only ones who can do that. The only real solutions lie in the ways we organize and run our social affairs. That becomes evident when you look at all the social problems that persist today, despite the clear presence of viable, technological solutions.

Overpopulation, for example, is a pressing problem in the world today. The number of people currently living on earth is severely taxing our planet's life support systems, and this number is rapidly increasing year after year. If you study the matter, however, you'll find that we already possess all the technological developments we need to stem population growth. It is technologically possible and feasible for us to stop population growth on the planet at whatever limit we want. Yet, overpopulation worsens each year.

Clearly, the solution to overpopulation is a social one. The causes of population growth lie in the norms, values, and customs that make up organized social life, and that is where the solutions are hidden. Ultimately, only social science can save us from overpopulation.

Or consider the problem of starvation on the planet. Each year, about fifteen million people die as a consequence of starvation. That amounts to 28 people a minute, every minute of every day, and 21 of them are children. Virtually everyone would agree that this situation is deplorable. All would prefer it otherwise. We tolerate this level of starvation on the planet in the belief that it is currently inevitable. Perhaps one day someone will invent a method of producing food that will defeat starvation once and for all.

When you study the issue of starvation in the world, however, you learn some astounding facts. First, you learn that the earth currently produces more than enough food to feed everyone without requiring sacrifices from those of us who are eating well. Moreover, this level of production does not even take account of farm programs that pay farmers *not* to plant and produce all the food they could.

Second, you learn that there are carefully worked out and tested methods for ending starvation. In fact, since World War II, some thirty countries have actually taken on and ended their own problem of starvation. Some did it through food distribution programs. Other focused on land reform. Some collectivized; others developed agribusiness. Many applied the advances of the Green Revolution. Taken together, these many proven solutions make it possible to totally eliminate starvation on the planet. Still, fifteen million die each year: 21 children every minute of every hour of every day.

Why haven't we ended starvation? The answer, again, lies in the organization and operation of our social life. New developments in food production will not end starvation any more than earlier ones have. People will continue starving on this planet until we are able to *master* our social affairs rather than being enslaved by them.

Possibly, the problems of overpopulation and starvation may seem distant to you, occurring somewhere "over there," on the other side of the globe. To save space, let me skip over the conclusion, increasingly reached, that there is no "over there" anymore: that there is only "over here" in today's world. Instead, I'll mention some social problems undeniably close to home.

In June 1978, California voters passed by a 2-to-1 margin a proposition setting a constitutional limit on property taxes in the state, effectively reducing municipal government revenues by almost two-thirds. As I write this prologue, the consequences of the measure are yet to be discovered, though official pronouncements predict chaos and disastrous reduction of government services, including fire and police protection. Despite such dire warnings, Proposition 13 passed on a wave of popular frustration with the uncontrollable growth of taxation, and there are predictions that many states will follow in California's footsteps.

The problems of contemporary American life are manifold. The tax revolt is not only financial but involves the feeling that tax revenues only buy red tape and corruption. It is also related to the general problem of inflation. Workers having trouble making ends meet win pay raises only to find that the cost of living has increased more than their pay, and the good life seems ever more distant.

In one sense, the workers who are losing the battle with inflation are the lucky ones. Millions of others are unable to get work at all, including a growing number of college graduates and even those with Ph.D.s. People who would prefer to support themselves and their families are forced to live on food stamps, welfare, and unemployment payments—at a cost to dignity as well as living standard. The welfare spinoff from unemployment, moreover, creates a heavier tax burden on those who are losing the battle with inflation already.

Crime thrives, and city streets are now considered hazardous to your health. Each day's crop of news carries stories of murder, robbery, and senior citizens being mugged and having their social security checks stolen. Most criminals who are apprehended never go to prison and those who do emerge more hardened than before.

Problems such as these—and hundreds more—cannot be dismissed as being "over there." They exist where you live. And problems like these are unlikely to be solved by technology. You and I are the only ones who can solve them. If we don't take on the challenge, no one will. The question is whether you and I will solve our social problems before they create a "final solution" for us. So, let's get on with it.

We can't solve our social problems until we understand how they come about and persist. Social science research offers a way of examining and understanding the operation of human social affairs. It provides points of view and technical procedures that uncover things that would otherwise escape our awareness. Often, as the cliché goes, "Things are not what they seem," and social science research can make that clear. One example ought to illustrate this fact.

For years, the general issues of race relations in America has often touched on the special problems facing the black American family. Most have agreed that the black family was "matriarchal," that is, dominated by the wife/mother. The white family, by contrast, has been widely recognized as "egalitarian" with "patriarchal" traces. The matriarchal pattern of the black family has been seem as a special barrier to the achievement of equality by blacks in America. Indeed, the controversial "Moynihan Report" stressed the need for changes in the black family.

Several surveys have supported the conclusion that the black family was matriarchal. Asked who made the most important decisions in their families when they were growing up, black respondents in the survey were most likely to say their mothers did. The majority said their mothers excercised more power in the family than their fathers did. Similarly, most black adults surveyed have reported that the wives in their own families make most of the important decisions. The pattern of black matriarchy has seemed clear and consistent.

This documented pattern has produced considerable discussion and disagreement over the years. Political conservatives have often cited it as evidence of an inherent weakness in the character of black males. How, they have asked, can blacks expect to achieve equality when the men are so weak and submissive? Such apparent character flaws, then, have been used for years to explain and justify why blacks have fared so badly in American society.

From a liberal point of view, the facts have been explained quite differently. The pattern of matriarchy has been explained as a product of slavery—when families were forcibly separated—and of modern welfare laws that often force husbands/fathers to desert their families as the only means of obtaining government assistance for them.

These two ideological points of view present the facts of the matter quite differently, then, and the years of debate have not significantly altered their points of view or the facts. In 1969, however, two sociologists took a look at the matter from a totally different point of view. What they did exemplifies the social scientific approach, and what they discovered demonstrates the value of that approach.

Herbert Hyman and John Shelton Reed began by confirming that the surveys did indeed suggest a matriarchal pattern in the black American family.[1] As expected, they found consistent reports from blacks that wives/mothers were more powerful in family life than husbands/fathers. Then they looked at something others had overlooked: the answers given by *white respondents* in the same surveys. What do you suppose they discovered? *The answers given by white men and women were the same as those given by blacks!* Thus, Hyman and Reed concluded that if the black family is a matriarchy, so is the white family in America. Women seem to dominate white families to the same degree that they seem to dominate black ones. Thus, if black men are weak and submissive through some sort of character defect, then the same must be said of white men.

Many of the things social scientists study—including all the social problems we

[1] "Black Matriarchy Reconsidered: Evidence from Secondary Analysis of Sample Surveys," *Public Opinion Quarterly*, Vol. 33 (1969), pp. 346–354.

intend to solve—are a source of deep emotion and firm conviction for people generally. The depth of feeling and firmness of position in such cases makes effective inquiry into the facts difficult at best. All too often, we only manage to confirm our initial prejudices. The special value of social science research methods is that they offer a way of addressing such issues with logical and observational rigor. They let us pierce through our personal viewpoints and get a look at the world that lies beyond our normal vision. And it is that "world beyond" that holds the solutions to the social problems we face today.

At a time of increased depression and disillusionment, we are tempted daily to retreat from confronting social problems into the concerns of an ever-narrowed self-interest, despite the cost of becoming insignificant specks of protoplasm on a dust ball whirling through space. Social science research offers an opportunity to take on those problems and discover the experience of making a difference after all. The choice is yours, and I invite you to take on the challenge. Your instructor and I would like to share the excitement of social science with you.

THE PRACTICE OF SOCIAL RESEARCH
Second Edition

PART ONE

An Introduction to Inquiry

Science is a familiar word used by everyone. Yet images of science differ greatly. For some, science is mathematics; for others it is white coats and laboratories. It is often confused with technology or equated with difficult high school or college courses.

Science is, of course none of these things per se. It is difficult, however, to specify exactly what science is. Scientists would, in fact, disagree on the proper definition. For the purposes of this book, however, we shall look at science as a method of inquiry—a way of learning and knowing things about the world around us. Contrasted with other ways of learning and knowing about the world, science has some special characteristics, and we'll examine these traits in this opening set of chapters.

Dr. Benjamin Spock, the renowned author-pediatrician, begins his books on child care by assuring new mothers that they already know more about child care than they think they do. I want to begin this book on social scientific research methods on the same note. It will become clear to you before you've read very far that you *do* know a great deal about the practice of scientific social research already. In fact, you've been conducting scientific research all your life. From that perspective, the purpose of this book is to assist you in sharpening skills you already have and perhaps to show you some tricks that may not have occurred to you.

Part One of the book is intended to lay the groundwork for the discussions that follow in the rest of the book—to examine the fundamental characteristics and issues that make science different from other ways of knowing things. In Chapter 1, we'll begin with a look at native human inquiry, the sort of thing you've been doing all your life. In the course of that examination, we'll see some of the ways people go astray in trying to understand the world around them, and I'll summarize the primary characteristics of scientific inquiry that guard against those errors.

Chapter 2 deals specifically with social scientific inquiry. The lessons of Chapter 1 are applied in the study of human social behavior. You will discover that, although special considerations arise in studying people, the basic logic of all science is the same.

In Chapter 3, we'll look at science from a somewhat different point of view. As we'll see, the scientific study of social life occurs within a social context, and it is important for you to be aware of the political and ethical considerations that influence social research.

The overall purpose of Part One is to construct a backdrop against which to view more specific aspects of research design and execution. By the time you complete Part One, you should be ready to look at some of the more concrete aspects of social research.

CHAPTER 1

Human Inquiry and Science

INTRODUCTION

This book is about knowing things. Although you will probably come away from the book knowing some things you don't know right now, my primary purpose is to assist you in looking at *how* you know things, not what you know. Let's start out by examining a few of the things you probably know already.

You probably know that you have to breathe to live. Obviously, if you stopped breathing, you'd die. You probably also know that it's cold on the dark side of the moon, and you know that people speak Chinese in China.

How do you know? In asking such a question, I have no doubt that you *do* know those things. I'm not even interested in challenging the *accuracy* of what you know. But *how* do you know? If you reflect on it for a minute, you'll see that you know these things because someone told them to you, and you *believed* them. You may have read in *National Geographic* that people speak Chinese in China, and that made sense to you, so you didn't question it. Perhaps your physics or astronomy instructor told you that it was cold on the dark side of the moon, or maybe you read it in *Newsweek*. That's *how* you know.

Some of the things you know seem absolutely obvious to you. If I were to ask you how you knew that you have to breathe to live, you'd think I was kidding. If I pressed on in asking, you'd probably say, "Everybody knows that." There are a lot of things that everybody knows. Everybody knows that the world is round, for example. Of course, a few hundred years ago, everybody knew that the world was flat.

Much of what you know is a matter of agreement and belief. Little of it is based on your own personal experience and discovery. A big part of growing up in any society, in fact, is the process of learning to accept what everybody around you "knows" is so. If you don't know those same things, you can't really be a part of the group. If you were to start seriously questioning whether you have to breathe to live, you'd quickly find yourself set apart from other people. You might be sent to live in a hospital with other people who ask questions like that.

Although it's important for you to see that most of what you know is a matter of believing what you've been told, I also want you to see that there's nothing wrong with *you* in that respect. That's simply the way we've structured human societies. The fundamental basis of knowledge is agreement. Since you couldn't learn all those things through personal experience and discovery alone, we've set things up so that you can simply believe what others tell you.

There are other ways of knowing things, however. In contrast to knowing things through agreement, it is also possible to know things through direct experience—through observation. If you dive into a glacial stream flowing down through the Canadian Rockies, you don't need anyone to tell you it's cold. You notice that all by yourself. The first time you stepped on a thorn as a little child, you knew that hurt even before anyone told you.

TWO REALITIES

Ultimately, you live in a world of two realities. Part of what you know could be called your *agreement reality*: the things you consider to be real because you've been told they are real. Another part is what could be called *experiential reality*: the things you know as a function of your direct experience. The first is a product of what people have told you, the second a product of your own experience. The problem is that both seem very real.

Let's take an example. Imagine that you've come to a party at my house. It's a high-class affair, and the drinks and food are excellent. In particular, you are taken by one of the appetizers I bring around on a tray. It's a breaded, deep-fried appetizer with an especially zesty taste. You have a couple and they are delicious! You have more. Soon, you are subtly moving around the room so as to be wherever I arrive with a tray of these nibblies.

Finally, you can't contain yourself any more. "What are they?" you ask. "How can I get the recipe?" And I let you in on the secret: "You've been eating breaded, deep-fried *worms*!" Your response is dramatic: you promptly throw up all over the living room rug. Awful! What a terrible thing to serve guests! Imagine how your stomach would feel if you learned that you'd been eating worms.

The point of the story is that both feelings about the appetizer would be very real. Your initial liking for them was certainly real, but so was the feeling you had when you found out what you'd been eating. It should be evident, however, that the feeling of disgust you had when you discovered you were eating worms would be strictly a product of the agreements you have with those around you that worms aren't fit to eat. That's an agreement you began entering into the first time your mother found you sitting in a pile of dirt with half of a wriggling worm dangling from your lips. You learned worms were not kosher in our society when she pried your mouth open and reached down your throat in search of the other half of the worm.

Aside from the agreements we have, what's wrong with worms? They are probably high in protein and low in calories. Bite-sized and easily packaged, they are a distributor's dream. As you've probably guessed, they are also a delicacy for some people who live in societies that lack our agreement that worms are disgusting. There are people who would love the worms but would be turned off by the deep-fried breadcrumb crust.[1]

Reality, then, is a tricky business. How can you know what's really real? People have grappled with that question for thousands of years. And science is one of the answers that has arisen out of that grappling.

Science offers an approach to both realities, agreement as well as experiential. Scientists have certain criteria that must be met before they will accept the reality of something they haven't personally experienced. In general, an assertion must have both logical and empirical support: it must make sense and it must align with observations in the world. Why do earth-bound scientists accept the assertion that it's cold on the dark side of the moon? First, it makes sense, since the surface heat of the moon comes from the sun's rays. Second, the scientific measurements made on the moon's dark side confirm the expectation. So, scientists accept the reality of things they don't personally experience—they accept an agreement reality—but they have special standards for doing so.

More to the point of this book, however, science offers a special approach to the *discovery* of reality through personal experience. It offers a special approach to the business of *inquiry*. Whereas *epistemology* is the science of knowing, *methodology* (a subfield of epistemology) might be called "the science of finding out." This book is an examination and presentation of social science methodology, and we're going to concern ourselves with how social scientists find out about human social life.

In the remainder of this chapter, we're going to look at inquiry as an activity. We'll begin by examining inquiry as a native, natural human activity. It is something you and I have engaged in every day of our lives. Next, we'll look at some of the kinds of errors we make in normal inquiry, and we'll conclude by examining what makes science different. We'll see some of the ways in which science guards against the common human errors in inquiry.

NATIVE HUMAN INQUIRY

Practically all people, and many lower animals as well, exhibit a desire to predict their future circumstances. We seem quite willing, moreover, to undertake this task using *causal* and *probabilistic* reasoning. First, we generally recognize that future circumstances are somehow caused or conditioned by present ones. We learn that getting an education will affect how much money we earn later in life, and that swimming beyond the reef may bring an unhappy encounter with a shark. Sharks, on the other hand, may learn that hanging around the reef may bring a happy encounter with unhappy swimmers. As students, we learn that studying hard will result in better examination grades.

People, and seemingly other animals, learn also that such patterns of cause and effect are probabilistic in nature: the effects occur more often when the causes occur

---

[1]One of my students has pointed out that some people might object that worms do not have a cloven hoof.

than when the causes are absent—but not always. Thus, students learn that studying hard produces good grades in most instances, but not every time. We recognize the danger of swimming beyond the reef without believing that every such swim will be fatal.

We will return to these concepts of causality and probability throughout the book. As we'll see, science makes them more explicit and provides techniques for dealing with them more rigorously than does casual human inquiry. It is these qualities that most distinguish science from casual inquiry. What I want to do, then, is to sharpen skills you already have, making you more conscious, rigorous, and explicit in your inquiries.

In looking at native human inquiry, it is important to distinguish between prediction and understanding. Often, we are able to predict without understanding —you may be able to predict rain when your trick knee aches. And often, even in the absence of understanding, we are willing to act on the basis of a demonstrated predictive ability. The race track buff who finds that the third-ranked horse in the third race of the day always wins will probably keep betting without knowing, or caring, why it works out that way.

Whatever the primitive drives or instincts are that motivate human beings and other animals, satisfying them depends heavily on the ability to predict future circumstances. For humans, however, the attempt to predict is often placed in a context of *understanding*. If you can understand *why* things are related to one another, why certain patterns of regularities occur, you can predict even better than if you simply observe and remember those patterns. Thus, human inquiry aims at answering both *what* and *why* questions, and we pursue these goals by observing and figuring out.

As I suggested earlier in the chapter, our attempts to learn about the world we live in are only partly linked to direct, personal inquiry. Only part of what we "know" comes to us through direct experience. Another part—a much larger one— comes from the agreed-upon knowledge that others give us. This agreement reality both assists and hinders our attempts to find out for ourselves. Two important sources of our secondhand knowledge deserve brief consideration here.

Tradition

Each of us inherits a culture made up, in part, of firmly accepted knowledge about the workings of the world. We may learn from others that planting corn in the spring will gain the greatest assistance from the gods, that sugar from too much candy will decay our teeth, that the circumference of a circle is approximately twenty-two sevenths of its radius, or that masturbation will make us blind. We may or may not test these "truths" on our own, but we simply accept the great majority of them. These are the things that everybody knows.

Tradition, in this sense of the term, has some clear advantages for human inquiry. By accepting what everybody knows, you are spared the overwhelming task of starting from scratch in your search for regularities and understanding. Knowledge is cumulative, and an inherited body of information and understanding is the jumping-off point for the development of more knowledge. We often speak of "standing on the shoulders" of previous generations.

At the same time, tradition is often detrimental to human inquiry. If you seek a fresh and different understanding of something that everybody already understands and has always understood, you may be marked the fool for your efforts. You may be sent to live in one of those special hospitals I mentioned earlier. More to the point, however, it will probably never occur to you to seek a different understanding of something that is already understood and obvious.

Authority

Despite the power of tradition, new knowledge appears every day. Quite aside from your own personal inquiries, throughout your life you will be the beneficiary of new discoveries and understandings produced by others. Often, acceptance of these new acquisitions will depend on the status of the discoverer. The biologist who declares that the common cold can be transmitted through kissing, for example, will probably be believed more than you'd believe your maiden aunt.

Like tradition, authority can both assist and hinder human inquiry. We do well to trust in the judgment of the person who has special training, expertise, and credentials in the matter, especially in the face of contradictory positions on a given question. At the same time, inquiry can be greatly hindered by the legitimate authority who errs within his or her own special province. Biologists, after all, do make mistakes in the field of biology. Biological knowledge changes over time.

Inquiry is also hindered when we depend on the authority of experts speaking outside their realm of expertise. For example, consider the political or religious leader, lacking any biochemical expertise, who declares marijuana to be a dangerous drug. The advertising industry plays heavily on this misuse of authority by having popular athletes discuss the nutritional value of breakfast cereals, having movie actors evaluate the performance of automobiles, and using other similar tactics.

Both tradition and authority, then, are two-edged swords in the search for knowledge about the world. Most simply put, they provide us with a starting point for our own inquiry, but they may lead us to start at the wrong point and push us off in the wrong direction.

ERRORS IN PERSONAL HUMAN INQUIRY

Quite aside from the potential dangers of tradition and authority, you and I often stumble and fall down when we set out to learn for ourselves. I'm going to mention some of the common errors we make in our casual inquiries, then we can look at the ways in which science provides safeguards against those errors.

Inaccurate Observation

The keystone of inquiry is observation. We can never understand the way things are without first having something to understand. We have to know *what* before we can explain *why*. On the whole, however, you and I are pretty sloppy, even unconscious, observers of the flow of events in life. Recall, for example, the last person you talked to today. What kind of shoes was that person wearing? Are you even certain the person was wearing shoes? On the whole, we are pretty casual in observing things, and as a result we make mistakes. We fail to observe things right in front of us and mistakenly observe things that aren't so.

An American tourist in France, for example, may be treated rudely by several strangers and conclude that the French are a rude people, even though the offenders were actually German tourists. A meteor streaking across the sky may be mistaken for a flying saucer and held responsible for the earthquake that occurs the following day.

Overgeneralization

When we seek to find patterns among the specific things we observe around us, we often fall into assuming that a few similar occurrences are evidence of a general pattern. Probably the tendency to overgeneralize is greatest when the pressure to arrive at a general understanding is high. Yet it also occurs casually in the absence of pressure. Whenever it does occur, it can misdirect or impede inquiry.

Imagine that you are a reporter assigned to cover a student demonstration at the local college campus. You have orders to turn in your story in just two hours, and you need to know why the students are demonstrating. Rushing to the scene, you start interviewing demonstrators, asking them for their reasons. If the first 2 you interview give you essentially the same reason, you may simply assume that the other 3,000 students are demonstrating for that reason. Unless you are careful, you may report that 3,000 students are demonstrating because of a difficult and unfair sociology exam.

Selective Observation

One danger of overgeneralization is that it may lead to selective observation. Once you have concluded that a particular pattern exists and have developed a general understanding of why, you will be tempted to pay attention to future events and situations that correspond with the pattern and ignore those that don't. Racial and ethnic prejudices depend heavily on selective observation for their persistence.

Suppose you were once cheated by a shopkeeper you thought to be Jewish. You might conclude from that one event that Jewish shopkeepers are dishonest in general. Subsequently, you'd probably take special note of dishonest actions by other Jewish shopkeepers, all the while ignoring honest Jews and dishonest non-Jews. This pattern is used by people who take special note of all the lazy blacks they come across while ignoring energetic blacks and lazy whites. Others take special note of irrational and emotional women while overlooking stable women as well as unstable men.

Deduced Information

Sometimes you just can't ignore the events that contradict your general conclusions about the way things are. Suppose, for example, you had decided that all Jewish shopkeepers were dishonest, and one you did business with walked four miles to return the wallet that you left on the store counter. What would you do? In our casual, day-to-day handling of such matters, we often make up information that would resolve the contradiction. Maybe the shopkeeper isn't really Jewish after all. Or maybe the shopkeeper was just casing your house with a later burglary in mind.

Perhaps that hard-working and energetic black at work is just trying to get promoted to a soft executive post. Perversely, people often doubt the general femininity of the woman who is tough-minded, logical, and unemotional in getting the job done. Concluding that she's not really a woman protects the general conclusion that women are irrational and flighty.

Illogical Reasoning

There are other ways of handling observations that contradict our conclusions about the way things are. Surely one of the most remarkable creations of the human mind is "the exception that proves the rule." That idea doesn't make any sense at all. An exception can draw attention to a rule or to a supposed rule, but there is no system of logic by which it can prove the rule it contradicts. Yet, we often use this pithy saying to brush away contradictions with a simple stroke of illogic.

What statisticians have called *the gambler's fallacy* is another illustration of illogic in day-to-day reasoning. A consistent run of either good or bad luck is presumed to foreshadow its opposite. An evening of bad luck at poker may kindle the belief that a winning hand is just around the corner, and many a poker player has stayed in a game much too long because of that mistaken belief. Or, conversely, an extended period of good weather may lead you to worry that it is certain to rain on the weekend picnic.

The simple fact is that even the best of us get a little funny in our reasoning from time to time. Worse yet, we can get defensive when others point out our error of logic.

Ego-Involvement in Understanding

The search for regularities and generalized understanding is not a trivial intellectual exercise. It critically affects our personal lives. Our understanding of events and conditions, then, is often of special psychological significance to us. If you lose your job or fail to get a promotion, you may be tempted to "understand" that as part of an insidious conspiracy. That explanation would save you from examining your own abilities and worth. You could simply conclude that you were the victim of a Wall-Street-communist-Jewish-Jesuit-homosexual conspiracy. Any challenge to that conclusion, consequently, is also a challenge to your abilities and worth.

In countless ways, we link our understandings of how things are to the picture of ourselves that we present to others. We set things up so that any disproof of these understandings will make us look stupid, gullible, and generally not okay. Whenever we do that, of course, we commit ourselves unwisely to our understanding of how things are and create a formidable barrier to further inquiry and more accurate understanding.

The Premature Closure of Inquiry

Overgeneralization, selective observation, deduced information, and the defensive uses of illogical reasoning all conspire to produce a premature closure of inquiry. This whole discussion began with our desire to understand the world around us, and the various errors detailed above often lead us to stop looking at it too soon.

The anti-Semite who says, "I already understand Jews, so don't confuse me with fact," has achieved a personal closure on the subject. Sometimes this closure of inquiry is a social, rather than individual, act. For example, the private foundation or government agency that refuses to support further research on a topic that is "already understood" effects closure as a social act, as does the denominational college that prohibits scholarship and research that might challenge the existence of God. Even more generally, we have all—individually and together—pretty much closed inquiry into gravity. After all, we know how *that* works.

The danger of premature closure of inquiry is obvious. It brings a halt to attempts to understand things before that understanding is complete. If you review the history of human knowledge, however, you will reach a startling conclusion: we keep changing the things we know—even the things we know for certain. In an important sense, then, any closure of inquiry is premature.

The Mystification of Residuals

None of us can hope to understand everything. No matter how intelligent or how diligent you and I may be in our inquiry, there will always be countless events and situations that we do not understand. We may never fully understand the origin of the universe; a particular individual may never know why he or she failed calculus in college.

One common response to this problem is to attribute those things to supernatural or mystical causes that humans cannot understand. I am not referring to religious or magical systems that offer reasonable, though supernatural, explanations for events. I mean the simple assertion that there are causes ultimately beyond human comprehension. Quite possibly that may be true of some events and situations; perhaps some things are totally random. Nonetheless, accepting that something is ultimately unknowable brings a halt to inquiry, whether the thing is actually knowable or not.

To Err Is Human

These, then, are some of the ways in which you and I go astray in our attempts to know and understand the world. The parts played by tradition, authority, and the other forms of knowledge by agreement can hinder as well as help us. And when we strike out to discover things on our own, several pitfalls are waiting for us. All of us fall into them from time to time.

Science is another way of knowing things, and social science is a way of knowing social things. Although science doesn't protect us perfectly from error, it offers considerable protection nonetheless. For the most part, science differs from our casual, day-to-day inquiry in two important respects. First, scientific inquiry is a *conscious* activity. Although you and I engage in continuous observation in daily life, much of it is unconscious or semiconscious. In scientific inquiry, we make a conscious decision to observe, and we stay awake while we do it. Second, scientific inquiry is more *careful* than our casual efforts. In scientific inquiry, we are more wary of making mistakes and take special precautions to avoid error. The following sections examine these aspects of science in more depth.

SCIENCE AS A FORM OF INQUIRY

People have many different images of what science is, and this section examines several of them. I'll begin with a general statement of the relationship between theory and research. Then, I'll describe a traditional model of science that is often presented in science courses. Although I'll suggest later that the traditional model is inaccurate, it is a useful model for you to have in mind.

In recent years, science has come under considerable criticism, and this section will look at some of the ways in which science has been debunked. The section will close with a discussion of science in practice, a more realistic look at what science is like in operation. As you'll see, science is neither the activity idealized in the traditional view, nor is it as bad as its debunkers sometimes suggest. You should come away from this section realizing that science is a human enterprise, with both the strengths and weaknesses its humanity brings to it.

Scientific Theory and Research

Science is sometimes characterized as *logico-empirical*. This ugly term carries an important message: the two pillars of science are (1) logic or rationality and (2) the observation of empirical facts. A scientific understanding of the world must make sense *and* correspond with what we observe. Both of these elements are essential to science.

As a gross generalization, scientific theory deals with the logical aspect of science, and research deals with the observational aspect. A scientific theory describes the logical relationships that exist among parts of the world, and research offers means for seeing whether those relationships actually exist in the real world. Though too simplistic, perhaps, this statement provides a useful jumping-off point for the examination of theory and research. Here's an illustration.

The early civil rights movement, beginning in the mid-1950s, was reasonably peaceful outside the Deep South, and even there the main acts of violence were perpetrated by whites against blacks. Blacks were, for the most part, nonviolent. All that changed during the summer of 1965. Beginning on August 11, 35 people died and about $200 million in damages were incurred in nearly a week of rioting, burning, and looting in the predominantly black suburb of Watts in Los Angeles.

Although the Watts rioting was specifically triggered by an incident involving black residents and white police, that event couldn't account for the extent of the rioting that followed. Most of those who participated in the rioting had nothing to do with the initial incident. Who were they, then, and why did they participate? Many people asked those questions. H. Edward Ransford, a sociologist, was one who suggested an answer.

As he addressed the aftermath of Watts, Ransford found a body of theoretical literature dealing with extreme political behavior.[2] Specifically, *social isolation* and *powerlessness* had been linked to political violence by previous scholars. As he surveyed the violent events of Watts, Ransford found it reasonable to expect that those two variables might lie at the base of participation in the rioting. It made sense to imagine that blacks who were isolated from the mainstream white society would feel they had little opportunity for communication. They would, moreover, have little investment in the system, so it was reasonable to expect that they would be more likely to riot than those blacks who were already participating in the mainstream society.

Similarly, the psychological feeling of being powerless to effect peaceful changes in society should further encourage them to seek violent redress of grievances. Thus, Ransford reasoned that blacks who felt powerless would be more likely to riot than those who felt they already had some chance of improving things.

Ransford, then, had theoretical grounds for expecting that isolation and powerlessness would produce political violence. When you think about it, the idea makes sense. That's only half of science, however. Very often, the things that seem to make sense don't turn out to be true. So Ransford undertook a research project to find out if his theoretical expectations were borne out by empirical reality.

Here's how he did it. Ransford chose to find out if isolation and powerlessness

[2]H. Edward Ransford, "Isolation, Powerlessness, and Violence: A Study of Attitudes and Participation in the Watts Riot," *American Journal of Sociology*, Vol. 73 (1968), pp. 581-591.

produced violence by interviewing a sample of black residents in Watts. To find out the extent to which the subjects in his study were isolated from the mainstream white society, Ransford had his interviewers ask about contacts with whites in the community. Subjects were asked about contacts with whites at work, in their neighborhoods, in organizations, and in other situations. Other questions probed the extent to which they socialized with whites.

Feelings of powerlessness were measured by other questions in the study. For example, subjects were asked whether they agreed or disagreed with the statement: "The world is run by the few people in power, and there is not much the little guy can do about it." Similar statements had been used in previous research projects and had been found to give a good indication of general feelings of powerlessness and alienation.

The answers that subjects gave to all these questions made it possible for Ransford to characterize each in terms of (1) isolation and (2) powerlessness. In the simplest characterization, any particular subject could be described as being high or low in terms of isolation from whites and high or low in the feeling of powerlessness. How did these characterizations relate to participation in the rioting?

It seemed unlikely that many subjects would admit to participating in the actual rioting in Watts, since they might fear criminal prosecution. Therefore, Ransford had his interviewers ask two questions. First, subjects were asked: "Would you be willing to use violence to get Negro rights?" About one-fourth of the subjects said they would be willing. The second question asked if they *had ever* done so. Only 5 percent said they had.

If Ransford's theoretical expectations were correct, he should have found that subjects with high isolation and high powerlessness would be more likely to report a willingness to resort to violence and to report actually doing so than those who rated low on isolation and powerlessness. That's precisely what he found. Of the subjects rated high on isolation, 44 percent said they would be willing to use violence, contrasted with only 17 percent of those rated low on isolation. Similarly, 41 percent of those rated high on powerlessness and only 16 percent of those rated low said they would be willing to use violence.

As further confirmation of his theoretical expectations, Ransford found that the reports of actually using violence were strongly related to isolation and powerlessness. Of the 16 people who said they had used violence, for example, all but 1 scored high on powerlessness, and 11 of the 15 scored high on isolation from whites.

Ransford's conclusions regarding the causes of political violence had both logical and empirical support. His theoretical expectations made sense, and their sense was borne out by the facts. That's not always the case, however, as the next illustration shows.

During World War II, Samuel Stouffer, one of the greatest of social science researchers, organized a research branch in the United States Army for the purpose of conducting studies in support of the war effort. Many of the studies concerned the morale among soldiers. Stouffer and his colleagues found there was a great deal of "common wisdom" regarding the bases of military morale. Much of their research was devoted to testing some of the things that "everybody knew."

For example, it has been recognized for a long time that promotions affect morale in the military. When people get promotions and the promotion system seems a fair one, morale rises. Moreover, it makes sense that people who are getting promoted will tend to think the system is fair, whereas those passed over are likely to think the system unfair. By extension, it would make sense to suppose that those soldiers in units with slow promotion rates would tend to think the system unfair, while those in units with rapid promotions would think the system fair. Does it seem obvious? Stouffer decided to find out.

Stouffer and his colleagues asked soldiers whether they felt the Army's promotion system was fair. They focused their studies on two units: the Military Police (MPs), where promotions were the slowest in the army, and the Army Air Corps (forerunner of the United States Air Force), which had the fastest promotions. It stood to reason that those in the MPs would say the promotion system was unfair, while those in the Air Corps would say it was fair. The studies, however, showed just the opposite.

Notice the dilemma faced by a researcher in a situation such as this one. On the one hand, the observations don't make any sense. On the other hand, what makes obvious good sense isn't supported by the facts. A lesser person would set such a problem aside "for further study." Stouffer, however, asked why it was so.

Eventually he found the answer. Robert Merton and some other sociologists at Columbia had begun thinking and writing about something they called *reference group theory*. People judged their lot in life, they suggested, not so much by objective conditions as through a comparison of themselves with others around them—those people who constituted their reference group. You might think that earning $50,000 a year would be a decent salary, and certainly if you lived among poor people, that salary would make you feel like a millionaire. If you lived among people who earned $500,000 a year, however, you'd probably feel impoverished.

Stouffer applied this line of reasoning to the soldiers he had studied. Even if a particular MP had not been promoted for a long time, it was unlikely that he knew someone else—less deserving—who had gotten promoted faster. Nobody got promoted in the MPs. Had he been in the Air Corps—even if he had gotten several promotions in rapid succession—he would probably be able to point to someone less deserving who had gotten even faster promotion. An MP's reference group, then, was his fellow MPs, while the air corpsman compared himself with fellow corpsmen. Ultimately, then, Stouffer reached an understanding of soldiers' attitudes toward the promotion system that (1) made sense and (2) corresponded to the facts.

There are two important elements in science, then: logical integrity and empirical verification. Both are essential to scientific inquiry and discovery. Logic alone is not enough, since what initially seems a logical expectation may not be the case in fact. On the other hand, the mere observation and collection of empirical facts does not provide understanding—the telephone directory, for example, is not a scientific conclusion.

Although theory corresponds generally to the logical component of science and research corresponds generally to the empirical component, this pattern is—as I said above—an overgeneralization. As we'll see later in the book, the execution of scientific research must follow logical rules of its own. And the logical manipulation of empirical data can produce understanding. The interrelationship between theory and research, then, is more complex than it might seem initially, and that relationship has often been misunderstood and misrepresented.

The Traditional Model of Science

One model of science has been taught for years in introductory science classes. Although I am going to point out shortly that it is not an accurate model of science in the real world, it provides a useful starting point for our examination. If you can balance this presentation with later discussions of science, you will have a healthy understanding of what science is and what it does. More to the point, you will be in a good position to begin learning the methods of social scientific research.

There are three main elements in the traditional model of science, which are typically presented in a chronological order of execution. They are theory, operationalization, and experimentation. Let's look at each in turn.

Theory   According to the traditional model of science, the scientist begins with an interest in some aspect of the real world. Suppose, for example, you were interested in discovering some of the broad social factors that affect the stability of families. What kinds of major events in society at large threaten the stability and survival of existing families and produce marriages that do not last? You could have any number of reasons for wanting to know the answer to such questions.

As you thought about those questions, you'd probably come eventually to "mass crises" as one possible answer. Wars, droughts, floods, mass unemployment, and similar society-wide problems would seem to be an important source of instability in marriages and families. That's an idea Sam Stouffer had when he looked at the topic. Stouffer found a number of logical reasons why mass crises could affect family stability. Most obviously, major crises required a great many adjustments in the daily lives of individuals and families. To the extent that stability is supported by routine and habit, mass crises would upset that pattern. Moreover, in some crises, such as disasters, government and other agencies often step in to take over some of the functions of families and family members. When the disaster results in families' being unable to support themselves economically, the government—through welfare or similar programs—may take on the job of economic support. Since that takes away the customary function of the family's breadwinner, it is likely to produce repercussions.

Stouffer's primary interest, however, concerned the formation of new families. Did broad social crises lead to marriages that would not last? Even more specifically, he was interested in what he called *impulsive marriages*: those entered into "mainly as a device to legalize sexual intercourse, carrying few obligations and no necessary expectation of union or of children to carry on the family name."[3] In addition, Stouffer wanted to know whether crises produced more mixed marriages—those that crossed religious, ethnic, and socioeconomic lines—and whether there were more forced marriages, those in which the bride was pregnant at the time of marriage.

If you had been Sam Stouffer studying this matter in the late 1930s, you would have had little trouble selecting a particular crisis for testing your ideas. The Great Depression of 1929 and the early 1930s would have been your obvious choice, as it was Stouffer's. On a theoretical level, Stouffer found it was possible to derive two

---

[3]Samuel Stouffer, "Effects of the Depression on the Family," *Social Research to Test Ideas* (New York: Free Press of Glencoe, 1962), p. 138.

contradictory expectations regarding the relationship between the depression and impulsive marriages.

On the one hand, "The depression presumably weakened the respect for custom and tradition with respect to economic matters; therefore it might be inferred that this weakening carried over to other aspects of life."[4] In addition, he reasoned that the depression could have weakened parental authority, through the increase of mobility and other factors. It could produce more marriages entered into without the knowledge of the brides' or grooms' parents. Finally, with the assurance of "relief" (the forerunner of welfare), young people might get married even if they were not sure they could afford it. Thus, there were a number of reasons for expecting that the depression would produce an increase in the number of impulsive marriages.

At the same time, Stouffer saw a counter-argument. The same factors that produced a weakening of young people's commitment to tradition and custom might lead them to avoid marriage altogether. Stouffer reasoned:

> Why, indeed, it may be asked, should couples whose principal object in marriage was the legalization of sexual intercourse bother about those legalities, once the older conceptions of marriage had been altered? Would not the effect of the depression be to increase casual and extra-legal unions rather than marriages with lightly assumed obligations?[5]

In terms of theoretical logic, two contradictory expectations could be argued for. It could be argued that the depression would increase or decrease the number of impulsive marriages. Although Stouffer's theoretical analysis had greatly clarified the possible relationships among variables, the theoretical reasoning had not been sufficient to provide certainty. Empirical observation was all the more important in order to answer his original research interest.

Operationalization To settle the question of depressions and impulsive marriages, then, it would make sense to simply observe whether more such marriages happen during depressions. But how would you recognize an impulsive marriage if you saw one? Even if you thought you'd recognize one, where would you look for it? The second step in the traditional model of science is addressed to such questions.

Operationalization refers simply to a specification of the steps, procedures, or operations that you will go through in actually measuring and identifying the variables you want to observe. In the present example, it involves (1) how you'll go about looking for an impulsive marriage and (2) how you'll know one when you find it. Let's begin with the strategy for looking.

When Stouffer initially conceived of doing his study on families and the depression, he planned to undertake a large-scale survey. He would have selected a large sample of people—perhaps a sample purposely designed to include people who got married before, during, and after the depression. He would have designed a questionnaire asking them about their marriages and the events leading up to these marriages, and he would have then been in a position to see any changes that took place during the depression. Like other researchers, he requested a research grant to

[4]*Ibid.*, p. 139.
[5]*Ibid.*

cover the costs of his proposed study. Like many other researchers, he was turned down. No money.

It was now clear to Stouffer that he wouldn't be able to conduct the study he had envisioned. Still, he was interested in answering his research question. What Sam Stouffer did next is a mark of his special genius as a researcher—he turned his attention to thinking up studies he *could* conduct. Would it be possible, he asked, to recognize impulsive marriages among all the marriages routinely reported in official government statistics? He found that a reasonable approximation was at least possible, as the following statement shows:

> No single index would seem adequate. Only if all, or most, of several indexes showed a strong tendency in the same direction, would there be a basis for inference that the shift during the depression was toward, or away from, "impulsive" marriages. Among such indexes might be the following:
>
> 1. Marriage in a community other than residence of the bride and groom. . . .
> 2. Marriage by a magistrate rather than a clergyman.
> 3. Divorce or separation within five years of marriage, especially if no children had been born.[6]

Stouffer undertook the same operationalization process with regard to mixed and forced marriages. In each case, he was able to find *indicators* of what he had in mind. Some were to be found in regularly published government statistics (foreign, United States, state, local); some, such as indicators for religiously mixed marriages, were to be found in nongovernment publications.

In operationalizing his inquiry into the effects of the depression on the family, Stouffer had to handle one additional problem. Many of the indicators he intended to examine had been changing steadily over time, quite aside from the depression. The number of religiously mixed marriages had been increasing, for example. His research question, then, had to be refined: Did the *rate* of increase go up during the depression years? Ultimately, Stouffer became clear about how to look for the answer to his research questions and how to recognize and interpret the answers once he found them.

Observation   The final step in the traditional model of science involves actual observation. Having developed theoretical clarity and expectations and having created a strategy for looking, all that remains is to look at the way things are. Sometimes, this step involves conducting experiments, sometimes interviewing people, sometimes visiting what you're interested in and watching it. In Stouffer's case, it meant poring through published statistics in search of data relevant to his operationalization.

In the case of nonresident marriages, he found what he was looking for in the state of Massachusetts. As expected, he discovered a long-run trend toward more marriages in which one or both of the parties were from out of town. During the depression years, however, he found a greater increase, followed by a reversal as the depression receded. Regarding civil marriages (as distinguished from religious ones), he found that although the information was recorded on marriage licenses, it was not tabulated and reported in published statistics. He discovered that such statistics were reported in Australia, however. There, moreover, the percentage of civil

[6]*Ibid.*, p. 140.

marriages increased rapidly during the depression years and decreased as the depression waned.[7] Other variables were found in data relating to other states and countries.

Notice the format of Stouffer's research at this point. As he approached each set of statistics, he had certain expectations about the pattern he would find in the numbers if a particular theoretical explanation was accurate. He had operationalized forced marriages, for example, as those that resulted in births within seven months. He found data on this question available in Australia. If the depression increased forced marriages, he would expect to find a higher percentage of marriages resulting in early births during the depression years. Here's what he found:

Year	Percentage
1921	22.2
1922	21.6
1923	21.0
1924	20.8
1925	20.9
1926	21.4
1927	22.0
1928	23.5
1929	23.3
1930	25.7
1931	27.6
1932	24.3
1933	23.6
1934	20.8

Source: Stouffer, *op. cit.*, p. 151.

The dramatic increase in the number of forced marriages—as operationalized by Stouffer—in the years immediately following the onset of the depression (1930 and 1931) supported the theoretical expectation. In and of itself, of course, these particular data did not prove the case; they did not provide definitive evidence that the depression weakened the stability of the family. These data, however, were part of a weight of evidence that Stouffer amassed. To recall his earlier words, he discovered that "several indexes showed a strong tendency in the same direction."

I have chosen this illustration for several reasons. First, it demonstrates the traditional model of scientific research, moving from theory to observation. Second, it is more realistic than the hypothetical example of a simple physics experiment. Primarily, I suppose, I have wanted to share Stouffer's special genius with you.

Figure 1-1 provides a schematic diagram of the traditional model of scientific inquiry. In it, we see the researcher beginning with an interest in something or an

[7]Americans sometimes forget that the Great Depression was not our property alone. It actually swept most of the Western world.

idea about it. Next comes the development of a theoretical understanding. The theoretical considerations result in hypotheses or expectations about the way things ought to be in the world if the theoretical expectations are correct. The notation $Y = f(X)$ is a conventional way of saying that Y (for example, forced marriages) is a function of (is in some way affected by) X (for example, the depression). At that level, however, X and Y have general rather than specific meanings.

Figure 1-1   The Traditional Image of Science

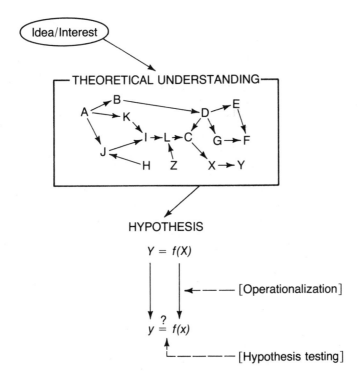

I have represented the operationalization process as one in which the general concepts are translated into specific indicators and procedures. The lowercase x, for example, is a concrete indicator of capital X. This operationalization process results in the formation of a testable hypothesis: for example, did the percentage of marriages resulting in early births actually increase with the onset of the depression? Observations aimed at finding out are part of what is typically called **hypothesis testing.**

Although this traditional model of science provides a clear and understandable guide of how you could study something carefully and logically, it has drawbacks. First, it is inaccurate as a description of research in the real world. As we shall see, the research process is more open-ended and flexible than the traditional model suggests. Second, the lockstep nature of the model (1) can make scientific research seem a pretty routine and even dull undertaking and (2) can stifle imagination and innovation. Not surprisingly, therefore, the scientific model just presented—as well as science itself—has come under criticism from many quarters in recent years. Let's look at some of those criticisms, then we'll examine a more realistic view of science in practice.

The Debunking of Science

In recent years, some students have been given an image of science and of scientists that is quite different from the traditional perspective. This more icono-clastic view of science has a number of dimensions.

First, this view points out that scientists are motivated by the same human emotions and hindered by the same human frailties as are other human beings. Scientists, we are told, frequently select their subjects of study on the basis of personal biases, and some may devote all their energies to proving some pet hunch. Rather than framing and executing experiments objectively, they design research as a continuing search for data to substantiate their prejudices.

Similarly, the cults and cliques of the scientific world have been held up to public view. A scientific paper submitted for publication may be judged more on the basis of the researcher's credentials (degrees, schools, and so forth) than on the intrinsic merits of the paper itself. A journal editor trained under Professor X may tend to reject all papers submitted by students of Professor Y. Moreover, accepted ideas in scientific disciplines are very difficult to challenge. A research paper present-ing a radically new perspective on an old and presumably settled issue may never see publication.

We are told that grantsmanship has replaced scholarship in science—that many researchers evaluate a prospective research project more in terms of the likelihood of foundation funding than in terms of its possible contributions to understanding. From this viewpoint, a researcher may be judged by the number of research assis-tants employed rather than by the quality of the research findings.

Since so much scientific research is conducted within universities, the growing criticism of the publish-or-perish norm attributed to most contemporary academic departments is worth noting. Faculty members are often expected to publish re-search reports in academic journals or as books in order to gain promotion, tenure, or even renewal of contract. Under the pressure of this nonscientific norm of the scientific community, researchers sometimes look more toward the quantity than the quality of research projects and reports. A forthright rejection of the norm may deny them the basic resources for research altogether.

Finally, scientific researchers—social and other—have been on the receiving end of growing criticism regarding participation in research that carries negative social implications. Researchers have been criticized for directly or indirectly supporting national war efforts or colonialism or for providing the tools of social control that may be used to subjugate people at home or abroad. Some people are demanding that scientific researchers exercise a social conscience in their scientific research.

These criticisms of modern science have been fueled by a number of candid research biographies published in recent years by noted scientists.[8] Increasingly, practicing scientists have attempted to place their findings in proper perspective and to give guidance to aspiring researchers. Since these accounts have pointed to errors, oversights, and other practical problems, many of the contemporary critics of science have taken these as inside admissions that all of science is bunk.

The recent criticism of science is probably a healthy turn of events. For too long, science has been regarded as a mystical enterprise and scientists as infallible super-humans. If science is a rational and objective activity, then it should withstand objective and rational evaluation. Those aspects that do not survive such scrutiny should probably not remain a part of science.

There is a danger inherent in the current widespread criticisms of science: they may serve as an excuse for dismissing science altogether. If you have difficulty understanding science the first time you approach it, you may dismiss the whole thing as meaningless, ritualistic, and even evil, rather than master it and make it better. Many people do that, and I don't want to contribute to your doing it.

I am, of course, biased on this topic. (See how candid scientists have become?) I regard science as a distinctive form of human inquiry. It has special strengths and special advantages over other forms of human inquiry. Those special strengths, however, are not necessarily the ones suggested by the traditional model of science. Let me describe some of the ways science in practice differs from that model.

Science in Practice

Although the traditional model suggests that the scientist moves directly from an interest in some subject to the logical derivation of a theory and/or hypothesis, that is seldom the case. As a researcher, your initial interest in the subject often stems from some previous empirical research, perhaps some curious findings that cropped up in your own research or that of some other researcher. Thus, for example, you might have noticed that dentists have a particularly high suicide rate in America, and you might set out to derive a more general understanding of why that is the case. Is the dental suicide rate an example of something even more general? What are the implications of that more general pattern?

Theories are almost never the result of a totally deductive process—logically figuring things out. They are more typically the end result of a long chain of observation and interpretation, looking and thinking. At one point, you may have a tentative explanation for an empirical relationship; you may test it partially through the collection of more data, use the results to modify your explanation, collect more data, and so forth.

Theories are seldom confirmed at a specific time because there are few *critical experiments* in science—experiments upon which a whole theory stands or falls. Instead, evidence is built up over time to lend support to a continually modified

[8]See, for example, James D. Watson, *The Double Helix* (New York: New American Library, 1968) for a candid account of the research that resulted in the discovery of the DNA molecule. For other candid research biographies, see Phillip E. Hammond, ed., *Sociologists at Work* (New York: Basic Books, 1964), and M. Patricia Golden, ed., *The Research Experience* (Itasca, Ill.: F. E. Peacock Publishers, 1976).

theory. Some form of a theory may eventually become generally accepted, but we can seldom point to a specific time at which it was proven. Moreover, all theories continue to undergo modifications even after they have been generally accepted.

In the discussion of the design and execution of empirical studies earlier, it may have looked as though researchers are successful in finding indicators in the world of the concepts they have in their heads. This process is seldom clear-cut. Most of the interesting scientific concepts lend themselves to a variety of interpretations and measurements. Therefore, when you settle on a particular way (or set of ways) of measuring something, the results of your studies reflect as much on your measurements as on the patterns of relationships that you are examining.

Even when you can create measurements that are clear and unambiguous, the empirical relationships you'll find in the world are never as clear and absolute as those you construct in your head. You may be able to construct a model of occupational satisfaction involving factors that would obviously and certainly increase worker satisfaction, but you will inevitably find cases that contradict your model. Someone with all the factors leading to satisfaction will commit suicide out of extreme job dissatisfaction. And people who should commit suicide because their work conditions are so bad, in terms of your model, will forsake their families in order to spend more time on the job. In short, things never turn out quite the way you expect; your theories are never absolutely confirmed or rejected. Virtually all research findings fall in the "gray area."

These latest comments should undermine the mistaken impression that science is straightforward, routine, and dull. Scientific research is anything but a cut-and-dried progression of steps in the search for truth. It is a constant adventure and a constant challenge.

I think it would be useful to sum up this discussion by likening scientific inquiry to the work of a detective. Like detectives, scientists work at finding the answers to questions: Who killed Cock Robin? What causes cancer? Why are some people prejudiced? It is essential to recognize that *finding the answer* is what makes a good scientist, just as it makes a good detective. Merely going through a set of steps generally associated with science or criminal investigation does not make you a good scientist or a good detective.

In one sense, how you get the answer is irrelevant as long as you can substantiate the soundness of that answer. Intuition, for example, is perfectly acceptable in science as in detective work. An answer to a problem is no less valid because it came to you originally through intuition. As a detective, you might get a feeling that the butler did it; as a scientist you might get a feeling that harsh toilet training produces prejudice.

Luck is perfectly all right in science and in detective work, too. The detective who just happens to be at the scene of the murder when the murderer sneaks back to erase a clue is simply lucky. The scientist who accidentally spills one substance into another and thereby creates an important new compound is also lucky. Luck counts just as much as brilliance, and such lucky events do not diminish the validity of the answers they provide.

If intuition and luck are acceptable, you may ask, why worry about specialized methods of scientific and detective work? The specialized methods and logic underlying them serve two important functions in inquiry. First, the methods typically followed by professional scientists and detectives increase the likelihood that intuition, insight, and good luck will occur. The detective's standard methods of criminal investigation place him or her at the scene of the crime. Similarly, the standard procedures of science place the scientist in the position of dealing with important substances.

Second, although intuition is legitimate in obtaining the answer to a problem, it is not sufficient to demonstrate that you really have the answer. The detective may feel that the butler is guilty, but such a feeling is not sufficient—nor should it be—for conviction. A gut feeling that harsh toilet training produces prejudice is not acceptable as scientific proof. Instead, the detective might be led by intuition to look for hard evidence showing the butler's guilt, and the scientist might be led to conduct rigorous scientific experiments on the consequences of harsh toilet training.

Implicit in these latest comments is the view that scientific methods of inquiry are more trustworthy than the casual, human inquiry described earlier. Let's see what makes that so. How does scientific inquiry avoid the common pitfalls that produce error in nonscientific inquiry?

SAFEGUARDS AGAINST ERROR

To look at what is special about scientific inquiry, I'm going to use the list of errors discussed earlier in connection with casual, human inquiry. In each case, we'll see that science offers *some* protection, and I want to be clear that the protection is never total. Scientists make mistakes, too.

Inaccurate Observation

Science is based on careful observation and measurement, and the care with which scientific observations are made is an important norm of science—one that students of science are taught early in their training. In contrast to casual, human inquiry, scientific observation is a *conscious* activity. Simply making observation more deliberate reduces many errors. You probably don't recall, for example, what your instructor was wearing on the first day of this class. If you had to guess now, you'd probably make a mistake. If you had gone to the first class meeting with a conscious plan to observe and record what your instructor was wearing, however, you'd have been more accurate.

In many cases, both simple and complex measurement devices help to guard against inaccurate observations. At the same time, they add a degree of precision well beyond the capacity of the unassisted human senses. Suppose, for example, that you had taken color photographs of your instructor that day.

Overgeneralization

In the attempt to develop general understanding of what is going on around us, we often draw conclusions on the basis of a few observations—conclusions that don't really apply much beyond those specific observations themselves. Science must guard against this danger, since generalizing is one of its primary goals.

The **replication** of inquiry is perhaps the chief safeguard. Basically, this means repeating a study, checking to see if the same results are produced each time. Then, the study may be repeated under slightly varied conditions. Thus, when a social scientist discovers that educated people are less prejudiced than uneducated people, that's only the beginning. Is the relationship true among men and women both? Among old and young? Among people from different regions of the country? This extension of the inquiry would point to the breadth and the limits of the generalization about education and prejudice.

Totally independent replications by other researchers extend the safeguards. Suppose that I do the original study that shows education and prejudice to be related. Later, you might conduct a study of your own. You would study different people, and perhaps you'd measure education and prejudice somewhat differently. If your independent study produced exactly the same conclusion as mine, we'd both feel more confident in the generalizability of the relationship. If you obtained somewhat different results or found a subgroup of people among whom it didn't hold at all, you'd have saved me from overgeneralizing.

Selective Observation

You'll recall that selective observation is an error that often follows overgeneralization. Once we've decided how things are in general, we pay attention to subsequent observations that confirm our conclusion and ignore those that contradict it. Science offers some protection against that, also.

Usually, a research design will specify in advance the number and nature of observations to be made as a basis for reaching a conclusion. If you and I wanted to learn whether men were more likely than women to support keeping women in their traditional sex roles, we'd commit ourselves to making a specified number of observations on that question in a research project. Even if the first ten men favored limiting women and the first ten women opposed it, we'd keep observing (that is, interviewing the sample), recognizing and recording each new observation in turn. Then, we'd base our conclusion on an analysis of all the observations.

There is a second safeguard against selective observation in science that has parallels in most of the other pitfalls. If you should happen to overlook something that contradicts your conclusion about the way things are, your colleagues will notice it and bring it to your attention. That's a service scientists provide to one another and—more seriously—to the enterprise of science itself.

Deduced Information

Just as you and I make up probable information in our day-to-day inquiries as a way of explaining away confusion, scientists engaged in scientific inquiry do also. When our scientific observations and analyses don't turn out the way we expect, we often think up other reasons to explain away the surprise.

Suppose, for example, that you and I had the idea that people who knew a lot about world affairs would feel less alienated politically than people who knew little or nothing about world affairs. We might test that idea by administering a questionnaire to a group of college students. In the questionnaire, we'd find out (1) how much they knew about world affairs and (2) how politically alienated they felt. We'd then examine the relationship between those two variables. But suppose further that we found no relationship between the two. The informed and uninformed turned out to be equally alienated. What a disappointment. "Aha!" you say, "The reason for that is that college students are generally quite knowledgeable about world affairs, so our distinction between the 'informed' and 'uninformed' wasn't much of a distinction after all. Surely the expected relationship would hold among the general public, where we'd find some people who were *really* uninformed."

The exercise I've just described is sometimes called *ex post facto hypothesizing*, and it's perfectly acceptable in science *if it doesn't stop there*. The argument you would have made clearly suggests that we need to test our hypothesis among a broader spectrum of people. The line of reasoning doesn't prove our hypothesis is correct, only that there's still some hope for it. Subsequent observations may prove its accuracy. Thus, scientists very often engage in deducing information, and they follow up on that by looking at the facts again.

Illogical Reasoning

Although we sometimes fall into embarrassingly illogical reasoning in day-to-day life, scientists avoid this pitfall by using systems of logic consciously and explicitly. I've already touched on this process in earlier discussions in this chapter, and subsequent discussions will go into the matter in more depth. For now, it is sufficient to note that logical reasoning is a conscious activity for scientists, and they always have their colleagues around to keep them honest in that regard as in others.

Ego-Involvement in Understanding

Scientists, being human, run the risk of becoming personally involved in and committed to the conclusions they reach in scientific inquiry. Sometimes it's worse than in nonscientific life. Imagine, for example, that you have discovered an apparent cure for cancer and have been awarded the Nobel prize. How do you suppose you'll feel when somebody else publishes an article arguing that your cure doesn't really work? You might not be totally objective.

A firm commitment to the other norms of science that we have been examining would work against too much ego-involvement. Failing that, you would at least find your colleagues less attached to your cure; they would be able to evaluate the basis of the critical article more objectively than you. Ultimately, then, although ego-involvement is a problem sometimes for individual scientists, it is less of a problem for science in general.

The Premature Closure of Inquiry

At its base, science is an open-ended enterprise in which conclusions are constantly being modified. That is an explicit norm of science. *Experienced* scientists, therefore, accept it as a fact of life and expect established theories to be overturned eventually. And if one scientist considers a line of inquiry to be completed forever, others will not. Even if a whole generation of scientists closes inquiry on a given topic, a later generation of scientists is likely to set about testing the old ideas and changing many of them.

In part, the reward structure of science supports this openness. While you may have to overcome a great deal of initial resistance and disparagement, imagine how famous you would be if you could *demonstrate* persuasively that something people have always believed simply isn't true. What if you could *prove* that carbon monoxide was really *good* for people? The potential rewards for astounding discoveries keep everything fair game for inquiry in science.

The Mystification of Residuals

The same comments just made in connection with the premature closure of inquiry can be made about the mystification of residuals. It is an article of faith in science that everything is knowable, or—waffling slightly—that everything is *potentially* knowable. Even if one scientist is willing to concede that a particular phenomenon is beyond human comprehension, another will recognize the rewards to be gained in making that phenomenon comprehensible. If I were to publicly announce my feeling that we can never hope to understand something, that would probably give you an added incentive to find a way to understand it.

Scientists Are Human Beings

I want to conclude this discussion with an illustration of the rigorous, scientific logic I've mentioned from time to time above:

1. To err is human.

2. Scientists are human.

Therefore:

3. Scientists screw up, too.

Nothing I've said should lead you to conclude that science offers total protection against the errors that nonscientists commit in casual, day-to-day inquiry. Not only do individual scientists make every kind of error we've looked at, scientists as a group—science as a collective enterprise—fall into the pitfalls and stay trapped for long periods of time.

Not long ago, when most of us felt it would be extremely difficult for people to travel to the moon, it was the physicists who could *prove* that such a trip would be *impossible*. I think it had something to do with the weight of the fuel it would take to lift the amount of fuel it would take to lift the amount of fuel it would take. . . . Only the physicists really understood it.

But who put us on the moon in 1969? The physicists! In fact it was the same physicists who could prove it was impossible. The NASA story provides an excellent illustration of how science operates. The scientists involved were able to view the proven impossibility of going to the moon within a larger context. Given that it's impossible, how can we do it?

SUMMARY

The purpose of this chapter has been to start you thinking about scientific research. It began with a discussion of native human inquiry, then we looked at some popular models of what science is all about. We saw that the traditional view of science as pretty cut-and-dried was not altogether accurate, and we saw that many people have criticized science and scientists in recent years. The sacred-cow status of science has come under attack, probably for the best.

Against this backdrop, I have attempted to provide a description of what science is like in practice. I have shown both the similarities and the differences between scientific and nonscientific inquiry, emphasizing the safeguards that science offers as protection against the common errors people make in attempting to understand the world around them. Although we've seen that scientists are not free from error, it should have become apparent that the *consciousness* of scientific inquiry and the protection scientists provide one another go a long way toward reducing error. In the next chapter, we are going to get more deeply into the nature of science—especially *social* science—and we'll see many of those safeguards in action.

MAIN POINTS

1. Inquiry is a natural human activity.

2. People seek general understanding about the world around them.

3. To understand, we observe and seek to find patterns of regularities in what we observe.

4. Science represents a special form of human inquiry.

5. The traditional image of science includes theory, operationalization, and observation.

6. The traditional image of science is not a very accurate picture of how scientific research is actually done.

7. The special character of science can best be seen in relation to the common errors people make in casual, day-to-day inquiry: inaccurate observation, over-generalization, selective observation, deduced information, illogical reasoning, ego-involvement in understanding, the premature closure of inquiry, and the mystification of residuals.

8. Though science gives no sure guarantee against such errors, it does offer important protection by making inquiry a conscious activity and by providing a community of colleagues who check up on one another.

ANNOTATED BIBLIOGRAPHY

Babbie, Earl, *Society by Agreement* (Belmont, Calif.: Wadsworth, 1977). A really dynamite introduction to sociology. (What did you expect I'd say?) Since I've suggested that you should have a sense of the "agreement reality" that makes up so much of what we "know," I wanted to tell you where to learn more about that.

Butterfield, Herbert, *The Origins of Modern Science* (New York: Macmillan, 1960). An excellent, readable history of the development of science that illustrates many of the central issues involved in scientific inquiry. Understanding some of the stages through which science has passed can clarify what it is that now distinguishes scientific inquiry from nonscientific inquiry.

Irvine, William, *Apes, Angels, and Victorians* (New York: Meridian Books, 1959). An account of the social and religious furor that surrounded Darwin's publications on evolution and natural selection and Thomas Huxley's propounding of Darwin's ideas. In addition to casting science within a social context, this engaging little book offers excellent insights into the personal doubts and vacillations of a great scientist at work.

Kaplan, Abraham, *The Conduct of Inquiry* (San Francisco: Chandler, 1964). A standard reference volume on the logic and philosophy of science and social science. Though rigorous and scholarly, it is eminently readable and continually related to the real world of inquiry.

Kuhn, Thomas, *The Structure of Scientific Revolution* (Chicago: University of Chicago Press, 1962). An exciting and innovative recasting of the nature of scientific development. Kuhn disputes the notion of gradual change and modification in science, arguing instead that established "paradigms" tend to persist until the weight of contradictory evidence brings their rejection and replacement by new paradigms. This short book is at once stimulating and informative.

Toben, Bob, *Space-Time and Beyond* (New York: E. P. Dutton, 1975). An absolutely delightful look at the tentativeness of what we know about physical reality. Using a cartoon format, Toben has presented some of the frontier issues of contemporary physics. I've included this book both because it's so much fun and because it fosters a healthy openness as you set about mastering the logic and skills of social science.

Watson, James, *The Double-Helix* (New York: New American Library, 1968). An informal and candid research biography describing the discovery of the DNA molecule, written by a principal in the drama. This account should serve as a healthy antidote to the traditional view of science as totally cool, rational, value-free, and objectively impersonal.

CHAPTER 2

Social Scientific Inquiry

INTRODUCTION

One of the livelier academic debates of recent years has concerned the scientific status of those disciplines gathered under the rubric of the social sciences—typically including sociology, political science, social psychology, economics, anthropology, and sometimes fields such as geography, history, communications, and other composite and specialty fields. Basically at issue is whether human behavior can be subjected to scientific study. Since the previous chapter has pointed to the confusion that surrounds the term *science* in general, it should come as no surprise that academicians have disagreed about the social sciences.

Opposition to the idea of social sciences has risen both within the fields and outside them. Within the fields, the movement toward social science has represented a redirection and, in some cases, a renaming of established academic disciplines. Increasingly, departments of government have been replaced by departments of political science. There are today few university departments of social studies, while sociology departments abound.

In many cases, the movement toward social science has represented a greater emphasis on systematic explanation where the previous emphasis was on description. In political science, it has meant a greater emphasis on explaining political behavior rather than describing political institutions. In anthropology, it has represented a lessening of the emphasis on ethnography. The growth of such subfields as econometrics has had this effect in economics, as has historiography in history. Some geographers have moved from the enumeration of imports and exports to mathematical models of migration. Quite understandably, professionals trained and experienced in the more traditional methods of these fields have objected to the new orientations.

Outside the social science departments, similar opposition has come from the physical sciences: from physicists, biologists, chemists, and so forth. Sometimes informed by the traditional image of science discussed in the previous chapter, the physical scientists have often objected that the scientific method cannot be applied to human social behavior.

A part of the objection to social *science* clearly has come from the traditional view of what science is. Much of what social scientists have done does not follow the routinized steps from theory, through operationalization, to observation. But then, a great deal of physics does not follow that pattern either.

This book is grounded in the position that human social behavior can be subjected to scientific study as legitimately as can atoms, cells, and so forth. This view needs to be seen in the context of the earlier discussion of what science is, however. The remainder of the present chapter is devoted to describing the nature of social scientific inquiry, focusing first on the foundations of social scientific theory, then on the foundations of social scientific research. By the time you complete this chapter, you should have a clear understanding of what is meant by the phrase "social science" and of what can and cannot be done in social scientific inquiry.

THE FOUNDATIONS OF SOCIAL THEORY

Chapter 1 has already introduced the topic of social scientific theory, giving examples of how it can operate in practice. In this section, I want to take a closer, more rigorous look at that. In particular, I want to draw your attention to some of the fundamental bases of social theory as they affect social science. Let's start that discussion by clearing up a common misunderstanding.

Theory, Not Philosophy or Belief

Social scientific theory has to do with what *is*, not with what *should be*. I point that out at the start, since social theory for many centuries combined these two orientations. Social philosophers mixed liberally their observations of what happened around them, their speculations as to why, and their ideas about how things ought to be. Although modern social scientists may do the same from time to time, it is important to realize that social *science* has to do only with how things are and why.

This means that scientific theory—and, more broadly, science itself—cannot settle debates on value. Science cannot determine whether capitalism is better or worse than socialism except in terms of some set of agreed-on criteria. We could only determine scientifically whether capitalism or socialism most supported human dignity and freedom if we were able to agree on some measures of dignity and freedom, and our conclusion in that case would depend totally on the measures we had agreed on. The conclusions would have no general meaning beyond that.

By the same token, if we could agree that suicide rates, say, or perhaps giving to charity were good measures of a religion's quality, then we would be in a position to determine scientifically whether Buddhism or Christianity was the better religion. Again, however, our conclusion would be inextricably tied to the criteria agreed on. As a practical matter, people are seldom able to agree on criteria for determining issues of value, so science is seldom of any use in settling such debates. Moreover, people's convictions in matters of value are more nonrational than rational, making science, which deals in rational proofs, all the more inappropriate.

This issue will be made more pointedly in Chapter 11 when we look at *evaluation research*. As you'll see, social scientists have become increasingly involved in studies of programs that often reflect ideological points of view, and one of the biggest problems faced by researchers is getting people to agree on criteria of success and failure. Yet such criteria are essential if social scientific research is to tell us anything useful in relation to matters of value. By analogy, a stopwatch cannot tell us if one sprinter is better than another unless we can agree that speed is the critical criterion.

Thus, social science can assist us in knowing only what is and why. It can be used to address the question of what ought to be only when there is agreement on the criteria for deciding what's better than something else. Furthermore, this agreement seldom occurs. With that understanding, let's turn now to some of the fundamental bases upon which social science allows us to develop theories about what is and why.

Social Regularities

Ultimately, social scientific theory aims at the determination of logical and persistent patterns of regularities in social life. Lying behind that aim is the fundamental assumption that life *is* regular, not totally chaotic or random. That assumption, of course, applies to all science, but it is sometimes a barrier for people when they first approach *social* science.

Certainly at first glance, it would appear that the subject matter of the physical sciences is more regular than that of the social sciences. A heavy object, after all, falls to earth *every* time we drop it, while a person may vote for a particular candidate in one election and against that same candidate in the next election. Similarly, ice *always* melts when heated, while seemingly honest people sometimes steal. Examples like these, although true, can lead us to lose sight of the high degree of regularity in social affairs.

To begin, a vast number of formal norms in society create a considerable degree of regularity. For example, only persons of a certain age or older are permitted to vote in elections. In American society previously, men were drafted into the armed forces, but women were not. And even after the end of conscription, only men were allowed to train for and participate in combat. Such formal prescriptions, then, regulate, or regularize, social behavior.

Aside from formal prescriptions, other social norms can be observed that create more regularities. Registered Republicans are more likely to vote for Republican candidates than are registered Democrats. University professors tend to earn more money than unskilled laborers. Men earn more than women. Whites earn more than blacks. The list of regularities could go on and on.

To review, all science is based on the fundamental assumption that regularity exists in what is to be studied, and we have noted that regularities exist in social life. Therefore, logically, social behavior would appear to be susceptible to scientific analysis. But is that necessarily the case? Are the kinds of regularities we've just looked at really dependable enough for scientific study? After all, you probably know an unskilled laborer who earns more than most college professors. Or are those kinds of regularities worthy of scientific study? So Republicans vote for Republicans more than Democrats do. So what. Isn't that pretty obvious? We don't need scientific theories to understand something like that.

There are three major objections that might be raised in regard to the kinds of social regularities that we've been looking at, and those should be dealt with before we proceed. First, some of the regularities may seem trivial, everyone is aware of them. Second, contradictory cases may be cited, indicating that the "regularity" isn't totally regular anyway. And third, it may be argued that the people involved in the regularity could upset the whole thing if they wanted to.

Let's handle the business of triviality first, those things that "everybody knows." The main problem with what everyone knows is that it may not be so. Recall the earlier example of Stouffer's study of attitudes toward promotion in the army? Sometimes, methods instructors play a game with that finding and others from the army research. They begin their classes by revealing a set of "important discoveries" that have come from social science: (1) Army air corpsmen with rapid promotions were more likely to think the promotion system was fair than were MPs who had slow rates of promotions. (2) Black soldiers were happier training in Northern camps than in Southern ones. (3) Educated soldiers were more likely to resent being drafted than were less educated soldiers. By the time these important discoveries have been revealed, most students have begun playing with their pencils and talking to each other about how obvious and trivial all that is. Then—Shazam!—the instructor points out dramatically that all three "findings," as we saw in the promotion example, are *false*. The actual research disproved each, and Stouffer was able to create a logical theoretical explanation for each being the way it was.

The point of all this is that documenting the obvious is a valuable function of any science, physical or social. All too often, the obvious turns out to be wrong, and apparent triviality is not a legitimate objection to any scientific endeavor. (Darwin coined the phrase "fool's experiment" in ironic reference to much of his own research—research in which he tested things that everyone else already knew.)

The objection that there are always exceptions to any social regularity is also inappropriate. It is not important that a particular woman earns more money than a particular man if men earn more than women overall. The pattern still exists. Social regularities represent *probabilistic* patterns, and a general pattern need not be reflected in 100 percent of the observable cases.

This rule applies in the physical sciences as well as in social science, by the way. In genetics, for example, the mating of a blue-eyed person with a brown-eyed person will *probably* result in a brown-eyed offspring. The birth of a blue-eyed offspring does not challenge the observed regularity, however, since the geneticist states only that the brown-eyed offspring is more likely and, further, that brown-eyed offspring will be born in a certain percentage of the cases. The social scientist makes a similar, probabilistic prediction—that women overall will be likely to earn less than men. And the social scientist has grounds for asking why that is the case.

Finally, the objection that observed social regularities could be upset through the conscious will of the actors is not a sufficient challenge to social science, even though there does not seem to be a parallel situation in the physical sciences. (Presumably an object cannot resist falling to earth "because it wants to.") There is no denying that the religious, right-wing bigot could go to the polls and vote for an agnostic, left-wing radical black if he or she wanted to upset the political scientist studying the election. All voters in an election could suddenly switch to the underdog so as to frustrate the pollster. Similarly, workers could go to work early or stay home from work and thereby prevent the expected rush-hour commuter traffic. But these things do not happen sufficiently often to seriously threaten the observation of social regularities.

The fact remains that social norms do exist, and the social scientist can observe those norms. When norms change over time, the social scientist can observe and explain those changes. Ultimately, social regularities persist because they tend to make sense for the people involved in them. When the social scientist suggests that it is logical to expect a given type of person to behave in a certain manner, that type of person may very well agree with the logical basis for the expectation. Thus, although the religious, right-wing bigot *could* vote for the agnostic, left-wing radical black candidate, such a voter would be the first to consider it stupid to do so.

Aggregates, Not Individuals

Social regularities do exist, then, and they are both susceptible to and worthy of theoretical and empirical study. Implicit in the above comments, however, is a point that needs to be made explicit. Social scientists study *social* patterns rather than individual ones. All the regular patterns I've mentioned have reflected the *aggregated* actions and situations of many individuals. Although social scientists often deal in the motivations that affect individuals, the individual per se is seldom the subject of social science. We do not create theories about an individual person, only about the nature of group life.

Sometimes the aggregated regularities are amazing. Consider the birthrate, for example. People have babies for an incredibly wide range of personal reasons. Some do it because their own parents want them to. Some feel it's a way of completing their womanhood or manhood. Others want to hold their marriages together. Still others have babies by accident.

If you have had a baby, you could probably tell a much more detailed, idiosyncratic story. Why did you have the baby when you did, rather than a year earlier or later? Maybe your house burned down and you had to delay a year before you could afford to have the baby. Maybe having the baby was related to your television set being in for repair. Maybe you felt that being a family person would demonstrate maturity that would support a promotion at work. If you've had a baby—or if you haven't—your particular set of reasons for having or not having a baby is not matched exactly by anyone else's.

Everyone who had a baby last year had a different set of reasons for doing so. Yet despite this vast diversity, despite the idiosyncrasy of each individual's reasons, the overall birthrate in a society is remarkably consistent from year to year. If the rate is 19.1 per 1,000 this year, it is likely to be very close to 19.1 per 1,000 next year, even though the rate may be gradually rising or declining over a longer period of time. If the birthrate of a society were to be 19.1, 35.6, 7.8, 28.9, and 16.2 in five successive years, demographers would begin dropping like flies.

Ultimately, then, social scientific theories deal with aggregated, not individual, behavior. Their purpose is to explain, for example, why aggregated patterns of behavior are so regular even when the individuals participating in them may change over time. In another important sense, social science doesn't even seek to explain *people*. Our aim is to understand the *systems* within which people operate, the systems that explain why people do what they do. The elements in such systems are not people but *variables*.

A Variable Language

The idea of a system composed of variables is somewhat complex, and I want to introduce this subtle aspect of social scientific theory with an analogy that tells the story. The subject of a physician's attention is the patient. The patient may be ill, and the physician's purpose is to assist that patient in getting well. By contrast, a medical researcher's subject matter is different: a disease, for example. The medical researcher may study the physician's patient, but for the researcher that patient is relevant only as a carrier of the disease, which is what the researcher is really studying.

That is not to say that medical researchers don't care about real people. They certainly do. Their ultimate purpose in studying diseases is to protect people from them. But in their actual research, patients are directly relevant only for what they reveal about the disease under study. In fact, when a disease can be studied meaningfully without studying actual patients, medical researchers do so.

By the same token, social science involves the study of *variables* and the *attributes* that compose them. Social scientific theories are written in a variable language, and people get involved only as the carriers of those variables. Here's what social scientists mean by variables and attributes.

Attributes are characteristics or qualities that describe an object—in this case, a person. Examples would include *female, Oriental, alienated, conservative, dishonest, intelligent, farmer*, and so forth. Anything you might say to describe yourself or someone else would involve an attribute.

Variables, on the other hand, are logical groupings of attributes. Thus, for example, *male* and *female* would be attributes, while *sex* or *gender* would be the variables composed of those two attributes. The variable *occupation* would be composed of attributes such as *farmer, professor, truck driver*, and so forth. *Social class* would be a variable composed of a set of attributes such as *upper class, middle class, lower class*, or some similar set of divisions.

The relationship between attributes and variables lies at the heart of both description and explanation in science. For example, we might describe a college class in terms of the variable *sex* by reporting the observed frequencies of the attributes *male* and *female*: "The class is 60 percent men and 40 percent women." An unemployment rate can be thought of as a description of the variable *employment status* of a labor force in terms of the attributes *employed* and *unemployed*. Even the report of family income for a city is a summary of attributes composing that variable: $3,124, $10,980, $35,000, and so forth.

The relationship between attributes and variables is more complicated in the case of explanation and gets to the heart of the variable language of scientific theory. Here's a simple example, involving two variables, *education* and *prejudice*. For the sake of simplicity, let's assume that the variable *education* has only two attributes: *educated* and *uneducated*. (Chapters 5 and 6 will address the issue of how such things are defined and measured.) Similarly, let's give the variable *prejudice* two attributes: *prejudiced* and *unprejudiced*.

Now let's suppose that 90 percent of the people who have the attribute *uneducated* also have the attribute *prejudiced*, while the other 10 percent have the attribute *unprejudiced*. And let's suppose that 30 percent of the *educated* people have the attribute *prejudiced*, while 70 percent have the attribute *unprejudiced*. Figure 2-1 presents a graphic illustration of this situation.

Figure 2-1   Illustration of Relationship between Two Variables

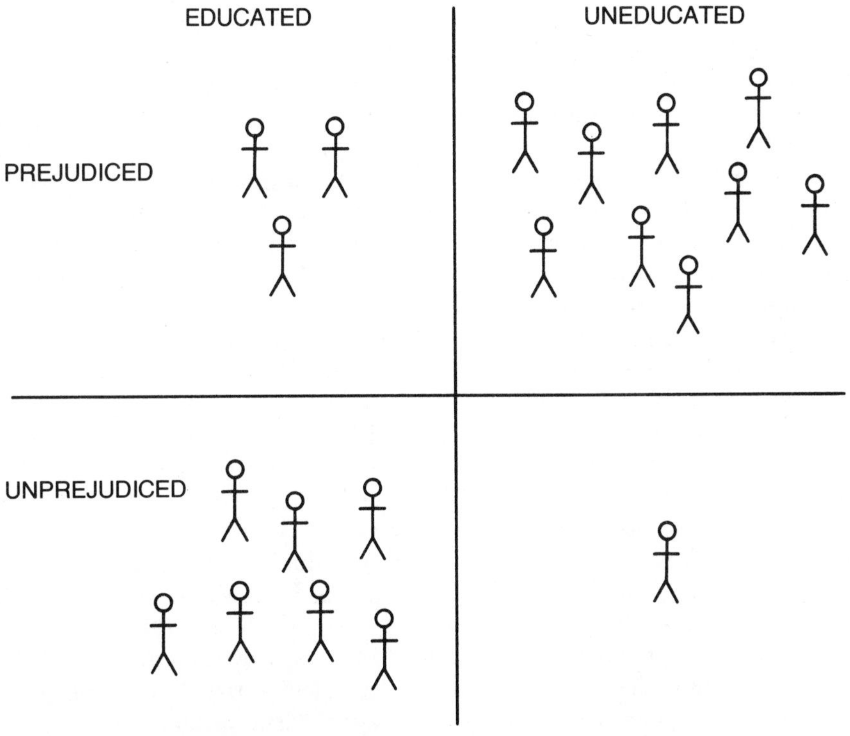

The figure illustrates a *relationship* or *association* between the variables *education* and *prejudice*. This relationship can be seen in terms of the pairings of attributes on the two variables. There are two predominant pairings: (1) those who are educated and unprejudiced and (2) those who are uneducated and prejudiced. Here are two other useful ways of seeing that relationship.

First, let's suppose that we play a game in which we bet on your ability to guess whether a person I pick from the figure is prejudiced or unprejudiced. I'll pick the people one at a time (not telling you which one I've picked) and you have to guess whether the person is prejudiced. We'll do it for all 20 people in the figure. Your best strategy in that case would be to always guess *prejudiced*, since 12 out of the 20 are categorized that way. Thus, you'll get 12 right and 8 wrong, for a net success of 4.

Now let's suppose that when I pick a person from the figure, I have to tell you whether the person is educated or uneducated. That information can be very valuable to you. Your best strategy now would be to guess *prejudiced* for each uneducated person and *unprejudiced* for each educated person. If you followed that strategy, you'd get 16 right and 4 wrong. Your improvement in guessing prejudice by knowing education is an illustration of what I mean by the variables being related. (This procedure, by the way, provides the basis for the statistical calculation, *lambda*, to be discussed in Chapter 18.)

Second, by contrast, let's consider how the 20 people would be distributed in the figure if education and prejudice were *unrelated* to one another. Notice that half the people are educated and half are uneducated. Also notice that 12 of the 20 are prejudiced. If 6 of the 10 educated and 6 of the 10 uneducated people were prejudiced (60 percent of each group), we would conclude that the two variables were unrelated to each other. If that were the case, knowing a person's education would not be of any value to you in guessing whether that person was prejudiced or not. (This approach provides the basis for the calculation of the statistic, *chi square*, also discussed in Chapter 18.)

We're going to be looking at the nature of relationships between variables in some depth in Part Four of this book. In particular, we'll see some of the ways in which relationships can be discovered and interpreted in research analysis. It is important that you have a general understanding of relationships now, however, in order to appreciate the logic of social scientific theories.

Theories describe the relationships that might logically be expected among variables. Often, the expectation involves the notion of *causation*. A person's attributes on one variable are expected to cause, predispose, or encourage a particular attribute on another variable. In the example just illustrated, it appeared that a person's being educated or uneducated caused that person to be unprejudiced or prejudiced, respectively. It seems that there is something about being educated that leads people to be less prejudiced than if they are uneducated.

As I'll discuss in more detail later in the book, education and prejudice in this example would be regarded as *independent* and *dependent* variables, respectively. These two concepts are implicit in deterministic, causal models. In this example, we assume that levels of prejudice are determined or caused by something; prejudice depends on something, hence it is called the dependent variable. That which the dependent variable depends on is called the independent variable; in this case, prejudice depends on education. Although the educational levels of the people being studied vary, that variation is independent of prejudice.

Notice, at the same time, that educational variations can be found to depend on something else—such as our subjects' parents' educational levels. People whose parents have a lot of education are more likely to get a lot of education themselves than those whose parents have little education. In this latter relationship, the subject's education would be the dependent variable, and the parents' education would be the independent variable.

Returning to our example, the discussion of Figure 2-1 has involved the interpretation of data. We looked at the distribution of the 20 people in terms of the two variables. In the construction of a social scientific theory, we would derive an expectation regarding the relationship between the two variables based on what we know about each. We know, for example, that education exposes people to a wide range of cultural variation, to diverse points of view—in short, it broadens their perspectives. Prejudice, on the other hand, represents a narrower perspective. Logically, then, we would expect that education and prejudice would be somewhat incompatible. We might arrive at an expectation, therefore, that increased education would lead to a reduction of prejudice, an expectation that would be supported by the observations to be made, perhaps later, in Figure 2-1.

Notice that the theory has to do with the two variables, education and prejudice, not with people per se. People are, as I indicated before, the carriers of those two variables, so the relationship between the variables can only be seen through an observation of people. Ultimately, however, the theory is constructed of a variable language. It describes the associations that might logically be expected to exist between particular attributes of different variables.

Determinism and Human Behavior

My introduction of the idea of causation, or determinism, points to another of the foundations of social scientific theory. Science is based on the assumption that all events have antecedent causes that can be identified and logically understood. For the scientist, nothing just happens; it happens for a reason. If a man catches a cold, if it rains today, if a ball seems to roll uphill, the scientist assumes that each of these events is susceptible to rational explanation.

Several caveats should be entered in this regard, however. First, scientists do not know, nor do they pretend to know, the specific causes of all events. They simply assume that such causes exist and can be discovered. Second, science accepts multiple causation. A given event may have several causes; the voting decision may have resulted from a number of different factors. And one event may have one cause, while a similar event may have a different cause. Two people may vote for the same candidate for different reasons, but it is assumed that reasons exist in each case.

Finally, much science is based on a probabilistic form of determinism. Thus, Event A may result in Event B 90 percent of the time, or 70 percent of all Republicans may vote for a given political candidate, while only 23 percent of the Democrats do so. In this sense, then, political party affiliation would be said to determine voting behavior, even though the determination is not complete. (Other factors might be introduced to explain the discrepancies.)

This characteristic of social science seems often at odds with common sense, as some earlier discussions in this chapter have indicated. The social scientist may conclude that a group of people behave in a certain fashion because of a number of prior events and conditions: for example, recall the voting behavior of the religious, right-wing bigot in an earlier discussion. In this sense, the conditions of religiosity, prejudice, right-wing political orientations *determine* the person's voting behavior. This is not to deny that the voter in question *could* vote for the agnostic, left-wing radical black candidate; such a person is simply unlikely to do so.

The deterministic posture of the social sciences represents its most significant departure from more traditional, humanistic examinations of social behavior. A biographer, for example, might consider the soul-searching and agonies by which a given person will weigh the relative merits and demerits of a given action, arriving at a considered decision, but the social scientist would more typically look for the general determinants of such a decision among different aggregates of persons. Where the biographer would argue that the decision reached by each individual person represented the outcome of an idiosyncratic process, the social scientist would say it could be fit into a much simpler, general pattern.

In Chapter 16, which deals with the logic of causation, we'll see how determinism provides the logical basis for the examination of cause and effect in social scientific analyses. We'll also consider how determinism relates to the charge of dehumanization in social science.

These, then, are some of the fundamental elements in social scientific theory. Basically, theory is aimed at making sense out of the world and involves the development of logical explanations and expectations. To review, theory deals with what is, not what ought to be. It is based on an assumption that social life, in the aggregate, possesses order, that our social affairs are not totally chaotic or random. That order, however, is to be found in the relationships among variables; people are involved only as the manifest carriers of those variables. Thus, we study people for the purpose of seeing how variables are related to one another.

The relationships among variables, however, are not irrelevant to people by any means. From the social scientific point of view, what we do, think, and feel reflects the impact of social variables on us. Whether you participate in a riot may be importantly affected by your feelings of alienation and powerlessness, feelings that have their own causes in the social conditions around you. Whether you enter into an unstable marriage may be importantly affected by gross economic conditions in the society. Social science is not possible without this deterministic point of view, and we'll consider it in more detail in Chapter 16.

As I've indicated earlier, theory is only a part of social scientific inquiry. While it is vital that we make sense out of the world, some of the earlier examples have already shown that what makes sense isn't always so in the real world. It made sense for the MPs to resent the army's promotion system and feel it was unfair—except they didn't feel that way. Ultimately, it made sense for them to think the system was fair, but we never would have reached that level of understanding without knowing the facts of the matter. Let's turn now to the foundations of social scientific research and see how it supports theory and vice versa.

THE FOUNDATIONS OF SOCIAL RESEARCH

Chapter 1 has already presented some of the fundamental characteristics of social scientific research in the context of errors we often make in more casual inquiry. In this section, I want to look at those characteristics, and others, from a more positive point of view and in more detail. To begin that examination, let's examine the way logical reasoning links theory and research together.

Two Logical Systems

In Chapter 1, I criticized the traditional model of science for its portrayal of scientific inquiry as a cut-and-dried process of steps from theory, through operationalization, to observation. As we'll see now, that is *one* of the ways in which scientific inquiry operates.

Logic is a difficult and complex branch of philosophy, and a full delineation of systems of logic is well beyond the scope of this textbook. Perhaps a few examples will illustrate what we mean by saying science is logical. For example, a given event cannot, logically, cause another event that occurred earlier in time. The movement of a bullet cannot cause the explosion of the gunpowder propelling it. Thus science takes a different approach from the views sometimes taken by religions. For example, some Christians believe that Jesus was destined to be crucified, and that this destiny caused him to be betrayed and tried. Such a view could not be accepted within the logic of science.

In the logic of science, it is impossible for an object to have two mutually exclusive qualities. The flip of a coin cannot result in both a head and a tail. By contrast, we might note that many deeply prejudiced people argue that Jews are both clannish (refusing to mix with non-Jews) and pushy (forcing themselves in with non-Jews). Faced with such an assertion, the scientist would suggest that either one or both of the characterizations of Jews are untrue or that the two characteristics are being defined in such a way that they are not mutually exclusive.

Similarly, a given event cannot have mutually exclusive results. Thus, getting a college education cannot make a given person both wealthier and poorer at the same time. It is possible for a college education to result in wealth for one person and poverty for another, just as some Jews might be described as clannish and others pushy, but contradictory results or descriptions fly in the face of logic and are intolerable to science.

This is not to say that science in practice is wholly devoid of illogical assertions. Many readers will already realize that physicists currently regard light as both particles and waves, even though these are contradictory descriptions of the nature of light. This particular contradiction exists in science because light behaves as particles under some conditions and as waves under others. As a result of this situation, physicists continue to use the two contradictory conceptualizations as they may be appropriate in given conditions. Nevertheless, such a situation represents a strain for the logic of science.

Beyond this common-sense notion of logic, there are two distinct logical systems important to the scientific quest: *deductive logic* and *inductive logic*. Beveridge describes them as follows:

> Logicians distinguish between inductive reasoning (from particular instances to general principles, from facts to theories) and deductive reasoning (from the general to the particular, applying a theory to a particular case). In induction one starts from observed data and develops a generalization which explains the relationships between the objects observed. On the other hand, in deductive reasoning one starts from some general law and applies it to a particular instance.[1]

The classical illustration of deductive logic is the familiar syllogism: "All men are mortal; Socrates is a man; therefore Socrates is mortal." You might then follow up this deductive exercise with an empirical test of Socrates' mortality. That is essentially the approach discussed as the traditional perspective of science in Chapter 1.

Using inductive logic, you might begin by noting that Socrates is mortal and observing a number of other men as well. You might then note that all the *observed* men were mortals, thereby arriving at the tentative conclusion that *all* men are mortal.

Figure 2-2 shows a graphic comparison of the deductive and inductive methods. In both cases, we are interested in the relationship between the number of hours spent studying for an exam and the grade earned on that exam. Using the deductive method, we would begin by examining the matter logically. Doing well on an exam reflects a student's ability to recall and manipulate information. Both of these abilities should be increased by exposure to the information before the exam. In this sort of fashion, we would arrive at a *hypothesis* that would suggest a positive relationship between the number of hours spent studying and the grade earned on the exam. The hypothesis is represented by the line in part I(a) of Figure 2-2.

Our next step, using the deductive method, would be to make observations relevant to testing our hypothesis. The shaded area in part I(b) of the figure represents perhaps hundreds of observations of different students, noting how many hours they studied and what grades they got. Finally, in part I(c) of the figure, we compare the hypothesis and the observations. Since observations in the real world seldom if ever match our expectations perfectly, we must decide whether the match is close enough to consider the hypothesis confirmed. Put differently, can we conclude that the hypothesis describes the *general* pattern that exists, granting some variations in real life?

Now let's turn to addressing the same research question, using the inductive method. In this case, we would begin—as in part II(a) of the figure—with a set of observations. Curious about the relationship between hours spent studying and grades earned, we might simply arrange to collect some data relevant to that. Then we'd look for a pattern that best represented or summarized our observations. In part II(b) of the figure, the pattern is shown as a curved line running through the center of the curving mass of points.

The pattern found among the points in this case suggests that with 1 to 15 hours

---

[1]W. I. B. Beveridge, *The Art of Scientific Investigation* (New York: Vintage Books, 1950), p. 113.

Figure 2-2 Deductive and Inductive Methods

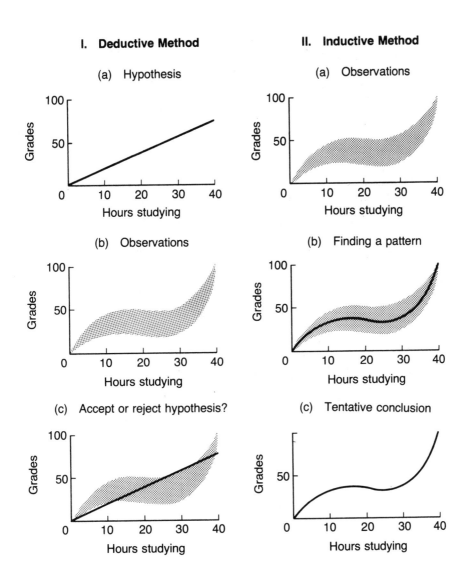

I. **Deductive Method**

(a) Hypothesis

II. **Inductive Method**

(a) Observations

(b) Observations

(b) Finding a pattern

(c) Accept or reject hypothesis?

(c) Tentative conclusion

of studying, each additional hour generally produces a higher grade on the exam. With 15 to about 25 hours, however, more study seems to slightly lower the grade. Studying more than 25 hours, on the other hand, results in a return to the initial pattern: more hours produce higher grades. Using the inductive method, then, we end up with a *tentative* conclusion as to the pattern of the relationship between the two variables. It is a tentative conclusion, since the observations we have made cannot be taken as a test of the pattern—those observations are the *source* of the pattern we've created.

What do you suppose would happen next in an actual research project? We'd try to find a logical explanation for the pattern discovered in the data, just as Stouffer tried to find a logical explanation for the discovery that MPs were more likely than air corpsmen to think the promotion system was fair. Eventually, we'd arrive at an explanation—one that would generate further expectations about what should be observed in the real world. Then, we'd look again.

In actual practice, then, theory and research interact through a never-ending alternation of deduction, induction, deduction, and so forth. Walter Wallace has represented this process nicely as a circle, which is presented in a modified form in Figure 2-3.

In the Wallace model, theories generate hypotheses, hypotheses suggest observations, observations produce generalizations, and those generalizations result in modifications of the theory. The modified theory then suggests somewhat modified hypotheses and a new set of observations, which produce somewhat revised generalizations, further modifying the theory. What I like most about this model is that there is clearly no beginning or ending point. You can begin anywhere in examining what interests you.

Thus, when Stouffer began wondering whether the Great Depression would have any consequences on the stability of families, he turned to a logical derivation of hypotheses, making observations later for the purpose of testing those hypotheses. When Emile Durkheim looked at suicide, on the other hand, he pored through table after table of official statistics on suicide rates in different areas, and he was struck by the fact that Protestant countries consistently had higher suicide rates than Catholic ones.[2] Why should that be the case? His initial observations led him to create a theory of religion, social integration, anomie, and suicide. His theoretical explanations led to further hypotheses and further observations.

In summary, the scientific norm of logical reasoning provides a bridge between theory and research—a two-way bridge. Scientific inquiry in practice typically involves an alternation between deduction and induction. During the deductive phase, we reason *toward* observations; during the inductive phase, we reason *from* observations. Both logic and observation are essential. Let's look a little more closely into the business of observations in social scientific research.

Empirical Verification

Science at its best results in the formulation of general laws or equations describing the world around us. Such formulations, however, are not useful unless they can be verified through the collection and manipulation of empirical data. A general theory of prejudice would be useless unless it suggested ways in which data might be collected and unless it predicted the results that would be obtained from the analysis of those data.

There is another way of viewing this characteristic, however. In a sense, no scientific theory can ever be *proved*. Let's consider the case of gravity. Physicists tell

[2]Emile Durkheim, *Suicide* (Glencoe, Ill.: Free Press, 1951). Originally published in 1897.

Figure 2-3 The Wheel of Science. *Source*: Adapted from Walter Wallace, *The Logic of Science in Sociology* (New York: Aldine Publishing Co.; copyright © 1971 by Walter L. Wallace).

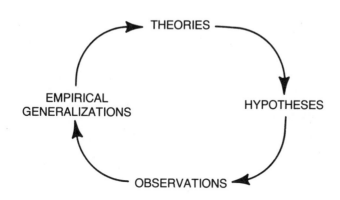

us that a body falls to earth because of the general attraction that exists between physical bodies and that this relationship is affected by the mass of the bodies involved. Since Earth has a vast mass, a ball thrown out a window will move toward Earth.

Such an explanation of gravity is empirically verifiable. A researcher can throw a ball out a window and observe that it falls to the earth. That does not prove the truth of the theory of gravity, however. Rather, the researcher specifies that if the ball does *not* fall to the earth, then the theory of gravity is incorrect. Since the ball is, in fact, observed to behave as expected, the theory of gravity *has not been disconfirmed*.

Thus, when we say that a scientific explanation must be subject to empirical testing, we mean, more precisely, that the researcher must be able to specify conditions under which the theory would be disproved. As we consistently fail to disprove the theory, then, we may become confident that the theory is correct. But it is important to realize that we will never have proved it.

In the example of falling bodies, another theorist might note that the experimental ball was of the same color as the ground to which it fell. This theorist might suggest, therefore, that bodies of the same color are attracted to each other—for whatever reason he or she might devise. The initial experiment, then, would lend confirmation to both of the competing theories. The second theory, however, suggests a method of disconfirmation. If a ball differing in color from the earth were thrown out the window, it should not fall to the earth. To do so would disconfirm the second theory. An appropriate second experiment could result in an empirical disconfirmation of the color attraction theory.

To be useful, social scientific propositions and theories must also be testable in the real world. Thus it is useless to assert that conservatism is positively associated with prejudice without suggesting ways in which the two variables might be measured and the proposition tested. As in the physical sciences, the social scientist must be able to describe empirical conditions under which a given proposition would be judged incorrect, ways in which it might be disproved.

Religious beliefs, such as the existence of God, for example, are not susceptible to empirical verification. Similarly, the assertion that members of a religious or racial group are disloyal "in their hearts" even when they appear to act in a loyal manner is not subject to empirical verification. The same would be true of propositions predicting human social behavior in the event that the sun did not rise on a given morning.

At the same time, a great many hypotheses about human social affairs *can* be tested empirically. For example, it has been commonly believed in America that women were incapable of reasoning as logically as men. Instead, women have been characterized as flighty and emotional in their thinking processes. This notion—so comfortable for American men—could be tested empirically. Moreover, the recent success of women in the thinking professions suggests that a controlled empirical test would wipe out the common, comfortable (for men) belief.

As indicated elsewhere in this book, much social research is addressed to testing, with empirical data, those items of "common sense" that "everybody knows are true." Where commonsense notions are imprecise, the social scientist doggedly specifies them in a testable form and tests them. Then, we respecify them in another testable form and retest them. Frequently, we discover that "common sense" doesn't make much sense in terms of the empirical reality.

I've already indicated that observation is no casual matter in science; it is a conscious and deliberate act. The brief discussions of operationalization earlier alluded to some of the steps in the observation process, and later chapters will examine them in detail. It would be appropriate to preview some of those steps here as a way of rounding out your understanding of empirical verification in science.

What I've been loosely calling observation is, in science, more a matter of *measurement*: the rigorous classification or quantification of things observed. To study the effects of the depression on the stability of families, then, Stouffer had to measure forced marriages, for example. As you recall, he defined forced marriages operationally as those resulting in a birth within the first seven months of marriage. That was the way he chose for recognizing a forced marriage when he saw one.

Two important criteria are applied to measurements in science: **validity** and **reliability**. Validity refers to the extent that the measurement procedures accurately reflect the concept under study. In the Stouffer example, his measurement method seems to have a certain basic validity—that is, an early birth, strongly suggesting that the bride was pregnant at the time of marriage, pretty much squares with our general understanding of the term *forced marriage*. At the same time, its validity is not perfect.

Suppose that the marrying couple didn't *know* the bride was pregnant at the time of marriage. In that case, her pregnancy couldn't have entered into their decision, and the early birth wouldn't really indicate a forced marriage. Or suppose the bride simply had a premature delivery? Or, maybe the couple dated for several years, reached a responsible and mature decision to marry, and then decided to get a head start on their family. That early birth wouldn't really represent a forced marriage either.

On the other hand, a couple might erroneously think they had started a family and rush into marriage. Their failure to have an early birth would conceal the fact that theirs was a forced marriage. Also, at the time Stouffer was studying the matter, merely having sexual relations was sometimes enough to force a marriage, with or without pregnancy.

Each of these possibilities weakens the validity of Stouffer's measurement procedure for identifying forced marriages. On the whole, however, the measure seems a generally valid way of recognizing forced marriages in the real world.

Whereas validity concerns the match between a mental concept and the operational definition used in measurement, reliability concerns the match between the operational definition and the actual measurements that are made. Continuing the Stouffer example, it is possible that the government records on time of birth in relation to time of marriage were pretty sloppy. Suppose the government made some "adjustments" to birth dates. That's not as farfetched as it may seem. In Japan, for example, certain years (in terms of astrological signs) are considered particularly unlucky, while others are considered lucky. It is a common practice, therefore, to fudge a little in recording the birth dates of children born near the end or the beginning of such years—a practice that makes demographers gray before their time. The research procedures related to validity and reliability are discussed further in Chapters 5 and 6.

Even when we have arrived at observation-measurement procedures that seem adequately valid and reliable, we often face the problem of having *too much* to observe and measure. Suppose you wanted to study the relationship between education and alienation, for example. Even if you were satisfied that you could adequately measure both a person's education and his or her level of alienation, you'd be left with 4 *billion potential observations*! Not wanting to observe every single man, woman, and child in the world, you'd have to decide on some method for picking a reasonable number of people whom you *would* observe. The selection of observations in this sense is called *sampling*, and you may recall this aspect of the Ransford study mentioned in Chapter 1. The logic and methods of sampling are discussed in detail in Chapter 7.

Conscious, controlled measurement and sampling, then, are two of the key elements of empirical verification that distinguish social scientific inquiry from the casual inquiry that marks much of our day-to-day activities. Let's turn more briefly to some other distinguishing characteristics of scientific inquiry.

Generalization

Science aims at general understanding rather than at the explanation of individual events. The scientist is typically less interested in understanding why a given ball falls to the earth when released from a height than in understanding why all such balls tend to do so. Similarly, the scientist is less interested in explaining why a given person voted as he or she did than in understanding why large groups of people voted as they did.

This characteristic of science is related to its probabilistic determinism. It is conceivable that we could completely explain the reasons lying behind a given event

—why a given man voted for Candidate X. We might conceivably discover every single factor that went into the voting decision. If we were successful, then presumably we would predict the voting behavior of identical persons with perfect accuracy. In the long run, however, such a capability would not give much useful information about voting behavior in general. First, it is doubtful that we would ever find another person with exactly the same characteristics. More important, our discoveries might help us very little in understanding the voting behavior of people with other characteristics. We would be happier with less than 100 percent understanding if we were able to understand voting behavior in general.

That is the sense in which the scientist and the historian differ in their approaches to the same subject matter. The historian aims at understanding everything about a specific event, while the scientist is more interested in generally understanding a class of similar, though not identical, events. By the same token, the psychologist and the therapist differ in their approaches to human behavior. The psychologist examines schizophrenic behavior among several individuals in an effort to arrive at a general understanding of schizophrenia, while the therapist takes advantage of existing general knowledge in an effort to help a specific individual.

Generalizability, thus, is an important characteristic of scientific discoveries. The discovery that red balls fall to earth at a given acceleration is less useful than the discovery that balls of all colors do so. Similarly, it is less useful to know that balls fall with a given acceleration at sea level, than to know that the acceleration of all falling balls can be determined from their altitude.

To the social scientist, a theory of voting behavior that applies only to whites is less useful than one that applies to voters of all races. A theory of religiosity that applies only to Christians is less useful than one that applies to people of all religions —or people with no religion at all.

While the social scientist often begins with an attempt to explain a more limited range of social behavior or the behavior of a limited subset of the population, the goal is normally to expand the findings to explain other forms of behavior and other subsets of the population.

Parsimony

As the previous sections indicate, scientists spend much of their effort in the attempt to discover the factors that determine types of events. At the same time, they attempt to discover those factors that do not determine the events. Thus, in determining the acceleration of a falling object, we discount its color as being irrelevant. In this sense, we say that science is parsimonious—representing a balance between power and efficiency in explanation.

Like the physical scientist, the social scientist attempts to gain the most explanatory power out of the smallest number of variables. In many cases, the additional consideration of new variables adds explanatory and predictive power, but it also results in a more complicated model. And, in practice, the addition of more variables often reduces the generalizability of the explanation, since certain variables may have one effect among members of one subset of the population and a different effect among those of other subsets.

It should be noted that the parsimonious character of social science, like its deterministic posture, opens it to criticism from those holding a more individualistic view of human behavior. Whereas they would tend to explore the depths of idiosyncratic factors resulting in a decision or action on the part of a given person, the social scientist consciously attempts to limit such inquiry.

The social scientist, then, might attempt to explain overall voting behavior through the observation of, say, three or four variables. The critic might object that all the voters had many other, individual, reasons for voting as they did, that the limited number of variables did not adequately explain the depth of decision making for any of the subjects under study. The problem here is that the social scientist has a special goal: consciously attempting to gain the greatest amount of understanding from the smallest number of variables. Neither the scientist nor the critic in such a case is more correct than the other; they simply have different goals. We must fully understand the scientist's goal, however, in order to recognize that this criticism is not a valid one.

Ultimately, the scientist attempts to understand the reasons for the events, using as few explanatory factors as possible. In practice, of course, the number of explanatory factors taken into account typically increases the degree of determination achieved. One political scientist may achieve a certain degree of explanation of voting behavior through the use of only two factors, say party affiliation and social class. Another might achieve a more complete understanding by also taking into account such other factors as race, region of upbringing, sex, education, and so forth. Frequently, the scientist is forced to choose between simplicity, on the one hand, and degree of explanation on the other. Ideally, we try to maximize both. In part, this accounts for the elegance of Einstein's famous equation: $E = mc^2$.

Specificity

The social scientist, like the physical scientist, must specify his or her methods of measurement. Perhaps this specificity is especially important in the social sciences, since they deal with concepts more vaguely defined in common discourse. Although the physicist defines *acceleration* more rigorously than the lay person, the scientific definition is not greatly at variance with the common understanding of the term. Concepts such as *religiosity* and *prejudice*, however, have such varied meanings in common language that their rigorous definitions are not readily apparent.

In conducting a research project on the topic of prejudice, then, the scientist must generate a *specific* operationalization of the concept prejudice: for example, agreement with several questionnaire statements that seem to indicate prejudice. In reporting your research, you must be careful to describe your operationalizations in detail so that the reader will know precisely how the concept has been measured. Although a given reader may disagree with the operationalization, he or she will at least know what it is.

Often the generalizability of a given discovery is substantiated through the use of different operationalizations of the concepts involved. If a given set of factors results in prejudice as measured in a number of different ways, the researcher (or the scientific community) may conclude that those factors result in prejudice *in general*, even though prejudice itself is not susceptible to a single measurement that would be accepted by everyone.

Intersubjectivity

Finally, it is frequently asserted that science is "objective," but such an assertion typically results in a good deal of confusion as to what objectivity is. Moreover, it has been noted increasingly in recent years that no scientist is completely objective in his or her work. All scientists are subjective to some extent—influenced by their personal motivations.

In saying that science is *intersubjective*, I mean that two scientists with different subjective orientations would arrive at the same conclusion if each conducted the same experiment. An example from political science should clarify this idea.

The tendency for intellectuals in America to align themselves more with the Democratic Party than with the Republican Party has led many people to assume that Democrats as a group are better educated than Republicans. It is reasonable to assume that a Democratic scientist would be happy with this view while a Republican scientist would not. Yet, it would be possible for the two scientists to agree on the design of a research project that would collect data from the American electorate relating to party affiliation and educational levels. The two scientists could then conduct independent studies of the subject, and both would discover that Republicans as a whole have a higher educational level than do Democrats. (That is due to the fact that the Democratic Party also attracts a larger proportion of working-class voters than does the Republican Party in America, while businessmen are more attracted to the Republican Party.) Both scientists—with opposite subjective orientations—would arrive at the same empirical conclusion. That is what is meant by the *intersubjectivity* of science.

SUMMARY

This chapter completes your introduction to the nature of social scientific inquiry and the ways in which it differs from the more casual inquiry you and I practice in our daily lives. It should be clear to you that scientific inquiry is really just a refinement of what you have been doing all your life—but it is a *refinement*. In science—physical or social—inquiry is a conscious and deliberate activity, and as such it avoids many of the common pitfalls that cause us to fall short of understanding what's going on around us.

The discussion in this chapter has been organized around the foundations of theory and research. We began by examining some of the bases of social scientific theory: what it is and isn't. Then we saw how theory is linked to research through the interplay of logic and observation. We concluded with an examination of some of the special characteristics of social scientific research, subjects that will be expanded on in later chapters of the book.

Before turning to the detailed discussions of specific research techniques, I think it would be useful for you to see social research in a broader perspective. After all, science is conducted *in* the world as well as about the world. Although this book focuses on the logical-technical aspects of research, you should be aware of some of the political and ethical elements as well. That's the purpose of Chapter 3, which follows.

MAIN POINTS

1. Whether human social behavior can be studied "scientifically" has been debated for some time. It can.

2. Social scientific theory concerns understanding what *is*, not proposing what ought to be. Thus, theory differs from philosophy or belief.

3. In examining what is, social scientific theory mainly addresses the regular patterns that appear in our social life.

4. Social scientists are primarily interested in group or aggregate behavior, not individual behavior.

5. An *attribute* is a characteristic or quality that can be used to describe something: for example, *female*.

6. A *variable* is a logical set of attributes: for example, *sex*. It is composed of the attributes *male* and *female*.

7. The aim of social science is to understand the relationships among variables as manifested in social life. Theories are written in a variable language.

8. In particular, social scientists are interested in causal relationships among variables. This interest is based on a fundamental view that human behavior is determined rather than totally free.

9. Social scientific theory and research are linked through two logical methods:
   a. *Deduction* involves the derivation of expectations or hypotheses from theories.
   b. *Induction* involves the development of generalizations from specific observations.

10. Science is a process involving an alternation of deduction and induction.

11. *Empirical verification* refers to the observational element in science. In addition to figuring out what might be logically expected, scientists look to see if the expected is actually so.

12. *Measurement* refers to the rigorous classification or quantification of things observed.

13. *Validity* refers to the match between a mental concept and the way it is measured.

14. *Reliability* refers to the match between the plan for measurement and the actual measurements.

15. *Sampling* involves the selection of a few observations that will serve as the basis for general conclusions.

16. Both *generalization* and *specificity* are important aspects of science. *Parsimony* is a matter of getting the most out of the least.

17. Despite its advanced publicity, science is seldom if ever objective; it is *intersubjective*, however, in the sense that different scientists—having different subjective positions—ought to arrive at the same conclusion if they execute the same research design.

ANNOTATED BIBLIOGRAPHY

Babbie, Earl, *Survey Research Methods* (Belmont, Calif.: Wadsworth, 1973), Chapter 3. An application of the basic ideas developed in this chapter to the method of survey research. This short discussion should further clarify your understanding of the characteristics of science and social science as these appear in practice.

Campbell, Donald, and Stanley, Julian, *Experimental and Quasi-Experimental Designs for Research* (Chicago: Rand McNally, 1963). A somewhat different approach to the logic of social science than has been presented in this chapter. The authors begin with the logic of the controlled experiment and show how it is approximated in other social research designs.

Franklin, Billy, and Osborne, Harold (eds.), *Research Methods: Issues and Insights* (Belmont, Calif.: Wadsworth, 1971), Parts One and Two. An excellent collection of papers dealing with various aspects of social research. The selections in Parts One and Two provide a variety of stimulating perspectives on the general logic of social research, asking whether social science is "scientific," where it fits into our comprehensive understanding of people, and the links between theory and research in the social sciences.

Glazer, Myron, *The Research Adventure: Promise and Problems of Field Work* (New York: Random House, 1972). An eminently readable and informal biography of social research. I've included this book among the more technical and theoretical references to give you a flavor of what social inquiry is like in the flesh.

Wallace, Walter, *The Logic of Science in Sociology* (Chicago: Aldine-Atherton, 1971). An eminently readable overview of the logic connecting the several stages of social research. This remarkable little book leads you around the unending circle of observation to generalization to theory to hypothesis to observation and on and on.

CHAPTER 3

The Ethics and Politics of Social Research

INTRODUCTION

For the most part, this book deals with the scientific aspects of social research. Although this approach is obviously appropriate, to deal with that aspect *only* would be inappropriate in a book that has the purpose of presenting a realistic and useful introduction to social research. The scientific aspect of social research is only one of four that must be considered in actually doing research.

The second essential consideration involves *administrative* matters. Very often, the type of study design that would be ideal from a purely scientific standpoint would be too expensive or time-consuming to be practical. If you wanted to examine the effects of society-wide economic situations on family life, it wouldn't even occur to you to interview every family in America at length. It simply wouldn't be feasible to do that. Thus, throughout this book, we're going to be looking at both scientific and administrative considerations. Every time we examine the alternative ways of handling a particular aspect of a research project, we'll look at both the logical and practical sides of the matter.

There are two other important considerations in doing research in the real world: *ethics* and *politics*. Since they are somewhat subtler and less obvious, I want to devote this chapter to them. Just as there are certain procedures that wouldn't be used in research because they are scientifically unsound, and others that wouldn't be used because they are impractical, so there are procedures you couldn't use because of ethical considerations and others that would be politically difficult or impossible. Two illustrations will show you what I mean.

Several years ago, I was invited to sit in on a planning session to design a study of legal education in California. It was to be a joint project involving a university research center and the state bar association. The purpose of the project was to improve legal education by learning those aspects of the law school experience that were related to success on the bar exam. Essentially, the plan was to prepare a questionnaire that would get detailed information about the law school experiences of individuals. The questionnaire would be administered to people when they took the bar exam. By analyzing how people with different kinds of law school experiences did on the bar exam, it would be possible to find out what sorts of things worked and what didn't. The findings of the research could be made available to law schools, and ultimately legal education could be improved.

The exciting thing about collaborating with the bar association was that all the normally aggravating logistical hassles would be handled. There would be no problem getting permission to administer questionnaires in conjunction with the exam, for example. In fact, one major problem could be eliminated altogether. As we'll see later in this book, *nonresponse* is always a problem in studies of this sort—to the extent that not everyone selected for study actually participates, the generalizability of the results is in question. The bar association officials had an easy answer to that problem: "We'll simply require the questionnaire as a part of the bar exam. That way, there'll be no nonresponse problem."

I left the meeting excited about the prospects for the study. When I told a colleague about it, I glowed about the absolute handling of the nonresponse problem. Her immediate comment turned everything around completely. "That's unethical. There's no law requiring the questionnaire, and participation in research has to be voluntary." The study wasn't done.

In retelling this story, it is obvious to me that it would have been inappropriate to require participation as suggested. You may have seen that before I told you about my colleague's comment. I still experience a little bit of embarrassment over the matter. Yet, I have a specific purpose in telling this story about myself.

All of us consider ourselves to be ethical; not perfect perhaps, but more ethical than the rest of humanity. The problem in social research—and probably in life—is that ethical considerations are not always apparent to us. As a result, we often plunge into things without seeing ethical issues that may be apparent to others and may even be cut-and-dried for us when they are pointed out. When I reported back to the others in the planning group, for example, no one disagreed with the inappropriateness of requiring participation. Everyone was a bit embarrassed about not having seen it.

All of us could immediately see the ethical aspect in a study that would require the torturing of small children. I know you'd speak out immediately if I suggested we interview people about their sex lives and then publish what they said in the local newspaper. But, as ethical as you are, you'd totally miss the ethical issue in other situations—not because you're bad, but because we all do that.

The first half of this chapter, then, deals with the ethics of social research. In part, I'll present some of the broadly agreed-on norms describing what's ethical and what's not. More importantly, however, my purpose is to *sensitize* you to the ethical component in research so that you'll become accustomed to looking for it whenever you plan a study. Even when the ethical aspects of a situation are arguable, you should know there's something to argue about.

Political considerations in research are also subtle, ambiguous, and arguable. Notice that the law school example described above involves politics as well as ethics. Although social scientists have an ethical norm that participation in research should be voluntary, that norm clearly grows out of our political norms protecting civil liberties. In other nations, the proposed study would not have been considered unethical at all.

In the second half of this chapter, we'll look at a number of cases of social research projects that were crushed or nearly crushed by political considerations. As with ethical concerns, there is often no "correct" answer to the situation. People of goodwill disagree. Again, however, my purpose is to assist you in becoming more sensitive to the political considerations involved without giving you a party line of what's politically acceptable or unacceptable.

ETHICAL ISSUES IN SOCIAL RESEARCH

In most dictionaries and in common usage, ethics is typically associated with morality, and both concern matters of right and wrong. But what *is* right and what wrong? What is the source of the distinction? For individuals, the sources vary. They may be religions, political ideologies, or the pragmatic observation of what seems to work and what doesn't.

Webster's New World Dictionary is typical among dictionaries in defining ethical as "conforming to the standards of conduct of a given profession or group." Although the idea may frustrate those in search of moral absolutes, what we regard as morality and ethics in day-to-day life is a matter of agreement among members of a group. And, not surprisingly, different groups have agreed on different codes of conduct. If you are going to live in a particular society, then, it is extremely useful for you to know what that society considers ethical and unethical. The same holds true for the social research "community."

If you are going to do social scientific research, you should be aware of the general agreements shared by researchers as to what's proper and improper in the conduct of scientific inquiry. The section that follows summarizes some of the more important ethical agreements that prevail in social research. Realize that there is some disagreement among researchers on the specifics of some general issues. Still, the discussion will give you some useful guidelines.

Voluntary Participation

Social research often, though not always, represents an intrusion into the lives of people. The interviewer's knock on the door or the arrival of a questionnaire in the mail signals the beginning of an activity that the respondent has not requested and one that may require a significant portion of his or her time and energy. Participation in a social experiment represents a disruption in the subject's regular activities. The arrival of the participant observer can and often does interfere with the social process under study.

Social research, moreover, often requires that people reveal personal information about themselves—personal things that may be unknown to their friends and associates. And social research often requires that such information be revealed to strangers.

Other professionals, such as physicians and lawyers, also require such information. Their requests may be justified, however, on the grounds that the information is required for them to serve the personal interests of the respondent. The social researcher can seldom make this claim. Like medical scientists, we can only argue that the research effort may ultimately help all humanity.

A major tenet of medical research ethics is that experimental participation must be *voluntary*. (Interestingly, the indictment of Nazi medical experimentation was based not so much on the cruelty of the experiments—such research is often unavoidably cruel—but on the fact that prisoners were forced to participate.) The same norm applies to social research. No one should be forced to participate. This norm is far easier to accept in theory than to apply in practice, however.

Again, medical research provides a useful parallel. Many experimental drugs are tested on prisoners. In the most rigorously ethical cases, the prisoners are told the nature—and the possible dangers—of the experiment; they are told that participation is completely voluntary; and they are further instructed that they can expect no special rewards—such as early parole—for participation. Even under these conditions, it is often clear that volunteers are motivated by the belief that they will personally benefit from their cooperation.

When the instructor in an introductory sociology class asks students to fill out a questionnaire that he or she hopes to analyze and publish, it should always be impressed upon the students that their participation in the survey is completely voluntary. Even so, it should be clear that most students will fear that nonparticipation will somehow affect the grades they receive in the course. In such a case, the instructor should be especially sensitive to the implied sanctions, and make special provisions to obviate them. For example, the instructor could leave the room while the questionnaires are completed and dropped in a box. Or, students could be asked to return the questionnaires by mail, or put them in a box near the door upon arriving at the next meeting of the course.

You should be clear that this norm of voluntary participation goes directly against a number of scientific concerns. In the most general terms, the scientific goal of *generalizability* is threatened if experimental subjects or survey respondents are all the kinds of people who willingly participate in such things. This orientation probably reflects more general personality traits; possibly, then, the results of the research will not be generalizable to all kinds of people. Most clearly, in the case of a descriptive survey, a researcher cannot generalize the sample survey findings to an entire population unless a substantial majority of the scientifically selected sample actually participate—the willing respondents and the somewhat unwilling.

As will be discussed in Chapter 8, field research has its own ethical dilemmas in this regard. Very often, the researcher cannot even reveal that a study is being done, for fear that that revelation might significantly affect the social processes being studied. Clearly, the subjects of study in such cases are not even given the opportunity to volunteer or refuse to participate.

You should realize that the norm of voluntary participation is an important one, and you should also know that it is often impossible to follow it. In those cases where you feel ultimately justified in violating it, it is all the more important that you observe the other ethical norms of scientific research, such as bringing no harm to the people under study.

No Harm to the People Being Studied

Social research should never injure the people being studied, regardless of whether they volunteer for the study. Perhaps the clearest instance of this norm in practice concerns the revealing of information that would embarrass them or endanger their home life, friendships, jobs, and so forth. This norm is discussed more fully in the next section.

It is possible for subjects of study to be harmed psychologically in the course of a study, however, and the researcher must be aware of the often subtle dangers and guard against them. Very often, research subjects are asked to reveal deviant behavior, attitudes they feel are unpopular, or demeaning personal characteristics such as low income, the receipt of welfare payments, and the like. Revealing such information is very likely to make them feel at least uncomfortable.

Often, social research projects force participants to face aspects of themselves that they do not normally consider. That can happen even when the information is not revealed directly to the researcher. In retrospect, a certain past behavior may appear unjust or immoral. The project, then, can be the source of a continuing, personal agony for the subject. Suppose, for example, that the study concerns codes of ethical conduct. The subject may begin questioning his or her own morality, and that personal concern may last long after the research has been completed and reported.

By now, you should have realized that just about any research you might conduct runs the risk of injuring other people in some of these regards. My purpose in discussing these issues is not to paralyze you, to prevent you from ever doing research. I would just like you to be sensitive to these problems and be aware constantly that you are intruding in the lives of other human beings—usually uninvited.

There is no way for the researcher—whose study design involves the collection of information from and about people directly—to insure against all these possible injuries. Yet, some study designs make such injuries more likely than others. If a particular research procedure seems likely to produce unpleasant effects for subjects —asking survey respondents to report deviant behavior, for example—the researcher should have the firmest of scientific grounds for doing it. Unless it is vital to your research aims, you should not do it. If it is essential and also likely to be unpleasant for subjects, you will find yourself in an ethical nether world and may find yourself forced to do some personal agonizing. Although agonizing has little value in itself, it may be a healthy sign that you have become sensitive to the problem.

Although the fact often goes unrecognized, subjects can be harmed by the analysis and reporting of data. Every now and then, research subjects read the books published about the studies they participated in. Reasonably sophisticated subjects will be able to locate themselves in the various indexes and tables. Having done so, they may find themselves characterized—though not identified by name—as bigoted, unpatriotic, irreligious, and so forth. At the very least, such characterizations are likely to trouble them and threaten their self-images. Yet the whole purpose of the research project may be to explain why some people are prejudiced while others are not.

I conducted a survey some years back of churchwomen. Ministers in a sample of churches were asked to distribute questionnaires to a specified sample of members, collect them, and return them to the research office. One of these ministers read through the questionnaires from his sample before returning them, and then proceeded to deliver a hell-fire and brimstone sermon to his congregation, saying that many of them were atheists and going to hell. Even though he could not know or identify the respondents who gave particular responses, it seems certain that many respondents were personally harmed by the action.

Like voluntary participation, not harming people is an easy norm to accept in theory, but it is often difficult to insure in practice. Sensitivity to the issue and experience with its applications, however, should improve the researcher's tact in delicate areas of research.

Increasingly, in recent years, social researchers have been getting support for abiding by this norm. Federal and other funding agencies typically require an independent evaluation of the treatment of human subjects for research proposals, and most universities now have human subject committees to serve that evaluative function. Although sometimes troublesome and inappropriately applied, such requirements not only guard against unethical research but can also reveal ethical issues overlooked by the most scrupulous of researchers.

Anonymity and Confidentiality

The clearest concern in the protection of the subjects' interests and well-being is the protection of their identity, especially in survey research. If revealing their survey responses would injure them in any way, adherence to this norm becomes all the more important. Two techniques—*anonymity* and *confidentiality*—assist you in this regard, although the two are often confused.

Anonymity   A respondent may be considered *anonymous* when you as researcher cannot identify a given response with a given respondent. This means that an interview survey respondent can never be considered anonymous, since an interviewer collects the information from an identifiable respondent. (I assume here that standard sampling methods are followed.) An example of anonymity would be the mail survey in which no identification numbers are put on the questionnaires before their return to the research office.

Assuring anonymity creates logistical problems that will be discussed in later chapters on specific modes of data collection. Despite these problems, there are some situations in which the researcher may be advised to pay the necessary price. In a recent study of drug use among university students, the researchers decided that they specifically did not want to know the identity of respondents. There were two reasons for this decision. First, they felt that honestly assuring anonymity would increase the likelihood and accuracy of responses. Second, they did not want to be in the position of being asked by authorities for the names of drug offenders. In the few instances in which respondents volunteered their names, such information was immediately obliterated on the questionnaires.

Confidentiality   In a *confidential* survey, the researcher is able to identify a given person's responses but essentially promises not to do so publicly. In an interview survey, for example, the researcher would be in a position to make public the income reported by a given respondent, but the respondent is assured that this will not be done.

You can use a number of techniques to insure better performance on this guarantee. To begin, interviewers and others with access to respondent identifications should be trained in their ethical responsibilities. As soon as possible, all names and addresses should be removed from questionnaires and replaced by identification numbers. A master identification file should be created linking numbers to names to permit the later correction of missing or contradictory information, but this file should not be available except for legitimate purposes.

Whenever a survey is confidential rather than anonymous, it is the responsibility of the researcher to make that fact clear to the respondent. The use of the term *anonymous* to mean *confidential* should never be tolerated.

The Researcher's Identity

We've seen that the handling of subjects' identities is an important ethical consideration. Handling your own identity as a researcher can be tricky also. Sometimes it's useful and even necessary to identify yourself as a researcher to those you want to study. You'd have to be a master con artist to get people to participate in a laboratory experiment or complete a lengthy questionnaire without letting on that you were conducting research.

Even when it's possible to conceal your research identity—and it's sometimes important to do that, as we'll see in Chapter 8—there is an important ethical dimension to be considered. In terms of our most general social norms, deceiving people is unethical, and within social research, deception needs to be justified by compelling scientific or administrative concerns. Even then, the justification will be arguable.

Sometimes researchers admit that they are doing research but fudge about why they are doing it or for whom. Suppose you've been asked by a public welfare agency to conduct a study of living standards among aid recipients. Even if the agency is looking for ways of improving conditions, the recipient-subjects are likely to suspect that the motivation is otherwise, fearing a witch-hunt for "cheaters." They might be tempted, therefore, to give answers making them seem more destitute than they really are. Unless they provide truthful answers, however, the study will not produce accurate data that will contribute to an effective improvement of living conditions. What do you do? One solution would be to tell subjects that you are conducting the study as part of a university research program—concealing your affiliation with the welfare agency. Doing that improves the scientific quality of the study, but it raises a serious ethical issue in the process.

Analysis and Reporting

As a social researcher, then, you have a number of ethical obligations to your subjects of study. At the same time, you have ethical obligations to your colleagues in the scientific community, and a few comments on those are in order.

In any rigorous study, the researcher should be more familiar than anyone else with the technical shortcomings and failures of the study. You have an obligation to make those shortcomings known to your readers. Even though you may feel foolish admitting mistakes, you should do it anyway.

Negative findings should be reported if they are at all related to your analysis. There is an unfortunate myth in scientific reporting that only positive discoveries are worth reporting (and journal editors are sometimes guilty of believing that as well). From the standpoint of the scientific community, however, it is often as important to know that two variables are *not* related to each other as to know that they are. Recall the earlier discussion of Stouffer's examination of attitudes toward the promotion system in the army. It was a mark of his caliber as a researcher that he insisted on finding out *why* the MPs thought the system was fair while the air corpsmen didn't. Had he simply set the puzzling findings aside for later analysis, our understanding of reference groups and relative deprivation would have been held back.

Similarly, it is important to avoid the temptation to save face by describing your findings as the product of a carefully preplanned analytical strategy when that is not the case. It is simply a fact of life that many findings arrive unexpectedly—even though they may seem obvious in retrospect. So you uncovered an interesting relationship by accident—so what. Embroidering such situations with descriptions of fictitious hypotheses is dishonest and tends to mislead inexperienced researchers into thinking that all scientific inquiry is rigorously preplanned and organized.

In general, science progresses through honesty and openness, and it is retarded by ego-defenses and deception. You can serve your fellow researchers—and scientific discovery as a whole—by telling the truth about all the pitfalls and problems you have experienced in a particular line of inquiry. Perhaps you'll save them from the same problems.

A Professional Code of Ethics

Because of both the importance and the ambiguities of ethical issues in social research, most of the professional associations have created and published formal codes of conduct describing what is considered acceptable and unacceptable professional behavior. As an illustration, I have presented the code of conduct adopted by the American Association for Public Opinion Research, since AAPOR is an interdisciplinary research association in the social sciences (see Figure 3-1).

TWO ETHICAL CONTROVERSIES

As you may have already guessed, the adoption and publication of professional codes of conduct have not totally resolved the issue of research ethics. Social scientists still disagree on some general principles, and those who seem to agree in principle debate specifics.

In this section, I am going to describe briefly two research projects that have provoked ethical controversy and discussion in recent years. Please realize that these are not the only two controversial projects that have been done; they simply illustrate ethical issues in the real world, and I thought you'd find them interesting and perhaps provocative. The first project involved the study of homosexual behavior in public restrooms, and the second examined obedience in a laboratory setting.

Trouble in the Tearoom

As a graduate student, Laud Humphreys became interested in the study of homosexuality. Beyond the study of homosexuals, however, Humphreys developed a special interest in looking at the casual and fleeting homosexual acts engaged in by some nonhomosexuals. In particular, his research interest focused on homosexual acts between strangers meeting in the public restrooms in parks, called "tearooms" among homosexuals. The result was the publication in 1970 of *Tearoom Trade*.[1]

What particularly interested Humphreys about the tearoom activity was that the participants seemed to live "normal" lives otherwise, as family men and as accepted members of the community. They did nothing else that might qualify them as homosexuals. Thus, it was important to them that they remain anonymous in their tearoom visits. How would you study something like that? It probably wouldn't work for you to bounce out of a stall and conduct interviews with the participants.

To study the tearoom action, Humphreys took advantage of the social structure of the situation. Typically, the tearoom encounter involved three people: the two men actually engaged in the homosexual act and a lookout, called the "watch-queen." Thus, Humphreys began showing up at public restrooms, offering to serve as watchqueen whenever it seemed appropriate. Since the watchqueen's payoff was the chance to watch the action, Humphreys was able to conduct field observations as he would in a study of political rallies or jaywalking behavior at intersections.

To round out his understanding of the tearoom trade, Humphreys needed to

[1]Laud Humphreys, *Tearoom Trade: Impersonal Sex in Public Places* (Chicago: Aldine, 1970). For a criticism of Humphreys's study, see Nicholas von Hoffman, "Sociological Snoopers," *Washington Post*, January 30, 1970. For a criticism of von Hoffman's criticism of Humphreys, see Irving Louis Horowitz and Lee Rainwater, "Journalistic Moralizers," *Transaction* (May 1970). The latter two pieces, plus excerpts from the first, may also be found in George Ritzer, *Social Realities* (Boston: Allyn & Bacon, 1974), pp. 46-48, 49-56.

CODE OF PROFESSIONAL ETHICS AND PRACTICES

We, the members of the American Association for Public Opinion Research, subscribe to the principles expressed in the following code.

Our goal is to support sound practice in the profession of public opinion research. (By public opinion research we mean studies in which the principal source of information about individual beliefs, preferences, and behavior is a report given by the individual himself or herself.)

We pledge ourselves to maintain high standards of scientific competence and integrity in our work, and in our relations both with our clients and with the general public. We further pledge ourselves to reject all tasks or assignments which would be inconsistent with the principles of this code.

THE CODE

I. *Principles of Professional Practice in the Conduct of Our Work*

A. We shall exercise due care in gathering and processing data, taking all reasonable steps to assume the accuracy of results.

B. We shall exercise due care in the development of research designs and in the analysis of data.

1. We shall employ only research tools and methods of analysis which, in our professional judgment, are well suited to the research problem at hand.
2. We shall not select research tools and methods of analysis because of their special capacity to yield a desired conclusion.
3. We shall not knowingly make interpretations of research results, nor shall we tacitly permit interpretations, which are inconsistent with the data available.
4. We shall not knowingly imply that interpretations should be accorded greater confidence than the data actually warrant.

C. We shall describe our findings and methods accurately and in appropriate detail in all research reports.

Figure 3-1   Code of Conduct of the American Association for Public Opinion Research. *Source:*   Reprinted from the American Association for Public Opinion Research, *By-Laws* (May 1977).

know something more about the people who participated. As I've already indicated, however, it is unlikely that the men would have been thrilled about being interviewed, so Humphreys developed a different solution. Whenever possible, he noted down the license numbers of participants' cars and tracked down their names and addresses through the police. Humphreys then visited the men at their homes, disguising himself enough to avoid recognition, and announced that he was conducting a survey. In that fashion, he collected the personal information he was unable to get in the restrooms.

If you've been thinking that social science research is dull and unexciting, this illustration may have altered your view somewhat. That's not my main purpose,

II. *Principles of Professional Responsibility in Our Dealings with People*

A. The Public:

1. We shall cooperate with legally authorized representatives of the public by describing the methods used in our studies.
2. We shall maintain the right to approve the release of our findings, whether or not ascribed to us. When misinterpretation appears, we shall publicly disclose what is required to correct it, notwithstanding our obligation for client confidentiality in all other respects.

B. Clients or Sponsors:

1. We shall hold confidential all information obtained about the client's general business affairs and about the findings of research conducted for the client, except when the dissemination of such information is expressly authorized.
2. We shall be mindful of the limitations of our techniques and facilities and shall accept only those research assignments which can be accomplished within these limitations.

C. The Profession:

1. We shall not cite our membership in the Association as evidence of professional competence, since the Association does not so certify any persons or organizations.
2. We recognize our responsibility to contribute to the science of public opinion research and to disseminate as freely as possible the ideas and findings which emerge from our research.

D. The Respondent:

1. We shall not lie to survey respondents or use practices and methods which abuse, coerce, or humiliate them.
2. We shall protect the anonymity of every respondent, unless the respondent waives such anonymity for specified uses. In addition, we shall hold as privileged and confidential all information which tends to identify the respondent.

however. Humphreys's research provoked considerable controversy both within and outside the social scientific community. A great many ethical issues were raised and concerns expressed, and it will be useful to look at some of those now.

Some critics charged Humphreys with a gross invasion of privacy in the name of science. What men did in public restrooms was their own business and not Humphreys's. Others were mostly concerned about the deceit involved—Humphreys had lied to the participants by leading them to believe he was only a voyeur-participant.

People who felt that the tearoom participants, because they were doing their stuff in a public facility, were fair game for observation nonetheless protested the follow-up survey. They felt it was unethical for Humphreys to trace the participants to their homes and to interview them under false pretenses.

Still others justified Humphreys's research. The topic, they said, was worth study. It couldn't be studied any other way, and they regarded the deceit practiced by Humphreys to be essentially harmless, noting that he was careful not to harm his subjects by disclosing their tearoom activities.

The tearoom trade controversy, as you might imagine, has never been resolved. It is still debated, and it probably always will be, since it provokes emotions and contains ethical issues people disagree about. What do you think? Do you think Humphreys was ethical in doing what he did? Are there parts of the research that you feel were acceptable and other parts that were not? Whatever you feel in the matter, you are sure to find others to disagree with you.

Observing Human Obedience

The second illustration differs from the first in many ways. Whereas Humphreys's study involved field observations (participant observation), this study has its setting in the laboratory. The first study was sociological, this one psychological. And where the first examined a form of human deviance, the study we're going to look at now examined conformity.

One of the more unsettling clichés to come out of World War II was the German soldier's common excuse for atrocities: "I was only following orders." From the point of view that gave rise to this comment, any behavior—no matter how reprehensible—could be justified if someone else could be assigned responsibility for it. If a superior officer ordered a soldier to kill a small baby, the fact of the *order* was said to exempt the soldier from personal responsibility for the action.

Although the military tribunals that tried the war crime cases did not accept the excuse, social scientists and others have recognized the extent to which this point of view pervades social life. Very often people seem willing to do things they know would be considered wrong by others, *if* they can cite some higher authority as ordering them to do it. Such was the pattern of justification in the My Lai tragedy of Viet Nam, and it appears less dramatically in day-to-day civilian life.

Stanley Milgram, a psychologist, felt the topic of human obedience was worth careful study.[2] If we could understand the manner in which people were willing to obey orders to harm others, we might be able to defuse that danger in real life. Few would disagree with that sentiment, yet Milgram's study of the topic provoked considerable controversy.

To observe people's willingness to harm others when following orders, Milgram brought 40 adult men—from many different walks of life—into a laboratory setting designed to create the phenomenon under study. If you had been a subject in the experiment, you would have had something like the following experience.

You would have been informed that you and another subject were about to participate in a learning experiment. Through a draw of lots, you would have been assigned the job of "teacher" and your fellow subject the job of "pupil." He would

[2]Stanley Milgram, "Behavioral Study of Obedience," *Journal of Abnormal and Social Psychology*, Vol. 67 (1963), pp. 371–378; and Stanley Milgram, "Some Conditions of Obedience and Disobedience to Authority," *Human Relations*, Vol. 18 (1965), pp. 57–76.

have then been led into another room, strapped into a chair, and had an electrode attached to his wrist. As the teacher, you would have been seated in front of an impressive electrical control panel covered with dials, gauges, and switches. You would have noticed that each of the switches had a label giving a different number of volts, ranging from 15 to 315. The switches would have had other labels, too, some with the ominous phrases "Extreme-Intensity Shock," "Danger—Severe Shock," and "XXX."

The experiment would run like this. You would read a list of word pairs to the learner, and then test his ability to match them up. Since you couldn't see him, a light on your control panel would indicate his answer. Whenever the learner made a mistake, you would be instructed by the experimenter to throw one of the switches —beginning with the mildest—and administer a shock to your pupil. Through an open door between the two rooms, you'd hear your pupil's response to the shock. Then you'd read another list of word pairs and test him again.

As the experiment progressed, you'd be administering ever more intense shocks, until your pupil was screaming for mercy and begging for the experiment to end. You'd be instructed to administer the next shock anyway. After awhile, your pupil would begin kicking the wall between the two rooms and screaming. You'd be told to give the next shock. Finally, you'd read a list and ask for the pupil's answer—and there would be no reply whatever, only silence from the other room. The experimenter would inform you that no answer was considered an error and instruct you to administer the next higher shock. This would continue up to the "XXX" shock at the end of the series.

What do you suppose you would have done when the pupil first began screaming? When he began kicking on the wall? Or when he became totally silent and gave no indication of life? You'd refuse to continue giving shocks, right? Of the first 40 adult men Milgram tested, nobody refused to administer the shocks until the pupil began kicking the wall between the two rooms. Of the 40, 5 did so then. Two-thirds of the subjects, 26 of the 40, continued doing as they were told through the entire series—up to and including the administration of the highest shock.

As you've probably guessed, the shocks were phony, and the "pupil" was another experimenter. Only the "teacher" was a real subject in the experiment. You wouldn't have been hurting another person, even though you would have been led to think you were. The experiment was designed to test your *willingness* to follow orders, to the point of presumably killing someone.

A number of criticisms have been raised against the Milgram experiments, some methodological and some ethical. In the latter area, particular concerns have been expressed about the effects of the experiment on the subjects. Many seem to have personally experienced about as much pain as they thought they were administering to someone else. They pleaded with the experimenter to let them stop giving the shocks. They became extremely upset and nervous. Some had uncontrollable seizures.

How do *you* feel about this research? Do you think the topic was important enough to justify such measures? Can you think of other ways in which the researcher might have examined obedience?

DISCUSSION EXAMPLES

Research ethics, then, is an important though very ambiguous topic. The difficulty of resolving ethical issues should not be an excuse for ignoring them. To further sensitize yourself to the ethical component in social research, I've prepared a list of real and hypothetical research situations. See if you can see the ethical component in each. How do you feel about it? Do you feel the procedures described are ultimately acceptable or unacceptable? It would be useful to discuss some of these with others in your methods course.

1. A psychology instructor asks students in an introductory psychology class to complete questionnaires that the instructor will analyze and use in preparing a journal article for publication.

2. After a field study of deviant behavior during a riot, law enforcement officials demand that the researcher identify those people who were observed looting. Rather than risk arrest as an accomplice after the fact, the researcher complies.

3. After completing the final draft of a book reporting a research project, the researcher-author discovers that 25 of the 2,000 survey interviews were falsified by interviewers—but chooses to ignore that fact and publish the book anyway.

4. Researchers obtain a list of right-wing radicals they wish to study. They contact the radicals with the explanation that each has been selected "at random" from among the general population to take a sampling of "public opinion."

5. A college instructor administers an hour exam to both sections of a specific course. The overall performance of the two sections is essentially the same. The grades of one section are artificially lowered, however, and the instructor berates them for performing so badly. The purpose of this experiment is to test the effect of such berating. The instructor then administers the same final exam to both sections and discovers that the performance of the unfairly berated section is worse. The hypothesis is confirmed, and the research report is published.

6. In a study of sexual behavior, the investigator wants to overcome subjects' reluctance to report what they might regard as deviant behavior. To get past their reluctance, subjects are asked: "Everyone masturbates now and then; about how much do you masturbate?"

7. A researcher discovers that 85 percent of the university student body smoke marijuana regularly. Publication of this finding will probably create a furor in the community. Since no extensive analysis of drug use is planned, the researcher decides to ignore the finding and keep it quiet.

8. To test the extent to which people may try to save face by expressing attitudes on matters they are wholly uninformed about, the researcher asks for their attitudes regarding a fictitious issue.

9. A research questionnaire is circulated among students as part of their university registration packet. Although students are not told they must complete the questionnaire, the hope is that they will believe they must—thus insuring a higher completion rate.

10. A participant-observer pretends to join a radical, political group in order to study it and is successfully accepted as a member of the inner planning circle. What should the researcher do if the group makes plans for:
    a. a peaceful, though illegal, demonstration?
    b. the bombing of a public building during a time it is sure to be unoccupied?
    c. the assassination of a public official?

THE POLITICS OF SOCIAL RESEARCH

As I've indicated earlier, both ethics and politics hinge on ideological points of view. What is unacceptable from one point of view will be acceptable from another. Thus, we are going to see that people disagree on political aspects of research just as they disagree on ethical ones. As we change topics now, I want to distinguish ethical from political issues in two ways.

First, although ethics and politics are often closely intertwined, the ethics of social research deals more with the methods employed, whereas political issues are more concerned with the substance and use of research. Thus, for example, some critics raise ethical objections to the Milgram experiments, saying that the methods used harmed the experimental subjects. A political objection would be that obedience is not a worthy topic for study: either that (1) we should not tinker with people's willingness to follow orders from higher authority or, from the opposite political point of view, (2) that the results of the research could be used to make people *more* blindly obedient.

The second thing that distinguishes ethical from political aspects of social research is that there are no formal codes of accepted political conduct comparable to the codes of ethical conduct that we've discussed earlier. Although some of the ethical norms have political aspects—for example, not harming subjects clearly relates to our protection of civil liberties—no one has developed a set of political norms that could be agreed on by social researchers.

The only partial exception to the lack of political norms is to be found in the generally accepted view that a researcher's personal, political orientations should not interfere or unduly influence his or her scientific research. It would be considered improper for you to employ shoddy techniques or lie about your research as a way of furthering your political views. Although you were permitted to *have* political views, you are expected to hold them aside when you enter the realm of science. It is in this context that science is idealized as apolitical, amoral, and objective.

Objectivity and Ideology

As you'll recall from Chapter 2, I've suggested that social research can never be totally objective, since researchers are humanly subjective. Science, as a collective enterprise, achieves the equivalent of objectivity through intersubjectivity. That is, different scientists, having different subjective views, can and should arrive at the same results when they employ accepted research techniques. Essentially, that will happen to the extent that each is able to set personal values and views aside for the duration of the research.

The classic statement on objectivity and neutrality in social science is Max Weber's 1918 lecture on "Science as a Vocation."[3] In his talk, Weber coined the phrase "value-free sociology," urging that sociology, like other sciences, needed to be unencumbered by personal values if it was to make a special contribution to society. Liberals and conservatives alike could recognize the "facts" of, say, biology or mathematics, and they needed to be able to recognize the "facts" of social science, regardless of how those facts accorded with their personal politics.

For the most part, this abstract ideal has been agreed to in the social sciences— but not totally so. Increasingly in recent years, Marxist and neo-Marxist scholars have argued that social science and social action cannot and should not be separated. Explanations of the status quo in society, they contend, shade subtly into defenses of that same status quo. Simple explanations of the social functions of, say, discrimination can easily become justifications for its continuance. By the same token, merely studying society and its ills without a commitment to making society more humane has been called irresponsible.

Quite aside from abstract disagreements about whether social science can or should be value free, there have been numerous disagreements about whether particular research undertakings *are* value free or whether they represent an intrusion of the researcher's own political values. Typically, researchers have denied the intrusion, and the denial has been denied. Let's look at some examples of the controversies that have raged and continue to rage over this issue.

Social Research and Race

Nowhere have social research and politics been more controversially intertwined than in the area of race relations. Social scientists have been studying the topic for a very long time, and often the products of the social research have found their way into the arena of practical politics. A few brief references should illustrate the point.

When the United States Supreme Court, in 1896, established the principle of "separate but equal" as a means of reconciling the Fourteenth Amendment's guarantee of equality to blacks with the norms of segregation, it neither asked for nor cited social science research. Nonetheless, it is widely believed that the Court was influenced by the writings of sociologist William Graham Sumner. Sumner, a leading

[3]Max Weber, "Science as a Vocation," in Hans Gerth and C. Wright Mills (eds.), *From Max Weber: Essays in Sociology* (New York: Free Press, 1946).

social scientist of his era, was noted for his view that the mores and folkways of a society were relatively impervious to legislation and social planning. His view has often been paraphrased as "stateways do not make folkways." Thus the Court ruled that it could not accept the assumption that "social prejudices may be overcome by legislation" and denied the wisdom of "laws which conflict with the general sentiment of the community"[4]

This example illustrates one of the problems in the relationship between politics and science. As Robert Oppenheimer and other atomic scientists were to discover years later, scientific findings can be used for purposes that the scientists themselves might oppose. We shall see this concern raised again shortly in the case of Camelot.

Returning specifically to research and race, there is no doubt that Gunnar Myrdal's classic two-volume study of race relations in America had a significant impact on the topic of his research.[5] Entitling the work *An American Dilemma*, Myrdal amassed a great volume of data to show that the position of black Americans presented a direct contradiction to American values of social and political equality. And, Myrdal did not attempt to hide his own point of view in the matter.

When the doctrine of "separate but equal" was overturned in 1954 (*Brown* v. *Board of Education of Topeka*), the new Supreme Court decision was based in part on the conclusion that segregation had a detrimental effect on black children. In drawing that conclusion, moreover, the Court cited a number of sociological and psychological research reports.[6]

For the most part, social scientists in this century have supported the cause of black equality in America. Many have been actively involved in the civil rights movement, some more radically than others. Thus, social scientists have been able to draw research conclusions supporting the cause of equality without fear of criticism from colleagues. It has been acceptable to conduct research on prejudice with the avowed aim of ultimately eradicating it. No reasonable and humane person could object to that, right? I don't. You wouldn't.

To recognize the solidity of the general social science position in the matter of equality, we need only examine a few research projects that have produced conclusions disagreeing with the predominant ideological position. Most social scientists have—overtly, at least—supported the end of even de facto school segregation. Thus, an immediate and heated controversy was provoked in 1966 when James Coleman, a respected sociologist, published the results of a major national study of race and education.[7] Contrary to general agreement, Coleman found little difference between the academic performance of black students attending integrated schools and the performance of those attending segregated ones. Indeed, such obvious things as libraries, laboratory facilities, and high expenditures per student made little difference. Instead, Coleman reported that family and neighborhood factors had the most influence on academic achievement.

[4]See Albert Blaunstein and Robert Zangrando (eds.), *Civil Rights and the Black American* (New York: Washington Square Press, 1970) p. 308.
[5]Gunnar Myrdal, *An American Dilemma: The Negro Problem and Modern Democracy* (New York: Harper & Row, 1944).
[6]See Blaunstein and Zangrando, *op. cit.*
[7]James Coleman, *Equality of Educational Opportunity* (Washington, D.C.: U.S. Government Printing Office, 1966).

Coleman's findings were not well received by many of the social scientists who had been active in the civil rights movement, since the results of Coleman's research findings were seen as ammunition for those intent on thwarting school desegregation. After all, if integrated schools didn't benefit black children, why integrate? Although some scholars criticized Coleman's work on methodological grounds, many objected hotly on the grounds that the findings would have segregationist political consequences. The controversy that raged around the Coleman report was reminiscent of that provoked earlier by Daniel Moynihan in his critical analysis of the black family in America.[8]

The last example of political controversy surrounding social research in connection with race concerns the issue of IQ scores of black and white people. In 1969, Arthur Jensen, a Harvard psychologist, was asked to prepare an article for the *Harvard Educational Review* examining the data on racial differences in IQ test results.[9] In the ensuing article, Jensen concluded that genetic differences between blacks and whites accounted for the lower average IQ scores of blacks. Jensen was to become so identified with that position that he was soon to appear on college campuses across the country discussing it.

The Jensen position has been attacked on numerous methodological bases. It was charged that much of the data upon which Jensen's conclusion was based were inadequate and sloppy—there are many IQ tests, some worse than others. Similarly, it was argued that Jensen had not taken social-environmental factors sufficiently into account. Other social scientists raised other methodological objections, and appropriately so.

Beyond the scientific critique, however, Jensen was condemned by many as a racist. He was booed and his public presentations drowned out by hostile crowds. The reception Jensen received from several university audiences was not significantly different from the reception received by abolitionists a century before.

Please understand that many social scientists limited their objections to the Moynihan, Coleman, and Jensen research to scientific, methodological grounds. The purpose of the foregoing account, however, is to point out that political ideology often gets involved in matters of social research. Although the abstract model of science is divorced from ideology, the practice of science is not.

Project Camelot

Among social scientists *Camelot* is a household term in discussions of research and politics. Today, it is frequently referenced with no further description, it is so well known. Irving Louis Horowitz, a man who has criticized government agencies on occasion, said that Project Camelot "has had perhaps the worst public relations

[8]Daniel Moynihan, *The Negro Family: The Case for National Action* (Washington, D.C.: Government Printing Office, 1965).
[9]Arthur Jensen, "How Much Can We Boost IQ and Scholastic Achievement?" *Harvard Educational Review*, Vol. 39 (1969), pp. 1–123.

record of any agency or subagency of the U.S. government."[10] What provoked such a stir?

On December 4, 1964, the Special Operations Research Office of American University sent an announcement to a number of social scientists about a project being organized around the topic of internal war. The announcement contained, in part, the following description:

> Project CAMELOT is a study whose objective is to determine the feasibility of developing a general social systems model which would make it possible to predict and influence politically significant aspects of social change in the developing nations of the world. Somewhat more specifically, its objectives are:
> *First*, to devise procedures for assessing the potential for internal war within national societies;
> *Second*, to identify with increased degrees of confidence those actions which a government might take to relieve conditions which are assessed as giving rise to a potential for internal war.[11]

Of course, few people are openly in favor of war, and most would support research aimed at ending or preventing war. By the summer of 1965, however, with the national debate on Viet Nam gaining momentum, Camelot was being hotly argued in social science circles as a Department of Defense attempt to co-opt scientists into a *counterinsurgency* effort in Chile. It was claimed that the Defense Department intended to sponsor social scientific research with the direct purpose of putting down political and potentially revolutionary dissatisfaction in that volatile Latin American nation. Whatever the motivations of the social scientists, it was feared that the result of their research would be the strengthening of established regimes and the thwarting of popular reformist and revolutionary movements in foreign countries.

Many social scientists who had agreed in principle to participate in the project soon felt they were learning a lesson learned decades before them by Robert Oppenheimer and the atomic scientists. Charges and countercharges were hurled around professional circles. Names were called, motives questioned. Old friendships ended. The Defense Department was roundly damned by all for attempting to subvert social research. Foreign relations with Latin America simultaneously chilled and got hot. Finally, under the cloud of growing criticism, Camelot was cancelled and dismantled.

It is interesting, in the present context, to imagine what might have happened to Project Camelot had it been proposed to a steadfastly conservative and anticommunist social research community. I think there is no doubt but that it would have been supported, executed, and completed without serious challenge or controversy. Certainly war per se was not the issue. There was no serious criticism when Sam Stouffer organized the research branch in the army during World War II to conduct research aimed at *supporting* the war effort, making our soldiers more effective fighters. Ultimately science is neutral on the topics of war and peace, but scientists are not.

[10]Irving Louis Horowitz, *The Rise and Fall of Project Camelot* (Cambridge: M.I.T. Press, 1967), p. vi.
[11]*Ibid.*, p. 47.

Politics in Perspective

There is no end to the list of illustrations that might appropriately be introduced in this section. Edward Banfield's *The Unheavenly City*[12] stirred up a hornets' nest of protest with its conclusion that the urban lower classes in America were beyond help or redemption, that nothing would serve them better than "benign neglect." The developing field of *sociobiology* has become a constant source of controversy as its practitioners announce inherent, genetic universals in human nature—especially those dealing with the inherent nature of men and women.

The role of politics and related ideologies in social research is not unique in science. The natural sciences have experienced and continue to experience similar situations. The preceding discussion has three main purposes in a textbook on the *practice* of social research.

First, it seems important to me that you realize that science is not untouched by politics. Social science, in particular, is a part of social life. We study things that matter to people, things they have firm, personal feelings about, and things that affect their lives. Scientists are human beings, and their human feelings often show through in their professional lives. To think otherwise would be naive.

Second, I'd like you to see that science does proceed even under political controversy and hostility. Even when researchers get angry and call each other names, or when the research community comes under attack from the outside, the job of science gets done anyway. Scientific inquiry persists, studies are done, reports are published, and new things are learned. In short, ideological disputes do not bring science to a halt but simply make it more exciting.

Finally, I want you to make ideological considerations a part of the backdrop you create—a backdrop that will increase your awareness as you learn the various techniques of social science methods. As I've already suggested in Chapters 1 and 2, many of the established techniques of science function to cancel out or hold in check our human shortcomings, especially those we are unaware of. Otherwise, we might look into the world and never see anything but ourselves—our personal biases and beliefs.

SUMMARY

This chapter has addressed some of the nonscientific aspects of social research. It is useful for you to have these in mind as we prepare now to dive into the technical aspects of scientific social research.

We began with some ethical concerns, looking at some of the norms social scientists have developed as a framework for the humane study of humans. Three broad topics were covered.

First, we looked at the requirement that participation in research be voluntary. On the face of it, that is an obvious necessity in humane research, and it would seem

[12]Edward Banfield, *The Unheavenly City: The Nature and Future of our Urban Crisis* (Boston: Little, Brown, 1968.)

easy to comply with. We saw, however, that it is trickier in practice. It can sometimes be difficult to weed out implied pressure to participate, as in the case of prisoners and students.

The second broad topic had to do with harming subjects in social research. The general norm, as you would guess, is against doing that. But there are subtle ways of harming people inadvertently, and it is often difficult to anticipate and avoid them all. In this context, we saw that the norms of anonymity and confidentiality play a part in protecting subjects from harm.

Finally, we looked at the broad topic of honesty. On the one hand, we looked at the deceptions that researchers sometimes feel are required. At times it seems essential to mislead subjects as to the nature of a research project or even as to whether research is being conducted at all. In this latter respect, we found that field researchers must decide whether to identify themselves as researchers or just pretend to be one of the gang.

We also saw that honesty in reporting research findings is a consideration. As with the other ethical issues, the need for honest reporting is clearer in the abstract than in practical situations. Outright lying would probably be unanimously condemned, but there are many shades of fudging.

The effect of political beliefs is the other nonscientific aspect of social research. Here we saw that political ideologies of the general society and of subgroups within it can create special problems for "objective" scientific research. All of us—scientists included—have our own explicit and implicit points of view. Ultimately, it is impossible to divorce those points of view from our research altogether. At the very least, however, we can (1) be conscious of potential biases and (2) be honest in reporting the points of view that we do have.

MAIN POINTS

1. In addition to technical, scientific considerations, social research projects are likely to be shaped by administrative, ethical, and political considerations.

2. What's ethically "right" and "wrong" in research is ultimately a matter of what people *agree* is right and wrong.

3. Scientists agree that participation in research should, as a general norm, be voluntary. This norm, however, can conflict with the scientific need for generalizability.

4. Probably all scientists agree that research should not harm those that participate in it, unless they willingly and knowingly accept the risks of harm.

5. *Anonymity* refers to the situation in which even the researcher cannot identify specific information with the individuals it describes.

6. *Confidentiality* refers to the situation in which the researcher—although knowing which data describe which subjects—agrees to keep that information confidential.

7. Although science is neutral on political matters, scientists are not.

8. Even though the norms of science cannot force individual scientists to give up their personal values, the intersubjective character of science provides a guard against "scientific" findings being the product of bias only.

ANNOTATED BIBLIOGRAPHY

Golden, M. Patricia (ed.), *The Research Experience* (Itasca, Ill.: Peacock, 1976). An excellent collection of pieces about *doing* research in a social context. The book presents an excerpt from a published report and follows it with a more informal account by the researcher. In several of the informal accounts, you will get an inside view of the way political and ethical issues are involved in social research.

MacRae, Duncan, Jr., *The Social Function of Social Science* (New Haven: Yale University Press, 1976). A historical analysis of the interplay of social science and social reform in America. Both the values of the general community and the values of the social scientists themselves are examined.

Richter, Maurice, Jr., *Science as a Cultural Process* (Cambridge, Mass.: Schenkman, 1972). A sociological analysis of science as a human process, occurring within a sociocultural context. Richter provides both a historical and contemporary picture of the interplay between science and society.

Ritzer, George (ed.), *Social Realities: Dynamic Perspectives* (Boston: Allyn & Bacon), 1974. A lively collection of views regarding political and ethical issues in social science. Ritzer has done an excellent job of presenting widely divergent views regarding the same issue. This book not only portrays "social realities," it will also give you an opportunity to make up your own mind in these matters.

PART TWO
The Structuring of Inquiry

Posing problems properly is often more difficult than answering them. Indeed, a properly phrased question often seems to answer itself. You may have discovered the answer to a question just in the process of making the question clear to someone else.

At base, scientific research is a process for achieving generalized understanding through observation. Part Three of this book describes some of the specific methods of social scientific observation. Part Two deals with what should be observed. Put differently, Part Two considers the posing of proper scientific questions, the structuring of inquiry.

Chapter 4 addresses the beginnings of research. It examines some of the purposes of inquiry, the units of analysis and topics of social scientific research, and the reasons scientists get involved in research projects.

Chapter 5 deals with the specification of what it is you want to study—a process called *conceptualization*. We're going to look at some of the terms that you and I use quite casually in everyday life—terms like *prejudice*, *liberalism*, *happiness*, and so forth—and we're going to see how essential it is to get clear about what we really mean by such terms when we do research.

Chapter 6 is an extension of Chapter 5. Once we have gotten clear on what we mean when we use certain terms, we are then in a position to create measurements of what those terms refer to. The process of devising steps or operations for measuring what we want to study is called *operationalization*. Chapter 6 deals with the topic of operationalization in general and with the concrete application of the process in the framing of questions to ask people.

Finally, we'll look at how social scientists go about selecting people or things for observation. Chapter 7, on *sampling*, addresses the fundamental scientific issue of *generalizability*. As we'll see, it is possible for us to select a few people or things for observation and then apply what we observe to a much larger group of people or things than we actually observed. It is possible, for example, to ask 1,000 Americans whom they favor for President of the United States and accurately predict how tens of millions will vote.

What you learn in Part Two will bring you to the verge of making controlled social scientific observations. Part Three will then show you how to take that next step.

CHAPTER 4
Research Design

INTRODUCTION

Science is an enterprise dedicated to "finding out." No matter what you want to find out, though, there are likely to be a great many ways of doing it. That's true in life generally. Suppose, for example, that you want to find out whether a particular automobile—say, the new Burpo-Blasto—would be a good car for you. You could, of course, buy one and find out that way. You could talk to a lot of B-B owners, or talk to people who considered buying one and didn't. You might check the classified ads to see if there were a lot of B-Bs being sold cheap. You could read a consumer magazine evaluation of Burpo-Blastos, or you could find out in a number of other ways. The same situation occurs in scientific inquiry.

Research design, the topic of this chapter, addresses the planning of scientific inquiry—designing a strategy for finding out something. Although the special details vary according to what you wish to study, there are two major aspects of research design. First, you must specify precisely what it is you want to find out. Second, you must determine the best way to do that. Interestingly, if you can handle the first consideration fully, you'll probably handle the second in the same process. Mathematicians point that out when they say that a properly framed question contains the answer within it.

Ultimately, scientific inquiry comes down to making observations and interpreting what you've observed. Parts Three and Four of this book deal with those two major aspects of social research. Part Three examines the various modes of observation available to the social researcher, and Part Four deals with data analysis. Before you can observe and analyze, however, you need a plan. You need to determine what you're going to observe and analyze: why and how. That's what research design is all about.

Let's say that you are interested in studying corruption in government. That's certainly a worthy and appropriate topic for social research. But what *specifically* are you interested in? What do you mean by *corruption*? What kinds of behavior do you have in mind? An essential step in your research design, then, would be the clarification of what you mean by corruption. And what do you mean by *government*? *Who* do you want to study: all public employees? only civilian employees? elected officials? civil servants? Finally, what is your purpose? Do you want to find out how much corruption there is? Do you want to learn why corruption exists? These are the kinds of questions that need to be answered in the course of research design.

This chapter provides a general introduction to research design, and subsequent chapters in Part Two elaborate on the specific aspects. We'll start with a brief examination of some main purposes for social research. Then, we'll consider **units of analysis**—the what or whom you want to study. This topic will be elaborated further in Chapter 7, which deals with sampling.

Next, we'll look at some topics of research. We'll see some of the things you can study when you observe the units of analysis you've chosen. Chapters 5 and 6 elaborate on this topic by discussing the process of refining your measurements of the things you want to study. As we'll see, this aspect of research design is inextricably tied to the method of observation that you'll use.

In practice, *all* the aspects of research design are interrelated. I have separated them here to permit a reasonably coherent presentation, but I want to warn you that I've created a somewhat artificial picture of research by doing that. In this chapter, I want to lay out the various possibilities for social research. In later chapters, the interrelationships among parts will become clearer.

The chapter concludes with two additional topics dealing with research design and a brief overview of the whole process. First, I want to draw your attention to alternative ways of handling *time* in social research. As we'll see, it is sometimes appropriate to examine a static cross section of social life, but other studies follow social processes across time.

Next, I've presented some discussions of the various motivations that can and do lie behind social research. Although these do not represent design decisions in the way that the other topics of the chapter do, I think it will be useful for you to have a broader understanding of the reasons social researchers have for engaging in social research.

Finally, the brief overview of the research process serves two purposes: (1) I want to give you a sense of how *you* might go about designing a study, and (2) I want to give you a map to the remainder of this book.

So, let's get started. We'll begin with the various purposes of social research.

PURPOSES OF RESEARCH

Social research, of course, serves many purposes. In this section, I want to mention three purposes that make a useful beginning for our discussion of research design. These three general purposes are *exploration*, *description*, and *explanation*. Although a given study can have more than one of these purposes—and most do—it will be useful to examine them separately because each has different implications for other aspects of research design.

Exploration

A great deal of social research is conducted to explore a topic, to provide a beginning familiarity with that topic. This purpose is typical when a researcher is examining a new interest or when the subject of study is itself relatively new and unstudied.

As an example, let's suppose that widespread taxpayer dissatisfaction with the government erupts into a taxpayers' revolt. People begin refusing to pay their taxes and they organize themselves around that issue. You might like to learn more about the movement: How widespread is it? What levels and degrees of support are there within the community? How is the movement organized? What kinds of people are active in it? You might undertake an exploratory study to obtain at least approximate answers to some of these questions. You might check figures with tax-collecting officials, collect and study the literature of the movement, and attend meetings and interview leaders.

Exploratory studies are also appropriate in the case of more persistent phenomena. Perhaps a college student is unhappy with the college's dormitory regulations and wants to work toward changing them. He or she might study the history of dormitory regulations at the college, meet with college officials to learn the reasons for the regulations, and talk to a number of students to get a rough idea of student sentiments on the subject. This latter activity would not necessarily yield a precise and accurate picture of student opinion, but it would give some guide to what probably would be discovered in a more careful study.

Exploratory studies are most typically done for three purposes: (1) simply to satisfy the researcher's curiosity and desire for better understanding, (2) to test the feasibility of undertaking a more careful study, and (3) to develop the methods to be employed in a more careful study. As an example of the last of these, a number of researchers at a major university, during the mid-to-late 1960s, were interested in studying the extent, sources, and consequences of the changes in student attitudes occurring at about that time. It was evident to a casual observer that many students were becoming active in radical politics, others were becoming "flower children," and still others seemed to have maintained a commitment to the more traditional collegiate orientations. The researchers were interested in learning the relative proportions of the student body in each category, the reasons for commitment to the various positions, and the possible consequences in terms of school performance, occupational plans, and so forth.

A large-scale survey of students was planned ultimately, but a difficulty was foreseen in devising a questionnaire to measure the several student orientations. In view of this difficulty, a small-scale exploratory study was made in which open-ended interviews were conducted with approximately 50 students who were selected so that some seemed to fit into each of the categories initially considered. In the interviews, respondents were asked very general questions about their orientations to college and to the society and were encouraged to give their answers in depth and in their own words. The answers given in the exploratory study provided many insights as to the complexities of the different major orientations and suggested ways in which those complexities could be tapped in a more structured questionnaire to be administered to a much larger sample.

Exploratory studies are very valuable in social scientific research. They are essential whenever a researcher is breaking new ground, and they can almost always yield new insights into a topic for research. The chief shortcoming of exploratory studies is that they seldom provide satisfactory answers to research questions. They can hint at the answers and can give insights into the research methods that could provide definitive answers. The reason exploratory studies are seldom definitive in themselves is the issue of representativeness, discussed at length in Chapter 7 in connection with sampling. Once you understand sampling and representativeness, you will be able to know whether a given exploratory study actually answered a given research problem or only pointed the way toward an answer.

Description

A major purpose of many social scientific studies is to describe situations and events. The researcher observes and then describes what was observed. Since scientific observation is careful and deliberate, however, scientific descriptions are typically more accurate and precise than casual descriptions.

The United States Census is an excellent example of a descriptive social scientific research project. The goal of the census is to describe accurately and precisely a wide variety of characteristics of the United States population, as well as the populations of smaller areas such as states and counties. Other examples of descriptive studies are the computation of age-sex profiles of populations done by demographers and the computation of crime rates for different cities.

A Gallup Poll conducted during a political election campaign has the purpose of describing the voting intentions of the electorate. A product marketing survey has the purpose normally of describing the people who use, or would use, a particular product. A researcher who carefully chronicles the events that take place during a student political demonstration has, or at least serves, a descriptive purpose. A researcher who computes and reports the number of times individual legislators voted for or against organized labor also has or serves a descriptive purpose.

Two aspects of social scientific description discussed in more detail in later chapters are worth mentioning at this point. They are the *quality* of descriptions and the *generalizability* of them. The first of these considerations will be examined in Chapter 5, which deals, among other things, with the quality criteria for measurement. The second consideration will be dealt with in Chapter 7 on sampling.

Explanation

The third general purpose of social scientific research is to explain things. Reporting the voting intentions of an electorate is a descriptive activity, but reporting *why* some people plan to vote for Candidate A and others for Candidate B is an explanatory activity. Reporting *why* some cities have higher crime rates than others is a case of explanation, but simply reporting the different crime rates is a case of

<u>description</u>. A researcher has an explanatory purpose if he or she wishes to know why a student demonstration ended in a violent confrontation with police, as opposed to simply describing that it happened.

The logic of explanation is the subject of several chapters in Part Four of this book, and it is much too complicated to be summarized here. It is sufficient now for us to realize that explanation normally involves the examination of many different aspects of a situation or event simultaneously. In the design of a research project, then, it is essential that all those aspects be incorporated in the plan for observation and analysis.

Although it is useful to distinguish the three purposes of research, it bears repeating that most studies will have elements of all three. Suppose, for example, that you have set out to evaluate a new form of psychotherapy. There will be exploratory aspects to the study, as you map out the impacts of the therapy. You will want to describe recovery rates, and you will undoubtedly seek to explain why the therapy works better for some types of people than for others.

You will see these several purposes at work in the following discussions of other aspects of research design. Let's turn now to a consideration of whom or what you want to explore, describe, and explain.

UNITS OF ANALYSIS

In social scientific research, there is a wide range of variation in what or whom is studied. By this, I do not mean the *topics* of research but what are technically called the *units of analysis*. To clarify this further, I may note that social scientists most typically perhaps have individual people as their units of analysis. You may make observations describing the characteristics of a large number of individual people, such as their sexes, ages, regions of birth, attitudes, and so forth. You then aggregate the descriptions of the many individuals so as to provide a descriptive picture of the population that those several individuals comprise. For example, you may note the age and sex of each individual student enrolled in Political Science 110 and then characterize the students as a group as being 53 percent men and 47 percent women, and as having a mean age of 18.6 years.

What I have just described would be a descriptive analysis of the students taking Political Science 110. Although the final description would be of the class as a whole, the individual students in it would be the units of analysis, the units whose individual characteristics are aggregated for purposes of describing some larger group.

The same situation would exist in an explanatory study. Suppose that you wished to discover whether students with a high grade point average received better grades in Political Science 110 than did students with a low grade point average. A relevant study would measure the grade point averages and the P.S. 110 grades of individual students. You might then aggregate all those students with a high grade point average and aggregate all those with a low grade point average and see which group received the best grades in the course. The purpose of the study would be to explain why some students do better in the course than others (looking at overall grade point averages as a possible explanation), but individual students would still be the units of analysis.

Units of analysis, then, are those units that we initially describe for the ultimate purpose of aggregating their characteristics in order to describe some larger group or explain some abstract phenomenon. This concept should be clarified further as we now consider some possible social science units of analysis.

Individuals

As mentioned above, individual human beings are perhaps the most typical units of analysis for social scientific research. We tend to describe and explain social groups and interactions by aggregating and manipulating the descriptions of individual persons.

Any variety of individuals may be the unit of analysis for social scientific research. This point is more important than it may seem at first reading. The norm of *generalized understanding* in social science would suggest that scientific findings are most valuable when they apply to *all* kinds of people. In practice, however, social scientists seldom study all kinds of people. At the very least, their studies are typically limited to the people living in a single country, though some comparative studies stretch across national boundaries. Often, our studies are even more circumscribed.

Examples of circumscribed groups whose members may be units of analysis—at the individual level—would be students, residents, workers, voters, parents, and faculty members. Note that each of these terms implies some population of individual persons. The term *students* implies some population of *all* students (at a given school, in a given class, and so forth); *residents* implies a population of all residents (of a certain place). The term *population* will be considered in some detail in Chapter 7 on sampling. At this point, it is sufficient to realize that descriptive studies that have individuals as their units of analysis typically aim at describing the population that those individuals comprise, whereas explanatory studies aim at discovering the social dynamics operating within that population.

Groups

Social groups may also be the units of analysis for social scientific research. Realize that this case is not the same as studying the individuals within a group. Families, for example, might be the units of analysis in a study. You might describe each family in terms of its total annual income and according to whether or not it had a color television set. You could aggregate families and describe the mean income of families and the percentage with color television sets. You would then be in a position to determine whether families with higher incomes were more likely to have color television sets than those with lower incomes. The individual *family* in such a case would be the unit of analysis.

Other units of analysis—at the group level—could be friendship cliques, street gangs, married couples, census blocks, cities, or geographical regions. Realize that each of these terms also implies some population. *Street gangs* implies some population that includes all street gangs. The population of street gangs could be described, say, in terms of its geographical distribution throughout a city, and an explanatory study of street gangs might discover, say, whether large gangs were more likely to engage in intergang warfare than were small ones.

When social groups are the unit of analysis, their characteristics may be derived from the characteristics of their individual members. Thus, a family might be described in terms of the age, race, or education of its head. In a descriptive study, then, we might examine and report the percentage of all families that have a college-educated head of family. In an explanatory study, we might determine whether families with a college-educated head have, on the average, more or fewer children than families with heads who have not graduated from college. In each of these examples, however, the family would be the unit of analysis. (Had we asked whether college graduates—college-educated *individuals*—have more or fewer children than their less educated counterparts, then the individual *person* would have been the unit of analysis.)

Social groups, and also individuals, may be characterized in other ways: for instance, in terms of their environments or their membership in larger groupings. Families, for example, might be described in terms of the type of dwelling unit they reside in, and we might want to determine whether rich families are more likely to reside in single-family houses (as opposed, say, to apartments) than are poor families. The unit of analysis would still be the family.

Individuals, as the units of analysis, may be characterized in terms of their membership in social groupings. Thus, an individual may be described as belonging to a rich family or to a poor one, or a person may be described as having a college-educated mother or not having one. We might examine in a research project whether people with college-educated mothers are more likely to attend college than are those with non-college-educated mothers, or whether high school graduates in rich families are more likely to attend college than are those in poor families. In each case, the individual would be the unit of analysis—not the mother or the family.

Organizations

Formal social organizations may also be the units of analysis in social scientific research. An example would be corporations, implying, of course, a population of all corporations. Individual corporations might be characterized in terms of their number of employees, their net annual profits, gross assets, number of defense contracts, percentage of employees who are from racial or ethnic minority groups, and so forth. In a descriptive study, we might examine the average net profit of all corporations. In an explanatory study, we might determine whether large corporations employ a larger percentage of minority group employees or a smaller percentage than is true of small corporations.

Other examples of formal social organizations suitable as units of analysis would be churches, colleges, army divisions, academic departments, and super-markets. Each of these units of analysis could be characterized in terms of its organizational characteristics, descriptions of its elements, or descriptions of larger groupings to which it belonged.

A further set of related examples should point out the possible complexity of the issue of units of analysis. If you ask whether companies whose employees have many preschool-age children are more likely to establish day-care programs than com-panies whose employees have few preschool-age children, this question suggests that your unit of analysis is the company. If you ask whether workers with many preschool-age children are more likely to work at companies with day-care pro-grams than are workers with fewer preschool-age children, this question suggests your unit of analysis is the individual worker. If, finally, you ask whether children whose parents work for companies with day-care programs are more likely to attend *some* day-care program than are children whose parents do not work at such com-panies, this question suggests that the unit of analysis is the individual child.

If all this seems unduly complicated, you may take some assurance that in most research projects you are likely to undertake, the unit of analysis will be relatively clear to you. When the unit of analysis is not so clear, however, it is absolutely essential to determine what it is; otherwise, it will be impossible to determine what observations are to be made about whom or what.

Some studies have the purpose of making descriptions or explanations pertain-ing to more than one unit of analysis. In these cases, it is imperative that the re-searcher anticipate what conclusions he or she wishes to draw with regard to what units of analysis.

Social Artifacts

Another large group of possible units of analysis may be referred to generally as *social artifacts*, or the products of social beings or their behavior. One class of artifacts would include social objects such as books, poems, paintings, automobiles, buildings, songs, pottery, jokes, and scientific discoveries.

Each of these objects implies a population of all such objects: all books, all novels, all biographies, all introductory sociology textbooks, all cookbooks. A description of an individual book might characterize it in terms of its size, weight, length, price, content, number of pictures, volume of sale, or descriptions of its author. The population of all books or of a particular kind of book could be analyzed for the purpose of description or explanation.

A social scientist could analyze whether paintings by Russians, Chinese, or American artists showed the greatest degree of working-class consciousness, taking paintings as the units of analysis and describing each, in part, by the nationality of its creator. You might examine a local newspaper's editorials regarding a local univer-sity for purposes of describing, or perhaps explaining, changes in the newspaper's editorial position on the university over time; individual editorials would be the units of analysis.

Social interactions form another class of social artifacts suitable for social scientific research. Weddings would be an example. Weddings might be characterized as racially or religiously mixed or not, religious or secular in ceremony, resulting in divorce or not, or they could be characterized in terms of descriptions of one or both of the marriage partners. Realize that when a researcher reports that weddings between partners of different religions are more likely to be performed by secular authorities than those between partners of the same religion, the weddings are the units of analysis and not the individual partners to them.

Other examples of social interactions that might be the units of analysis in social scientific research are friendship choices, court cases, traffic accidents, divorces, fistfights, ship launchings, airline hijackings, race riots, and congressional hearings.

Summary

The purpose of this section has been to stretch your imagination somewhat regarding possible units of analysis for social scientific research. Although individual human beings are typically the units of analysis, that need not be the case. Indeed, many research questions could more appropriately be answered through the examination of other units of analysis.

The concept of the unit of analysis may seem more complicated than it needs to be. It is irrelevant whether you classify a given unit of analysis as a group, a formal organization, or a social artifact. It is essential, however, that you be able to identify what your unit of analysis *is*. You must decide whether you are studying marriages or marriage partners, crimes or criminals, corporations or corporate executives. Unless you keep this point in mind constantly, you run the risk of making assertions about one unit of analysis based on the examination of another.

At this point it is appropriate to introduce briefly two important concepts related to units of analysis: the *ecological fallacy* and *reductionism*. The first of these concepts, the *ecological fallacy*, means the danger, just mentioned, of making assertions about one unit of analysis based on the examination of another. Let's consider a hypothetical illustration of this fallacy.

Suppose we are interested in learning something about the nature of electoral support received by a female political candidate in a recent city-wide election. Let's assume that we have the vote tally for each precinct so that we can tell which precincts gave her the greatest support and which gave her the least. Assume also that we have census data describing some of the characteristics of those precincts.

Our analyses of such data might show that those precincts whose voters were relatively young gave the female candidate a greater proportion of their votes than those precincts whose voters had an older average age. We would be tempted to conclude from these findings that young voters were more likely to vote for the female candidate than were older voters—that age affected support for the woman. In reaching such a conclusion, we run the risk of committing the *ecological fallacy* because it may have been the older voters in those "young" precincts who voted for the woman. Our problem is that we have examined *precincts* as our units of analysis and wish to draw conclusions about *voters*.

The same problem would arise if we discovered that crime rates were higher in cities having large black populations than in those with few blacks. We would not know if the crimes were actually committed by blacks. Or if we found suicide rates higher in Protestant countries than in Catholic ones, we still could not know for sure that more actual suicides were committed by Protestants than Catholics.

In another example, let's assume that the students attending High School A come from families having a higher average income than those students attending High School B. Assume further that High School A sends a higher proportion of its students on to college than does High School B. That, in and of itself, does not necessarily mean that students from wealthy families are more likely to attend college than those from poor families. It is possible—in both schools—that rich and poor students have the same likelihood of attending college, and that those in High School A are more likely overall to attend college than those in High School B.

Notice that very often the social scientist must address a particular research question through an ecological analysis such as those mentioned above. Perhaps the most appropriate data are simply not available. For example, the precinct vote tallies and the precinct characteristics mentioned in our initial example might be easily obtained, but we may not have the resources necessary to conduct a postelection survey of individual voters. In such cases, we may reach a tentative conclusion, recognizing and noting the risk we run in terms of the ecological fallacy.

The second concept that I wish to mention at this point is *reductionism*. Basically, *reductionism* refers to an overly strict limiting of the kinds of concepts and variables to be considered in understanding a broad range of human behavior. Sociologists may tend to consider only sociological variables (values, norms, roles); economists may consider only economic variables (supply and demand, marginal value); psychologists may consider only psychological variables (personality types, traumas). For example, what caused the American Revolution? a shared commitment to the value of individual liberty? the economic plight of the colonies in relation to Britain? the megalomania of the Founding Fathers? Scientists from different disciplines would tend to look at different types of answers and would ignore others. Explaining all or most human behavior in terms of economic factors is called *economic reductionism*; explaining all or most human behavior in terms of psychological factors is called *psychological reductionism*; and so forth.

This concept is related to our present discussion, since reductionism of any type tends to suggest particular units of analysis as being more relevant than others. If we were to regard shared values as the cause of the American Revolution, our unit of analysis would be the individual colonist. An economist, on the other hand, might choose the thirteen different colonies as units of analysis and examine the economic organizations and conditions of each colony. The psychologist might choose individual leaders as the units of analysis for purposes of examining their personalities.

This fault, like the ecological fallacy, occurs with the use of inappropriate units of analysis. The appropriate unit of analysis for a given research question, however, is not always clear, and it is often debated by social scientists, especially across disciplinary boundaries.

TOPICS FOR RESEARCH

The preceding discussion of different possible units of analysis has frequently mentioned their *characteristics*. Now let's turn to the range of possible characteristics, seen as *topics* for research. In order to present a general overview of this range, I'll consider three classes: *conditions*, *orientations*, and *actions*.

Conditions

To begin, the various units of analysis may be characterized in terms of their conditions or their states of being. Individual persons might be characterized by such states as sex, age, height, marital status, deformities, region of origin, or hearing ability. Social groups and formal organizations might be characterized, fo: example, by their size, structure, location, and aggregated descriptions of their members. Physical objects as social artifacts might be described in terms of their physical characteristics such as size, weight, and color, or by the characteristics of the humans associated with them. Social interactions as units of analysis might be characterized in terms of where they occur, when they occur, or what the people involved are like.

These examples are not intended to represent an exhaustive list of possibilities. Nevertheless, they should suggest the kinds of conditions that may be used to characterize the units of analysis.

Orientations

In the study of individual people as the units of analysis, we frequently investigate what are called *orientations*: attitudes, beliefs, personality traits, prejudices, predispositions, and the like. Individuals might be characterized as religious, politically liberal, anti-Semitic, intellectually sophisticated, superstitious, scientific.

Social groups and formal organizations, similarly, might be characterized in terms of their purposes, policies, regulations, or procedures, or in terms of the aggregated orientations of their members.

Social interactions might be similarly characterized. Airline hijackings might be characterized as politically or nonpolitically motivated. So could court cases and congressional hearings.

Actions

Sometimes social *action* is the focus of research. We may observe directly or accept secondhand accounts of individual human actions such as voting, bond buying, investing, striking, dropping out of school, going to church, or buying Brand X toothpaste. Secondhand accounts of actions may be obtained from the participants themselves or from other sources. Thus, to find out whether people have registered to vote, we might ask them, or we might check the list of registered voters.

Social groups and formal organizations act as well. Families may go on picnics, pray together, fight over money, or move to another city. Fraternities may sponsor concerts; sororities may collect money to send girls to camp. Corporations may contribute to political campaigns, merge with other corporations, fix prices, or go bankrupt.

Since social interactions are actions themselves, it is a little more difficult to imagine them engaging in actions. Nevertheless, marriages succeed or fail, court cases result in conviction or acquittal, and fistfights cool off or get out of hand.

Summary

Like the earlier discussion of units of analysis, the present section on topics for research is intended as a mind-expanding exercise, not as a definitive statement of all the possible or legitimate topics. It matters little at this point whether you regard a person's score on an IQ test as a condition, an orientation, or an action—only that you recognize it as a possible focus of study.

Chapters 5 and 6 will return to these issues with a more rigorously analytical perspective.

THE TIME DIMENSION

Time plays a number of roles in the design and execution of research, quite aside from the time it takes to do research. When we examine causation in detail in Part Four, we'll find that the time sequence of events and situations is a critical element in determining causation. Time is also involved in the issue of the generalizability of research findings. Do the descriptions and explanations that result from a particular study accurately represent the situation of 10 years ago, 10 years from now, or do they represent only the present state of affairs?

Thus far in this chapter, we have regarded research design as a process for deciding *what aspects* we shall observe, *of whom*, and *for what purpose*. Now we must consider another set of options that is time-related and that cuts across each of these earlier considerations. Our observations may be made at more or less one time, or they may be deliberately stretched over a longer period.

Cross-Sectional Studies

Many research projects are designed to study some phenomenon by taking a cross section of it at one time and analyzing that cross section carefully. Exploratory and descriptive studies are often **cross-sectional**. A single United States Census, for instance, is a study aimed at a description of the United States population at a given time.

Many explanatory studies are also cross-sectional. A researcher who conducted a large-scale national survey to examine the sources of racial and religious prejudice would, in all likelihood, be dealing with a single time frame in the ongoing process of prejudice.

Explanatory, cross-sectional studies have an inherent problem. Typically, they are directed at the understanding of causal processes that occur over time, yet the conclusions are based on observations made at only one time. This problem is somewhat akin to that of determining the speed of a moving object on the basis of a high-speed, still photograph that freezes the movement of the object. A following subsection of this chapter as well as Chapter 16 will present some of the ways in which you can deal with this difficult problem.

Longitudinal Studies

Other research projects are designed to permit observations over an extended period. An example of that is a researcher who participates in and observes the activities of a radical political group from the time of its inception to its demise. The analysis of newspaper editorials or Supreme Court decisions over time provides other examples. In the latter instances, it would be irrelevant whether the researcher's observations and analyses were made at one time or over the course of the actual events under study.

Three special types of **longitudinal studies** should be noted here. **Trend studies** are those that study changes within some general population over time. Examples would be a comparison of United States Censuses over time, showing growth in the national population, or a series of Gallup Polls during the course of an election campaign, showing trends in the relative strengths and standing of different candidates.

Cohort studies examine more specific subpopulations (cohorts) as they change over time. Typically, a cohort is an age group, such as those people born during the 1920s, but it can also be based on some other time grouping, such as people attending college during the Viet Nam war, people who got married in 1964, and so forth. Cohort studies follow such groups across time. An example would be a series of national surveys, conducted perhaps every 10 years, to study the economic attitudes of the cohort composed of those persons born during the depression of the early 1930s. A sample of persons 20–25 years of age might be surveyed in 1950, another sample of those 30–35 years of age in 1960, and another sample of those 40–45 years of age in 1970. Although the specific set of people studied in each of those surveys would be different, each sample would represent the survivors of the cohort born between 1930 and 1935.

Panel studies are similar to trend and cohort studies except that the same set of people is studied each time. One example would be a voting study in which the same sample of voters were interviewed every month during an election campaign and asked for whom they intended to vote. Such a study would make it possible to analyze overall trends in voter preferences for different candidates, but it would have the added advantage of showing the precise patterns of persistence and change in intentions. For example, a trend study which showed that Candidates A and B each had exactly half of the voters on September first and on October first as well could indicate that none of the electorate had changed voting plans, that all of the voters had changed their intentions, or something in between. A panel study would eliminate this confusion by showing what kinds of voters switched from A to B and what kinds switched from B to A, as well as other facts.

Longitudinal studies have an obvious advantage over cross-sectional ones in providing information describing processes over time. But very often this advantage comes at a heavy cost in both time and money, especially in a large-scale survey. Observations may have to be made at the time events are occurring, and the method. of observation may require the employment of many research workers.

Approximating Longitudinal Studies

Often it is possible to draw approximate conclusions about processes that take place over time even when only cross-sectional data are available. It is worth noting some of the ways to do that.

Sometimes, cross-sectional data imply processes over time on the basis of simple logic. For example, a study of student drug use was conducted at the University of Hawaii in 1969. Students were asked to report whether they had ever tried each of a number of illegal drugs. With regard to marijuana and LSD, it was found that some students had tried both drugs, some had tried only one, and others had not tried either. Since these data were collected at one time, and since some students presumably would experiment with drugs later on, it would appear that such a study could not tell the *order* in which students were likely to experiment with marijuana and LSD: were students more likely to try marijuana or LSD first?

A closer examination of the data showed, however, that although some students reported having tried marijuana but not LSD, there were no students in the study who had tried only LSD. From this finding it was inferred—as common wisdom suggested—that marijuana use preceded LSD use. If the process of drug experimentation occurred in the opposite time order, then a study at a given time should have found some students who had tried LSD but had not gone on to try marijuana, and it should have found no students who had tried only marijuana.

Logical inferences may also be made whenever the time order of variables is clear. If we discovered in a cross-sectional study of college students that those educated in private high schools received better college grades than those educated in public high schools, we would conclude that the type of high school attended affected college grades, not the other way around. Thus, even though our observations were made at only one time, we would feel justified in drawing conclusions about processes taking place across time.

Very often, age differences discovered in a cross-sectional study form the basis for inferring processes across time. Suppose you are interested in the pattern of worsening health over the course of the typical life cycle. You might examine that by studying the results of annual checkups in a large hospital. You could group the health records according to the ages of those examined and rate each age group in terms of several health conditions—sight, hearing, blood pressure, and so forth. By reading across the age group ratings for each health condition, you would have something approximating the health history of individuals. Thus, you might conclude that the average person develops vision problems earlier in life than hearing problems, for example.

Asking people to *recall* their pasts is another common way of approximating observations over time. We use that method when we ask people where they were born or when they graduated from high school or whom they voted for in 1976. The danger in this technique is evident. Sometimes people have faulty memories; sometimes they lie. When people are asked in postelection polls whom they voted for, the results inevitably show more people voting for the winner than did so on election day. Thus, although recall may be the only way of approximating observations across time, it must be used with caution.

These, then, are some of the ways in which time figures into social research and some of the ways social scientists have learned to cope with it. In designing any study, you need to look at both the explicit and implicit assumptions you are making about time in whatever you are studying. Are you interested in describing some process that occurs over time, or are you simply going to describe what exists now? If you want to describe a process occurring over time, will you be able to make observations at different points in the process, or will you have to approximate such observations—drawing logical inferences from what you can observe now? Unless you pay attention to questions like these, you are likely to end up in trouble.

MOTIVATIONS FOR RESEARCH

So far, I've sketched out some of the sets of options available to you in doing social research: some of the purposes that may be served by inquiry, the different units of analysis appropriate for observation and analysis, some types of topics you can study, and finally some of the choices you can make with regard to time. I've kept the discussion reasonably abstract so as to expand your perspective on what's possible and reasonable. There's a potential problem in this approach that I'd like to handle now.

Abstraction inevitably comes at a cost to concreteness. At this point, for example, you may have a broad view of the possibilities for social research, and you might be able to do well on a short-answer examination dealing with research design, but you may not have a very concrete picture of what research design looks like in practice. You might not feel too confident about how to *design* research. To remedy this possible situation, I want to give some illustrations of concrete research designs.

As a way of organizing the illustrations, we're going to take a somewhat different approach to the purposes social research can serve. The illustrations that follow are organized around the various *motivations* that researchers can have in designing and conducting research. Over the course of the several different illustrations, you should develop a clearer, more realistic sense of the ways in which social research gets started.

Testing Formal Theories

Sometimes, rather ambitious social scientists attempt to frame an understanding of all or a sizable portion of social reality. (That is not advisable as a class project.) For a hypothetical illustration of this process, discussed previously in Chapter 1, let's try our hands at deriving a comprehensive theory of social behavior.

A formal deductive theory begins with one or more postulates, or basic premises. (Realize, of course, that these will have grown out of prior observations, including, perhaps, rigorous empirical research.) Let's begin with the postulate: *All social behavior is based on self-interest.* We might further specify this postulate as follows: *Given a choice among alternative action possibilities, a person will choose that action which best corresponds to his or her own self-interest.*

No sooner have we printed this neatly at the top of a clean page in our Big 5 tablet than we immediately think of hundreds of examples of people acting in ways that go directly contrary to their self-interest. Further specification is clearly in order. We might begin by introducing the notion of *perceived* self-interest, thereby allowing a person to choose the "wrong" action thinking it was the "right" one. Correspondingly, we would want to introduce the notion of a *perceived* choice to take account of those who did not know they had a choice. We would want to be sure to build in *no action* as one of the choices for the situation in which a person does not perceive any one of the action possibilities as being more in his or her self-interest than the others.

Before long, we would be forced to delineate various types of perceived self-interest: biological, economic, psychological, and others. Having done that, we might address the issue of priority ranking of the different types, either as might apply universally among all people or as might apply among different kinds of people or under different conditions. This consideration would permit us to handle those situations in which one action most closely corresponds to economic self-interest while another corresponds most closely to psychological self-interest. (Will a person accept a promotion at work, acquiring a raise in pay but also the insecurity of added responsibilities?)

As we pursue this sort of activity, we shall develop two types of statements: those that we postulate as the basic premises upon which our theory is grounded, and those that are derived logically from the beginning premises. In this process, we'd have two goals: (1) to develop a comprehensive theory of social behavior, covering all its aspects, and (2) to arrive at more specific statements about the types of behavior to be expected in different types of situations. Statements of this latter kind are called *hypotheses*. In stating a hypothesis, the social scientist says that (a) if the basic premises are correct and (b) if the derivations are logically correct, then the behavior specified in the hypothesis should be observed in reality.

For purposes of illustration, let's suppose that our derivation of a self-interest theory of social behavior has progressed to the point at which we are prepared to state the following hypothesis: *Persons who experience economic deprivation during socialization will place a higher priority on economic self-interest later in life than will those persons who do not experience economic deprivation during socialization.* Now we would have a hypothesis, but one that could not be tested immediately. Before testing the hypothesis, we would have to (1) specify the several concepts contained in it, (2) select a research method and research setting appropriate to testing, and (3) determine and obtain the resources needed. In practice, these several decisions are interwoven, and their relative importance will vary from one situation to another.

The specification of our concepts, for example, might be already pretty clear in our minds. Indeed, the hypothesis may have been suggested in part by some real-life situation that could imply the most appropriate method and setting, and having settled these factors, we could determine the amount and kind of resources needed.

On the other hand, it might be that we were qualified in the use of only a particular research method, say, survey research, participant observation, or small-group experimentation. If so, we would be limited in the ways in which we might specify our concepts and test the hypothesis. Or we might find ourselves effectively limited to a particular research setting, say, students enrolled in a social science methods class. This latter example is a typical limit to the resources available for research.

Although a large, national grant-giving agency would be unlikely to be interested in funding a test of the particular hypothesis in our illustration, very frequently it would be appropriate to seek support for research. Possibly we could obtain support for basic research on a theory of social behavior, but we would be more likely to do so if we envisioned a more or less practical concern to which the hypothesis might be related. Typically, that would require testing the hypothesis within a broader setting, but since the hypothesis itself is already part of a broader theoretical context, a large-scale research project might test a substantial portion of the theory.

For purposes of our illustration, though, let's assume that there is no support for the research; we are, for some reason, interested in testing only our particular hypothesis; and we don't have much time to devote to it. (Please note: this exercise in realism is not intended as a lesson on how research ought to be done.) Thus, we test the hypothesis among that class of methodology students mentioned before.

Although these conditions do not inexorably fix the research method to be used, it seems likely that we would choose survey research because of economy and efficiency. We decide, therefore, to administer a questionnaire to the class. To do this, we must construct a questionnaire that will solicit data relevant to testing our hypothesis. There are, of course, many ways in which we might do this, but let's consider only one or two examples here.

Our hypothesis contains two key variables: *economic deprivation during socialization* and *current priority of economic self-interest*. Our questionnaire, then, should measure both variables among the students being studied. We might measure economic deprivation during socialization in a number of ways: ask for subjective assessments from the students, ask them for estimates of family income during the period in question, or ask for reports on various possessions of their families during the period. In the first of these, for example, we might ask: "During most of the time you were growing up, would you say your family was better off financially than other families, worse off, or about the same as other families?" As to specific possessions, we might ask: "How many cars, if any, did your family have when you started school?" In practice, we'd design several questions similar to these examples, attempting to tap several different aspects of economic deprivation and asking for both objective and subjective reports.

Current priority of economic self-interest might also be measured in a number of ways. Since the units of analysis are all students, we might ask: "In thinking of your future career, how important would you say it is for you to earn a high salary? Extremely important, very important, fairly important, or not very important?" Or, we might ask them to rank a high salary with other possible characteristics of their careers such as responsibility, helping people, or creativity.

These two sets of questions, and others, would permit us to classify students in terms of the two key variables in the hypothesis. They could be ranked in terms of their relative economic deprivation during socialization and in terms of their current concern over economic self-interest. We would, therefore, administer the questionnaire, process the data, and analyze the relationship between the two variables.

Although survey research seems to be the likely method in this situation, we might have tested the hypothesis in other ways. We might note that certain college majors are generally assumed to lead to higher-paying jobs than others: engineering is assumed to be better than English, for example. Moreover, we might surmise that students economically deprived during socialization would be more likely to need financial assistance during college than others. These premises would suggest, therefore, that engineering majors should be overrepresented among those seeking financial aid (loans, student jobs) and English majors should be underrepresented. Perhaps the student aid office at our university would provide us with a tally of the majors of loan and job applicants. Let's assume that engineering majors make up 10 percent of the total student body, but they make up 20 percent of the loan and job applicants; and let's assume that English majors make up 15 percent of the total student body but only 2 percent of the loan and job applicants. These findings would support our hypothesis.

I know that you may feel a little uneasy with this second test of our hypothesis; it is so indirect and involves additional assumptions that may not be so. Realize that this way of testing the hypothesis is not ideal. I've included it for two reasons. First, I want to be realistic, and you will often find that you lack the resources to conduct what would seem like the ideal study. Second, and related to the first reason, I want you to develop a facility for finding feasible approximations of ideal methods when the ideal methods are not feasible. Recall, for example, Stouffer's study of the effects of the depression on the family.

Although the research situation described above, testing a general theory, is perhaps the most well known, it is nonetheless the least typical. One good example, however, would be Samuel Stouffer's attempt to test a portion of Talcott Parsons's general theory of action: that portion dealing with *pattern variables*.[1]

In part, Parsons's theory dealt with standards that determine social action. He considered situations in which *universalistic* standards would be applied—standards that are the same regardless of which *social actors* are involved in a situation. For example, judges should apply the same standards to all defendants appearing before them in court. Parsons also considered situations in which *particularistic* standards would be applied—different standards for different people. In a family, for example, parents might have different standards for older children than for younger ones. (Realize that these concepts have far more general applicability than these specific examples suggest.)

Parsons was also concerned, at a general theoretical level, with situations in which universalistic and particularistic standards might conflict. Consider, for example, the policeman who discovers his own son burglarizing a store or speeding. His role as policeman would in all likelihood conflict with his role as father.

Stouffer directed his attention specifically to the question of role conflict with regard to particularistic and universalistic standards. His research, in this instance, consisted of a survey of Harvard students; in it they were presented with hypothetical situations in which they witnessed friends of theirs breaking laws and rules. Would they act in accord with the universalistic standards pertaining to law breaking, or in accord with the particularistic standards more appropriate to friendship relations?

Stouffer's research, while testing Parsons's theoretical derivations, contributed to the theory itself by pointing to additional specifications required for a full understanding of social behavior. In addition, it provides an excellent example of the procedures involved in making concrete measurements appropriate to abstract theoretical concepts (a topic to be addressed in detail in Chapters 5 and 6).

The Parsons-Stouffer example also illustrates the frequent division of labor in the social sciences. A separation of theory and research has characterized the social sciences in recent decades: some social scientists are primarily noted for the derivation of social theories, while others are primarily noted for their empirical research efforts. Thus, we frequently find some social scientists conducting research in order to test or refine the theories developed by others. To the extent that specialization promotes better theories and better research, this situation is advantageous to the progress of social science. At the same time, it can be dysfunctional. Researchers may not fully understand the theories they attempt to test; theorists might develop better theories if they more fully understood the logic of scientific research methods.

Testing Limited Hypotheses

In practice, few research projects in the social sciences seek to test substantial portions of general theories. Although some empirical research is aimed at testing

[1]See Talcott Parsons and Edward A. Shils, *Toward a General Theory of Action* (Cambridge: Harvard University Press, 1954), pp. 479–496.

portions of comprehensive theories, more research is concerned with developing and testing limited theoretical hypotheses. Often these hypotheses have no direct reference to general theories. Sometimes the social scientist will begin with a particular interest in some area of social life, attempt to derive a theoretical understanding of it, and then conduct research aimed at testing a limited hypothesis.

Let's suppose you have an interest in superpatriotic political movements in the United States. Whereas the desire to frame a general and comprehensive theory of social behavior would lead you to a consideration of first principles, a more limited interest such as this one would probably begin with a review of your own observations and previous research, perhaps by others, on the specific topic. You might then attempt to place the specific topic within a more general theoretical context. How do superpatriotic political movements fit into the context of political attitudes and movements of all types, and perhaps even nonpolitical attitudes and movements?

You might discard the notion that members of superpatriotic movements are simply more patriotic than other people, based on your interpretation of the idea of patriotism as loyalty to one's country. Thus, you would look for another explanation.

Being a good social scientist, you might note that group membership has as one of its functions an effect on the member's social identification. Thus, membership in a superpatriotic political movement would lead to a member's being identified as superpatriotic, or perhaps clearly and unquestionably patriotic to the United States. Such an identity might, of course, be desired by most if not all Americans, but why do only a small minority seek such identification through involvement in such a movement? You might conclude that some people feel a greater need for patriotic certification than others. "Aha!" you say, "Those people whose loyalty to the United States might be questioned by others will be more in need of certification of their loyalty than others. Therefore, they will be more likely to join a superpatriotic political movement."

This line of reasoning would lead you to think about the ways in which a person's loyalty to the United States might be subject to question. First, note that members of the New Left—often criticized as disloyal and subversive—are, by definition, absent from the movements under consideration. Then, especially if you are a sociologist, you ask whether there might be some other social statuses that might raise questions of loyalty.

"Aha!" you say again, knowingly, "Persons who feel they might be identified with some other nation might feel their loyalty to the United States could be doubted." Thus, you conclude that persons identified, by themselves or by others, as foreigners might feel their American loyalty was subject to doubt, and they might attempt to prove loyalty through participation in superpatriotic organizations.

Having framed your hypothesis, you would then set about specifying it in terms of some research methodology and study design. You might, for example, analyze the membership lists of superpatriotic organizations, identifying "hyphenated" Americans—Italian-Americans, German-Americans, Polish-Americans—and compare the proportion of such members with their proportion in the total population. In this manner, you might determine whether such people are disproportionately represented in superpatriotic organizations.

As an alternative approach, you might design and conduct a survey of the general population, asking questions about national origins and about participation in superpatriotic organizations. In this instance, you might wish to collect additional information about political attitudes in general and also information about respondents' perceptions of how others might view their loyalty.

The manner in which a limited hypothesis might be tested is the same as that described earlier in the case of a comprehensive theory. The only differences lie in the manner in which the hypothesis is derived and in the implications of the results of testing it. In the case of a comprehensive theory, the results will reflect on the theory from which the hypothesis is derived, while in a test of a limited hypothesis, the implications are for the hypothesis only. (If the hypothesis in our example were disconfirmed, you would begin again to look for reasons for participation in superpatriotic organizations.)

Exploring Unstructured Interests

Quite often, a scientist will take an interest in a topic without having any clear ideas about what to expect in the way of relationships among variables. Let's suppose that you are a social science graduate student who is particularly interested in the issue of student representation on the standing committees of the department in which you are enrolled. Perhaps you believe that students deserve representation and that they would be able to make meaningful contributions to the operation of the department. Each time the matter is raised, however, you may get the feeling that faculty members are generally opposed to the idea. You want to learn more about the situation and to understand the reasons for opposition if it really exists.

Initially, you have no general theory of behavior from which to derive formal hypotheses regarding faculty attitudes toward student participation. Probably you have no hypotheses relating to this particular issue. Let's assume that all you have are concern and curiosity. Since the situation is so unstructured, you can choose from a number of methods for beginning your inquiry. Let's consider a few of them briefly.

You could find out whether other researchers have examined this issue. You might begin with a review of appropriate literature, utilizing the various indexing sources of the campus library, academic journals, and so forth. If you find relevant prior research, you should assess its applicability to the situation in your own department. Do the conditions studied by the prior researchers seem similar to or different from the conditions in your own department? Do the findings of the earlier studies make sense intuitively as you attempt to apply them to your department? Perhaps this exercise will adequately satisfy your curiosity regarding faculty attitudes toward student participation. Perhaps you will decide to replicate one or more of the prior studies within your own department, or perhaps the prior studies will suggest elements of a rather different study design.

As a different approach, you might examine the several departments comprising your college. Contact with the various departmental offices, for example, might provide you with information about student representation on the committees of assorted departments. If you discover that students have representation in some departments but not in others, you would then begin investigating the characteristics of those departments granting representation and those not granting it. You might consider such variables as number of faculty members, their average age, academic field, and ethnic and sex composition of faculty. If this examination produces fairly clear patterns of differences between those departments with and those without student representation, such patterns may help to explain the situation in your own department.

If you have discovered that some departments have student representation on committees, you might undertake a historical study of how such representation came about in those cases. You might be given access to the minutes of departmental meetings on the issue of representation. If you are barred from that, you might be able to construct a history of events through informal interviews with the students and faculty members who are involved.

Coming closer to home, you might conduct unstructured interviews with *informants* (in the less sinister, anthropological, sense) in your own department. You may discover that some faculty members can give you a good picture of the situation, based on their knowledge of the faculty and discussions of the issue. Such interviews might be coupled with some careful observations at faculty meetings—if you are permitted to attend. (Bugging faculty meetings or faculty restrooms is not an acceptable research technique.)

Finally, you might feel the necessity of a formal study of faculty attitudes within your department. Having been properly socialized in social research techniques, you decide to conduct a survey to assess the nature of sources of faculty attitudes on the issue of student representation on departmental committees. The design and content of your survey questionnaire will reflect the various insights gained from the research methods and activities previously discussed. You may replicate portions of earlier surveys, if any, and you will attempt to collect data relevant to the possible explanations suggested by your examination of other departments and your informal examination of your own.

The analysis of data collected in such a survey would be necessarily open-ended, since you would have no formal hypotheses to test. For this situation, it is rather difficult to provide a set of guidelines for undertaking the analysis, but a few general comments may be made.

Typically, studies of this sort aim at determining the sources and consequences of something: what causes it and what does it cause? If there is no other specific design, the most useful analytical format would appear to be the following. The researcher begins by constructing a workable measure of the *something* that constitutes the primary focus of the study—in this case, faculty attitude toward student representation on committees. For example, you may have asked several questions in the questionnaire that reflect such attitudes. You might then construct an index or scale to measure such attitudes in general. (See Chapter 15 for methods of index and scale construction.)

Next you should examine the relationship between the *something*, on the one hand, and those variables that precede it in time. In our present example, you might look for a possible correlation between such variables as age, sex, academic rank, and tenure status and attitudes toward student representation. If you discover several variables related to the attitudes in question, you should ask what else those variables may have in common and attempt to develop a general understanding of the sources of the attitudes.[2]

In our present example, the analysis might conclude with the formulation of specific hypotheses about the sources of faculty attitudes toward student representation, but frequently the researcher goes on to explore how the key variable affects other things.[3] In this example, you might examine how faculty attitudes toward student representation are related to other attitudes and actions.

Since there is a tendency among social scientists to regard the exploration of unstructured ideas as inferior to more structured inquiries, I should note that I do not take that position. Often research efforts that are largely unstructured at the outset may be more fruitful ultimately than those that are prestructured. In a structured inquiry, analysis all too often concludes with the testing of a prespecified hypothesis. In an unstructured inquiry, however, it concludes with our satisfying ourselves that we have discovered the best available answer to our general research question or that we are presently unable to discover an answer. There is a constant danger that structured inquiries may overlook relationships not anticipated by formal hypotheses. These comments are not made to encourage chaos and anarchy among social researchers. Rather, they are meant to suggest that there are many legitimate paths to scientific discovery, perhaps thereby helping those who fear to take the first step in the belief that all empirical inquiries must be preceded by the framing of formal hypotheses.

Contracted Research

With increased frequency, social scientists are being commissioned to engage in specific research projects, usually of an applied nature. A city government may commission a survey of unemployment rates; a business firm may commission an evaluation of its new apprenticeship program; a political aspirant may commission a poll of voters. Although researchers may occasionally be asked to undertake research that will add to basic scientific knowledge, contracted research typically is predicated on a need for specific facts and findings with policy implications. In other words, persons or agencies requesting such research usually plan to determine future

[2]An example of this process may be found in Charles Y. Glock, Benjamin B. Ringer, and Earl R. Babbie, *To Comfort and to Challenge* (Berkeley: University of California Press, 1967). Having discovered church involvement to be affected by sex, age, family status, and socioeconomic status, we were forced to consider what those disparate variables had in common; the result was the concept of social deprivation.
[3]Having determined the sources of church involvement (*ibid.*), we then set about to determine what difference it made. What effect might it have on other orientations and behaviors? As another example of this general approach to analysis, see Earl R. Babbie, *Science and Morality in Medicine* (Berkeley: University of California Press, 1970), a study that attempted to (a) measure the scientific orientations of medical school faculty members, (b) discover why some of them were more scientifically oriented than others, and (c) determine the consequences of scientific orientations on such things as humanitarian patient care.

courses of action on the basis of the research results. (Whether they ultimately do so is quite another matter.)

This research situation differs importantly from the earlier ones discussed in the present chapter. Whenever you seek to test a formal theory or an isolated hypothesis or when you seek to explore an unstructured interest, you yourself decide what will be the focus of inquiry. In contracted research, this decision is made by someone else. Your response to a request for such research involves a number of considerations and decisions. The priority of considerations and the order of decisions will vary in different situations.

Chapter 11 is addressed specifically to *evaluation research* and examines in detail the kinds of problems and special considerations that mark this form of inquiry. In addition to looking at the particular demands for research design in evaluation research, we'll also look at the special complications created by the role of the people sponsoring the research.

HOW TO DESIGN A RESEARCH PROJECT

The preceding discussions of various motivations for research should have given you a broader picture of what social research is all about. At the same time, you may have gotten a pretty clear idea of how *you* might go about designing and executing a research project of your own. In this concluding section of the chapter, I want to address that latter issue directly. Suppose *you* were going to undertake social research. Where would you begin?

Although research design occurs at the beginning of a research project, it involves all the steps that will follow. The comments to follow, then, (1) should give you some guidance on how to start a research project and (2) will preview the topics that follow in later chapters of the book. Ultimately, the research process needs to be seen as a *whole*, and you need to grasp it as a whole in order to create a research design. Unfortunately, both textbooks and human cognition operate on the basis of sequential *parts*. To handle that problem, then, I want to give you a quick overview of the whole, then you can study the parts in more detail in the rest of the book.

Figure 4-1 presents a schematic view of the social science research process. I present this view reluctantly, since it may suggest more of a "cookbook" order to research than is the case in practice. Nonetheless, as I've said, it should be useful to you to have some overview of the whole process before we launch into the specific details of particular components of research.

At the top of the diagram, I've represented interests, ideas, and theories as possible beginning points for a line of research. The letters (A, B, X, Y, and so forth) represent variables or concepts such as prejudice, anomie, and so on. Thus, you might have a general *interest* in finding out what causes some people to be more prejudiced than others, or you might want to know some of the consequences of anomie, say.

Alternatively, your inquiry might begin with a specific *idea* about the way things are. You might have the idea that working on an assembly line causes anomie, for

Figure 4-1   The Research Process

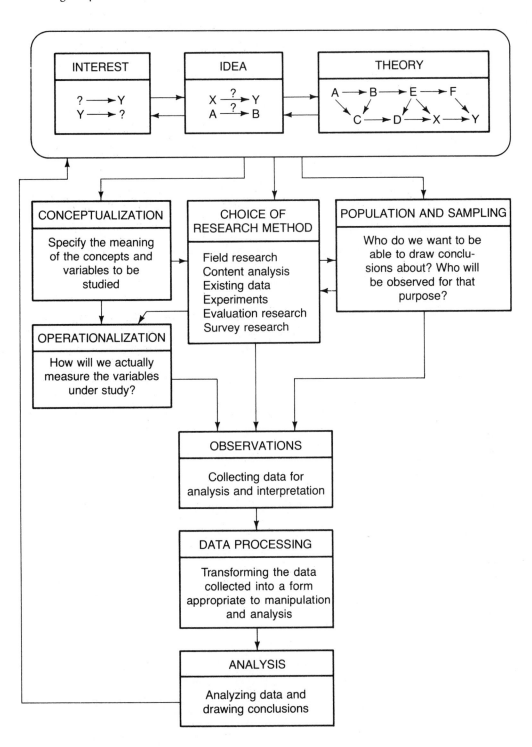

example. I have put a question mark in the diagram to indicate that you aren't sure things are the way you suspect they are.

Finally, I have represented a *theory* as a complex set of relationships among several variables. Notice, moreover, that there is a possible movement back and forth across these several possible beginnings. An initial interest may lead to the formulation of an idea, which may be fit into a larger theory, and the theory may produce new ideas and create new interests.

Any or all of these three may suggest the advisability of empirical research. As discussed earlier, the purpose of such research can be the exploration of an interest, the testing of a specific idea, or the validation of a complex theory. Whatever the purpose, a variety of decisions need to be made, as indicated in the remainder of the diagram.

Conceptualization. We tend to think loosely in terms of concepts such as *prejudice, anomie,* and so forth. but it's necessary to specify what we mean by these concepts in order to do research on them. Chapter 5 examines this process of conceptualization.

Choice of Research Method. As we'll see in Part Three of this book, there are a variety of research methods available to the social scientist. Each of those methods has its own special strengths and weaknesses, and certain concepts are more appropriately studied by some methods than by others.

Operationalization. Having specified the concepts to be studied and having chosen the research method to be used, we must create concrete measurement techniques. *Operationalization,* discussed in Chapter 6, refers to the concrete steps or operations that will be undertaken in measuring specific concepts.

Population and Sampling. In addition to refining concepts and measurements, decisions must be made in regard to *who* or *what* will be studied. The *population* for a study is that group (usually of people) about whom we want to be able to draw conclusions. The population might be all college students in America, marriages, or cities. We are almost never able to study all the members of the population that interests us, however. In virtually every case, then, we must sample subjects for study. Chapter 7 describes methods for selecting samples that give an adequate reflection of the whole population that interests us. Notice in the diagram that decisions about population and sampling are related to decisions about the research method to be used.

Observations. Having decided what to study among whom by what method, we are now ready to make observations—to collect empirical data. The chapters of Part Three, which describe the various research methods, give the different observation methods appropriate to each.

Data Processing. Depending on the research method chosen, you will have amassed a volume of observations in a form that probably isn't easily interpretable. Chapter 13 describes some of the ways in which social scientific data are processed or transformed for quantitative analysis.

Analysis. Finally we manipulate the collected data for the purpose of drawing conclusions that reflect on the interests, ideas, and theories that initiated the inquiry. Chapters 14 through 19 describe a few of the many options available to you in analyzing data. Notice that the results of your analyses feed back into your initial interests, ideas, and theories. In practice, this feedback may very well represent the beginning of another cycle of inquiry.

As this overview shows, research design involves a set of decisions regarding *what topic* is to be studied among *what population* with *what research methods* for *what purpose.* Whereas the earlier sections of this chapter—dealing with research purposes, units of analysis, topics—aimed at broadening your perspective in all these regards, research design is the process of narrowing, or focusing, your perspective for purposes of a particular study.

If you are doing a research project for a course you are taking, many aspects of research design may have been specified for you in advance. If you must do a project for a course in experimental methods, the method of research will have been specified for you. If the project is for a course in voting behavior, the research topic will have been somewhat specified. Since it would not be feasible for me to anticipate all such constraints, the following discussion will assume there are none.

In designing a research project, you will find it useful to begin by assessing three things: your own interests, your abilities, and the resources available to you. Each of these considerations will suggest a large number of possible studies.

Simulate the beginning of a somewhat conventional research project: ask yourself what you are interested in understanding. Surely there are several questions you have about social behavior and attitudes. Why are some people politically liberal and others politically conservative? Why are some people more religious than others? Are college students becoming more vocationally oriented or less so? Do colleges and universities still discriminate against women faculty members? Are interracial marriages more or less successful than others? Do students learn more in large classes or small ones? Is the United States' economy more or less dependent on war and defense than in the past? Sit for a while and think about the kinds of questions that interest and concern you.

Once you have a few questions you would be interested in answering for yourself, think about the kind of information that would be needed to answer them. What research units of analysis would provide the most relevant information: college students, corporations, voters, cities, or what? This question will probably be inseparable in your thoughts from the question of research topics. Then ask: what *aspects* of the units of analysis would provide the information you need to answer your research question?

Once you have some ideas about the kind of information relevant to your purpose, ask yourself how you might go about getting that information. Are the relevant data likely to be already available somewhere (say, in a government publication), or would you have to collect them yourself? If you think you would have to collect them, how would you go about doing that? Would it be necessary to interview a large number of people? Could you learn what you need to know by attending meetings of certain groups? Could you glean the data you need from books in the library?

As you answer these questions, you are well into the process of research design. Keep in mind your own research abilities and the resources available to you, however. Do not design the perfect study when you will be unable to carry it out. You may want to attempt to use research methods that you have not used before, since research should be a learning experience in many ways, but you should not put yourself at too great a disadvantage.

Once you have a general idea of what you want to study and how, you should carefully review previous research in journals and books to see how other researchers have addressed the topic and what they have learned about it. Your review of the literature may lead you to revise your research design: perhaps you will decide to use a previous researcher's method or even *replicate* an earlier study. The independent replication of research projects is a standard procedure in the physical sciences, and it is just as important in the social sciences, although we tend to overlook that. Or, you might want to go beyond replication and study some aspect of the topic that you feel previous researchers have overlooked.

Here's another approach you might take. Suppose a topic has been studied previously using field research methods. Can you design an experiment that would test the findings the earlier researchers produced? Or, can you think of existing statistics that could be used to test the conclusions reached? The use of several different research methods to test the same finding is sometimes called *triangulation*, and you should always keep it in mind as a valuable research strategy. Since each research method has its particular strengths and weaknesses, there is always a danger that research findings will reflect, at least in part, the method of inquiry. In the best of all worlds, your own research design should bring more than one research method to bear on the topic.

Having refined your ideas about what you will study and how, you should turn to the remaining chapters in this book and learn exactly how to proceed. If you have found a topic that really interests you, you will have made an excellent start on a successful project.

SUMMARY

This chapter has dealt with the process of research design. It has posed the question: what aspects of whom (or what) will be studied in what fashion and for what purpose? As we have seen, in social science the answers can be numerous.

We began by examining the three major purposes of research: exploration, description, and explanation. Then, we considered the variety of units of analysis appropriate to social scientific research: we saw that social scientists can study individual people, groups, social organizations, and social artifacts. Next, we examined the different aspects of those units of analysis that might serve as topics of study: the conditions in which people and groups exist, people's orientations, and their actions.

Social science methods can be used to study social phenomena at a particular time or across time. Different research designs serve these different approaches.

The chapter closed with a description of several motivations for undertaking social research and with an overview of the research process.

MAIN POINTS

1. Exploration is the attempt to develop an initial, rough understanding of some phenomenon.

2. Description is the precise measurement and reporting of the characteristics of some population or phenomenon under study.

3. Explanation is the discovery and reporting of relationships among different aspects of the phenomenon under study. Whereas descriptive studies answer the question "what's so?" explanatory ones tend to answer the question "why?"

4. Units of analysis are the people or things whose characteristics social researchers observe, describe, and explain. Typically, the unit of analysis in social research is the individual person, but it may also be a group, a formal organization, or a social artifact.

5. Cross-sectional studies are those based on observations made at one time. While such studies are limited by this characteristic, inferences can be made about processes that occur over time.

6. Longitudinal studies are those in which observations are made at many times. Such observations may be made of samples drawn from general populations (trend studies), samples drawn from more specific subpopulations (cohort studies), or the same sample of people each time (panel studies).

7. A theory is a general and more or less comprehensive set of statements relating different aspects of some phenomenon.

8. A hypothesis is a statement of specific expectations about the nature of things, derived from a theory. Much research is devoted to hypothesis testing to determine whether theoretical expectations are confirmed by what goes on in the real world.

ANNOTATED BIBLIOGRAPHY

Bart, Pauline, and Frankel, Linda, *The Student Sociologist's Handbook* (Morristown, N.J.: General Learning Press, 1976). A handy little reference book to assist you in getting started on a research project. Written from the standpoint of a student term paper, this volume gives a particularly good guide to the periodical literature of the social sciences that's waiting for you in your campus library.

Hammond, Phillip (ed.), *Sociologists at Work* (New York: Basic Books, 1964). A collection of candid research biographies written by several eminent social science researchers, discussing the studies that made them eminent. A variety of research motivations and designs are illustrated in these honest reports of how the research actually came about and unfolded. Take two chapters every four hours to relieve the discomfort of believing that social science research is routine and dull.

Miller, Delbert, *Handbook of Research Design and Social Measurement* (New York: David McKay, 1977). A useful reference book for introducing or reviewing numerous issues involved in design and measurement. In addition, the book contains a wealth of practical information relating to foundations, journals, and professional associations.

Stouffer, Samuel, *Social Research to Test Ideas* (New York: Free Press of Glencoe, 1962). A stimulating and downright inspirational posthumous collection of research articles by one of the giants of social research. In these reports, you will see how an ingenious man formulates an idea, designs the perfect study for testing it, is prevented from conducting the study, and then devises another feasible method for testing the same idea. Especially enlightening are Paul Lazarsfeld's introduction and Chapter 6 in which Stouffer reports on the effects of the Great Depression on the family.

CHAPTER 5

Conceptualization and Measurement

INTRODUCTION

This chapter is the first of two dealing with the process of moving from vague ideas about what you want to study to being able to recognize it and measure it in the real world. In this chapter we deal with the general issue of *conceptualization*, which sets up a foundation for the discussions of *operationalization* in Chapter 6.

I want to begin the chapter with a frontal attack on the hidden concern people sometimes have as to whether it's possible to measure the stuff of life: love, hate, prejudice, radicalism, alienation, and things like that. The answer is "yes," but it will take a few pages for me to make that point. Once you see that we can measure anything that exists, we'll turn to the steps involved in doing that.

MEASURING ANYTHING THAT EXISTS

It seems altogether possible to me that you may have some reservations about the ability of science to measure the really important aspects of human social existence. You may have read research reports dealing with something like liberalism or religion or prejudice, and you may have been dissatisfied with the way the researchers measured whatever they were studying. You may have felt they were too superficial, that they missed the aspects that really matter most. Maybe they measured *religiosity* as the number of times a person went to church, or maybe *liberalism* was measured in terms of whom people voted for in a single election. Your dissatisfaction would surely have been increased if you found yourself being misclassified by the measurement system. People often have that experience.

Or, you may have looked up the definition of a word like *compassionate* in the dictionary and found the definition wanting. You may have heard yourself muttering, "There's more to it than that." In fact, whenever you look up the definition of something you already understand well, you can probably see ways people might misunderstand the term if they had only that definition to go on.

Although measurement would seem to present a special problem for social science, this section of the chapter makes the point that *we can measure anything that exists*. There are no exceptions. If it exists, we can measure it. By the time you finish this section, moreover, you should see the accuracy of that assertion, and you ought to be relieved of your concerns in the matter.

How Do You Know?

To demonstrate to you that social scientists can measure anything that exists, I'd like you to imagine that we are discussing the matter. I'll write the script, but feel free to make substitutions for your side of the dialogue as you see fit. Here goes.

ME: Social scientists can measure anything that exists.

YOU: Hah! Betcha can't.

ME: Tell me something that exists and I'll tell you how to measure it.

YOU: Okay, let's see you measure prejudice.

ME: Good choice. Now, I'm not willing to waste our time trying to measure something that doesn't exist. So, tell me if it exists.

YOU: Yes, of course it exists. Everybody knows that.

ME: How do you *know* that prejudice exists.

YOU: *Everybody* knows that.

ME: Everybody used to think the world was flat, too. I want to know how *you* know that prejudice really exists.

YOU: I've seen it in action.

ME: What have you seen that proves prejudice exists?

YOU: Well, a businessman told me that he'd never hire a woman for an executive position because he thought all women were flighty and irrational. How's that?

ME: Great! That sounds like prejudice to me, so I guess we can assume that prejudice exists. I am now prepared to measure prejudice. Ready?

YOU: Ready.

ME: You and I will circulate quietly through the business community, talking to businessmen about hiring. Whenever a businessman tells us that he would never hire a woman for an executive position because he thinks all women are flighty and irrational, we'll count that as a case of prejudice. Whenever we are not told that, we'll count the conversation as a case of nonprejudice. When we finish, we'll be able to classify all the businessmen we've talked to as either prejudiced or nonprejudiced.

YOU: Wait a minute! That's not a very good measure of prejudice. We're going to miss a lot of prejudice that way. All we'll measure is blatant prejudice against women in hiring.

ME: I see what you mean. But your comment also means that the situation you described before proves only that blatant prejudice against women in hiring exists. We'd better reconsider whether *prejudice* exists. Does it?

YOU: Of course it does. I was just giving you one example. There are hundreds of other examples of prejudice.

ME: Give me one that proves prejudice exists.

YOU: Okay, try this for size. I was in a bar the other night, and two guys—one white and one black—were arguing about politics. Finally, the white guy got so angry, he yelled, "You stupid nigger. All you niggers ought to be sent back to Africa." Is that prejudiced enough for you?

ME: Suits me. That would seem to prove that prejudice exists, so I'm ready again to measure prejudice. This will be more fun. You and I will split up and start touring bars every night. We'll keep our ears open and listen for a white person saying, "You stupid nigger. All you niggers—"

YOU: Hold it! I see where this is headed, and that's not going to do it either. A person who said that would be prejudiced, but we're going to classify a lot of prejudiced people as nonprejudiced just because they don't happen to get carried away and talk dirty.

ME: All of which brings me back to my original question. Does prejudice really exist or have you been just stringing me along?

YOU: Yes it exists!

ME: Well, I'm not sure any longer. You persuaded me that businessmen who discriminate against women in hiring exist, because you saw that and I believe you. You persuaded me that there are people who call black people niggers and say they should all go back to Africa. But I'm not so sure *prejudice* exists. I'd sure like to track it down so I can show you that I can measure it. To be honest, though, I'm beginning to doubt that it really exists. I mean, have you ever seen a prejudice? What color are they? How much do they weigh? Where are they located?

YOU: What on earth are you talking about?

The point of this dialogue, as you may have guessed, is to demonstrate that *prejudice doesn't exist.* We don't know what a prejudice looks like, how big it is, or what color. None of us has ever touched a prejudice or ridden in one. But we do talk a lot about prejudice. Here's how that came about.

As you and I wandered down the road of life, we observed a lot of things and knew they were real through our observations. We heard about a lot of other things that other people said they observed, and those other things seemed to have existed. Someone reported seeing a lynching and described the whole thing in great detail.

With additional experience, we noticed something more. We noticed that people who participate in lynchings are also quite likely to call black people niggers. A lot of them, moreover, seemed to want women to "stay in their place." Eventually, we began to get the feeling that there was a certain kind of person running around the world that had those several tendencies. When we discussed the people we'd met, it was sometimes appropriate to identify someone in terms of those tendencies. We used to say a person was "one of those who participates in lynchings, calls black people niggers, and wouldn't hire a woman for an executive position." After a while, however, it got pretty clumsy to say all of that, and you had a bright idea: "Let's use the word *prejudiced* as a shorthand notation for people like that. We can use the term even if they don't do all those things—as long as they're pretty much like that."

Being basically agreeable and interested in efficiency, I agreed to go along with the system. That's where *prejudice* came from. It never really existed. We never saw it. We just made it up as a shortcut for talking behind people's backs. Ultimately, *prejudice* is merely a *term* we have agreed to use in communication: a term we use to represent a whole collection of apparently related phenomena that we've each observed in the course of life. Each of us developed his or her own mental image of what the set of real phenomena we've observed represent in general and what they have in common.

When I say the word *prejudice* I know that it evokes a mental image in your mind, just as it evokes a mental image for me. It's as though we have file drawers in our minds containing thousands of sheets of paper, and each sheet of paper has a label in the upper right-hand corner. One sheet of paper in your file drawer has the term *prejudice* on it, and I have one too. On your sheet are all the things you were told about *prejudice* the first time you heard the word, plus all the things you've observed since then that seemed to be examples of it. My sheet has what I was told about *prejudice* plus all the things I've observed that seemed to be examples of it.

Concepts

The technical term for those mental images, those sheets of paper in our mental file drawers, is *concept*. Each sheet of paper is a concept. Now, those mental images cannot be communicated directly. There is no way I can directly reveal to you what's written on my sheet of paper labeled *prejudice*, nor can you reveal directly what's written on yours. So we use the *terms* written in the upper right-hand corner as a way of communicating about our concepts and the things we observe that are related to those concepts.

Let's suppose that I'm going to meet someone named Pat whom you already know. I ask you what Pat is like. Now suppose that you have seen Pat help lost children find their parents and put a tiny bird back in its nest. Pat got you to take turkeys to poor families on Thanksgiving and to visit a children's hospital on Christmas. You've seen Pat weep in a movie about a mother overcoming adversities to save and protect her child. As you search through your mental file drawer, you may find all or most of those phenomena recorded on a single sheet labeled *compassionate* in the upper right-hand corner. You look over the other entries on the page, and you find they seem to provide an accurate description of Pat. So, you say, "Pat is compassionate."

Now I leaf through my own mental file drawer until I find a sheet marked *compassionate*. I then look over the things written on my sheet, and say, "Oh, that's nice." I now feel I know what Pat is like, but my expectations in that regard reflect the entries on *my* file sheet, not yours. Later, when I meet Pat, I may find that my own, personal experiences correspond to the entries I have on my *compassionate* file sheet, and I'll say you were sure right. Or, my observations of Pat may contradict the things I have on my file sheet, and I'll tell you that I don't think Pat is very compassionate. If the latter happens, we may begin to compare notes.

You say, "I once saw Pat weep in a movie about a mother overcoming adversity to save and protect her child." I look at my *compassionate* sheet and can't find anything like that. Looking elsewhere in my file, I locate that sort of phenomenon on a sheet labeled *sentimental*. I retort, "That's not compassion. That's just sentimentality."

To further strengthen my case, I tell you that I saw Pat refuse to give money to an organization dedicated to saving the whales from extinction. "That represents a lack of compassion," I argue. You search through your files and find saving the whales on a sheet marked *environmental activism*, and you say so. Eventually, we set about comparing the entries we have on our respective sheets labeled *compassionate*. We may discover that we have quite different mental images represented by that term.

In the big picture, language and communication only work to the extent that you and I have considerable overlap in the kinds of entries we have on our mental file sheets bearing a particular label. The similarities we have on those sheets represent the agreements existing in the society we both occupy. When we were growing up, we were both told approximately the same thing when we were first introduced to a particular term. Dictionaries give a formalization of the agreements our society has about such terms. Each of us, then, shapes his or her mental images to correspond with those agreements, but since all of us have different sets of experiences and observations, no two people end up with exactly the same set of entries on any sheet in our file systems.

Returning to the assertion made at the outset of this chapter, we *can* measure anything that is real. We can measure, for example, whether Pat actually puts the little bird back in its nest, visits the hospital on Christmas, weeps at the movie, or refuses to contribute to saving the whales. All of those things are real. They exist, so we can measure them. But is Pat really compassionate? We can't answer that question, we can't measure compassion in that sense, because compassion doesn't exist the way those things I just described exist.

Compassion as a *term* does exist; it's real. We can measure the number of letters it contains and agree that there are 10. We can agree that it has three syllables, and that it begins with the letter *c*. We can measure those aspects of it, in short, that are real.

Some aspects of our concepts are real, also. Whether you *have* a mental image associated with the term *compassion* is real. When an elementary school teacher asks a class how many know what *compassion* means, those who raise their hands can be counted. The presence of particular entries on the sheets bearing a given label is also real, and that can be measured. We could measure how many people do or do not associate giving money to save the whales with their concept of compassion.

About the only thing we cannot measure is what compassion really means, because compassion isn't real. Compassion exists only in the form of the agreements we have about how to use the term in communicating about things that are real. Happily, we *do* have such agreements, and those agreements make both communication and research possible.

Conceptualization

Day-to-day communication usually occurs through a system of vague and general agreements about the use of terms. Usually, people do not get exactly what we wish to communicate, but they get the general drift of our meaning. Although you and I do not agree completely about the use of the term *compassionate*, I'm probably safe in assuming that Pat won't pull the wings off flies. A wide range of misunderstandings and conflict—from the interpersonal to the international—is the price we pay for our imprecision, but somehow we muddle through. Science, however, aims at more than muddling, and it cannot operate in a context of such imprecision.

Conceptualization is the process through which we specify precisely what we will mean when we use particular terms. Suppose we want to find out, for example, whether women are more compassionate than men. I suspect most of us assume that is the case, but it might be interesting to find out if it's really so. We can't meaningfully study the question, let alone agree on the answer, without some precise working agreements as to the meaning of the term. They are working agreements in the sense that they allow us to work on the question. We don't need to agree or even pretend to agree that a particular specification captures the real meaning of the concept; we need only agree that the specification might be worth using.

Indicators and Dimensions

The end product of this conceptualization process is the specification of a set of _indicators_ of what we have in mind. Those indicators will be real and observable things that give evidence of the presence or absence of the concept we are studying. Thus, we may agree to use visiting children's hospitals at Christmas as an indicator of compassion. Putting little birds back in their nests may be agreed on as another indicator, and so forth. If the unit of analysis for our study were the individual person, we could then observe the presence or absence of each indicator for each person under study. Going beyond that, we could add up the number of indicators of compassion observed for each individual. We might agree on 10 specific indicators, for example, and find 6 present in our study of Pat, 3 for John, 9 for Mary, and so forth.

Returning to our original question, we might calculate that the women we studied had an average of 6.5 indicators of compassion, and the men studied had an average of 3.2. We might therefore conclude on the basis of that group difference that women are, on the whole, more compassionate than men. Usually, it's not that simple.

Very often, when we take our concepts seriously and set about specifying what we mean by them, we discover disagreements and inconsistencies. Not only do you and I disagree, but each of us is likely to find a good deal of muddiness within our own, individual mental images. If you take a moment to look at what *you* mean by compassion, you'll probably find that your image contains several *kinds* of compassion. The entries on your file sheet can be combined into groups and subgroups, and you'll even find several different strategies for making the combinations. For example, you might group the entries in terms of feelings, on the one hand, and actions, on the other hand. The technical term for such groupings is *dimension*, and we might speak of the feeling dimension of compassion and the action dimension of compassion.

Alternatively, we might organize the concept of compassion differently. It might make sense, for example, to distinguish religiously based compassion, politically based compassion, and so forth. Or, compassion might center on helping people be and have what *we* want for them or what *they* want for themselves. Thus, it would be possible for us to subdivide the concept of compassion according to several sets of dimensions. Specification of dimensions and the collecting of various indicators for each of those dimensions is all a part of conceptualization.

Specifying the different dimensions of a concept often paves the way for a more sophisticated understanding of what we are studying. We might observe, for example, that women are more compassionate in terms of feelings, and men are more compassionate in terms of actions—or vice versa. Noting that this was the case, we would not be able to say whether men or women are really more compassionate. Our research, in fact, would have shown that there is no single answer to the question.

The Interchangeability of Indicators

In spite of the preceding discussion, it is sometimes possible for research to answer a general question such as whether men or women are the more compassionate. That is possible, ironically, even when we cannot agree on the ultimate or even the best indicators of the general concept or any of its dimensions.

Suppose, for the moment, that you and I have compiled a list of 100 indicators of the concept *compassion* and its various dimensions. Suppose further that we disagree widely on which indicators give the clearest evidence of compassion or the absence of it. If there are some indicators we pretty much agree on, we could focus our attention on those, and we could probably agree on the answer they provided. But suppose we don't really agree on any of the possible indicators. It is still possible for us to reach an agreement on whether men or women are the more compassionate.

If we disagree totally on the value of the several indicators, one solution would be to study all of them. Now, suppose that women turn out to be more compassionate than men on all 100 indicators—on all the indicators you favor and on all of mine. Then we would be able to agree that women are more compassionate than men even though we still disagree on what compassion means in general.

The *interchangeability of indicators* means that if several different indicators all represent, to some degree, the same concept, then all of them will behave the same way that the concept would behave if it were real and could be observed. Thus, if women are generally more compassionate than men, we should be able to observe that difference by using any reasonable measure of compassion.

You now have the fundamental logic of conceptualization and measurement. The discussions that follow in this chapter and the next one are mainly refinements and extensions of what I've just presented. Before turning to more technical elaborations on the main framework, however, it may be useful to cover two more general topics.

First, I know that the discussions above may not fit exactly with your previous understanding of the meaning of such terms as *prejudice* and *compassion*. We tend to operate in daily life as though such terms have real, ultimate meanings. In the next subsection, then, I want to comment briefly on how we came to that understanding.

Second, lest this whole discussion create a picture of anarchy in the meanings of words, I will describe some of the ways in which scientists have organized the confusion so as to provide standards, consistency, and commonality in the meaning of terms. You should come away from this latter discussion with a recaptured sense of order—but one based on a conscious understanding rather than the casual acceptance of common usage.

The Confusion over Definitions and Reality

Reviewing briefly, our concepts are mental images that summarize collections of seemingly related observations and experiences. Although the observations and experiences are real, our concepts are only mental creations. The terms associated with concepts are merely devices created for purposes of filing and communication. The word *prejudice* is an example. Ultimately, that word is only a collection of letters and has no intrinsic meaning. We could have as easily and meaningfully created the word *slanderice* to serve the same purpose.

Very often, however, we fall into the trap of believing that terms have real meanings. That danger seems to grow stronger when we begin to take terms seriously and attempt to use them precisely. And the danger is all the greater in the presence of experts who appear to know more than you do about what the terms really mean. It's very easy to yield to the authority of experts in such a situation.

Once we have assumed that terms have real meanings, we begin the tortured task of discovering what those real meanings are and what would constitute a genuine measurement of them. Figure 5-1 illustrates the history of this process. We make up conceptual summaries of real observations because the summaries are convenient. They prove to be *so* convenient, however, that we begin tricking ourselves into thinking they are real. The process of regarding as real those things that are not is called *reification*, and the reification of concepts in day-to-day life is very common.

In all this confusion, logicians and scientists have found it useful to distinguish three kinds of definitions: *real*, *nominal*, and *operational*. The first of these reflects the reification of terms, and as Carl G. Hempel has cautioned:

Figure 5-1   The Process of Conceptual Entrapment

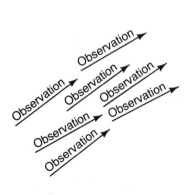

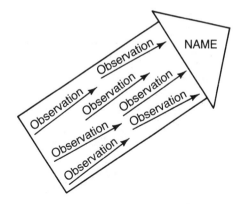

(a) Many of our observations in life seem to have something in common. We get the sense that they represent something more general than the simple content of any single observation. We find it useful, moreover, to communicate about the more general concept.

(b) It is inconvenient to keep describing all the specific observations whenever we want to communicate about the more general concept they seem to have in common, so we give a name to the general concept— to stand for whatever it is the specific observations have in common.

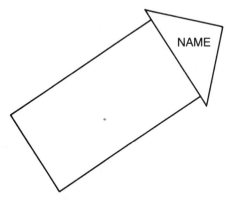

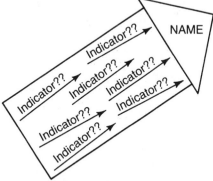

(c) As we communicate about the general concept, using its term, we begin to think that the concept is some*thing* that really exists, not just a summary reference for several concrete observations in the world.

(d) The belief that the concept itself is real results in irony. We now begin discussing and debating whether specific observations are "really" sufficient *indicators* of the concept.

A "real" definition, according to traditional logic, is not a stipulation determining the meaning of some expression but a statement of the "essential nature" or the "essential attributes" of some entity. The notion of essential nature, however, is so vague as to render this characterization useless for the purposes of rigorous inquiry.[1]

The idea of *real* definitions, then, is of no value to science. Whenever we seek to pin down the real meanings of words, we end up dissatisfied. Yet, the situation is not hopeless.

Creating Conceptual Order

The specification of concepts in scientific inquiry depends on nominal and operational definitions. A *nominal* definition is one that is *assigned* to a term. In the midst of disagreement and confusion over what a term really means, the scientist specifies a working definition for the purposes of the inquiry. Wishing to examine socioeconomic status (SES) in our study, for example, we may simply specify that we are going to treat it as a combination of income and educational attainment. In that definitional decision, we rule out many other possible aspects of SES: occupational status, money in the bank, property, lineage, life-style, and so forth.

The specification of nominal definitions focuses our observational strategy, but it does not allow us to observe. As a next step we must specify exactly what we are going to observe, how we will do it, and what interpretations we are going to place on various possible observations. All of these further specifications make up what is called the *operational* definition of the concept —a description of the operations that will be involved in measuring it.

Pursuing the case of SES, we might decide to ask the people we are studying two questions:

1. What was your total, family income during the past twelve months?

2. What is the highest level of school you completed?

Here, we would probably want to specify a system for categorizing the answers people give us. For income, we might want to use categories such as "under $5,000," "$5,000 to $10,000," and so forth. Educational attainment might be similarly grouped in categories. Finally, we would specify the manner in which a person's responses to these two questions would be combined in creating a measure of socioeconomic status. Chapter 15, on index and scale construction, will present some of the methods for doing that.

Ultimately, we would have created a working and workable definition of SES. Others might disagree with our conceptualization and operationalization, but the definition would have one essential scientific virtue: it would be absolutely specific and unambiguous. Even if someone disagreed with our definition, that person would have a good idea how to interpret our research results, since what we meant by the

---

[1]Carl G. Hempel, "Fundamentals of Concept Formation in Empirical Science," *International Encyclopedia of Unified Science II*, No. 7 (1952), p. 6.

term SES—reflected in our analyses and conclusions—would be clear.

I want to bring the preceding discussions together now through a brief history of a social scientific concept. You may recall from Chapter 1 that Edward Ransford, in his study of the Watts riots, was particularly interested in the part played by *anomie*. This term was first introduced into social science by Emile Durkheim, the great French sociologist, in his classic 1897 study of *Suicide*.[2]

Using only government publications on suicide rates in different regions and countries, Durkheim turned in a work of analytical genius. To determine the effects of religion on suicide, he compared the suicide rates of predominantly Protestant countries with predominantly Catholic ones, Protestant regions of Catholic countries with Catholic regions of Protestant countries, and so forth. To determine the possible effects of the weather, he compared suicide rates in northern and southern countries and regions, and he examined the different suicide rates across the months and seasons of the year. Thus, he was able to draw conclusions about a supremely individualistic and personal act without having any data about the individuals engaging in it.

At a more general level, Durkheim suggested that suicide also reflected the extent to which a society's agreements were clear and stable. Noting that times of social upheaval and change often presented the individual with grave uncertainties about what was expected of him or her, Durkheim suggested that such uncertainties could result in confusion, anxiety, and even self-destruction. To describe this societal condition of normlessness, Durkheim chose the term *anomie*. It is worth noting that Durkheim did not make this word up out of whole cloth. Used in both German and French, it meant, literally, *without law*, and the English term *anomy* had been used for at least three centuries before Durkheim to mean *disregard for Divine Law*. Still, Durkheim created *anomie* as a social scientific concept.

In the years that have followed the publication of *Suicide*, social scientists have found *anomie* a useful concept, and many have expanded on Durkheim's use. Robert Merton, in a classic article entitled "Social Structure and Anomie," concluded that *anomie* results from a disparity between the goals and means prescribed by a society.[3] Monetary success, for example, is a widely shared goal in our society, yet not all individuals have the resources appropriate to achieving it through acceptable means. An emphasis on the goal itself, Merton suggested, results in a situation of normlessness, because those denied the traditional avenues to wealth go about getting it through illegitimate means. Merton's discussion, then, could be considered a further conceptualization of the concept of *anomie*.

Although Durkheim originally intended the concept of anomie to be a characteristic of societies, as did Merton after him, other social scientists have found it useful as a description of individuals.[4] In a given society, then, some individuals experience *anomie*, while others do not. Elwin Powell, writing 20 years after Merton, provided the following conceptualization of *anomie* as a characteristic of individuals: "When the ends of action become contradictory, inaccessible or insignificant, a condition of

[2]Emile Durkheim, *Suicide* (Glencoe, Ill.: Free Press, 1951). Originally published in 1897.
[3]Robert K. Merton, "Social Structure and Anomie," *American Sociological Review*, Vol. 3 (1938), pp. 672–682.
[4]To clarify this distinction, some scholars have chosen to use the term *anomie* in its original, Durkheimian meaning and to use *anomia* in reference to the individual characteristic.

anomie arises. Characterized by a general loss of orientation and accompanied by feelings of 'emptiness' and apathy, anomie can be simply conceived as meaninglessness."[5]

Powell went on to suggest there were two distinct kinds of anomie and to examine how the two rose out of different occupational experiences to result, sometimes, in suicide. In his study, however, Powell did not measure *anomie* per se; he studied the relationship between suicide and occupation, making inferences about the two kinds of anomie. Thus, the study did not provide an operational definition of *anomie*, only a further conceptualization.

Many other researchers, however, have offered operational definitions. One name stands out over all the others in this regard, however. Two years before the Powell article appeared, Leo Srole published a set of questionnaire items that he said provided a good measure of *anomie* as experienced by individuals.[6] In the subsequent two decades, the Srole scale has become a research staple for social scientists. It consists of five statements that subjects are asked to agree or disagree with.

1. In spite of what some people say, the lot of the average man is getting worse.

2. It's hardly fair to bring children into the world with the way things look for the future.

3. Nowadays a person has to live pretty much for today and let tomorrow take care of itself.

4. These days a person doesn't really know who he can count on.

5. There's little use writing to public officials because they aren't really interested in the problems of the average man.[7]

I've presented this greatly abbreviated history of *anomie* as a social scientific concept for several reasons. First, it illustrates the process through which a general concept becomes an operationalized measurement, though I wouldn't want you to think that the issue of *anomie* has been handled once and for all. Scholars will surely continue to reconceptualize and reoperationalize it for years to come—continually seeking more useful views of it.

I've ended the story with the Srole scale, however, because it illustrates another important point. Despite open-endedness of conceptualization and operationalization, it does not necessarily produce the kind of anarchy and chaos you might fear. Order emerges. There are several elements in this order. First, although you *could* define *anomie* any way you chose—in terms of, say, shoe size—you are likely to define it in ways not too far removed from other people's mental images. If you were to use a really offbeat definition, you probably wouldn't have any impact; people would simply ignore you.

Second, as researchers discover the *utility* of a particular conceptualization and

[5]Elwin H. Powell, "Occupation, Status, and Suicide: Toward a Redefinition of Anomie," *American Sociological Review*, Vol. 23 (1958), p. 132.

[6]Leo Srole, "Social Integration and Certain Corollaries: An Exploratory Study," *American Sociological Review*, Vol. 21 (1956), pp. 709–716.

[7]*Ibid.*, p. 713.

operationalization of a concept, they are likely to adopt it, and standardized definitions of concepts appear. Examples, in addition to the Srole scale, include IQ tests and a whole host of demographic and economic measures developed by the Bureau of the Census. Using such established measures not only has the advantage of extensive pretesting and debugging, but also adds an advantage of comparability. If you and I do separate studies of two different groups, and if each of us uses the Srole scale, we will be able to compare our two groups on the basis of *anomie*.

Thus, in summary, social scientists can measure anything that's real, and we can even do a pretty good job of measuring things that aren't. Granting that such concepts as socioeconomic status, prejudice, compassion, and anomie aren't real ultimately, we've now seen that social scientists are able to create order in handling them. It is an order based on utility, however, and not on ultimate truth.

The remainder of this chapter is devoted to some of the considerations and alternatives involved in the creation of *useful* definitions and measurements. First, we're going to look at the relationship between definitions and research purposes, then the chapter concludes with an examination of some criteria used in determining the *quality* of the measurements we create.

DEFINITIONS AND RESEARCH PURPOSES

Recall from Chapter 4 that two of the general purposes of research are *description* and *explanation*. The distinction between them has important implications for the process of definition and measurement. If you have formed the opinion that description is a simpler task than explanation, you will be surprised to learn that definitions are more problematic for descriptive research than for explanatory research. This point will be discussed more fully in Part Four, but it is important that you have a basic understanding of why it is so before we turn to other aspects of measurement.

The importance of definitions for descriptive research should be clear. If our task is to describe and report the unemployment rate in a city, our definition of *being unemployed* is critical. That definition will depend on our definition of another term: the *labor force*. If it seems patently absurd to regard a 3-year-old child as being unemployed, it is because such a child is not considered a member of the labor force. Thus, we might follow the United States Census Bureau's convention and exclude all persons under 14 years of age from the labor force.

This convention alone, however, would not give us a satisfactory definition, since it would count as unemployed such people as high school students, the retired, the disabled, and housewives. We might follow the census convention further by defining the labor force as "all persons 14 years of age and over who are employed, looking for work, or waiting to be called back to a job from which they have been laid off or furloughed." Unemployed persons, then, would be those members of the labor force who are not employed. If a student, housewife, or retired person is not looking for work, such a person would not even be included in the labor force.

But what does "looking for work" mean? Would it be necessary for a person to register with the state employment service or go from door to door asking for employment? Would it be sufficient to want a job or be open to an offer of employment? Conventionally, "looking for work" is defined operationally as saying "yes" in response to an interviewer's asking "Have you been looking for a job during the past seven days?" (Seven days is the conventional time period specified, but for some research purposes it might make more sense to shorten or lengthen it.)

I have spelled out these considerations in some detail so that you will realize that the conclusion of a descriptive study about the unemployment rate, for example, depends directly on each of them. Increasing the period of time during which people are counted as looking for work would have the effect of adding more unemployed persons to the labor force as defined, thereby increasing the reported unemployment rate. If we follow another convention and speak of the *civilian* labor force and the *civilian* unemployment rate, we are excluding military personnel; that, too, increases the reported unemployment rate, since military personnel would be employed—*by definition.*

Thus the descriptive statement that the unemployment rate in a city is 3 percent, or 9 percent, or whatever it might be, depends directly on the specific operational definitions used. If that seems clear in this example, it is because there are a number of accepted conventions relating to the labor force and unemployment. Consider how difficult it would be to get agreement about the definitions you would need in order to make a descriptive statement such as "45 percent of the students are politically conservative." This percentage, like the unemployment rate above, would depend directly on your definition of what is being measured. A different definition might result if you said that "5 percent of the student body are politically conservative."

Ironically, definitions are less problematical in the case of explanatory research. Let's suppose that we are interested in explaining political conservatism. Why are some people conservative while others are not? More specifically, let's suppose we are interested in whether old people are generally more conservative than young people. What if you and I have 25 different operational definitions of *conservative,* and we can't agree on which definition is the best one? We would seem to have an insurmountable obstacle to our research *unless we discovered that the definition didn't really matter.* Suppose that we found old people generally more conservative than young people in terms of each of the 25 definitions! (Recall the earlier discussion of compassion in men and women?) Suppose that we found old people more conservative than young people in terms of *every* reasonable definition of conservatism we could think of. It wouldn't matter what our definition was. We would conclude that old people are generally more conservative than young people—even though we couldn't agree about what a conservative really was.

In practice, explanatory research seldom results in findings quite as unambiguous as the above example suggests; nonetheless, the general pattern is quite common in actual research. There *are* consistent patterns of relationships in human social life, and they result in consistent research findings. The important point here, however, is that such consistency would not appear in a descriptive situation. Changing definitions almost inevitably results in different descriptive conclusions.

CRITERIA FOR MEASUREMENT QUALITY

This chapter has come some distance. It began with the bald assertion that social scientists can measure anything that exists. Then we discovered that most of the things we might want to measure and study don't really exist. Next we learned that it is possible to measure them anyway. I want to conclude the chapter with a discussion of some of the yardsticks against which we judge our relative success or failure in measuring things—even things that don't exist.

To begin, measurements can be made with varying degrees of _precision._ The description of a woman as "43 years old" is more precise than "in her forties." Saying "11½ inches long" is a more precise description than "about a foot long."

As a general rule, precise measurements are superior to imprecise ones, as common sense would dictate. There are no conditions under which imprecise measurements would be intrinsically superior to precise ones. Precision is not always necessary or desirable, however. If your research purpose is such that knowing a woman to be in her forties is sufficient, then any additional effort invested in learning her precise age is wasted. The operationalization of concepts, then, must be guided partly by an understanding of the degree of precision required. If your needs are not clear, be more precise rather than less.

Don't confuse precision with _accuracy_, however. Describing someone as "born in Stowe, Vermont," is more precise than "born in New England"—but suppose the person in question was actually born in Boston. The less precise description would have been more accurate.

Precision and accuracy are obviously important qualities in research measurement, and they probably need no further explanation. When social scientists construct and evaluate measurements, however, they pay special attention to two technical considerations: _reliability_ and _validity._

Reliability

In the abstract, reliability is a matter of whether a particular technique, applied repeatedly to the same object, would yield the same result each time. Suppose, for example, that I asked you to estimate how much I weigh. You look me over carefully and guess that I weigh 165 pounds. (Thank you.) Now let's suppose I ask you to estimate the weights of 30 or 40 other people, and while you're engrossed in that, I slip back into line wearing a clever disguise. When my turn comes again, you guess 180 pounds. Gotcha! That little exercise would have demonstrated that having you estimate people's weights was not a very reliable technique.

Suppose, however, that I had loaned you my bathroom scale to use in determining people's weights. No matter how clever my disguise, you would presumably announce the same weight for me both times, indicating that the scale provided a more reliable measure of weight than guessing.

Reliability, however, does not insure accuracy any more than precision does.

Suppose I've set my bathroom scale to shave 5 pounds off my weight just to make me feel better. Although you would (reliably) report the same weight for me each time, you would always be wrong. This new element is called *bias*, and it is discussed in more detail in Chapter 7 on sampling. For now, just be warned that reliability does not insure accuracy.

Now let's see what reliability means in the context of a realistic social research inquiry. Let's suppose that we are interested in studying morale among factory workers in two different kinds of factories. In one set of factories, workers do very specialized jobs, reflecting an extreme division of labor. Each worker contributes a tiny part to the overall process performed on a long assembly line. In the other set of factories, each worker performs many tasks and small teams of workers complete the whole process. (This experiment is being run by Swedish auto makers.)

How should we measure morale? Following one strategy, we could spend more time observing the workers in each factory, noticing such things as whether they joke with one another, whether they smile and laugh a lot, and so forth. We could ask them how they like their work and even ask them whether they think they would prefer their current arrangement or the other one being studied. By comparing what we observed in the different factories, we might reach a conclusion as to which assembly process produced the higher morale.

Now let's look at some of the possible problems of reliability inherent in this method. First of all, how you and I are feeling when we do the observing is likely to color what we see. We may misinterpret what we see. We may see workers kidding each other and think they are having an argument. Or, maybe we'll catch them on an off day. If we were to observe the same group of workers several days in a row, we might arrive at different evaluations on each day. If several observers evaluated the same behavior, on the other hand, they too might arrive at different conclusions about the workers' morale.

Here's another strategy for assessing morale. Suppose we check the company records to see how many grievances have been filed with the union during some fixed period of time. Presumably that would be an indicator of morale: the more grievances, the lower the morale. This measurement strategy would appear to be more reliable: we could count up the grievances over and over and we should keep arriving at the same number.

If you find yourself saying, "Wait a minute," over the second measurement strategy, you're worrying about validity, not reliability. Let's complete the discussion of reliability, and then we'll handle validity.

Reliability problems crop up in many forms in social research. Survey researchers have known for a long time that different interviewers get different answers from respondents as a result of their own attitudes and demeanor. If we were to conduct a study of editorial positions on some public issue, we might create a team of coders to take on the job of reading hundreds of editorials and classifying them in terms of their position on the issue. Different coders would code the same editorial differently. Or we might want to classify a few hundred specific occupations in terms of some standard coding scheme, say a set of categories created by the Department of Labor or by the Bureau of the Census. You and I would not code all those occupations into the same categories.

Each of these examples illustrates problems of reliability. Similar problems arise whenever we ask people to give us information about themselves. Sometimes we ask questions that people don't know the answers to. (How many times have you been to church?) Sometimes we ask people about things that are totally irrelevant to them. (Are you satisfied with China's current relationship with Albania?) And sometimes we ask questions that are so complicated that a person who had a clear opinion in the matter might arrive at a different interpretation of the question upon being asked a second time.

How do you create reliable measures? There are a number of techniques. First, in asking people for information—if your research design calls for that—be careful to ask only about things the respondents are likely to know the answer to. Ask about things relevant to them, and be clear in what you're asking. The danger in these instances is that people *will* give you answers—reliable or not. People will tell you how they feel about China's relationship with Albania even if they haven't the foggiest idea what that relationship is.

In addition to this commonsense advice, there are a number of more technical methods for coping with the problem of reliability in asking people for information. Sometimes researchers ask for the same information more than once, using either the same or a similar question. By the same token, you should always ask several questions aimed at tapping a particular variable if it is attitudinal rather than factual—something like religiosity, alienation, prejudice, and so forth. Thus, if you ask ten questions aimed at measuring alienation, and one of them classifies people very differently from the other nine, that should be a tip-off that the variant item is unreliable (or invalid—coming up soon).

Sometimes, it will be appropriate for you to ask people questions at different times, and it may be possible to ask the same question each time, thereby testing the reliability of their answers. Experiments, for example, often involve a test and retest, and you might repeat some of the earlier questions the second time around. Be careful about those things that might actually change during the interval between the test and retest, however, or you could misjudge the reliability of your measure. Somebody might get married during the course of the study, and you'd then doubt the reliability of your data on marital status.

Another way to handle the problem of reliability in getting information from people is to use measures that have proven their reliability in previous research. If you want to measure anomie, for example, you might very well want to follow Srole's lead. There are other ways of handling this problem, and you'll probably be able to think of some new ones.

In the case of unreliability generated by research workers, there are also several solutions. To guard against interviewer unreliability, it is common practice in surveys to have a supervisor call a subsample of the respondents on the telephone and verify selected pieces of information. Replication works in other situations also. If you are worried that newspaper editorials or occupations may not be classified reliably, why not have each independently coded by several coders? Those that get the same classification from each coder are probably safe. Those that generate disagreement should be evaluated more carefully and resolved.

Finally, clarity, specificity, training, and practice will avoid a great deal of unreliability and grief. If you and I were to spend some time reaching a clear agreement on how we were going to evaluate editorial positions on an issue—discussing the various positions that might be represented and reading through several together—we'd probably be able to do a good job of classifying them in the same way independently.

We'll return to the issue of reliability more than once in the chapters ahead. For now, however, let's recall that even total reliability doesn't insure that our measures measure what we think they measure. Now let's plunge into the question of validity.

Validity

In conventional usage, the term *validity* refers to the extent to which an empirical measure adequately reflects the *real meaning* of the concept under consideration. (Whoops! I've already committed us to the view that concepts don't have real meanings) How can we ever say whether a particular measure adequately reflects the concept's meaning, then? Ultimately, of course, we can't. At the same time, I've already suggested some of the ways in which researchers deal with this issue.

First, there's something called *face validity*. Particular empirical measures may or may not jibe with our common agreements and our individual mental images associated with a particular concept. You and I might quarrel about the adequacy of measuring worker morale by counting the number of grievances filed with the union, but we'd surely agree that the number of grievances has *something* to do with morale. If I were to suggest that we measure morale by finding out how many books the workers took out of the library during their off-duty hours, you'd undoubtedly raise a more serious objection: that measure wouldn't have any face validity.

Second, I've already pointed to many of the more concrete agreements researchers have reached in the case of some concepts. The Bureau of the Census, for example, has created operational definitions of such concepts as family, household, and employment status that seem to have a workable validity in most studies using those concepts.

Finally, as I've hinted in the previous section and earlier in the chapter (see the discussion on interchangeability of indicators), whether a particular indicator produces the same conclusions as other indicators of the same concept is a good guide to its utility. We'll get into this in much more detail in Part Four, which deals with the analysis of data.

Tension between Reliability and Validity

As a footnote to these discussions, I want to point out briefly that a certain tension often exists between the criteria of reliability and validity. Often we seem to face a trade-off between the two.

If you'll recall for a moment the earlier example of measuring morale in different factories, I think you'll see that the strategy of immersing yourself in the day-to-day routine of the assembly line, observing what went on, and talking to the workers seems to provide a more valid measure of morale than counting grievances. It just seems obvious that we'd be able to get a clearer sense of whether the morale was high or low in that fashion than we would get from counting the number of grievances filed with the union.

As I pointed out earlier, however, the counting strategy would be more reliable. This situation reflects a more general strain in research measurement. Most of the really interesting concepts that we want to study have many subtle nuances, and it's hard to specify precisely what we mean by them. Researchers sometimes speak of such concepts as having a "richness of meaning." Scores of books and articles have been written on the topic of anomie, and they still haven't exhausted the interesting aspects of that concept.

Yet, science needs to be specific to generate reliable measurements. Very often, then, the specification of reliable operational definitions and measurements seems to rob such concepts of their richness of meaning. I mean, morale is much more than a lack of grievances filed with the union; anomie is much more than the five items created by Leo Srole.

That is a persistent and inevitable dilemma for the social researcher, and you will be importantly forearmed against it by being forewarned. Be prepared for it and deal with it. If there is no clear agreement on how to measure a concept, measure it several different ways. If the concept has several different dimensions, measure them all. And above all, know that the concept does not have any meaning other than what you and I give it. And the only justification for giving any concept a particular meaning is utility. Measure concepts in ways that help us understand the world around us.

SUMMARY

The purpose of this chapter has been to orient you to the process of defining and measuring the things social scientists study. Since people sometimes worry about whether it's possible to measure the really important things like prejudice, alienation, love, religiosity, and political orientations, I began by announcing that we can measure anything that's real—anything that exists.

As it turned out, you'll recall, most of the concepts we are interested in studying aren't real. Instead, they are vague mental images you and I use as summary devices for bringing together and filing sets of seemingly related things we experience and observe. We see one person call another a nigger, we hear about someone being denied an executive promotion because she's a woman, and we feel these things have something in common. We use the term *prejudice* as a summary device for holding them together. Unfortunately, however, prejudice per se doesn't exist, so we can't measure it directly.

More happily, though, we *can* measure anything that's real—including the sorts of things we've associated under the general heading of prejudice. Conceptualization is the process through which we specify what we are going to mean in our use of general conceptual terms in a research project and what specific kinds of real phenomena will be appropriate to our study.

In the remainder of the chapter, we looked at some of the guidelines and options that make conceptualization a pretty rigorous and effective enterprise. The fact that concepts don't really exist just makes research more exciting and challenging. It requires more consciousness and ingenuity than might otherwise be the case.

We've seen that the way concepts are defined depends on the purpose of the research. In particular, we've seen that descriptive studies present different definitional considerations than explanatory ones.

The chapter concludes with a discussion of the criteria for measurement quality. We looked at some of the considerations that separate good measurements from bad ones. Specifically, we examined and distinguished precision, accuracy, reliability, and validity. And I pointed out that the ultimate criterion of quality is *utility*. Will a particular way of measuring something tell you anything useful about the world?

The chapter that follows is a more concrete extension of the present one. Conceptualization and operationalization come as a set in social research, the way Laurel and Hardy came as a set in comedy. Conceptualization is the process of getting clearer about how you will define and mean particular terms, and operationalization completes that process by specifying the nitty-gritty details of actual observation and measurement.

MAIN POINTS

1. Concepts are mental images we use as summary devices for bringing together observations and experiences that seem to have something in common.

2. Our concepts do not exist in the real world, so they can't be measured directly.

3. It *is* possible to measure the things that our concepts summarize.

4. Conceptualization is the process of specifying the vague mental imagery of our concepts, sorting out the kinds of observations and measurements that will be appropriate for our research.

5. The interchangeability of indicators permits us to study and draw conclusions about concepts even when we can't agree on how those concepts should be defined.

6. Precision refers to the exactness of the measure used in an observation or description of an attribute. For example, the description of a person as being "six feet, one and three-quarters inches tall" is more precise than the description "about six feet tall."

7. Reliability refers to the likelihood that a given measurement procedure would yield the same description of a given phenomenon if that measurement were repeated. For example, estimating a person's age by asking his or her

friends would be less reliable than asking the person or checking the birth certificate.

8. Validity refers to the extent to which a specific measurement provides data that relate to commonly accepted meanings of a particular concept. For example, the frequency of church attendance would be a more valid measure of religiosity than would the frequency of a person's use of the word *God*, since this latter measure would result in attributing a high degree of religiosity to people who swear a lot.

9. The creation of specific, reliable measures often seems to diminish the richness of meaning our general concepts have. This problem is inevitable. The best solution is to use several different measures, tapping the different aspects of the concept.

ANNOTATED BIBLIOGRAPHY

Franklin, Billy, and Osborne, Harold (eds.), *Research Methods: Issues and Insights* (Belmont, Calif.: Wadsworth, 1971), Part 5A. Three articles providing different overviews of measurement in social research. The Lazarsfeld-Barton article on qualitative measurements offers a useful balance to the generally quantitative orientation of this chapter.

Gould, Julius, and Kolb, William, *A Dictionary of the Social Sciences* (New York: Free Press, 1964). A primary reference to the social scientific agreements on various concepts. Although the terms used by social scientists do not have ultimately "true" meanings, this reference book lays out the meanings social scientists have in mind when they use those terms.

Lazarsfeld, Paul, and Rosenberg, Morris (eds.), *The Language of Social Research* (New York: Free Press of Glencoe, 1955), Section I. An excellent and diverse collection of descriptions of specific measurements in past social research. These 14 articles present extremely useful accounts of actual measurement operations performed by social researchers as well as more conceptual discussions of measurement in general.

Wallace, Walter, *The Logic of Science in Sociology* (Chicago: Aldine-Atherton, 1971), Chapter 3. A brief and lucid presentation of concept formation within the context of other research steps. This discussion relates conceptualization to observation on the one hand and to generalization on the other.

CHAPTER 6

Operationalization

INTRODUCTION

The preceding chapter discussed and described various aspects of the conceptualization process. In the course of that discussion, we moved frequently into the business of operationalization, since the two are intimately linked. I have distinguished the two as follows: conceptualization is the refinement and specification of abstract concepts, and operationalization is the development of specific research procedures (operations) that will result in empirical observations representing those concepts in the real world.

The purpose of this chapter—moving squarely into the operationalization process—is to get closer to the nitty-gritty of concrete measurements in social research. Even so, our coverage here will still be a little abstract and general. Ultimately, operationalization is inseparable from actual data collection, and we'll get even more specific and concrete in this regard in the examinations of the different modes of observations available to social researchers in Part Three. In that sense, the present chapter is partly a preview of what is to come. Nonetheless, I'm going to present some issues in operationalization that apply to most or all types of studies you might undertake.

We'll begin with an overview of some of the operationalization choices you have in organizing the business of observation and measurement: how and what to measure, what range of variation to consider, what levels of measurement to use, and whether to depend on a single indicator or several. Then, I'll give you some illustrations of the different ways we might measure a given variable. The purpose of that will be to broaden your imagination and vision.

Next, since social research often involves asking people for information, I'll present some general guidelines for doing that in a useful way. As you'll see, there are many styles of questions—only some of which will give you useful information about how human social life operates. There is a danger in observation that your magnifying glass will turn into a mirror, and all you'll see is yourself.

The chapter ends with a discussion of operationalization as a continuing process throughout a research project. Although I've discussed it in the context of research design—gearing up for the collection of data—we'll see that concepts are also operationalized during the analysis of the data that are collected. This concluding discussion, then, should fully round out your understanding of how social scientists measure things—even things that don't really exist.

OPERATIONALIZATION CHOICES

As I've indicated above, the social researcher has a wide variety of options available when it comes down to measuring a concept. Although the several choices are intimately interconnected, I've separated them for purposes of discussion. Please realize, however, that operationalization does *not* proceed through a systematic checklist.

Modes of Observation

As I've suggested in earlier chapters, social scientists make observations and collect data in many different ways. There are many sources to draw on and special ways of tapping them. I'll distinguish three main types of observation.

First, it is sometimes appropriate to base your measurements on *direct observations*. You can learn a lot by just looking and listening to what's going on. Chapter 8 on field research focuses on this form of observation, as did Humphreys's tearoom trade study, which was described earlier. If you wanted to measure the size of a picket line day after day during a protracted strike, you'd do well to go there each day and count the picketers.

Social scientists, then, often learn about life by observing what goes on in the natural course of things. At other times, it is appropriate to structure the course of things and then observe what happens. That is particularly the case with experiments, which are discussed more fully in Chapter 10, and it was illustrated earlier in the examination of the Milgram experiment. This kind of structuring often occurs with evaluation research (Chapter 11) as well. An innovative work furlough program might be established at a prison, for example, and a part of your evaluation could be observing how many prisoners come back to prison (or don't) when they're supposed to.

The second general mode of observation involves the *examination of existing statistics and documents*. As in Stouffer's research on the effects of the depression on the family, the data you need are often already compiled and ready for interpretation. Other times you will find that you need to compile them from raw sources, as you do in content analysis, which is discussed in Chapter 9. This method is, of course, the mainstay of historians and anyone else who wants to study the past.

Finally, we often learn about human affairs by *asking questions*. This method is always used in survey research (Chapter 12), and it is often involved in other research methods as well. Sometimes, we ask individuals about themselves and aggregate their answers to create an overall picture of groups. We usually refer to these people as _respondents_. At other times, we ask some individuals to give us information about others or about group matters. In a study of newborn babies, for example, we wouldn't get anywhere asking _them_ questions, so we ask their parents, doctors, and so forth. By the same token, the Bureau of the Census asks one household member to report on everyone in the household. In such cases, we usually refer to those we question as _informants_. (_Informers_ has an unpleasant ring to it.)

To begin, then, you can usually measure particular variables in several different ways, using different sources of information and different observation techniques. Making that decision, however, still leaves a number of options open. Let's look at some of them.

Range of Variation

In operationalizing any concept, it is essential that you be clear about the range of variation that interests you in your research. What will be the extremes that you are interested in measuring and recording? To what extent are you willing to combine attributes in fairly gross categories?

Let's suppose you want to measure people's incomes in a study—either collecting the information from records or in interviews. The highest annual incomes people receive run into the millions of dollars, but not many people get that much. Unless you are studying the very rich, it probably wouldn't be worth much to allow for and keep track of extremely high categories. Depending on whom you are studying, you'll probably want to establish a highest income category with a much lower floor—maybe $50,000 or more. Although this decision will lead you to throw together people who earn a trillion dollars a year with paupers earning only $50,000, they'll survive it, and that mixing probably won't hurt your research any. The same decision faces you at the other end of the income spectrum. In studies of the general American population, a cutoff of $5,000 or less usually works just fine.

In the study of attitudes and orientations, the question of range of variation has another dimension. Unless you're careful, you may end up measuring only half an attitude without really meaning to. Here's an example of what I mean.

Suppose you're interested in people's attitudes toward the expanded use of the supersonic transport (SST) aircraft. You'd anticipate in advance that some people consider it the greatest thing since the wheel, while other people have absolutely no interest in it whatever. Given that anticipation, it would seem to make sense to ask people how much they favor expanding the use of the SST. You might give them answer categories ranging from "Favor it very much" to "Don't favor it at all."

This operationalization, however, conceals half of the attitudinal spectrum regarding the SST. Many people have feelings about the SST that go beyond simply not favoring it: they are absolutely _opposed_ to it. In this instance, there is considerable variation on the left side of zero. Some oppose it a little, some quite a bit, and others a great deal. To measure the full range of variation, then, you'd want to operationalize attitudes toward the SST with a range from favoring it very much, through no feelings one way or the other, to opposing it very much.

This consideration applies to many of the variables we study in social science. Virtually any public issue provokes both support and opposition, each in varying degrees. Political orientations range from very liberal to very conservative, and depending on the people you are studying, you may want to allow for radicals on one or both ends. People are not just more or less religious, some are antireligious.

I do not mean that you must measure the full range of variation in any given case. You should, however, consider that possibility in the light of your research purpose. If the difference between *not religious* and *antireligious* isn't relevant to your research, forget it. Someone has defined pragmatism as "any difference that makes no difference is no difference." Be pragmatic.

Finally, your decision on range of variation should be governed also by the expected distribution of attributes among your subjects of study. That is what I meant earlier when I said range depends on whom you are studying. In a study of college professors' attitudes toward the value of higher education, you could probably stop at *no value* and not worry about those who might consider higher education dangerous to students' health. (If you were studying students, however. . . .)

Variations between the Extremes

In Chapter 5, I briefly discussed precision as a criterion of quality in measurement. It arises again as a consideration in operationalizing variables. What it boils down to is how fine you will make distinctions among the various possible attributes composing a given variable. Does it really matter whether a person is 17 or 18 years old, or could you conduct your inquiry by throwing them together in a group labeled 10 to 19 years old? Don't answer too quickly. If you wanted to study rates of voter registration and participation, you'd definitely want to know whether the people you studied were old enough to qualify to vote.

If you are going to measure age, then, you must look at the purpose and procedures of your study and decide whether fine or gross differences in age are important to you. If you measure political affiliation, will it matter to your inquiry whether a person is a conservative Democrat rather than a liberal Democrat, or is it sufficient to know the party? In measuring religious affiliation, is it enough to know that a person is a Protestant, or do you need to know the denomination? Do you simply need to know whether a person is married or not, or will it make a difference to know if they have never married or are separated, widowed, or divorced?

There is, of course, no general answer to questions like these. The answers come out of the purpose of your study, the purpose you have in making a particular measurement. I can mention a useful guideline, however. Whenever you're not sure how much detail to get in a measurement, get too much rather than too little. During the analysis of data, it will always be possible to combine precise attributes into more general categories, but it will never be possible to separate out the variations that were lumped together during observation and measurement.

A Note on Dimensions

(When people get down to the business of creating operational measures of variables, they often discover—or worse, never notice—that they are not exactly clear about the dimension of a variable that they are really interested in.)In Chapter 5, I dealt with this to some degree, and now I want to look at it more closely. Here's one example to illustrate what I mean.

Let's suppose you and I are studying people's attitudes toward government, and we want to include an examination of how people feel about corruption. Here are just a few of the different dimensions we might examine:

Do people think there is corruption in government?

How much corruption do they think there is?

How certain are they in their judgment of how much corruption there is?

How do they feel about corruption in government as a problem in society?

What do they think causes it?

Do they think it's inevitable?

What do they feel should be done about it?

What are they willing to do personally to eliminate corruption in government?

How certain are they that they would be willing to do what they say they would do?

The list could go on and on. How people feel about corruption in government has many dimensions, and it's essential that you be clear about which ones are important in your inquiry. Otherwise, you may measure how people feel about it when you really wanted to know how much they think there is, or vice versa.

Once you have determined how you are going to make your observations—how you are going to collect data—and have decided on the relevant range of variation, the degree of precision needed between the extremes of variation, and the specific dimensions of the variables that interest you, you may have another choice: a mathematical-logical one. You may need to decide what level of measurement to use, and to discuss that question we need to take another look at attributes and their relationship to variables. (See Chapter 2 for the first discussion of this topic.)

Levels of Measurement

An attribute, you'll recall, is a characteristic or quality of something. *Female* would be an example. So would *old* or *student*. Variables, on the other hand, are logical sets of attributes. Thus, *sex* or *gender* is a variable composed of the attributes *female* and *male*.

The conceptualization and operationalization processes can be seen as the specification of variables and the attributes composing them. Thus, in one of the examples given in the preceding section, employment status would be a variable having the attributes *employed* and *unemployed* and perhaps expanded to include the other possibilities discussed.

Every variable should have two important qualities. First, the attributes composing it should be *exhaustive*. If the variable is to have any utility in research, you should be able to classify every observation in terms of one of the attributes composing the variable. You will run into trouble if you conceptualize the variable political party affiliation in terms of the attributes *Republican* and *Democrat*, because some of the people you set out to study will belong to the Socialist Workers Party, the American Independent Party, and the Peace and Freedom Party, or other party, and some (often a large percentage) will tell you they have no party affiliation. You could make the list of attributes exhaustive by adding *other* and *no affiliation*. Whatever you do, you must be able to classify every observation.

At the same time, attributes composing a variable must be *mutually exclusive*. You must be able to classify every observation in terms of one and *only one* attribute. Thus, for example, you need to define *employed* and *unemployed* in such a way that nobody can be both at the same time. That means being able to handle the person who is working at a job *and* is looking for work. (You might run across an employed economist who is looking for the glamor and excitement of being a sociologist.) In this case, you might define your attributes so that *employed* takes precedence over *unemployed* and anyone working at a job is employed regardless of whether he or she is looking for something better.

These structural qualities must be present among the attributes composing any variable. However, attributes form other structures as well. Because of these additional structural features, different variables may represent different *levels of measurement*. We are going to examine four levels of measurement in this section: *nominal*, *ordinal*, *interval*, and *ratio*.

Nominal Measures   Variables whose attributes have only the characteristics of exhaustiveness and mutual exclusiveness represent **nominal measures**. Examples of these would be sex, religious affiliation, political party affiliation, college major, hair color, and birthplace. Although the attributes composing each of these variables —*male* and *female* composing the variable *sex*—are distinct from one another (and exhaust the possibilities of gender among people), they have none of the additional structures mentioned below.

It might be useful to imagine a group of people being characterized in terms of one such variable and physically grouped by the applicable attributes. Imagine asking a large gathering of people to stand together in groups according to the states in which they were born: all those born in Vermont together in one group, those born in California in another, and so forth. (The variable would be *place of birth*; the attribute would be *born in California*, or *born in Vermont*.) All the people standing in a given group would share at least one thing in common; the people in any group would differ from the people in all the other groups in that same regard. Where the individual groups formed, how close they were to one another, or how the groups were arranged in the room, would all be irrelevant. All that would matter would be that all the members of a given group share the same state of birth, and that each group has a different shared state of birth.

Ordinal Measures (Variables whose attributes may be logically *rank-ordered* represent **ordinal measures.**)The different attributes represent relatively more or less of the variable. Variables of this type are social class, religiosity, conservatism, alienation, prejudice, intellectual sophistication, and the like.

Note that each of these examples would be subject to serious differences of opinion as to its definition. Many of the ordinal variables used in social scientific research have this quality, but that need not be the case. In the physical sciences, hardness is the most frequently cited example of an ordinal measure. We may say that one material (for example, diamond) is harder than another (say, glass) if the former can scratch the latter and not vice versa (that is, diamond scratches glass, but glass does not scratch diamond). By attempting to scratch various materials with other materials, we might eventually be able to arrange several materials in a row, ranging from the softest to the hardest. It would not ever be possible to say how hard a given material was in absolute terms, but only in relative terms—which materials it was harder than, and which it was softer than.

Let's pursue the earlier example of grouping the people at a social gathering and imagine that we asked all the people with a college education to stand in one group, all those with a high school education (but who were not also college graduates) to stand in another group, and all those who had not graduated from high school to stand in a third group. This manner of grouping people would satisfy the requirements for exhaustiveness and mutual exclusiveness discussed earlier. In addition, however, we might logically arrange the three groups in terms of the relative amount of formal education (the shared attribute) each had. We might arrange the three groups in a row, ranging from most to least formal education. This arrangement would provide a physical representation of an ordinal measure. If we knew which groups two individual people were in, we could determine that one had more, less, or the same formal education as the other; in a similar way, one individual object could be ranked as harder, softer, or of the same hardness as another object.

It is important to note that in this example it would be irrelevant how close or far apart the educational groups were from one another. They might stand 5 feet apart or 500 feet apart; the college and high school groups could be 5 feet apart, while the less-than-high-school group might be 500 feet farther down the line. These actual distances would not have any meaning. The high school group, however, should be between the less-than-high-school group and the college group, or else the rank order would be incorrect.

Interval Measures   For the attributes composing some variables, the actual distance separating those attributes has meaning. Such variables are interval **measures.** For these, the logical distance between attributes can be expressed in meaningful standard intervals. A physical science example would be the Fahrenheit (or the Celsius, but not the Kelvin) temperature scale. The difference, or distance, between 80 degrees and 90 degrees is the same as that which separates 40 degrees and 50 degrees. However, 80 degrees Fahrenheit is not twice as hot as 40 degrees, since the zero point in the Fahrenheit scale (and the Celsius, but not the Kelvin) is an arbitrary one; zero degrees does not really mean lack of heat, nor does −30 degrees represent 30 degrees less than no heat. (The Kelvin scale is based on an *absolute zero* that does mean—for a physicist at least—a complete lack of heat.)

About the only interval measures commonly used in social scientific research are those constructed measures such as standardized intelligence tests that have been more or less accepted. The interval separating IQ scores of 100 and 110 may be regarded as the same as the interval separating scores of 110 and 120 by virtue of the distribution of observed scores obtained by many thousands of people who have taken the tests over the years. (A person who received a score of 0 on a standard IQ test could not be regarded, strictly speaking, as having *no* intelligence, although we might feel he or she was unsuited to be a college professor or even a college student.)

Ratio Measures   Most of the social scientific variables meeting the minimum requirements for interval measures also meet the requirements for **ratio measures**. The attributes composing some variables, besides having all the structural characteristics mentioned above, are based on a true zero point. I have already mentioned Kelvin temperature scale in contrast to the Fahrenheit and Celsius scales. Examples from social scientific research would include age, length of residence in a given place, the number of organizations belonged to, the number of times attending church during a particular period of time, the number of times married, and the number of Arab friends.

Returning to the illustration of methodological party games at a social gathering, we might ask people to group themselves according to age. All the one-year-olds would stand (or sit or lie) together, the two-year-olds together, the three-year-olds, and so forth. The fact that members of a single group shared the same age and that different groups had different shared ages would satisfy the minimum requirements for a nominal measure. The several groups could be arranged in a line running from the youngest to the oldest, thereby meeting the additional requirements of an ordinal measure and permitting us to determine if one person was older, younger, or the same age as another. It would also be reasonable to arrange the groups in such a way as to have the same distance between each pair of adjacent groups, thereby satisfying the additional requirements of an interval measure and permitting us to say *how much* older one person was than another. Finally, since one of the attributes included in age represents a true zero (babies carried by women about to give birth), the phalanx of hapless party goers would also meet the requirements for a ratio measure, permitting us to say that one person was twice as old as another.

Implications of Levels of Measurement   Since it is unlikely that you will undertake the physical grouping of people described above (try it once, and you won't be invited to many parties), I should draw your attention to some of the practical implications of the differences that have been distinguished. Primarily, these implications appear in the analysis of data (discussed in Part Four), but those analytical implications should be anticipated in the structuring of your research project.

Certain analytical techniques require variables of certain minimum levels of measurement. To the extent that the variables to be examined in your research project are limited to a particular level of measurement—say, ordinal—you should plan your analytical techniques accordingly. More precisely, you should anticipate drawing research conclusions appropriate to the levels of measurement used in your variables. For example, you might reasonably plan to determine and report the mean age of a population under study (add up all the individual ages and divide by the number of people), but you should not plan on reporting the mean religious affiliation, since that is a nominal variable. (You could report the *modal*—the most common—religious affiliation.)

At the same time, it is important to realize that some variables may be treated as representing different levels of measurement. Ratio measures are the highest level, descending through interval and ordinal to nominal, the lowest level of measurement. A variable representing a given level of measurement—say, ratio—may also be treated as representing a lower level of measurement—say, ordinal. Recall for example, that age is a ratio measure. If you wished to examine only the relationship between age and some ordinal-level variable—say, self-perceived religiosity: high, medium, and low—you might choose to treat age as an ordinal-level variable as well. You might characterize the subjects of your study as being *young*, *middle-aged*, and *old*, specifying what age range composed each of those groupings. Finally age might be used as a nominal-level variable for certain research purposes. People might be grouped as being members of the post-World War II baby boom or not; they might be grouped as being born during the depression of the 1930s or not. Another nominal measurement, based on birth date rather than just age, would be the grouping of people by astrological signs.

The analytical uses planned for a given variable, then, should determine the level of measurement to be sought, with the realization that some variables are inherently limited to a certain level. If a variable is to be used in a variety of ways, requiring different levels of measurement, the study should be designed in such a fashion as to achieve the highest level required. (For example, if the subjects in a study are asked their exact ages, they can subsequently be organized into ordinal or nominal groupings.)

You need not necessarily measure variables at their highest level of measurement, however. If you are sure to have no need for ages of people at higher than the ordinal level of measurement, you may simply ask people which among several age ranges they belong in: their twenties, thirties, and so forth. In a study of the wealth of corporations, you may use Dun & Bradstreet reports, which list many United States corporations and classify them according to net worth. If your research purposes require only ordinal measurement of corporate wealth, you might choose to use Dun & Bradstreet data to rank corporations rather than seek more precise information. Whenever your research purposes are not altogether clear, however, it is advisable to seek the highest level of measurement possible. Although ratio measures can later be reduced to ordinal ones, it is not possible to convert an ordinal measure to a ratio one. That is a one-way street worth remembering.

Single or Multiple Indicators

In presenting so many alternatives and choices for you to make in operational-izing social scientific variables, I realize that I may create a sense of uncertainty and insecurity. You may find yourself worrying about whether you will make the right choices. To counterbalance this possible feeling, let me add a momentary dash of certainty and stability.

Many social scientific variables have pretty obvious, straightforward measures. No matter how you cut it, gender usually turns out to be a matter of male or female: a nominal-level variable that can be measured by a single observation—either look-ing or asking a question. Although you'll want to think about adopted and foster children, it's usually pretty easy to find out how many children a family has. And although some fine tuning is possible, for most research purposes, the resident population of a country is the resident population of that country—you can look it up in an almanac and know the answer. A great many variables, then, have obvious single indicators. If you can get one piece of information, you have what you need.

Sometimes, however, there is no single indicator that will give you the measure of a variable that you really want. As discussed in Chapter 5, many concepts are subject to varying interpretations—each with several possible indicators. In these cases, you will want to make several observations for a given variable. You can then combine the several pieces of information you've collected to create a *composite* measurement of the variable in question. All of Chapter 15 (Index and Scale Con-struction) is devoted to ways of doing that, so I'll give you only a simple illustration at this point.

Consider the concept *college performance*. All of us have noticed that some students do well in college and others don't do so well—in terms of their perfor-mance in courses. It might be useful to study that, perhaps asking what character-istics and experiences are related to high levels of performance, and many research-ers have done just that. How should we measure overall performance? Each grade in each course is a potential indicator of college performance, but we run a risk in using any single course grade that the one used will not be typical of the student's general performance. The solution to this problem is so firmly established that it is, of course, obvious to you: the *grade point average*. By assigning numerical scores to each letter grade, we total the points earned by each student and divide by the number of courses taken. This, then, is an example of a composite measure, and it is often appropriate to create such composite measures in social research.

SOME OPERATIONALIZATION ILLUSTRATIONS

To bring together all the operationalization choices available to the social researcher and to show you the potential in those possibilities, I want to take just a little time to illustrate some of the ways in which you might address certain research problems. My purpose here is to stretch your imagination just a bit further and demonstrate the challenge that social research can present to your ingenuity. To simplify matters, I have not attempted to describe all the research conditions that would make one alternative superior to the others, though you should realize that in a given situation, they would not all be equally appropriate. Let's look at specific research questions, then, and some of the ways you could address them. Let's begin with an example that was discussed at length in Chapter 5. It has the added advantage that one of the variables is reasonably straightforward.

1. *Are women more compassionate than men?*

  1a. Select a group of subjects for study. Present them with hypothetical situations that involve someone's being in trouble. Ask them what *they* would do if they were confronted with that situation. What would they do, for example, if they came across a small child who was lost and crying for its parents. Consider any answer that involves helping the child or comforting it to be compassionate, and count whether men or women are more likely to indicate they would be compassionate.

  1b. Set up an experiment in which you pay a small child to pretend that he or she is lost. Put the kid to work on a busy sidewalk, and count whether men or women are more likely to offer assistance. Be sure to count how many men and women walk by, also, since there may be more of one than the other. If that's the case, simply calculate the percentage of men and the percentage of women who help.

  1c. Select a sample of people and do a survey in which you ask them what organizations they belong to. Calculate whether women or men are more likely to belong to those that seem to reflect compassionate feelings. To take account of men belonging to more organizations than women in general—or vice versa—do this: for each person you study, calculate the *percentage* of his or her organizational memberships that reflect compassion. See if men or women have a higher average percentage.

  1d. Watch your local newspaper for a special feature on some issue involving compassion—the slaughter of baby seals, for example. In the days to follow, keep a record of all letters to the editor on the subject. See whether men or women are the more likely to express their compassion in the matter—making the necessary adjustments for one gender writing more letters to the editor than the other in general.

2. *Are sociology students or psychology students better informed about world affairs?*

  2a. Prepare a short quiz on world affairs and arrange to administer it to the students in a sociology class and in a comparable psychology class. If you want to compare sociology and psychology *majors*, be sure to ask them what they are majoring in.

  2b. Get the instructor of a course in world affairs to give the average grades of sociology and psychology students in the course.

  2c. Take a petition to sociology and psychology classes which urges that "the United Nations headquarters be moved to New York City." Keep a count of how many in each class sign the petition and how many inform you that the UN headquarters is already located in New York City.

3. *Do people consider New York or California the better place to live?*

    3a. Consulting the *Statistical Abstract of the United States* or a similar publication, check the migration rates into and out of each state. See if you can find the numbers moving directly from New York to California and vice versa.

    3b. The national polling companies—Gallup, Harris, Roper, and so forth—often ask people what they consider the best state to live in. Look up some recent results in the library or through your local newspaper.

    3c. Compare suicide rates in the two states.

4. *Who are the most popular instructors on your campus: those in the social sciences, the natural sciences, or the humanities?*

    4a. If your school has a provision for student evaluation of instructors, review some recent results and compute the average ratings given the three groups.

    4b. Begin visiting the introductory courses given in each group of disciplines and count the numbers of students attending classes. Get the enrollment figures for the classes you study and calculate the average absentee rates.

    4c. Around Christmas, select a group of faculty in each of the three divisions and ask them to keep a record of the numbers of cards and presents they receive from admiring students. See who wins.

    4d. Read the obituary column in your campus newspaper every day and keep a record of all the faculty who are lynched after class by mobs of irate students—taking care to always note their departmental affiliation. Be sure to adjust your figures to take account of the total number of faculty in each division: the percentages lynched is more appropriate than the numbers lynched.

We could continue moving from the ridiculous to the more ridiculous, but the point of the illustrations has been to broaden your vision of the many ways variables can be operationalized, not necessarily to suggest respectable research projects. When you think about it, absolutely everything you see around you is already an operationalized measure of some variable. Most are measures of more than one variable, so all you have to do is pick the ones you want and decide what they will represent in your particular study. Usually, you will want to use more than one measure for each variable in the inquiry.

GUIDELINES FOR ASKING QUESTIONS

In several of the illustrations above—and in the practice of actual social research —variables are often operationalized by asking people questions as a way of getting data for analysis and interpretation. That is always the case in survey research, and questions are often used in experiments, field research, and other modes of observation. Sometimes the questions are asked by an interviewer, sometimes they are written down and given to respondents for completion (these are called *self-administered questionnaires*).

Since questionnaires represent a common and concrete illustration of the operationalization process, they are a fit topic for completing our general examination. As we'll see, several general guidelines can assist you in framing and asking questions that serve as excellent operationalizations of variables. There are also pitfalls that can result in useless and even misleading information. This section should assist you in distinguishing the two. Let's begin with some of the options available to you in creating questionnaires.

Questions and Statements

The term *questionnaire* suggests a collection of questions, but an examination of a typical questionnaire will probably reveal as many statements as questions. That is not without reason. Often, the researcher is interested in determining the extent to which respondents hold a particular attitude or perspective. If you are able to summarize the attitude in a fairly brief statement, you will often present that statement and ask respondents whether they agree or disagree with it. Rensis Likert has greatly formalized this procedure through the creation of the Likert scale, a format in which respondents are asked to strongly agree, agree, disagree, or strongly disagree, or perhaps strongly approve, approve, and so forth.

Both questions and statements may be used profitably. Using both in a given questionnaire gives you more flexibility in the design of items and can make the questionnaire more interesting as well.

Open-Ended and Closed-Ended Questions

In asking questions, the researcher has two options. We may ask *open-ended* questions, in which case the respondent is asked to provide his or her own answer to the question. For example, the respondent may be asked, "What do you feel is the most important issue facing the United States today?"and be provided with a space to write in the answer (or be asked to report it verbally to an interviewer).

In the other case, *closed-ended* questions, the respondent is asked to select an answer from among a list provided by the researcher. Closed-ended questions are very popular, since they provide a greater uniformity of responses and are more easily processed. Open-ended responses must be coded before keypunching and there is a danger that some respondents will give answers that are essentially irrelevant to the researcher's intent. Closed-ended responses, on the other hand, can often be keypunched directly from the questionnaire and in some cases can be marked directly on optical-sensing sheets by respondents for automatic punching.

The chief shortcoming of closed-ended questions lies in the researcher's structuring of responses. When the relevant answers to a given question are relatively clear, that may present no problem. In other cases, however, the researcher's structuring of responses may overlook some important responses. In asking about "the most important issue facing the United States," for example, you might provide a checklist of issues, but in doing so you might overlook certain issues that respondents would have said were important.

In the construction of closed-ended questions, you should be guided by the two structural requirements discussed earlier. The response categories provided should be *exhaustive*: they should include all the possible responses that might be expected. Often, researchers insure this by adding a category labeled something like: Other (Please specify.) _____.

Second, the answer categories must be *mutually exclusive*: the respondent should not feel compelled to select more than one. (In some cases, you may wish to solicit multiple answers, but these may create difficulties in data processing and analysis later on.) To insure that your categories are mutually exclusive, you should carefully consider each combination of categories, asking whether a person could reasonably choose more than one answer. In addition, it is useful to add an instruction to the question asking the respondent to select the *one best* answer, but this technique is not a satisfactory substitute for a carefully constructed set of responses.

Make Items Clear

It should go without saying that questionnaire items should be clear and unambiguous, but the broad proliferation of unclear and ambiguous questions in surveys makes the point worth stressing here. Often you can become so deeply involved in the topic under examination that opinions and perspectives are clear to you but will not be clear to your respondents—many of whom have given little or no attention to the topic. Or, on the other hand, you may have only a superficial understanding of the topic and fail to specify the intent of your question sufficiently. The question "What do you think about the proposed antiballistic missile system?" may evoke in the respondent a counterquestion: "*Which* proposed antiballistic missile system?" Questionnaire items should be precise so that the respondent knows exactly what the researcher wants an answer to.

Avoid Double-Barreled Questions

Very frequently, researchers ask respondents for a single answer to a combination of questions. That seems to happen most often when the researcher has personally identified with a complex question. For example, you might ask respondents to agree or disagree with the statement "The United States should abandon its space program and spend the money on domestic programs." Although many people would unequivocally agree with the statement and others would unequivocally disagree, still others would be unable to answer. Some would want to abandon the space program and give the money back to the taxpayers. Others would want to continue the space program, but also put more money into domestic programs.

These latter respondents could neither agree nor disagree without misleading you.

As a general rule, whenever the word *and* appears in a question or questionnaire statement, you should check whether you are asking a double-barreled question.

Respondents Must Be Competent to Answer

In asking respondents to provide information, you should continually ask yourself whether they are able to do so reliably. In a study of child rearing, you might ask respondents to report the age at which they first talked back to their parents. Quite aside from the problem of defining *talking back to parents*, it is doubtful if most respondents would remember with any degree of accuracy.

As another example, student government leaders occasionally ask their constituents to indicate the manner in which students' fees ought to be spent. Typically, respondents are asked to indicate the percentage of available funds that should be devoted to a long list of activities. Wthout a fairly good knowledge of the nature of those activities and the costs involved in them, the respondents cannot provide meaningful answers. (*Administrative costs* will receive little support although they may be essential to the program as a whole.)

One group of researchers examining the driving experience of teenagers insisted on asking an open-ended question concerning the number of miles driven since receiving a license. Although consultants argued that few drivers would be able to estimate such information with any accuracy, the question was asked nonetheless. In response, some teenagers reported driving hundreds of thousands of miles.

Questions Should Be Relevant

Similarly, questions asked in a questionnaire should be relevant to most respondents. When attitudes are requested on a topic that few respondents have thought about or really care about, the results are not likely to be very useful. Of course, the respondents may express attitudes even though they have never given any thought to the issue, and you run the risk of being misled.

This point is illustrated occasionally when you ask for responses relating to fictitious persons and issues. In one study of political images, respondents were asked whether they were familiar with each of 15 political figures in the community. In regard to one purely fictitious figure, 9 percent of the respondents said they were familiar with her. Of those respondents, about half reported seeing her on television and reading about her in the newspapers.

When responses are obtained with regard to fictitious issues, you can disregard those responses. But when the issue is real, you may have no way of telling which responses genuinely reflect attitudes and which reflect meaningless answers to an irrelevant question.

Short Items Are Best

In the interest of being unambiguous and precise and pointing to the relevance of an issue, the researcher is often led into long and complicated items. That should be avoided. Respondents are often unwilling to study an item in order to understand it. The respondent should be able to read an item quickly, understand its intent, and select or provide an answer without difficulty. In general, you should assume that respondents *will* read items quickly and give quick answers; therefore, you should provide clear, short items that will not be misinterpreted under those conditions.

Avoid Negative Items

The appearance of a negation in a questionnaire item paves the way for easy misinterpretation. Asked to agree or disagree with the statement "The United States should not recognize Cuba," a sizable portion of the respondents will read over the word "not" and answer on that basis. Thus, some will agree with the statement when they are in favor of recognition, while others will agree when they oppose it. And you may never know which is which.

In a study of civil liberties support, respondents were asked whether they felt "the following kinds of people should be prohibited from teaching in public schools," and were presented with a list including such items as a Communist, a Ku Klux Klansman, and so forth. The response categories "yes" and "no" were given beside each entry. A comparison of the responses to this item with other items reflecting support for civil liberties strongly suggested that many respondents gave the answer "yes" to indicate willingness for such a person to teach, rather than to indicate that such a person should be prohibited. (A subsequent study in the series gave as answer categories "permit" and "prohibit" and produced much clearer results.)

Avoid Biased Items and Terms

Recall from the earlier discussion of conceptualization and operationalization that there are no ultimately true meanings for any of the concepts that we typically study in social science. *Prejudice* has no ultimately correct definition, and whether a given person is prejudiced depends on our definition of that term. This same general principle applies to the responses that we get from persons completing a questionnaire.

The meaning of someone's response to a question depends in large part on the wording of the question that was asked. That is true of every question and answer. Some questions would seem to encourage particular responses more than other questions. Questions that encourage respondents to answer in a particular way are called **biased**.

Most researchers would recognize the likely effect of a question that began "Don't you agree with the President of the United States in the belief that . . .," and no reputable researcher would use such an item. Unhappily, the biasing effect of items and terms is far subtler than this example suggests.

The mere identification of an attitude or position with a prestigious person or agency can bias responses. The item "Do you agree or disagree with the President's proposal to . . ." would have this effect. "Do you agree or disagree with the recent Supreme Court decision that . . ." would have a similar effect. I should make it clear that I am not suggesting that such wording will necessarily produce consensus or even a majority in support of the position identified with the prestigious person or agency, only that support would likely be increased over what would have been obtained without such identification.

Questionnaire items can be biased negatively as well as positively. "Do you agree or disagree with the position of Adolf Hitler when he stated that . . ." would be an example. In recent years in the United States, it has been very difficult to ask questions relating to China. Identifying the country as "China" would result in confusion between mainland China and Taiwan. Referring to "Red China" or "Communist China" would evoke a more negative response from many respondents. At the same time, of course, the researcher's purpose must be taken into account. Referring to "mainland China" might produce less hostile responses when anticommunist feelings were an important aspect of the research.

In this context, you need to be generally wary of what researchers call the *social desirability* of questions and answers. Whenever you ask people for information, they answer through a filter of what will make them look good. That is especially true if they are being interviewed in a face-to-face situation. Thus, for example, a particular man may feel that things would be a lot better if women were kept in the kitchen, not allowed to vote, forced to be quiet in public, and so forth. Asked whether he supports equal rights for women, however, he may want to avoid looking like a male chauvinist pig. Recognizing that his views might have been progressive in the fifteenth century but are out of step with current thinking, he may choose to say "yes." Perhaps the only guidance I can offer you in relation to this problem is to suggest that you imagine how *you* would feel giving each of the answers you offered to respondents. If you'd feel embarrassed, perverted, inhumane, stupid, irresponsible, or anything like that, you should give some serious thought to whether others will be willing to give those answers.

As in all other examples, you must carefully examine the purpose of your inquiry and construct items that will be most useful to it. You should never be misled into thinking there are ultimately "right" and "wrong" ways of asking the questions.

These, then, are some general guidelines for writing questions to elicit data for analysis and interpretation. I'll have more to say about questionnaires in Chapter 12 (Survey Research) when we look at some nitty-gritty details such as questionnaire layout, interviewing guidelines, and so forth. For now, the discussion of question construction should have filled out your understanding of the operationalization process. There's only one more general comment to be made.

OPERATIONALIZATION GOES ON AND ON

Although I've discussed conceptualization and operationalization as activities that precede data collection and analysis—you design your operational measures before you observe—you should realize that these two processes continue throughout a research project, even after data have been collected and analyzed. Here's what I mean by that.

You'll recall that I have repeatedly suggested that you measure a given variable in several different ways in your research. That is essential if the concept lying in the background is at all ambiguous and open to different interpretations and definitions. By measuring the variable in several different ways, you will be in a position to examine alternative operational definitions during your analysis. You will have several single indicators to choose from and many ways of creating different composite measures. Thus, you'll be able to experiment with different measures—each representing a somewhat different conceptualization and operationalization—to decide which gives the clearest and most useful answers to your research questions.

This doesn't mean that you should select the measurement that confirms your expectations or proves your point. That's clearly not appropriate and doesn't do much to advance our understanding of social life. Instead, operationalization is a continuing process, not a blind commitment to a particular measure that may turn out to have been poorly chosen. Suppose, for example, that you decide to measure compassion by asking people whether they give money to charity and everybody says "yes." Where does that leave you? Nowhere. Your study of why some people are more compassionate than others would be in deep trouble unless you had included some other possible measures in designing your observations.

The ultimate purpose of social research is to clarify the nature of social life. The validity and utility of what you learn in that regard doesn't depend on when you first figured out how to look at things, any more than it matters whether you got the idea from a learned textbook, a dream, or your brother-in-law.

SUMMARY

This chapter concludes the process of moving from an interesting idea to an empirical measurement. In Chapter 5 we dealt with the process of conceptualization—the refinement and specification of mental images. The discussion of operationalization in this chapter has extended the process so that we can now recognize indicators of our ideas when we see them. The chapter has presented a number of options available in operationalization.

First, we examined briefly some of the main modes of observation available. Essentially you can (1) observe what's happening, either in its natural state or under special conditions, (2) find indicators of concepts within the body of statistical and other materials already in existence, or (3) ask people questions.

Second, variation on a variable is the subject of two forms of options. You need to decide on the relevant range of variation: what extremes of variation will interest you? Do you want to measure both the concept and its opposite? To what extent does it make sense to group together differences near the extremes? And within the extreme categories of variation, you must also decide how finely or precisely you want to distinguish differences.

Third, some comments were made on the topic of dimensions of a variable. Often, it takes some careful thought to determine exactly what aspect of a concept is the most relevant to an inquiry.

Fourth, we looked at the different levels of measurement that can be used in the operationalization of different variables: nominal, ordinal, interval, and ratio. Each level of measurement has different implications for both observation and subsequent analysis.

Fifth, measuring variables with single indicators or composite measures such as indexes and scales was discussed briefly. This topic will be covered in more detail in Chapter 15. These various options were then illustrated in a number of examples.

Since asking questions is a common method of operationalizing variables, a special section was devoted to some general guidelines for doing it right. We saw some of the pitfalls awaiting the asker of social research questions, and we also saw some of the ways of detouring around those pitfalls. Chapter 12 includes a further discussion of questionnaire construction.

The chapter concludes with a discussion of operationalization as a continuing process. Though we have discussed it so far in the context of study design—getting ready for observations—I pointed out that the process continues into the analysis of data as well. In this sense, your whole research project has as its purpose the determination of useful ways of measuring variables.

MAIN POINTS

1. Operationalization is an extension of the conceptualization process.

2. In operationalization, concrete empirical procedures are specified that will result in measurements of variables.

3. Operationalization is the final specification of how we would recognize the different attributes of a given variable in the real world.

4. In determining the range of variation for a variable, be sure to consider the opposite of the concept. Will it be sufficient to measure *religiosity* from "very much" to "none" or should you go past "none" to measure "anti-religiosity" as well?

5. Nominal measures refer to those variables whose attributes are simply different from one another. An example would be *sex*.

6. Ordinal measures refer to those variables whose attributes may be rank-ordered along some progression from more to less. An example would be the variable *prejudice* as composed of the attributes "very prejudiced," "somewhat prejudiced," "slightly prejudiced," and "not at all prejudiced."

7. Interval measures refer to those variables whose attributes are not only rank-ordered but also are separated by a uniform distance between them. An example would be IQ.

8. Ratio measures are the same as interval measures except that ratio measures are also based on a true zero point. Age would be an example of a ratio measure, since that variable contains the attribute *zero years old*.

9. A given variable can sometimes be measured at different levels of measurement. Thus, age, potentially a ratio measure, may also be treated as interval, ordinal, or even nominal. The most appropriate level of measurement employed depends on the purpose of the measurement.

10. Questionnaires provide a method of collecting data by (a) asking people questions or (b) asking them to agree or disagree with statements representing different points of view.

11. Questions may be open-ended (respondents supply their own answers) or closed-ended (they select from a list of answers provided them).

12. Usually, short items in a questionnaire are better than long ones.

13. Negative items and terms should be avoided because they may confuse respondents.

14. *Bias* is the quality in questionnaire items that encourages respondents to answer in a particular way or to support a particular point of view. Avoid it.

15. Operationalization begins in study design and continues throughout the research project, including the analysis of data.

ANNOTATED BIBLIOGRAPHY

Miller, Delbert, *Handbook of Research Design and Social Measurement* (New York: David McKay, 1977). A useful reference work. This book, especially Part IV, cites and describes a wide variety of operational measures used in earlier social research. In a number of cases, the questionnaire formats used are presented. Though the quality of these illustrations is uneven, they provide excellent examples of the variations possible.

Oppenheim, A. N., *Questionnaire Design and Attitude Measurement* (New York: Basic Books, 1966). An excellent and comprehensive treatment of the construction of questionnaires and their relation to measurement in general. Although the illustrations of questionnaire formats are not always the best, this comes the closest of any book available to being the definitive work on questionnaires. Its coverage ranges from the theoretical to the nitty-gritty.

Payne, Stanley, *The Art of Asking Questions* (Princeton, N.J.: Princeton University Press, 1951). A dated but still instructive treatment of questionnaires. This book is decidedly practical, anecdotal, and folksy. Special attention is paid to the field of meanings of words and the implications of that on questionnaire construction. In that regard, it should be inspirational as well as specifically instructive.

CHAPTER 7

The Logic of Sampling

INTRODUCTION

In the preceding discussions, I have made frequent references to the observations that you will make in the course of social research. Part Three, which follows, will go into the details of several observational options available to you. The present chapter deals with the critical aspect of research that is intimately entwined with observation: who or what will you observe?

If you'll take a moment to glance around you, you'll see immediately that there are billions of things available for you to observe. Clearly, you cannot focus on all of them or even a significant portion of them. Not surprisingly, psychologists are very interested in the way people select what they will observe, and *selective perception* seems to be a fundamental component of our cognitive process.

Selective perception is also a fundamental component of scientific research. It occurs in two stages. First, the vast majority of things available for observation are irrelevant to any particular research project. If your research interest concerns the effectiveness of a new psychotherapeutic technique, you would probably do well to ignore economic cycles, subatomic particles, house-painting techniques, and a zillion other things. Earlier discussions in this book have dealt with some of the ways in which we focus on the set of possible observations relevant to a particular research interest. This first aspect of selective perception in research is probably obvious in principle, though it can be trickier and more ambiguous in practice.

Suppose, however, that you've been able to develop a conceptual limit to the observations relevant to your particular inquiry. Let's say that you want to study the economic status of the nation's elderly. Perhaps you want to undertake an evaluation of various private and government assistance programs. You would have narrowed down the focus of your subsequent observations—you need only to observe the elderly. There are, however, over 20 million Americans aged 65 and older. Clearly, you can't observe them all.

Sampling is the process of selecting a subset of observations—from among many possible observations—for the purpose of drawing conclusions about that larger set of possible observations. In terms of the above example, sampling would be the selection of, say, 1,000 or 2,000 older Americans in such a way that those selected will give us essentially the same information we would have obtained had we been able to study everyone. Thus, we are able to study a few and reach accurate conclusions about the many. This chapter discusses how that can be accomplished.

The key principle in sampling is *representativeness*. The purpose of scientific sampling is to select a few who can be taken to represent the many. If you wanted to draw conclusions about all American corporations, you'd want to select a sample of corporations that—taken together—were a replica of all corporations, in miniature. Thus if the average net profit among some 2 million corporations in the nation was, say, $70,000, then you'd want to select a sample of corporations with that same average net profit. If the nation's corporations spent about 1 percent of their receipts on advertising, your sample should also spend about 1 percent. The average number of employees in the sample of corporations, the average number of years in business, the distribution of sample corporations among various industries, and so forth should all be a close approximation of those characteristics among the larger group of 2 million.

To take a very different example, if you want to compare some aspect of French and Russian folk songs, you'll need to select a sample of each for study. You'll need to insure that the sample of Russian folk songs is representative of all Russian folk songs, and the same must be true of the sample of French folk songs.

As we'll see in Chapter 10 (Experiments), it is often important to compare two or more groupings that are the same except for the presence or absence of some experimental condition, such as receiving a psychotherapeutic treatment, for example. It is necessary, therefore, for each of the subgroups to be representative of the total group comprising all the individuals combined.

Suppose now that I gave you the task of selecting a sample of 2,000 voters to represent the tens of millions who make the total electorate. Our purpose is to predict how an upcoming election will turn out. Do you think you could do that? How would you begin? By the time you complete this chapter, you should have a clear view of how to proceed in solving that problem and similar ones.

Since social scientific sampling has largely developed in a context of opinion research in surveys, I want to start this discussion with a quick overview of that history. In the course of this overview, you should come to realize that all problems I posed above can be solved: that it is possible to select samples that accurately represent very large populations. Then, I'll show you the logic that lies behind scientific sampling and some of the specific techniques involved in accomplishing it.

Social Sampling's Checkered Past

You may have noticed an interesting irony in connection with the accuracy of sampling. As I've indicated, we typically select samples from large populations because it would not be feasible to observe all members of those total populations. The goal is to select samples that are representative of the larger populations. But, if we are unable to study the total populations that the samples are selected from, how can we ever determine if the samples are accurate?

Political pollsters are one group of survey researchers who are given an opportunity to check the accuracy of their sample findings. Election day is the final judgment for political pollsters, and their mixed experiences are instructive in the more general question of sample survey accuracy.

Most critics of sample survey methods are familiar with the 1936 *Literary Digest* poll that predicted Alfred M. Landon to win over Franklin D. Roosevelt by a landslide. Polling a sample of more than 2 million voters by mail, the *Digest* predicted that Landon would beat Roosevelt by nearly 15 percentage points. The primary reason for this failure lay in the *sampling frame* (see below) used by the pollsters. The *Digest* sample was drawn from telephone directories and automobile registration lists. This sampling procedure had seemed sufficient in the 1920, 1924, 1928, and 1932 elections, but by 1936 it did not provide a representative cross section of American voters. In the wake of the depression, and in the midst of the New Deal, unprecedented numbers of poor Americans came to the polls. These people, however, were not adequately represented by telephone directories and automobile registration lists, since they could not afford telephones and automobiles.

In 1936, George Gallup correctly predicted that Roosevelt would win the second term. Gallup's sampling procedures differed from those of the *Literary Digest*, however. Gallup's American Institute of Public Opinion had pioneered in the use of *quota sampling* (see below), which better insured that all types of American voters—rich and poor—would be adequately represented in the survey sample. Where the *Digest* poll failed to reach and question the poor—and predominantly Democratic—voters, Gallup's quota sampling succeeded.

Twelve years later Gallup, and most political pollsters, suffered the embarrassment of predicting victory for Thomas Dewey over Harry Truman. As Goodman Ace acidly noted, "Everyone believes in public opinion polls. Everyone from the man in the street . . . up to President Thomas E. Dewey."[1] A number of factors conspired to bring about the 1948 polling debacle. For one thing, most pollsters finished their polling too soon despite a steady trend toward Truman over the course of the campaign. The large numbers of voters who said they did not know whom they would vote for went predominantly to Truman. Most important, however, the failure in 1948 pointed to serious shortcomings inherent in quota sampling—the method that was such an improvement over the *Literary Digest* sampling methods. In 1948 a number of academic survey researchers had been experimenting with *probability sampling* methods. By and large, they were far more successful than the quota samplers, and probability sampling remains the most respected method used by survey researchers today.

This brief excursion into some of the more exciting moments in the history of political polling may have destroyed whatever faith you originally had in survey sampling, so let me rectify the situation. How have the samplers been doing lately? In the 1976 presidential election, Jimmy Carter received 51.1 percent of the two-party vote, and Gerald Ford received 48.9 percent. During the week just before the

[1]Requoted in *Newsweek*, July 8, 1968, p. 24.

election, national polls were conducted by George Gallup, Louis Harris, and Burns Roper, and by the *New York Times* in collaboration with CBS. Although a proportion of the respondents in each poll said they were still undecided, the polls estimated how the election would go. Discounting the "undecideds," the *Times*-CBS poll predicted 51.1 percent for Carter and 48.9 percent for Ford! A lucky guess? Hardly. The other three polls missed the vote by only .6 to 1.6 percentage points. And, in place of the 2 million voters polled by the *Literary Digest* in 1936, approximately 2,000 voters were sufficient to predict the voting of nearly 80 million who went to the polls in 1976.

The preceding short history should give you some confidence that sampling can provide accurate information about groups too large to observe in their entirety. You may conclude, therefore, that sampling is "almost as good" as studying whole populations. Ironically, there are many circumstances in which sample observations are *more* accurate descriptions of whole populations than would be provided by an attempt to observe everything. There are several reasons for this seemingly bizarre fact, growing out of the logistics of observation.

First, an enormous interviewing project would require a very large staff of interviewers. Although researchers typically attempt to limit their staffs to the best available interviewers, such a project would probably require them to employ everyone in sight, with the result that the overall quality of interviewers would be lower than usually achieved. The quality of data collected would be reduced by the decreased quality of interviewers. Also, a smaller-scale study would permit more diligent follow-up procedures, thereby increasing the rates of interview completion.

Second, interviewing all members of a given large population would require a lengthy interviewing period. As a result, it would be difficult if not impossible to specify the *time* to which the data refer. If the study were aimed at measuring the level of unemployment in a given large city, the unemployment rate produced by the survey data would not refer to the city as of the beginning of the interviewing or as of the end. Rather, the researcher would be forced to attribute the unemployment rate to some hypothetical date—representing perhaps the midpoint of the interviewing period. (Asking respondents to answer in terms of a uniform date introduces the problem of inaccurate recall.) Although this problem is inherent in any interviewing project that is not executed all in one moment, the seriousness of the problem grows with the duration of interviewing. If the interviewing were to take 10 years to complete—with the unemployment rate presumably changing during that period—the resultant rate would be meaningless.

Finally, the managerial requirements of a very large survey would be far greater than normally faced by survey researchers. Supervision, record keeping, training, and so forth would all be more difficult in a very large survey. Once again, the quality of data collected in a very large survey might be lower than that obtained in a smaller, more manageable one. (It is worth noting that the Bureau of the Census follows its decennial census with a sample survey for purposes of evaluating the data collected in the total enumeration.)

Sample surveys can be extremely accurate. At the same time, we should concede that they often are not, even today. The remainder of this chapter is devoted to presenting the reasons and rules for accuracy in sampling.

Two Types of Sampling Methods

It is useful to distinguish two major types of sampling methods: _probability_ sampling and _nonprobability_ sampling. The bulk of this chapter will be devoted to probability sampling, since it is currently the most respected and useful method. A smaller portion of this chapter will consider the various methods of nonprobability sampling.

I'll begin with a discussion of the logic of probability sampling, followed by a brief glossary of sampling concepts and terminology. Then we'll look at the concept of sampling distribution: the basis of estimating the accuracy of sample survey findings. Following these theoretical discussions, we'll turn to a consideration of populations and sampling frames—focusing on practical problems of determining the target group of the study and the way to begin selecting a sample. Next, we'll examine the basic types of survey designs: simple random samples, systematic samples, stratified samples, and cluster samples. Then, a short discussion and description of nonprobability sampling is presented.

Subsequent chapters in Part Three will consider nonsurvey uses of sampling methods in such fields as content analysis, participant observation, and historical analyses. I hope that you will become so familiar with the _logic_ of survey sampling that you'll be able to profit from that knowledge in a broader variety of situations.

THE LOGIC OF PROBABILITY SAMPLING

It should be apparent from the history of political polling that sample surveys can be very accurate. At the same time it should be equally apparent that samples must be selected in a careful fashion. We might consider briefly why that is the case.

The Implications of Homogeneity and Heterogeneity

If all members of a population were identical to one another in all respects, there would be no need for careful sampling procedures. In such a case, any sample would indeed be sufficient. In this extreme case of homogeneity, in fact, _one_ case would be sufficient as a sample to study characteristics of the whole population.

Before you dismiss this idea as impossible, recall that much scientific sampling is carried out on this basis. In the physical sciences, it is sometimes safe to make this assumption and proceed on the basis of it in research. The chemist who wishes to test certain properties of carbon, for example, need not undertake the painstaking enumeration of all the carbon molecules in the world and then carefully select a probability sample of carbon molecules for study.

Similarly, the medical scientist—or the practicing physician—who wishes to examine a person's blood need not draw out all of the person's blood and select a probability sample of blood cells. Again, for most purposes, any sample of blood from the person will suffice.

Faced with variation or heterogeneity in the population under study, however, more controlled sampling procedures are required. The broader applicability of this principle—beyond social research—is worth noting. The origins of modern sampling theory are to be found in agricultural research, especially in the work of R. A. Fisher whose name is still attached to some commonly used survey statistics.

For our purposes, it is more important to note the heterogeneity of social groups. People differ in many ways. A given human population, then, is composed of varied individuals. A sample of individuals from that population, if it is to provide useful descriptions of the total population, must contain essentially the same variation as exists in the population. Probability sampling provides an efficient method for selecting a sample that should adequately reflect the variation that exists in the population.

Conscious and Unconscious Sampling Bias

Of course anyone could select a survey sample, even without any special training or care. To select a sample of 100 university students, a person might go to the university campus and begin interviewing students found walking around campus. This kind of sampling method is often used by untrained researchers, but it has very serious problems.

To begin, there is a danger that the researcher's own personal biases may affect the sample selected in this manner—hence the sample would not truly represent the student population. Let's assume that you are personally somewhat intimidated by "hippie-looking" students, feeling that they would ridicule your research effort. As a result, you might consciously or semiconsciously avoid interviewing such people. Or, you might feel that the attitudes of "straight-looking" students would not be relevant to your research purposes and would avoid interviewing such students. Even if you sought to interview a balanced group of students, you probably would not know the proper proportions of different types of students making up such a balance, or you might be unable to identify the different types just by watching them walk by.

Even if you made a conscientious effort to interview every tenth student entering the university library, this would not insure you of a *representative* sample, since different types of students visit the library with different frequencies. Thus, the sample would overrepresent students frequenting the library more often.

Representativeness and Probability of Selection

Survey samples must represent the populations from which they are drawn if they are to provide useful estimates about the characteristics of those populations. Realize that they need not be representative in all respects; representativeness, as it has any meaning in regard to sampling, is limited to those characteristics that are relevant to the substantive interests of the study. (That will become more evident in the discussion of stratification below.)

A basic principle of probability sampling is that: *a sample will be representative of the population from which it is selected if all members of the population have an equal chance of being selected in the sample.*[2] Samples that have this quality are often labeled **EPSEM** samples (equal probability of selection method). I'll discuss variations of this principle later, but it is primary and forms the basis of probability sampling.

Moving beyond this basic principle, we must realize that samples—even carefully selected EPSEM samples—are seldom if ever *perfectly* representative of the populations from which they are drawn. Nevertheless, probability sampling offers two special advantages.

First, probability samples, although never perfectly representative, are typically *more representative* than other types of samples because the biases discussed in the preceding section are avoided. In practice, there is a greater likelihood that a probability sample will be representative of the population from which it is drawn than that a nonprobability sample will be.

Second, and more important, probability theory permits us to estimate the accuracy or representativeness of the sample. Conceivably, an uninformed researcher might, through wholly haphazard means, select a sample that nearly perfectly represents the larger population. The odds are against doing so, however, and we would be unable to estimate the likelihood that he or she has achieved representativeness. The probability sampler, on the other hand, can provide an accurate estimate of success or failure.

Following a brief glossary of sampling terminology, we'll examine the means the probability sampler uses to estimate the representativeness of the sample.

SAMPLING CONCEPTS AND TERMINOLOGY

The following discussions of sampling theory and practice use a number of technical terms. To make it easier for you to understand those discussions, it is important to quickly define these terms. For the most part, I'll employ terms commonly used in sampling and statistical textbooks so that readers may better understand those other sources.

In presenting this glossary of sampling concepts and terminology, I would like to acknowledge a debt to Leslie Kish and his excellent textbook on survey sampling.[3] Although I have modified some of the conventions used by Kish, his presentation is easily the most important source of this discussion.

---

[2]We'll see shortly that the size of the sample selected as well as the actual characteristics of the larger population affect the *degree* of representativeness.
[3]Leslie Kish, *Survey Sampling* (New York: John Wiley, 1965).

Element

An *element* is that unit about which information is collected and which provides the basis of analysis. Typically, in survey research, elements are people or certain types of people. It should be recognized, however, that other kinds of units might constitute the elements for a survey; families, social clubs, or corporations might be the elements of a survey. (*Note*: Elements and units of analysis are often the same in a given study.)

Universe

A *universe* is the theoretical and hypothetical aggregation of all elements, as defined for a given survey. If the individual American is the element for a survey, then *Americans* would be the universe. A survey universe is wholly unspecified as to time and place, however, and is essentially a useless term.

Population

A *population* is the theoretically specified aggregation of survey elements. While the vague term *Americans* might be the universe for a survey, the delineation of the population would include the definition of the element Americans (for example, citizenship, residence) and the time referent for the study (Americans as of when?). Translating the universe *adult New Yorkers* into a workable population would require a specification of the age defining *adult* and the boundaries of New York. Specifying the term *college student* would include a consideration of full-time and part-time students, degree candidates and nondegree candidates, undergraduate and graduate students, and similar issues.

While researchers must begin with careful specification of their population, poetic license usually permits them to phrase their reports in terms of the hypothetical universe. For ease of presentation, even the most conscientious researcher normally speaks of "Americans" rather than "resident citizens of the United States of America as of November 12, 1971." The primary guide in this matter, as in most others, is that you should not mislead or deceive your readers.

Survey Population

A *survey population* is that aggregation of elements from which the survey sample is actually selected. Recall that a population is a theoretical specification of the universe. As a practical matter, you are seldom in a position to guarantee that every element that meets the theoretical definitions laid down actually has a chance of being selected in the sample. Even where lists of elements exist for sampling purposes, the lists are usually somewhat incomplete. Some students are always omitted, inadvertently, from student rosters. Some telephone subscribers request that their names and numbers be unlisted. The survey population, then, is the aggregation of elements from which the sample is selected.

Often researchers may decide to limit their survey populations more severely than indicated in the above examples. National polling firms may limit their national samples to the 48 adjacent states, omitting Alaska and Hawaii for practical reasons. A researcher wishing to sample psychology professors may limit the survey population to psychology professors who are serving in psychology departments, omitting those serving in other departments. (In a sense, we might say that these researchers have redefined their universes and populations, in which case they must make the revisions clear to their readers.)

Sampling Unit

A *sampling unit* is that element or set of elements considered for selection in some stage of sampling. In a simple, single-stage sample, the sampling units are the same as the elements. In more complex samples, however, different levels of sampling units may be employed. For example, you might select a sample of census blocks in a city, then select a sample of households on the selected blocks, and finally select a sample of adults from the selected households. The sampling units for these three stages of sampling are, respectively, census blocks, households, and adults, of which only the last of these are the elements. More specifically, the terms *primary sampling units*, *secondary sampling units*, and *final sampling units* would be used to designate the successive stages.

Sampling Frame

A **sampling frame** is the actual list of sampling units from which the sample, or some stage of the sample, is selected. If a simple sample of students is selected from a student roster, the roster is the sampling frame. If the primary sampling unit for a complex population sample is the census block, the list of census blocks composes the sampling frame—either in the form of a printed booklet, a card file, or a magnetic tape file.

In a single-stage sample design, the sampling frame is a list of the elements composing the survey population. In practice, the existing sampling frames often define the survey population rather than the other way around. We often begin with a universe or perhaps a population in mind for our study; then we search for possible sampling frames. The frames available for our use are examined and evaluated, and we decide which frame presents a survey population most appropriate to our needs.

The relationship between populations and sampling frames is critical and one that has not been given sufficient attention. A later section of the present chapter will pursue this issue in greater detail.

Observation Unit

An *observation unit*, or unit of data collection, is an element or aggregation of elements from which information is collected. Again, often the unit of analysis and unit of observation are the same—the individual person—but that need not be the case. Thus the researcher may interview heads of households (the observation units) to collect information about all members of the households (the units of analysis).

Our task is simplified when the unit of analysis and observation unit are the same. Often that is not possible or feasible, however, and in such situations we need to exercise some ingenuity in collecting data relevant to our units of analysis without actually observing those units.

Variable

As discussed earlier, a *variable* is a set of mutually exclusive attributes: sex, age, employment status, and so forth. The elements of a given population may be described in terms of their individual attributes on a given variable. Typically, surveys aim at describing the distribution of attributes composing a variable in a population. Thus a researcher may describe the age distribution of a population by examining the relative frequency of different ages among members of the population.

It should be noted that a variable, by definition, must possess *variation*; if all elements in the population have the same attribute, that attribute is a *constant* in the population, rather than part of a variable.

Parameter

A *parameter is* the summary description of a given variable in a *population*. The mean income of all families in a city and the age distribution of the city's population are parameters. An important portion of survey research involves the estimation of population parameters on the basis of sample observations.

Statistic

A *statistic* is the summary description of a given variable in a survey sample. Thus the mean income computed from a survey sample and the age distribution of that sample are statistics. Sample statistics are used to make estimates of population parameters.

Sampling Error

Sampling error will be discussed in more detail later. Probability sampling methods seldom, if ever, provide statistics exactly equal to the parameters that they are used to estimate. Probability theory, however, permits us to estimate the degree of error to be expected for a given sample design.

Confidence Levels and Confidence Intervals

Confidence levels and *confidence intervals* will also be discussed more fully later. The computation of sampling error permits us to express the accuracy of our sample statistics in terms of a level of confidence that the statistics fall within a specified interval from the parameter. For example, we may say we are 95 percent confident that our sample statistics (for example, 50 percent favor Candidate X) are within plus or minus ($\pm$) 5 percentage points of the population parameter. As the confidence interval is expanded for a given statistic, our confidence increases and we may say that we are 99.9 percent confident that our statistic falls within ± 7.5 percentage points of the parameter.

PROBABILITY SAMPLING THEORY AND SAMPLING DISTRIBUTION

This section will examine the basic theory of probability sampling as it applies to survey sampling, and we'll consider the logic of sampling distribution and sampling error with regard to a binomial variable—a variable composed of two characteristics.

Probability Sampling Theory

The ultimate purpose of survey sampling is to select a set of elements from a population in such a way that descriptions of those elements (statistics) accurately portray the total population from which they are selected. Probability sampling enhances the likelihood of accomplishing this aim and also provides methods for estimating the degree of probable success.

Random selection is the key to this process. In random selection each element has an equal chance of selection that is independent of any other events in the selection process. Flipping a perfect coin is the most frequently cited example: the "selec-tion" of a head or a tail is independent of previous selections of heads or tails. Rolling a perfect set of dice is another example.

Such images of random selection seldom apply directly to survey sampling methods, however. The survey sampler more typically uses tables of random num-bers or computer programs that provide a random selection of sampling units. The wide availability of such research aids makes this an adequate beginning point for our discussion of random sampling.

The reasons for using random selection methods—using random-number tables or computer programs—are twofold. First, this procedure serves as a check on con-scious or unconscious bias on the part of the researcher. The researcher who under-takes the selection of cases on an intuitive basis might very well select cases that would support his or her research expectations or hypotheses. Random selection, then, erases this danger.

More important, random selection offers access to the body of probability theory, which provides the basis for estimates of population parameters and esti-mates of error. Let's turn now to an examination of this latter aspect.

Binomial Sampling Distribution

To discuss the concept of sampling distribution, it will be clearest to use a simple survey example. Let's assume for the moment that we wish to study the student population of State University to determine approval or disapproval of a student conduct code proposed by the administration. The survey population will be that aggregation of students contained in a student roster: the sampling frame. The elements will be the individual students at SU. The variable under consideration will be attitudes toward the code, a binomial variable: approve and disapprove. We'll select a random sample of students for purposes of estimating the entire student body.

Figure 7-1 presents an x axis that represents all possible values of this parameter in the population—from 0 percent approval to 100 percent approval. The midpoint of the axis—50 percent—represents half the students approving of the code and the other half disapproving.

Let's assume for the moment that we have given each student on the student

Figure 7-1   Range of Possible Sample Survey Results

roster a number and have selected 100 random numbers from a table of random numbers. The 100 students having their numbers selected are then interviewed and asked for their attitudes toward the student code: whether they approve or disapprove. Let's further assume that this operation gives us 48 students who approve of the code and 52 who disapprove. We may present this statistic by placing a dot on the x axis at the point representing 48 percent.

Now let's suppose that we select another sample of 100 students in exactly the same fashion and measure their approval or disapproval of the student code. Perhaps 51 students in the second sample approve of the code, and that might be represented by another dot in the appropriate place on the x axis. Repeating this

Figure 7-2   Results Produced by Three Hypothetical Surveys

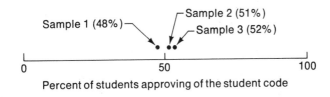

Percent of students approving of the student code

process once more, we may discover that 52 students in the third sample approve of the code.

Figure 7-2 presents the three different sample statistics representing the percentages of students in each of the three random samples who approved of the student code. The basic rule of random sampling is that such samples drawn from a population give estimates of the parameter that pertains in the total population. Each of the random samples, then, gives us an estimate of the percentage of students in the total student body who approve of the student code. Unhappily, however, we have selected three samples and now have three separate estimates.

To retrieve ourselves from this dilemma, let's go on to draw more and more samples of 100 students each, question each of the samples as to their approval or disapproval of the code, and plot the new sample statistics on our summary graph. In drawing many such samples, we will begin to discover that some of the new samples provide the same estimates given by earlier samples. To take account of this situation, we shall add a y axis to the figure, representing the number of samples providing a given estimate. Figure 7-3 is the product of our new sampling efforts.

The distribution of sample statistics shown in Figure 7-3 is called the *sampling distribution*. We note that by increasing the number of samples selected and interviewed, we have also increased the range of estimates provided by the sampling operation. In one sense we have increased our dilemma in attempting to guess the parameter in the population. Probability theory, however, provides certain important rules regarding the sampling distribution presented in Figure 7-3.

First, if many independent random samples are selected from a population, the sample statistics provided by those samples will be *distributed around the popula-*

Figure 7-3   The Sampling Distribution

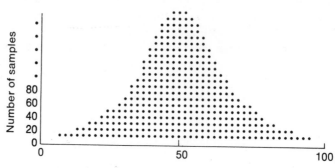

tion parameter in a known way. Although there is a wide range of estimates, more of them are in the vicinity of 50 percent than elsewhere in the graph. Probability theory tells us, then, that the true value is in the vicinity of 50 percent.

Second, probability theory gives us a formula for estimating *how closely* the sample statistics are clustered around the true value. This formula contains three factors: the parameter, the sample size, and the *standard error* (a measure of sampling error).

Formula: $S = \sqrt{\dfrac{PQ}{n}}$

Symbols: *P, Q*:   the population parameters for the binomial; if 60 percent of the student body approves of the code and 40 percent disapproves, *P* and *Q* are 60 percent and 40 percent, or .6 and .4. Note that $Q = 1 - P$ and $P = 1 - Q$.

     n: the number of cases in each sample.

     s: the standard error.

Let's assume that the population parameter in the study survey example is 50 percent approving of the code and 50 percent disapproving. Recall that we have been selecting samples of 100 cases each. When these numbers are put into the formula, we find that the standard error equals .05 or 5 percent.

In terms of probability theory, the standard error is a valuable piece of information, for it indicates the extent to which the sample estimates will be distributed around the population parameter. Specifically, probability theory indicates that certain proportions of the sample estimates will fall within specified increments of standard errors from the population parameter. Approximately 34 percent (.3413) of the sample estimates will fall within one standard error above the population parameter, and another 34 percent will fall within one standard error below the parameter. In our example, the standard error is 5 percent, so we know that 34 percent of our samples will give estimates of student approval between 50 percent (parameter) and 55 percent (one standard error above); another 34 percent of the samples will give estimates between 50 percent and 45 percent (one standard error below the parameter). Taken together, then, we know that roughly two-thirds (68 percent) of the samples will give estimates within (plus or minus) 5 percent of the parameter.

Moreover, probability theory dictates that roughly 95 percent of the samples will fall within plus or minus two standard errors of the true value, and 99.9 percent of the samples will fall within plus or minus three standard errors. In our present example, then, we know that only one sample out of a thousand would give an estimate lower than 35 percent approval or higher than 65 percent.

The proportion of samples falling within one, two, or three standard errors of the parameter are constants for any random sampling procedure such as the one just described, providing that a large number of samples are selected. The size of the standard error in any given case, however, is a function of the population parameter and the sample size. If we return to the formula for a moment, we note that the standard error will increase as a function of an increase in the quantity: P times Q. Note further that this quantity reaches its maximum in the situation of an even split in the population. If $P = .5, PQ = .25$; if $P = .6, PQ = .24$; if $P = .8, PQ = .16$; if $P = .99, PQ = .0099$. By extension, if P is either 0.0 or 1.0 (either 0 percent or 100 percent approve of the student code), the standard error will be 0. If everyone in the population has the same attitude (no variation), then every sample will give exactly that estimate.

The standard error is also a function of the sample size—an *inverse* function. As the sample size increases, the standard error *decreases*. As the sample size increases, the several samples will be clustered nearer to the true value. Another rule of thumb is evident in the formula: because of the square root formula, the standard error is reduced by half if the sample size is *quadrupled*. In our present example, samples of 100 produce a standard error of 5 percent; to reduce the standard error to 2.5 percent, it would be necessary to increase the sample size to 400.

All of this information is provided by established probability theory in reference to the selection of large numbers of random samples. If the population parameter is known and very many random samples are selected, we are able to predict how many of the samples will fall within specified intervals from the parameter. These conditions do not typically pertain in survey sampling, however.

Typically, we do not know the parameter, but we conduct a sample survey in order to estimate that value. Moreover, we do not typically select large numbers of samples; we select only one sample. Nevertheless, the preceding discussion of probability theory provides the basis for inferences about the typical survey situation.

Whereas probability theory specifies that 68 percent of the samples will fall within one standard error of the parameter, the survey sampler infers that a given random sample has a likelihood of 68 percent of falling within that range. In this regard we speak of **confidence levels**: we are 68 percent confident that our sample estimate is within one standard error of the parameter. Or we may say that we are 95 percent confident that the sample statistic is within two standard errors of the parameter, and so forth. Quite reasonably, our confidence increases as the margin for error is extended. We are virtually positive (99.9 percent confident) that we are within three standard errors of the true value.

Although we may be confident (at some level) of being within a certain range of the parameter, we have already noted that we seldom know what the parameter is. To resolve this dilemma, we substitute our sample estimate for the parameter in the formula; lacking the true value, we substitute the best available guess.

The result of these inferences and estimations is that we are able to estimate a population parameter and also the expected degree of error on the basis of one sample drawn from a population. Beginning with the question "What percentage of the student body approves of the student code?" you could select a random sample of 100 students and interview them. You might then report your best estimate is that 50 percent of the student body approves of the code, and that you are 95 percent confident that between 40 and 60 percent (plus or minus two standard errors) approve. The range from 40 to 60 percent is called the **confidence interval**.

This then is the basic logic of probability sampling. Random selection permits the researcher to link sample survey findings to the body of probability theory for purposes of estimating the accuracy of those findings. All statements of accuracy in sampling must specify both a confidence level and a confidence interval. The researcher may report that he or she is x percent confident that the population parameter is between two specific values. It does not make sense, however, for a researcher to report that the findings are x percent accurate.

The foregoing discussion has considered only one type of statistic: the percentages produced by a *binomial* or dichotomous variable. The same logic, however, would apply to the examination of other statistics, such as mean income for example. Since the computations are somewhat more complicated in such a case, I have chosen to consider only binomials in this introduction.

You should be cautioned that the survey uses of probability theory as discussed above are not wholly justified technically. The theory of sampling distribution, for example, makes assumptions that almost never apply in survey conditions. The number of samples contained within specified increments of standard errors, for example, assumes an infinitely large population, an infinite number of samples, and sampling with replacement. Moreover, the inferential jump from the distribution of several samples to the probable characteristics of one sample has been grossly oversimplified in the above discussion.

These cautions are offered to give you perspective. Researchers often appear to overestimate the precision of estimates produced by the use of probability theory in connection with survey research. As will be mentioned elsewhere in this chapter and throughout the book, variations in sampling techniques and nonsampling factors may further reduce the legitimacy of such estimates. Nevertheless, the calculations discussed in this section can be extremely valuable to you in understanding and evaluating your data. Although the calculations do not provide as precise estimates as some researchers might assume, they can be quite valid for practical purposes; they are unquestionably more valid than less rigorously derived estimates based on less rigorous sampling methods.

Most important, you should be familiar with the basic *logic* underlying the calculations. If you are so informed, you will be able to react sensibly to your own data and to those reported by others.

POPULATIONS AND SAMPLING FRAMES

The immediately preceding section has dealt with the theoretical model for survey sampling. Although it is necessary for the survey consumer, student, and researcher to understand that theory, it is no less important that they appreciate the less-than-perfect conditions that exist in the field. The present section is devoted to a discussion of one aspect of field conditions that requires a compromise with regard to theoretical conditions and assumptions. Here we'll consider the congruence of or disparity between populations of sampling frames.

Simply put, a sampling frame is the list, or reasonable facsimile, of elements from which a probability sample is selected. The following section will deal with the methods for selecting samples, but we must first consider the sampling frame itself. Properly drawn samples will provide information appropriate for describing the population of elements composing the sampling frame—nothing more. It is necessary to make this point in view of the all-too-common tendency for researchers to select samples from a given sampling frame and then make assertions about a population similar to, but not identical to, the survey population defined by the sampling frame. The problem involved here is the broader social scientific one of generalization and is akin to studying a small Lutheran church in North Dakota for purposes of describing religion in America.

In the remainder of this section, we'll examine different survey purposes and discuss the good and bad sampling frames that might be used to satisfy those purposes.

Surveys of organizations are often the simplest from a sampling standpoint because organizations typically have membership lists. In such cases, the list of members constitutes an excellent sampling frame. If a random sample is selected from a membership list, the data collected from that sample may be taken as representative of all members—*if all members are included in the list*. If some members are omitted from the membership list, an effort must be made to sample those nonlisted members, or else the sample survey findings can be taken as representative only of those members on the list.

Populations that often can be sampled from good organizational lists include elementary school, high school, and university students and faculty; church members; factory workers; fraternity or sorority members; members of social, service, or political clubs; and members of professional associations.

The above comments apply primarily to local organizations. Often statewide or national organizations do not have a single membership list easily available. There is, for example, no single list of Episcopalian church members. However, a slightly more complex sample design could take advantage of local church membership lists by first sampling churches, and then subsampling the membership lists of those churches selected. (More about that below.)

Other lists of individuals may be especially relevant to the research needs of a particular survey. Government agencies maintain lists of registered voters, for example, that might be used if you wanted to conduct a preelection poll or a more detailed examination of voting behavior—but you must insure that the list is up-to-date. Similar lists contain the names of automobile owners, welfare recipients, taxpayers, business permit holders, licensed professionals, and so forth. Although it may be difficult to gain access to some of these lists, they may provide excellent sampling frames for specialized research purposes.

Realizing that the sampling elements in a survey need not be individual persons, we may note that the lists of other types of elements also exist: universities, businesses of various types, cities, academic journals, newspapers, unions, political clubs, professional associations, and so forth.

Telephone directories are frequently used for "quick and dirty" public opinion polls. Undeniably they are easy and inexpensive to use, and that is no doubt the reason for their popularity. And, if you want to make assertions about telephone subscribers, the directory is a *fairly* good sampling frame.[4] Unfortunately, telephone directories are all too often taken to be a listing of a city's population or of its voters. There are many defects in this reasoning, but the chief one involves a social-class bias. Poor people are less likely to have telephones; a telephone directory sample, therefore, is likely to have a middle- or upper-class bias.

The class bias inherent in telephone directory samples is often hidden. Preelection polls conducted in this fashion are sometimes quite accurate. The reason for that would seem to be in the class bias evident in voting itself: poor people are less likely to vote. Frequently, then, these two biases nearly coincide and the results of a telephone poll may come very close to the final election outcome. Unhappily, the pollster never knows for sure until after the election. And sometimes, as in the case of the 1936 *Literary Digest* poll, you may discover that the voters have not acted according to the expected class biases. The ultimate disadvantage of this method, then, is the researcher's inability to estimate the degree of error to be expected in the sample findings.

Street directories and tax maps are often used for easy samples of households, but they may suffer from some of the same disadvantages as the telephone directory: incompleteness and possible bias. For example, in strictly zoned urban regions, illegal housing units are unlikely to appear on official records. As a result, such units would have no chance for selection, and sample findings could not be representative of those units, which are often poorer and more overcrowded than the average.

Review of Populations and Sampling Frames

Surprisingly little attention has been given to the issues of populations and sampling frames in survey research literature. With this in mind, I've devoted special attention to them here. To further emphasize the point, it seems appropriate to list, in review, the main guidelines to be borne in mind.

1. Sample survey findings can be taken only as representative of the aggregation of elements that compose the sampling frame.

[4]Realize, of course, that a given directory will not include new subscribers or those who have requested unlisted numbers. Sampling is further complicated by the inclusion in directories of nonresidential listings.

2. *Often, sampling frames do not truly include all the elements that their names might imply. (Student directories do not include all students; telephone directories do not include all telephone subscribers.) Omissions are almost inevitable. Thus a first concern of the researcher must be to assess the extent of the omissions and to correct them if possible. (Realize, of course, that the researcher may feel he or she can safely ignore a small number of omissions that cannot easily be corrected.)*

3. *Even to generalize to the population composing the sampling frame, it is necessary for all elements to have equal representation to the frame: typically, each element should appear only once. Otherwise, elements that appear more than once will have a greater probability of selection, and the sample will, overall, overrepresent these elements.*

Other, more practical, matters relating to populations and sampling frames will be treated elsewhere in this book. For example, the form of the sampling frame is very important: a list in a publication, a 3×5 card file, mailing address plates, machine-readable cards, or magnetic tapes. It should be noted here that such considerations may often take priority over scientific considerations: an "easier" list may be chosen over a "harder" one, even though the latter is more appropriate to the target population. We should not take a dogmatic position in this regard, but every researcher should carefully weigh the relative advantages and disadvantages of such alternatives.

TYPES OF SAMPLING DESIGNS

Introduction

You may have reached this point in your reading somewhat aghast at the importance and difficulties of organizing your sampling frame, and such a feeling would probably be appropriate and healthy. Once it has been established, you must then move along and actually select a sample of elements for study.

Up to this point, we have focused on *simple random sampling*. And, indeed, the body of statistics typically used by survey researchers assumes such a sample. As we shall see shortly, however, you have a number of options in choosing your sampling method, and you will seldom if ever choose simple random sampling. There are two reasons for that. First, with all but the simplest sampling frame, simple random sampling is not possible. Second, and probably surprisingly, simple random sampling may not be the best (most accurate) method available. Let's turn now to a discussion of simple random sampling and the other options available.

Simple Random Sampling

As noted above, **simple random sampling (SRS) is the basic sampling** method assumed in survey statistical computations. The mathematics of random sampling are especially complex, so we'll detour around them in favor of describing the field methods of employing this method.

Once a sampling frame has been established in accord with the discussion above, the researcher may then assign numbers to each of the elements in this list —assigning one and only one number to each and not skipping any number in the process. A table of random numbers could then be used in the selection of elements for the sample. (See Appendex C.) The boxed description on pages 180 and 181 explains how to use the table of random numbers.

If your sampling frame is in a machine-readable form—cards or magnetic tape —a simple random sample could be selected automatically by computer. (In effect, the computer program would number the elements in the sampling frame, generate its own series of random numbers, and print out the list of elements selected.)

Systematic Sampling

Simple random sampling is seldom used in practice. As we shall see in later sections, it is not usually the most efficient sampling method, and as we have already seen, it can be rather laborious if done manually. SRS typically requires a list of elements; when such a list is available, researchers usually employ a *systematic* sampling method rather than simple random sampling.

In systematic sampling, every *k*th element in the total list is chosen (systematically) for inclusion in the sample. If the list contains 10,000 elements and you want a sample of 1,000, you would select every tenth element for your sample. To insure against any possible human bias in using this method, you should select the first element at random. Thus, in the above example you would begin by selecting a random number between 1 and 10; the element having that number would be included in the sample, plus every tenth element following it. This method is technically referred to as a *systematic sample with a random start*.

Two terms are frequently used in connection with systematic sampling. The **sampling interval** is the standard distance between elements selected in the sample: 10 in the sample above. The *sampling ratio* is the proportion of elements in the population that are selected: 1/10 in the example above.

In practice, systematic sampling is virtually identical to simple random sampling. If, indeed, the list of elements is randomized in advance of sampling, one might argue a systematic sample drawn from that list is in fact a simple random sample. By now, debates over the relative merits of simple random sampling and systematic sampling have been resolved largely in favor of the simpler method: systematic sampling. Empirically, the results are virtually identical. And, as we shall see in a later section, systematic sampling, in some instances, is slightly more accurate than simple random sampling.

There is one danger involved in systematic sampling. The arrangement of elements in the list can make systematic sampling unwise. Such an arrangement is usually referred to as *periodicity*. If the list of elements is arranged in a cyclical pattern that coincides with the sampling interval, it is possible that a grossly biased sample may be drawn. Two examples will illustrate.

In one study of soldiers during World War II, the researchers selected a systematic sample from unit rosters. Every tenth soldier on the roster was selected for the study. The rosters, however, were arranged in a table of organizations: sergeants first, then corporals and privates, squad by squad—and each squad had 10 members. As a result, every tenth person on the roster was a squad sergeant. The systematic sample selected contained only sergeants. It could, of course, have been the case that no sergeants were selected for the same reason.

As another example, suppose we wish to select a sample of apartments in an apartment building. If the sample were drawn from a list of apartments arranged in numerical order (for example, 101, 102, 103, 104, 201, 202, and so on), there would be a danger of the sampling interval coinciding with the number of apartments on a floor or some multiple thereof. In such a case, the samples might include only northwest-corner apartments or only apartments near the elevator. If these types of apartments had some other particular characteristic in common (for example, higher rent), the sample would be biased. The same danger would appear in a systematic sample of houses in a subdivision arranged with the same number of houses on a block.

In considering a systematic sample from a list, then, you should carefully examine the nature of that list. If the elements are arranged in any particular order, you should ascertain whether that order will bias the sample to be selected and take steps to counteract any possible bias (for example, take a simple random sample from cyclical portions).

In summary, however, systematic sampling is usually superior to simple random sampling, in convenience if nothing else. Where problems exist in the ordering of elements in the sampling frame, these can usually be remedied quite easily.

Stratified Sampling

In the two preceding sections we have discussed two alternative methods of sample selection from a list. Stratified sampling is not an alternative to these methods, but it represents a possible modification in their use.

Simple random and systematic sampling are important in that they insure a degree of representativeness and permit an estimate of the error present. Stratified sampling is a method for obtaining a greater degree of representativeness—decreasing the probable sampling error. To understand why that is the case, we must return briefly to the basic theory of sampling distribution.

We recall that sampling error is reduced by two factors in the sample design. First, a large sample produces a smaller sampling error than does a small sample. Second, a homogeneous population produces samples with smaller sampling errors than does a heterogeneous population. If 99 percent of the population agree with a certain statement, it is extremely unlikely that any probability sample will greatly misrepresent the extent of agreement. If, on the other hand, the population is split 50-50 on the statement, then the sampling error will be much greater.

Stratified sampling is based on this second factor in sampling theory. Rather than selecting your sample from the total population at large, you would insure that

---

USING A TABLE OF RANDOM NUMBERS

In social research, it is often appropriate to select a set of random numbers from a table such as the one presented in Appendix C. Here's how to do that.

Suppose that you want to select a simple random sample of 100 people (or other units) out of a population totaling 980. Let's say there are 980 members of the senior class on your campus, and you want to select a sample of 100.

1. To begin, number the members of the population: in this case, from 1 to 980. Now the problem is to select 100 random numbers. Once you've done that, your sample will consist of the people having the numbers you've selected (*Note*: It's not essential to actually number them, as long as you're sure of the total. If you have them in a list, for example, you can always count through the list after you've selected the numbers.)

2. The next step is to determine the number of digits you will need in the random numbers you select. In our example, there are 980 members of the population, so you will need to select 3-digit numbers in order to give everyone a chance of selection. (If there were 11,825 members of the population, you'd need to select 5-digit numbers.) Thus, we want to select 100 random numbers in the range from 001 to 980.

3. Now turn to the first page of Appendix C. Notice that there are several rows and columns of 5-digit numbers, and there are several pages. (There's no scarcity of random numbers.) These tables represent a series of random numbers in the range from 00001 to 99999. To use the tables to serve your hypothetical sampling purpose, you have to answer three questions:

    a. How will you create 3-digit numbers out of 5-digit numbers?
    b. What pattern will you follow in moving through the tables to select your numbers?
    c. Where will you start?

Each of these questions has several satisfactory answers. The key is that you must create a plan and follow it. Here's an example.

---

appropriate numbers of elements were drawn from homogeneous subsets of that population. In a study of university students, for example, you would first organize your population by college class and draw appropriate numbers of freshmen, sophomores, juniors, and seniors. In a nonstratified sample, representation by class would be subjected to the same sampling error as other variables. In a sample stratified by class, the sampling error on this variable is reduced to zero.

Sometimes, you may want to use an even more complex stratification method. In addition to stratifying by class, you might also stratify by sex, by grade point average, and so forth. In this fashion you might be able to insure that your sample would contain the proper numbers of freshman men with a 4.0 average, of freshman women with a 4.0 average, and so forth.

The ultimate function of stratification, then, is to organize the population into homogeneous subsets (with heterogeneity between subsets) and to select the appro-

4. To create 3-digit numbers from 5-digit numbers, let's agree to select 5-digit numbers from the table but only consider the leftmost 3 digits in each case. If we picked the first number on the first page—10480— we would only consider the 104. (We could agree to take the digits furthest to the right, 480, or the middle three digits, 048, and any of those plans would work. The key is to make a plan and stick with it. For convenience, then, let's use the leftmost 3 digits.

5. We could choose to progress through the tables any way we wanted, also: down the columns, up them, across to the right or to the left, or diagonally. Again, any of these plans would work just fine, as long as we created some plan and stuck to it. For convenience, let's agree to move down the columns; when we get to the bottom of one column, we'll go to the top of the next; when we exhaust a given page, we'll start at the top of the first column of the next page.

6. Now, where do we start? First, you can close your eyes and stick a pencil into the table and start wherever the pencil point lands. (I know it doesn't sound scientific, but it works.) Or, if you're afraid you'll hurt the book or miss it altogether, close your eyes and make up a column number and a row number. ("I pick the number in the fifth row of column 2.") Start with that number.

7. Let's suppose we decided to start with the fifth number in column 2. Now we're on our way. If you look on the first page of Appendix C, you'll see that the starting number is 39975. In terms of our earlier agreement, we have selected 399 as our first random number, and we have 99 more to go. Moving down the second column, we select 069, 729, 919, 143, 368, 695, 409, 939, and so forth. At the bottom of column 2, we select number 104 and continue to the top of column 3: 015, 255, and so on.

8. See how easy it is? But trouble lies ahead. When we reach column 5, we are speeding along, selecting 816, 309, 763, 078, 061, 277, 988. . . . Wait a minute! 988? There are only 980 students in the senior class. How can we pick number 988? The solution is simple: ignore it. Any time you come across a number that lies outside your range, skip it and continue on your way: 188, 174, and so forth.

9. That's it. You keep up the procedure until you've selected 100 random numbers. Returning to your list, you find your random sample consists of person number 399, person number 69, person number 729, and so forth.

priate number of elements from each. To the extent that the subsets are homogeneous on the stratification variables, they may also be homogeneous on other variables as well. Since age is related to college class, a sample stratified by class will be more representative in terms of age as well. Since occupational aspirations still seem to be related to sex, a sample stratified by sex will be more representative in terms of occupational aspirations.

The choice of stratification variables typically depends on what variables are available. Sex can often be determined in a list of names. University lists are typically arranged by class. Lists of faculty members may indicate their departmental affiliation. Government agency files may be arranged by geographical region. Voter registration lists are arranged according to precinct.

In selecting stratification variables from among those available, however, you should be concerned primarily with those that are presumably related to variables that you want to represent accurately. Since sex is related to many variables and is often available for stratification, it is often used. Education is related to many variables, but it is often not available for stratification. Geographical location within a city, state, or nation is related to many things. Within a city, stratification by geographical location usually increases representativeness in social class, ethnic group, and so forth. Within a nation, it increases representativeness in a broad range of attitudes as well as in social class and ethnicity.

Methods of stratification in sampling vary. When you are working with a simple list of all elements in the population, two are predominant. First, you can group the population elements into discrete groups based on whatever stratification variables are being used. On the basis of the relative proportion of the population represented by a given group, you select—randomly or systematically—a number of elements from that group constituting the same proportion of your desired sample size. For example, if freshman men with a 4.0 average compose 1 percent of the student population and you desire a sample of 1,000 students, you would select 10 students from the group of freshman men with a 4.0 average.

As an alternative method, you could group students as described above and then put those several groups together in a continuous list: beginning with all freshman men with 4.0 average and ending with all senior women with a 1.0 or below. You would then select a systematic sample, with a random start, from the entire list. Given the arrangement of the list, a systematic sample would select proper numbers (within an error range of 1 or 2) from each of the subgroups. (*Note*: A simple random sample drawn from such a composite list would cancel out the stratification.)

The effect of stratification is to insure the proper representation of the stratification variables to enhance representation of other variables related to them. Taken as a whole, then, a stratified sample is likely to be more representative on a number of variables than would be the case for a simple random sample. Although the simple random sample is still regarded as somewhat sacred, it should now be clear that you can often do better.

Implicit Stratification in Systematic Sampling

It was mentioned above that systematic sampling can, under certain conditions, be more accurate than simple random sampling. That is the case whenever the arrangement of the list is such as to create an implicit stratification. As already noted, if a list of university students is already arranged by class, then a systematic sample will provide a stratification by class where a simple random sample would not. Other typical arrangements of elements in lists can provide the same feature.

If a list of names composing the sampling frame for a study is arranged alphabetically, then the list is somewhat stratified by ethnic origins. All the McTavishes are collected together, for example, as are the Lees, Wongs, Yamamuras, Schmidts, Whitehalls, Weinsteins, Gonzaleses, and so forth. To the extent that any of these groups is a substantial subset of the total population, that group will be properly represented in a systematic sample drawn from an alphabetical list.

In a study of students at the University of Hawaii (to be described shortly), after stratification by school class, the students were arranged by their student identification numbers. These numbers, however, were their social security numbers. The first three digits of the social security number indicate the state in which the number was issued. As a result, within a class, students were arranged by the state in which they were issued a social security number, providing a rough stratification by geographical origins.

You should realize, therefore, that an ordered list of elements may be more useful to you than an unordered, randomized list. This point has been stressed here in view of an unfortunate belief that lists should be randomized before systematic sampling. Only if the arrangement presents the problems discussed earlier should the list be rearranged.

ILLUSTRATION: SAMPLING UNIVERSITY STUDENTS

Let's put these principles into practice. Let's look at an actual sampling design used to select a sample of university students. The purpose of this study was to survey, with a self-administered instrument, the representative cross section of students attending the main campus of the University of Hawaii in 1968. The following sections will describe the steps and decisions involved in selecting that sample.

Survey Population and Sampling Frame

The obvious sampling frame available for use in this sample selection was the magnetic registration tape maintained by the university administration. The tape contained students' names, local and permanent addresses, social security numbers, and a variety of other information such as field of study, class, age, sex, and so forth.

The registration tape, however, contains files on all persons who could, by any conceivable definition, be called students, many of whom seemed inappropriate to the purposes of the study. As a result, it was necessary to define the *survey population* in a somewhat more restricted fashion. The final definition included those 15,225 day-program degree candidates registered for the fall 1968 semester on the Manoa campus of the university, including all colleges and departments, both undergraduate and graduate students, and both American and foreign students. The computer program used for sampling, therefore, limited consideration to students fitting this definition.

Stratification

The sampling program also permitted stratification of students before sample selection. In this instance, it was decided that stratification by college class would be sufficient, although the students might have been further stratified within class if desired, by sex, college, major, and so forth.

Sample Selection

Once the students had been arranged by class (by the sampling program), a systematic sample was selected across the entire rearranged list. The sample size for the study was initially set at 1,100. To achieve this sample, the sampling program was set to employ a 1/14 sampling fraction. The program, therefore, generated a random number between 1 and 14; the student having that number and every fourteenth student thereafter were selected in the sample.

Once the sample had been selected in this fashion, the computer was instructed to print each student's name and mailing address on six self-adhesive mailing labels. These labels were then simply transferred to envelopes for mailing the questionnaires.

Sample Modification

This initial design of the sample for the study of the university students had to be modified. Before the mailing of questionnaires, it was discovered that unexpected expenses in the production of the questionnaires made it impossible to cover the costs of mailing to some 1,100 students. As a result, one-third of the mailing labels were systematically selected (with a random start) for exclusion from the sample. The final sample for the study was thereby reduced to about 770.

This modification to the sample is mentioned here to illustrate the frequent necessity to change aspects of the study plan in midstream. Since a systematic sample of students was omitted from the initial systematic sample, the resulting 770 students could still be taken as reasonably representing the survey population. The reduction in sample size did, of course, increase the range of sampling error.

MULTISTAGE CLUSTER SAMPLING

The preceding sections have dealt with reasonably simple procedures for sampling from lists of elements. Such a situation is ideal. Unfortunately, however, much interesting social research requires the selection of samples from populations that cannot be easily listed for sampling purposes. Examples would be the population of a city, of a state, or of a nation, all university students in the United States, and so forth. In such cases, it is necessary to create and execute a more complex sample design. Such a design typically involves the initial sampling of *groups* of elements— clusters—followed by the selection of elements within each of the selected clusters.

Cluster sampling may be used when it is either impossible or impractical to compile an exhaustive list of the elements composing the target population. All church members in the United States would be an example of such a population. It is often the case, however, that the population elements are already grouped into subpopulations, and a list of those subpopulations either exists or can be created practically. Thus, church members in the United States belong to discrete churches, and it would be possible to discover or create a list of those churches. Following a cluster sample format, then, the list of churches would be sampled in some manner as discussed above (for example, a stratified, systematic sample). Next, you would obtain lists of members from each of the selected churches. Each of the lists obtained would then be sampled, to provide samples of church members for study.[5]

Another typical situation concerns sampling among population areas such as a city. Although there is no single list of a city's population, citizens reside on discrete city blocks or census blocks. It is possible, therefore, to select a sample of blocks initially, create a list of persons living on each of the selected blocks, and subsample persons on each block.

In a more complex design, you might sample blocks, list the households on each selected block, sample the households, list the persons residing in each household, and, finally, sample persons within each selected household. This multistage sample design would lead to the ultimate selection of a sample of individuals but would not require the initial listing of all individuals composing the city's population.

Multistage cluster sampling, then, involves the repetition of two basic steps: listing and sampling. The list of primary sampling units (churches, blocks) is compiled and, perhaps, stratified for sampling. Then a sample of those units is selected. The selected primary sampling units are then listed and perhaps stratified. The list of secondary sampling units is then sampled, and so forth.

Cluster sampling is highly recommended by its efficiency, but that efficiency comes at a price in terms of accuracy. Whereas a simple random sample drawn from a population list is subject to a single sampling error, a two-stage cluster sample is subject to two sampling errors. First, the initial sample of clusters will represent the population of clusters only within a range of sampling error. Second, the sample of elements selected within a given cluster will represent all the elements in that cluster only within a range of sampling error. Thus, for example, you run a certain risk of selecting a sample of disproportionately wealthy city blocks, plus a sample of disproportionately wealthy households within those blocks. The best solution to this problem lies in the number of clusters selected initially and the number of elements selected within each.

Typically, you'll be restricted to a total sample size; for example, you may be limited to conducting 2,000 interviews in a city. Given this broad limitation, however, you have several options in designing your cluster sample. At the extremes you might choose one cluster and select 2,000 elements within that cluster; or you might

[5]For an example, see Charles Y. Glock, Benjamin B. Ringer, and Earl R. Babbie, *To Comfort and to Challenge* (Berkeley: University of California Press, 1967), App. A.

select 2,000 clusters with one element selected within each. Of course, neither of these extremes is advisable, but you are faced with a broad range of choices between them. Fortunately, the logic of sampling distributions provides a general guideline to be followed.

Recall that sampling error is reduced by two factors: an increase in the sample size and an increased homogeneity of the elements being sampled. These factors operate at each level of a multistage sample design. A sample of clusters will best represent all clusters if a large number are selected and if all clusters are very much alike. A sample of elements will best represent all elements in a given cluster if a large number are selected from the cluster and if all the elements in the cluster are very much alike.

With a given total sample size, however, if the number of clusters is increased, the number of elements within a cluster must be decreased. In this respect, the representativeness of the clusters is increased at the expense of more poorly representing the elements composing each of those clusters, or vice versa, Fortunately, the factor of homogeneity can be used to ease this dilemma.

Typically, the elements composing a given natural cluster within a population are more homogeneous than are all elements composing the total population. The members of a given church are more alike than are all church members; the residents of a given city block are more alike than are all the residents of a whole city. As a result, relatively fewer elements may be needed to adequately represent a given natural cluster, while a larger number of clusters may be needed to adequately represent the diversity found among the clusters. This fact is most clearly seen in the extreme case of very different clusters that are composed of exactly identical elements within each. In such a situation, a large number of clusters would adequately represent the variety among clusters, while only one element within each cluster would adequately represent all its members. Although this extreme situation never exists in reality, it is closer to the truth in most cases than its opposite: identical clusters composed of grossly divergent elements.

The general guideline for cluster design, then, is to maximize the number of clusters selected while decreasing the number of elements within each cluster. It must be noted, however, that this scientific guideline must be balanced against an administrative constraint. The efficiency of cluster sampling is based on the ability to minimize the listing of population elements. By initially selecting clusters, you only need to list the elements composing the selected clusters, not all elements in the entire population. Increasing the number of clusters, however, goes directly against this efficiency factor in cluster sampling. A small number of clusters may be listed more quickly and more cheaply than a large number. (Remember that all the elements in a selected cluster must be listed even if only a few are to be chosen in the sample.)

The final sample design will reflect these two constraints. In effect, you will probably select as many clusters as you can afford. Lest this issue be left too open-ended at this point, one rule of thumb may be presented. Population researchers conventionally aim for the selection of 5 households per census block. If a total of 2,000 households are to be interviewed, you would aim at 400 blocks with 5 household interviews on each.

Before turning to more detailed procedures available to cluster sampling, it bears repeating that this method almost inevitably involves a loss of accuracy. The manner in which this appears, however, is somewhat complex. First, as noted earlier, a multistage sample design is subject to a sampling error at each of its stages. Since the sample size is necessarily smaller at each stage than the total sample size, the sampling error at each stage will be greater than would be the case for a single-stage random sample of elements. Second, sampling error is estimated on the basis of observed variance among the sample elements. When those elements are drawn from among relatively homogeneous clusters, the estimates of sampling error will be too optimistic and must be corrected in the light of the cluster sample design. (This will be discussed in detail in the later consideration of univariate analysis.)

Multistage Cluster Sampling, Stratification

Thus far, we have looked at cluster sampling as though a simple random sample were selected at each stage of the design. In fact, it is possible to employ stratification techniques as discussed earlier to refine and improve the sample being selected.

The basic options available are essentially the same as those possible in single-stage sampling from a list. In selecting a national sample of churches, for example, you might initially stratify your list of churches by denomination, geographical region, size, rural or urban location, and perhaps by some measure of social class. United States Census information might be used by population researchers to stratify quality of structures, nature of property ownership, and size.

Once the primary sampling units (churches, blocks) have been grouped according to the relevant, available stratification variables, either simple random or systematic sampling techniques could be used to select the sample. You might select a specified number of units from each group or *stratum*, or you might arrange the stratified clusters in a continuous list and systematically sample that list.

To the extent that clusters are combined into homogeneous strata, the sampling error at this stage will be reduced. The primary goal of stratification, as before, is homogeneity.

There is no reason why stratification could not take place at each level of sampling. The elements listed within a selected cluster might be stratified before the next stage of sampling. Typically, however, that is not done. (Recall the assumption of relative homogeneity within clusters.)

Probability Proportionate to Size (PPS) Sampling

In this section, I want to give you an introduction to a more sophisticated form of cluster sampling that is used in many large-scale survey sampling projects. In the discussion above, I talked about selecting a random or systematic sample of clusters and then a random or systematic sample of elements within each cluster that was selected. Notice that this would produce an overall sampling scheme in which every element in the whole population would have the same probability of selection.

Let's say that we are selecting households within a city. If there are 1,000 city blocks and we initially select a sample of 100, that means that each block had a 100/1,000 or .1 chance of being selected. If we next selected 1 household in 10 from those residing on the selected blocks, each household would have a .1 chance of selection within its block. To calculate the overall probability of a household being selected, we simply multiply the probabilities at the individual steps in sampling. That is, each household had a 1/10 chance of its block being selected and a 1/10 chance of that specific household being selected *if* the block is one of those chosen. Each household, in this case, would have a $1/10 \times 1/10 = 1/100$ chance of selection overall. Since each household would have the same chance of selection, the sample so selected should be representative of all households in the city.

There are dangers in this procedure, however. In particular, the varying sizes of blocks (measured in numbers of households) present a problem. Let's suppose that half of the city's population resided in 10 densely packed blocks filled with high-rise apartment buildings, and suppose that the rest of the population lived in single-family dwellings spread out over the remaining 900 blocks. When we first selected our sample of 1/10 of the blocks, it is quite possible that we'll miss all of the 10 densely packed high-rise blocks. No matter what happens in the second stage of sampling, our final sample of households will be grossly unrepresentative of the city, being composed only of single-family dwellings.

Whenever the clusters sampled are of greatly differing sizes, it is appropriate to use a modified sampling design called *probability proportionate to size*—PPS. This design (1) guards against the problem I've just described and (2) still produces a final sample in which each element has the same chance of selection.

As the name suggests, each cluster is given a chance of selection proportionate to its size. Thus, a city block with 200 households has twice the chance of selection as one with only 100 households. The method for doing this is demonstrated in the illustration that follows in the next section. Within each cluster, however, a fixed *number* of elements is selected, say, 5 households per block. Notice how this procedure results in each household having the same probability of selection overall.

Let's say that Household A is located on a block containing 100 households altogether, and Household B is located on a block containing 25 households. Suppose that we plan to select 5 households from whatever blocks are picked. This means that if the block containing Household A is picked, that household has a 5/100 chance of selection in the second stage of sampling. If the block containing Household B is picked, it has a 5/25 or 20/100 chance of being selected in the second stage of sampling. At the second stage of sampling, then, Household B has four times as good a chance of having its block selected in the first stage as did Household B. In the overall sampling design, then, both Household A and Household B have the same chance of being selected.

In a PPS sample design, the overall probability of selection for elements is calculated as follows:

1. The probability of a cluster being selected is equal to its proportional share of all the elements in the population *times* the number of clusters to be selected.

2. The probability of an element being selected within a cluster is equal to the number to be selected within each cluster divided by the number of elements contained within that particular cluster.

3. The overall probability of an element being selected equals (1) times (2).

Here's an example. Suppose a city is composed of 2,000 blocks and 100,000 households. Suppose further that we want to select 1,000 households. That means that each household should have a 1,000/100,000 or .01 chance of selection. We decide to accomplish this by picking 200 blocks PPS and selecting 5 households on each of the blocks chosen.

Now consider a block containing 100 households. The block has a probability of selection equal to:

$$\begin{matrix} .200 \\ \text{Blocks} \\ \text{to be} \\ \text{chosen} \end{matrix} \times \frac{100 \text{ (households on the block)}}{100,000 \text{ (households in the city)}} = .2$$

If that block is selected, each household has a second-stage probability of selection equal to:

$$\frac{5 \text{ (to be selected on each block)}}{100 \text{ (households on that block)}} = .05$$

Multiplying .2 times .05, we get an overall probability of selection equal to .01, as required.

Now let's consider a block with only 20 households on it. The block's chance of selection is only 200 × 20/100,000 or .04, much less than the earlier example. If this block is selected, however, each household has a chance of 5/20 or .25 of selection in the second stage. Overall, its probability of selection is .04 times .25, or .01: the same as the earlier case and as required by the overall sample design.

If you examine the method for calculating overall probabilities carefully, you'll see why the result is always going to be the same.

$$\text{Example 1:} \quad 200 \times \frac{100}{100,000} \times \frac{5}{100} = .01$$

$$\text{Example 2:} \quad 200 \times \frac{20}{100,000} \times \frac{5}{20} = .01$$

The only thing that differs in the two examples is the number of households on the blocks, and that number appears in both numerator and denominator, thus cancelling itself out. No matter what the block size, then, the overall probability of a household being selected will be equal to 200 times 5/100,000, or .01. See how neat and clean it is?

As a practical matter, PPS cluster sampling is never quite this neat in the field.

For example, the estimates of the number of households on blocks are seldom totally accurate, so that blocks are given too high or too low probabilities of selection. There are several statistical solutions to this problem, however, although it's probably not necessary for you to know them for purposes of this introduction to sampling. Other problems arise because some households selected cannot be interviewed—either the people are never home or they refuse to be interviewed. Again, the structure of PPS sampling makes adjustments possible, so that the data collected from those households that are selected and interviewed can be taken as representative of all households in the city.

I began this section on PPS sampling by pointing to the danger of missing very large blocks altogether. There is another benefit inherent in this more sophisticated design. If you recall the earlier discussion of homogeneity and heterogeneity, you'll remember that sampling is less of a problem if all the elements being selected are pretty much alike, that is, homogeneous. PPS sampling takes advantage of that fact, in the sense that households composing a single city block or similar geographical groupings are likely to be quite similar to one another, as are the families residing in them. Specifically, the similarity of households on a block is greater than the similarity among households in a whole city. This means that it takes relatively few households on a single block to describe all the households on that block. As a rule of thumb, 5 is usually enough in the context of a large multistage cluster sample. Observing more than 5 households on a single block would improve the description of the block slightly, but the description of the city as a whole would be better improved by adding more blocks to the sample than adding more households on a fewer number of blocks. Given that you can only interview, say 1,000 households altogether, it would be better to interview 5 each on 200 blocks than to interview 20 each on 50 blocks. In addition to guarding against specific dangers, then, PPS sampling is an efficient use of limited resources.

Disproportionate Sampling and Weighting

Ultimately, a probability sample is representative of a population if all elements in the population have an equal chance of selection in that sample. Thus, in each of the preceding discussions we have noted that the various sampling procedures result in an equal chance of selection—even though the ultimate selection probability is the product of several partial probabilities.

More generally, however, a probability sample is one in which each population element has a _known nonzero_ probability of selection—even though different elements may have different probabilities. If controlled probability sampling procedures have been used, any such sample may be representative of the population from which it is drawn if each sample element is assigned a weight equal to the inverse of its probability of selection. Thus, where all sample elements have had the same chance of selection, each is given the same weight: 1. (This is called a _self-weighting_ sample.)

Disproportionate sampling and weighting come into play in two basic ways. First, you may sample subpopulations disproportionately to insure sufficient numbers of cases from each for analysis. For example, a given city may have a suburban area containing one-fourth of its total population. Yet you might be especially interested in a detailed analysis of households in that area and may feel that one-fourth of this total sample size would be too few. As a result, you might decide to select the same number of households from the suburban area as from the remainder of the city. Households in the suburban area, then, are given a disproportionately better chance of selection than those located elsewhere in the city.

As long as you analyze the two area samples separately or comparatively, you need not worry about the differential sampling. If you want to combine the two samples to create a composite picture of the entire city, however, you must take the disproportionate sampling into account. If n is the number of households selected from each area, then the households in the suburban area had a chance of selection equal to n divided by one-fourth of the total city population. Since the total city population and the sample size are the same for both areas, the suburban-area households should be given a weight of $\frac{1}{4}n$ while the remaining households should be given a weight of $\frac{3}{4}n$. This weighting procedure could be simplified by merely giving a weight of 3 to each of the households selected outside the suburban area. (This procedure would give a *proportionate* representation to each sample element. The population figure would have to be included in the weighting if population estimates were desired.)

Degrees of Precision in Weighting

In any complex sample design, you face a number of options with regard to weighting in connection with purposively or inadvertently disproportionate sampling. You may compute weights for each element to several decimal places, or you may assign rough weights to account for only the grossest instances of disproportionate sampling. In the previous case of the city in which the suburban area was oversampled, it is unlikely that the population of that area was exactly one-fourth of the city's population: suppose it actually was .25001, .2600, or .2816 of the total population. In the first instance, it seems quite likely that you would choose to apply the rough overall weighting of cases described if no other disproportionate sampling were involved at other stages in the sampling design. Perhaps you would do the same in the second and third instances as well. The precision you will seek in weighting should be commensurate with the precision you will desire in your findings. If your research purposes can tolerate errors of a few percentage points, you will probably not waste your time and effort in weighting exactly. In deciding the degree of precision required, moreover, you should take into account the degree of error to be expected from normal sampling distribution, plus all the various types of nonsampling error.

Ultimately, there is no firm guideline for you to follow in determining the precision to be sought in weighting. As in so many other aspects of survey design, you are afforded considerable latitude. At the same time, however, you should bear your decision in mind when reporting your findings. You should not employ only a rough weighting procedure and then suggest that your findings are accurate within a minuscule range of error.

Methods for Weighting

Having outlined the scientific concerns for determining the degree of precision desired in weighting, I should note that the choice will often be made on the basis of available methods for weighting. There are three basic methods for weighting.

1. For the rough weighting of samples drawn from subpopulations, weighting tables can be constructed from the unweighted tables for each of the subsamples. In the earlier example, you could create a raw table of distributions for the suburban sample and for the nonsuburban sample separately, triple the number of cases in each cell of the nonsuburban table, add the cases across the two tables, and compute percentages for the composite table.

2. For more extensive and faster, though still rough, weighting, machine-readable cards can be mechanically reproduced for those cases requiring weights. In the previous example two additional copies of each card relating to a non-suburban household could be made (for a total of three each), the enlarged nonsuburban file could then be combined with the suburban file, and the entire card file could be analyzed as though three times as many nonsuburban house-holds had been studied.

3. If the data are to be analyzed by computer, a special program may be designed to assign a precise weight to each case in the original data file. Only this latter method is appropriate to refined weighting, since it is impossible to reproduce fractions of cards with any meaning.

As mentioned at the outset of this section, scientific concerns in weighting are usually subjugated to practical concerns as in other instances. If the analysis is to be conducted through cards only, weighting must of necessity be approximate rather than precise.

ILLUSTRATION: SAMPLING CHURCHWOMEN

Now let's see what cluster sampling looks like in practice. The illustration that follows is not as complex as the area probability samples that are employed in studies of geographic areas such as cities, states, or the nation. Nonetheless, it should be a useful example of the various principles of cluster sampling.

The purpose of this study was to examine the attitudes of women members of churches in a diocese of the Episcopal church. A representative sample of all church-women in the diocese was desired. As you will by now expect, there was no single list of such women, so a multistage sample design was created. In the initial stage of sampling, churches were selected with probability proportionate to size (PPS), and then women were selected from each.

Selecting the Churches

The diocese in question publishes an annual report that contains a listing of the 100 or so churches composing it with their respective sizes in terms of membership. This listing constituted the sampling frame for the first stage of sampling.

A total of approximately 500 respondents was desired for the study, so the decision was made to select 25 churches with probability proportionate to size and take 20 women from each of those selected. To accomplish this, the list of churches was arranged geographically, and then a table was created similar to the partial listing shown in Table 7-1.

Table 7-1   Form Used in Listing of Churches

Church	Membership	Cumulative Membership
Church A	3,000	3,000
Church B	5,000	8,000
Church C	1,000	9,000

Beside each church in the table, its membership was entered, and that figure was used to compute the cumulative total running through the list. The final total came to approximately 200,000. The object at this point was to select a sample of 25 churches in such a way that each would have a chance of selection proportionate to the number of members in it. To accomplish this, the cumulative totals were used to create ranges of numbers for each church equaling the number of members in that church. Church A in the table above was assigned the numbers 1 through 3,000; Church B was assigned 3,001 through 8,000; Church C was assigned 8,001 through 9,000; and so forth.

By selecting 25 numbers ranging between 1 and 200,000, it would be possible to select 25 churches for the study. The 25 numbers were selected in a systematic sample as follows. The sampling interval was set at 8,000 (200,000/25) and a random start was selected between 1 and 8,000. Let us say the random number was 4,538. Since that number fell within the range of numbers assigned to Church B (3,001–8,000), Church B was selected.

Increments of 8,000 (the sampling interval) were then added to the random start, and every church within whose range one of the resultant numbers appeared was selected into the sample of churches. It should be apparent that in this fashion, each church in the diocese had a chance of selection directly proportionate to its membership size. A church with 4,000 members had twice the chance of selection as a church of 2,000 and 10 times the chance of selection as one with only 400 members.

Selecting the Churchwomen

Once the sample of churches was selected, arrangements were made to get lists of the women members of each. It is worth noting here that in practice the lists varied greatly in their form and content. In a number of cases, lists of all members (men and women) were provided, and it was necessary to sort out the women before sampling the lists. The form of the lists varied from typed lists to 3 × 5 cards printed from mailing address plates.

As the list arrived from a selected church, a sampling interval for that church was computed on the basis of the number of women members and the number desired (20). If a church contained 2,000 women, the sample interval, therefore, was set at 100. A random number was selected and incremented by the sampling interval to select the sample of women from that church. This procedure was repeated for each church.

Note that this sample design ultimately gives every woman in the diocese an equal chance of selection *only* if the assumption is made that half the members of each church are women (or if a constant proportion of them are). That is due to the fact that churches were given a chance of selection based on their *total* membership (numbers of women were not available). Given the aims of this particular study, the slight inequities of selection were considered insignificant.

A more sophisticated sample design for the second stage would have resolved this possible problem. Since each church was given a chance of selection based on an assumed number of women (assuming 1,000 women in a church of 2,000), the sampling interval could have been computed on the basis of that assumption rather than on the actual number of women listed. If it were assumed in the first stage of sampling that a church had 1,000 women (out of a membership of 2,000), the sampling interval could have been set at 50 (1,000/20). Then this interval could have been used in the selection of respondents regardless of the actual number of women listed for that church. If 1,000 women were in fact listed, then their church had the proper chance of selection and 20 women would be selected from it. If 1,200 women were listed, that would mean that the church had too small a chance of selection, but this would have been remedied through the selection of 24 women using the preestablished sampling interval. If only 800 women were listed, on the other hand, only 16 would have been selected.

Probability Sampling in Review

The preceding lengthy and detailed discussions have been devoted to the key sampling method used in controlled survey research: probability sampling. In each of the variations examined, we have seen that elements are chosen for study from a population on a basis of random selection with known nonzero probabilities.

Depending on the field situation, probability sampling can be very simple, or it can be extremely difficult, time-consuming, and expensive. Whatever the situation, however, it remains the most effective method for the selection of study elements. There are two reasons for this.

First, probability sampling avoids conscious or unconscious biases in element selection on the part of the researcher. If all elements in the population have an equal (or unequal and subsequently weighted) chance of selection, there is an excellent chance that the sample so selected will closely represent the population of all elements.

Second, probability sampling permits estimates of sampling error. Although no probability sample will be perfectly representative in all respects, controlled selection methods permit the researcher to estimate the degree of expected error in that regard.

In spite of the above comments, it is sometimes not possible to use standard probability sampling methods. Sometimes it wouldn't even be appropriate to do so. In those cases, nonprobability sampling is used. The remainder of this chapter is devoted to a brief discussion of the different forms of nonprobability sampling available to you as a researcher.

NONPROBABILITY SAMPLING

I'm sure you can envision situations in which it would be either impossible or grossly unfeasible to select the kinds of probability samples described above. In addition, as I've suggested in the preceding paragraph, there are times when a probability sample wouldn't be appropriate even though possible. I'll begin this section with a discussion of that situation, then we'll look at some other forms of nonprobability sampling.

Purposive or Judgmental Sampling

Occasionally it may be appropriate for you to select your sample on the basis of your own knowledge of the population, its elements, and the nature of your research aims. Especially in the initial design of your questionnaire, you might wish to select the widest variety of respondents to test the broad applicability of questions. Although the survey findings would not represent any meaningful population, the test run might effectively uncover any peculiar defects in your research instrument. This situation would be referred to as a pretest, however, rather than a survey proper.

In some instances, you may wish to study a small subset of a larger population in which many members of the subset are easily identified but the enumeration of all would be nearly impossible. For example, you might want to study the leadership of a student protest movement; many of the leaders are easily visible, but it would not be feasible to define and sample all leaders. In studying all or a sample of the most visible leaders, you may collect data sufficient for your purposes.

In a multistage sample design, you might want to compare left-wing and right-wing students. Since you may not be able to enumerate and sample from all such students, you might decide to sample the memberships of Students for a Democratic Society and Young Americans for Freedom. Although such a sample design would not provide a good description of either left-wing or right-wing students as a whole, it might suffice for general comparative purposes.

Sampling of *selected precincts* for political polls is a somewhat refined judgmental process. On the basis of previous voting results in a given area (city, state, nation), you purposively select a group of voting precincts that, in combination, produces results similar to those of the entire area. Then, in subsequent polls, you select your samples solely from those precincts. The theory is, of course, that the selected precincts provide a cross section of the entire electorate, so you need to know what you're doing.

Each time there is an election that permits you to evaluate the adequacy of your group of precincts, you would consider revisions, additions, or deletions. Your goal is to update the group of precincts to insure that it will provide a good representation of all precincts.

To be done effectively, selected precinct sampling requires considerable political expertise. You should be well versed in the political and social history of the area under consideration so that the selection of precincts is based on an *educated* guess as to its persistent representativeness. In addition, this system of sampling requires continuing feedback to be effective. You must be in a position to conduct frequent polls and must have periodic electoral validations.

Quota Sampling

Quota sampling was mentioned earlier, in the discussion of political polling. It's the method that helped George Gallup avoid disaster in 1936—and set up the disaster of 1948. It addresses the issue of representativeness that was discussed in connection with probability sampling, though quota sampling handles the issue quite differently.

Quota sampling begins with a matrix describing the characteristics of the target population. You need to know what proportion of the population is male and what proportion female, for example, and for each sex, what proportions fall into various age categories, educational levels, ethnic groups, and so forth. In establishing a national quota sample, you would need to know what proportion of the national population is urban, eastern, male, under 25, white, working class, and the like, and all the other permutations of such a matrix.

Once such a matrix has been created and a relative proportion assigned to each cell in the matrix, you collect data from persons having all the characteristics of a given cell. All the persons in a given cell are then assigned a weight appropriate to their portion of the total population. When all the sample elements are so weighted, the overall data should provide a reasonable representation of the total population.

There are a number of inherent problems in quota sampling. First, the quota frame (the proportions that different cells represent) must be accurate, and it is often difficult to get up-to-date information for this purpose. The Gallup failure to predict Truman as the presidential victor in 1948 was due partly to this problem.

Second, biases may exist in the selection of sample elements within a given cell —even though its proportion of the population is accurately estimated. An interviewer, instructed to interview five persons meeting a given, complex set of characteristics, may still avoid persons living at the top of seven-story walk-ups, having particularly run-down homes, or owning vicious dogs.

In recent years, attempts have been made to combine probability and quota sampling methods, but the effectiveness of this effort remains to be seen. At present, you would be advised to treat quota sampling warily.

Reliance on Available Subjects

Stopping people at a street corner or some other location is almost never an adequate sampling method, although it is employed all too frequently. It would be justified only if the researcher wanted to study the characteristics of people passing the sampling point at specified times.

University researchers frequently conduct surveys among the students enrolled in large lecture classes. The ease and inexpense of such a method explains its popularity, but it seldom produces data of any general value. It may serve the purpose of a pretest of a questionnaire, but such a sampling method should not be used for a study purportedly describing students as a whole.

SUMMARY

Chapter 7, a rather lengthy one, has presented the basic logic and some of the techniques of probability sampling. In addition, it has discussed, more briefly, some methods for nonprobability sampling. Since rigorous sampling methods have been developed and used primarily within the context of survey research, most of the discussions have focused on that method. It is important for you to realize, however, that the basic logic and many of the specific techniques of sampling discussed in this chapter are equally applicable to other research methods, such as content analysis, experimentation, and even field research.

The chapter began with an introductory discussion of what sampling is and why sampling methods are used. We noted that social researchers are often interested in describing and explaining certain characteristics of very large populations. Since it is often impossible—in terms of time and money—to observe all the members of such populations, you may select a smaller subset—a sample—of members from that population. You then observe your sample and infer that what you learn about the sample will also be true of the population from which it is drawn.

We noted that the history of sampling in social research has been a rather spotty one, containing the well-known snafus of the *Literary Digest* poll of 1936 and the Gallup poll of 1948. More recently, however, sampling techniques have yielded results that are extremely accurate reflections of the characteristics of large populations.

Most of the chapter dealt with the logic of probability sampling, based on probability theory. We noted that these controlled sampling methods have three basic advantages: (1) they rule out the human biases that might be involved in the more casual selection of people to be observed, (2) they enhance the likelihood that a sample drawn from a population will be representative, that is, it will have essentially the same distribution of characteristics as the population from which it is drawn, and (3) probability theory provides a set of computational methods for estimating the degree of error to be expected in a given sample. The basic principle involved in probability sampling is that every member of the total population will have a known nonzero probability of being selected into the sample. In the simplest case, each member will have the same probability of being selected.

The chapter then illustrated the logic of probability sampling by introducing the notion of a sampling distribution, the expected variety of samples that would be drawn from a given population. Although none of the samples would be likely to reflect *perfectly* all the characteristics of the total population, we saw the distribution of different degrees of error (sampling error) in such samples. This model was then turned inside out to permit the estimation of the accuracy of a single sample in describing the larger population.

Next, the chapter turned to an examination of sampling frames, the lists or quasi-lists of population members that constitute the fundamental resource in the selection of a sample. We discussed the relative quality of several commonly used sampling frames.

The remainder of the chapter was devoted to some of the many concrete sampling techniques that are used in sample selection. Most of this discussion focused on different types of probability sampling techniques, with less attention given to some of the available nonprobability sampling techniques.

MAIN POINTS

1. A sample is a special subset of a population that is observed for purposes of making inferences about the nature of the total population itself.

2. Although the sampling methods used earlier in this century often produced misleading inferences, current techniques are far more accurate and reliable.

3. The chief criterion of the quality of a sample is the degree to which it is representative—the extent to which the characteristics of the sample are the same as those of the population from which it was selected.

4. Probability sampling methods provide one excellent way of selecting samples that will be quite representative.

5. The most carefully selected sample will almost never provide a perfect representation of the population from which it was selected. There will always be some degree of sampling error.

6. Probability sampling methods make it possible for you to estimate the amount of sampling error that should be expected in a given sample.

7. The chief principle of probability sampling is that every member of the total population must have some known nonzero probability of being selected into the sample.

8. An EPSEM sample is one in which every member of a population has the same probability of being selected.

9. A sampling frame is a list or quasi-list of the members of a population. It is the resource used in the selection of a sample. A sample's representativeness depends directly on the extent to which a sampling frame contains all the members of the total population that the sample is intended to represent.

10. Simple random sampling is logically the most fundamental technique in probability sampling, though it is seldom used in practice.

11. Systematic sampling involves the selection of every kth member from a sampling frame. This method is functionally equivalent to simple random sampling, with a few exceptions, and it is a more practical method.

12. Stratification is the process of grouping the members of a population into relatively homogeneous strata before sampling. This practice has the effect of improving the representativeness of a sample by reducing the degree of sampling error.

13. Multistage cluster sampling is a more complex sampling technique that is frequently used in those cases in which a list of all the members of a population does not exist. An initial sample of groups of members (clusters) is selected first. Then, all the members of the selected cluster are listed, often through direct observation in the field. Finally, the members listed in each of the selected clusters are subsampled, thereby providing the final sample of members.

14. Probability proportionate to size (PPS) is a special efficient method for multistage cluster sampling.

15. If the members of a population have unequal probabilities of selection into the sample, it is necessary to assign weights to the different observations made in order to provide a representative picture of the total population. Basically, the weight assigned to a particular sample member should be the inverse of its probability of selection.

16. Purposive sampling is a type of nonprobability sampling method in which the researcher uses his or her own judgment in the selection of sample members. It is sometimes called a judgmental sample.

17. Quota sampling is another nonprobability sampling method. You begin with a detailed description of the characteristics of the total population (quota

matrix) and then select your sample members in such a fashion as to include different composite profiles that exist in the population. The representativeness of a quota sample depends in large part on the accuracy of the quota matrix as a reflection of the characteristics of the population.

18. In general, nonprobability sampling methods are regarded as less reliable than probability sampling methods. On the other hand, they are often easier and cheaper to use.

ANNOTATED BIBLIOGRAPHY

Kish, Leslie, *Survey Sampling* (New York: John Wiley, 1965). Unquestionably the definitive work on sampling in social research. Let's not beat around the bush: if you need to know something more about sampling than was contained in this chapter, there is only one place to go. Kish's coverage ranges from the simplest matters to the most complex and mathematical. He is both highly theoretical and downright practical. Easily readable and difficult passages intermingle as Kish exhausts everything you could want to need to know about each aspect of sampling. It seems to me altogether possible that nobody will ever write another book on this subject.

PART THREE

Modes of Observation

I have a hunch that you may have grown impatient. If you began this book with a view that doing research means making observations and analyzing what you've observed, the preliminary discussions of various aspects of research design may have seemed overlong. It bears repeating, however, that the structuring of inquiry is an integral part of research. With that point firmly in mind, let's dive into the various observational techniques available to social scientists.

Chapter 8, on field research, examines what is perhaps the most natural form of data collection employed by social scientists: the direct observation of social phenomena in natural settings. As we shall see, some researchers go beyond mere observation to participate in what they are studying so as to get a more intimate view and fuller understanding.

Chapter 9 discusses two forms of data collection that take advantage of some of the data that are available all around us. Content analysis is a method of collecting social data through carefully specifying and counting social artifacts such as books, songs, speeches, and paintings. Without making any personal contact with people, you can use this method to examine a wide variety of social phenomena. The analysis of existing statistics offers another way of studying people without having to talk to them. Governments and a variety of private organizations regularly compile great masses of data, and these data can often be used with little or no modification to answer properly posed questions.

Experiments are usually thought of in connection with the physical sciences. In Chapter 10 we will see how social scientists use experiments. This is the most rigorously controllable of the methods we'll examine, and you should come away from this chapter with a better understanding of the general logic of social scientific research.

Chapter 11, on evaluation research, looks at a rapidly growing subfield in social science, involving the application of experimental and quasi-experimental models to the testing of social interventions in real life. Evaluation research, for example, might be used to test the effectiveness of a drug rehabilitation program or the efficiency of a new school cafeteria. In the same chapter, we'll look briefly at social indicators as a way of assessing broader social processes.

Finally, Chapter 12 will describe survey research, one of the most popular of methods in social science. As we'll see, this type of research involves collecting data through asking people questions—either in self-administered questionnaires or through interviews.

Before we turn to the actual descriptions of the several methods, two points should be made. First, you will probably discover that you have been using these scientific methods quite casually in your daily life for as long as you can remember. You use some form of field research every day. You are employing a crude form of content analysis every time you judge an author's motivation or orientation from his or her writings. You engage in at least casual experiments frequently. The chapters in Part Three will show you how to improve your use of these methods so as to avoid the pitfalls and casual, uncontrolled observation.

Second, none of the data-collection methods described in the following chapters is appropriate to all research topics and situations. I have tried to give you some ideas, early in each chapter, of when a given method might be appropriate. Still, it would not be possible to anticipate all the possible research topics that may one day interest you. As a general guideline, it is always best to employ a variety of techniques in the study of any topic. Since each of the methods has its weaknesses, the use of several methods can help fill in any gaps; and, if the different, independent approaches to the topic all yield the same conclusion, that can constitute a form of replication.

CHAPTER 8

Field Research

INTRODUCTION

Several chapters ago, I said that you had been doing social research all your life. That should become even clearer to you as we turn now to what probably seems like the most obvious methods of making observations: field research. If you want to know about something, why not just go where it's happening and watch it happen? That's what this chapter is all about. I have used the term *field research* to include methods of research sometimes referred to as *participant observation*, *direct observation*, and *case studies.*

Field research is at once very old and very new in social science. It is very old in that many of the techniques to be discussed in this chapter have been used by social researchers for centuries. It is very new in that it has received increasing methodological attention and has been refined in recent years. It should be noted, moreover, that this method is employed by many people who might not, strictly speaking, be regarded as social science researchers. Newspaper reporters are one example; welfare department case workers are another.

It bears repeating that field research is constantly used in everyday life, by all of us. In a sense, we do field research whenever we observe or participate in social behavior, whether at a corner tavern, in a doctor's waiting room, on an airplane, or anywhere. Whenever we look around us and observe what is happening and try to understand it, we are engaging in field research. Whenever we report our observations to others, we are reporting our field research efforts. The purpose of this chapter is to discuss this method in some detail, providing a logical overview of the method, and suggesting some of the specific skills and techniques that make scientific field research more useful than the casual observation we all engage in.

Field observation differs from some other models of observation in that it is not only a data-collecting activity. Frequently, perhaps typically, it is a theory-generating activity as well. As a field researcher you will seldom approach your task with precisely defined hypotheses to be tested. More typically, you will attempt to make sense out of an ongoing process that cannot be predicted in advance—making initial observations, developing tentative general conclusions that suggest particular types of further observations, making those observations and thereby revising your conclusions, and so forth. The alternation of induction and deduction discussed in Part One of this book is perhaps nowhere more evident and essential than in good field research.

TOPICS APPROPRIATE TO FIELD RESEARCH

One of the key strengths of field research, as will be discussed at the close of this chapter, is the comprehensiveness of perspective it gives the researcher. By going directly to the social phenomenon under study and observing it as completely as possible, you can develop a deeper and fuller understanding of it. This mode of observation, then, is especially, though not exclusively, appropriate to those research topics and social studies that appear to defy simple quantification. The field researcher may recognize several nuances of attitude and behavior that might escape researchers using other methods.

Somewhat differently, field research is especially appropriate to the study of those topics for which attitudes and behaviors can best be understood within their natural setting. Experiments and surveys, for example, may be able to measure behaviors and attitudes in somewhat artificial settings, but not all behavior is best measured this way. For example, field research provides a superior method for studying the dynamics of religious conversion at a revival meeting.

Finally, field research is especially appropriate to the study of social processes over time. Thus, for example, the field researcher might be in a position to examine the rumblings and final explosion of a riot as events actually occur rather than trying to reconstruct them afterwards.

Other good studies for field research methods would be campus demonstrations, courtroom proceedings, labor negotiations, public hearings, or similar events taking place within a relatively limited area and time. Several such observations must be combined in a more comprehensive examination across time and space.

John Lofland, in his *Analyzing Social Settings*, has suggested six different types of social phenomena that might be addressed by the field researcher.

> In thinking about presenting the examples in an orderly fashion, it seemed best to arrange them along a continuum from the most *microscopic* social phenomenon to the most *macroscopic*. While the materials in fact shade one into another, in order to be more precise, I have chopped the continuum into six categories. Ranging from microscopic to macroscopic, these are as follows:
>
> 1. *Acts*. Action in a situation that is temporally brief, consuming only a few seconds, minutes, or hours.
>
> 2. *Activities*. Action in a setting of more major duration—days, weeks, months—constituting significant elements of persons' involvements.
>
> 3. *Meanings*. The verbal productions of participants that define and direct action.

4. *Participation*. Persons' holistic involvement, or adaptation to, a situation or setting under study.

5. *Relationships*. Interrelationships among several persons considered simultaneously.

6. *Settings*. The entire setting under study conceived as the unit of analysis.[1]

Let me give you a concrete example of how field research can reveal things that would not otherwise be apparent. Recently, I've become increasingly interested in the nature of responsibility for public matters: Who's responsible for having the things we share work? Who's responsible for keeping public spaces—parks, malls, buildings, and so on—clean? Who's responsible for seeing to it that broken street signs get fixed? Or, if a strong wind knocks over garbage cans and rolls them around the street, who's responsible for getting them out of the street?

On the surface, the answer to these questions is pretty clear. We have formal and informal agreements in our society that assign responsibility for these activities. Government custodians are responsible for keeping public places clean. Transportation department people are responsible for the street signs, and perhaps the police are responsible for the garbage cans rolling around the street on a windy day. And when these responsibilities are not fulfilled, we tend to look around for someone to blame.

What has fascinated me is the extent to which the assignment of responsibility for public things to specific individuals not only relieves others of the responsibility but actually *prohibits* them from *taking* responsibility. It's been my notion, for example, that it has become unacceptable for someone like you or me to take personal responsibility for public matters that haven't been assigned to us.

Let me illustrate what I mean. If you were walking through a public park and you threw down a bunch of trash, you'd discover that your action was unacceptable to those around you. People would glare at you, grumble to each other, and perhaps someone would say something to you about it. Whatever the form, you'd be subjected to definite, negative sanctions for littering. Now here's the irony. If you were walking through that same park, came across a bunch of trash that someone else had dropped there, and took responsibility for cleaning it up, that would also be unacceptable to those around you. You'd be subjected to definite, negative sanctions for taking responsibility for cleaning it up.

When I first began discussing this pattern with students, most felt the notion was absurd. Although we would be negatively sanctioned for littering, cleaning up a public place would obviously bring positive sanctions. People would be pleased with us for doing it. Certainly, all my students said *they* would be pleased if someone cleaned up a public place. It seemed likely that everyone else would be pleased, too, if we asked them how they would react to someone's taking responsibility for cleaning up litter in a public place or otherwise taking personal responsibility for fixing some social problem.

To settle the issue, I suggested that my students start fixing the public problems they came across in the course of their everyday activities. As they did so, I asked them to note the answers to two questions:

[1]John Lofland, *Analyzing Social Settings* (Belmont, Calif.: Wadsworth, 1971), pp. 14-15.

1. How did they feel while they were fixing a public problem they had not been assigned responsibility for?

2. How did others around them react?

My students then set out to take personal responsibility for having public things work. They picked up litter, fixed street signs, put knocked-over traffic cones back in place, cleaned and decorated communal lounges in their dorms, trimmed trees that blocked visibility at intersections, repaired public playground equipment, cleaned public restrooms, and took care of a hundred other public problems that weren't "their responsibility."

In answer to my first question, most reported feeling very uncomfortable doing whatever they did. They felt foolish, goody-goody, conspicuous, and all the other feelings that keep us from performing these activities normally. In almost every case, their personal feelings of discomfort were increased by the reactions of those around them. One student was removing a damaged and long-unused newspaper box from the bus stop where it had been a problem for months when the police arrived, having been summoned by a neighbor. Another student decided to clean out a clogged storm drain on his street and found himself being yelled at by a neighbor who insisted that the mess should be left for the street cleaners. Everyone who picked up litter was sneered at, laughed at, and generally put down. One young man was picking up litter scattered around a trash can when a passerby sneered, "Clumsy!" It became clear to us that there are only three acceptable explanations for picking up litter in a public place:

1. You did it and got caught—somebody forced you to clean up your mess.

2. You did it and got a guilty conscience.

3. You're stealing litter.

In the normal course of things, it is simply not acceptable for people to take responsibility for public things.

Clearly, we could not have discovered the nature and strength of agreements about taking personal responsibility for public things except by field research. The formal norms of society would suggest that taking such responsibility was a good thing—sometimes referred to as *good citizenship*. Asking people what they thought about it would have produced a solid consensus that it was good. Only going out into life, doing it, and watching what happened gave an accurate picture.

As an interesting footnote to this story, we found that whenever people could get past their initial reactions and discover that the students were simply taking responsibility for fixing things for the sake of having them work, the tendency was for the passersby to join in and assist. Although there are some very strong agreements making it "unsafe" to take responsibility for public things, the willingness of one person to rise above those agreements seemed to make it safe for others to do so, and they did.

In summary, then, field research offers the advantage of probing social life in its natural habitat. Although some things can be studied adequately in questionnaires or in the laboratory, others cannot be. And direct observation in the field lets you observe subtle communications and other events that might not be anticipated or measured otherwise.

THE VARIOUS ROLES OF THE OBSERVER

In the illustration of students fixing public things, they were definitely *participating* in what they wanted to observe. In this chapter, I have used the term *field research* rather than the frequently used term *participant observation*, since field researchers need not always participate in what they are studying, though they usually will study it directly at the scene of the action. Raymond Gold has discussed four different roles that field researchers may play in this regard: *complete participant*, *participant-as-observer*, *observer-as-participant*, and *complete observer*.[2]

Gold described the complete participant as follows:

The true identity and purpose of the complete participant in field research are not known to those whom he observes. He interacts with them as naturally as possible in whatever areas of their living interest him and are acceptable to him in situations in which he can play or learn to play requisite day-to-day roles successfully.[3]

The complete participant, in this sense, may be a genuine participant in what he or she is studying (for example, a participant in a campus demonstration) or may pretend to be a genuine participant. In any event, if you are acting as the complete participant you let people see you *only* as a participant, not a researcher.

Clearly, if you are not a genuine participant in that which you are studying, you must learn to behave as though you were. If you are studying a group made up of uneducated and inarticulate people, it would not be appropriate for you to talk and act like a university professor or student.

Here let me recall your attention to an ethical issue involved in the research situation under discussion. Social researchers themselves are divided on this issue. Is it ethical to deceive the people you are studying in the hope that they will confide in you as they will not confide in an identified researcher? Do the interests of science—the scientific values of the research—offset such ethical considerations? Although many professional associations have addressed this issue, the norms to be followed remain somewhat ambiguous when applied to specific situations.

Related to this ethical consideration is a scientific one. No researcher deceives his or her subjects solely for the purpose of deception. Rather, it is done in the belief that the data will be more valid and reliable, that the subjects will be more natural and honest if they do not know that the researcher is doing a research project. If the people being studied know they are being studied, they might modify their behavior in a variety of ways. First, they might expel the researcher. Second, they might

[2]Raymond L. Gold, "Roles in Sociological Field Observation," in George J. McCall and J. L. Simmons (eds.), *Issues in Participant Observation* (Reading, Mass.: Addison-Wesley, 1969), pp. 30–39.
[3]*Ibid.*, p. 33.

modify their speech and behavior so as to appear more respectable than would otherwise be the case. Third, the social process itself might be radically changed. Students making plans to burn down the university administration building, for example, might give up the plan altogether once they learn that one of their group is a social scientist conducting a research project.

On the other side of the coin, if you are a complete participant, you may affect what you are studying. To play the role of participant, you must *participate*. Yet, your participation may importantly affect the social process you are studying. Suppose, for example, that you are asked for your ideas as to what the group should do next. No matter what you say, you will affect the process in some fashion. If you make a suggestion that is followed by the group, your influence on the process is obvious. If you make a suggestion that is not followed, the process whereby the suggestion is rejected may importantly affect what happens next. Finally, if you indicate that you just don't know what is to be done next, that may add to a general feeling of uncertainty and indecisiveness in the group.

Ultimately, *anything* that the participant observer does or does not do will have some effect on that which is being observed; it is simply inevitable. More seriously, what you do or do not do may have an *important* effect on what happens. There is no complete protection against this effect, though sensitivity to the issue may provide a partial protection. (This influence, called the Hawthorne effect, is discussed more fully in Chapter 10.)

Because of these several considerations, ethical and scientific, the field researcher frequently chooses a different role from that of complete participant. In Gold's terminology, you might choose the role of participant-as-observer. In this role, you would participate fully with the group under study, but you would make it clear that you were also undertaking research. There are dangers in this role also, however. First, the people being studied may shift much of their attention to the research project rather than focusing on the natural social process, and the process being observed may no longer be typical. (Or, conversely, you yourself may come to identify too much with the interests and viewpoints of the participants. You may begin to "go native" and lose much of your scientific objectivity.)

The observer-as-participant is one who identifies himself or herself as a researcher and interacts with the participants in the social process but makes no pretense of actually being a participant. A good example of that would be a newspaper reporter who is learning about a social movement, for instance, the unionization of migrant farm workers. The reporter might interview leaders and also visit workers where they live, watch strawberry picking, go with an injured worker to the hospital, and so on.

The complete observer, at the other extreme, is one who only observes a social process without becoming a part of it in any way. Quite possibly, the subjects of study might not realize they are being studied because of the researcher's unobtrusiveness. Sitting at a bus stop for the purpose of observing jaywalking behavior at a nearby intersection would be an example. While the complete observer is less likely to affect that which is being studied and less likely to "go native" than the complete participant, he or she is also less likely to develop a full appreciation of what is being studied. Observations may be more sketchy and transitory.

It bears repeating that different situations require different roles for the researcher. Unfortunately, there are no clear guidelines for making this choice, and you must rely on your understanding of the situation and your own good judgment. In making your decision, however, you must be guided by both methodological and ethical considerations. Since these often conflict with one another, your decision will frequently be a difficult one, and you may find sometimes that your role limits your study.

PREPARING FOR THE FIELD

Let's assume for the moment that you have decided to undertake field research regarding a campus political organization. Let's assume further that you are not a member of that group, that you do not know a great deal about it, and that you will identify yourself to the participants as a researcher. This section will discuss some of the ways in which you might prepare yourself before undertaking direct observation of the group.

As is true of all research methods, you would be well advised to begin with a search of the relevant literature. Depending on the popularity and the age of the group, there may be published material about it. Perhaps the group itself has published something. It would be wise, as a beginning, to read everything you can find relating to the group. Whether or not there are writings available on this specific group, you surely will find some that are at least indirectly relevant. There has been a large volume of research on student politics in general; there is an even larger volume of research literature on social movements. Reviewing such literature will assist you in refining whatever theoretical framework you may bring to your particular study, thereby attuning you to the most relevant things to observe.

The review of literature in connection with a research project has two phases: (1) finding a relevant starting point and (2) expanding the search in a "snowball" fashion. To find a relevant beginning, you probably can't do any better than ask the reference desk librarian for assistance. Describe what you are interested in, and the librarian will probably refer you to several of the useful indexes that provide a roadmap through the information contained in the library. The subject matter card file indexes books. The *Social Science Index* and various abstracts, such as *Psychological Abstracts* and *Sociological Abstracts*, are a guide to journal articles. There are many other indexes, and your reference desk librarian can assist you in finding those most appropriate to your interests and the organization and holdings of your particular library.

The reference section of the library, then, is the starting point for your search. Once you've found several books and articles that are relevant to your interests, read them. As you get into your reading, you can expand your search in two ways. First, each of the books and articles you read will have bibliographic references. Look through those to see what additional publications are likely to be relevant to your research. Pay special attention to books and articles that are cited in several of the things you read. They are probably important.

Second, whenever you go to the library shelves to get a particular book or journal, take a minute to scan other nearby volumes. Since library holdings are shelved by subject matter, you may stumble across relevant books and articles that escaped your search through the various indexes. These two techniques make up what I called the "snowball" expansion of your literature search.

These remarks about the importance of library research before study design and data collection are part of the common sense of scientific research in general, and they would apply to all types of research methods. There is a sense in which it might be argued that they should be *ignored* in the case of field research, however. Since this method is less structured than others, field researchers have a greater danger of unconsciously observing only what they *expect* to find: *selective perception* is the term normally used for this tendency. There is a danger, in other words, that you may familiarize yourself with previous research on a topic, accept the conceptual frameworks and the conclusions of past studies as reasonable, and observe only those things that confirm the earlier studies. That would not happen, of course, if you were unfamiliar with the earlier research.

Again, I can provide no handy guideline. "To read or not to read" is not a question I can answer for you. As with all other gray areas in social research, I can only suggest that sensitivity to the problem should help to alleviate it. Certainly, no one should avoid a review of literature on a topic out of laziness, but you should know that there may be legitimate scientific grounds for doing so.

In the next phase of your research, you may wish to make use of *informants*. You might wish to discuss the student political group with others who have already studied it, or with anyone else who is likely to be familiar with it. In particular, you might find it useful to discuss the group with a member of it. Perhaps you have a friend who is a member, or you can meet someone who is. This aspect of your preparation is likely to be more effective if your relationship with the informant extends beyond your research role. In dealing with members of the group as informants, you should take care that your initial discussions do not compromise or limit later aspects of your research. Realize that the impression you make on the member-informant, the role you establish for yourself, may carry over into your later effort. For example, creating the initial impression that you may be an undercover FBI agent is unlikely to facilitate later observations of the group.

Before making your first contact with the student group, then, you should be already quite familiar with it, and you should understand the general, theoretical context within which it exists.

There are a variety of ways in which to establish your initial contact with the people you plan to study. How you do it will depend, in part, on the role you intend to play. Especially if you are to take on the role of complete participant, you must find a way of developing an identity with the people to be studied. If you wish to study dishwashers in a restaurant, the most direct method would be to get a job as a dishwasher. In the case of the student political group, you might simply join the group.

Many of the social processes appropriate to field research are sufficiently open to make your contact with the people to be studied rather simple and straightforward. If you wish to observe a mass demonstration, just be there. If you wish to observe patterns in jaywalking, hang around busy streets.

Whenever you wish to make a more formal contact with the people and wish to identify yourself as a researcher, you must be able to establish a certain rapport with them. You might contact a participant with whom you feel comfortable and gain that person's assistance. If you are studying a formal group, you might approach the group leaders. Or you may find that one of your informants who has studied the group is able to introduce you to it.

In making a direct, formal contact with the people you want to study, you will be required to give them some explanation of the purpose of your study. Here again, you face an ethical dilemma. Telling them the complete purpose of your research might lose you their cooperation altogether or importantly affect their subsequent behavior. On the other hand, giving only what you believe would be an acceptable explanation may involve outright deception. Realize in all this that your decisions— in practice—may be largely determined by the purpose of your study, the nature of what you are studying, observations you wish to use, and other such factors.

Previous field research offers no fixed rule—methodological or ethical—to be followed in this regard. Your appearance as a researcher, regardless of stated purpose, may result in a warm welcome from people who are flattered that a scientist finds them important enough to study. Or, it may result in your being totally ostracized or worse. (Do not, for example, burst into a meeting of an organized crime syndicate and announce that you are writing a term paper on organized crime.)

SAMPLING IN FIELD RESEARCH

Earlier chapters of this book discussed the logic and the more conventional techniques involved in probability sampling in social research. Although the general principles of representativeness in that context should be remembered in field research, controlled sampling techniques are normally inappropriate. This section will discuss the matter of sampling as it typically applies in field research.

To begin, the population and the units of analysis in the field research project may be somewhat ambiguous. In studying the campus political group mentioned above, are you interested in studying that group only, the members of the group, student political behavior in general, political behavior more generally, or what? If you are studying three juvenile gangs in a particular city, are the gangs your units of analysis, the individual juveniles, or the city? Are you interested only in describing the gangs under study, or does your interest extend to juvenile peer relations in general? It is important that you ask yourself what population you wish to make general assertions about when you are finished with your research. The answer to this question will not always be obvious to you, and it may change over the course of your research. A limited initial concern may be expanded later, as you conclude that certain of the phenomena that you are observing apply well beyond your specific subjects of study. Although this general issue may not be easily resolved in practice, sensitivity to it should help clarify your goals and methods.

Field researchers attempt to observe everything within their field of study; thus, in a sense, they do not sample at all. In reality, of course, it is impossible to observe everything. To the extent that field researchers observe only a portion of what transpires, then, that which they do observe is a de facto sample of all the possible observations that might have been made.

The concept of sampling, in connection with field research, is more complicated than in the situation dealt with in the earlier chapters. Of the communications and behaviors under study, those observed represent a sample of all those that occur. If several people are shouting support for the speaker in a religious revival meeting, those shouts that the researcher hears and understands represent a sample of all such shouts. Or if a researcher observes acts of violence during a riot, the observed acts are a sample of all such acts of violence. You will seldom be able to select a controlled sample of such observations, but you should bear in mind the general principles of representativeness and interpret your observations accordingly.

Sometimes, however, you will be in a position to sample among possible observations. If you are studying the development of a student political organization over time, for example, you may choose to interview different members of that organization by making a list of all the members and then selecting a probability sample. This might not be the best method of sampling for your purposes, however. McCall and Simmons suggest three types of sampling methods that are specifically appropriate to field research: the *quota* sample, the *snowball* sample, and *deviant cases.*[4]

To begin, if the group or social process under study has fairly clearly defined categories of participants, some kind of quota sample might be employed: persons representing all different participation categories should be studied. (See Chapter 7 for a more detailed discussion of quota sampling as a general procedure.) In the study of a formal group, for example, you might wish to interview both leaders and nonleaders. In studying a student political organization, it might be useful to interview both radical and more moderate members of that group. In general, whenever representativeness is desired, you should use quota sampling and interview both men and women, young people and old people, and the like.

Second, McCall and Simmons mentioned the snowball sample. If you wish to learn, for example, the pattern of recruitment to a religious organization over time, you might begin by interviewing fairly recent converts, asking them who introduced them to the group. You might then interview the persons named, asking, in part, who introduced *them*. In studying a loosely structured political group, you might ask one of the participants who he or she believes to be the most influential members of the group. You might interview those people and, in the course of the interviews, ask who *they* believe to be the most influential. In each of these examples, your sample would "snowball" as each of your interviewees suggested others.

Finally, McCall and Simmons draw attention to the importance of *deviant cases*. Often, our understanding of fairly regular patterns of attitudes and behaviors is further improved through the examination of those cases that do not fit into the regular pattern. Thus, for example, you might gain important insights into the nature of school spirit as exhibited at a pep rally by interviewing those people who did not appear to be caught up in the emotions of the crowd, or by interviewing students who did not attend the rally at all.

Aside from sampling individuals for interviewing, there are other field research situations in which it may be possible to undertake a conscious sampling procedure. In a study of jaywalking, you might wish to make observations on a number of

[4]McCall and Simmons, *op. cit.*, pp. 64–67 (see footnote 2 on page 209).

different city streets. You might pick the sample of locations through standard probability methods; or, more likely, you might employ a rough quota system, observing wide streets and narrow ones, busy streets and quiet ones, or including samples from different times of day, or of common types of pedestrians. In a study of the way in which people interact or fail to interact at a bus stop, you would make observations at a number of different kinds of bus stops and of other variations in that situation.

In practice, controlled probability sampling is seldom employed in field research. To the extent that you may consciously sample at all, you are more likely to employ what has been called a **purposive sample**. You select a sample of observations that you believe will yield the most comprehensive understanding of your subject of study, based on the intuitive feel for the subject that comes from extended observation and reflection. Nonetheless, understanding the principles and logic of more formal sampling methods is likely to result in more effective intuitive sampling in field research.

In field research, bear in mind two stages of sampling. First, to what extent are the total situations *available* for observation representative of the more *general class* of phenomena you wish to describe and explain? Are the three juvenile gangs you are observing representative of all gangs? Second, are your *actual* observations within those total situations representative of all the *possible* observations? Have you observed a representative sample of the members of the three gangs, have you observed a representative sample of the interactions that have taken place? Even when controlled probability sampling methods are impossible or inappropriate, the logical link between representativeness and generalizability still holds.

ASKING QUESTIONS

In part, field research is a matter of going where the action is and simply watching and listening. You can learn a lot merely by being attentive to what's going on. At the same time, as I've already indicated, field research can involve more active inquiry. Sometimes it's appropriate to ask people questions and record their answers. Your on-the-spot observations of a full-blown riot will lack something if you don't know why people are rioting. Ask somebody.

Asking questions and noting answers is a natural process for us all, and it seems simple enough to add that to your bag of tricks as a field researcher. Be a little *Be careful.* cautious, however. There is a danger that, to paraphrase comedian Flip Wilson, "what you ask is what you get." As I've already discussed in Chapter 6, question wording is a tricky business. All too often, the way we ask questions subtly biases the answers we get. Sometimes we put the person responding under pressure to look good. Sometimes we put the question in a particular context that omits altogether the most relevant answers.

Pursuing the above example, suppose you want to find out why a group of students is rioting and pillaging on campus. You might be tempted to focus your questioning on how students feel about the dean's recent ruling to require that students always carry *The Practice of Social Research* with them on campus. (Makes sense to me.) Although you may succeed in collecting a great deal of information about students' attitudes toward the infamous ruling, they may be rioting for some other reason. Or perhaps most are simply joining in for the excitement.

In preparing to interview people in connection with a field research project, you should review two other sections of this book. First, as I've mentioned, Chapter 6 deals with wording questions in general, and most of what is discussed there is appropriate to field research. Second, Chapter 12 on survey research has a section on interviewing, much of which applies equally to field research. The main difference is that in survey research, interviewers use standardized questionnaires to collect information. They don't have to worry about wording questions. That's not the case with field research typically.

Although you may set out to conduct interviews with a pretty clear idea of what you want to ask, one of the special strengths of field research is the possibility of flexibility in the field. The answers evoked by your initial questions should shape your subsequent ones. It doesn't work, in this situation, to merely ask preestablished questions and record the answers. You need to ask a question, hear the answer, interpret its meaning for your general inquiry, frame another question either to dig into the earlier answer in more depth or to redirect the person's attention to an area more relevant to your inquiry. In short, you need to be able to think and talk almost at the same time.

The discussion of *probes* in Chapter 12 provides a useful guide to getting answers in more depth without biasing the subsequent answers. Learn the skills of being a good listener. Be more interested than interesting. Learn to say things like "How is that?", "In what ways?", "How do you mean that?", "What would be an example of that?" Learn to look and listen expectantly, and let the person you are interviewing fill in the silence.

Interviewing needs to be an integral part of your whole field research process. Later, I stress the need to review your notes every night—making sense out of what you've observed, getting a clearer feel for the situation you're studying, and finding out what you should pay more attention to in further observations. In this same fashion, you need to review your notes on interviews, detecting all those things you should have asked but didn't. Start asking those things when you next interview people.

As with all other aspects of field research, interviewing improves with practice. Fortunately, it is something you can practice any time you want. Practice on your friends. You'll probably become a valued conversationalist.

RECORDING OBSERVATIONS

Finally, the basic tools of field research are the notebook—or *field journal*—and a pencil. Even tape recorders and cameras cannot capture all the relevant aspects of social processes. The greatest advantage of the field research method is the presence of an observing, thinking researcher on the scene of the action. If possible, you should take notes on your observations *as you observe*. When that is not possible, you should write down your notes as soon as possible afterwards.

Your notes should include both your empirical observations and your interpretations of them. You should record what you "know" has happened and what you "think" has happened. It is important, however, that these different kinds of notes be identified for what they are. For example, you might note that Person X spoke out in opposition to a proposal made by a group leader, that you *think* this represents an attempt by Person X to take over leadership of the group, and you *think* you heard the leader comment to that effect in response to the opposition.

Just as you cannot hope to observe everything, neither can you record everything that you do observe. Whereas your observations represent a de facto sample of all possible observations, so do your notes represent a sample of your observations. Rather than recording a random sample of your observations, however, you should, of course, record your most important observations.

Some of the most important observations can be anticipated in advance of beginning the study; others will become apparent as your observations progress. Sometimes your note taking can be facilitated by the advance preparation of standardized forms for recording. In a study of jaywalking, for example, you might anticipate the characteristics of pedestrians that are the most likely to be useful for analysis—age, sex, social class, ethnicity, and so forth—and prepare a form in which actual observations can be recorded easily. Or, you might develop a symbolic shorthand in advance to speed up recording. For studying audience participation at a mass meeting, you might want to construct a number grid representing the different sections of the meeting room; then, you would be able to record the location of participants easily, quickly, and accurately.

None of this advance preparation should limit your recording of unanticipated events and aspects of the situation. Quite the contrary, speeding up the handling of anticipated observations can give you more freedom to observe the unanticipated.

I know that you are at least somewhat familiar with the process of taking notes. Every student is. And as I've said earlier, everybody is somewhat familiar with field research in general. Like *good* field research, however, *good* note taking requires more careful and deliberate attention, and there are some specific skills that can be learned in that regard. I'll provide some guidelines below, and you can learn more about this in John Lofland's *Analyzing Social Settings*, which was mentioned earlier in the chapter.[5]

First, as I suggested earlier in this section, don't trust your memory any more than you have to; it's untrustworthy. If I'm being too unkind to your mind, try this experiment. Recall the last few movies you saw that you really liked. Now, name five of the actors or actresses. Which one had the longest hair? Which was the most likely to start conversations? Which was the most likely to make suggestions that others followed? ("Quick! Bring the wagons into a circle!") Now, if you didn't have any trouble answering any of those questions (and think you outsmarted me), how *sure* are you of your answers? Would you be willing to bet a hundred dollars that a panel of impartial judges would observe what you recall? If you are absolutely certain of your answers, then what color socks or stockings was your methods instructor wearing three class meetings ago? Gotcha!

[5]Lofland, *op. cit.*, pp. 101–108.

Even if you pride yourself on having a photographic memory, it's a good idea to take notes either during the observation or as soon afterward as possible. If you are taking notes during observation, however, do it as unobtrusively as possible, since people are likely to behave differently if they see you taking down everything they say or do.

Second, it's usually a good idea to take notes in stages. In the first stage, you may need to take sketchy notes (words and phrases) in order to keep abreast of what's happening. Then get off by yourself and rewrite your notes in more detail. If you do this soon after the events you've observed, the sketchy notes should allow you to recall most of the details. Notice, however, that the longer you delay, the less likely it is that you'll recall things accurately and fully.

I know this method sounds logical, and you've probably made a mental resolve to do it that way if you're ever involved in field research. Let me warn you, however, that you'll need some self-discipline to keep your resolution in practice. Careful observation and note taking can be tiring, especially if it involves excitement or tension and if it extends over a long period of time. If you've just spent eight hours straight observing and making notes on how people have been coping with a disastrous flood, your first thought afterward is likely to be directed toward getting some sleep, dry clothes, or a drink. You may need to take some inspiration from newspaper reporters who undergo the same sorts of hardships, then write their stories and meet their deadlines.

Third, you will inevitably wonder *how much* you should record. Is it really worth the effort to write out all the details you can recall right after the observation session? The general guideline here is: *yes*. There are several reasons for that. Generally, in field research you can't be really sure of what's important and what's unimportant until you've had a chance to review and analyze a great volume of information, so you should record things that don't seem important at the outset. They may turn out to be significant after all. Also, the act of recording the details of something "unimportant" may jog your memory on something that *is* important.

You should realize that *most* of your field notes will not be reflected in your final report on the project. Put more harshly, most of the notes you take will be "wasted." But take heart: even the richest gold ore yields only about 30 grams of gold per metric ton, meaning that 99.997 percent of the ore is wasted. Yet, that 30 grams of gold can be hammered out to cover an area 18 feet square—the equivalent of about 685 book pages. So take a ton of notes and plan to select and use only the gold.

Finally, here are a few suggestions on the mechanics of handling your notes. To begin, it's far, far better to type up your full notes than to write them longhand. They'll be more legible, and as your typing improves it will be faster than longhand. Also, you should make every effort to have at least two copies, whether carbons, photocopies, or dittos. When you analyze your data and prepare your report, you will need to be able to cut and paste without losing information. With at least two copies, you can cut up one and have the other as backup.

Like other aspects of field research (and all research for that matter), proficiency comes with practice. The nice thing about field research is that you can begin practicing now and can continue practicing in almost any situation you find yourself in.

You don't have to be engaged in an organized research project in order to practice observation and recording.

DATA PROCESSING

Chapter 13 of this textbook describes the process social scientific researchers use to transform their original observations into something that can be manipulated by card sorters and computers. Those remarks are appropriate to *quantitative* social scientific analyses, and they may sometimes apply to portions of field research projects. At the same time, field research is more typically an example of *qualitative social scientific research,* and the comments in Chapter 13 regarding mechanized data processing are inappropriate to much of what field researchers do. Therefore, I'll cover the processing of qualitative, field research data here.

The preceding section of this chapter dealt with the ways you, as a field researcher, would make observations and record them. Now, we're going to look at what you might do with those recorded observations afterward. In large part, this discussion will focus on the process of *filing* and organizing. I'll give you a brief overview of the process, but you'd do well to study some of the specific techniques field researchers have developed also before actually undertaking a project. An excellent source of nitty-gritty, detailed suggestions can be found in John Lofland's *Analyzing Social Settings.* [6]

Rewriting Your Notes

Hot on the trail of some social phenomenon, you are likely to end a day of observations with a mass of scribbled notes in your notebook and on the backs of envelopes and wine-stained cocktail napkins. Depending on how late in the day or night you complete your observations, you may be tempted to set the notes aside and sleep on them. Don't. Field researchers can't work on a 9 to 5 schedule, and it is vital that you rewrite your notes as soon as possible after making a set of observations.

Ideally, you should get away by yourself and *type* your notes. Use your notes as a stimulus to recreate as much of the details of the day's experiences as possible. Your goal should be to produce a set of typed notes as comprehensive and detailed as you would have taken in the first place if it had been possible to record everything that seemed relevant. If you regard your scribbled on-the-spot notes as a trigger for your memory, then you'll see the importance of retyping each night and you'll have a clear sense of how to proceed.

Before you put that paper in the typewriter, however, stock up on carbon paper, unless you have access to a photocopying machine. As we'll see next, you will need multiple copies of your typed notes.

[6]*Ibid.*, pp. 116–121.

Creating Files

Your typed notes will probably represent a more or less chronological record of your observations in the project, and you should be sure to include notations of the dates and times you made them. You should keep one complete set of notes in this form. It will serve as a master file that you can fall back on to establish the chronological order of events later on and to get more copies of certain notes if you need them. You don't need to store your master file in a bank safe-deposit box, but you should take care of it.

The carbon copies of your typed notes are for cutting up, underlining, scribbling on, circling, and *filing*. So far in this chapter, we have focused on the making of observations. A mass of raw observations, however, doesn't tell us much of general value about social life. Ultimately, you must analyze and interpret your observations, discerning *patterns* of behavior, finding the underlying *meaning* that was manifested in the things you observed. The organization and filing of your notes is the first step in discovering that meaning.

Files can be organized in an endless variety of ways, so what I'll do here is suggest some possibilities you might otherwise overlook. As you undertake your own research project, however, you'll find that deciding what files to create is a part of your analysis of the data.

As a start, you should create some background files. If you are studying a social movement, for example, it would be useful to have a separate file on its history. You'll probably begin the file with notes from your initial reading about the movement: When and where did it begin? How many people were in it initially? What has been the history of its subsequent membership size? What have been the major events in the history of the movement? What were the dates? Although you'll probably begin this file before making observations in the field, you should plan to add to it over the course of your study, since you'll be continually learning more about the history of your subject.

You'll probably want to create a biographical file, too. Who are the key figures in the movement? You may want to have separate files for the most important figures. In any event, you should keep all the information on a particular individual together. That will allow you to get a fuller sense of the person, and it may also help you to understand the links between diverse events.

Lest you forget, you should also create a bibliographical file to keep track of all the things you will have read in the course of your study. When you set about writing up your report, you will want to make references to what other people have written, and it will be both wasteful and frustrating if you have to return continually to the library to relocate sources.

The creation of background files represents a pretty straightforward housekeeping function, but the creation of *analytical* files depends more on the nature of what you are studying and what you "see" in what you observe. As you begin to develop a sense of the different aspects of what you're observing, you'll want to establish files to deal with those different aspects.

Suppose, for example, that you begin to sense that the political movement you're studying has a religious or quasi-religious significance for the people participating in it. You'll want to establish a file for data relating to that aspect. You might do that as follows. Write "Religious Significance" on a manila file folder. Every time you find an entry in your notes that's relevant to the religious aspect of the movement—perhaps a participant will tell you that the movement has provided a new meaning to life—you should cut out that entry (recall the multiple copies?) and stick it in the file folder.

Perhaps one of your interests in the political movement concerns the varying degrees of violence considered, proposed, or engaged in by movement members. Sometimes they seem peaceful and willing to compromise; at other times they are more oriented toward hard-line aggression. Perhaps you will want to explain why those differences occur. Create a file on "Degrees of Violence" and clip and file all entries from your notes that are relevant.

I could continue endlessly with illustrations of the kinds of analytical files you might want to create, but I think you've gotten a sense of what's involved. I can't give you a blueprint of what files will be appropriate in your project—you get to do that. I should add, however, that the creation of analytical files is a continuous process. Do not create a filing system at the beginning of the project and stick doggedly to it throughout. Stay flexible and keep modifying the system as new topics appear to be relevant.

The flexibility of your filing system suggests another important step in the data processing of field research notes and other materials. As you modify your view of how best to organize your files, you should frequently review the materials already filed to see if certain notes should be moved to a newly created file. Sometimes, it will work to merely *cross-reference* your notes. You can jot a note to yourself indicating that the notes on X in File A are also relevant to the topic in File G. Stick the jotted note in File G.

As I've indicated, the creation and use of analytical files is part and parcel of the interpretation of your data. Let's turn now to that topic specifically.

DATA ANALYSIS

Throughout the previous discussions, I have omitted a direct discussion of the most critical aspects of field research: how you determine what is important to observe, and how you formulate your analytical conclusions on the basis of those observations. I have indicated that observation and analysis are interwoven processes in field research. Now it is time to say something about that interweaving.

As perhaps the most general guide, you look especially for *similarities* and *dissimilarities*. (That just about covers everything you are likely to see.) On the one hand, you look for those patterns of interaction and events that are generally common to what you are studying. In sociological terms, you look for *norms* of behavior. What do all the participants in a situation share in terms of behavior patterns? Do all jaywalkers check for police officers before darting across the street? Do all the participants in a campus political rally join in the same forms of supportive behavior during speeches? Do all the participants in a religious revival meeting shout "amen" at the appropriate times? Do all prostitutes dress seductively? In this sense, then, the field researcher is especially attuned to the discovery of *univer-sals*. As you first notice these, you become more deliberate in observing whether they are truly universal in the situation you are observing. If they are essentially universal, you ask why that should be the case. What function do they serve, for example? This explanation may suggest conditions under which the "universals" would not appear, and you may look around for those conditions in order to test your expectations.

On the other hand, the field researcher is constantly alert to *differences*. You should be on the watch for deviation from the general norms you may have noted. Although most of the participants in a religious revival meeting murmur "amen" throughout the leader's sermon, you may note a few who do not. Why do they deviate from the norm? In what other ways are they different from the other participants?

Sometimes you will find aspects of behavior that are more characterized by dissimilarity and similarity in general; there is no easily identifiable norm. How do different people handle the problem of standing in a line for tickets at a movie theater? Some stare into space, some strike up conversations with strangers, some talk to themselves, some keep standing on tiptoes to see if the line is really moving, some keep counting their money, some read, and so forth. An important part of the field researcher's initial task in such situations is to create a *taxonomy* of behaviors: an organized listing of the variety of types. Having done that, you then seek to discover other characteristics associated with those different types of behavior. Are the "rich-looking" or "poor-looking" moviegoers more likely to recount their money? Do men strike up more conversations with strangers than women? Do old people talk to themselves more than young people? Your purpose is to discover general patterns.

To the field researcher, the formulation of theoretical propositions, the observation of empirical events, and the evaluation of theory are typically all part of the same ongoing process. While your actual field observations may be preceded by deductive theoretical formulas, you seldom if ever merely test a theory and let it go at that. Rather, you develop theories, or generalized understandings, over the course of your observations. About each new set of empirical observations, you ask what it represents in terms of general social scientific principles. Your tentative conclusions, so arrived at, then provide the conceptual framework for further observations. In the course of your observations of jaywalking, for example, it may strike you that whenever a well-dressed and important-looking person jaywalks, others are encouraged to follow suit. Having noticed this apparent pattern, you might pay more attention to this aspect of the phenomenon, thereby testing more carefully your initial impression. You might subsequently observe that your initial impression held true only when the jaywalking "leader" was also middle-aged, for example, or perhaps only if he or she were Caucasian. These more specific impressions would simultaneously lead you to pay special attention to the new variables and require that you consider what general principle might be underlying the new observations.

There is an inherent advantage in field research in that interaction between data collection and data analysis affords a greater flexibility than is typically found in connection with other research methods. Survey researchers, for example, must at some point commit themselves to a questionnaire, thus limiting the kind of data that will be collected. If subsequent analyses indicate that they have overlooked the most important variable of all, they are out of luck. The field researcher, on the other hand, is in a position to modify continually the research design as indicated by the observations, the developing theoretical perspective, or changes in what he or she is studying.

This advantage in field research comes at the price of an accompanying danger. As you develop theoretical understanding of what you are observing, there is a constant risk that you will observe only those things that support your theoretical conclusions. You'll recall that this problem has already been discussed in connection with selective perception.

This danger may be at least partially avoided in a number of ways. First, you can augment your qualitative observations with quantitative ones. If you expect religious proselytization to be greater under some conditions than under others, you might formulate a concrete operational definition of proselytization and begin counting under the different conditions. For example, you might note the number of group members who raised this topic, the number of members assigned to the task, or perhaps the number of new converts added to the group. Even rough quantifications such as these might provide a safeguard against selective perception and misinterpretation.

Second, we should recall that one of the norms of science is its *intersubjectivity*. As a field researcher, then, you might enlist the assistance of others as you begin to refine your theoretical conclusions. In the case of religious conversion, for example, you might ask colleagues to attend several meetings of the group over time and indicate their observations as to the relative stress placed on proselytization in each of the meetings.

Finally, as with all such problems, sensitivity and awareness may provide sufficient safeguards. Merely by being aware of the problem, you may be able to avoid it.

This last comment points to a more general aspect of field research analysis. By virtue of your very closeness to the stuff of human behavior, *introspection* is a natural and crucial process for understanding what you observe. Since you will have been observing social life close up and in all its details, you should be able to put yourself in the place of those you are studying—George Herbert Mead called this "taking the role of the other"—and ask yourself how you would have felt and behaved. Can you imagine yourself acting the way the person you observed acted? Why do you suppose you would have done that?

Introspection, then, can protect against many of the pitfalls of inquiry. And, when leavened with some role taking, it can give you insights into what you see going on around you.

In connection with the combined process of data collection and data analysis, the following general procedure usually would be advisable. As already mentioned, you should record your observations in detail either during or immediately after making them. Following each period of observation and notation, you should review your notes, adding recollections and interpretations. After spending the day with jaywalkers, for example, you might spend the evening reviewing, revising, and interpreting your notes. It is important that this review process be carried on continually. Reviewing your notes while an event is still fresh in your mind will be of far greater value than doing so once the event has dimmed in your memory.

In all social science research methods, there is a large gap between understanding the skills of data analysis and actually using those skills effectively. Typically, experience is the only effective bridge across the gap. This situation applies more to field research than to any other method. It is worth recalling the parallel between the activities of the scientist and those of the investigative detective. While fledgling detectives can be taught technical skills and can be given general guidelines, insight and experience separate good detectives from mediocre ones. The same is true of field researchers.

ILLUSTRATIONS OF FIELD RESEARCH

I have a fear that technical discussions of research methods—no matter how clear, charming, and witty—tend to take the life out of what is really an exciting enterprise. In each of the chapters in Part Three, therefore, I want to give you some illustrations of the method under consideration, adding a little more reality and life to it. In the case of field research, I have already given you one fairly detailed description: Laud Humphreys's study of the tearoom trade, discussed in Chapter 3. Here are two more.

Analyzing Lucifer's Legions

As a part of a broad-based study of the "new religious consciousness," sociology graduate student Randy Alfred was given the task of studying and reporting on the Church of Satan.[7] Pronouncing itself in league with Satan and opposed to Christ, the church is headquartered in San Francisco and operates under the charismatic leadership of Anton LaVey. You can probably imagine how you'd handle an assignment to study the local Methodist or Episcopalian congregation, but how would you go about studying the Satanists? Here's what Randy Alfred did:

> I approached the group in April 1968 as an outsider and indicated an immediate interest in joining. My feigned conversion to Satanism was accepted as genuine and I made rapid progress in the group, as measured by my advancement in ritual rank, my being given administrative as well as magical responsibilities, and my appointment to the "ruling" body of the church.
>
> From April 1968 to August 1969 I attended fifty-two of the group's weekly rituals, participating in all but eight of these early on. I was also present at twelve meetings of the ruling council, at twelve classes on various aspects of Satanism, and at six parties.[8]

Alfred continued studying the church until 1973, having some one hundred contacts with members, lasting a total of perhaps 600 hours and resulting in about as

[7]Randall Alfred, "The Church of Satan," in Charles Glock and Robert Bellah (eds.), *The New Religious Consciousness* (Berkeley: University of California Press, 1976), pp. 180–202.
[8]*Ibid.*, pp. 183–184.

many pages of notes. In addition, he read books and articles about the group, including publications of the church itself. Right up until the end, he played the role of complete participant, concealing his research identity from those he was studying. (More about this in a moment.)

Alfred's total immersion in church life gave him insights into the nature of Satanism that would have been hard to gain from the outside. He was able to discover and distinguish the variety of motivations that led people to the group. Some were attracted by the prospect of sexual indulgence, others by the powers they might gain from magic, and others seemed primarily intent on rebelling against conventional religiosity and conventionality even more generally. Still others saw Satanism as a wave of the future, a new millennium. All told, Alfred found six distinct categories of reasons for joining the church.

Through his *participation* in the church—he ultimately became the official church historian—Alfred was able to learn details of rituals and other practices that would have been kept secret from outsiders. He was able to observe LaVey and other church leaders close up and was able to study the dynamics of interpersonal relations in the church. There simply would have been no other way of gaining such information.

In reading Alfred's report, you also have the sense that many of his analytical insights would have escaped an outsider. For example, the popular view of Satanism is one of total self-indulgence. Freed from all conventional social norms, Satanists would be expected to be completely hedonistic, indulging their every urge and desire. That is not what Alfred observed, however. In the case of sex, for example, Satanists limit sexual indulgence to those acts that don't hurt others against their will. LaVey further distinguishes between indulgence freely chosen and compulsive acts. Satanists should be free to indulge their desires, but they should not be run by those desires. By the same token, Satanists have a negative view of drug use. Even more unexpectedly, perhaps, LaVey strongly urges his followers to work hard at their jobs and succeed.

As a closing note, Alfred reports that he eventually found himself regretting the initial decision to conceal his research identity—he felt increasingly unethical. After all, he had been admitted into the inner circles of the church and given a position of trust and responsibility. As he approached the final stages of wrapping up and reporting the project, he went to LaVey to tell him the truth and to request permission to publish an article about what he had learned. LaVey indicated that he had suspected all along that Alfred was doing research. Did he feel Alfred had been unethical in attempting deception? Not at all: it was an appropriately satanic thing to do!

Studying the Street Scene

Elliot Liebow's modern classic study of *Tally's Corner*[9] differs from Alfred's study in many ways. There is an initial similarity, however. Like Alfred, Liebow was assigned to his task as part of a larger research project. In this instance, Liebow, an

[9]Elliot Liebow, *Tally's Corner* (Boston: Little, Brown, 1967).

anthropology graduate student, was hired to work on an ongoing study of child-rearing practices among low-income families in the District of Columbia. Liebow's task was to do field work among low-income adult males to fill out the picture created by numerous interviews with families.

Liebow prepared for the fieldwork through a series of meetings with the project staff, learning the kinds of materials that were needed. He read the reports already written on the project. Then, one day,

> having partially digested the project literature, I told the director that I was ready to get started. He suggested a neighborhood that might be "a good place to get your feet wet." His instructions were: "Get out there and make like an anthropologist."[10]

Arriving in the suggested neighborhood, Liebow discovered a white police detective scuffling with an angry black woman. Approaching two black, male onlookers, Liebow asked them what happened. They answered cautiously. The conversation continued, warming somewhat as each expressed negative feelings about the police. Eventually convinced that Liebow was not himself a policeman, one of the men spent the next several hours talking to him over coffee.

Unlike Alfred, Liebow revealed his identity as a researcher and the purpose of his research from the start. Himself white, Liebow wisely did not attempt to feign conversion to being black. Though recognized as an "outsider," he was accepted as a friend, and he became more and more a part of the street corner life as the research progressed. Like Alfred, Liebow soon found himself deeply involved in the lives of his subjects. He reports:

> I went to three different jails during this time, sat through one murder trial and two hearings in judges' chambers, testifying at one of them. I went to bondsmen's offices, to the United Employment Service, to the Blessed Martin de Porres Hostel (for homeless men) and into several private homes.[11]

Whenever his new friends ran afoul of the law, Liebow's legal advice was sought and respected. He reports that he stayed in close touch with the project director about this participation, weighing the consequences of his actions for his research. There was certainly a danger that his own participation would change the character of the events and situations he had set out to study in the first place.

Liebow's description of his record keeping nicely illustrates the procedures described earlier in this chapter:

> Throughout this period, my field observations were focused on individuals: what they said, what they did, and the contexts in which they said them or did them. I sought them out and was sought out by them.
>
> My field notes contain a record of what I saw when I looked at Tally, Richard, Sea Cat and the others. I have only a small notion—and one that I myself consider suspect—of what they saw when they looked at me.[12]

Ultimately, Liebow was able to gain a personal experience of street corner life in

[10]*Ibid.*, p. 245.

[11]*Ibid.*, p. 245.

[12]*Ibid.*, p. 248.

a black, urban ghetto that few white people ever have. To an unusual extent, he was able to see and understand the men as they saw and understood themselves. He was able to learn their views and experiences of family life, employment, and—more to the point—unemployment.

These two short accounts scarcely do justice to the projects they describe, but they should give you a more concrete view of what field research entails. Both of the original reports are interesting and eminently readable, so you might like to read them for yourself.

THE STRENGTHS AND WEAKNESSES OF FIELD RESEARCH

It's time now to wrap up the discussion of field research and move on to some of the other methods available to social researchers. I want to conclude the chapter by assessing the relative strengths and weaknesses of this particular method, and I'll repeat the practice in subsequent chapters. In evaluating each of the different research methods, we'll be referring back to the pitfalls of inquiry and the safeguards provided by science, as discussed in Chapters 1 and 2.

As indicated earlier, field research is especially effective for studying the subtle nuances of attitudes and behaviors, and for examining social processes over time. For these reasons, the chief strength of this method lies in the depth of understanding that it may permit. Although other research methods may be challenged as "superficial," that charge is seldom lodged against field research.

Flexibility is another advantage of field research. In this method, you may modify your research design at any time, as discussed earlier. Moreover, you are always prepared to engage in field research, whenever the occasion should arise, whereas you could not as easily initiate a survey or an experiment.

Field research can be relatively inexpensive. Other social scientific research methods may require expensive equipment or an expensive research staff, but field research typically can be undertaken by one researcher with a notebook and a pencil. This is not to say that field research is never expensive. The nature of the research project, for example, may require a large number of trained observers. Expensive recording equipment may be needed. Or the researcher may wish to undertake participant observation of interactions in expensive Paris nightclubs.

Field research has a number of weaknesses as well. First, being qualitative rather than quantitative, it seldom yields precise descriptive statements about a large population. Observing casual political discussions in laundromats, for example, would not yield trustworthy estimates of the future voting behavior of the total electorate. Nevertheless, the study could provide important insights into the process of political attitude formation.

More generally, the conclusions drawn from qualitative field research are often regarded as suggestive rather than definitive. In part that is a function of the informal sampling and uncertain representativeness of the observations made and recorded. Also involved is the nature of operational definition and measurement in field research. Since field research depends so heavily on the judgments and total comprehension of the researcher, operating within the context of the phenomenon under study, field research seldom involves the uniform application of precise operational definitions. Thus, for example, you might draw general conclusions regarding the "radical" and the "moderate" members of a student political organization, based on your overall assessment of the attitudes and actions of individuals. You might be unable, ultimately, to specify your definitions and to tell exactly why you labeled a given student as "radical" and another as "moderate"; another observer might draw different conclusions.

The chief weaknesses of field research, then, are in relation to the scientific norms of *generalizability* and *intersubjectivity*. This is not to say that a particular set of field research conclusions are not generally applicable, nor that two field researchers would not arrive at the same research conclusion. We simply have less assurance in these regards than would be the case for more structured research methods. In terms of measurement quality, this point might be made by saying that field research seems stronger on validity than on reliability.

Overall, field research is an excellent vehicle for exploratory research, and it is quite weak in terms of descriptive research as discussed in Chapter 4. As to explanatory research, it has the great advantage of dealing with processes occurring over time, though it is advisable to replicate the explanatory conclusions of field research by using more rigorously controlled research designs.

SUMMARY

Chapter 8 has described some of the characteristics and techniques involved in one particular method of observation, or data collection, in social research: field research. Basically, this technique is the direct observation of events by the researcher at the scene of the action. As noted at the outset, this is a research method that you have been using all your life and one that is used by other professionals such as newspaper reporters.

The chapter began with a discussion of the topics most appropriate to field research. First, it is effective in the study of those phenomena that can be understood adequately only in their full, natural settings. Moreover, we noted that it is especially useful for the study of some processes taking place over time, such as the development and course of a riot.

One of the procedural options open to the field researcher is the choice of several different *roles* that he or she may assume. Essentially, these choices revolve around (1) whether you identify yourself as a researcher to those people you are observing and (2) whether you participate in the events under study. The several different possibilities in these regards were discussed in terms of their ethical and scientific aspects.

Next, the chapter took up the details of getting ready for field research and beginning to make observations. We saw some of the preparatory steps, such as library research and the interviewing of informants, that can make for more fruitful subsequent observations in the field.

Sampling in field research is usually handled differently than in other methods of observation. Although field researchers are guided by the same basic concern as other researchers for representativeness, they may achieve it differently. In particular, they are likely to pay more attention to unusual or deviant cases than other researchers. The different types of sampling methods employed in field research were described.

The specific techniques for making and recording observations were the next focus of the chapter. Note taking, we saw, is an essential skill in field research, yet it is a difficult skill to master. It is important to take inclusive notes and to type up your notes, adding to them, while details are still fresh in your mind.

In field research, observation, data processing, and analysis are interrelated activities far more than is the case for other social research methods. The field researcher makes and records a set of observations, reviews and organizes them, and looks for meaningful patterns in what has been observed; the recognition of patterns and the development of generalized understanding then suggest a modified strategy for subsequent observations. The new observations may then reveal new patterns, modifying the researcher's understanding further, and revising the observational strategy.

Following two illustrations of the method in practice, the chapter concluded with a discussion of the special strengths and weaknesses of field research. We found it especially useful as a way of developing a fuller comprehension of social processes in their natural settings but discovered that it is weakest in terms of scientific norms of *generalizability* and *intersubjectivity*.

MAIN POINTS

1. Field research is a social research method that involves the direct observation of social phenomena in their natural settings.

2. You may or may not identify yourself as a researcher to the people you are observing. Identifying yourself as a researcher may have some effect on the nature of what you are observing, but concealing your identity may involve deceit.

3. You may or may not participate in that which you are observing. Participating in the events may make it easier for you to conceal your identity as a researcher, but participation is likely to affect what is being observed.

4. Since controlled probability sampling techniques are usually impossible in field research, a rough form of quota sampling may be used in the attempt to achieve better representativeness in observations.

5. Snowball sampling is a method through which you develop an ever-increasing set of sample observations. You ask one participant in the event under study to recommend others for interviewing, and each of the subsequently interviewed participants is asked for further recommendations.

6. Often, the careful examination of deviant cases in field research can yield important insights into the "normal" patterns of social behavior.

7. The field journal is the backbone of field research, for that is where the researcher records his or her observations. Journal entries should be detailed, yet concise. If possible, observations should be recorded as they are made; otherwise, they should be recorded as soon afterward as possible.

8. Field research is a form of qualitative research, although it is sometimes possible to quantify some of the observations that are being recorded.

9. In field research, observation, data processing, and analysis are interwoven and cyclical processes.

ANNOTATED BIBLIOGRAPHY

Becker, Howard; Geer, Blanche; Hughes, Everett; and Strauss, Anselm, *Boys in White: Student Culture in Medical School* (Chicago: University of Chicago Press, 1961). An excellent and important illustration of field research methods. This study, involving continued interaction with medical school students over the course of their professional training, examines the impact of their experiences on their values and orientations. An informal biography of this project, by Blanche Geer, may be found in Phillip Hammond (ed.), *Sociologists at Work* (New York: Basic Books, 1964) and is also reprinted in McCall and Simmons (see below).

Lofland, John, *Analyzing Social Settings* (Belmont, Calif.: Wadsworth, 1971). An unexcelled presentation of field research methods from beginning to end. This eminently readable little book manages successfully to draw the links between the logic of scientific inquiry and the nitty-gritty practicalities of observing, communicating, recording, filing, reporting, and everything else involved in field research. In addition, the book contains a wealth of references to field research illustrations.

Lofland, John, *Doomsday Cult: A Study of Conversion, Proselytization, and Maintenance of Faith* (Englewood Cliffs, N.J.: Prentice Hall, 1966). Another excellent illustration of field research methods in practice. This study examines the dynamic development of a deviant religious movement still active today. A shorter report of this study may be found in John Lofland and Rodney Stark, "Becoming a World-Saver: Conversion to a Deviant Perspective," *American Sociological Review*, Vol. 30 (December 1965), pp. 862–875.

McCall, George, and Simmons, J. L., (eds.), *Issues in Participant Observation: A Text and Reader* (Reading, Mass.: Addison-Wesley, 1969). An excellent collection of important articles dealing with field research. The 32 selections cover most aspects of field research, both theoretical and practical. Moreover, many of the selections provide illustrations of actual research projects.

Shostak, Arthur, (ed.), *Our Sociological Eye: Personal Essays on Society and Culture* (Port Washington, N.Y.: Alfred, 1977). An orgy of social scientific introspection. This delightful collection of first-person research accounts offers concrete, inside views of the thinking process in sociological research, especially field research.

CHAPTER 9
Content Analysis and the Analysis of Existing Data

INTRODUCTION

As we saw in the preceding chapter, social research can be quite unobtrusive—it's often possible for social scientists to simply sit back and observe what's going on. That pattern continues in the present chapter as we focus on *content analysis* and the analysis of *existing data*. Like field research, these two new methods are based on the observation of what's already there. In contrast, however, these methods are more *indirect* than field research. If you recall the short discussion of artifacts in Chapter 4 (artifacts are what's left over after people have done what they were doing), that's what we'll be looking at in this chapter.

Although I'll consider content analysis and the analysis of existing data separately, I think you'll see that they have a great deal in common, both in their strengths and in their weaknesses. I want to point out one particular advantage of the two methods as you begin your reading of the chapter: both are readily available to *you* even if you don't happen to have a half-million-dollar research grant to play around with. Put another way: they're cheap. At the same time, however, you can undertake some fairly sophisticated social scientific inquiries with them, as the examples I'll give illustrate.

We'll begin now with an examination of content analysis: the topics appropriate to it, sampling methods, and the process of *coding* and its implications for validity and reliability. Then, I'll present some illustrations of the use of this research method, and the treatment will conclude with an examination of the strengths and weaknesses of content analysis. Next, I'll talk about the analysis of existing data, following essentially the same format, though more briefly. Finally, I want to conclude the chapter with a general comment on *unobtrusive measures*.

TOPICS APPROPRIATE TO CONTENT ANALYSIS

Content analysis methods may be applied to virtually any form of communication. Among the possible artifacts for study are books, poems, newspapers, songs, paintings, speeches, letters, laws, and constitutions, as well as any components or collections thereof. Are popular French novels more concerned with love than American ones? Was the popular American music of the 1960s more politically cynical than the popular German music during that period? Do political candidates who primarily address "bread and butter" issues get elected more often than those who address issues of principle? Each of these questions addresses a social scientific research topic: the first might address national character, the second political orientations, and the third political process. While such topics might be studied through the observation of individual people, content analysis provides another approach.

Some topics are more appropriately addressed by content analysis than by any other method of inquiry. Suppose for a moment that you're interested in violence on television. Maybe you have a suspicion that the manufacturers of men's products are more likely to sponsor violent TV shows than are other kinds of sponsors. Content analysis would be the best way of finding out if it's true.

Briefly, here's what you would do. First, you'd develop operational definitions of the two key variables in your inquiry: *men's products* and *violence*. The section on coding, later in this chapter, will discuss some of the ways you could do that. Ultimately, you'd need a plan that would allow you to watch television, classify sponsors, and rate the degree of violence on particular shows.

Next, you'd have to decide what to watch. Probably you would decide (1) what stations to watch, (2) for what days or period, and (3) at what hours. Then, you'd stock in some beer and potato chips and start watching, classifying, and recording. Once you had completed your observations, you'd be able to analyze the data you collected and determine whether men's product manufacturers sponsored more blood and gore than other sponsors.

Content analysis, then, is particularly well suited to the study of communications and to answering the classic question of communications research: "Who says what, to whom, how, and with what effect?"[1] as well as to the more recently added "why?"[2] As a mode of observation, content analysis requires a considered handling of the *what*, and the analysis of data collected in this mode, as in others, addresses the *why* and *with what effect.*

SAMPLING IN CONTENT ANALYSIS

In the study of communications, as in the study of people, it is often impossible to observe directly all that you are interested in. If you were interested in the question of television violence and sponsorship, I'd advise against attempting to

[1] See Harold B. Lasswell, Daniel Lerne, and I. de S. Pool, *The Comparative Study of Symbols* (Stanford: Stanford University Press, 1952).
[2] Ole R. Holsti, *Content Analysis for the Social Sciences and Humanities* (Reading, Mass.: Addison-Wesley, 1969).

watch everything that's broadcast. It wouldn't be possible, and your brain would probably short-circuit before you got close to discovering that for yourself. Usually, then, it's appropriate to sample.

As we'll see shortly, the logic and techniques of sampling in content analysis closely parallel those described in Chapter 7. Let's begin by looking again at *units of analysis* and then review some of the sampling techniques that might be applied to them in content analysis.

Units of Analysis

You'll recall from Chapter 7 that the units of analysis are the individual units about which or whom descriptive and explanatory statements are to be made. If we wished to examine the orientation of American voters, for example, the individual American voter would be the unit of analysis in that study. If we wished to compute the average family income, the individual family would be the unit of analysis. If we wished to compare divorce rates between religiously mixed and unmixed marriages, the individual marriage would be the unit of analysis.

It was pointed out in Chapter 7 that determining the appropriate unit of analysis is not always a simple task. For example, in computing the average family income, we might ask individual members of families how much money they make. Individual people, then, would be the units of observation, but the individual family would still be the unit of analysis. Similarly, we may wish to compare crime rates of different cities in terms of their sizes, geographical regions, racial composition, and other differences. Even though the characteristics of these cities are partly a function of the behaviors and characteristics of their individual residents, cities would ultimately be the units of analysis.

The complexity of this issue is often more apparent in content analysis than in other research methods. That is especially the case when the units of observation differ from the units of analysis. A few examples should clarify this distinction.

Let's suppose we are interested in learning about sex discrimination and the legal system in America. Suppose, as a start, that we want to find out whether criminal law or civil law makes the most distinctions between men and women. In this instance, individual laws would be both the units of observation and the units of analysis. We might select a sample of, say, a state's criminal and its civil laws, and we might then categorize each law in the sample in terms of whether it makes a distinction between men and women. In this fashion, we would be able to determine whether criminal or civil law distinguishes most by sex.

Somewhat differently, we might wish to determine whether states that enact laws distinguishing between different racial groups were more likely to enact laws distinguishing between men and women than was true of states that did not distinguish races. Although the examination of this question would involve, like the previous one, the examination and coding of individual acts of legislation, the unit of analysis in this latter case would be the individual state.

Or, changing topics radically, let's suppose we are interested in representationalism in painting. If our interest is in comparing the relative popularity of representational and nonrepresentational paintings, the individual paintings would be our units of analysis. If, on the other hand, we wish to discover whether representationalism in painting is more characteristic of wealthy or impoverished painters, of educated or uneducated painters, of capitalist or socialist painters, individual painters would be our units of analysis.

It is essential that this issue be clear, since sample selection depends largely on what the unit of analysis is. If individual writers are the units of analysis, the sample design should select all or a sample of the writers appropriate to the research question. If books, on the other hand, are the units of analysis, we would select a sample of books, regardless of their authors.

I am not suggesting that sampling is to be based solely on the units of analysis. Indeed, we may often subsample—select samples of subcategories—for each individual unit of analysis. Thus, if writers are the units of analysis, we might (1) select a sample of writers from the total population of writers, (2) select a sample of books written by each writer selected, and (3) select portions of each selected book for observation and coding.

Finally, let's look at a trickier example: the study of television violence and sponsors. What is the unit of analysis for the research question, "Are men's products manufacturers more likely to sponsor violent shows than other sponsors?" Is it the TV show? the sponsor? the instance of violence? In the simplest study design, it would be none of these.

Though you might structure your inquiry in various ways, the most straightforward design would be based on the *commercial* as the unit of analysis. Ultimately, each commercial would be classified in terms of whether it was on behalf of a men's product manufacturer and whether it was associated with violent programming. Here's how you might proceed.

For the purpose of this study, TV broadcasting can be broken into two kinds of observational units: the commercial and the program (the show that gets squeezed in between commercials). You'd want to observe both units. You would classify commercials in terms of whether they were sponsored by men's products manufacturers. The programs would be classified in terms of violence, and those classifications would be transferred to the commercials occurring near them. Figure 9-1 is an example of the kind of record you might keep.

Notice that in the research design illustrated in Figure 9-1, all the commercials occurring together are bracketed and get the same scores. Also, the number of violent instances recorded as following one commercial is the same as the number preceding the next commercial. This simple design, then, would allow us to classify each commercial in terms of its sponsorship and the degree of violence associated with it. Thus, for example, the first Grunt Aftershave commercial is coded as being a men's product and as having 10 instances of violence associated with it. The Buttercup Bra commercial is coded as not being a men's product and as having no violent instances associated with it.

In the illustration, we have four men's product commercials with an average of 7.5 violent instances each. The four commercials classified as definitely not men's products have an average of 1.75, and the two that might or might not be considered men's products have an average of 1 violent instance each. If this pattern of differences persisted across a much larger number of observations, we'd probably con-

Figure 9-1 Example of Recording Sheet for TV Violence

Sponsor	Men's Product?			Number of instances of violence	
	Yes	No	?	Before	After
Grunt Aftershave	✓			6	4
Brute Jock Straps	✓			6	4
Roperot Cigars	✓			4	3
Grunt Aftershave	✓			3	0
Snowflake Toothpaste		✓		3	0
Godliness Cleanser		✓		3	0
Big Thumb Hammers			✓	0	1
Snow flake Toothpaste		✓		1	0
Big Thumb Hammers			✓	1	0
Buttercup Bras		✓		0	0

clude that men's products manufacturers are more likely to sponsor TV violence than other sponsors.

The point of this illustration is to demonstrate how units of analysis figure into the data collection and analysis. You need to be clear about your unit of analysis before planning your sampling strategy, but in this case you can't sample commercials. Unless you have access to the stations' broadcasting logs, you won't know when the commercials are going to occur. Moreover, you need to observe the programming as well as the commercials. As a result, you must set up a sampling design that will include everything you need to observe.

In designing the sample, you would need to establish the universe to be sampled from. In this case, what TV stations will you observe? What will be the period of the study—the number of days? And what hours of each day will you observe? Then, how many commercials do you want to observe and code for analysis? Watch television for a while and find out how many commercials occur each hour, then you can figure out how many hours of observation will be needed.

Now you're ready to design the sample selection. As a practical matter, you wouldn't have to sample among the different stations if you had assistants—each of you could watch a different channel during the same time periods. But let's suppose you are working alone. Your final sampling frame might look something like this:

Jan. 7, Channel 2, 7–9 P.M.
Jan. 7, Channel 4, 7–9 P.M.
Jan. 7, Channel 9, 7–9 P.M.
Jan. 7, Channel 2, 9–11 P.M.
Jan. 7, Channel 4, 9–11 P.M.
Jan. 7, Channel 9, 9–11 P.M.
Jan. 8, Channel 2, 7–9 P.M.
Jan. 8, Channel 4, 7–9 P.M.
Jan. 8, Channel 9, 7–9 P.M.
Jan. 8, Channel 2, 9–11 P.M.
Jan. 8, Channel 4, 9–11 P.M.
Jan. 8, Channel 9, 9–11 P.M.
Jan. 9, Channel 2, 7–9 P.M.
Jan. 9, Channel 4, 7–9 P.M.
etc.

Notice that I've made several decisions for you in the illustration. First, I have assumed that channels 2, 4, and 9 are the ones appropriate to your study. I've assumed that you found the 7 to 11 P.M. prime time hours to be the most relevant, and that two-hour periods would do the job. I picked January 7 out of the hat for a starting date. In practice, of course, all of these decisions should be based on your careful consideration of what would be appropriate to your particular study.

Once you have become clear as to your units of analysis and the observations appropriate to those units and have created a sampling frame like the one I've illustrated, sampling is simple and straightforward. The alternative procedures available to you are the same ones described earlier, in Chapter 7: random, systematic, stratified, and so on.

Sampling Techniques

In content analysis of written prose, sampling may occur at any or all of the following levels: words, phrases, sentences, paragraphs, sections, chapters, books, writers, or the contexts relevant to the works. Other forms of communication may also be sampled at any of the conceptual levels appropriate to them.

Any of the conventional sampling techniques discussed in Chapter 7 may be employed in content analysis. We might select a _random_ or _systematic_ sample of French and American novelists, of laws passed in the state of Mississippi, or of Shakespearean soliloquies. We might select (with a random start) every twenty-third paragraph in Tolstoy's _War and Peace_. Or, we might number all of the songs recorded by the Beatles and select a random sample (using a random number table) of 25.

Stratified sampling is also appropriate to content analysis. To analyze the editorial policies of American newspapers, for example, we might first group all newspapers by region of the country, size of the community in which they are published, frequency of publication, or average circulation. We might then select a stratified random or systematic sample of newspapers for analysis. Having done so, we might select a sample of editorials from each selected newspaper, perhaps stratified chronologically.

Cluster sampling is equally appropriate to content analysis. Indeed, if individual editorials were to be the unit of analysis in the previous example, then the selection of newspapers at the first stage of sampling would be a cluster sample. In an analysis of political speeches, we might begin by selecting a sample of politicians; each politician would represent a cluster of political speeches. The TV commercial study described above is another example of cluster sampling.

It should be repeated that sampling need not end when we reach the unit of analysis. If novels are the unit of analysis in a study, we might select a sample of novelists, subsamples of novels written by each selected author, and a sample of paragraphs within each novel. We would then analyze the content of the paragraphs for the purpose of describing the novels themselves.

Let us turn now to a more direct examination of analysis, which has been mentioned so frequently in the previous discussions. At this point, *content analysis* will refer to the coding or classification of material being observed. Part Four of this book will deal with analysis in terms of manipulating those classifications to draw descriptive and explanatory conclusions.

CODING IN CONTENT ANALYSIS

As a mode of observation, content analysis is essentially an operation of coding. Communications—oral, written, or other—are coded or classified in terms of some conceptual framework. Thus, for example, newspaper editorials may be coded as liberal or conservative. Radio broadcasts might be coded as propagandistic or not. Novels might be coded as romantic or not. Paintings might be coded as representational or not. Political speeches might be coded as containing character assassinations or not. Recall that terms such as these are subject to many interpretations, and the researcher must specify definitions clearly.

Coding in content analysis involves the logic of conceptualization and operationalization as these have been discussed in Chapters 5 and 6. In content analysis, as in other research methods, you must refine your conceptual framework and develop specific methods for observing in relation to that framework. This section discusses those processes in the context of content analysis.

Manifest and Latent Content

In the earlier discussions of field research, we found that the researcher faces a fundamental choice between *depth* and *specificity* of understanding. Often, this represents a choice between *validity* and *reliability*, respectively. Typically, field researchers opt for the former, preferring to base their judgments on a broad range of observations and information, even at the risk that another observer might reach a different judgment of the situation. In Chapter 12, we'll see that survey research—through the use of standardized questionnaires—represents the other extreme: total specificity, even though the specific measures of variables may not be fully satisfactory as valid reflections of those variables. The content analyst has more of a choice in this matter.

Coding the **manifest content** of communication would more closely approximate the use of standardized questionnaires. To determine, for example, how erotic certain novels are, you might simply count the number of times the word *love* appears in each novel, or the average number of appearances per page. Or, you might use a list of words, such as *love*, each of which might serve as an indicator of the erotic nature of the novel. This method would have the advantages of ease and *reliability* in coding and of letting the reader of the research report know precisely how eroticism was measured. It would have a disadvantage, on the other hand, in terms of *validity*. Surely the term *erotic novel* conveys a richer and deeper meaning than the number of times the word *love* is used.

Alternatively, you may code the **latent content** of the communication. In the present example, you might read an entire novel or a sample of paragraphs or pages and make an overall assessment of how erotic the novel was. Although your total assessment might very well be influenced by the appearance of words such as *love* and *kiss*, it would not depend fully on the frequency with which such words appeared.

Clearly, this second method would appear better designed for tapping the underlying meaning of communications, but this advantage comes at a cost of reliability and specificity. Especially if more than one person is coding the novel, somewhat different definitions or standards may be employed. A passage that may be regarded as erotic by one coder may seem nonerotic to another. Even if you do all of the coding yourself, there is no guarantee that your definitions and standards will remain constant throughout the enterprise. Moreover, the reader of your research report would be generally uncertain as to the definitions you have employed.

Wherever possible, the best solution to this dilemma is to use *both* methods. A given unit of observation should receive the same characterization from both methods if coding *manifest* content has validity and coding *latent* content has reliability. If the agreement produced by the two methods is fairly close, though imperfect, the final score might reflect the scores assigned in the two independent methods. If, on the other hand, coding manifest and latent content produces gross disagreement, you would be well advised to reconsider your theoretical conceptualization.

Conceptualization and the Creation of Code Categories

In all research methods, conceptualization and operationalization typically involve the interaction of theoretical concerns and empirical observations. If, for example, you believe some newspaper editorials to be liberal and others to be conservative, ask yourself *why* you believe that to be the case. Read some editorials, asking yourself which ones are liberal and which ones are conservative. Why did you feel that way? Was the political orientation of a particular editorial most clearly indicated by its manifest content or by its tone? Was your decision based on the use of certain terms (for example, *pinko*, *right-winger*, and so on) or on the support or opposition given to a particular issue or political personality?

Both inductive and deductive methods should be used in this activity. If you are testing theoretical propositions, your theories should suggest empirical indicators of concepts. If you have begun with specific empirical observations, you should attempt to derive general principles relating to them and then apply those principles to the other empirical observations.

Throughout this activity, you should remember that the operational definition of any variable is composed of the *attributes* included in it. Such attributes, moreover, should be mutually exclusive and exhaustive. A newspaper editorial, for example, should not be described as both liberal and conservative, though you should probably allow for some to be "middle-of-the-road." It may be sufficient for your purposes to code novels as being erotic or nonerotic, but you may also want to consider the range of variation in this extending to novels that are antierotic. Paintings might be classified as representational or not, if that satisfied your research purpose, or you might wish to further classify them as impressionistic, abstract, allegorical, and so forth.

Realize, further, that different levels of measurement may be employed in content analysis. You may, for example, use the *nominal* categories of liberal and conservative for characterizing newspaper editorials, or you might wish to use a more refined *ordinal* ranking ranging from extremely liberal to extremely conservative. It is important that you bear in mind, however, that the level of measurement implicit in your coding methods does not necessarily represent that level of measurement in terms of your variables. If you were to count the number of times the word *love* appeared in a novel, the raw score assigned to that novel would be a *ratio* measurement. If the word *love* appeared 100 times in novel A and 50 times in novel B, you would be justified in saying that the word *love* appeared twice as often in novel A, but not that novel A was twice as erotic as novel B. This is true for the same reason that agreeing with twice as many anti-Semitic statements in a questionnaire does not make one twice as anti-Semitic.

No coding scheme should be used in content analysis until it has been carefully pretested. You should decide what manifest or latent contents of communications will be regarded as indicators of the different attributes composing your research variable, write down these operational definitions, and then use them in the actual coding of several units of observation. If more than one person is to be engaged in the coding phase of the final project, each of them should independently code the same set of observations. With several coders, you should then determine the extent of agreement produced. In any event, you should take special note of any difficult cases: those observations that were not easily classified in terms of the operational definition. Finally, you should review the overall results of the pretest effort to insure that such results will be appropriate to your analytical concerns. If, for example, all of the pretest newspaper editorials have been coded as liberal, you may want to reconsider your definition of that attribute.

As with other types of quantitative research, it is not essential that you commit yourself in advance to a specific definition of each concept. Often you will do better to devise the most appropriate definition of a concept on the basis of your subsequent quantitative analyses. In the case of erotic novels, for example, you might do well to count separately the frequency with which different erotic words appear. This procedure would provide you with the resources for determining, during your later analysis, which of the words, if any, or which combination thereof provided the most useful indication of your variable. (Part Four—especially Chapter 15—of this book will tell you how to do that.)

Counting and Record Keeping

If a quantitative analysis of your content analytic data is to be undertaken, it is essential that your coding operation be amenable to data processing. Chapter 13 of this book will explain the requirements of data processing, but some specific comments are in order at this point.

First, the end product of your coding must be *numerical*. If you are counting the frequency of appearance of certain words, phrases, or other manifest content, that will necessarily be the case. Even if you are coding latent content on the basis of overall judgments, it will be necessary to represent your coding decision numerically: 1 = very liberal, 2 = moderately liberal, 3 = moderately conservative, and so on.

Second, it is essential that your record keeping clearly distinguishes between your units of analysis and your units of observation, especially if these two are different. Your initial coding, of course, must relate to your units of observation. If novelists are your units of analysis, for example, and you wish to characterize them through a content analysis of their novels, your primary records will represent novels. You may then combine your scoring of individual novels for purposes of characterizing each of the individual novelists.

Third, when counting, it will normally be important to record the *base* from which the counting is done. It would probably be useless to know the number of realistic paintings produced by a given painter without knowing the number that he or she had painted altogether; the painter would be regarded as realistic if a high percentage of paintings were of that genre. Similarly, it would tell us little that the word *love* appeared 87 times in a novel if we did not know about how many words there were in the novel altogether.

The issue of observation base is most easily resolved if *every* observation is coded in terms of one of the attributes making up the variables in question. Rather than simply counting the number of liberal editorials in a given collection, for example, code each editorial examined in terms of its political orientation, even if it must be coded "no apparent orientation."

In all cases, the end product of coding should be essentially the same. A set of numerical scores must be assigned to each of the units of analysis, as will be discussed in greater detail in Chapter 13. Figure 9-2 is a hypothetical illustration of a portion of a tally sheet that might result from the coding of newspaper editorials.

Note in the illustration that newspapers are the units of analysis. Our purpose in this hypothetical project is to describe and explain the editorial policies of different newspapers. Each newspaper has been assigned an identification number to facil-

Figure 9-2 Sample Tally Sheet (partial)

Newspaper ID	Number of editorials evaluated	SUBJECTIVE EVALUATION 1. Very liberal 2. Moderately liberal 3. Middle-of-road 4. Moderately conservative 5. Very conservative	Number of "anticommunist" editorials	Number of "pro-UN" editorials	Number of "anti-UN" editorials
001	37	2	0	8	0
002	26	5	10	0	6
003	44	4	2	1	2
004	22	3	1	2	3
005	30	1	0	6	0

itate mechanized processing. In the second column in the illustration, we have a space for indicating the number of editorials coded for each newspaper. That will be an important piece of information, since we want to be able to say "22 percent of all the editorials were pro-United Nations," not just "there were eight pro-United Nations editorials."

There is a column in the illustration for assigning a subjective overall assessment of the newspapers' editorial policies. (Such assignments might subsequently be compared with the several objective measures.) Other columns provide space for recording the numbers of editorials reflecting specific editorial positions. In a real content analysis, there would be additional spaces for recording other editorial positions as well as other noneditorial information about each newspaper, such as region in which published, circulation, and so forth.

ILLUSTRATIONS OF CONTENT ANALYSIS

Let's look at some actual examples of content analysis in action. The first illustration uses content analysis in conjunction with public opinion polling to find out what the key issues of the 1960s were in America. The second example represents a content analysis of the underground press to shed some light on the nature of the early counterculture movement of the 1960s.

Isolating Issues

The 1960s were turbulent years for the United States. The decade opened with a civil rights movement in full swing. Midway, popular attention turned to the war in Vietnam, and the decade ended with the appearance of social movements focused on the environment and on equality for women. The decade began with the romantic Camelot period of the Kennedy administration, experienced the tragedy of assassination, and witnessed a steady decline in popular faith in government. If you were a historian writing the history of the 1960s, what would you cite as the *key* issues of the decade? Or, more to the point in this discussion, how would you go about *finding* the key issues?

For G. Ray Funkhouser, a communications researcher, the problem was that of finding the key *public opinion* issues of the 1960s. He approached the problem from two independent directions, using two different research methods: survey research and content analysis.[3] For the survey research portion, Funkhouser turned to the Gallup Polls conducted during the decade, looking at answers people gave when asked for "the most important problem facing America." The three issues cited most often during the 1960s were: (1) the Vietnam war, (2) race relations (and urban riots), and (3) crime.

In addition to checking public opinion, Funkhouser turned his attention to an important source of public opinion: the mass media, in particular weekly news

[3]G. Ray Funkhouser, "The Issues of the Sixties: An Exploratory Study," *Public Opinion Quarterly*, Vol. 37, (Spring 1973), pp. 62–75.

magazines. His intention here was to discover which issues were given the most coverage by weekly news magazines during the decade—and compare that with the results shown in the Gallup Polls.

Here are the decisions Funkhouser had to make:

1. What period would be covered?
2. What magazines would be observed?
3. What sampling design would be used?
4. What issues would be considered?
5. How would the issues be coded?

The period to be covered was already specified in Funkhouser's research purpose: the 1960s. More specifically, he looked at 1960 through 1970. As to magazines, he chose to examine the three most popular weekly news magazines: *Newsweek*, *Time*, and *U.S. News and World Report*. His sampling design was simplicity itself: he took 'em all, every edition of each magazine during the period specified.

Funkhouser discusses his decision to focus on news magazines from among the many forms of mass media:

> It would clearly be impossible to carry out a completely representative, content-analytic study of the full range of informational stimuli carried by television and newspapers to the nationwide public during the years 1960 through 1970. The sheer volume of material *available* would overwhelm, to say nothing of the material no longer available (for example, the nightly network newscasts) or the problem of generalizing from the available (mostly local) material to the potential nationwide audience. Therefore, a strategy of indicators was used. Although news magazines are not cited as primary sources of information by most people, it seems likely that their content reflects the nationwide content of the prominent news media—television and newspapers. That is, if television and newspapers were presenting abundant material concerning ecology (or drugs, or whatever), the news magazines probably would be doing so also.[4]

Given the decisions made so far, you can probably envision the observation procedures appropriate once the code categories were established: scan some 1,716 magazines, coding each of the thousands of articles. Suddenly content analysis may not seem so much fun. Actually, Funkhouser handled the creation of code categories and grossly simplified the observation procedures at the same time. I'll let him tell you what he did.

> The source of data for the content analysis of these publications was the *Reader's Guide to Periodical Literature.* Articles (but not book reviews) were tallied, by publication and by year, for the following issues (using *only* the topics listed under the headings):
>
> VIETNAM: *Vietnam* . . . American participation . . . peace and mediation (except negotiation meetings) . . . politics and government . . . protests, demonstrations, etc., against . . . public opinion
>
> RACE RELATIONS: *Negro* . . . militants . . . students . . . student demonstrations . . .

[4]*Ibid.*, p. 64.

student militants . . . in U.S. . . . civil rights . . . culture . . . education . . . history . . . politics and suffrage . . . segregation . . . resistance to segregation . . . social conditions . . . *Race Relations* . . . in U.S. . . . prejudice

INFLATION: *Inflation (financial)*

CRIME: *Crime and Criminals* . . . in U.S. . . . prevention . . . procedure . . . criminal statistics . . . *Law Enforcement*

URBAN RIOTS (covering the general topic only—not specific cities, which were in some years listed separately): *United States* . . . riots

CAMPUS UNREST: *Student* . . . demonstrations . . . militants . . . movement . . . SDS . . . SNCC . . . opinion (all in U.S. only) . . . *Kent State* (in 1970 only)

ENVIRONMENT: *Ecology* . . . study and teaching . . . *Environment* . . . environmental movement . . . environmental policy . . . pollution . . . control . . . laws and legislation . . . *Air Pollution* . . . *Water Pollution*

DRUGS: *Drugs* . . . abuse . . . laws and legislation . . . *Hallucinogenic Drugs* . . . *LSD* . . . *Marijuana* . . . *Narcotics* . . . habit . . . addicts . . . control of . . . and youth

SEX: *Sex* . . . (psychology) . . . in literature . . . in moving pictures . . . in art and the arts . . . in the performing arts . . . instruction . . . and laws . . . relations . . . sexual behavior . . . sexual ethics

MASS MEDIA: *Mass Media* . . . *Television Broadcasting* . . . and children . . . censorship . . . moral aspects . . . news . . . in politics . . . laws and regulations . . . in U.S. . . . social aspects

POPULATION: *Population* . . . overpopulation . . . increase of . . . distribution of

POVERTY: *Poor* . . . in U.S. . . . *Poverty* . . . *Slums*

SMOKING: *Smoking* . . . *Cigarettes* . . . advertising

SCIENCE: *Research* . . . federal aid . . . in U.S. . . . *Science* . . . and civilization . . . social aspects . . . and state . . . *Technology* . . . technological change . . . and civilization

WOMEN'S RIGHTS: *Woman, Women* . . . equal rights . . . in U.S. . . . and men . . . social and moral questions . . . liberation movement . . . marches, rallies . . . suffrage [5]

Rather than creating his own coding scheme and poring through thousands of magazine articles, Funkhouser chose to use the coding scheme developed by the *Reader's Guide* editors, and he used their coding of articles as well. All he needed to do, then, was count the number of entries under each code category for the three magazines.

In simplifying the research effort, of course, Funkhouser ran certain risks, and he discussed those in his report. He had no control over the validity and reliability of what the editors had done. Similarly, he noted the difficulty involved in multiple entries—a single article being listed under more than one heading. All in all, however, he felt that the data generated from the index listings gave him a good measure of the mass media coverage of various issues during the 1960s.

Table 9-1 presents his summary data. In addition to showing the number of articles and ranking of issues in terms of news magazine coverage, the table also presents the ranking of issues as indicated by the Gallup Poll. Notice the close—though imperfect—correspondence between the two rankings.

I think the Funkhouser study is a perfect example for this chapter, since it

[5]*Ibid.*, pp. 64–65.

Table 9-1   News Magazine Coverage of Various Issues during the 1960s and Importance Ranking of the Issues

Issue	Number of Articles	Coverage Rank	Importance Rank
Vietnam war	861	1	1
Race relations (and urban riots)	687	2	2
Campus unrest	267	3	4
Inflation	234	4	5
Television and mass media	218	5	12*
Crime	203	6	3
Drugs	173	7	9
Environment and pollution	109	8	6
Smoking	99	9	12*
Poverty	74	10	7
Sex (declining morality)	62	11	8
Women's rights	47	12	12*
Science and society	37	13	12*
Population	36	14	12*

Source: Taken from Funkhouser, *op. cit.*, p. 66.

Note: Rank-order correlation between coverage and importance = .78 (p = .001).

*These items were never noted as "the most important problem" in the Gallup findings, so are ranked equally below the items that were.

combines content analysis and the analysis of existing data, demonstrating how a social researcher can find out about social life through an examination of information already collected and compiled by others. The next illustration focuses solely on content analysis.

Understanding the Underground

Growing up in the 1940s and 1950s, Jack Levin and James Spates attended college and graduate school during the appearance and development of the hippie movement of the 1960s. Not surprisingly, they found themselves personally interested in that social movement and its implications for mainstream American culture. As their sociological training progressed in graduate school, they were able to use their new professional skills to pursue their personal interest and contribute to our scientific understanding of the hippie movement.[6]

[6]The discussion that follows is taken from two articles by Levin and Spates. "Hippie Values: An Analysis of the Underground Press" was published in *Youth and Society* (Vol. 2, pp. 59–72) in 1970 and was reprinted in M. Patricia Golden (ed.), *The Research Experience* (Itasca, Ill.: Peacock, 1976), pp. 390–399. The second article is a research autobiography, "Through the Looking Glass of Time: Personal Reflections on Researching the Hip Counterculture," written by Levin and Spates especially for *The Research Experience* (pp. 400–411). Subsequent page references are for that book.

The thing that most interested Levin and Spates was a value difference that had been discussed on a general theoretical level by Talcott Parsons and others years before: the difference between *instrumental* and *expressive* values and orientations. To put it simply, instrumental values are those having to do with rationality and achievement, and expressive values lie more in the realm of feelings. Thus, an engineer building a bridge is engaged in an instrumental activity, and the profession of engineering is heavily imbued with instrumental values. A romantic poet writing of love, on the other hand, is engaged in a more expressive activity.

Though not simply favoring poetry over engineering, the hippie movement— like the beat movement before it—represented a challenge to the predominant emphasis on instrumental achievement that has characterized mainstream American society throughout our national history. The movement produced critics who spoke of the meaningless superficiality of middle-class American concerns for material possessions and social status. It was often charged that Americans had for the most part lost touch with their feelings and were unable to relate to one another in a meaningful, human way. Clearly, it looked as though the hippie movement represented a commitment to expressive values, in contrast to the instrumental values of mainstream American society. Levin and Spates wanted to find out if that was so, and—if it was—whether the hippie movement was having any impact on the values of the host society. Here's how they did it.

One place where the movement values could be observed would be in its literature—for example, in the underground press made up of such newspapers as the *East Village Other*, *Avatar*, the *San Francisco Oracle*, and others. If the hippie movement was oriented toward expressive values, it should be evidenced in the movement newspapers. But two problems immediately arose: (1) How would the authors recognize an expressive orientation in contrast to an instrumental one? (2) *How much* expressiveness would be "really" expressive? Put differently, they needed some definitions of expressiveness and instrumentality and a standard for comparison.

They found the answer to their first need in the research literature. Ralph White had published a value catalog several years before that seemed to specify the different orientations sufficiently for the research project.[7] Levin and Spates adapted White's work to create the following definitions and categories:

Instrumental

a. Achievement: Values which produce achievement motivation for the individual in terms of hard work, practicality, or economic value are often expressed by means of contributions to society through occupation and high regard for ownership.

b. Cognitive: These represent the drive for learning as an end in itself as well as the means for achieving success, welfare, or happiness.

c. Economic: Economic values are at the collective level (such as national, state, industrial), thus differing from individual goals such as achievement.

---

[7]Ralph White, *Value-Analysis: The Nature and Use of the Method* (New York: Society for the Psychological Study of Social Issues, 1951).

Expressive

d. Self-expressive: This area includes all the self-expressive values and goals. The main ones are humor, play, and fun in general, relaxation, or exciting new discoveries, and travel. Art and beauty are included as well as other creative-expressive activities.

e. Affiliative: These may be the product of social conditioning, or a result of the need to belong to a group, to affiliate with another person. This category focuses upon the gregariousness of individuals and the friendships which they develop. These affiliative aims may be expressed as conformity, loyalty to the group, friendship, or other-directedness.

f. Concern for others: Concern for others does not depend upon a drive to interact. Unlike the affiliative values, this category focuses upon attitudes and feelings toward particular groups or toward humanity in general. Therefore, this category tends to include more abstract objectives than those associated with affiliation.

g. Religious-philosophical: This category includes goals dealing with ultimate meaning in life, the role of deity, concerns with after-life, and so on.

Other

h. Individualistic: This category is concerned with values which stress the importance of the individual, the development of his unique personality, individual independence, and the achievement of individualized personal fulfillment including rebellion.

i. Physiological: These are goals created by simple physiological drives such as hunger, sex, physical health, and physical safety.

j. Political: This category includes collective goals (such as state, community, national, international objectives) in their central reference to group decision-making processes.

k. Miscellaneous: Any other goals not covered above (such as hope, honesty, purity, modesty, and manners).[8]

Notice that the categorization scheme was not totally specific, calling for the coding of latent more than manifest content. Although this lack of specificity perhaps strengthened the *validity* of the coding, it presented a potential problem in terms of *reliability*, as discussed earlier in this chapter. To check this danger, the researchers selected 30 sample articles and had three coders independently code each. In 90 percent of the cases, two out of three coders agreed as to whether a particular article was *expressive*, *instrumental*, or *other*; in 78 percent, all three agreed in their coding. On the basis of this test, the researchers concluded that the coding scheme provided a sufficiently high reliability to permit a meaningful study and analysis.

To satisfy their second need—that for a way of determining how much expressiveness ought to be considered expressive—they turned to the mainstream periodical literature of America. Specifically, they chose to compare the underground press with the *Reader's Digest*. If the common assumptions about the predominantly instrumental orientation of mainstream American society and about the contrasting expressive orientation of the hippie movement were true, the difference should show up in the comparison proposed.

Here is the authors' description of how they specified their sampling design for the study:

[8]Levin and Spates, *op. cit.*, p. 395.

To obtain a representative sample of underground newspapers, the following most widely circulated periodicals were selected from major centers of . . . hippie activities, including both eastern and western regions: *Avatar* (Boston), *Distant Drummer* (Philadelphia), *East Village Other* (New York), *Los Angeles Free Press*, *San Francisco Oracle*, and *Washington Free Press*. A single issue of each UPS periodical from every second month in the period from September 1967 to August 1968 was selected on a random basis. Every second nonfictional article appearing in this sample of issues, excluding poetry and letters to the editor, was subjected to analysis ($n = 316$).

To provide a comparable sample of articles representative of middle-class values, an analysis was also conducted of concurrently published issues of the *Reader's Digest*, selected for its variety of middle-class articles from diverse sources. . . . Excluding fiction and poetry, each article appearing in every other issue of *Reader's Digest* was studied ($n = 162$).[9]

Table 9-2 presents the results of the comparison. As expected, the sample of underground press papers was clearly and strongly more expressive than was the *Reader's Digest*. The initial question asked by Levin and Spates was thus answered.

But how about the possibility that the hippie movement would have an impact on the mainstream values of American society? The impact on music, dress, and other aspects of culture was too obvious to require study. But would the movement bring about a trend toward expressiveness and away from instrumentalism?

To gauge the historical consequences, the researchers subsequently repeated their study on a larger scale, examining three time periods: 1957 to 1959 (the "beat" era), 1967 to 1969, and 1970 to 1972. If the hippie movement—through the underground press and in other ways—was strengthening expressive values in America, the predominance of expressive values in the underground press should have been maintained over time, and the mainstream media, such as the *Reader's Digest*, should be found to have shifted from instrumental to expressive values.

For purposes of the expanded study, *Life*, *Look*, *True*, *Redbook*, and *Cosmopolitan* were added to the *Reader's Digest*. A sampling design was created to produce a larger number of observations from both the underground press and mainstream magazines, running to several thousand observations altogether. To further refine the study design, the researchers shifted from articles to paragraphs as the unit of analysis. In the initial study, they had coded whole articles as either expressive, instrumental, or other. Now they selected a sample of paragraphs from articles in both the underground press and mainstream magazines, and coded the paragraphs.

Once the sampling and coding were complete, the tabulations were done, and the surprises appeared. First, no significant change was found in the value orientations of the mainstream magazines over the course of the three time periods. They stayed predominantly instrumental. However, Levin and Spates discovered that "the real *coup de grace* concerning our high hopes for the counterculture came in the underground press figures themselves. These indicated that a major value priority shift had occurred within the counterculture *itself*."[10] Table 9-3 presents the data producing that conclusion.

[9]*Ibid.*, p. 394.
[10]*Ibid.*, p. 408.

Table 9-2   Value-Themes in the Underground Press and *Reader's Digest*

Value-Theme	Underground Press		*Reader's Digest*	
Expressive	46%		23%	
Self-expressive		28%		9%
Concern for others		8		6
Affiliative		4		3
Religious-philosophical		6		5
Instrumental	10		42	
Achievement		3		28
Cognitive		5		7
Economic		2		7
Other	44		35	
Individual		20		10
Political*		19		12
Physiological†		4		12
Miscellaneous		1		1
Total		100		100
(*n* = 478)		(316)		(162)

Source: Adapted from Levin and Spates, *op. cit.*, p. 396.

Note: A chi-square analysis was conducted by comparing the underground press and *Reader's Digest* on the two major value-themes, Expressive and Instrumental ($\chi^2 = 61.17$, *df* = 1, *p* < .001).

*The distribution of political values reveals an important aspect of the nature of the underground press: a secondary appeal of these newspapers is often to politically radical or New Left types, though most of the material is designed for hippie consumption . . . a group known for its apolitical stance. . . .

† In the *Reader's Digest*, this category consisted primarily of health-related topics such as methods of weight reduction, physical diseases such as cancer, and aging. In the underground press, it contained references to physiological sex.

Table 9-3   Changes in Value Orientations

	Percentage of Instrumental Paragraphs from Those Coded as Either Instrumental or Expressive	
	Underground Press	Mainstream Magazines
1957–1959	25%*	73%
1967–1969	30%	78%
1970–1972	55%	78%

Source: Adapted from Levin and Spates, *op. cit.*, pp. 407–408.

*The authors report this figure is "approximately one-quarter instrumental" in the text of their report, and I have taken the liberty of showing it as 25% for the sake of readability in the table.

Rather than finding the mainstream American press moved from instrumental to expressive concerns, the researchers discovered that the underground press had moved in an instrumental direction. The underground press had shifted toward greater agreement with the mainstream, as expressive values were significantly replaced by instrumental ones. As the researchers noted in their second report, this finding from the content analysis was supported by other observations. In particular, it was being widely reported that the leaders of the counterculture were dropping back into the mainstream society as they reached their late twenties and early thirties.

These two illustrations of content analysis in action should give you a clearer picture of the procedures and potential that characterize this research method. Let's conclude the discussion of content analysis with an overview of its particular strengths and weaknesses.

STRENGTHS AND WEAKNESSES OF CONTENT ANALYSIS

Probably the greatest advantage of content analysis is its economy in terms of both time and money. It might be feasible for a single college student to undertake a content analysis, whereas undertaking a survey, for example, might not be feasible. There is no requirement for a large research staff; no special equipment is required. As long as you had access to the material to be coded, you could undertake content analysis.

Safety is another advantage of content analysis. If you discover that you have botched up a survey or an experiment, you may be forced to repeat the whole research project with all the attendant costs in time and money. If you botch up your field research, it may be impossible to redo the project; the event under study may no longer exist. In content analysis, although you might be forced to repeat a portion of the study, that more likely would be feasible than in the case of other research methods. You might be required, moreover, to recode only a portion of your data rather than to repeat the entire enterprise.

Another important, and nearly unique, strength of content analysis has to do with *historical research*. As long as historical records exist, content analysts easily may study past periods of history or make comparisons over time. You might focus on the imagery of blacks conveyed in American novels of 1850 to 1860, for example, or you might examine changing imagery from 1850 to the present.

Finally, content analysis has the advantage of being *unobtrusive* (see later discussion in this chapter.) That is, the content analyst seldom has any effect on that which *is being studied*. Since the novels have already been written, the paintings already painted, the speeches already presented, subsequent content analyses can have no effect on them. This advantage is not present in all research methods.

Content analysis has disadvantages as well. For one thing, content analysis is limited to the examination of *recorded* communications. Such communications may be oral, written, or graphic, but they must be recorded in some fashion to permit analysis.

2   Finally, I have already discussed the considerations of validity and reliability in terms of content analysis. Here, we find both advantages and disadvantages. In terms of validity, problems are likely unless you happen to be studying communication processes per se. For example, did the appearance of expressive/instrumental values in the underground press represent the most valid measure of those values in the hippie movement in general? Probably not. Even if the researchers achieved a high degree of validity in their coding of value orientations in the underground press and mainstream magazines, there's still a question of whether they had a valid measure of the *cultures* those media were taken to represent. This, then, is a common problem with content analysis.

On the other side of the ledger, the concreteness of materials studied in content analysis strengthens the likelihood of reliability. You can always code and recode and even recode again if you want, making certain that the coding is consistent. In field research, by contrast, there's probably nothing you can do after the fact to insure greater reliability in observation and categorization.

Let's move from content analysis now and turn to a related research method: the analysis of existing data. Although numbers rather than communications are the substance analyzed in this case, I think you'll see the similarity to content analysis.

ANALYZING EXISTING STATISTICS

Frequently it is possible or necessary to undertake social scientific inquiry through the use of official or quasi-official statistics. I've already given some illustrations of this method. Earlier in this chapter, you'll recall, the Funkhouser study of the issues of the 1960s employed Gallup Poll findings on public opinion. And in the beginning of the book, we looked at Samuel Stouffer's study of the consequences of the Great Depression on the family, which used government statistics on marriages, divorces, and the like.

Before getting into the nuts and bolts of this research method, I'd like to point out that existing statistics should always be considered as at least a *supplemental* source of data. If you were planning a survey of political attitudes, for example, you would do well to examine and present your findings within a context of voting patterns, rates of voter turnout, or similar statistics relevant to your research interest. Or, if you were doing evaluation research on an experimental morale-building program on an assembly line, probably statistics on absenteeism, sick leave, and so on would be interesting and revealing in connection with the data your own research would generate. Existing statistics, then, can very often provide a historical or conceptual context within which to locate your original research.

Existing statistics can also provide the main data for a social scientific inquiry. In contrast to the structure of preceding discussions, I want to begin here with an illustration: Durkheim's classic study of *Suicide*.[11] Then, we'll look at some of the special problems this method presents in terms of units of analysis, validity, and reliability. I'll conclude the discussion by mentioning some useful sources of data.

[11]Emile Durkheim, *Suicide* (Glencoe, Ill.: Free Press, 1951). Originally published in 1897.

Studying Suicide

Why do people kill themselves? Undoubtedly every suicide case has a unique history and explanation, yet all such cases could no doubt be grouped according to certain common causes: financial failure, trouble in love, disgrace, and other kinds of personal problems. Emile Durkheim had a slightly different question in mind when he addressed the matter of suicide, however. He was particularly interested in discovering the environmental conditions that encouraged or discouraged it, especially social conditions.

As he examined the data, one of the first things that attracted Durkheim's attention was the relative *stability* of suicide rates. Looking at several countries, he found suicide rates to be about the same year after year. Now, if there had been a particular group of diehards committing suicide year after year, it would have made some sense, but that explanation was ruled out.

The more he examined the available records, the more patterns of differences became apparent to Durkheim. All of these patterns interested Durkheim. He discovered, for example, that a disproportionate number of suicides occurred during the hot summer months, leading him to hypothesize that temperature might have something to do with suicide. If that were the case, however, we should expect to find higher suicide rates in the southern European countries than in the temperate ones. Testing this hypothesis, though, he discovered that the highest rates were found in countries in the central latitudes, so temperate couldn't be the answer.

He explored the role of age (35 was the most common suicide age), sex (men outnumbered women by around four to one), and numerous other factors. Eventually, a general pattern emerged from different sources.

In terms of the stability of suicide rates over time, for instance, Durkheim found the pattern was not *totally* stable. In particular, he found spurts in the rates during times of political turmoil, which occurred in a number of European countries around 1848. This observation led him to hypothesize that suicide might have something to do with "breaches in social equilibrium." Put differently, social stability and integration seemed to be a protection against suicide.

This general hypothesis was substantiated and specified through Durkheim's analysis of a different set of data. The different countries of Europe had radically different suicide rates. The rate in Saxony, for example, was about ten times that of Italy, and the relative ranking of the various countries persisted over time. As Durkheim considered other differences in the various countries, he eventually noticed a striking pattern: predominantly Protestant countries had consistently higher suicide rates than Catholic ones. The predominantly Protestant countries had 190 suicides per million population; mixed Protestant-Catholic countries, 96; and predominantly Catholic countries, 58.[12]

It was possible, Durkheim reasoned, that some other factor, such as level of economic and cultural development, might explain the observed differences. If religion had a genuine effect on suicide, then, the religious difference would have to be found *within* given countries. To test this idea, Durkheim first noted that the German state of Bavaria had both the most Catholics and the lowest suicide rates in that country, whereas heavily Protestant Prussia had a much higher suicide rate. Not

[12]*Ibid.*, p. 152.

content to stop there, however, Durkheim went on to examine the provinces composing each of those states. Table 9-4 shows what he found.

As you can see, in both Bavaria and Prussia, those provinces with the highest proportion of Protestants also had the highest suicide rates. Increasingly, Durkheim became confident that religion played a significant role in the matter of suicide.

Returning eventually to a more general theoretical level, Durkheim combined the religious findings with the earlier observation about increased suicide rates during times of political turmoil. Put most simply, Durkheim suggested that many suicides are a product of *anomie*, "normlessness," or a general sense of social instability and disintegration. During times of political strife, people might feel that the old ways of society were collapsing. They would become demoralized and depressed, and suicide was one answer to the severe discomfort. Seen from the other direction, social integration and solidarity—reflected in personal feelings of being part of a coherent, enduring social whole—would offer protection against depression and suicide. That was where the religious difference fit in. Catholicism, as a far more structured and integrated religious system, would give people a greater sense of coherence and stability than would the more loosely structured Protestantism.

From these theories, Durkheim created the concept of *anomic suicide* and, more importantly, added the concept of *anomie* to the lexicon of the social sciences. Please realize that I have given you only the most superficial picture of Durkheim's classic study, and I think you'd enjoy looking through the original. In any event, this study gives you a good illustration of the possibilities for research contained in the masses of data regularly gathered and reported by government agencies.

Units of Analysis

As we have already seen in the case of *Suicide*, the unit of analysis involved in the analysis of existing statistics is often *not* the individual. Thus, Durkheim was required to work with political-geographical units: countries, regions, states, and cities. The same situation would probably appear if you were to undertake a study of crime rates, accident rates, disease, and so forth. By their nature, most existing statistics are *aggregated*: they describe groups.

The aggregate nature of existing statistics can present a problem, though not an insurmountable one. As we saw, for example, Durkheim wanted to determine whether Protestants or Catholics were the more likely to commit suicide. None of the records available to him indicated the religion of those people who committed suicide, however. Ultimately, then, it was not possible for him to say whether Protestants committed suicide more often than Catholics, though he *inferred* as much. Since Protestant countries, regions, and states had higher suicides than Catholic countries, regions, and states, he drew the obvious conclusion.

There's a danger in drawing that kind of conclusion, however. It is always possible that patterns of behavior at a group level do not reflect corresponding patterns on an individual level. Such errors are said to be due to an *ecological fallacy*. It was altogether possible, for example, that it was Catholics who committed suicide in the predominantly Protestant areas. Think about it for a minute, and you

Table 9-4 Suicide Rates in Various German
Provinces, Arranged in Terms of Religious Affiliation

Religious Character of Province	Suicides per Million Inhabitants
Bavarian Provinces (1867–1875)*	
Less than 50% Catholic	
Rhenish Palatinate	167
Central Franconia	207
Upper Franconia	204
Average	192
50% to 90% Catholic	
Lower Franconia	157
Swabia	118
Average	135
Over 90% Catholic	
Upper Palatinate	64
Upper Bavaria	114
Lower Bavaria	19
Average	75
Prussian Provinces (1883–1890)	
More than 90% Protestant	
Saxony	309.4
Schleswig	312.9
Pomerania	171.5
Average	264.6
89% to 68% Protestant	
Hanover	212.3
Hesse	200.3
Bradenberg and Berlin	296.3
East Prussia	171.3
Average	220.0
40% to 50% Protestant	
West Prussia	123.9
Silesia	260.2
Westphalia	107.5
Average	163.6
32% to 28% Protestant	
Posen	96.4
Rhineland	100.3
Hohenzollern	90.1
Average	95.6

Source: Adapted from Emile Durkheim, *op. cit.*, p. 153.
*Note: The population below 15 years has been omitted.

can probably come up with a story to support that possibility. Perhaps, the Protestants in the areas Durkheim studied were more religiously intolerant than Catholics. If that were the case, we'd expect that Catholics in predominantly Protestant areas would be badly persecuted—perhaps leading them into despair and suicide. It would be possible, then, for Protestant countries to have high suicide rates without any Protestants committing suicide.

Durkheim avoided the danger of the ecological fallacy in two ways. First, his general conclusions were based as much on rigorous, theoretical deductions as on the empirical facts. The correspondence between theory and fact made a counter-explanation, such as the one I just made up, less likely. Second, by extensively retesting his conclusions in a variety of ways, Durkheim further strengthened the likelihood that they were correct. Suicide rates were higher in Protestant countries than in Catholic ones; higher in Protestant regions of Catholic countries than in Catholic regions of Protestant countries; and so forth. The replication of findings added to the weight of evidence in support of his conclusions.

Problems of Validity

Whenever you base your research on an analysis of data that already exist, you are obviously limited to what exists. Often, what exists isn't exactly what you are interested in, and your measurements may not be altogether valid representations of the variables and concepts you want to draw conclusions about.

You'll recall that Stouffer wanted to look at the consequences of the depression on what he called "impulsive marriages." Had he been able to interview married couples at length, he probably would have been able to categorize each couple as representing an impulsive marriage or not, and we might have all agreed that his categorizations were valid ones. In working with official statistics, however, he discovered that the government officials neither asked nor recorded whether the couples were getting married impulsively. As a result, he had to find data that *were* recorded and could be taken as an *indicator* of impulsiveness. In this case, he chose to analyze rates of out-of-state marriages.

Notice that this procedure involves the following line of reasoning:

1. Assume that out-of-state marriages are more impulsive than in-state marriages.

2. If the depression produced a greater number of impulsive marriages, then we should expect to find more out-of-state marriages during the depression.

3. Finding that out-of-state marriages *did* increase during the depression confirms the hypothesis about impulsive marriages *only if* the assumption about out-of-state marriages being impulsive is correct.

Two additional characteristics of science are used to handle the problem of validity in the analysis of existing statistics: logical reasoning and replication. First, you'll recall that Stouffer didn't grab out-of-state marriages out of the hat; he had a carefully reasoned theoretical basis for assuming that they could be taken to represent impulsiveness. Second, the increase in out-of-state marriages during the depression was only one of several findings supporting Stouffer's general conclusions about the consequences of the depression on the family. Had none of his other hypotheses turned out as expected, he would have questioned whether the increase in out-of-state marriages really meant what he thought it did.

Replication, in this sense, is a general solution to problems of validity in social research. Recall the earlier discussion of the interchangeability of indexes. Crying in sad movies isn't necessarily a valid measure of compassion, so if women cry more than men, that doesn't *prove* they are more compassionate. Neither is putting little birds back in their nests a valid measure of compassion, so that wouldn't *prove* women to be more compassionate. And giving money to charity could represent something other than compassion, and so forth. None of these things, *taken alone*, would prove that women were more compassionate than men. But if women appeared more compassionate than men on *all* of them, that would create a weight of evidence in support of the conclusion. In the analysis of existing statistics, a little ingenuity and reason can usually turn up several independent tests of your hypothesis, and if all the tests seem to confirm it, that produces a weight of evidence in support of the view you are advancing.

Problems of Reliability

The analysis of existing statistics depends heavily on the quality of the statistics themselves: are they accurate reports of what they claim to report? That can be a substantial problem sometimes, since the weighty tables of government statistics are sometimes grossly inaccurate.

Since a great deal of the research into crime is dependent on official crime statistics, this body of data has come under critical evaluation. The results have not been too encouraging. Suppose, for purposes of illustration, that you were interested in tracing the long-term trends in marijuana use in the United States. Official statistics on the numbers of people arrested for selling or possessing it would seem to be a reasonable measure of use. Right? Not necessarily.

To begin, you face a hefty problem of validity. Before the passage of the Marihuana Tax Act in 1937, grass was legal in the United States, so arrest records would not give you a valid measure of use. But let's suppose that you were willing to limit your inquiry to the post-1937 era. You would still have problems of reliability, stemming from the nature of law enforcement and crime record keeping.

Law enforcement, for example, is subject to various pressures. A public outcry against marijuana, led perhaps by a vocal citizens' group, often results in a police "crackdown on drug trafficking"—especially if it occurs during an election or budget year. A sensational story in the press can have a similar effect. In addition, the volume of other business facing police has an effect on marijuana arrests.

Lois DeFleur, for example, has traced the pattern of drug arrests in Chicago between 1942 and 1970 and has demonstrated that the official records present a far more accurate history of police practices and political pressures on police than a history of drug use.[13] On a different level of analysis, Donald Black and others have analyzed the factors influencing whether an offender is actually arrested by police or let off with a warning.[14] Ultimately, official crime statistics are influenced by whether specific offenders are well or poorly dressed, whether they are polite or abusive to police officers, and so forth. Consider also the whole matter of unreported crimes, sometimes estimated to be as much as ten times the number of crimes known to police, and the reliability of crime statistics gets even shakier.

These comments concern crime statistics at a local level. Often it is useful to analyze national crime statistics, such as those reported in the FBI's *Uniform Crime Reports*. Additional problems are introduced at the national level. Different local jurisdictions define crimes differently. Also, participation in the FBI program is voluntary, so the data are incomplete.

Finally, the process of record keeping affects the records that are kept and reported. Whenever a law enforcement unit improves its record-keeping system—computerizing it, for example—the apparent crime rates always increase dramatically. That can happen even if the number of crimes committed, reported, and investigated does not increase.

Your first protection against the problems of reliability in the analysis of existing statistics is awareness—knowing that the problem may exist. Investigating the nature of the data collection and tabulation may enable you to assess the nature and degree of unreliability so that you can judge its potential impact on your research interest. If you also use logical reasoning and replication, as discussed above, you can usually cope with the problem.

Sources of Existing Statistics

It would take a whole book just to list the sources of data available for analysis. In this section, I want to mention a few sources and point you in the direction of finding others relevant to your research interest.

Undoubtedly, the single most valuable book you can buy is the annual *Statistical Abstract of the United States*, published by the United States Department of Commerce. It is unquestionably the single best source of data about the United States, and it includes statistics on the individual states and (less extensively) cities as well as on the nation as a whole. Where else can you learn the number of work stoppages in the country year by year, residential property taxes of major cities, the number of water pollution discharges reported around the country, the number of business proprietorships in the nation, and hundreds of other such handy bits of information? To make things even better, Grosset & Dunlap, a commercial publisher, currently offers the same book in soft cover for $3.95. (You get around 700 facts per penny.) The commercial version is entitled *The U.S. Fact Book: The American Almanac* and

[13]Lois DeFleur, "Biasing Influences on Drug Arrest Records: Implications for Deviance Research," *American Sociological Review*, Vol. 40 (February 1975), pp. 88–103.
[14]Donald Black, "Production of Crime Rates," *American Sociological Review*, Vol. 35 (August 1970), pp. 733–748.

shouldn't be confused with other almanacs that are less reliable and less useful for social scientific research.

Federal agencies—the Departments of Labor, Agriculture, Transportation, and so forth—publish countless data series. To find out what's available, go to your library, find the government documents section, and spend a few hours browsing through the shelves. You'll come away with a clear sense of the wealth of data available for your insight and ingenuity.

World statistics are available through the United Nations. Its *Demographic Yearbook* presents annual vital statistics (births, deaths, and other data relevant to population) for the individual nations of the world. Other publications report a variety of other kinds of data. Again, a trip to your library is the best introduction to what's available.

The amount of data provided by nongovernment agencies is as staggering as the amount your taxes buy. Chambers of commerce often publish data reports on business, as do private consumer groups. Ralph Nader has information on automobile safety, and *Common Cause* covers politics and government. And, as mentioned earlier, George Gallup publishes reference volumes on public opinion as tapped by Gallup Polls since 1935.

My temptation is to continue listing data sources, but I suspect that you have already gotten the idea. The lack of funds to support expensive data collection is no reason for not doing good and useful social research. The data are as close as your university library.

A COMMENT ON UNOBTRUSIVE MEASURES

Both content analysis and the analysis of existing statistics are examples of what Eugene Webb and his colleagues have referred to as *unobtrusive measures*.[15] Some field research provides other examples. The term refers to social research that has no impact on what is being studied. Whereas surveys, experiments, and "obtrusive" field research may influence the behavior of the people being studied, coding English novels doesn't affect either the novels or the novelists. Analyzing traffic accident statistics neither increases nor decreases accidents.

Webb and his colleagues, in a delightful and ingenious book, have played freely with the task of learning about human behavior by observing what people inadvertently leave behind them. Want to know what exhibits are the most popular at a museum? You could conduct a poll, but people might tell you what they thought you wanted to hear or what might make them look more intellectual and serious. You could stand by different exhibits and count the viewers that came by, but people might come over to see what you were doing. Webb and his colleagues suggest that you check the wear and tear on the floor in front of various exhibits. Those where the tiles have been worn down the most are probably the most popular. Want to know which exhibits are popular with little kids? Look for mucus on the glass cases.

[15]Eugene J. Webb, Donald T. Campbell, Richard D. Schwartz, and Lee Sechrest, *Unobtrusive Measures: Nonreactive Research in the Social Sciences* (Chicago: Rand McNally, 1966).

To get a sense of the most popular radio stations, you could arrange with an auto mechanic to check the radio dial settings on cars brought in for repair. The possibilities are limitless. Like the investigative detective, the social researcher looks for clues, and the clues of social behavior are all around you. In a sense, everything you see represents the answer to some important social scientific question—all you have to do is think of the question.

While problems of validity and reliability crop up in unobtrusive measures like those mentioned above, a little ingenuity can either handle them or put them in perspective. I'd encourage you to look at the Webb book. It's enjoyable reading, and it should be a source of stimulation and insight for you in taking on social inquiry through the use of the data that already exist.

SUMMARY

This chapter has focused on two forms of social research: content analysis and the analysis of existing statistics. We saw that content analysis is different from most other research methods in that it does not focus on people per se but on social artifacts, very often on social communications such as books, songs, paintings, and so forth. While content analysis is often used in the study of communication processes, it is also appropriate to the study of other social phenomena. The chapter began with a discussion of some of the topics appropriate to content analysis.

The sampling methods employed in content analysis are essentially those discussed in Chapter 7. Only the units of analysis and sampling units are importantly different. The content analyst may sample words, sentences, paragraphs, books, or similar units of communication, whereas the survey researcher would sample people. The logic and techniques for sampling are the same, however.

Conceptualization and operationalization are essential in content analysis, and these processes must be carried out more explicitly than in field research. The content analyst can develop operational definitions based on either the *manifest* or the *latent* content of communications.

Coding is the primary observation and recording process in content analysis. Coding is an important element in data processing, no matter by what mode of observation the data have been produced.

This section concluded with a discussion of the special strengths and weaknesses of content analysis. It is an economical and unobtrusive research method, but one that is limited to the analysis of recorded communications.

Next, we looked at the various uses of existing statistics in social research. The world around us is filled with collected and published data, in the form of government and nongovernment reports. The social researcher can often obtain and analyze such data for the purpose of answering important research questions.

The term *unobtrusive measures* refers to a wide variety of research methods, including content analysis and some types of field research. The term refers to all those modes of observation that have no impact on what is being observed. Although surveys and experiments, for example, represent a clear intrusion into what is being studied, a little ingenuity can often suggest ways of getting relevant data without intruding.

MAIN POINTS

1. Content analysis is a social research method appropriate for studying human communications. Besides being used to study communication processes, it may be used to study other aspects of social behavior.

2. Units of communication, such as words, paragraphs, and books, are the usual units of analysis in content analysis.

3. Standard probability sampling techniques are appropriate in content analysis.

4. *Manifest content* refers to the directly visible, objectively identifiable characteristics of a communication, such as the specific words in a book, the specific colors used in a painting, and so forth. That is one focus for content analysis.

5. *Latent content* refers to the meanings contained within communications. The determination of latent content requires judgments on the part of the researcher.

6. *Coding* is the process of transforming raw data—either manifest or latent content—into standardized, quantitative form.

7. A variety of government and nongovernment agencies provide aggregate data for studying aspects of social life.

8. The *ecological fallacy* refers to the possibility that patterns found at a group level differ from those that would be found on an individual level; thus we can be misled when we analyze aggregated data for the purpose of understanding individual behavior.

9. The problem of validity in connection with the analysis of existing statistics can usually be handled through logical reasoning and replication.

10. Existing statistics often have problems of reliability, and it is necessary to use them with caution.

11. *Unobtrusive measures* are ways of studying social behavior without affecting it in the process.

ANNOTATED BIBLIOGRAPHY

Berelson, Bernard, "Content Analysis," in Lindzey, Gardner, (ed.), *Handbook of Social Psychology* (Reading, Mass.: Addison-Wesley, 1954), Vol. 1, pp. 488–522. A somewhat dated but classic overview of content analysis. The author discusses the various aspects of content analysis, describing the options available to the analyst, and provides many illustrations and citations of the use of this method.

Durkheim, Emile, *Suicide*, John Spalding and George Simpson (trans.), (Glencoe, Ill.: Free Press, 1951). A classic study. Durkheim set out to understand the reasons for suicide, analyzing the suicide rates for different types of areas. For example, Durkheim examined the effects of religion by analyzing the suicide rates of Catholic and Protestant countries and regions of countries.

Funkhouser, G. Ray, "The Issues of the Sixties: An Exploratory Study of the Dynamics of Public Opinion," *Public Opinion Quarterly*, Vol. 37 (Spring 1973), pp. 62–75. An illustration of content analysis. This article reports a content analysis of the most prominent issues of the 1960s. News articles appearing in *Time*, *Newsweek*, and *U.S. News and World Report* provide the basis for the analysis. In addition, Gallup Polls of the period are analyzed to determine the issues considered most important by the general public. The relationships between these two rankings are compared. (Vietnam was number one in both.)

Holsti, Ole, *Content Analysis for the Social Sciences and Humanities* (Reading, Mass.: Addison-Wesley, 1969). A more recent comprehensive overview of content analysis as a method. This excellent book examines the place of content analysis within the context of studying communication processes, discusses and illustrates specific techniques, and cites numerous reports utilizing this method. This book concludes with a substantial discussion of the use of computers in both the coding and analysis of content.

Stouffer, Samuel, *Social Research to Test Ideas* (New York: Free Press of Glencoe, 1962), Chapter 6: "Effects of the Depression on the Family." A minor, little-known study by a master that illustrates what can be done with existing statistics when specially collected data are not available. Wishing to learn whether the depression of the 1930s had substantially altered traditional marriage and family patterns, Stouffer asks how such an alteration would show up in regularly compiled government statistics and then looks to see. Also instructive is Chapter 7, which examines the effects of radio on newspaper circulation.

The U.S. Fact Book: The American Almanac (New York: Grosset & Dunlap, 1979). A commercial reprinting of *Statistical Abstract of the United States*, compiled and published by the United States Department of Commerce, Bureau of the Census. This is absolutely the best book bargain available (present company excluded). Although the hundreds of pages of tables of statistics are not exciting bedtime reading—the plot is a little thin—it is an absolutely essential resource volume for every social scientist.

Webb, Eugene; Campbell, Donald; Schwartz, Richard; and Sechrest, Lee, *Unobtrusive Measures: Nonreactive Research in the Social Sciences* (Chicago: Rand McNally, 1966). A stimulating and delightful statement on unobtrusive measures. As noted in the present book, there are many unobtrusive ways of studying social phenomena, and many of those have been discussed separately: for example, content analysis, participant observation, historical research, and the analysis of existing statistics may be regarded as unobtrusive. The book by Webb *et al.*, however, examines the general notion of unobtrusiveness, and the many ingenious illustrations provide a perfect portrayal of the social researcher as a detective.

Zuckerman, Harriet, "Nobel Laureates in Science: Patterns of Productivity,

Collaboration, and Authorship," *American Sociological Review*, Vol. 32 (June 1967), pp. 391–403. Another illustration of the use of content analysis. The author examines aspects of professional behavior among the nation's most eminent scientists through a content analysis of, among other things, whether Nobel laureate co-authors list themselves as "first" authors on articles or whether they give this status to their collaborators.

CHAPTER 10
Experiments

INTRODUCTION

Chapter 8 discussed a research method most closely associated with natural human inquiry; this chapter addresses a research method that is probably most frequently associated with structured science in general. Here, we'll discuss the *experiment* as a mode of scientific observation.

It is worth noting at the outset that experiments also are used often in nonscientific human inquiry. We experiment copiously in our attempt to develop generalized understanding about the world we live in. All adult skills are learned through experimentation: eating, walking, talking, riding a bicycle, swimming, and so forth. Students discover how much studying is required for academic success through experimentation. Professors learn how much preparation is required for successful lectures through experimentation.

At base, experiments involve (1) taking action and (2) observing the consequences of that action. In preparing a stew, for example, we add salt, taste, add more salt, and taste again. In defusing a bomb, we clip a wire, observe whether the bomb explodes, and clip another.

This chapter will discuss some of the ways in which social scientists may employ experiments in the development of generalized understandings. We'll see that, like other methods available to the social scientist, experimenting has special strengths and weaknesses.

TOPICS APPROPRIATE TO EXPERIMENTS

Experiments are especially well suited to research projects involving relatively limited and well-defined concepts and propositions. The traditional image of science, discussed earlier in this book, and the *experimental model* are closely related to one another. Experimentation, then, is especially appropriate for hypothesis testing. It is better suited to explanatory than to descriptive purposes.

Let's assume, for example, that we are interested in studying antiblack prejudice and in discovering ways of reducing it. We might hypothesize that acquiring an understanding of the contribution of blacks to American history might have the effect of reducing prejudice. We might test this hypothesis experimentally. To begin, we might test the level of antiblack prejudice among a group of experimental subjects. Next, we might show them a documentary film depicting the many ways in which blacks have contributed importantly to the scientific, literary, political, and social development of the nation. Finally, we might remeasure the levels of antiblack prejudice among our subjects to determine whether the film has actually reduced prejudice.

Experimentation would also be appropriate and has been successful in the study of small group interaction. Thus, we might bring together a small group of experimental subjects and assign them a task, such as making recommendations for popularizing carpools. We might observe, then, the manner in which the group organizes itself and deals with the problem. Over the course of several such experiments, we might vary the nature of the task or the rewards for handling the task successfully. By observing differences in the way groups organize themselves and operate under these varying conditions, we would learn a great deal about the nature of small group interaction.

We typically think of experiments as being conducted in laboratories. Indeed, most of the examples to be used in this chapter will involve such a setting. That need not be the case, however. As we'll see, social scientists often study what are called *natural experiments*: "experiments" that occur in the regular course of social events. The latter portion of this chapter will deal with such research.

THE CLASSICAL EXPERIMENT

The most conventional type of experiment, in the natural as well as social sciences, involves three major components: (1) independent and dependent variables, (2) experimental and control groups, and (3) pretesting and posttesting. This section of the chapter will deal with each of those components and the way they are put together in the execution of the experiment.

Independent and Dependent Variables

Essentially, an experiment examines the effect of an **independent variable** on a **dependent variable**. (Typically, the independent variable takes the form of an experimental stimulus, which is either present or absent; that is, it is typically a *dichotomous variable*—having two attributes. That need not be the case, however, as later sections of this chapter will indicate.) In the example concerning antiblack prejudice mentioned above, prejudice would be the dependent variable, and exposure to black history would be the independent variable. The researcher's hypothesis would suggest that prejudice depends, in part, on a lack of knowledge of black history. The purpose of the experiment would be to test the validity of this hypothesis. The independent and dependent variables appropriate to experimentation are nearly limitless. It should be noted, moreover, that a given variable might serve as an independent variable in one experiment and as a dependent variable in another.

It is essential that both independent and dependent variables be operationally defined for purposes of experimentation. Such operational definitions might involve a variety of observation methods. Responses to a questionnaire, for example, might be the basis for defining antiblack prejudice. Speaking to black subjects, agreeing with the black subjects, disagreeing with black subjects, or ignoring the comments of black subjects might be elements in the operational definition of interaction with blacks in a small group setting.

Conventionally, the experimental model has required the operational definition of such variables in advance of the experiment. That need not be the case, however. As was seen with content analysis and will be seen in connection with survey research, it is sometimes appropriate to make a wide variety of observations during data collection and determine the most useful operational definitions of variables during the subsequent analyses. Ultimately, however, experimentation, like other quantitative methods, requires specific and standardized measurements and observations.

Pretesting and Posttesting

In the classical experimental model, subjects are measured in terms of a dependent variable, are exposed to a stimulus representing an independent variable, and then are remeasured in terms of the dependent variable. Differences noted between the first and last measurements on the dependent variable are then attributed to the influence of the independent variable.

In the example of antiblack prejudice and exposure to black history, we might begin by measuring the extent of prejudice among our experimental subjects. Using a questionnaire asking about attitudes toward blacks, for example, we would be able to measure the extent of prejudice exhibited by each individual subject and the average prejudice level of the whole group. After exposing the subjects to the black history film, we might then administer the same questionnaire again. Responses given in the second administration of the questionnaire would permit us to measure the later extent of prejudice for each subject and the average prejudice level of the group as a whole. If we discovered a lower level of prejudice during the second administration of the questionnaire, we might conclude that the film had indeed reduced prejudice.

In the experimental examination of attitudes such as prejudice, we face a special practical problem relating to validity. As you may have already imagined, it is possible that the subjects would respond differently to the questionnaires the second time, even if their attitudes remained unchanged. During the first administration of the questionnaire, the subjects may have been unaware of its purpose. By the time of the second measurement, they might have figured out that the researchers were interested in measuring their prejudice. Since no one wishes to seem prejudiced, the subjects might "clean up" their answers the second time around. Thus, the film would seem to have reduced prejudice, although, in fact, it had not.

This is an example of a more general problem that plagues many forms of social scientific research. The very act of studying something may change it. As we'll see in the following subsection, and elsewhere in this chapter, there are a variety of techniques for dealing with this problem in the context of experimentation.

Experimental and Control Groups

The foremost method of offsetting the effects of the experiment itself is the use of a *control* group. Laboratory experiments seldom if ever involve only the observation of an experimental group to which a stimulus has been administered. In addition, observations are made of a control group to which the experimental stimulus has *not* been administered.

In the example of prejudice and black history, two groups of subjects might be examined. To begin, each group would be administered a questionnaire designed to measure their antiblack prejudice. Then, one of the groups—the experimental group—would be shown the film. Subsequently, the researcher would administer a post-test of the prejudice of *both* groups. Figure 10-1 presents a diagrammatic illustration of this basic experimental design.

Figure 10-1   Diagram of Basic Experimental Design

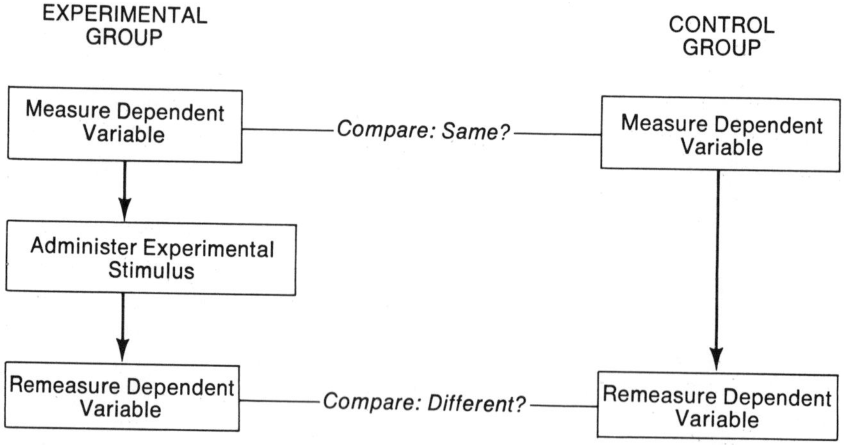

The use of a control group serves the purpose of ruling out, or "controlling," the effects of the experiment itself. If participation in the experiment were to lead the subjects to exhibit, or even to have, less prejudice against blacks, that should occur in both experimental and control groups. If the overall level of prejudice exhibited by the control group were reduced between the pretest and posttest as much as for the experimental group, then the apparent reduction in prejudice would be a function of the experiment per se or some external factor rather than a function of the film specifically. If, on the other hand, prejudice were reduced *only* in the experimental group, such reduction would seem to be a consequence of exposure to the film. Or, alternatively, if prejudice were reduced *more* in the experimental group than in the control group, that, too, would be grounds for assuming that the film reduced prejudice.

The need for control groups in social research became clear in connection with a series of studies of employee satisfaction conducted by F. J. Roethlisberger and W. J. Dickson in the late 1920s and early 1930s.[1] These two researchers undertook a series of experiments concerning working conditions in the telephone "bank wiring room" of the Western Electric Hawthorne Works in Chicago, attempting to discover what changes in working conditions would improve employee satisfaction and productivity.

To the researchers' great satisfaction, they discovered that making working conditions better consistently increased satisfaction and productivity. As the workroom was brightened up through better lighting, for example, productivity went up. Lighting was further improved, and productivity went up again. To further substantiate their scientific conclusion, the researchers then dimmed the lights: *productivity again improved*!

It became evident that the wiring room workers were responding more to the *attention* given them by the researchers than to the improvements of working conditions. As a result of this phenomenon, often referred to as the *Hawthorne effect*, social researchers have become more sensitive to and cautious about the possible effects of experiments themselves. The use of a proper control group—studied intensively without any of the working conditions changed otherwise—would have pointed to the existence of this effect in the wiring room study.

The need for control groups in experimentation has been nowhere more evident than in medical research. Time and again, patients have appeared to improve by participation in medical experiments, and it has been unclear how much of the improvement has been due to the experimental treatment and how much to the experiment. In testing the effects of new drugs, then, medical researchers frequently administer a *placebo* (for example, sugar pills) to a control group. Thus, the control group of patients believe they, like the experimental group, are receiving an experimental drug. Often, they improve. If the new drug is effective, however, those receiving that drug will improve more than those receiving the placebo.

In social scientific experiments, control groups are important as a guard not only against the effects of the experiments themselves but also against the effects of events that may occur outside the laboratory during the course of experiments. In the example of the study of antiblack prejudice, suppose that a relatively popular black leader were assassinated in the middle of, say, a week-long experiment. Such an event might very well horrify the experimental subjects, requiring them to examine their own attitudes toward blacks, with the result of reduced prejudice.

[1]F. J. Roethlisberger and W. J. Dickson, *Management and the Worker* (Cambridge: Harvard University Press, 1939).

Since such an effect should happen about equally for members of the control and experimental groups, a *greater* reduction of prejudice among the experimental group would, again, point to the impact of the experimental stimulus: the documentary film.

The Double-Blind Experiment

Mention was made earlier of the problem in medical experimentation that patients often improve when they *think* they are receiving a new drug; thus it is often necessary to administer a placebo to a control group.

Sometimes, experimenters are subject to this same tendency to prejudge results. In medical research, the experimenters are sometimes more likely to "observe" improvement among patients receiving the experimental drug than among those receiving the placebo. (That would be most likely, perhaps, for the researcher who developed the drug.) The double-blind experiment is one in which neither the experimental subjects nor the experimenters know which is the experimental group and which the control. In the medical case, those researchers who were responsible for administering the drug and for noting improvements would not be told which subjects were receiving the drug and which were receiving the placebo. Conversely, the researcher who knew which subjects were in which group would not be responsible for the administration of the experiment.

In social scientific experiments, as in medical experiments, the danger of experimenter bias is further reduced to the extent that the operational definitions of the dependent variables are clear and precise. Thus, medical researchers would be less likely to unconsciously bias their reading of a patient's temperature than they would be to unconsciously bias their assessment of how lethargic the patient was. For the same reason, the small group researcher would be less likely to misperceive which subject spoke, or to whom he or she spoke, than whether the subject's comments were in a spirit of cooperation or competition.

As indicated several times already in this book, it is seldom possible to devise operational definitions and measurements that are wholly precise and unambiguous. It may be appropriate sometimes, therefore, to employ a double-blind design in social research experiments.

SELECTING SUBJECTS

It seems very likely that most social scientific laboratory experiments are conducted with college undergraduates as subjects. Typically, the experimenter asks students enrolled in his or her classes to participate in experiments or advertises for subjects in a college newspaper. Subjects may or may not be paid for participation in such experiments.

In relation to the norm of *generalizability* in science, it is clear that this tendency represents a potential defect in social scientific research. Most simply put, college undergraduates are not typical of the public at large. There is a danger, therefore, that we may become knowledgeable about the attitudes and actions of college undergraduates without learning very much about social attitudes and actions in general.

However, this potential defect is less significant in terms of explanatory research than it would be in the case of description. Having noted the level of antiblack prejudice that existed among a group of college undergraduates, we would have little confidence that the same level existed among the public at large. If a documentary film, on the other hand, were found to reduce prejudice among those undergraduates, we would have more confidence—without being certain—that it would have a similar effect in the community at large. Social processes and *patterns* of causal relationships appear to be more generalizable and more stable than *specific* characteristics.

Aside from the question of generalizability, the cardinal rule of subject selection and experimentation concerns the comparability of experimental and control groups. Ideally, the control group represents what the experimental group would have been like had it not been exposed to the experimental stimulus. It is essential, therefore, that experimental and control groups be as similar as possible. There are several ways of accomplishing that.

Probability Sampling

The earlier discussions of the logic and techniques of probability sampling offer one method of selecting two groups of people very similar to each other. Beginning with a sampling frame composed of all the people in the population under study, the researcher might select two probability samples. If two probability samples each resemble the total population from which they are selected, they should also resemble each other.

Recall also, however, that the degree of resemblance (representativeness) achieved by probability sampling is largely a function of the sample size. As a rule of thumb, probability samples of less than 100 are not likely to be terribly representative, and social scientific experiments seldom involve that many subjects in either experimental or control groups. As a result, then, probability sampling is seldom used in the selection of subjects for experiments, except in the following way.

Randomization

Frequently, a somewhat special use of probability sampling is employed in experimentation. Having recruited, by whatever means, a total group of subjects, the experimenter may *randomly* assign those subjects to either the experimental or control group. That might be accomplished by numbering all of the subjects serially and selecting numbers by means of a random number table, or the experimenter might assign the odd-numbered subjects to the experimental group and the even-numbered subjects to the control group.

Let's return again to the basic concept of probability sampling. If the experimenter has recruited a group of forty subjects altogether, in response to a newspaper advertisement, for example, there is no reason to believe that the forty subjects are necessarily representative of the entire population from which they have been drawn. Nor can we assume that the twenty subjects randomly assigned to the experimental group represent that larger population. We may have greater confidence, however, that the twenty subjects randomly assigned to the experimental group will be reasonably similar to the twenty assigned to the control group.

All this notwithstanding, the *number* of subjects involved is important. In the extreme, if we recruited only two subjects and assigned, by the flip of a coin, one as the experimental subject and one as the control, there would be no reason to assume that the two subjects would be similar to each other. With larger numbers of subjects, however, randomization makes more sense.

Matching

The comparability of experimental and control groups can sometimes be achieved more directly through a **matching** process similar to the *quota sampling* methods discussed in Chapter 7.

If twelve of your subjects were young white men, you might assign six of those at random to the experimental group and the other six to the control group. If fourteen were middle-aged black women, you might assign seven to each of the groups. The overall matching process could be most efficiently achieved through the creation of a *quota matrix* constructed of all the most relevant characteristics. (Figure 10-2 provides a simplified illustration of such a matrix.) Ideally, the quota matrix would be so constructed as to result in an even number of subjects in each cell of the matrix. Then, half the subjects in each cell would go into the experimental group, and half into the control group.

Alternatively, you might recruit more subjects than are required by your experimental design. You might then examine many characteristics of the large initial group of subjects. Whenever you discover a pair of very similar subjects, you might assign one at random to the experimental group and the other to the control group. Potential subjects who were unlike anyone else in the initial group might be left out of the experiment altogether.

Whatever method is employed, the end result desired is the same. The overall average description of the experimental group should be the same as that of the control group. For example, they should have about the same average age, the same sex composition, the same racial composition, and so forth. (*Note*: This same test of comparability should be employed whether the two groups are created through probability sampling or through randomization.)

Thus far, I have referred to the "important" variables without saying clearly what those variables are. I cannot, of course, give a definitive answer to this question, any more than I could specify, earlier, which variables should be used in stratified sampling. The answer, ultimately, depends on the nature and purpose of the experiment. As a general rule, however, the two groups should be comparable in

Figure 10-2 Quota Matrix Illustration

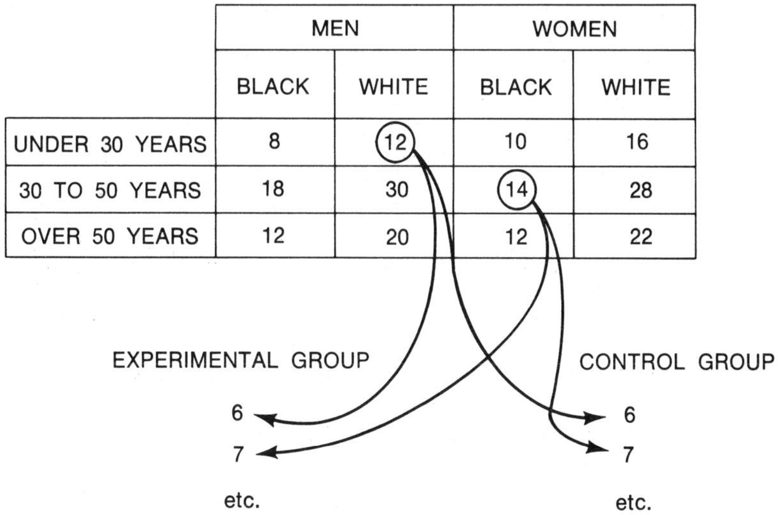

	MEN		WOMEN	
	BLACK	WHITE	BLACK	WHITE
UNDER 30 YEARS	8	(12)	10	16
30 TO 50 YEARS	18	30	(14)	28
OVER 50 YEARS	12	20	12	22

EXPERIMENTAL GROUP   CONTROL GROUP

6   6

7   7

etc.   etc.

terms of those variables that are likely to be related to the dependent variable under study. In some cases, moreover, you may delay the assignment of subjects to experimental and control groups until you have initially measured the dependent variable. Thus, for example, you might administer a questionnaire measuring subjects' prejudice and then undertake a matching of experimental and control groups so as to assure yourself, additionally, that the resulting two groups exhibited the same overall level of prejudice.

When considering the assignment of subjects to the experimental and control groups, you should be aware of two arguments in favor of randomization over matching. On the one hand, as I have already noted, you may not be in a position to know in advance what the relevant variables are for the matching process. While matching would probably not hurt, it wouldn't help either. Second, there's a more technical reason for randomization. Most of the statistics used to evaluate the results of experiments assume randomization. Failure to design your experiment that way, then, makes your subsequent use of those statistics less meaningful.

Sometimes it is possible to combine matching and randomization. When conducting an experiment in the educational enrichment of young adolescents, Milton Yinger and his colleagues needed to assign a large number of students, aged 13 and 14, to several different experimental and control groups so as to insure the comparability of students composing each of the groups.[2] They achieved this goal by the following method.

Beginning with a pool of subjects, the researchers first created strata of students nearly identical to one another in terms of some fifteen variables. From each of the strata, students were randomly assigned to the different experimental and control

[2]J. Milton Yinger, Kiyoshi Ikeda, Frank Laycock, and Stephen J. Cutler, *Middle Start: An Experiment in the Educational Enrichment of Young Adolescents* (London: Cambridge University Press, 1977).

groups. In this fashion, the researchers actually improved on conventional randomization. Essentially, they had used a *stratified* sampling procedure (recall Chapter 7), except that they had employed far more stratification variables than are typically used in, say, survey sampling.

Thus far, I have described the classical experiment—the experimental design that best represents the logic of causal analysis in the laboratory. In practice, however, social researchers use a great variety of experimental designs. Let's look at some of the variations on the basic theme.

VARIATIONS ON EXPERIMENTAL DESIGN

Donald Campbell and Julian Stanley, in an excellent little book on research design, describe some 16 different experimental and quasi-experimental designs.[3] In this section, I'm going to describe some of those briefly to give you a broader view of the potential for experimentation in social research.

To begin, Campbell and Stanley discuss three pre-experimental designs, not to recommend them but because they are frequently used in less than professional research. In the first such design—the *one-shot case study*—a single group of subjects are measured on a dependent variable following the administration of some experimental stimulus. Suppose, for example, that we show the black history film mentioned earlier to a group of people and then administer a questionnaire that seems to measure antiblack prejudice. Suppose further that the answers given to the questionnaire seem to represent a low level of prejudice. We might be tempted to conclude that the film reduced prejudice. Lacking a pretest, however, we can't be sure. Perhaps the questionnaire doesn't really represent a very sensitive measure of prejudice, or perhaps the group we are studying was low in prejudice to begin with. In either case, the film might have made no difference, though our experimental results might have misled us into thinking it did.

The second pre-experimental design discussed by Campbell and Stanley adds a pretest for the experimental group but lacks a control group. This design—which the authors call the *one-group pretest-posttest design*—suffers from the possibility that some other factor might cause a change in the posttest results (compared to the pretest), as in the case of the assassination of a respected black leader mentioned earlier.

To round out the possibilities for pre-experimental designs, Campbell and Stanley point out that some research is based on experimental and control groups but has no pretests. They call this design the *static-group comparison*. In the case of the black history film, we might show the film to one group and not to another; then measure prejudice in both groups. If the experimental group had less prejudice, we might assume the film was responsible, but we would have no way of knowing that the two groups had the same degree of prejudice initially.

Figure 10-3 gives a graphic illustration of these three pre-experimental research

[3]Donald Campbell and Julian Stanley, *Experimental and Quasi-Experimental Designs for Research.* Copyright 1963, American Educational Research Association, Washington, D.C.

designs. See if you can visualize where the potentially confounding and misleading factors could intrude into each design.

Figure 10-3   Three Pre-Experimental Research Designs. *Source*: Adapted from Campbell and Stanley, *op. cit.*, pp. 6–13.

1.   THE ONE-SHOT CASE STUDY

Administer the experimental stimulus to a single group and measure the dependent variable in that group afterward. Make an intuitive judgment as to whether the posttest result is "high" or "low."

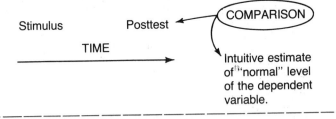

2.   THE ONE-GROUP PRETEST-POSTTEST DESIGN

Measure the dependent variable in a single group, administer the experimental stimulus, and then remeasure the dependent variable. Compare pretest and posttest results.

3.   THE STATIC-GROUP COMPARISON

Administer the experimental stimulus to one group (the experimental group), then measure the dependent variable in both the experimental group and a control group.

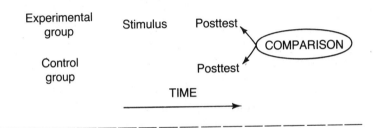

In discussing the disadvantages or weaknesses of the three pre-experimental research designs and in the initial discussion of the classical experiment, I have pointed to a number of factors impinging on experimental research. Now, I want to review those, adding additional factors, in a more systematic fashion. We are going to look at what Campbell and Stanley call the *sources of internal invalidity*. Having examined those, we will be in a position to appreciate the advantages of some of the more sophisticated experimental and quasi-experimental designs social researchers sometimes use.

Sources of Internal Invalidity

The problem of **internal invalidity** refers to the possibility that the conclusions drawn from experimental results may not accurately reflect what has gone on in the experiment itself. (Later, we shall look at the problem of generalizing experimental results to the "real" world, referring to **external invalidity**.) Campbell and Stanley point to eight sources of the problem.[4]

1. *History*. Historical events may occur during the course of the experiment that will confound the experimental results. The previously mentioned assassination of a black leader during the course of an experiment on reducing anti-black prejudice would be an example.

2. *Maturation*. People are continually growing and changing, whether in an experiment or not, and those changes may affect the results of the experiment. In a long-run experiment, the fact that they grow older (and wiser?) may have an effect. In shorter experiments, they will grow tired, sleepy, bored, or hungry or change in other ways that may affect their behavior in the experiment.

3. *Testing*. Often the process of testing and retesting will influence people's behavior, thereby confounding the experimental results. Suppose we administer a questionnaire to a group as a way of measuring their prejudice. Then we administer an experimental stimulus and remeasure their prejudice. By the time we conduct the posttest, the subjects will probably have gotten more sensitive to the issue of prejudice and will be more thoughtful in their answers. Possibly, in fact, they will have figured out that we are trying to find out how prejudiced they are, and, since none of us likes to appear prejudiced, they will be on their best behavior and give answers that they think we want or that will make them look good.

4. *Instrumentation*. Thus far, I haven't said very much about the process of measurement in pretesting and posttesting, and it's appropriate to remind you of the problems of conceptualization and operationalization discussed earlier. If we use different measures of the dependent variable, how can we be sure that they are comparable to one another? Perhaps prejudice will seem to have decreased simply because the pretest measure was more sensitive than the posttest measure. Or if the measurements are being made by the experimenters, their

---

[4]*Ibid.*, pp. 5–6.

standards or their abilities may change over the course of the experiment. Here we have the problem of reliability.

5. *Statistical regression.* Sometimes it's appropriate to conduct experiments on subjects who start out with extreme scores on the dependent variable. If you were testing a new method for teaching math to hard-core failures in math, you'd want to conduct your experiment on people who have done extremely poorly in it previously. But consider for a minute what is likely to happen to the math achievement of such people over time without any experimental interference. They are starting out so low that they can only stay at the bottom or improve: they can't get worse. Without any experimental stimulus, then, the group as a whole is likely to show some improvement over time. (Referring to a *regression to the mean*, statisticians often point out that a group of extremely tall people are likely to have children shorter than themselves, whereas a group of extremely short people are likely to have children taller than themselves.) There is a danger, then, that changes occurring by virtue of subjects starting out in extreme positions will be attributed erroneously to the effects of the experimental stimulus.

6. *Selection biases.* We discussed bias in selection earlier when we examined different ways of selecting subjects for experiments and assigning them to experimental and control groups. Comparisons don't have any meaning unless the groups are *compare-able*.

7. *Experimental mortality.* Although some social experiments could, I suppose, kill subjects, this problem refers to a more general and less extreme form of mortality. Often, experimental subjects will drop out of the experiment before it is completed, and the statistical comparisons and conclusions drawn can be affected by that. In the classical experiment involving an experimental and a control group, each with a pretest and posttest, suppose that the bigots in the experimental group are so offended by the black history film that they tell the experimenter to forget it and leave. Those subjects sticking around for the posttest will have been less prejudiced to start with, and the group results will reflect a substantial "decrease" in prejudice.

8. *Selection-maturation and other interactions.* In addition to each of the individual sources of internal invalidity described above, it is always possible that some combination of two or more sources may present a more sophisticated problem. Suppose, for example, that the experimental group had a lower boredom threshold than the control group. Or, perhaps the experimental stimulus itself proved tiring, so that the experimental group was more weary than the control group at the time of posttesting. Either of these possibilities could produce misleading experimental results.

These, then, are the sources of internal invalidity cited by Campbell and Stanley. Aware of these, experimenters have devised designs aimed at handling some or all of them. The classical experiment, discussed earlier in the chapter, if coupled with proper subject selection and assignment, handles each of the eight problems of internal invalidation. Let's look again at that study design, presented graphically in Figure 10-4.

Figure 10-4   Another Look at the Classical Experiment

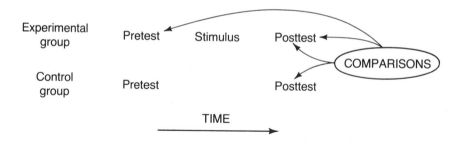

Pursuing the example of the black history film as an attempt to reduce antiblack prejudice, we should expect two findings from the experimental design shown in Figure 10-4. In the experimental group, the level of prejudice measured in the posttest should be less than was found in the pretest. In addition, when the two posttests are compared, less prejudice should be found in the experimental group than in the control.

This design guards against the problem of history in that anything occurring outside the experiment that might affect the experimental group should also affect the control group, and there should still be a difference in the two posttest results. The same comparison guards against problems of maturation as long as the subjects have been randomly assigned to the two groups. Testing and instrumentation can't be problems, since both the experimental and control groups are subject to the same tests and experimenter effects. If the subjects have been assigned to the two groups randomly, statistical regression should affect both equally, even if people with extreme scores on prejudice (or whatever the dependent variable is) are being studied. Selection bias is ruled out by random assignment of subjects. The problems of experimental mortality and the interaction of selection-maturation and other factors are more complicated to handle, but the data provided in the study design offer a number of ways for dealing with them. Slight modifications to the design— administering a placebo to the control group, for example—can make the problems even more easily managed.

Sources of External Invalidity

The problems of internal invalidity are only a part of the complications faced by experimenters, however. In addition, there are problems of what Campbell and Stanley call *external invalidity*. This second class of problems relates to the *generalizability* of experimental findings. Even if the results of the experiment are an accurate gauge of what happened during the experiment, do they really tell us anything about life in the wilds of society?

Campbell and Stanley describe four forms of this problem, and I want to present one of them to you as an illustration. The generalizability of the experimental findings are jeopardized, as the authors point out, if there is an interaction between the testing and the experimental stimulus.[5] Here's an example of what they mean.

Staying with the study of prejudice and the black history film, let's suppose that our experimental group—in the classical experiment—has less prejudice in its posttest than in its pretest and its posttest shows less prejudice than that of the control group. We can be confident that the film actually reduced prejudice among our experimental subjects. But would it have the same effect if the film were shown in theaters or on television? We can't be sure, since the film might only be effective when people have been sensitized to the issue of prejudice, as may have happened in the course of the pretest in our experiment. That is an example of interaction between the testing and the stimulus. The classical experimental design cannot control for that possibility. Fortunately, experimenters have devised other designs that can.

The *Solomon four-group design*[6] handles the problem of testing interaction with the stimulus. As the name suggests, it involves four groups of subjects, assigned randomly from a pool. Figure 10-5 presents this design graphically.

Figure 10-5   The Solomon Four-Group Design

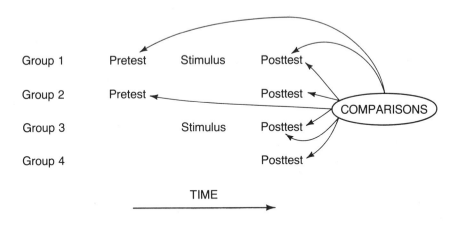

Notice that Groups 1 and 2 in Figure 10-5 compose the classical experiment. In addition, Group 3 is administered the experimental stimulus without a pretest and Group 4 is only posttested. This latest experimental design permits four meaningful comparisons. If the black history film really reduces prejudice—unaccounted for by

[5]*Ibid.*, p. 18.
[6]*Ibid.* pp. 24–25.

the problems of internal validity *and* unaccounted for by an interaction between the testing and the stimulus—we should expect four findings:

1. In Group 1, posttest prejudice should be less than pretest prejudice.

2. There should be less prejudice evident in the Group 1 posttest than in the Group 2 posttest.

3. The Group 3 posttest should show less prejudice than the Group 2 pretest.

4. The Group 3 posttest should show less prejudice than the Group 4 posttest.

Notice that findings (3) and (4) rule out any interaction between the testing and the stimulus. And remember that these comparisons are meaningful only if subjects have been assigned randomly to the different groups, thereby providing groups of equal prejudice initially, even though their pre-experiment prejudice is only measured in Groups 1 and 2.

There is a side benefit to this research design, as the authors point out. Not only does the Solomon four-group design rule out interactions between testing and the stimulus, it provides data for comparisons that will reveal the amount of such interaction that occurs in the classical experimental design. This knowledge would allow a researcher to review and evaluate the value of any prior research using that simpler design.

The last experimental design I want to mention is what Campbell and Stanley call the *posttest-only control group design*,[7] and it consists of the second half—Groups 3 and 4—of the Solomon design. As the authors argue persuasively, with proper randomization, only Groups 3 and 4 are needed for a true experiment that controls for the problems of internal invalidity as well as the interaction between testing and the stimulus. With randomized assignment to experimental and control groups (which distinguishes this design from the static-group comparison discussed earlier), the subjects will be initially comparable on the dependent variable—comparable enough to satisfy the conventional statistical tests used to evaluate the results—and it is not necessary to measure them. Indeed, Campbell and Stanley suggest the only justification for pretesting in this situation is tradition. Experimenters have simply grown accustomed to pretesting and feel more secure with research designs that include it.

I trust that this discussion has given you a sense of the intricacies of experimental design, its problems, and some solutions. There are, of course, a great many other possible experimental designs in use. Some involve more than one stimulus and combinations of stimuli. Others involve several tests of the dependent variable over time and the administration of the stimulus at different times for different groups. If you are interested in pursuing this topic, you should look at the Campbell and Stanley book, since such variations go beyond the scope of this discussion.

[7]*Ibid.*, 25–26.

AN ILLUSTRATION OF EXPERIMENTATION

Having thrust you into the logical maneuvering of complex and sophisticated experimental design, I'd like to change the pace now and describe an example of experimentation that I think you'll find interesting and stimulating. It differs from the neat rigor of the previous discussions, and I have chosen it because it seems to give an excellent picture of how logical-empirical inquiry can progress along the path to understanding social life. In the process, it demonstrates how experiments can be incorporated into a broader package of research methods, and you should get a sense of how the appropriateness of experimentation can crop up in the course of tracking down elusive explanations of social phenomena.

Which Women Were Wooed?

In the folklore of courtship, there is a long and cross-cultural tradition concerning the desirability of the hard-to-get woman. Sages have advised young men to seek her out and win her heart, and young women, in turn, have been encouraged to play the part. By contrast, the too-easy woman is likely to be scorned, spurned, and slandered. But why, exactly, is that the case? That's the question that started Elaine Walster, Jane Allyn Piliavin, and G. William Walster off on a winding and often frustrating search.[8]

They began in a logical enough fashion: they asked a number of college men what they found so attractive about hard-to-get women. The answers came easily. If a woman could afford to play hard-to-get, she must be very popular and have desirable characteristics. Moreover, she was a challenge to male egos. Winning her brought fame if not fortune. Aside from the reports of college men, a number of psychological theories supported the desirability of the hard-to-get woman. People most appreciate those things they have to work hardest for. Also, sexual frustration can provide a strong motivation and hot passion. In short, everything supported the notion that hard-to-get women were especially desirable. But the researchers wanted a clearer understanding of the phenomenon.

In their initial experiment, the researchers showed pictures and biographies of teenage couples to a group of high school juniors and seniors. The key element in the biographies concerned the extent to which one member of the couple "liked" the other. Then, students were asked how desirable the various partners pictured and described were. Everything suggested, of course, that those who were described as not caring very much for his or her partner would be the most desirable. Everything, that is, except the results of the experiment. Consistently, those described as caring very much were said to be the most desirable by the student-subjects.

Back at the drawing boards, the researchers decided to approach the matter from a different direction and in a different fashion. Rather than using pictures and stories, they chose to be more realistic. Teaming up with a computer dating service,

[8]Elaine Walster, Jane Allyn Piliavin, and G. William Walster, "The Hard-to-Get Woman," *Psychology Today* (September 1973), pp. 80–83.

they hired as experimenters a number of women recently enrolled in the program. When the women began receiving calls and offers of dates from men matched with them, they had specific instructions on how to behave. Half the time, they were to pause three seconds before accepting; half the time they were to accept right away. It was expected, then, that the men would develop a greater liking for the dates who had subjected them to three seconds of being hard to get than for those who had been easy. Not so. It didn't seem to make any difference.

Rethinking the problem, and getting increasingly frustrated with the repeated failures, the researchers added two new dimensions. On the one hand, they wanted to rule out the actual experience of the date, forcing their subjects to react only to others' assessments of the woman. Second, they began to think that men's own self-esteem and self-confidence might matter. Specifically, they hypothesized that men lacking in self-confidence would be the most susceptible to the judgments of others that a woman was hard to get and thereby desirable. Here's how they tested that hypothesis.

This time, each man was given a standard test of self-esteem when he signed up for the dating service. All his data were entered into the computer, and the counselor then gave him a telephone number, saying it was that of a woman the computer had matched him with. The man then called the woman for a date, and, after talking to her, reported his first impressions to the counselor. As you might guess, all the "dates" were members of the research team. Half the time, the "dates" accepted eagerly. The other half, they responded to the invitation saying "Mmmm. (slight pause). No, I've got a date then. It seems like I signed up for that Date Match thing a long time ago and I've met more people since then. . . . I'm really busy this week." [9] If the man suggested another time, she paused slightly and then agreed. If he didn't, she suggested getting together the next week and accepted whatever time he proposed.

Alas, no positive results were forthcoming from the new experiment. The men did not have a more favorable impression of the hard-to-get women than of the others, and their own level of self-esteem didn't make the difference. The desirability of the hard-to-get woman was now becoming an increasingly hard-to-get research finding. But the researchers persevered.

It next occurred to them that the experiment needed a heavier sexual component. After all, much of the folklore surrounding the hard-to-get woman had to do with sexuality and sexual attractiveness. So they set about adding sex to the study. How do you suppose you would do that? Walster, Piliavin, and Walster hired a prostitute as a new member of the research team.

The easy-to-get condition was operationalized as the prostitute's normal mode of business. When playing hard-to-get, on the other hand, she would mix her client-subject a drink and warn him that she wasn't necessarily going to let him call her any time he wanted, adding that she was starting school soon and would only be able to see the men she liked best. She measured her perceived desirability on the basis of (1) how much she got paid by the man and (2) the number of times he returned during the next month.

Though the experimentation was certainly getting more exciting, it didn't get

[9]*Ibid.*, p. 82.

any more successful. Being hard-to-get didn't seem to make the prostitute any more desirable. If anything, it seemed to put a chill on business.

At this point, the researchers concluded that the desirability of the hard-to-get woman was at least more complicated than they had imagined. Perhaps it only appeared under particular conditions. Not knowing what new dimensions to pursue, they went back to interviewing college men on the subject. But this time, there was an important difference in their questioning. Instead of merely asking what made the hard-to-get woman desirable, they asked about both the advantages and disadvantages she presented, and they repeated the expanded question in reference to the easy-to-get woman. It quickly became apparent that men perceived advantages and disadvantages in both kinds of women. While there was certainly prestige to be gained by dating a woman generally regarded as hard-to-get, there was the accompanying danger that she'd stand her date up or call him a turkey in front of his friends. Eventually the full picture began to emerge.

A man was most likely to consider a woman desirable if she was impossibly hard-to-get for all other men but easy for *him*, subsequently labeled the *selectively elusive* woman. Now they were ready to conduct what would be the final experiments in the study.

Returning to the computer-dating gambit, 71 college men were asked to participate in a test of computer matching as compared with random matching. Initially, each man completed a form describing himself. Then, later, he returned to the office to examine the files of some (fictitious) women in the study. Each man was given five folders, and each of the folders contained a woman's self-description plus her evaluations of five men, including the subject. Each of the self-descriptions was close enough to what the subject had said about himself to make each woman a reasonable date. The five files differed from one another as follows:

- One woman indicated she was willing to date any of the five men but was not very enthusiastic about any of them.

- One woman was enthusiastic about all the men, including the subject.

- One woman gave low marks to all the men *except* the subject, about whom she was really enthusiastic.

- The other two women were described, but the subject was told they had not returned to the office to evaluate the prospective dates.

Virtually every man in the experiment picked the selectively elusive woman: the one who liked him but didn't like any of the other men. They tended to reject the uniformly hard-to-get woman as too picky or stuck up, and they tended to suspect that the uniformly easy-to-get woman must have trouble getting dates. The selectively elusive woman was sometimes complimented for her good judgment, and some men simply said, "She made me feel good."

As I indicated at the outset of this section, the study of the hard-to-get woman has a special merit for my purpose here. It demonstrates nicely the pursuit of understanding in real-life social research. Failing repeatedly to confirm their hypothesis, the researchers returned again and again, rethinking their topic, adding new dimensions, and redesigning their observations. This is the process—often frustrating, always challenging—that can give social research the fascination and excitement of detective work.

I'm going to conclude the discussion of experimentation with some brief comments on what are sometimes called *natural experiments*. Then we'll review the strengths and weaknesses of experiments as a mode of observation and wrap up.

NATURAL EXPERIMENTS

Although we tend to equate the terms *experiment* and *laboratory experiment*, many important social scientific experiments occur outside of laboratories, often in the course of normal social events. Sometimes nature designs and executes experiments that we are able to observe and analyze; sometimes social and political decision makers serve this natural function.

Let's imagine, for example, that a hurricane has struck a particular town. Some residents of the town suffer severe financial damages while others escape relatively lightly. What, we might ask, are the behavioral consequences of suffering a natural disaster? Are those who suffer most more likely to take precautions against future occurrences than are those who suffer less? To find the answers to these questions, we might interview residents of the town at some time after the hurricane. We might question them regarding their precautions before the hurricane and precautions that they are currently taking, comparing those who suffered greatly from the hurricane with those who suffered relatively little. In this fashion, we might take advantage of a natural experiment, which we could not have arranged even if we were perversely willing to do so.

A similar example may be taken from the annals of social research surrounding World War II. Following the end of the war, social researchers undertook retrospective surveys of wartime morale among civilians in a number of German cities. One of the chief purposes of this research was to determine the effect of mass bombing on the morale of civilians, and the reports of wartime morale were compared for residents of heavily bombed cities and cities that received relatively little bombing. (*Note*: Bombing did not reduce morale.)

There is another form of natural experiment that we'll consider in some detail in Chapter 11: *evaluation research*. As we'll see, it involves taking the logic of experimentation into the field to observe and evaluate the effects of stimuli in real life. Since it is an increasingly important form of social research, I want to devote a whole chapter to it.

STRENGTHS AND WEAKNESSES OF THE EXPERIMENTAL METHOD

The chief advantage of a controlled experiment lies in the isolation of the experimental variable and its impact over time. That is seen most clearly in terms of the basic experimental model. A group of experimental subjects are found, at the outset of the experiment, to have a certain characteristic; following the administration of an experimental stimulus, they are found to have a different characteristic. To the extent that subjects have experienced no other stimuli, we may conclude that the change of characteristics is attributable to the experimental stimulus.

Another advantage is that, since individual experiments are often rather limited in scope, requiring relatively little time and money, it is often possible to replicate a given experiment several times, utilizing several different groups of subjects. (That is not always the case, of course, but it is usually easier to repeat experiments than, say, survey research.) As in all other forms of scientific research, replication of research findings strengthens our confidence in the validity and generalizability of those findings.

The greatest weakness of laboratory experiments lies in their artificiality. Social processes observed to occur within a laboratory setting might not necessarily occur within more natural social settings. If we may return to the example used frequently in this chapter, a black history film might genuinely reduce prejudice among a group of experimental subjects. That would not necessarily mean, however, that the same film shown in neighborhood movie theaters throughout the country would reduce prejudice among the general public. Artificiality is not as much a problem, of course, in the case of natural experiments as in the case of those conducted in the laboratory.

I've already discussed several of the sources of internal and external invalidity mentioned by Campbell and Stanley. As we saw in that context, it is possible to create experimental designs that logically control those problems. This possibility points to one of the great advantages of experiments: they lend themselves to a logical rigor that is often much more difficult to achieve in other modes of observation.

SUMMARY

The experiment is a frequently used research method in the physical sciences and an important method in social research as well. Experiments are especially appropriate to explanatory research purposes, particularly when the number of variables is rather limited.

We noted that the sampling considerations in experiments are somewhat different from those in surveys or content analysis. In part, that is because experiments seldom have a descriptive purpose. Hence, it is less important that the group of subjects studied in an experiment be representative of some real population.

The chief sampling concern in experiments is the presumed similarity of the experimental and control groups. Unless these groups are the same in terms of all variables save the experimental ones, the researcher cannot be sure that observed effects are attributable to the experimental stimuli. *Randomization* and *matching* are two common methods for insuring the similarity of control and experimental groups, but randomization is generally preferred for statistical and other reasons.

The classical experimental model is as follows. Subjects are divided into two groups: an experimental group and a control group. A pretest administered to both groups insures that both groups are the same in terms of some dependent variable.

Then, an experimental stimulus is administered to the experimental group only. Subsequently, a posttest determines any differences between the experimental and control groups in terms of the dependent variable. Finally, any observed difference is then attributed to the effects of the experimental stimulus.

Having examined the classical experiment, we looked at it in a broader context, building on the work of Donald Campbell and Julian Stanley. First, we examined three pre-experimental models, seeing the problems inherent in each. Then, we looked more systematically at the sources of internal and external invalidity: those confounding factors that might produce misleading conclusions about what occurred within the experiment itself and that might limit the generalizability of the experimental findings. Two variations on the classical experiment were discussed in terms of how they handle the problems of internal and external invalidity.

After looking at an illustration of social experimentation in practice—the case of the hard-to-get woman—I made a few comments on natural experiments, showing that it's sometimes possible to impose the logic of experimental design on real-world events. Finally, we reviewed some of the main strengths and weaknesses of experiments as a mode of observation in social research.

MAIN POINTS

1. Experiments are an excellent vehicle for the controlled testing of causal processes.

2. The classical experiment tests the effect of an experimental stimulus on some dependent variable through the pretesting and posttesting of experimental and control groups.

3. It is generally less important that a group of experimental subjects be representative of some larger population than that experimental and control groups be similar to one another.

4. Randomization is the generally preferred method for achieving comparability in the experimental and control groups.

5. Campbell and Stanley describe three forms of pre-experiments: the one-shot case study, the one-group pretest-posttest design, and the static-group comparison.

6. There are eight sources of internal invalidity in experimental design:
   a. history
   b. maturation
   c. testing
   d. instrumentation
   e. regression
   f. selection
   g. mortality
   h. interaction of selection and maturation, and so on.

7. The classical experiment with random assignment of subjects guards against each of the sources of internal invalidity.

8. Experiments also face problems of external invalidity: experimental findings may not reflect real life.

9. The interaction of testing with the stimulus is an example of external invalidity, and the classical experiment does not guard against that problem.

10. The Solomon four-group design and other variations on the classical experiment can safeguard against the problems of external invalidity.

11. Campbell and Stanley suggest that, given proper randomization in the assignment of subjects to the experimental and control groups, there is no need for pretesting in experiments.

12. Natural experiments often occur in the course of social life in the real world, and social researchers can study those in somewhat the way they would design and conduct laboratory experiments.

ANNOTATED BIBLIOGRAPHY

Anderson, Barry, *The Psychology Experiment* (Monterey, Calif.: Brooks/Cole, 1971). An excellent overview of experimental methods. This readable little book begins with an examination of scientific inquiry in general, then describes the specific techniques available to the experimenter. Considerable attention is given to the analysis of experimental data.

Bales, Robert, *Interaction Process Analysis: A Method for the Study of Small Groups* (Reading, Mass.: Addison-Wesley, 1950). An old but classic overview of small group research. Bales discusses the theory and techniques appropriate to the examination of social interaction in small groups under controlled laboratory conditions.

Campbell, Donald, and Stanley, Julian, *Experimental and Quasi-Experimental Designs for Research* (Chicago: Rand McNally, 1963). An excellent analysis of the logic and methods of experimentation in social research. This book is especially useful in its application of the logic of experiments to other social research methods.

Graham, Kenneth, *Psychological Research: Controlled Interpersonal Interaction* (Monterey, Calif.: Brooks/Cole, 1977. A comprehensive treatment on the experimentation process, from initial curiosity to written report. This book presents psychological experimentation within theoretical, ethical, and technical contexts. It also gives a good guide to all the issues and problems that are likely to come up in the course of actually doing experiments.

CHAPTER 11
Evaluation Research

INTRODUCTION

In this chapter, we're going to look at social experimentation from a different point of view than that of Chapter 10. You'll recall that one of the characteristics of experiments was bringing social life into the laboratory. Here, we'll look at some of the ways in which social researchers take the lab into life, conducting experiments in the field.

Evaluation research, loosely defined, is probably as old as social research generally. Whenever people have instituted a social reform for a specific purpose, they have paid some attention to the actual consequences of it, even if they have not always done so in a conscious, deliberate, or sophisticated fashion. In recent years, however, the field of evaluation research has become an increasingly popular and active research specialty, which has been reflected in textbooks, courses, and projects. The growth of evaluation research also indicates a more general trend in the social sciences.

Social scientists, like physical scientists, have tended to distinguish between "pure" and "applied" research. The former has sought fundamental knowledge and understanding, whether of immediate value or not: knowledge for the sake of knowledge. Applied research, as the name implies, has addressed specific, real issues; its justification has depended on the immediate utility of its results. And, as in the physical sciences, pure research has generally been accorded the greater prestige within university communities, whereas applied research has been looked down on as intellectually inferior. The growth of evaluation research in the social sciences is nested within a trend toward greater respectability and acknowledgment for applied research generally.

As I have mentioned, evaluation research has grown enormously in recent years. In part, this growth no doubt reflects social scientists' increasing desire to make an actual difference in the world. At the same time, we cannot discount the influence of (1) increased federal requirements for program evaluations to accompany the implementation of new programs and (2) the availability of research funds to fulfill that requirement. Whatever the mixture of these influences, it seems clear that social scientists will be bringing their skills into the real world more in the future than ever before.

In this chapter, we're going to look at some of the key elements in this form of social research. We'll start by considering the kinds of topics most appropriate to evaluation, and then we'll move through some of the main operational aspects of it: measurement, study design, and execution. As we'll see, formulating questions is as important as answering them.

Evaluation research, since it occurs within real life, has special problems, and we're going to look at some of those. There are particular logistical problems, and we'll see that there are also special ethical issues involved in evaluation research generally and in its specific, technical procedures.

Since evaluation is a form of applied research, it will be useful to consider whether and how it is actually applied. As will become evident, the clear and obvious implications of an evaluation research project do not necessarily have any impact on real life. They may become the focus of ideological, rather than scientific, debates. They may simply be denied out of hand, which occurred when former President Nixon summarily dismissed the conclusions drawn by his commission on pornography. Or, perhaps most typically, they are simply ignored and forgotten, left to warp shelves and collect dust in bookcases across the land.

After presenting some illustrations of evaluation research, I'm going to change topics slightly by focusing on a particular resource for large-scale evaluation—*social indicators* research. This type of research is also a rapidly growing specialty. Essentially this method involves the creation of aggregated indicators of the "health" of society, similar to the economic indicators that give diagnoses and prognoses of economies.

The chapter concludes with an examination of the salient strengths and weaknesses of evaluation research.

TOPICS APPROPRIATE TO EVALUATION RESEARCH

Most fundamentally, evaluation research is appropriate whenever some *social intervention* occurs or is planned. It is specifically appropriate whenever a new social program or process is introduced for the purpose of achieving a particular result. In its simplest sense, evaluation research is a process of determining whether the intended result was produced.

Suppose, for example, that we have the good idea that conjugal visits would improve morale at a prison. (In such programs, prisoners are permitted to have sex periodically with their spouses.) If we were to institute such a program, it would be nice to know if morale actually improved. Conceivably, the program might have no overall effect on morale and it could even make matters worse than before. An evaluation research project could be designed to test the impact of the program. Essentially, it would involve devising some measure of morale, creating experimental and control groups of prisoners, letting the experimental group have conjugal visits for a while, then measuring the levels of morale in the two groups. If morale was significantly higher in the experimental group, we might conclude that conjugal visits did the trick. As we'll see in the following discussions of this chapter, there's much more to evaluation research than this simple illustration suggests, but you should get the general idea of what's involved.

To take another example, you might believe, as some educational reformers do, that grading in schools is counterproductive to the process of real learning. If you were in a position to do something about it, you might be tempted to put a halt to grading. Again, however, it would be nice to know if the innovation produced the intended result, did nothing, or even produced some unintended result that you'd prefer not to have.

The substantive topics appropriate to evaluation research are limitless. When the federal government abolished the selective service system, military researchers began paying special attention to the impact on enlistments. As individual states have greatly liberalized their marijuana laws, researchers have sought to learn the consequences, both in terms of marijuana use and in terms of other forms of social behavior. Do no-fault divorce reforms increase the number of divorces, and are related social problems lessened or increased? Has no-fault automobile insurance really brought down insurance policy premiums? As you can see, the questions appropriate to evaluation research are of great practical significance. Let's turn now to an examination of how these questions are answered—how evaluations are conducted.

FORMULATING THE PROBLEM

Several years ago, I headed an institutional research office that had the task of conducting research of direct relevance to the operation of the university. Often, we were asked to evaluate new programs in the curriculum. The following description is fairly typical of the problem that arose in that context, and it points to one of the key barriers to good evaluation research.

Faculty members would appear at my office to say they had been told by the university administration to arrange to have evaluations made of new programs they had been given permission to try. The way I've put that points to a very common problem: often the people whose programs are being evaluated aren't thrilled at the prospect. For them, an independent evaluation poses a threat to the survival of the program and perhaps an even more far-reaching occupational threat. Forced evaluation, though quite common, presents special problems that we'll discuss later on.

The main problem I want to introduce, however, has to do with the purpose of the intervention that is to be evaluated. The question "What is the intended result of the new program?" often produced a rather vague response; for example, "Students will get an in-depth and genuine understanding of mathematics, instead of simply memorizing methods of calculation." Fabulous! And how could we measure that "in-depth and genuine" understanding? Often, I was told that the program aimed at producing something that could not be measured by conventional aptitude and achievement tests. No problem there; that's to be expected when we're innovating and being unconventional. What would be an unconventional measure of the intended result? Sometimes, this discussion came down to an assertion that what was to be produced by the program was "unmeasurable."

There's the common rub in evaluation research: measuring the "unmeasurable." Whereas evaluation as a psychosocial process involves matters of "right" and "wrong," "good" and "bad," and so forth, evaluation research as a scientific undertaking is a matter of finding out whether something is there or not there, whether something happened or didn't happen. In order to conduct evaluation research, it must be possible to operationalize, observe, and recognize the presence or absence of what is under study.

In the case of the innovative math program, it would be possible to measure (1) increased mathematical achievement, (2) increased subjective enjoyment of mathematics, (3) a greater likelihood of students selecting mathematics as a college major, (4) a greater sense of the value of mathematics as a logical approach to living, and any number of other possible outcomes. To conduct evaluation research, however, it is necessary to devise a measure of what is to be evaluated and to create a research design that frames the meaning of such measurements. Ultimately, we must create a research design that specifies the conditions under which various evaluations (for example, successful/unsuccessful, functional/dysfunctional) will be the conclusions associated with specified research outcomes. Let's see some of the ways of making such a design.

Measurement

Earlier chapters in this book have already discussed *how* to measure in some depth, and those earlier discussions apply to evaluation research. In the present case, it will be more useful to focus our attention on *what* to measure.

Clearly, a key variable to be measured is the *outcome* or *response* variable. If a social program is intended to accomplish something, we must be able to measure that something. If we want to reduce prejudice, we need to be able to measure prejudice. If we want to increase marital harmony, we need to be able to measure that. The way I've put it is a little too simplistic, however. As Riecken and Boruch point out, there are usually multiple responses to consider, and some of them are negative in relation to the program's purpose.[1]

When, for example, Meyer and Borgatta set out to evaluate the effects of a mental rehabilitation program, they created a list of behaviors and conditions to specify the general goal of "patient recovery." The list included the following dimensions and aspects of recovery:

- Not being recommitted to an institution.
- Being independent of rehabilitation agencies.
- Being effective in social relations.
- Being economically independent.

[1]Henry W. Riecken and Robert F. Boruch, *Social Experimentation: A Method for Planning and Evaluating Social Intervention* (New York: Academic Press, 1974), p. 118 ff.

- Being oriented toward reality.
- Enjoying a general well-being.[2]

Notice the value of specifying several different aspects of the desired outcome. If the rehabilitation program achieved one of these goals at the expense of others, it might be considered unsuccessful. If patients, for example, were saved from being recommitted to mental health institutions at the expense of making them dependent on, say, welfare agencies, that would probably be regarded as simply trading one problem for another. It is essential, therefore, that the researcher recognize and take account of all possible aspects of the program's outcomes.

Intended outcomes such as those listed above, of course, are not specified sufficiently for measurement. How much *well-being* is enough? And what would *well-being* look like in real life? How could we tell if it occurred or not? Even something like not being recommitted to an institution is subject to varied interpretations. Suppose a patient stayed overnight for follow-up observation? That probably wouldn't be considered recommitment. But suppose it was three days of observation, or seven days? And suppose the observation was ordered by authorities because of the patient's behavior on the outside? You can see how the line between recommitment and nonrecommitment can become fuzzy. Even where medical or legal definitions of commitment exist, they might not be appropriate to the evaluation of the program.

Measuring the dependent variables directly involved in the experimental program is only a beginning. As Riecken and Boruch point out, it is often appropriate and important to measure "complementary" variables.[3] These are variables external to the experiment itself, yet consequential to it. Suppose, for example, that you are evaluating a program aimed at training unskilled people for employment. Your primary outcome measure would be their success at gaining employment after completing the program. While you would, of course, observe and calculate your subjects' employment rate, you should also determine what has happened to the employment/unemployment rates of the society at large during the time of your evaluation. If there is a general slump in the job market, that should be taken into account in assessing what might otherwise seem a pretty low employment rate for subjects. Or, on the other hand, all of your experimental subjects might get jobs following the program, but that might be more due to a general increase in available jobs than to the value of the program itself. Combining complementary measures with proper control group designs should allow you to pinpoint the effects of the program you are evaluating.

In addition to making measurements relevant to the outcomes of the experiment, you must also measure the experimental stimulus. In part, this measurement will be handled by the assignment of subjects to experimental and control groups, if that's your research design. Assigning a person to the experimental group is the same as scoring that person "yes" on the stimulus, and assignment to the control group represents a score of "no." In practice, however, it's seldom that simple and straightforward.

[2]H. J. Meyer and E. F. Borgatta, *An Experiment in Mental Patient Rehabilitation* (New York: Russell Sage Foundation, 1959), cited by Riecken and Boruch, *op. cit.*, p. 119.
[3]Riecken and Boruch, *op. cit.*, pp. 120-121.

Let's stick with the job-training example mentioned above. Some people will participate in the program, others will not. But imagine for a moment what job-training programs are probably like in practice. Some participants will participate fully, others will miss a lot of sessions or fool around when they are present. It might be appropriate, therefore, to have additional measures of the extent or quality of participation in the program. If the program is effective, then, we should expect to find those participating fully to have higher employment rates than those who participated less.

Other factors may further confound the administration of the experimental stimulus. Suppose you are evaluating a new form of psychotherapy. Several therapists administer it to subjects composing an experimental group. The recovery rate of the experimental group will be compared with that of a control group (a group receiving some other therapy or none at all). It might be very useful to include the names of the specific therapists treating specific subjects in the experimental group, since some may be more effective than others. If that turns out to be the case, your job now becomes one of finding out why it worked better for some therapists than for others. What you learn about that question will further elaborate your understanding of the therapy itself.

It is usually necessary to make certain measurements regarding the nature of the population of subjects involved in the program being evaluated. To start, it will be appropriate to define and measure those characteristics that determine who the program is appropriate for. If you are evaluating a new form of psychotherapy, it's probably appropriate for people with mental problems, but how will you define and measure mental problems more specifically? The job-training program mentioned above is probably intended for people who are having trouble finding work, but a more specific definition would be needed.

This process of definition and measurement has two aspects. First, the population of possible subjects for the evaluation must be defined. Then, ideally, all or a sample of appropriate subjects would be assigned to experimental and control groups as warranted by your study design. Beyond defining the relevant population, however, it is usually wise to make fairly precise measurements on the variables considered in your definition for the specific subjects in the study. Even though the randomization of subjects in the psychotherapy study would insure an equal distribution of those with mild and severe mental problems in the experimental and control groups, you'd do well to keep track of the relative severity of different subjects' problems in case the therapy turns out to be effective only for those with mild cases. Similarly, you should measure such demographic variables as sex, age, race, and so forth in case it only works for women, the elderly, or whatever.

Second, in providing for the measurement of these different kinds of variables, you have a continuing choice: to create new measures or use some that have already been devised and used by other researchers. If you need to measure something that's never been measured before, your choice is an easy one. If not, you'll have to evaluate the relative worth of various existing measurement devices in the context of your specific research situations and purpose. And you'll recall, this is a general issue in social research—applying well beyond evaluation research. Let me review briefly the advantages of the two options.

Creating measurements specifically for your own study has the advantage of greater possible relevance and validity. If the psychotherapy you are evaluating is aimed at a specific aspect of recovery, you can create measures that pinpoint that aspect. You might not be able to find any standardized psychological measures that hit that aspect right on the head. On the other hand, however, creating your own measure would cost you the advantages to be gained from using preexisting measures. Creating good measures takes time and energy, both of which could be saved by adopting an existing technique. Of greater scientific significance, measures that have been used frequently by other researchers carry a body of possible comparisons that might be important to your evaluation. If the experimental therapy raises scores by an average of, say, 10 points on a standardized test, you would be in a position to compare that therapy with others that had been evaluated using the same standardized measure. Finally, measures with a long history of use usually have known degrees of validity and reliability, whereas newly created measures will require pretesting or, worse, will be used with considerable uncertainty.

As you can see, measurement is something to be taken very seriously in evaluation research. You need to be careful in determining all the variables that should be measured and get appropriate measures for each. I should mention that such decisions are typically not purely scientific ones. As an evaluation researcher, you will probably work out your measurement strategy with those people who are responsible for the program that is being evaluated. In one sense, of course, it would be stupid not to do so. It usually doesn't make sense to determine whether a program achieves Outcome X when its purpose is to achieve Outcome Y. (Realize, however, that you may sometimes have the purpose of testing for unintended consequences.)

There is a political aspect in these choices, also. Since evaluation research often affects other people's professional interests—their pet program may be halted, or they may be fired or lose professional standing—the results of evaluation research are often argued about. We'll look at this aspect more fully in a later section. For now, however, you should recognize the advantage of gaining agreement as to appropriate measures in advance. Many subsequent headaches can be avoided or lessened if those running the experimental program will agree in advance on the criteria of success or failure as indicated by specific measurements.

Experimental Designs

Chapter 10 has already given you a good introduction to the variety of experimental designs that social researchers use in studying social life. Many of those same designs are appropriate to evaluation research. By way of illustration, let's see how the classical experimental model might be applied to an evaluation of the new psychotherapy mentioned above.

Let's imagine that the therapy is designed to cure sexual impotence. To begin, then, it would be necessary to identify a population of patients relevant to the therapy. This identification might be made by the group planning to experiment with the new therapy. Let's say we are dealing with a clinic that already has

100 patients being treated for sexual impotence. We might take that existing identification-definition as a starting point, and we should maintain any existing assessments of the severity of the problem for each specific patient.

For purposes of the evaluation research, however, we'll need to develop a more specific measure of impotence. Maybe it will involve whether patients have sexual intercourse at all (within a specified time), how often they have intercourse, or whether and how often they reach orgasm. Taking a very different tack, the outcome measure might be based on the assessments of independent therapists who would not be involved in the therapies but would interview the patients subsequently. In any event, we would need to reach an agreement on the measures to be used.

In the simplest of designs, we would assign the 100 patients randomly to experimental and control groups; the former would receive the new therapy and the latter would be taken out of therapy altogether for the course of the experiment. Since that is unlikely, however, the control group might continue to receive whatever conventional therapy they are already receiving. (Notice the ethical issue that would probably prevent withdrawing therapy altogether from the control group. Also notice the political issue: continuing their regular therapy avoids the embarrassing possibility that *no* therapy might prove more effective than the new one.)

Having assigned subjects to the experimental and control groups, we would need to agree on the length of the experiment. Perhaps the dsigners of the new therapy would feel it ought to be effective within two months, and an agreement could be reached. The duration of the study doesn't need to be rigid, however. One purpose of the experiment and evaluation might be to determine how long it actually takes for the new therapy to be effective. Conceivably, then, an agreement could be struck to measure recovery rates weekly, say, and let the ultimate length of the experiment rest on a continual review of the results.

Let's suppose that the new therapy involves showing pronographic movies to patients. We'd need to specify that stimulus. How often would patients see the movies and how long would each session be? Would they see the movies in private or in groups? Should therapists be present? Perhaps it would be appropriate to observe the patients during the showing of the movies and include those observations in the measurements related to the administration of the experimental stimulus. Do some patients watch the movies eagerly and others keep looking away from the screen? These are the kinds of questions that would need to be asked, and specific measurements would have to be created.

Having thus designed the study, all we have to do is "roll 'em." The study is set in motion, the observations are made and recorded, and the mass of data is accumulated for analysis. Once the study has run its course, we would be in a position to determine whether the new therapy had its intended—or perhaps some unintended —consequences. We could tell whether the movies were most effective on patients with mild problems or severe ones, whether it worked for men but not women, and so forth.

This simple illustration should show you how the standard experimental designs presented in Chapter 10 can be used in evaluation research. Being nested in real life, however, evaluation research often calls for what are called *quasi-experimental* designs. Let's see what that means.

Quasi-Experimental Designs

Quasi-experiments are primarily distinguished from "true" experiments by the lack of random assignment of subjects to an experimental and a control group. In evaluation research, it is often impossible to achieve such an assignment of subjects. Rather than forego evaluation altogether in such instances, it is sometimes possible to create and execute research designs that give some evaluation of the program in question. In this section, I'll briefly describe some of the designs used.

Time-Series Designs   To illustrate the time-series design, I want to begin by asking you to assess the meaning of some hypothetical data. Suppose I come to you with what I say is an effective technique for getting students to *participate* in classroom sessions of a course I am teaching. To prove my assertion, I tell you that on Monday, only four students asked questions or made a comment in class; on Wednesday I devoted the class time to an open discussion of a controversial issue raging on campus (an issue having nothing to do with the subject matter of the course); and on Friday, when we returned to the subject matter of the course, eight students asked questions or made comments. In other words, I contend, the discussion of a controversial issue on Wednesday has doubled classroom participation. This simple set of data is presented graphically in Figure 11-1.

Figure 11-1   Two Observations of Class Participation: Before and After an Open Discussion

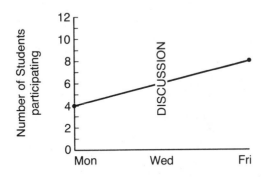

Have I persuaded you that the open discussion on Wednesday has had the consequence I say it has? Probably, you'd object that my data don't prove the case. Two observations (Monday and Friday) aren't really enough to prove anything. Ideally I should have had two classes, with students assigned randomly to each, held an open discussion in only one, and then compared the two on Friday. I don't have two classes with random assignment of students. *But*, I tell you that I've been keeping a record of class participation throughout the semester for the one class. This record would allow you to conduct a time-series evaluation.

Figure 11-2 presents three different patterns that might be discovered when we looked at the level of class participation over time—both before and after the open discussion on Wednesday. Which of these patterns would give you some confidence that the discussion had the impact I contend it had?

Figure 11-2   Three Patterns of Class Participation in a Longer Historical Perspective

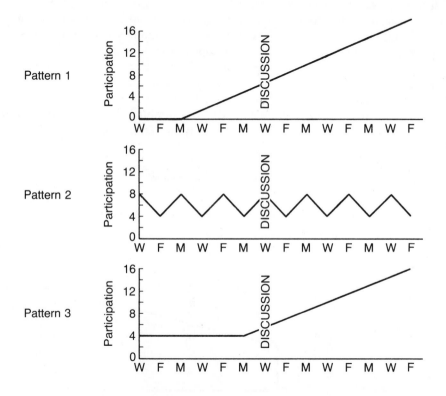

If the time-series results looked like Pattern 1 in Figure 11-2, you'd probably conclude that a process of even greater class participation had begun on the Wednesday before the discussion and that the process had continued, unaffected, after the day devoted to the discussion. The long-term data seem to suggest that the trend would have occurred even without the discussion on Wednesday. Pattern 1, then, contradicts my assertion that the special discussion increased class participation.

Pattern 2 contradicts my assertion also. It indicates that class participation has been bouncing up and down in a regular pattern through the whole semester. Sometimes it increases from one class to the next, and sometimes it decreases; the open discussion on that Wednesday simply came at a time when the level of participation was due to increase. More to the point, we noted that class participation decreased again at the next class following the alleged postdiscussion increase.

Only Pattern 3 in Figure 11-2 would support my contention that the open discussion mattered. As we see, the level of discussion before that Wednesday had been a steady four students per class. Not only did the level of participation double following the day of discussion, but it continued to increase further afterward. Although these data do not protect us against the possible influence of some extraneous factor (I might have also mentioned that participation would figure into students' grades), it does guard against a process of maturation (indicated in Pattern 1) or the regular fluctuations indicated in Pattern 2.

Multiple Time-Series Designs   Sometimes the evaluation of processes occurring outside of "pure" experimental controls can be facilitated through the use of several different time-series analyses. Carol Weiss has presented a useful example of this design:

> An interesting example of multiple time series was the evaluation of the Connecticut crackdown on highway speeding. Evaluators collected reports of traffic fatalities for several periods before and after the new program went into effect. They found that fatalities went down after the crackdown, but since the series had had an unstable up-and-down pattern for many years, it was not certain that the drop was due to the program. They then compared the statistics with time-series data from four neighboring states where there had been no changes in traffic enforcement. Those states registered no equivalent drop in fatalities. The comparison lent credence to the conclusion that the crackdown had had some effect.[4]

Nonequivalent Control Groups   The two time-series designs just described only involve an "experimental" group, and you'll recall the value to be gained from having a control group. Sometimes, when it's not possible to create experimental and control groups by random assignment from a common pool, it is nonetheless possible to find a "control" group already in existence that appears to be similar to the experimental group. If an innovative foreign language program is being tried in one class in a large high school, for example, you may be able to find another foreign language class in the same school that has a very similar student population: one that has about the same composition in terms of grade in school, sex, ethnicity, IQ, and so forth. The second class, then, could provide a point of comparison. At the end of the semester, both classes could be given the same foreign language test, and you could compare performances.

Although this study design is not as good as one in which students are assigned randomly, it is nonetheless an improvement over assessing the experimental group's performance without any comparison. That's what makes these designs quasi-*experiments* instead of just fooling around.

---

[4]Carol H. Weiss, *Evaluation Research* (Englewood Cliffs, N.J.: Prentice-Hall), 1972, p. 69.

Operationalizing Success/Failure

Potentially, one of the most taxing aspects of evaluation research is determining whether the program under review succeeded or failed. The purpose of the foreign language program mentioned above may be to help students do better in learning the language, but how much better is *better enough*? The purpose of the conjugal visit program at a prison may be to raise morale, but *how high* does morale need to be raised to justify the program?

As you may anticipate, there are almost never clear-cut answers to questions like these. This dilemma has surely been the source of what is generally called *cost/ benefit analysis*. How much does the program cost in relation to what it returns in benefits? If the benefits outweigh the cost, keep it. If the reverse, junk it. That's simple enough, and it seems to apply in straightforward economic situations: if it costs you $20 to produce something and you can only sell it for $18, there's no way you can make up for that in volume.

Unfortunately, the situations usually faced by evaluation researchers are seldom amenable to straightforward economic accounting. The foreign language program may cost an extra $100, and it may raise students' performances on tests by an average of 15 points. Since the test scores can't be converted into dollars, there's no obvious grounds for weighing the costs and benefits.

Sometimes, as a practical matter, the criteria of success and failure can be handled through competition among programs. If a second foreign language program only costs $50 and produces an increase of 20 points in test scores, it would undoubtedly be considered more successful than the first program—assuming that test scores were seen as an appropriate measure of the purpose of both programs.

Ultimately, the criteria of success and failure are often a matter of agreement. The person responsible for the program may commit himself or herself in advance to a particular outcome that will be regarded as an indication of success. If that's the case, all you, as the evaluation researcher, need do is make absolutely certain that your research design will permit a measurement of the specified outcome. I mention something as obvious as this requirement simply because researchers sometimes fail to meet it, and there's little or nothing more embarrassing than that.

THE SOCIAL CONTEXT

Many of the comments in previous sections have hinted at the possibility of problems in the actual execution of evaluation research projects. Of course, all forms of research can run into problems, but evaluation research has a special propensity for it, and I want to draw your attention to some of these difficult aspects. We're going to look at some of the logistical problems that can hinder evaluation research. Then, we'll consider some of the special ethical issues evaluation touches. Finally, I want to make a few comments about the utilization of evaluation research results.

Logistical Problems

In a military context, *logistics* refers to moving supplies around—making sure people have food, guns, and tent pegs when they need them. In this context, I use it to refer to getting subjects to do what they're supposed to do, getting research instruments distributed and returned, and other seemingly unchallenging tasks. These tasks are more challenging than you would guess!

The special, logistical problems of evaluation research grow out of the fact that it occurs within the context of real life. Although evaluation research is modeled after the experiment—which suggests that we have control over what happens—it takes place within frequently uncontrollable daily life. Of course, the participant observer in field research doesn't have control over what is observed either, but that method does not strive for control. If you realize the importance of this lack of control, I think you'll start to understand the dilemma facing the evaluation researcher.

Let's suppose you're evaluating the conjugal visit program I've referred to earlier. On the fourth day of the program, a male prisoner knocks out his wife, dresses up in her clothes, and escapes. Although you might be tempted to assume that his morale was greatly improved by escaping, that turn of events would complicate your study design in many ways. Perhaps the warden will terminate the program altogether, and where's your evaluation then? (You'll *never* complete a dissertation.) Or, if the warden is braver, he or she may review the files of all those prisoners you selected randomly for the experimental group and veto the "bad risks." There goes the comparability of your experimental and control groups. As an alternative, stricter security measures may be introduced to prevent further escapes, and the security measures may have a dampening effect on morale. Not only has the experimental stimulus changed, it has changed in the middle of your research project. Some of your data will reflect the original stimulus, other data will reflect the modification. Although you'll probably be able to sort it all out, your carefully designed study has become a logical snakepit.

Maybe you've been engaged to evaluate the effect of race relations lectures on prejudice in the army. You've carefully studied the soldiers available to you for study, and you've randomly assigned some to attend the lectures and others to stay away. The rosters have been circulated weeks in advance, and at the appointed day and hour, the lectures begin. Everything seems to be going smoothly, until you begin processing the files: the names don't match. Checking around, you discover that military field exercises, KP duty, and a variety of emergencies required some of the experimental subjects to be elsewhere at the time of the lectures. That's bad enough, but then you learn that helpful commanding officers sent others to fill in for the missing soldiers. And whom do you suppose they picked to fill in? Soldiers who didn't have anything else to do or who couldn't be trusted to do anything important. You might learn this bit of information a week or so before the deadline for submitting your final report on the impact of the race relations lectures.

In most evaluation research you are working for someone else and with the cooperation of others. Those you need to depend on may not be fully versed in the niceties of research design, and they may often make changes or refuse cooperation in ways they feel to be inconsequential, but your evaluation may fall apart as a result.

Some Ethical Issues

In part, the ethical issues of evaluation research are the issues engaged by the social interventions being evaluated. Doing an evaluation of the impact of busing schoolchildren to achieve educational integration will throw you directly into the political, ideological, and ethical issues of busing itself. You can't evaluate a sex education program in elementary schools without becoming involved in the heated issues surrounding sex education per se, and your involvement is by no means just that of an impartial observer. Your evaluation study design will *require* that some children be exposed to sex education—in fact, you may very well be the one who decides which children are exposed. (From a scientific standpoint, you *should* be in charge of selection.) That means that when parents become outraged that *their* child is being taught about sex, you will be the one directly responsible.

If the program you are evaluating turns out to have negative side effects for the participants, guess who shares in the responsibility for that. You do. There you are evaluating the morale value of a pottery class at the state prison, and one of the prisoners gets stuffed in the kiln by an enemy. Who selected the victim and his enemy for the class? You and your table of random numbers.

Now, let's look on the "bright" side. Maybe the experimental program is of great value to those participating in it. Let's say you've found that the new industrial safety program you're evaluating reduces injuries dramatically. What about the control group members who were deprived of the program by you and your table of random numbers? Your actions as an evaluator are an important part of the reason that a control group subject suffered an injury.

My purpose in these comments has not been to discourage you from doing evaluation research or to make you feel bad when you do it. Rather, I want to bring home the real-life consequences of the evaluation researcher's actions. Otherwise, you might find yourself unhappily surprised by the way things turn out. As with so many other potential problems in social research, advance warning and awareness may be a sufficient safeguard.

Finally, all the ethical issues raised in Chapter 3 are especially real for evaluation researchers. The problems of deception, confidentiality, and so forth crop up in most evaluation projects. The safeguards and guidelines presented in Chapter 3 should be reviewed whenever you design and launch any evaluation research project.

Utilization of Research Results

There's one more facts-of-life aspect of evaluation research that you should be aware of. Recalling that the purpose of evaluation research is to determine the success or failure of social interventions, it would seem reasonable that the continuation or termination of such interventions should follow automatically from the results of the research. If a particular program is seen to be enormously successful in achieving its objective, then it should be continued. If it fails, it should bite the dust.

In practice, however, things are not that simple and reasonable. Other factors intrude on the assessment of evaluation research results, sometimes blatantly and sometimes more subtly. As president, Richard Nixon appointed a blue-ribbon national commission to study the consequences of pornography. After a diligent, multifaceted evaluation, the commission reported that pornography didn't appear to have any of the negative social consequences often attributed to it. Exposure to pornographic materials, for example, didn't increase the likelihood of sex crimes. You might have expected liberalized legislation to follow from the research. Instead, the president said they were wrong.

Less dramatic examples of the failure to follow the implications of evaluation research could be listed endlessly. Undoubtedly every evaluation researcher can point to studies he or she conducted—studies providing clear research results and obvious policy implications—that were subsequently ignored.

There are three important reasons why the implications of the evaluation research results are not always put into practice. First, the implications are not always presented in a way that can be understood by nonresearchers. It is worth bearing in mind that the clear communication of findings is as critical a part of effective research as the careful designing of the study.

Second, evaluation results, like other social science findings, sometimes contradict deeply held beliefs. That was certainly evident in the case of the pornography commission mentioned above. If everybody *knows* that pornography is bad, that it causes all manner of sexual deviance, then it is likely that research results to the contrary will have little immediate impact. By the same token, people thought Copernicus was crazy when he said the earth revolved around the sun. Anybody could tell the earth was standing still.

The third barrier to the utilization of evaluation results has been hinted at above from time to time: *vested interests*. If I have devised a new rehabilitation program that I'm convinced will keep exconvicts from returning to prison, and if people have taken to calling it "The Babbie Plan," how do you think I'm going to feel when you conduct an evaluation that suggests the program doesn't work? I might apologize for misleading people, fold up my tent, and go into another line of work. Or, more likely, I might call your research worthless and begin intense lobbying with the appropriate authorities to have the program continue.

Realize therefore that the utilization of evaluation research findings is by no means automatic or assured. At the same time, I don't want to create an image of evaluation as inconsequential. In fact, the first illustration below should demonstrate just the opposite.

ILLUSTRATIONS OF EVALUATION RESEARCH

In this section, I'm going to present two examples of evaluation research. The first example concerns the use of bail in releasing criminal defendants before trial, and I think you'll find the results of the study interesting. The second example is taken from the realm of mental health, and in the process of presenting it, I'll point you toward many other illustrations of evaluation research.

Bye-Bye Bail Bonds

The Manhattan Bail Project is a frequently cited example of evaluation research in action.[5] It's a reasonably neat and clean illustration, and it has the added appeal that the program under evaluation proved an effective alternative to what many regard as a social problem. The problem, in this case, is the system of bail bonds, a traditional element in our legal system. People awaiting trial are often allowed to spend the waiting time outside of jail if they can post a substantial amount of money to insure that they will not skip town. The profession of bail bondsman has grown up and flourished around that system. Those who cannot afford, say, a $10,000 bond may be able to pay a bondsman 10 percent of that sum, $1,000. The bondsman then puts up the other $9,000. Once the accused appears for trial, the bond— all $10,000 of it—is returned to the bondsman, and the accused gets nothing.

Many people have criticized the bail system. Some people object to the economic discrimination it fosters. Others have complained that judges sometimes use it in an inappropriate manner: they may set extremely high bail in notorious cases, even though the crime alleged is relatively minor.

Other people have contended that the bail system is not really necessary, or at least that it need not be used as widely as it is. The Manhattan Bail Project, initiated by the Vera Institute in New York, was designed as a test of that contention. The purpose of the project was to determine whether certain kinds of defendants—those with close ties to the community—could be released without bail and still be counted on to appear for their trials.

To undertake the study, the Vera Institute staff interviewed thousands of defendants and examined their files. A scoring system allowed them to rate each defendant's integration into the community so as to identify those expected to stick around even if they were released without bail. Those scored as "good risks" were randomly divided into two groups, an experimental and a control group. The staff recommended release without bail for all those in the experimental group and made no recommendations for those in the control group.

Ideally, of course, all those recommended for release without bail would have gotten it, and all those not recommended wouldn't have. Naturally, it didn't turn out exactly that way. In the first year of study, the judges granted release without bail to 59 percent of those recommended by the researchers and to 16 percent of the control group. In spite of this variation, it was still possible to determine the impact of releasing defendants without bail. More than 99 percent appeared in court for trial at the appropriate time! This level of appearance was easily as high as the normal level under the bail system.

Given the powerful and obvious success of the experiment, the program of release without bail has expanded in a number of ways. First, with increased expe-

[5]See B. Botein, "The Manhattan Bail Project: Its Impact in Criminology and the Criminal Law Process," *Texas Law Review*, Vol. 43 (1965), pp. 319–331.

rience, the Vera staff has gotten better at evaluating defendants and has improved the validity and reliability of its scoring systems. Second, the staff has found it feasible to lower the threshold of "good risk," thus recommending larger portions of defendants for release without bail. The judges, for their part, have steadily increased their reliance on the Vera staff recommendations, going along with a larger proportion of them. Finally, the program has spread to many other jurisdictions, and the bail system in America has been significantly changed as a result of the project.

Mending Mental Health at Home

The second illustration concerns the problem of schizophrenia and its treatment. By way of presentation this time, I want to simply reproduce the project abstract prepared by Robert Boruch for publication in *Social Experimentation*. I have two purposes in presenting this abstract. First, it will introduce you to a brief and systematic way in which evaluation studies are often reported in the literature—particularly when several studies on a given topic are being compared in order to reach a general conclusion. Second, this presentation may encourage you to look at the Riecken and Boruch book firsthand. If you do so, you will discover a fascinating collection of project abstracts as well as an excellent book on evaluation research per se.

Abstract of: *Schizophrenics in the community: an experimental study in the prevention of hospitalization*, by B. Pasemanick, F. R. Scarpetti, and S. Dinitz; with J. Abini, and M. Lefton. New York: Appleton-Century-Crofts, 1967.

Objectives: The study was designed to assess the feasibility and the effectiveness of home care treatment for schizophrenics. The home care, one of a number of possible elements in larger-scale (planned) community health centers, was regarded as a potentially effective substitute for long-term hospitalization.

Description of Program: Home care consisted of regular visits by public health nurses, visits by staff psychiatrists as needed (mainly for diagnostic purposes), and drug medication. Drug treatment was maintained to alleviate acute symptoms and to ameliorate patient difficulties in holding jobs and maintaining relations with family. The main point of the home care effort was to prevent the alienation of patients from society and their families that frequently characterizes long-term hospitalization and to facilitate rehabilitation. Specialized methods were used to introduce the program to the community and to circumvent institutional blocks to the program.

Study Design: Subjects were randomly chosen and assigned to treatment (home care) and control (hospitalization) groups from schizophrenics who had just been admitted to a state mental hospital. Ninety-eight people were eventually assigned to the experimental group and 54 people were assigned to the control condition.

Response Variables: The physical outcome variables included day of hospitalization, days until rehospitalization, and similar indicators. Assessment of functional behavior of patients was accomplished through a battery of four psychological tests, two types of psychiatric evaluations, and ratings of patient functioning by nursing and psychiatric staff.

Results: On the average, control group patients required rehospitalization after release more frequently than the experimental group members did. The program was successful in maintaining at-home treatment and in preventing long-term hospitalization of home care patients. Patient improvement on the psychological measures did not differ across experimental and control groups.[6]

SOCIAL INDICATORS RESEARCH

Let's take a minute now to consider a special form of evaluation research—one hinted at in the earlier discussion of existing statistics. Another rapidly growing field in social research involves the development and monitoring of *social indicators*. Just as economists use indexes such as gross national product (GNP) per capita as an indicator of a nation's economic development, we can monitor other aspects of society in a similar fashion.

If we wanted to compare the relative health conditions in different societies, we could compare their death rates (number of deaths per 1,000 population). Or, more specifically, we could look at infant mortality: the number of infants who die during the first year of life among every 1,000 live births. Depending on the particular aspect of health conditions we were interested in, we could devise any number of other measures: physicians per capita, hospital beds per capita, days of hospitalization per capita, and so forth. Notice that intersocietal comparisons are facilitated by calculating per capita rates (dividing by the size of the population or by some fixed unit such as 1,000s of population).

Before we go further with social indicators, I'd like you to recall the Chapter 9 discussion of the various problems involved in existing statistics. In a word, they are often unreliable, reflecting their modes of collection, storage, and calculation. Bearing that caution in mind, we'll look at some of the ways in which social indicators can be used for purposes of evaluation research on a large scale.

Does the death penalty deter capital crimes such as murder? That question is hotly debated every time a state considers eliminating or reinstating capital punishment. Those supporting capital punishment often argue that the threat of execution will keep potential murderers from killing people. Opponents of capital punishment often argue that it has no effect in that regard. Social indicators can be used to shed some light on the question.

If capital punishment actually deters people from committing murder, then we should expect to find murder rates lower in those states that have the death penalty than in those that do not. The relevant comparisons in this instance are not only possible, they have been compiled and published. Table 11-1 presents data compiled by William Bailey that directly contradict the view that the death penalty deters murderers.[7] In both 1967 and 1968, those states with capital punishment had dramatically *higher* murder rates than those without capital punishment. Some

[6]Riecken and Boruch, *op. cit.*, p. 298.
[7]William C. Bailey, "Murder and Capital Punishment," in William J. Chambliss (ed.), *Criminal Law in Action* (New York: John Wiley, 1975).

people criticized the interpretation of Bailey's data, saying that most states have not used the death penalty in recent years, even when they had it on the books. That could explain why it hasn't seemed to work as a deterrent. Further analysis, however, contradicts that explanation. When Bailey compared those states that hadn't used the death penalty with those that *had*, he found no real difference in murder rates.

Table 11-1   Average Rate per 100,000 Population of First- and Second-Degree Murders for Capital-Punishment and Non-Capital-Punishment States, 1967 and 1968

	Non-Capital-Punishment States		Capital-Punishment States	
	1967	1968	1967	1968
First-degree murder	.18	.21	.47	.58
Second-degree murder	.30	.43	.92	1.03
Total murders	.48	.64	1.38	1.59

Source: Adapted from William C. Bailey, "Murder and Capital Punishment," in William J. Chambliss (ed.), *Criminal Law in Action*. Copyright © 1975 by John Wiley & Sons, Inc. Reprinted by permission of John Wiley & Sons, Inc.

Another counter-explanation is possible, however. It could be the case that the interpretation given Bailey's data was *backwards*. Maybe the existence of the death penalty as an option was a consequence of high murder rates: those states with high rates instituted it, those with low rates didn't institute it or repealed it if they had it on the books. It could be the case, then, that instituting the death penalty would bring murder rates down, while repealing it would increase murders and still produce—in a broad aggregate—the data presented in Table 11-1. Not so, however. Analyses over time do not show an increase in murder rates when a state repeals the death penalty nor a decrease in murders when one is instituted.

Notice from the discussion above that it's possible to use social indicators data either for comparisons across groups at one time or within a particular length of time. And often doing both sheds the most light on the subject.

At present, work on the use of social indicators is proceeding on two fronts. On the one hand, researchers are developing ever more refined indicators—finding which indicators of a general variable are the most useful in monitoring social life. At the same time, research is being devoted to discovering the relationships among variables within whole societies.

One of the more exciting prospects for social indicators research is in the area of *computer simulation*. As we begin compiling mathematical equations describing the relationships that link social variables to one another (for example, what is the relationship between population growth and increases in the number of automobiles?), those equations can be stored and linked to one another in a computer. With a sufficient number of sufficiently accurate equations on tap, it will one day be possible to test the implications of specific social changes by computer rather than in real life. Suppose a state contemplated doubling the size of its tourism industry, for example. It would be possible to enter that proposal into a computer simulation model and receive in seconds or minutes a description of all the direct and indirect consequences of it. It would be possible to know what new public facilities would be required, which public agencies such as police and fire departments would have to be increased and by how much, what the labor force would look like, what kind of training would be required to provide it, how much new income and tax revenue would be produced, and so forth through all the intended and unintended consequences of the action. Depending on the results, the public planners might say, "Suppose we only increased the industry by half," and have a new printout of consequences immediately.

An excellent illustration of computer simulation linking social and physical variables is to be found in the research of Donella and Dennis Meadows and their colleagues at Dartmouth and Massachusetts Institute of Technology.[8] They have taken as input data known and estimated reserves of various nonreplaceable natural resources (for example, oil, coal, iron), past patterns of population and economic growth, and the relationships between growth and use of resources. Using a complex computer simulation model, they have been able to project, among other things, the probable number of years various resources will last in the face of alternative usage patterns in the future. Going beyond the initially gloomy projections, such models also make it possible to chart out less gloomy futures, specifying the actions required to achieve them. Clearly, the value of computer simulation is not limited to evaluation research, though it can serve an important function in that regard.

This potentiality points to the special value of evaluation research in general. Throughout human history, we have been tinkering with our social arrangements, seeking better results. Evaluation research provides a means for us to learn right away whether a particular tinkering really makes things better. Social indicators allow us to make that determination on a broad scale, and coupling them with computer simulation opens up the possibility of knowing how much we would like a particular intervention without having to suffer through it for real.

STRENGTHS AND WEAKNESSES OF EVALUATION RESEARCH

For the most part, the strengths and weaknesses of evaluation research are those of experiments more generally, as already discussed in Chapter 10. And the peculiar strengths and weaknesses of social indicators are those of existing statistics as discussed in Chapter 9. There are some differences, too.

One of the key weaknesses of the experiment, you'll recall, was its artificiality. Bringing behavior into the laboratory has a tendency to change it in the process. What you learn in the laboratory may not accurately represent what would happen in similar circumstances in real life. We saw in Chapter 10 that certain experimental designs can alleviate that problem, and evaluation research—when it is conducted in real social settings—can provide even further protection. Just the fact that an evaluation is being conducted in real social settings, however, is not enough to solve the problem in all cases. As you'll recall from the Hawthorne study, workers became

[8] See Donella Meadows *et al.*, *The Limits to Growth* (New York: Universe Books, 1972), and Dennis Meadows *et al.*, *The Dynamics of Growth in a Finite World* (Cambridge, Mass.: Wright-Allen, 1973).

more productive whenever they were studied, regardless of whether their working conditions were improved or worsened.

The use of social indicators for purposes of evaluation, of course, erases the influence of the research itself. Scrutinizing murder rates has never been found to increase or decrease the number of murders committed (though scrutiny may point to a need to change the *figures* reported). This advantage comes at a cost in terms of both validity and reliability, however. Reported murder rates may underestimate the number of actual murders, and hospital beds per capita may not be a valid indicator of what we mean by *health care* in a society.

Finally, a special appeal of evaluation research is its utility or potential utility. While pure research is exciting and ultimately useful, there is a special satisfaction to be gained from seeing research have an impact in your own lifetime. Evaluation research is one way that you can take a direct responsibility for how your own society turns out.

SUMMARY

This chapter has focused on a particularly practical aspect of social research. As we saw, evaluation research represents the use of an experimental model to examine social intervention and social conditions in the real world. Potentially at least, it allows us to monitor the course of our social life and work rationally toward its improvement.

As is often the case with scientific research generally, we saw that *formulating* the question in evaluation research is a very big part of answering it. In part, that is a matter of measurement, and we saw the kinds of variables that need to be conceptualized and operationalized. Those variables can be manipulated and observed in a variety of ways, and researchers can use both experimental and quasi-experimental designs. An important goal running through the design process is the operationalization of what will be considered success or failure for the program being evaluated.

Evaluation research, through its direct involvement in real life, faces particular problems. Often the operations of the program itself or of the host organization conflict with the scientific design requirements of the evaluation. Often the evaluation loses reliability and validity, particularly when the researcher does not have control. Similarly, evaluation presents special ethical problems and dilemmas. The researcher is often in a damned if you do and damned if you don't position. The program being evaluated may produce harmful effects for subjects, and the evaluation researcher will have been the one to choose who got harmed. On the other hand, if the program under study actually benefits people, the evaluation researcher will be the one to have chosen who was denied those benefits. If the program saves lives, you will be the one who put people in the control group where lives were lost.

Although evaluation research is conducted for the explicit purpose of pointing to policy actions, we saw that those actions do not automatically flow from the results of the study. Deeply ingrained beliefs and feelings as well as special vested interests can get in the way.

Social indicators research offers a different approach to evaluation. Based on existing data, it is unobtrusive and thus avoids the problem of influencing what is being studied. At the same time, social indicators research has the same problems of validity and reliability that apply to the analysis of existing statistics in general. One prospect for the future links social indicators with computer simulation, making it ultimately possible to experiment with whole societies by imitating real-world conditions before committing ourselves to actual decisions that may cause unintended and unexpected consequences.

MAIN POINTS

1. Evaluation research is a good example of applied research in social science.

2. Evaluation research is especially appropriate whenever a *social intervention* is undertaken.

3. A careful formulation of the problem, including relevant measurements and criteria of success or failure, is essential in evaluation research.

4. Evaluation researchers typically use experimental or quasi-experimental designs.

5. A *time-series* design involves the observation of an experimental group over time. It is a weak design in that something other than the experimental stimulus may explain any observed change.

6. Evaluation research entails special logistical and ethical problems because it is embedded in the day-to-day events of real life.

7. It cannot be assumed that the implications of evaluation research will necessarily be put into practice, especially if they conflict with official points of view.

8. *Social indicators* are aggregated descriptions of populations. They can provide an understanding of broad social processes.

9. Sometimes, *computer simulation models* can be constructed so as to point to the possible results of social intervention without having to experience those results in real life.

ANNOTATED BIBLIOGRAPHY

Bennett, Carl A., and Lumsdaine, Arthur A. (eds.), *Evaluation and Experiment* (New York: Academic Press, 1975). Packed with illustrative examples, this reader digs into a number of special aspects of evaluation research. About every problem you are likely to hit is discussed in the book.

Riecken, Henry W., and Boruch, Robert F. (eds.), *Social Experimentation: A Method for Planning and Evaluating Social Intervention* (New York: Academic Press, 1974). As my several references to this book throughout the chapter suggest, it is an excellent basic text for the serious evaluation researcher. It is an especially appropriate companion piece for the Bennett-Lumsdaine book listed above. If you were to master both, you'd be ready to set about some serious (or fun) evaluations.

Weiss, Carol, *Evaluation Research* (Englewood Cliffs, N.J.: Prentice-Hall, 1972). Here's a quicker and easier introduction to evaluation research. In a short paperback, the author gives a good overview of the method and points you toward aspects you might want to learn more about. It is an especially good beginning if you don't have any prior experience in social research in general. This introduction may let you discover that you'd like to get some experience.

Wilcox, Leslie D., *et al.*, *Social Indicators and Societal Monitoring* (New York: Elsevier, 1972). This is not a textbook on social indicators or even an example of their use. Rather, it is a seemingly exhaustive, annotated *bibliography* on the subject. Although it is now a few years old, it provides an excellent entry into further study. Whatever your particular substantive interest, this book will direct you to those studies that have addressed that interest through social indicators research.

CHAPTER 12
Survey Research

INTRODUCTION

This last chapter on modes of observation is addressed to what is perhaps the most frequently used method in the social sciences: *survey research*. I am certain that you have been a respondent in a survey more than once, and it is quite possible that you have done a survey of your own. In a typical survey, the researcher selects a sample of respondents and administers a standardized questionnaire to them.

Chapter 7 has already covered the topic of sampling, referring most often to survey situations. In this chapter, we look at questionnaire construction and then at the two primary methods for administering questionnaires. Sometimes it's appropriate to have respondents complete questionnaires themselves, and other times it's more appropriate to have interviewers ask the questions and record the answers given. We'll examine both methods and then compare their relative advantages and disadvantages.

The chapter concludes with a short discussion of *secondary analysis*: the analysis of survey data collected by someone else, perhaps for some purpose other than that of subsequent analyses. This use of survey results has become an important aspect of survey research in recent years, and it's especially useful for students and others with scarce research funds.

Let's begin by looking at the kinds of topics you could study using survey research.

TOPICS APPROPRIATE TO SURVEY RESEARCH

Surveys may be used for descriptive, explanatory, and exploratory purposes. They are chiefly used in studies that have individual people as the units of analysis. Although this method can be used for other units of analysis, such as groups or interactions, it is necessary that some individual persons are used as respondents or informants. Thus, it would be possible to undertake a survey in which divorces were the unit of analysis, but the survey questionnaire would need to be administered to the participants in the divorces (or to some other informants).

Survey research is probably the best method available to the social scientist interested in collecting original data for purposes of describing a population too large to observe directly. Careful probability sampling provides a group of respondents whose characteristics may be taken as representative of those of the larger population, and carefully constructed standardized questionnaires provide data in the same form from all respondents. Formal government censuses differ from surveys only in that all members of the larger population are studied rather than a sample.

Surveys are also excellent vehicles for the measurement of attitudes and orientations prevalent with a large population. Public opinion polls are a well-known example of this use. Probability sampling and standardized questionnaires provide the means of discovering the prevailing attitudes among a large population.

QUESTIONNAIRE CONSTRUCTION

Questionnaires are used in connection with many modes of observation in social research, but they are essential to and most directly associated with survey research. Thus, it's appropriate that questionnaires be dealt with in this chapter, though you should bear in mind that what you learn here might be useful in doing experiments, field research, and so forth.

This section is, in a sense, a continuation of the operationalization discussion in Chapter 6. You recall that I covered some of the guidelines and techniques for writing *questions* as a culmination of the conceptualization-operationalization process. This section will continue that discussion, showing some of the ways questions are organized and presented in a questionnaire.

As in the earlier discussion of question wording, I'll run the risk of offending you, perhaps, by presenting some nitty-gritty details that may seem unworthy of scientific attention and other details that seem so obvious as to be not worth mentioning. I take the risk, however, because I have made each of the mistakes I'll warn against and have seen others do the same. Let's begin with some issues concerning questionnaire *format*.

General Questionnaire Format

The format of a questionnaire can be just as important as the nature and wording of the questions asked. An improperly laid out questionnaire can lead respondents to miss questions, can confuse them as to the nature of the data desired, and in the extreme, can lead to respondents throwing the questionnaire away. Both general and specific guidelines can be suggested.

As a general rule, the questionnaire should be spread out and uncluttered. You should maximize the white space in your instrument. Inexperienced researchers tend to fear their questionnaire will look too long, and as a result, they squeeze several questions on a single line, abbreviate questions, and try to use as few pages as possible. All these efforts are ill-advised and even dangerous. Putting more than one question on a line will result in some respondents skipping the second question. Abbreviating questions will result in misinterpretations. And more generally, respondents who find they have spent considerable time on the first page of what seemed a short questionnaire will be more demoralized than respondents who quickly completed the first several pages of what initially seemed rather long. Moreover, the latter will have made fewer errors and will not have been forced to reread confusing, abbreviated questions. Nor will they have been forced to write a long answer in a tiny space.

The desirability of spreading questions out in the questionnaire cannot be overemphasized. Squeezed-together questionnaires are disastrous whether they are to be completed by the respondents themselves or to be administered by trained interviewers.

Formats for Respondents

A variety of methods are available for presenting a series of response categories for the respondent to check in answering a given question. It has been my experience that *boxes* adequately spaced apart are the best. If the questionnaire is to be set in type, this can be accomplished easily and neatly. It is also possible to do this with a typewriter, however.

If the questionnaire is typed on a typewriter with brackets, excellent boxes can be produced by a left-bracket, a space, and a right-bracket: [   ]. If brackets are not available, parentheses work reasonably well in the same fashion: ( ). I'd discourage the use of slashes and underscores, however. First, this technique will require considerably more typing effort; and second, the result is not very neat, especially if the response categories must be single-spaced. Figure 12-1 provides a comparison of the different methods.

Figure 12-1   Three Answer Formats

```
[ ] Yes
[ ] No
[ ] Don't know

( ) Yes
( ) No
( ) Don't know
```

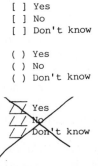

Of the three methods shown, the brackets and the parentheses are clearly the neatest; the slash-and-underscore method simply looks sloppy. Since every typewriter at least has parentheses, there is no excuse for using the slashes and underscores. (It is also much easier to type the brackets or parentheses.)

The worst method of all is to provide open blanks for check marks, since respondents will often enter rather large check marks and it will not be possible to determine which response was intended. As a general rule, moreover, it is always best to double-space between response categories to avoid ambiguous check marks.

A very different method might also be considered. Rather than providing boxes to be checked, the researcher might consider entering code numbers beside each response and asking the respondent to *circle* the appropriate number. This method has the added advantage of specifying the number to be punched later in the processing stage. I have had little experience with this method, but my initial experimentation has been favorable. If it is used, however, the researcher should provide clear and prominent instructions to the respondent, because many will be tempted to cross out the appropriate number, thereby making punching even more difficult. (*Note*: The technique can be used more safely in those studies in which interviewers will administer the questionnaires, since they can be specially instructed and supervised.) Figure 12-2 illustrates this last method.

Figure 12-2   Circling the Answer

```
            1.   Yes
          ( 2.)  No
            3.   Don't know
```

Contingency Questions

Quite often in questionnaires, certain questions will clearly be relevant only to some of the respondents and irrelevant to others. In a study of birth control methods, for instance, you would probably not want to ask men if they take birth control pills.

Frequently, this situation will arise when you wish to ask a series of questions about a certain topic—realizing that the topic is relevant only to some respondents. You may want to ask whether your respondents belong to a particular organization and, if so, how often they attend meetings, whether they have held office in the organization, and so forth. Or, you might want to ask whether respondents have heard anything about a certain political issue and then learn the attitudes of those who have heard of it.

The subsequent questions in series such as these are called **contingency questions** (or filter questions)—whether they are to be asked and answered is contingent on responses to the first question in the series. The proper use of contingency questions can facilitate the respondents' task in completing the questionnaire in that they are not faced with the problem of answering questions that are irrelevant to them.

There are several formats for contingency questions. The one shown in Figure 12-3 is probably the clearest and most effective. Note two key elements in this format. First, the contingency question is isolated from the other questions by being set off to the side and by being enclosed in a box. Second, an arrow connects the contingency question to the answer upon which it is contingent. In the illustration, only those respondents answering "yes" are expected to answer the contingency question. The rest of the respondents should simply skip it.

It should be noted that the questions shown in Figure 12-3 could have been dealt with in a single question. The question might have read: "How many times, if any, have you smoked marijuana?" The response categories, then, might have read: "Never," "Once," "2 to 5 times," and so forth. Such a single question, then, would apply to all respondents, and each would find an appropriate answer category. Such a question, however, would appear to put some pressure on respondents to report having smoked marijuana, since the main question asks how many times they have smoked it, even though it allows for those *exceptional cases* who have *never smoked marijuana even once*. (The emphases used in the previous sentence give a fair indication of how respondents might read the question.) The contingency question format illustrated in Figure 12-3 should reduce the subtle pressure on respondents to report having smoked marijuana. The foregoing discussion should show how seemingly theoretical issues of *validity* and *reliability* are involved in so mundane a matter as how to put questions on a piece of paper.

Figure 12-3   Contingency Question Format

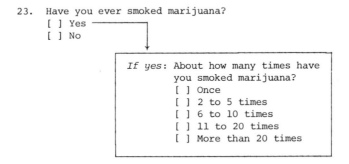

Used properly, even rather complex sets of contingency questions can be constructed without confusing the respondent. Figure 12-4 illustrates a more complicated example.

Sometimes it may be the case that a set of contingency questions is so long as to extend over several pages. Suppose you were studying political activities of college students, and you wished to ask a large number of questions of those students who had voted in a national, state, or local election. You could separate out the relevant

Figure 12-4   Complex Contingency Question

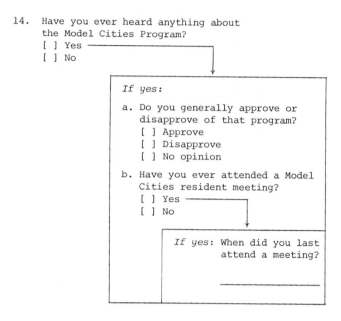

14. Have you ever heard anything about
    the Model Cities Program?
    [ ] Yes
    [ ] No

> **If yes:**
>
> a. Do you generally approve or
>   disapprove of that program?
>   [ ] Approve
>   [ ] Disapprove
>   [ ] No opinion
>
> b. Have you ever attended a Model
>   Cities resident meeting?
>   [ ] Yes
>   [ ] No
>
> > **If yes:** When did you last
> > attend a meeting?
> >
> > _____

respondents with an initial question such as "Have you ever voted in a national, state, or local election?" but it would not make sense to place all the contingency questions in a box stretching over several pages. Instead, it would make more sense to enter instructions in parentheses after each answer telling respondents whether to answer or skip the contingency questions. Figure 12-5 provides an illustration of this method.

Figure 12-5   Instructions to Skip

13. Have you ever voted in a national, state, or local
    election?
    [ ] Yes   (Please answer questions 14-25)
    [ ] No   (Please skip questions 14-25. Go directly
              to question 26 on page 8.)

In addition to these instructions, it would be of additional value to place an instruction at the top of each of the subsequent pages containing only the contingency questions. For example, you might say, "This page is only for respondents who have voted in a national, state, or local election." Clear instructions such as these spare respondents the frustration of reading and puzzling over questions that are irrelevant to them as well as increasing the likelihood of responses from those for whom the questions are relevant.

Figure 12-6 Matrix Question Format

```
17.  Beside each of the statements presented below,
     please indicate whether you Strongly Agree (SA),
     Agree (A), Disagree (D), Strongly Disagree (SD),
     or are Undecided (U).

                          SA   A    D    SD   U
     a. What this country
        needs is more law and
        order. . . . . . . . [ ]  [ ]  [ ]  [ ]  [ ]
     b. The police should be
        disarmed in America. . [ ]  [ ]  [ ]  [ ]  [ ]
     c. During riots, looters
        should be shot on
        sight. . . . . . . . [ ]  [ ]  [ ]  [ ]  [ ]
     etc.
```

Matrix Questions

Quite often, you will want to ask several questions that have the same set of answer categories. This is typically the case whenever the Likert response categories are used. In such cases, it is often possible to construct a matrix of items and answers as illustrated in Figure 12-6.

This format has a number of advantages. First, it is efficient in its use of space. Second, respondents will probably find it faster to complete a set of questions presented in this fashion. In addition, this format may increase the comparability of responses given to different questions for the respondent as well as the researcher. Since the respondents can quickly review the answers given to earlier items in the set, they might choose between, say, "strongly agree" and "agree" on a given statement by comparing their strength of agreement with their earlier responses in the set.

There are some dangers inherent in using this format as well. Its advantages may encourage you to include items in a matrix that might be more appropriately presented in a different format. For example, you might try to structure the item so as to use the response being called for in the matrix when a different, more idiosyncratic, set of responses might be more appropriate.

Also, the matrix-question format can foster a *response-set* among some respondents—they may develop a pattern of, say, agreeing with all the statements. That would be especially likely if the set of statements began with several that indicated a particular orientation (for example, a liberal political perspective) with only a few, later ones that represented the opposite orientation. Respondents might assume that all the statements represented the same orientation and, reading quickly, misread some of them, thereby giving the wrong answers. This problem can be reduced somewhat by alternating statements representing different orientations and by making all statements short and clear.

Ordering Questions in a Questionnaire

The *order* in which questions are asked can also affect the answers given. First, the appearance of one question can affect the answers given to subsequent ones. For example, if a number of questions have been asked about the dangers of communism to the United States and a subsequent question asks respondents to volunteer (open-ended) what they believe to represent dangers to the United States, communism will receive more citations than would otherwise be the case.

If respondents are asked to assess their overall religiosity ("How important is your religion to you in general?"), their responses to later questions concerning specific aspects of religiosity will be aimed at consistency with the prior assessment. The converse would be true as well. If respondents are first asked specific questions about different aspects of their religiosity, their subsequent overall assessment will reflect the earlier answers.

Some researchers attempt to overcome this effect by randomizing the order of questions. This is usually a futile effort. To begin, a randomized set of questions will probably strike respondents as chaotic and worthless. It will be difficult to answer, moreover, since they must continually switch their attention from one topic to another. And, finally, even a randomized ordering of questions will have the effect discussed above—except that you will have no control over the effect.

The safest solution is sensitivity to the problem. Although you cannot avoid the effect of question order, you should attempt to estimate what that effect will be. Thus, you will be able to interpret results in a meaningful fashion. If the order of questions seems an especially important issue in a given study, you might construct more than one version of the questionnaire containing the different possible orderings of questions. You would then be able to determine the effects. At the very least, you should pretest your questionnaire in the different forms.

The desired ordering of questions differs somewhat between self-administered questionnaires and interviews. In the former, it is usually best to begin the questionnaire with the most interesting set of questions. The potential respondents who glance casually over the first few questions should *want* to answer them. Perhaps the questions will ask for attitudes that they are aching to express. At the same time, however, the initial questions should not be threatening. (It might be a bad idea to begin with questions about sexual behavior or drug use.) Requests for duller, demographic data (age, sex, and the like) should generally be placed at the end of the self-administered questionnaire. Placing these questions at the beginning, as many inexperienced researchers are tempted to do, gives the questionnaire the initial appearance of a routine form, and the person receiving it may not be motivated to complete it.

Just the opposite is generally true for interview surveys. When the potential respondent's door first opens, the interviewer must begin quickly gaining rapport. After a short introduction to the study, the interviewer can best begin by enumerating the members of the household, getting demographic data about each. Such questions are easily answered and generally nonthreatening. Once the initial rapport has been established, the interviewer can then move into the area of attitudes and more sensitive matters. An interview that began with the question "Do you believe in God?" would probably end rather quickly.

Instructions

Every questionnaire, whether it is to be completed by respondents or administered by interviewers, should contain clear instructions and introductory comments where appropriate.

It is useful to begin every self-administered questionnaire with basic instructions to be followed in completing it. Although many people these days are pretty familiar with forms and questionnaires, you should begin by telling them exactly what you want: that they are to indicate their answers to certain questions by placing a check mark or an X in the box beside the appropriate answer, or by writing in their answer when asked to do so. If many open-ended questions are used, respondents should be given some guide as to whether brief or lengthy answers are expected. If you wish to encourage written-in answers to elaborate on responses given to closed-ended questions, that should be noted.

If a questionnaire is arranged into content subsections—political attitudes, religious attitudes, background data—it is useful to introduce each section with a short statement concerning its content and purpose. For example, "In this section, we would like to know what people around here consider the most important community problems." Demographic items at the end of a self-administered questionnaire might be introduced thus: "Finally, we would like to know just a little about you so we can see how different types of people feel about the issues we have been examining."

Short introductions such as these help make sense out of the questionnaire for the respondent. They make the questionnaire seem less chaotic, especially when it taps a variety of data. And they help put the respondent in the proper frame of mind for answering the questions.

Some questions may require special instructions to facilitate proper answering. That is especially true if a given question varies from the general instructions pertaining to the whole questionnaire. Some specific examples will illustrate this situation.

Despite the desirability for mutually exclusive answer categories in closed-ended questions, it is often the case that more than one answer will apply for respondents. If you want a single answer, you should make this perfectly clear in the question. An example would be, "From the list below, please check the *primary* reason for your decision to attend college." Often the main question can be followed by a parenthetical note: "Please check the *one* best answer." If, on the other hand, you want the respondent to check as many answers as apply, that should be made clear as well.

When a set of answer categories are to be rank-ordered by the respondent, the instructions should indicate as much, and a different type of answer format should be used (for example, blanks instead of boxes). These instructions should indicate how many answers are to be ranked (for example, all, first and second, first and last, most important and least important) and the order of ranking (for example, "place a 1 beside the most important, a 2 beside the next most important, and so forth").

(*Note*: Rank-ordering of responses is often difficult for respondents, since they may have to read and reread the list several times.)

In multiple-part matrix questions, it is useful to give special instructions unless the same format is used throughout the questionnaire. Sometimes respondents will be expected to check one answer in each *column* of the matrix, while in other questionnaires they will be expected to check one answer in each *row*. Whenever the questionnaire contains both types, it will be useful to add an instruction clarifying which is expected in each case.

There are countless other tips and guidelines that I feel I should give you in connection with questionnaire construction, but this section of this single chapter would soon be longer than the rest of the book. There is also the danger that you'd be bored silly. Somewhat reluctantly, then, I'm going to complete this discussion with an illustration of a questionnaire, showing you how some of these comments find substance in practice.

Before turning to the illustration, however, I want to mention a critical aspect of questionnaire design that I will delay discussing until Chapter 13: *precoding*. Since the information collected by questionnaires is typically transformed into punch cards and magnetic tapes, it is usually appropriate to include data-processing instructions on the questionnaire itself. These instructions indicate where specific pieces of information will be stored in the machine-readable data files. In Chapter 13, I'll discuss the nature of such storage and point out the kinds of questionnaire notations that would be appropriate. As a preview, however, notice that the illustration that follows has been precoded with the mysterious numbers that appear near questions and answer categories.

A Composite Illustration

As mentioned above, I want to conclude this section with an illustration of a real questionnaire similar to one you might construct. Figure 12-7 is a portion of a 30-page questionnaire developed by University of Hawaii students for the purpose of a student survey in 1969. The purpose of the survey was to create a comprehensive file of information about student attitudes and orientations in a variety of areas: politics, religion, education, and others.

I have chosen this questionnaire because it employed no expensive production techniques—it was typed and then photo-offset—and because it covers subject matter that you might want to study sometime yourself. On the whole, it is a pretty good questionnaire. Still, it is not perfect. As you read through the questionnaire, you will find marginal notations (NOTE 1 and so on). Whenever such a notation appears, you might try to figure out how the questionnaire could have been improved at that point. In the notes below the illustration questionnaire, I have told how I feel it could have been improved.

To improve your critical skills in questionnaire construction, you should also look for mistakes that I have *not* marked.

Figure 12-7   A Sample Questionnaire

GENERAL INSTRUCTIONS: Either a pen or pencil may be used
to complete this questionnaire. Most of the questions may be
answered by simply placing an X in the appropriate box; other
questions ask for written-in answers. However, you may write
in additional comments whenever you wish to do so. Please ignore
the numbers beside the questions and answers; they are for machine
tabulation only.

<table>
<tr><td>A. POLITICAL ORIENTATIONS</td><td>NOTE 1</td></tr>
</table>

(1-4, 5/1)

1. Beside each of the statements listed below, please indicate
   whether you strongly agree (SA), agree (A), disagree (D),
   strongly disagree (SD), or don't know (DK).

(6-15)	SA 1	A 2	D 3	SD 4	DK 5
a. It would be a good thing if the United Nations were someday converted into a world government. .	[ ]	[ ]	[ ]	[ ]	[ ]
b. People who defile the American flag should be put in prison. . .	[ ]	[ ]	[ ]	[ ]	[ ]
c. The United States is too ready to interpret the actions of communist nations as threatening . . .	[ ]	[ ]	[ ]	[ ]	[ ]
d. The United States is spending too much money on defense	[ ]	[ ]	[ ]	[ ]	[ ]
e. Communism is probably the best form of government for some countries	[ ]	[ ]	[ ]	[ ]	[ ]
f. The Central Intelligence Agency has too much power.	[ ]	[ ]	[ ]	[ ]	[ ]
g. The NLF (Viet Cong) are mostly invaders from North Vietnam . . .	[ ]	[ ]	[ ]	[ ]	[ ]
h. The United States was justified in using nuclear weapons against Japan in 1945	[ ]	[ ]	[ ]	[ ]	[ ]
i. If it were not for the power of the United States, most nations of the world would be taken over by the communists	[ ]	[ ]	[ ]	[ ]	[ ]
j. We should support our country's policies even when they are wrong	[ ]	[ ]	[ ]	[ ]	[ ]

Note 1   This is not a serious problem, but since the full questionnaire dealt
with a variety of topics, it would have been useful to insert a short introductory
comment at this point to inform respondents of what was contained in the section.
Such introductions would have been even more useful in later sections, where
respondents were asked implicitly to switch their thinking to different topics. An
appropriate introduction might have been, "In this first section, we are interested in
learning how you feel about a variety of foreign and domestic political issues."

Figure 12-7 (Continued)

2. In general, how do you feel about each of the following possible U.S. policies regarding the war in Vietnam? Please
   indicate beside each whether you approve (A), disapprove (D),
   or don't know (DK).

	A 1	D 2	DK 3
(16-25)			
a. Maintenance of present level of U.S. military activities	[ ]	[ ]	[ ]
b. Immediate beginning of unilateral withdrawal of U.S. forces	[ ]	[ ]	[ ]
c. Withdrawal of U.S. forces into strategic hamlets in South Vietnam.	[ ]	[ ]	[ ]
d. Bombing of strategic targets in North Vietnam	[ ]	[ ]	[ ]
e. Invasion of North Vietnam by U.S. ground forces.	[ ]	[ ]	[ ]
f. Invasion of North Vietnam by South Vietnamese ground forces.	[ ]	[ ]	[ ]
g. Use of nuclear weapons against North Vietnam if recommended by U.S. military leaders	[ ]	[ ]	[ ]
h. Cessation of all U.S. bombing in South Vietnam	[ ]	[ ]	[ ]
i. Granting U.S. military leaders complete freedom to handle the war as they see fit .	[ ]	[ ]	[ ]
j. Continuation of the Paris peace talks . . .	[ ]	[ ]	[ ]

3. As a general rule, do you personally tend to believe or doubt
   the validity of *official* U.S. government reports regarding
   the following aspects of the war in Vietnam?

	Believe 1	Doubt 2	Don't know 3
(26-28)			
a. Reports of enemy casualties	[ ]	[ ]	[ ]
b. Reports of Viet Cong atrocities . .	[ ]	[ ]	[ ]
c. Proclamations of U.S. goals in Vietnam	[ ]	[ ]	[ ]

4. Is there anything else you would like to say about the war in
   Vietnam? (Additional space is provided at the end of the
   questionnaire.)
   (29-30)

Note 2   Since Question 5 has its answer spaces to the right of the answers, it
would have been better to follow the same pattern with Questions 6 and 7. Switch-
ing the placement of answer spaces on the same page will make processing somewhat difficult for keypunchers and will increase the likelihood of errors.

Figure 12-7   (Continued)

5. Listed below are some statements people have made regarding
    the student peace movement in America. Beside each, please
    indicate whether you strongly agree (SA), agree (A), disagree
    (D), strongly disagree (SD), or don't know how you feel (DK).

	(31-36)	SA 1	A 2	D 3	SD 4	DK 5
a.	Peace demonstrators threaten the peace more than they enhance it .	[ ]	[ ]	[ ]	[ ]	[ ]
b.	A person's moral convictions should take precedence over na- tional policies of war.	[ ]	[ ]	[ ]	[ ]	[ ]
c.	Peace demonstrators are primarily interested in personal publicity.	[ ]	[ ]	[ ]	[ ]	[ ]
d.	Pacifism is simply not a practi- cal philosophy in the world today.	[ ]	[ ]	[ ]	[ ]	[ ]
e.	Burning one's draft card should *not* be considered a crime	[ ]	[ ]	[ ]	[ ]	[ ]
f.	Peace demonstrators should be drafted and sent to Vietnam . . .	[ ]	[ ]	[ ]	[ ]	[ ]

6. In November, 1968, two U.S. Marines sought sanctuary on the
    UH campus as a protest against the war in Vietnam. Which of
    the following do you believe *should* have been the policy of
    the university administration?   NOTE 2
    (37)
        1 [ ] The university should have granted official sanctuary.
        2 [ ] The university should have permitted them to stay on
               campus without granting official sanctuary.
        3 [ ] The university should have forced them to leave the
               campus.
                                                                              NOTE 3
7. There has been disagreement recently as to whether the uni-
    versity should permit military recruiters and antidraft
    counselors to come on the UH campus to talk with students.
    Do you personally feel the university should permit both,
    only one, or neither to come on campus to talk with students?
    (38)
        1 [ ] Should permit *both* military recruiters and antidraft
               counselors
        2 [ ] Should permit only *military* recruiters
        3 [ ] Should permit only *antidraft* counselors
        4 [ ] Should permit *neither*
        5 [ ] I don't know

Note 3   The list of response categories for Question 6 is probably not exhaustive. In fact, some respondents wrote in answers of their own. It would have been
better to provide an "Other (Please specify:) _____" category
for this purpose. (Incidentally, the university administration chose the second alternative, and everything worked out just fine.)

Figure 12-7   (Continued)

8. Which of the following, if any, do you believe should be suf-
    ficient grounds for exemption from military service? (Please
    check 'yes' if you believe it should be sufficient and 'no'
    if you believe it should not be sufficient.)

	(39-43)	Yes 1	No 2	Don't know 3
a.	Membership in a religious group with strong pacifist principles.	[ ]	[ ]	[ ]
b.	Strong personal religious pacifist principles.	[ ]	[ ]	[ ]
c.	Strong personal moral or philosophical (nonreligious) pacifist principles. . . .	[ ]	[ ]	[ ]
d.	Strong objections to a particular war . .	[ ]	[ ]	[ ]
e.	Other (Please specify: _____ _____) . .	[ ]	[ ]	[ ]

9. Have you personally supported the current peace movement in
    any of the following ways?

	(44-50)	Yes 1	No 2
a.	Attended a peace rally.	[ ]	[ ]
b.	Participated in a peace march	[ ]	[ ]
c.	Written a letter intended for publication . . .	[ ]	[ ]
d.	Spoken at a peace rally	[ ]	[ ]
e.	Written a letter to a public official	[ ]	[ ]
f.	Campaigned for a peace candidate.	[ ]	[ ]
g.	Distributed peace literature.	[ ]	[ ]
h.	Participated in *mild* direct action subject to arrest (trespassing, disturbing the peace, etc.)	[ ]	[ ]
i.	Participated in *strong* direct action subject to arrest (destruction of property, inter- fering with military operations, etc.).	[ ]	[ ]
j.	Was arrested for peace movement activities. . .	[ ]	[ ]
k.	Other (Please specify: _____ _____)	[ ]	[ ]

10. Which government would you prefer to have represented in the
     United Nations: the Nationalist government on Taiwan or the
     Communist government on the mainland of China?

(55)   <u>NOTE 4</u>

    1 [ ] Only the Nationalist government on Taiwan
    2 [ ] Only the Communist government on the mainland
    3 [ ] Both governments should be represented

Note 4   Rather whimsically, the answer spaces for Question 10 have been
placed to the left, while those for Questions 11 and 12 are on the right. See Note 2
above if you've forgotten why this is a bad idea.

Figure 12-7   (Continued)

11. Please indicate whether you agree (A), disagree (D), or are
     undecided (U) about each of the following possible United
     States' policies toward mainland China.

	A	D	U
(56-61)	1	2	3

	A	D	U
a. Granting diplomatic recognition to China. .	[ ]	[ ]	[ ]
b. Seeking economic trade with China	[ ]	[ ]	[ ]
c. Offering economic aid to China.	[ ]	[ ]	[ ]
d. Seeking cultural exchange programs with China	[ ]	[ ]	[ ]
e. Seeking to contain China militarily	[ ]	[ ]	[ ]
f. Seeking to destroy China's military power .	[ ]	[ ]	[ ]

12. The question of military intervention has come up many times
     in the past. The following is a list of instances in which
     the U.S. had to decide whether or not to intervene militar-
     ily. In each case, please indicate whether or not you feel
     the U.S. should have intervened with military force.

(62-72)	Should have intervened	Should not have intervened	Not sure
	1	2	3
a. Chinese Communist Revolu- tion, 1948-49	[ ]	[ ]	[ ]
b. Korean conflict, 1950	[ ]	[ ]	[ ]
c. Hungarian revolt, 1956. . . .	[ ]	[ ]	[ ]
d. Bay of Pigs invasion, 1961. .	[ ]	[ ]	[ ]
e. Vietnam buildup, 1964-65. . .	[ ]	[ ]	[ ]
f. Dominican Republic revolt, 1965.	[ ]	[ ]	[ ]
g. Rhodesian independence, 1965.	[ ]	[ ]	[ ]
h. Greek military coup d'etat, 1965.	[ ]	[ ]	[ ]
i. Israeli-Arab conflict, 1967 .	[ ]	[ ]	[ ]
j. Capture of U.S.S. Pueblo, 1968.	[ ]	[ ]	[ ]
k. Russian occupation of Czecho- slovakia, 1968.	[ ]	[ ]	[ ]

Note 5   "Very liberal" is missing from the list of response categories. As a
result, the spectrum of political orientations is unbalanced. This omission is the
result of a simple typing error and the failure to proofread the questionnaire
carefully enough. It is worth noting that this error occurred after hours of considered debate over the proper terms to be used in labeling different political orientations—especially the extremes. The most careful conceptualization can go for naught
unless every step in the research process is taken with sufficient caution.

Figure 12-7   (Continued)

13. In general, how would you characterize your own political
     orientation? How would you characterize the political orien-
     tations of your parents? (Please answer for each.)

	Yourself	Your Father	Your Mother	NOTE 5
Right radical.	1 [ ]	1 [ ]	1 [ ]	
Very conservative.	2 [ ]	2 [ ]	2 [ ]	
Moderately conservative.	3 [ ]	3 [ ]	3 [ ]	
Moderately liberal	4 [ ]	4 [ ]	4 [ ]	
Left radical	5 [ ]	5 [ ]	5 [ ]	
Other (Please specify: _____				
_____). .	6 [ ]	6 [ ]	6 [ ]	
Don't know	7 [ ]	7 [ ]	7 [ ]	

14. Do you normally identify yourself with any particular politi-
     cal party? (Please indicate *which party*, if any, you identi-
     fy with.)
     (76)   NOTE 6
         1 [ ] Democratic party
         2 [ ] Republican party
         3 [ ] American Independent party
         4 [ ] Peace and Freedom party
         5 [ ] Other (Please specify: _____)
         6 [ ] No party identification, independent

15. Were you eligible to vote in the November, 1968, general
     election?
     (77-78)   NOTE 7
         1 [ ] Yes**
         2 [ ] No   15a. ** If *yes*, did you vote? 1 [ ] Yes
                                                        2 [ ] No

16. Whether or not you were eligible to vote in November, 1968,
     which of these Presidential candidates, if any, did you
     prefer?
     (79)
         1 [ ] Hubert Humphrey
         2 [ ] Richard Nixon
         3 [ ] George Wallace
         4 [ ] Eldridge Cleaver
         5 [ ] None of these

     (80/R)

Note 6   There go the answer spaces across the page again. Since Question 15
contains a contingency question, making it awkward to place the answer spaces to
the right, it would have been better to place those for Question 13 on the left.

Note 7   This is not a very good format for the contingency question. See Figure
12-5 earlier in this chapter for a better format. Also, note how crowded the questionnaire is at this point. There is a danger that many respondents would get
confused and miss the contingency question altogether. Can you determine why the
researchers crowded questions together so much here?

SELF-ADMINISTERED QUESTIONNAIRES

There are two main methods of administering survey questionnaires to a sample of respondents. This section will deal with the method in which respondents are asked to complete the questionnaires themselves—*self-administered* questionnaires —and the following section will deal with surveys that are administered by staff interviewers.

Although the mail survey is the typical method used in self-administered studies, there are several additional methods commonly used. In some cases, it may be appropriate to administer the questionnaire to a group of respondents gathered at the same place at the same time. A survey of students taking Introductory Psychology might be conducted in this manner during class. High school students might be surveyed during homeroom period.

Some recent experimentation has been conducted with regard to the home delivery of questionnaires. A research worker delivers the questionnaire to the home of sample respondents and explains the study. Then, the questionnaire is left for the respondent to complete, and it is picked up later by the researcher.

Home delivery and the mail can be used in combination as well. In many parts of the country, the 1970 United States Census was conducted in this fashion. Questionnaires were mailed to families, and then census enumerators visited homes to pick up the questionnaires and check them for completeness. In just the opposite method, questionnaires have been hand delivered by research workers with a request that the respondents mail the completed questionnaires to the research office.

On the whole, the appearance of a research worker, either delivering the questionnaire, picking it up, or both, seems to produce a higher completion rate than is normally true for straightforward mail surveys. Additional experimentation with this method is likely to point to additional techniques for improving completion while reducing costs.

Mail surveys are the typical form of self-administered survey, however, and the remainder of this section is devoted specifically to that type of study.

Mail Distribution and Return

The basic method for data collection through the mail has been transmittal of a questionnaire, accompanied by a letter of explanation and a return envelope. I would imagine you have received one or two in your lifetime. As a respondent, you are expected to complete the questionnaire, put it in the return envelope, and return it. If, by any chance, you've received such a questionnaire and failed to return it, it would be extremely valuable for you to recall the reasons you had for *not* returning it—and keep those in mind any time you plan to send questionnaires to others.

One big reason for not returning questionnaires is that it can seem like too much trouble. To overcome this problem, researchers have developed a number of ways to make the return of questionnaires easier. One development is a *self-mailing* questionnaire, requiring no return envelope. The questionnaire is designed so that when it is folded in a particular fashion, the return address appears on the outside. That way, the respondent doesn't have to worry about losing the envelope.

Use this method with caution, however. One of the first surveys I conducted was an enormous one with some 70,000 respondents. To save money and simplify the logistics, I had the questionnaire printed on a long sheet of paper and had it prefolded so that my return address and business-reply postage permit showed on the outside. To facilitate several follow-up mailings (see below), I had nearly a quarter of a million questionnaires printed. Since we were going to be receiving a lot of mail, we thought it would be nice to warn the local post office and see if we could arrange to have it delivered to us in mail bags. When the postal officials saw the questionnaire, they immediately concluded that it violated postal regulations! Since I had made no provisions for the folded questionnaire to be sealed (required for first class mail), the local officials indicated that they couldn't handle it. Only an inspirational discussion of social research and a tearful appeal to save my graduate career got the questionnaires into the mail.

More elaborate designs are available, also. The student questionnaire described and illustrated earlier in this chapter was bound in a booklet with a special, two-panel back cover. Once the questionnaire was completed, the respondent needed only to fold out the extra panel, wrap it around the booklet, and seal the whole thing with the adhesive strip running along the edge of the panel. The foldout panel contained my return address and postage. When I repeated the study a couple of years later, I improved on the design further. Both the front and back covers had foldout panels: one for sending the questionnaire out and the other for getting it back—thus avoiding the use of envelopes altogether.

The point here is that anything you can do to make the job of completing and returning the questionnaire easier will improve your study. At the opposite extreme, imagine receiving a questionnaire that made no provisions for its return to the researcher. Suppose you had to (1) find an envelope, (2) write the address on it, (3) figure out how much postage it required, and (4) put the stamps on it. How likely is it that you would return the questionnaire?

A few brief comments are in order here on the postal options available to you. You have options for mailing questionnaires out and for getting them returned. On outgoing mail, your choices are essentially between first-class postage and *bulk rate*. The first is more certain, but the second is far cheaper. (Check your local post office for rates and procedures.) On return mail, your choice is between postage stamps and business-reply permits. Here, the cost differential is more complicated. If you use stamps, you pay for them whether people return their questionnaires or not. With the business-reply permit, you only pay for those that are used, but you pay an *extra* surcharge of about a nickel. This means that stamps are cheaper if a lot of questionnaires are returned, but business-reply permits are cheaper if fewer are returned. (And you won't know in advance how many will be returned.)

There are many other considerations involved in choosing among the several postal options. Some researchers, for example, feel that the use of postal stamps communicates more "human-ness" and sincerity than bulk rate and business reply permits. Others worry that respondents will steam off stamps and use them for some purpose other than returning the questionnaire. Since both bulk rate and business-reply permits require establishing accounts at the post office, you'll probably find stamps much easier in small surveys.

Monitoring Returns

The mailing of questionnaires sets up a new research question that may prove very valuable to the study. As questionnaires are returned, you should not sit back idly, but should undertake a careful recording of the varying rates of return among respondents.

An invaluable tool in this activity will be a return rate graph. The day on which questionnaires were mailed should be labeled Day 1 on the graph; and, every day thereafter, the number of returned questionnaires should be logged on the graph. Since this is a rather minor activity, it is usually best to compile two graphs. One should show the number returned each day—rising, then dropping. Another should report the *cumulative* number or percentage. In part, this activity provides you with gratification as you get to draw a picture of your successful data collection. More important, however, it is your guide to how the data collection is going. If you plan follow-up mailings, the graph provides a clue as to when such mailings should be launched. (The dates of subsequent mailings should be noted on the graph.)

As completed questionnaires are returned, each should be opened, perused, and assigned an identification number. These numbers should be assigned serially as the questionnaires are returned—even if other identification (ID) numbers have already been assigned. Two examples should illustrate the important advantages of this procedure.

Let's assume that you are studying attitudes toward a political figure. In the middle of the data collection, let's further assume that the figure in question is discovered to be supporting a mistress. By knowing the date of that public disclosure and the dates when questionnaires have been received, the researcher is in a position to determine the effects of the disclosure. (Recall the discussion of history in connection with experiments.)

In a less sensational way, serialized ID numbers can be valuable in estimating nonresponse biases in the survey. Barring more direct tests of bias, you may wish to assume that those respondents who failed to answer the questionnaire will be more like those who delayed answering than like those who answered right away. An analysis of questionnaires received at different points in the data collection might then be used for estimates of sampling bias. For example, if grade point averages (GPA) reported by students decrease steadily through the data collection, with those replying right away having higher GPAs and those replying later having lower GPAs, then you might tentatively conclude that those who failed to answer at all have lower GPAs yet. Although it would not be advisable to make statistical estimates of bias in this fashion, you could take advantage of approximate estimates.

If respondents have been identified for purposes of follow-up mailing, then preparations for those mailings should be made as the questionnaires are returned. The case study that follows in this chapter will discuss this process in greater detail.

Follow-up Mailings

The methodological literature on follow-up mailings strongly suggests this is an effective method for increasing return rates in mail surveys. In general, the longer a potential respondent delays replying, the less likely he or she is to do so at all. Properly timed follow-up mailings, then, provide additional stimuli for responding.

The effects of follow-up mailings will be seen in the response rate curves recorded during data collection. The initial mailing will be followed by a rise and subsequent subsiding of returns; the follow-up mailing will spur a resurgence of returns; and more follow-ups will do the same. In practice, three mailings (an original and two follow-ups) seem the most efficient.

The timing of follow-up mailings is also important. Here the methodological literature offers less precise guides, but it has been my experience that two or three weeks is a reasonable space between mailings. (This period might be increased by a few days if the mailing time—out and in—is more than two or three days.)

When researchers conduct several surveys over time of the same population, such experience should help to develop more specific guidelines in this regard. The Survey Research Office at the University of Hawaii conducts frequent student surveys and has been able to refine the mailing and remailing procedure considerably. Indeed, a consistent pattern of returns has been found, which appears to transcend differences of survey content, quality of instrument, and so forth. Within two weeks after the first mailing, approximately 40 percent of the questionnaires are returned; within two weeks after the first follow-up, an additional 20 percent are received; and within two weeks after the final follow-up, an additional 10 percent are received. There are no grounds for assuming that a similar pattern would appear in surveys of different populations, but this illustration should indicate the value of carefully tabulating return rates for every survey conducted.

Follow-up mailings may be administered in a number of ways. In the simplest, nonrespondents are simply sent a letter of additional encouragement to participate. A better method, however, is to send a new copy of the survey questionnaire with the follow-up letter. If potential respondents have not returned their questionnaires after two or three weeks, there is a good likelihood that the questionnaires will have been lost or misplaced. Receiving a follow-up letter might encourage them to look for the original questionnaire, but if it is not easily found, the letter may go for naught. (The response rates reported in the above paragraph all involved the sending of additional questionnaires.)

If the individuals in the survey sample are not identified on the questionnaires, it may not be possible to remail only to nonrespondents. In such a case, you should send your follow-up mailing to all initial members of the sample, thanking those who may have already participated and encouraging those who have not to do so. (The case study reported in a later section of this chapter describes another method that may be used in an anonymous mail survey.)

Acceptable Response Rates

A question that new survey researchers frequently ask concerns the percentage return rate that should be achieved in a mail survey. It should be pointed out here that the body of inferential statistics used in connection with survey analysis assumed that *all* members of the initial sample complete and return their questionnaires. Since this almost never happens, response bias becomes a concern, with the researcher testing (and hoping for) the possibility that the respondents are essentially a random sample of the initial sample, and thus a somewhat smaller random sample of the total population.[1]

Nevertheless, overall response rate is one guide to the representativeness of the sample respondents. If a high response rate is achieved, there is less chance of significant response bias than if a low rate is achieved. But what is a *high* response rate?

A quick review of the survey literature will uncover a wide range of response rates. Each of these may be accompanied by a statement something like "This is regarded as a relatively high response rate for a survey of this type." (A United States senator made this statement regarding a poll of constituents that achieved a 4 percent return rate.) Despite the great variety of actual return rates and reactions to those rates, there are some rules of thumb that might be followed.

I feel that a response rate of at least 50 percent is *adequate* for analysis and reporting. A response rate of at least 60 percent is *good*. And a response rate of 70 percent or more is *very good*. You should bear in mind, however, that these are only rough guides; they have no statistical basis, and a demonstrated lack of response bias is far more important than a high response rate.

As you can imagine, one of the more persistent discussions among survey researchers concerns ways of increasing response rates. You'll recall that this was a chief concern in the earlier discussion of options for mailing out and receiving questionnaires. Survey researchers have developed a number of ingenious techniques addressing this problem.[2] Some have experimented with novel formats. Others have tried paying respondents to participate. The problem with paying, of course, is that it's expensive to make a meaningfully high payment to hundreds or thousands of respondents, but some imaginative alternatives have been used. Some researchers have said, "We want to get your two-cents worth on some issues, and we're willing to pay"—enclosing two pennies. Another enclosed a quarter, suggesting that the respondent make some little child happy.

A Case Study

The steps involved in the administration of a mail survey are many and can best be appreciated in a walk-through of an actual study. I'll conclude this section, then, with a detailed description of a survey conducted among University of Hawaii students in the spring of 1969. As you'll see shortly, the study did not represent the theoretical ideal for such studies, but in that regard it serves present purposes all the

[1]For more detailed examinations of nonresponse biases, see Marjorie N. Donald, "Implications of Nonresponse for the Interpretation of Mail Questionnaire Data," *Public Opinion Quarterly*, Vol. 24, No. 1 (1960), pp. 99–114, and K. A. Brownlee, "A Note on the Effects of Nonresponse on Surveys," *Journal of the American Statistical Association*, Vol. 52, No. 227 (1957), pp. 29–32.

[2]For a review of these techniques, see Joseph Horowitz and William Sedlacek, "Initial Returns on Mail Questionnaires: A Literature Review and Research Note," *Research in Higher Education*, Vol. 2 (1974), pp. 361–367.

better. The study was conducted by the students in my graduate seminar in survey research methods.

By way of general overview, approximately 1,100 students were selected from the university registration tape through a stratified, systematic sampling procedure. For each student so selected, six self-adhesive mailing labels were printed by the computer.

By the time we were prepared to distribute the questionnaires, it became apparent that our meager research funds were inadequate to cover several mailings to the entire sample of 1,100 students. (Questionnaire printing costs were higher than anticipated.) As a result, a systematic two-thirds sample of the mailing labels was chosen, yielding a subsample of 770 students.

An earlier decision had been made to keep the survey anonymous in the hope of encouraging more candid responses to some sensitive questions. (Subsequent surveys of the same issues among the same population indicate this anonymity was unnecessary.) Thus, the questionnaires would carry no identification of students on them. At the same time, it was hoped that follow-up mailing costs could be reduced by remailing only to nonrespondents.

To achieve both of these aims, a special postcard method was devised. Each student was mailed a questionnaire that carried no identifying marks, plus a postcard addressed to the research office—with one of the student's mailing labels affixed to the reverse side of the card. The introductory letter asked the student to complete and return the questionnaire—assuring anonymity—and to return the postcard simultaneously. Receipt of the postcard would tell us that the student had returned his or her questionnaire—without indicating *which* questionnaire it was. This procedure would then facilitate follow-up mailings. (See below.)

The 32-page questionnaire was printed in the form of a booklet (photo-offset and saddle-stitched). A three-panel cover—described elsewhere in this chapter—permitted the questionnaire to be returned without an additional envelope.

A letter introducing the study and its purposes was printed on the front cover of the booklet. It explained why the study was being conducted (to learn how students feel about a variety of issues), how students had been selected for the study, the importance of each student's responding, and the mechanics of returning the questionnaire.

Students were assured that the study was anonymous, and the postcard method and rationale were explained. A statement followed about the auspices under which the study was being conducted, and a telephone number was provided for those who might want more information about the study. (About five students called for information.)

By printing the introductory letter on the questionnaire, we avoided the necessity of enclosing a separate letter in the outgoing envelope, thereby simplifying the task of assembling mailing pieces.

The assembly of materials for the initial mailing involved the following steps. (1) One mailing label for each student was stuck on a postcard. (2) Another label was stuck on an outgoing manila envelope. (3) One postcard and one questionnaire were placed in each envelope—with a glance to insure that the name on the postcard and on the envelope were the same in each case.

These steps were accomplished through an assembly line procedure involving the several members of the research team. Although the procedure was somewhat organized in advance, it should be noted that a certain amount of actual practice was required before the best allocation of tasks and persons was discovered.

It is also worth noting that the entire process was delayed several days while the initial batch of manila envelopes was exchanged for larger ones. This delay could have been avoided if a walk-through of the assembly process had been carried out in advance.

The distribution of the survey questionnaires had been set up for a bulk-rate mailing. Once the questionnaires had been stuffed into the envelopes, they were grouped by zip codes, tied in bundles, and delivered to the post office.

Shortly after the initial mailing, questionnaires and postcards began arriving at the research office. Questionnaires were opened, perused, and assigned identification numbers as described earlier in the chapter. For every postcard received, a search was made for that student's remaining labels, and they were destroyed.

After a period of two or three weeks, all the mailing labels remaining were used to organize a follow-up mailing. The assembly procedures described above were repeated with one exception. A special separate letter of appeal was prepared and included in the mailing piece. The new letter indicated that many students had returned their questionnaires already, but that it was very important for all others to do so as well.

The follow-up mailing stimulated a resurgence of returns as expected, and the same logging procedures were continued. The returned postcards told us which additional mailing labels to destroy. Unfortunately, time and financial pressures made it impossible to undertake a third mailing as had been initially planned, but the two mailings resulted in an overall return rate of 62 percent.

I trust this illustration will give you a fairly good sense of what's involved in the execution of mailed self-administered questionnaires—a very popular survey method. Let's turn now to the other method of conducting surveys.

INTERVIEW SURVEYS

This section essentially parallels the prior one; it describes an alternative method of data collection through surveys. Rather than asking respondents to read questionnaires and enter their own answers, researchers send interviewers to ask the questions orally and record respondents' answers. **Interviewing** is typically done in a face-to-face encounter, and this section will focus on such interviewing situations. However, telephone interviewing, as we'll see, follows most of the same guidelines. Also, most interview surveys require more than one interviewer, although you might undertake a small-scale interview survey yourself. Portions of this section will discuss methods for training and supervising a staff of interviewers assisting you on the survey.

The Role of the Interviewer

There are a number of advantages in having a questionnaire administered by an interviewer rather than the respondent. To begin, interview surveys typically attain higher response rates than mail surveys. A properly designed and executed interview survey ought to achieve a completion rate of at least 80 to 85 percent. (Federally funded surveys often require this response rate.) It would seem that respondents are more reluctant to turn down an interviewer standing on their doorstep than they are to throw away a mail questionnaire.

Within the context of the questionnaire, the presence of an interviewer generally decreases the number of "don't knows" and "no answers." If minimizing such responses is important to the study, the interviewer can be instructed to probe for answers. ("If you had to pick one of the answers, which do you think would come closest to your feelings?")

Interviewers can also provide a guard against confusing questionnaire items. If the respondent clearly misunderstands the intent of a question or indicates that he or she does not understand, the interviewer can clarify matters, thereby obtaining relevant responses. (Such clarifications must be strictly controlled, however, through formal *specifications*. See below.)

Finally, the interviewer can observe as well as ask questions. For example, the interviewer can note the respondent's race if this is considered too delicate a question to ask. Similar observations can be made regarding the quality of the dwelling, the presence of various possessions, the respondent's ability to speak English, the respondent's general reactions to the study, and so forth. In one survey of students, respondents were given a short self-administered questionnaire to complete—concerning sexual attitudes and behavior—during the course of the interview. While a student completed the questionnaire, the interviewer made detailed notes regarding the dress and grooming of the respondent.

Neutral Role of Interviewer   Survey research is of necessity based on an unrealistic *stimulus-response* theory of cognition and behavior. It must be assumed that a questionnaire item will mean exactly the same thing to every respondent, and every given response must mean the same when given by different respondents. Although this is an impossible goal, survey questions are drafted in such a way as to closely approximate the ideal.

The interviewer must also fit into this ideal situation. The interviewer's presence should not affect a respondent's perception of a question or the answer given. The interviewer, then, should be a *neutral* medium through which questions and answers are transmitted.

If this goal is successfully accomplished, different interviewers would obtain exactly the same responses from a given respondent. This neutrality has a special importance in area samples. To save time and money, a given interviewer is typically assigned to complete all the interviews in a particular geographical area—a city block or a group of nearby blocks. If the interviewer does anything to affect the responses obtained, then the bias thus interjected might be interpreted as a characteristic of the area under study.

Let's suppose that a survey is being done to determine attitudes toward low-cost housing, to help in the selection of a site for a new government-sponsored development. An interviewer assigned to a given neighborhood might—through word or gesture—communicate his or her own distaste for low-cost housing developments. Respondents might therefore tend to give responses generally in agreement with the interviewer's own position. The results of the survey would indicate that the neighborhood in question would strongly resist construction of the development in its area.

General Rules for Interviewing

The manner in which interviews ought to be conducted will vary somewhat by survey population and will be affected somewhat by the nature of the survey content as well. Nevertheless, it is possible to provide some general guidelines that would apply to most if not all interviewing situations.

Appearance and Demeanor   As a general rule, the interviewer should dress in a fashion similar to that of the people he or she will be interviewing. A richly dressed interviewer will probably have difficulty getting good cooperation and responses from poorer respondents. And a poorly dressed interviewer will have similar difficulties with richer respondents.

To the extent that the interviewer's dress and grooming differ from those of the respondents, it should be in the direction of cleanliness and neatness in modest apparel. If cleanliness is not next to godliness, it appears to be next to neutrality. Although middle-class neatness and cleanliness may not be accepted by all sectors of American society, they remain the primary norm and are more likely to be acceptable to the largest number of respondents.

Dress and grooming are typically regarded as signals to a person's attitudes and orientations. At the time this is being written, a man wearing colorful clothes, beads, and sandals, and sporting long hair, sideburns, and a beard communicates— correctly or incorrectly—that he is politically on the left, sexually permissive, favorable to drug use, and so forth. His appearance will communicate these orientations to a respondent as much as if he began the interview by saying "Hi there, I'm a hippie!"

In demeanor, interviewers should be pleasant if nothing else. Since they will be prying into the respondent's personal life and attitudes, they must communicate a genuine interest in getting to know the respondent without appearing to be spies. They must be relaxed and friendly without being too casual or clinging. One of the most important natural abilities that interviewers must have is the ability to determine very quickly the kind of person the respondent will feel most comfortable with; the kind of person the respondent would most enjoy talking to. There are two aspects of this. Clearly, the interview will be more successful if the interviewer can become the kind of person the respondent is comfortable with. Second, since respondents are asked to volunteer a portion of their time and to divulge personal information about themselves, they deserve the most enjoyable experience that the researcher and the interviewer can provide.

Familiarity with Questionnaire   If the interviewer is unfamiliar with the questionnaire, the study suffers and an unfair burden is placed on the respondent. In the latter respect, the interview is likely to take more time than necessary and be generally unpleasant. Moreover, the interviewer cannot acquire familiarity by skimming through the questionnaire two or three times. It must be studied carefully, question by question, and the interviewer must practice reading it aloud. (See the discussion on coordination and control later in this chapter.)

Ultimately, the interviewer must be able to read the questionnaire items to respondents without error, without stumbling over words and phrases. A good model for interviewers is the actor reading lines in a play or motion picture. The lines must be read as naturally as though they constituted a natural conversation, but that conversation must follow exactly the language set down in the questionnaire. Of course, the interviewer should not attempt to memorize the questionnaire.

By the same token, the interviewer must be familiar with the specifications (to be discussed shortly) prepared in conjunction with the questionnaire. Inevitably some questions will not exactly fit a given respondent's situation, and the interviewer must determine how the question should be interpreted in that situation. The specifications provided to the interviewer should give adequate guidance in such cases, but the interviewer must know the organization and contents of the specifications sufficiently to permit efficient reference to them. It would be better for the interviewer to leave a given question unanswered than to spend five minutes searching through the specifications for clarification or trying to interpret the relevant instructions.

Following Question Wording Exactly   In Chapter 6 I have already discussed the significance of question wording for the responses obtained. A slight change in the wording of a given question may lead a respondent to answer "yes" rather than "no."

Although you will very carefully phrase your questionnaire items in such a way as to obtain the information you need to insure that respondents will interpret items in a manner appropriate to those needs, all this effort will be wasted if interviewers rephrase questions in their own words.

Recording Responses Exactly   Whenever the questionnaire contains open-ended questions, those soliciting the respondent's own answer, it is very important that the interviewer record that answer exactly as given. No attempt should be made to summarize, paraphrase, or correct bad grammar. The response should be written down exactly as given.

This exactness is especially important because the interviewer will not know how the responses are to be coded before processing—indeed, you may not know the coding until you have had an opportunity to read a hundred or so responses. For example, the questionnaire might ask respondents how they feel about the traffic situation in their community. One respondent might answer that there were too many cars on the roads and that something should be done to limit their numbers. Another might say there was a need for more roads. If the interviewer recorded these two responses with the same summary—"congested traffic"—you would not be able to take advantage of the important differences in the original responses.

Sometimes, the respondent may be so inarticulate that the verbal response is too ambiguous to permit interpretation. However, the interviewer may be able to understand the intent of the response through the respondent's gestures or tone. In such a situation, the exact verbal response should still be recorded, but the interviewer should add marginal comments giving both the interpretation and the reasons for arriving at it.

More generally, it will be useful for you to have any marginal comments explaining aspects of the response not conveyed in the verbal recording, such as the respondent's apparent uncertainty in answering, anger, embarrassment, and so forth. In each case, however, the exact verbal response should also be recorded.

Probing for Responses   Sometimes respondents will respond to a question with an inappropriate answer. For example, the question may present an attitudinal statement and ask the respondent to strongly agree, agree somewhat, disagree somewhat, or strongly disagree. The respondent, however, may reply: "I think that's true." The interviewer should follow this reply with: "Would you say you strongly agree or agree somewhat?" If necessary, interviewers can explain that they must check one or the other of the categories provided. If the respondent adamantly refuses to choose, the interviewer should write in the exact response given by the respondent.

Probes are more frequently required in eliciting responses to open-ended questions. For example, in response to the previous question about traffic conditions, the respondent might simply reply, "Pretty bad." The interviewer could obtain an elaboration on this response through a variety of probes. Sometimes the best probe is silence; if the interviewer sits quietly with pencil poised, the respondent will probably fill the pause with additional comments. (This is a technique used effectively by newspaper reporters.) Appropriate verbal probes might be "How is that? In what ways?" Perhaps the most generally useful probe is "Anything else?"

It is frequently necessary to probe for answers that will be sufficiently informative for analytical purposes. In every case, however, it is imperative that such probes be completely *neutral*. The probe must not in any way affect the nature of the subsequent response. Whenever you anticipate that a given question may require probing for appropriate responses, you should present one or more useful probes next to the question in the questionnaire. This practice has two important advantages. First, you will have more time to devise the best, most neutral probes. Second, all interviewers will use the same probes whenever they are needed. Thus, even if the probe is not perfectly neutral, all respondents will be presented with the same stimulus. This is the same logical guideline discussed for question wording. Although a question should not be loaded or biased, it is essential that every respondent be presented with the same question, even a biased one.

Coordination and Control

As indicated earlier in this section, most interview surveys require the assistance of several interviewers. In large-scale surveys, of course, such interviewers are hired and paid for their work. As a student researcher, you might find yourself recruiting friends to assist you in interviewing. Whenever more than one interviewer is involved in a survey, it is essential that their efforts be carefully controlled. There are two aspects of this control: training interviewers and supervising them after they begin work.

Interviewer training should be done in a group, rather than individually. The latter approach will inevitably result in more superficial training.

The interviewer training session should begin with the description of what the study is all about. Even though the interviewers may be involved only in the data collection phase of the project, it will be useful to them to understand what will be done with the interviews they conduct and what purpose will be served. Morale and motivation are usually low when interviewers do not know what is going on.

The training on how to interview should begin with a discussion of general guidelines and procedures, such as those discussed earlier in this chapter. Then, you should turn to the questionnaire itself. The whole group should go through the questionnaire together—question by question. Do not simply ask if anyone has any questions about the first page of the questionnaire. Read the first question aloud, explain the purpose of the question, and then entertain any questions or comments the interviewers may have. Once all their questions and comments have been handled, go on to the next question in the questionnaire.

It is always a good idea to prepare what are called *specifications* to accompany an interview questionnaire. Specifications are explanatory and clarifying comments about the handling of difficult or confusing situations that may occur with regard to specific questions in the questionnaire. When you are drafting the questionnaire, you should try to think of all the problem cases that might arise—the bizarre circumstances that might make a question difficult to answer. The survey specifications should provide detailed guidelines on how to handle such situations. As an example, such a simple matter as age might present problems. Suppose a respondent says he or she will be 25 next week. The interviewer might not be sure whether to take the respondent's current age or the nearest one. The specifications for that question should explain what should be done. (Probably, you would specify that age as of last birthday should be recorded in all cases.)

If you have prepared a set of specifications, you should go over them with the interviewers at the same time that you go over the individual questions in the questionnaire. Make sure that your interviewers fully understand the specifications as well as the questions themselves.

This portion of the interviewer training is likely to generate a number of troublesome questions from your interviewers. They will ask: "What should I do if . . . ?" In such cases, you should never give a quick answer. If you have specifications, be sure to show how the solution to the problem could be determined from the specifications. If you do not have specifications prepared, show how the preferred handling of the situation fits within the general logic of the question and the purpose of the study. Giving offhand, unexplained answers to such questions will only confuse the interviewers, and they will probably not take their work very seriously. If you do not know the answer to such a question when it is asked, you would do well to admit that and ask for some time to decide on the best answer. Then think out the situation carefully and be sure to give all the interviewers your answer, explaining your reasons.

Once you have gone through the whole questionnaire as described above, you should conduct one or two demonstration interviews in front of everyone. Preferably, *you* should interview someone else. Realize that your interview will be a model for those you are training, and make it good. It would be best, moreover, if the demonstration interview were done as realistically as possible. Do not break up the course of the demonstration to point out how you have handled a complicated situation; handle it, and then explain later. It is irrelevant if the person you are interviewing gives real answers or takes on some hypothetical identity for the purpose, just so long as the answers are consistent.

After the demonstration interviews, you should pair off your interviewers and have them practice on each other. When they have completed the questionnaire, have them reverse roles and do it over again. Interviewing is the best training for interviewing. As your interviewers are practicing on each other, you should try to wander around, listening in on the practice so that you will know how well they are doing. Once the practice is completed, the whole group should discuss their experiences and ask any additional questions they may have.

The final stage of the training for interviewers should involve some "real" interviews. Have them conduct some interviews under the actual conditions that will pertain to the final survey. You may want to assign them people to interview, or perhaps they may be allowed to pick people themselves. Do not have them practice on people you have selected in your sample, however. After each interviewer has completed three to five interviews, have him or her check back with you. Look over the completed questionnaires to see if there is any evidence of misunderstanding. Again, answer any questions that individual interviewers may have. Once you are convinced that a given interviewer knows what is to be done, assign some actual interviews—using the sample you have selected for the study.

It is essential that you continue supervising the work of interviewers over the course of the study. It is probably unwise to let them conduct more than 20 or 30 interviews without seeing you. You might assign 20 interviews, have the interviewer bring back those questionnaires when they are completed, look them over, and assign another 20 or so. Although that may seem overly cautious, you must continually protect yourself against misunderstandings that may not be evident early in the study.

If you are the only interviewer in your study, these comments may not seem relevant to you. That is not wholly the case, however. You would be advised, for example, to prepare specifications for potentially troublesome questions in your questionnaire. Otherwise, you run the risk of making ad hoc decisions during the course of the study that you will later regret or forget. Also, the emphasis that has been placed on *practice* applies equally to the one-person project and to the complex funded survey with a large interviewing staff.

Telephone Surveys

I want to conclude the discussion of interview surveys with some comments on an increasingly popular technique, sometimes ironically called *telephone polls*. For years, telephone surveys had a rather bad reputation among professional researchers. There were diverse sources of the bad press.

To begin, there were the sampling problems discussed in Chapter 7. Telephone surveys are limited by definition to those people who have telephones. Years ago, then, this method produced a substantial social-class bias in that poor people were excluded from such surveys. Over time, however, the telephone has become a standard fixture in almost all American homes. The class bias, then, has been substantially reduced.

A related sampling problem involved unlisted numbers. If the survey sample was selected from the pages of a local telephone directory, it would totally omit all those people—typically richer—who requested that their numbers not be published. A rather ingenious solution to this problem has emerged, however. Instead of selecting numbers from the directory, it is possible to generate *random numbers* for this purpose, giving listed and unlisted numbers an equal chance of selection. This process requires knowing the exchanges (first three digits) in use and the range of numbers being used in each exchange.

The final sampling problem concerns *who* should be interviewed at the number selected and called. There are a variety of ways for handling this decision. Carefully selecting the hours for calling will increase the chances of all family members being at home and will guard against interviewing only housewives. Going even further, a quota-sampling design can insure that you interview sufficient numbers of all kinds of family members overall. Or, finally, you can specify, through random assignment, who is to be interviewed at each specific number called.

As a general rule, telephone interviews need to be shorter than face-to-face, household interviews. As a rough rule of thumb, you should limit telephone interviews to 10 to 15 minutes at most, although it is sometimes possible to conduct longer ones.

Telephone surveys have many advantages that underlie the growing popularity of this method. Probably the greatest advantages are money and time, in that order. In a face-to-face, household interview, you may drive several miles to a respondent's home, find no one there, return to the research office, and drive back the next day—possibly finding no one there again. It's cheaper and quicker to let your fingers make the trips.

Interviewing by telephone, you can dress any way you please without affecting the answers respondents give. And, sometimes, respondents will be more honest in giving socially disapproved answers if they don't have to look you in the eye. Similarly, it may be possible to probe into more sensitive areas, though that is not necessarily the case. (People are, to some extent, more suspicious when they can't see the person asking them questions—probably a legacy, in part, of "surveys" aimed at selling magazine subscriptions.)

Finally, telephone surveys can give you greater control over data collection if several interviewers are engaged in the project. If all the interviewers are calling from the research office, they can get clarification from the person in charge whenever problems occur, as they inevitably do. Alone in the boondocks, an interviewer may have to wing it between weekly visits with the interviewing supervisor.

COMPARISON OF TWO SURVEY METHODS

We have now examined two methods of data collection appropriate for survey research. Although I have touched on some of the relative advantages of each, it will be worth looking at this issue directly.

Self-administered questionnaires have the advantages of being generally cheaper and quicker than interview surveys. These considerations are likely to be important for an unfunded student wishing to undertake a survey in connection with a term paper or a thesis. Moreover, if you use the self-administered mail format, it costs no more to conduct a national survey than a local one; the cost difference between a local and a national interview survey would be enormous. Also, mail surveys typically require a small staff: one person can conduct a reasonably good mail survey alone, although you should not underestimate the work involved.

Finally, self-administered surveys are more appropriate in dealing with especially sensitive issues, if they offer complete anonymity. Respondents might be reluctant to report controversial or deviant attitudes or behavior in a face-to-face interview, but might do so more willingly in response to an anonymous self-administered questionnaire.

Interview surveys have many advantages, also. As touched on earlier, interview surveys generally produce fewer incomplete questionnaires. Although respondents may skip questions in a self-administered questionnaire, interviewers are trained not to do so. Interview surveys, moreover, typically achieve higher return rates than self-administered ones.

Although self-administered questionnaires may be more effective in dealing with sensitive issues, interview surveys are definitely more effective in dealing with complicated ones. The prime example of that would be the enumeration of household members and the determination as to whether a given household address contained more than one housing unit. Although the concept *housing unit* has been refined and standardized by the Bureau of the Census, and interviewers can be trained to deal with the concept in the field, it would be extremely difficult to devise a self-administered questionnaire dealing with this issue that could be understood by respondents. This advantage of interview surveys pertains more generally to all complicated contingency questions.

With interviewers, it is possible to conduct a survey based on a sample of addresses. An interviewer can arrive at an assigned address, introduce the survey, and even—following instructions—choose the appropriate person at that address to respond to the survey. Self-administered mail questionnaires addressed to "occupant" receive a notoriously low response.

Finally, interviewers are able to make important observations aside from responses to questions asked in the interview. They may, in a household interview, note the characteristics of the neighborhood, the dwelling unit, and so forth. They may note characteristics of the respondents or their interaction with the respondents, such as that a respondent had difficulty communicating or was hostile.

Ultimately, you must balance all these advantages and disadvantages of the two methods in relation to (1) your research needs and (2) your resources.

STRENGTHS AND WEAKNESSES OF SURVEY RESEARCH

Like other modes of observation in social scientific research, surveys have special strengths and weaknesses. It is important to know these in determining whether the survey format is appropriate to your research goals.

As noted earlier in this chapter, surveys are particularly useful in describing the characteristics of a large population. A carefully selected probability sample in combination with a standardized questionnaire offers the possibility of making refined descriptive assertions about a student body, a city, a nation, or other large population. Surveys determine unemployment rates, voting intentions, and the like with uncanny accuracy. Although the examination of official documents—such as marriage, birth, or death records—can provide such accuracy in regard to a few topics, no other method of observation can provide this general capability.

Surveys—especially self-administered ones—make very large samples feasible. Surveys of 2,000 respondents are not unusual. A large number of cases is very important for both descriptive and explanatory analyses. Whenever several variables are to be analyzed simultaneously, it is essential to have a large number of cases.

In one sense, surveys are flexible. Many questions may be asked on a given topic, giving you considerable flexibility in your analyses. Although experimental design may require you to commit yourself in advance to a particular operational definition of a concept, surveys let you develop operational definitions on the basis of actual observations.

Finally, standardized questionnaires have an important strength in regard to measurement generally. Earlier chapters have discussed the ambiguous nature of most concepts: they have no ultimately *real* meanings. One person's religiosity is quite different from another's. Although you must be able to define concepts in ways most relevant to your research goals, you may not find it easy to apply the same definitions uniformly to all subjects. The survey researcher is bound to this requirement by having to ask exactly the same questions of all subjects and having to impute the same intent to all respondents giving a particular response.

Survey research has a number of weaknesses. First, the requirement for standardization just mentioned often seems to result in the fitting of round pegs into square holes. Standardized questionnaire items often represent the least common denominator in assessing people's attitudes, orientations, circumstances, and experiences. By designing questions that will be at least minimally appropriate to all respondents, you may miss what is most appropriate to many respondents. It is in this sense that surveys often appear superficial in their coverage of complex topics. Although this problem can be partly offset through sophisticated analyses, it is inherent in survey research.

Similarly, survey research can seldom deal with the *context* of social life. Although questionnaires can provide information in this area, the survey researcher can seldom develop the feel for the total life situation in which respondents are thinking and acting that, say, the participant observer can.

Although surveys are flexible in the sense mentioned earlier, they are inflexible in other ways. Studies involving direct observation can be modified as field conditions warrant, but surveys typically require that an initial study design remain unchanged throughout. As a field researcher, for example, you can become aware of an important new variable operating in the phenomenon you are studying and begin making careful observations of it. The survey researcher would likely be unaware of the new variable's importance, and could do nothing about it in any event.

Finally, surveys are subject to the artificiality mentioned earlier in connection with experiments. Few studies are aimed at the act of completing questionnaires or of being interviewed, and yet finding out that a person gives conservative answers to a questionnaire does not necessarily mean the person is conservative; finding out that a person gives prejudiced answers to a questionnaire does not necessarily mean that the person is prejudiced. This shortcoming is especially salient in the realm of action. Surveys cannot measure social action; they can only collect self-reports of recalled past action, or of prospective or hypothetical action. There are two aspects of this problem. First, the topic of study may not be amenable to measurement through questionnaires. Second, the act of studying that topic—an attitude, for example—may affect it. A survey respondent may have given no thought to whether the governor should be impeached until asked for his or her opinion by an interviewer. He or she may, at that point, form an opinion on the matter.

In the context of our earlier discussions of validity and reliability, survey research might be seen as generally weak on the former and strong on the latter. In comparison with field research, for example, the artificiality of the survey format puts a strain on validity. As an illustration, people's opinions on issues seldom take the form of strongly agreeing, agreeing, disagreeing, or strongly disagreeing with a specific statement. Their survey responses in such cases, then, must be regarded as approximate indicators of what we have in mind initially in framing the questions. This comment, however, needs to be held in the context of earlier discussions of the ambiguity of *validity* itself. To say something is a valid or invalid measure assumes the existence of a "real" definition of what is being measured, and many scholars now reject that assumption.

Reliability is a clearer matter. Survey research, by presenting all subjects with a standardized stimulus, goes a long way toward eliminating unreliability in observations made by the researcher. Moreover, careful wording of the questions can also reduce significantly the subjects' own unreliability.

As with all methods of observation, a full awareness of the inherent or probable weaknesses of survey research can partially resolve them in some cases. Ultimately, you are on the safest ground when you are able to employ a number of different research methods in studying a given topic.

SECONDARY ANALYSIS

As a mode of observation, survey research involves the following steps: (1) questionnaire construction, (2) sample selection, and (3) data collection, through either interviewing or self-administered questionnaires. As you will have gathered, surveys are usually major undertakings. It is not unusual for a large-scale survey to take several months or even more than a year to progress from conceptualization to having data in hand. (Smaller-scale surveys can, of course, be done more quickly.) At the same time, however, it is possible for you to pursue your particular social research interests, analyzing survey data from, say, a national sample of 2,000 respondents—all the while avoiding the enormous expenditure of time and money such a survey entails. I want to conclude this chapter with a short discussion of *secondary analysis*, which makes the kind of analysis I just mentioned possible.

With the development of computer-based analyses in social research, it has become easily possible for social researchers to *share* their data with one another. Suppose, for example, that I have been able to obtain the money and time to conduct large-scale surveys on the topic of political socialization and the nature of political participation in five different nations. Perhaps I want to learn something about the various faces of democracy as a form of political organization in the United States, Germany, Mexico, England, and Italy. It has taken me a few years and a very large, international staff to design and execute such a set of surveys. Once the interviews are completed, I process the data (see Chapter 13) and analyze them, answering the research questions that led to the study in the first place.

Now suppose further that you have some research interests in the same general area as mine. You have questions you would have addressed had you been able to get the resources necessary for the five-nation survey I conducted. Unfortunately, you couldn't get the money to do such a survey. But here's what you *can* do. For very little money—and assuming my cooperation—you can get a copy of the punch cards or magnetic tape that contains all the data collected in my study. If I have collected the data appropriate to answering your research questions, you are off and running.

The hypothetical situation I've just been describing is not hypothetical at all. In the later 1950s and early 1960s, Gabriel Almond and Sidney Verba designed and executed the five-nation study I've been describing. They reported their research results in 1963 in a book called *The Civic Culture*.[3] Once their own analyses were completed, the researchers made the data available to others for what is appropriately called *secondary analysis*. In the years that followed, the Almond-Verba data have probably become the most analyzed set of data in existence. Individual researchers have pursued particular research interests, and the data have also been used for teaching purposes in research methods classes. Let me illustrate this use with a short personal example.

As a graduate student at Berkeley, I became interested in Charles Glock's notions about the causes of religious involvement. In part, Glock had suggested that people who saw, and felt capable of achieving, secular solutions to social problems would seek those means. Those who did not see secular solutions would turn to the Church. I wanted to test that notion, though I didn't have the resources necessary to conduct a large-scale survey. The Almond-Verba data, however, contained information about both religious and political activities—and about people's perceptions of political solutions to problems. As a result, I was able to examine whether those people who did not see political solutions were more religiously involved than those who did see political solutions. Since the data set had been purchased for use in my research methods class, I was able to undertake my study at absolutely no cost to me.

Beginning in the 1960s, the potential for secondary analysis was developed on an international scale. A consortium of research centers collaborated with one another to form a network of *data archives*, each of which would collect and administer data sets from various parts of the United States and the world. Decks of punch cards and magnetic tapes were shelved the way books are shelved in a conven-

[3]Gabriel Almond and Sidney Verba, *The Civic Culture* (Princeton, N.J.: Princeton University Press, 1963).

tional library, and the holdings were available for broad circulation and use. Whereas library books are loaned, however, the data sets are reproduced and sold—you get to keep your copy and use it again and again for as long as you find new things to study.

The advantages of secondary analysis are obvious and enormous. There are disadvantages, however. The key problem involves the recurrent question of validity. When one researcher collects data for one particular purpose, you have no assurance, of course, that those data will be appropriate to *your* research interests. Typically, you'll find that the original researcher asked a question that comes close to measuring what you are interested in, but you'll wish the question had been asked just a little differently—or that another, related, question had been asked. Your question, then, is whether the question that *was* asked provides a valid measure of the variable you want to analyze.

Notice that this problem resembles closely one of the key problems in the analysis of existing statistics. Recall that Stouffer had to ask whether out-of-state marriages provided a valid measure of what he was calling, on theoretical grounds, impulsive marriages. As in the case of existing statistics, this dilemma in secondary analysis can be lessened through replication. Perhaps a particular set of data do not provide a totally satisfactory measure of what interests you. But there are other sets of data available. Even if no one set of data provides totally valid measures, you can build up a weight of evidence by analyzing all the possibilities. If each of the imperfect measures points to the same research conclusion, you will have developed considerable support for its accuracy.

In the context of the present book, the discussion of secondary analysis has a special purpose. As we conclude our examination of modes of observation in social research, you should have developed a full appreciation of the range of possibilities available to you in finding the answers to questions about social life. There is no single method of getting information that unlocks all puzzles. Yet, on the other hand, there is no limit to the ways you can find out about things. And, more powerfully, you can zero in on an issue from several independent directions, gaining an even greater mastery of it.

SUMMARY

This chapter has concluded the discussion of data collection methods—ways of getting information for the purpose of answering questions about the nature of social life. This lengthy discussion has ended with a look at what is perhaps the most popular form of social research: surveys.

Survey research involves the administration of standardized questionnaires to a relatively large sample of respondents drawn carefully from some relevant population. Our examination of the method began as a continuation of the discussion of operationalization and question wording in Chapter 6. Continuing that earlier discussion, we looked at some of the considerations involved in the format of a questionnaire. The physical layout of questions is sometimes as important as the wording of the questions themselves in assuring that the information elicited will be that which is needed for the research purposes. Several different types of question formats were discussed.

Also important is the order in which questions are asked in a questionnaire. The act of thinking about and answering one question may affect the answers given to subsequent questions. For example, if people are asked to rank the importance of, say, ten problems facing the nation, and are then asked to indicate, in their own words, what they believe to be the one most important national problem, they will very likely pick one from the earlier list.

There are two basic methods for the administration of questionnaires to respondents. *Self-administered* questionnaires may be mailed or handed to respondents who then complete them on their own. The chapter covered some of the considerations involved in this form of questionnaire administration, discussing such matters as various postal options, methods for monitoring the returned questionnaires, follow-up mailings, and response rates. A case study was provided to give a clearer picture of the several steps involved in the use of a self-administered questionnaire.

Sometimes, questionnaires are administered by *interviewers* — specially trained people who contact respondents, read the questionnaire items to them, and record respondents' answers. I discussed the role of the interviewer in this research process and provided a set of general guidelines for interviewing. In addition, I made some suggestions for the coordination and control of interviewers, just in case you find yourself supervising a team of interviewers.

The relative advantages of these two methods of survey administration were then discussed, and, finally, the special strengths and weaknesses of survey research were presented. Against the advantages of economy and standardization, we noted that surveys can be somewhat artificial and superficial.

The chapter concluded with a look at secondary analysis. We saw that the data one researcher collects through interviews or mailed questionnaires can be analyzed over and over by other researchers with somewhat different research interests. A network of data archives has grown up to support this research capability.

MAIN POINTS

1.   Survey research, a popular social research method, is the administration of questionnaires to a sample of respondents selected from some population.

2.   Survey research is especially appropriate for making *descriptive* studies of large populations; survey data may be used for *explanatory* purposes as well.

3.   Contingency questions are those that should be answered only by those persons giving a particular response to some preceding question. The contingency question format is very useful in that it saves asking people to answer questions that have no meaning for them. For example, a question about the number of times a person has been pregnant should be asked only of women.

4.   Matrix questions are those in which a standardized set of closed-ended response categories are to be used in answering several questionnaire items. This format can facilitate the presentation and completion of items.

5.   Questionnaires may be administered in two basically different ways: *self-*

administered questionnaires may be completed by the respondents themselves; *interviewers* may administer questionnaires, reading the items to respondents and recording the answers.

6.   It is generally advisable to plan *follow-up* mailings in the case of self-administered questionnaires: sending new questionnaires to those respondents who fail to respond to the initial appeal.

7.   A proper monitoring of questionnaire returns will provide a good guide as to when a follow-up mailing is appropriate.

8.   The essential characteristic of interviewers is that they be *neutral*; their presence in the data-collection process must not have any effect on the responses given to questionnaire items.

9.   Interviewers must be carefully trained to be familiar with the questionnaire, to follow the question wording and question order exactly, and to record responses exactly as they are given.

10.   A *probe* is a neutral, nondirective question designed to elicit an elaboration on an incomplete or ambiguous response, given in an interview in response to an open-ended question. Examples would include: "Anything else?" "How is that?" "In what ways?"

11.   The advantages of a self-administered questionnaire over an interview survey are: economy, speed, lack of interviewer bias, and the possibility of anonymity and privacy to encourage more candid responses on sensitive issues.

12.   The advantages of an interview survey over a self-administered questionnaire are: fewer incomplete questionnaires and fewer misunderstood questions, generally higher return rates, and greater flexibility in terms of sampling and special observations.

13.   Survey research in general has advantages in terms of economy and the amount of data that can be collected. The standardization of the data collected represents another special strength of survey research.

14.   Survey research has the weaknesses of being somewhat artificial and potentially superficial. It is difficult to gain a full sense of social processes in their natural settings through the use of surveys.

15.   Secondary analysis refers to the analysis of data collected earlier by another researcher for some purpose other than the topic of the current study.

ANNOTATED BIBLIOGRAPHY

Babbie, Earl, *Survey Research Methods* (Belmont, Calif.: Wadsworth, 1973). A comprehensive overview of survey methods. (You thought I'd say it was lousy?) This textbook, although overlapping somewhat with the present one, covers aspects of survey techniques that are omitted here.

Glock, Charles (ed.), *Survey Research in the Social Sciences* (New York: Russell

Sage Foundation, 1967). An excellent collection of essays on the use of survey methods in the several social sciences. This book is especially useful in illustrating the somewhat different ways in which different disciplines regard and utilize a given research method. The several chapters also provide extensive bibliographies, citing examples of survey projects.

Hyman, Herbert, *Survey Design and Analysis* (New York: Free Press, 1955). An old but classic and important overview of survey methods. Although incomplete or outdated in its treatment of survey techniques, it provides an excellent statement of the logic of survey in social research, illustrating the logic with several research examples. Paul Lazarsfeld's foreword is especially important.

Hyman, Herbert, *Secondary Analysis of Sample Surveys* (New York: John Wiley, 1972). A comprehensive overview of secondary analysis. Hyman examines the role of this method within the broader context of social scientific inquiry, discusses methods of secondary analysis, and provides many illustrations.

Lazarsfeld, Paul; Berelson, Bernard; and Gaudet, Hazel, *The People's Choice* (New York: Columbia University Press, 1948). An old but classic survey. This panel survey, conducted in Erie County, Ohio, examined the ways in which voters reached their final presidential preference during the 1940 election campaign. Survey research is currently so popular in the social sciences that citing recent examples is at once very easy and very difficult. I have chosen, therefore, to cite this one for its historical value and because its methodological and substantive values remain current several decades later.

Stouffer, Samuel, *Communism, Conformity, and Civil Liberties* (New York: John Wiley, 1955). Another old but classic survey. This massive survey examined the impact of (Joe) McCarthyism on the attitudes of both the general public and community leaders, asking whether the repression of the early 1950s affected support for civil liberties. Like *The People's Choice* (see above), this book maintains its methodological and substantive importance today.

PART FOUR

Analysis of Data

In this final part of the book, we'll be discussing several aspects of what is the most exciting portion of the research process: the analysis of data and the development of generalized understanding about social phenomena. In the chapters composing Part Four, we'll examine the steps that separate observation from the final reporting of findings.

Chapter 13 is addressed to the quantification of the data collected through the modes of observation discussed in Part Three. Today, much social science data is analyzed by machine: computers and other data-processing devices. Chapter 13 provides a brief overview of some of the equipment involved and describes the processes required to convert observations into forms suitable for machine processing.

The first of several discussions on the logic of data analysis is presented in Chapter 14. We'll begin with an examination of methods of analyzing and presenting the data related to a single variable. Then we'll turn to the relationship between two variables and learn how to construct and read simple percentage tables. The chapter ends with a preview of multivariate analysis.

Chapter 15 is addressed to measurement, a matter that has been discussed several times earlier in the book. This chapter specifically examines techniques of constructing indexes and scales—composite measures of variables.

In their attempt to develop generalized understanding, scientists seek to discover patterns of interrelationships among variables. Very often, these interrelationships take a cause-and-effect form. Chapter 16 is addressed to the logic of causation as appropriate to social scientific research. This theoretical chapter lays the basis for the following ones on analytical techniques.

Chapter 17 describes the elaboration model of data analysis developed by Paul Lazarsfeld at Columbia University. The concluding theme in Chapter 14 will be picked up again and developed further. This chapter will present the logic of causal analysis through the use of percentage tables. The same logic will then be applied in the use of other statistical techniques in subsequent chapters.

Chapter 18 provides an introduction to some of the more commonly used statistical methods in social science research. Rather than merely showing how to compute statistics by these methods (computers can do that), I have attempted to place them in the context of earlier theoretical and logical discussions. Thus, you should come away from this chapter knowing when to use various statistical measures as well as how to compute them.

The book ends with an overview of some of the more advanced methods of multivariate analysis. Again, the emphasis is on understanding the logic of their use rather than how to compute them.

CHAPTER 13

Quantifying Data

INTRODUCTION

The chapters of Part Three have dealt with a variety of methods of collecting social science data through direct or indirect observation. Chapter 13 will deal with the steps involved in converting such data into a form appropriate to *quantitative* analyses.

Put somewhat differently, the purpose of this chapter is to describe methods of converting social science data into a *machine-readable* form—a form that can be read and manipulated by computers and similar machines used in data analysis. Although earlier discussions have touched on this subject, we'll carry it through to its termination here. Once the steps described in this chapter have been completed in a real research project, you will have converted your data into the form of data cards (sometimes known by the trade name, IBM cards), magnetic tape, or something similar.

To insure that you understand what machine-readable data look like, the first section of this chapter will present a brief overview of common data-processing and analysis hardware. Then I'll discuss coding and, finally, the several options available for keypunching.

A QUICK LOOK AT HARDWARE

People often object to social research for attempting to reduce living, breathing human beings to holes in punched cards. Part One of this book dealt with this objection as a philosophical issue; this section and the rest of this chapter will deal with the mechanics of accomplishing the reduction.

An IBM card (Figure 13-1) is divided into 80 vertical columns, which are usually numbered, running from left to right. All of the mechanized data-processing equipment is designed to locate (and read) any specified columns. Data are stored on cards by punching holes within the columns. Each vertical column is further divided into 12 spaces. Ten of those spaces are numbered: 0, 1, 2, 3, 4, 5, 6, 7, 8, 9, from top to bottom. Above the 0 space, two unnumbered spaces are provided: moving up from 0, they are designated minus (−) and plus (+) or sometimes called 11 and 12, or X and Y, respectively.

Figure 13-1   Standard Punch Card for Recording Data

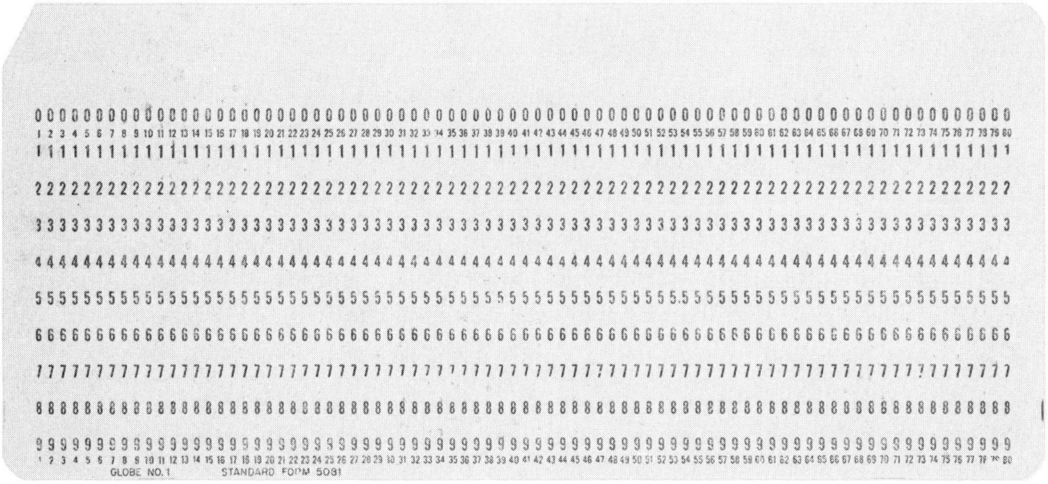

A keypunch machine punches holes in the spaces in columns of IBM cards. Using a keyboard similar to that of a typewriter, the keypunch operator can punch specified holes (0, 1, 2, . . .) into specified columns of a given card. Alphabetical letters and special characters may also be punched, in the form of multiple punches in a column, as illustrated in Figure 13-1. But for our purposes, we'll consider only single-punch, numerical data.

The keypunch machine also has the capacity to read the punches in a given column of one card and transfer those punches to the same column of the card following it in the deck (duplicate option). Finally, the keypunch machine may be programmed to carry out certain operations automatically; these will be mentioned in a later section of this chapter.

Data are put in machine-readable form by assigning one or more specific columns of a data card (a *field*) to a variable, and assigning punches within that column to the various attributes composing that variable. For example, an experimental subject's sex might be recorded in column 5 of the card. If the subject were male, a 1 might be punched in that column; if a female, a 2. The subject's age might be assigned to columns 6 and 7 (a two-column code); if the subject were 35 years of age, 3 and 5, respectively, would be punched in those columns. Or ages could be recorded in categories'and stored in a single column: for example, 1-punch for under 20, 2-punch for 20 to 29, and so forth.

A given card, then, represents the data provided by or about a given subject — the unit of analysis. If the units of analysis were newspaper editorials being examined in a content analysis, each data card would represent an editorial. The columns of each card would be assigned to specific variables describing that editorial. For example, two columns might be assigned to storing the last two digits of the year in which the editorial appeared.

The *precoding* of questionnaires and other data collection documents, which was mentioned in Chapter 12, is nothing more than the specification of card and column assignments to specific data items. If you'll turn back to the first page of Figure 12-7, you'll see what I mean. Notice the notation "(6-15)" in question A-1. This means that the answers to items a-j in question 1 will be stored in columns 6-15. The numbers 1, 2, 3, 4, and 5 printed under the answer categories indicate the answer "SA" (Strongly agree) will be stored as a 1-punch, the answer "A" (Agree) will be stored as a 2-punch, and so forth. The notation "(1-4,5/1)," which identifies case and deck, will be explained later in this chapter.

In survey research, a data card may stand for a questionnaire, with columns assigned to the various items contained in the questionnaire. Column 34 might store answers to the question "Have you ever smoked marijuana?" A 1-punch could represent "yes," and a 2-punch represent "no." The key ideas for you to grasp are that each card represents a single research unit of analysis, and that each *field* of one or more card columns is used for storing the same variable on each card. For example, each survey respondent may have his or her answer to the marijuana question stored in column 34.

Several pieces of equipment are capable of reading data cards. The simplest machine among these is the counter-sorter. This machine may be set to read a given column. Then when the cards are fed into it, they are sorted into pockets corresponding to the punches found in the column, and a counter indicates the number having each of the punches. If sex is recorded in column 5, the sorter would be set on that column, and men and women would be sorted into the 1 and 2 pockets, respectively.

The counter-sorter can be used for tabulating the distributions of responses given to questions in a survey simply by counting the punches to be found in the columns assigned to the questions. The counter-sorter can also be used to examine the relationships between variables.

Suppose you want to determine whether men or women attend church more often. Having separated the respondents by sex as described above, the counter-sorter should then be set to read the column containing responses to the question asking about church attendance. All the men would then be rerun through the counter-sorter to determine the frequency of church attendance as indicated by the punches contained in that column. The same procedure would be repeated for the women, and the distributions of responses would then be compared. Figure 13-2 illustrates the steps in this process.

Figure 13-2   Graphic Illustration of the Analysis of Data by Using a Counter-Sorter

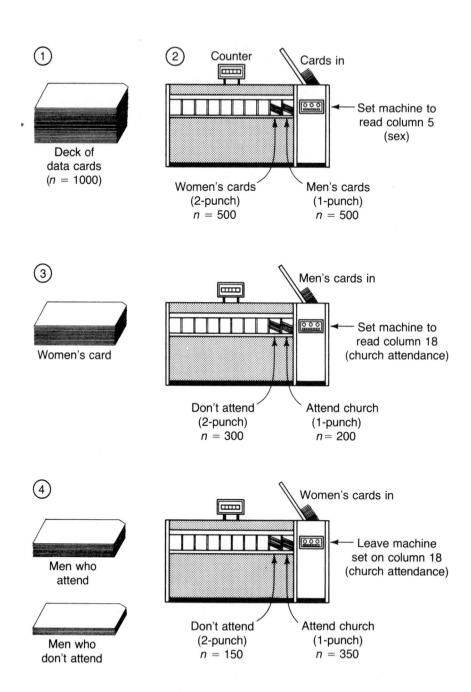

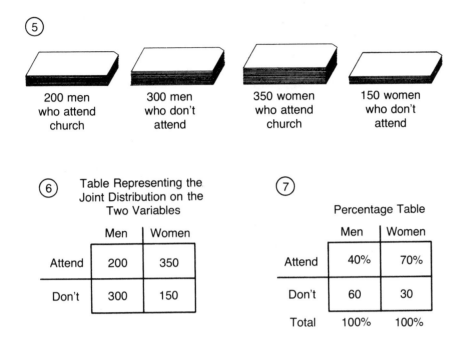

⑤

200 men
who attend
church

300 men
who don't
attend

350 women
who attend
church

150 women
who don't
attend

⑥ Table Representing the
Joint Distribution on the
Two Variables

	Men	Women
Attend	200	350
Don't	300	150

⑦ Percentage Table

	Men	Women
Attend	40%	70%
Don't	60	30
Total	100%	100%

Conclusion: Women are more likely to attend church than men.

The counter-sorter has three basic limitations for the analysis of data. First, it is limited to counting and sorting cards. Although you may use these capabilities for extremely sophisticated analyses, the machine itself cannot perform sophisticated manipulations of data. Second, the counter-sorter is rather slow in comparison with other available machines. Third, it is limited to the examination of one card per unit of analysis in the analysis of relationships among variables. In effect, you are thereby limited to 80 columns of data per unit of analysis (*Note*: Other machines provide for the construction of "work-decks" containing all the data required for a particular phase of the analysis. Data contained on several different cards can be transferred to a single deck, thereby permitting the use of the counter-sorter.)

Most sophisticated analysis today is conducted by the use of computers. The computer—through manipulation programs—can solve all the limitations of the counter-sorter. First, it can go beyond simple counting and sorting to perform intricate computations and provide sophisticated presentations of the results. The computer can be programmed to examine several variables simultaneously and to compute a variety of statistics. Second, if the data are stored on magnetic tape or magnetic disc rather than on cards, those data can be passed through the machine much faster than is possible by the use of cards and the counter-sorter. Moreover, the capability for simultaneous extensive manipulations and computations further speeds the overall analysis. Finally, the computer can analyze data contained on several cards per unit of analysis.

Today, most quantitative social scientific data analyses are achieved through the use of canned programs that cause the computer to simulate the steps illustrated in Figure 13-2 and much more. Essentially, you would take the deck of cards shown in step 1 of Figure 13-2, punch an additional card specifying that you would like to have the percentage table showing the relationship between the data stored in columns 5 and 18, and the computer would subsequently print out a table something like the one shown in step 7 of the figure. You still get to supply step 8.

There are a number of canned programs available for social scientists today. Appendix H of this book gives some information and instructions about the use of one of the more popular of these: SPSS. If you can get a sense of how SPSS works, you will understand the general logic of using computer programs to carry out data analyses.

This chapter will discuss the steps (and options) involved in converting data into forms amenable to the use of counter-sorter and computers. Following a brief presentation of selected data-processing terminology, we'll discuss the coding process and then turn to an enumeration of the several methods of keypunching the data.

SELECTED DATA-PROCESSING TERMINOLOGY

The present section defines some of the terms commonly used in data processing. The later sections of this chapter will utilize those terms that are most likely to be familiar to inexperienced researchers. Nonetheless, you should become familiar with the other terms frequently used.

File   A file is the collection of data pertaining to a given case. Thus, all the information obtained from or about a survey respondent, for example, would constitute his or her data file. All the data describing the experiences and behavior of an experimental subject over the course of an experiment would constitute that subject's file.

Case   The term *case* refers to a concrete instance of the unit of analysis in a study. For example, in a survey, each respondent would be a case. In a content analysis of popular songs, each song would be a case. Each subject in an experiment would be a case. The *number of cases* (typically designated by the letter *n*) is the number of respondents in a survey, subjects in an experiment, and so forth.

Record   A file is composed of one or more records. Typically, a record is a data card, and the data file for a particular subject might be recorded on one or more cards. When data are stored on magnetic tapes or discs, the term *card* becomes somewhat artificial, and records may have different configurations (see *record length* below). Even when tapes and discs are used, however, the card format is often maintained.

Whenever a file contains more than one record, a description of the location of a specific data item (for example, a questionnaire item) must include an indication of the appropriate record. Let's imagine a study in which each case is assigned three cards for the storage of its data file. These cards would be identified as card 1, card 2, and card 3. Each such card would contain a specified set of information. Thus, for example, the length of time required for an experimental subject to complete a given task on a particular trial might be stored in column 30 of card 2. This piece of information would be stored in column 30 of card 2 for each experimental subject. Column 30 of card 1 would contain some other piece of information.

Deck   A deck is a set of records containing the same items of information—for all subjects. *Deck 1*, then, would consist of all the card 1's punched for all subjects. In the coding and keypunching of data consisting of more than one record per case, a deck identification is required to distinguish the different records composing each case's file. (This process will be illustrated in the discussion of codebooks later in this chapter.)

Byte   *Byte* is a technical computer term that generally corresponds to the notion of a data card column in the present context. It specifies a location within a record. Whenever data are stored on magnetic tapes or discs, and the punch-card format is abandoned, the term *column* becomes somewhat anachronistic, and *byte* is more appropriate.

Code   *Code* is also a technical term; it generally corresponds to the notion of *punch* in the language surrounding data cards. Since magnetic tapes and discs do not have holes punched in them, the term *punch* seems as inappropriate as *card* and *column*. (*Note*: The coding process discussed in connection with content analysis and to be discussed again in this chapter refers to the assignment of numerical codes to represent the several attributes composing variables.)

Record Length

Whenever the data record is a card, the record length is 80 columns or 80 bytes, regardless of whether all 80 are actually used. Using tapes and discs, however, the researcher need not be constrained by the conventional 80-column format. With your data initially punched on, say, three cards per case, you might create, on tape or disc, files each composed of one record, 240 bytes in length. It would be as though you had manufactured a long card with 240 columns. A given data item, then, might be located at byte 200 rather than at column 40 of card 3.

CODING

To permit quantitative analyses, data must be converted to the form of numerical codes representing attributes of variables which, in turn, are assigned for storage in specified locations in data files. The conversion of data into this form is called **coding.**

The discussion of content analysis in Chapter 9 dealt with the coding process in a manner very close to our present concern. Recall that the content analysis must develop methods of assigning individual paragraphs, editorials, books, songs, and so forth with specific classifications or attributes. In content analysis, the coding process is inherent in data collection or observation.

When other research methods are employed, it is often necessary to engage in a coding process after the data have been collected. For example, open-ended questionnaire items result in nonnumerical responses, which must be coded before analysis. Or a field researcher might wish to undertake a quantitative analysis based on qualitative field notes. You might wish, for example, to quantify the open-ended interviews you conducted with participants in some social event under study.

As with content analysis, the task here is one of reducing a wide variety of idiosyncratic items of information to a more limited set of attributes composing a variable. Suppose, for example, that a survey researcher has asked respondents "What is your occupation?" The responses to such a question would vary considerably. Although it would be possible to assign each separate occupation reported a separate numerical code, this procedure would not facilitate analysis, which typically depends on several subjects having the same attribute.

In the matter of occupation, there are a number of preestablished coding schemes (none of them very good, however). One such scheme would distinguish professional and managerial occupations, clerical occupations, semiskilled occupations, and so forth. Another scheme distinguishes among different sectors of the economy: manufacturing, health, education, commerce, and so forth. Still others combine both.

The occupational coding scheme used should be appropriate to the analyses intended in the study. From one perspective, it might be sufficient to code all occupations as either white-collar or blue-collar. From another perspective, self-employed and not self-employed might be sufficient. Or a peace researcher might wish to know only whether the occupation was dependent on the defense establishment or not.

Although the coding scheme ought to be tailored to meet particular requirements of the analysis, one general rule of thumb should be kept in mind. If the data are coded so as to maintain a great deal of detail, code categories can always be combined during an analysis that does not require such detail. If the data are coded into relatively few, gross categories, however, there is no way during analysis for recreating the original detail. Thus, you would be well advised to code your data in somewhat more detail than you plan to use in the analysis.

There are two basic approaches to the coding process. First, you may begin with a relatively well-developed coding scheme, derived from your research purpose. Thus, as suggested above, the peace researcher might want to code occupations in terms of their relationship to the defense establishment. Or let's suppose, for example, that you have been engaging in participant observation of an emerging new religion. You have been keeping very careful notes of the reasons new members have given for joining. Perhaps you have developed the impression that new members seem increasingly to regard the religion as a substitute for a family. You might, then, wish to review your notes more carefully—coding each new member's comments in terms of whether this aspect of the religion was mentioned. You might also wish to code their comments in terms of their own family status: whether they have a family or not.

If you are fortunate enough to have assistance in the coding process, your task would be to refine your definitions of code categories and train your coders so that they will be able to assign given responses to the proper categories. You should explain the meaning of the code categories you have developed and give several examples of each. To insure that your coders fully understand what you have in mind, it would be useful for you to code several cases. Then your coders should be asked to code the same cases, without knowing how you coded them, and your coders' work should be compared with your own. Any discrepancies will indicate an imperfect communication of your coding scheme to your coders. Even if there is perfect agreement between you and your coders in this regard, you should still continue to *check-code* at least a portion of the cases throughout the coding process.

If you are not fortunate enough to have assistance in coding, it is still important to obtain some verification of your own reliability as a coder. Nobody is perfect, especially a researcher hot on the trail of a finding. In the case of the participant observer quantifying notes regarding reasons for joining a new religion, let's suppose further that you have the impression that persons who do not have a regular family will be more likely to regard the new religion as a family substitute. There is a danger, then, that whenever you discover a subject who reports no family, you will unconsciously try to find some evidence in the subject's comments that the religion is a family substitute. If at all possible, then, you should try to get someone else to code a portion of your cases—explaining the meaning of your coding scheme—to see if someone else would make the same assignments that you have made. (Note how this relates to the characteristic of *intersubjectivity* in science.)

The second approach to coding is appropriate whenever you are not sure initially how your data should be coded—you do not know what variables they represent among your subjects of study. Suppose, for example, that you have asked, in a questionnaire, "What do you think about the John Birch Society?" Although you might anticipate coding responses as being positive, negative, or neutral, it is unlikely that you would be able to anticipate the full range of variation in responses. In such a situation, it would be useful to prepare a list of perhaps 50 or 100 actual responses to this open-ended question. You could then review that list, noting the different dimensions that those responses reflect. Perhaps you would find that several of the positive responses contained references to the fight against domestic communism; perhaps a number of the negative responses referred to racial prejudice.

Once you have developed a coding scheme based on the list of 50 or 100 responses, you should insure that each of the listed responses would fit into one of the code categories so developed. Then you would be ready to begin coding the remainder of the responses. If you have coding assistance, the previous comments regarding the training and checking of coders would apply here; if you do not, the comments on having your own work checked apply.

Like the set of attributes composing a variable, and like the response categories in a closed-ended questionnaire item, code categories should be both exhaustive and mutually exclusive. Every piece of information being coded should fit into *one and only one* code category. Problems arise whenever a given response appears to fit equally into more than one code category, or when it fits into none.

Since code category assignments for individual cases will ultimately be converted into punches in specific columns of cards, it is essential that you understand that you should *never* punch more than one punch in a given column for a given case —that is, do not plan on *multiple punching*. Most computer programs that you might use simply do not accept multiple punches, and complications arise even in the use of those machines, such as the counter-sorter, that do read multiple punches. Assign a single code category to each observation being coded; punch a single punch in each column being punched. You'll find this one-on-one method will lighten your life once you get your coding going.

Notice that if a subject has two jobs—one within the defense establishment and one outside it—or if a questionnaire respondent checks both "strongly agree" and "agree," you cannot assign both codes to that case. There are a number of methods of resolving such situations. For example, you may be able to establish a logical order of priorities among code categories. In the example of defense-related occupations, you might wish to code a case as having a defense-related occupation even if there is also a nondefense-related occupation. In the example of Likert items, you might want to code multiple answers to the extremes, coding "strongly agree" in the above example.

Another solution to this problem is the assignment of a special code for multiple classifications. In the example of the defense-related occupation, you might want to assign a code of 1 for those with such an occupation *only*, a code of 2 for those without a defense-related occupation, and a code of 3 for those with both kinds.

Sometimes you may want to allow for more than one code category for each case. Let's suppose you are conducting a laboratory experiment in which subjects are given a difficult task to perform, and you wish to analyze their emotional responses to that difficulty. Perhaps you are interested in such reactions as anger, sorrow, humor, violence, resignation, diligence, and so forth. During the course of the experiment, you have noted that many subjects exhibit more than one of these reactions, and you have recorded all that appear. You should not attempt to punch several punches, representing different reactions, in a single column assigned to this variable. There are two ways in which you might handle this situation.

First, you might assign a single column to each of the possible reactions to the situation, and code each subject in terms of whether or not each reaction was exhibited. You might assign column 28 to anger, and use a code of 1 to indicate that the subject exhibited anger and a code of 2 to indicate that he or she did not. Column 29 might be assigned to sorrow, and so forth. This procedure will require the assignment of several columns to subjects' reactions to the experimental situation, but data card columns are about the cheapest resource in research.

As an alternative, you might assign only as many columns to this piece of information as there are different code categories applicable to a given case. Suppose that three reactions was the largest number exhibited by a single subject. Three columns might then be assigned a numerical code: anger could be 1, sorrow could be 2, humor could be 3, and so forth. If a given subject exhibited anger and sorrow, a 1-punch could be put in the first column assigned, a 2-punch could be put in the second column, and the third column could be left blank. If a subject exhibited only humor, then a 3-punch should be put in the first of the columns and the other two should be left blank. This method for handling multiple classifications is most effective if you have access to a computer program that has a capacity to read several columns simultaneously—treating them as a multiple-punched, single column. If you do not have access to such a program, you would do better to use the first alternative described.

Finally, a comment on the use of "blanks" is in order. If you are planning to analyze your data using a counter-sorter, blanks in columns being analyzed present no immediate problem. If you plan to use computer programs, however, you should be warned against the use of blanks. Leaving a column blank (unless it is assigned as a blank column for all cases) is inadvisable for two reasons. First, this procedure creates a quality control problem in data processing. Discovering that a given case is blank in a particular column, you will not be sure whether the blank occurred intentionally or is the result of an error—that the keypuncher failed to punch the appropriate punch in the column. Even "no answer" should be assigned a numerical punch, then.

The second difficulty created by the use of blanks is more technical. Some computers or computer programs assign a special value to blanks as part of their internal operations. Depending on the type of analysis being conducted, a blank may confuse or abort the desired computations.

In the previous example relating to the solution of multiple classifications through the assignment of, say, three columns for coding emotional reactions to an experimental situation, it would be more appropriate to enter a standard punch such as 0 in each column in which no reaction is coded.

CODEBOOK CONSTRUCTION

The end product of the coding process is the conversion of data items into numerical codes representing attributes composing variables, which, in turn, are assigned card and column locations within a data file. A codebook is a document that describes the locations of variables and the code assignments to the attributes composing those variables. A codebook serves two essential functions. First, it is the primary guide used in the coding process. Second, it is your guide for locating variables and interpreting punches in your data file during analysis. If you decide to correlate two variables as a part of your analysis of your data, the codebook tells you where to find the variables and what the punches represent.

Figure 13-3 illustrates portions of the codebook appropriate to the survey questionnaire illustrated in Chapter 12, a questionnaire requiring more than one card per case for data storage. (It would be useful for you to refer back to the questionnaire—paying special attention to the precoding notations.)

Note that columns 1 through 4 of *each deck* have been assigned to the respondent's identification number (case ID). Since there is more than one card per case, this number would be punched into each card so as to permit us to relate all the cards making up a single respondent's data file. Column 5 in the example has been assigned for recording the card or deck identification. Column 5 is used for this purpose in each card, but the number punched is different: appropriately, a 1 is punched in all the card 1's, a 2 in all the card 2's, and so forth.

Figure 13-3   Partial Example of a Codebook

DECK 1 CODEBOOK

COLUMN	DESCRIPTION
1-4	Respondent identification number
5	Deck identification number: 1
6	A-1a. "It would be a good thing if the United Nations were someday converted into a world government." 1. Strongly agree 2. Agree 3. Disagree 4. Strongly disagree 5. Don't know 0. no answer
7	A-1b. "People who defile the American flag should be put in prison." 1. Strongly agree 2. Agree 3. Disagree 4. Strongly disagree 5. Don't know 0. no answer

. . . .

DECK 3 CODEBOOK

COLUMN	DESCRIPTION
1-4	Respondent identification number
5	Deck identification number: 3
6	B-9. "How important is it to you to have the instructor comment on your remarks in class?" 1. Very important 2. Fairly important 3. Not very important 4. Not at all important 0. no answer
7	B-10. "In terms of your own personal satisfaction, how much importance do you attach to getting good grades?" 1. A great deal of importance 2. A fair amount of importance 3. Only a little importance 4. No importance at all 0. no answer

. . . .

DECK 5 CODEBOOK

COLUMN	DESCRIPTION
1-4	Respondent identification number
5	Deck identification number: 5

E-1. "In general, how would you characterize your
       participation in the following activities
       during the time you have been in college?"

6   E-1a. "Varsity athletics"
            1. Much
            2. Some
            3. Little
            4. None
            0. no answer

7   E-1b. "Intramural athletics"
            1. Much
            2. Some
            3. Little
            4. None
            0. no answer

8   E-1c. "Social action or political groups"
            1. Much
            2. Some
            3. Little
            4. None
            0. no answer

. . . .

Only portions of only three of the six decks have been illustrated here. The actual codebook was, of course, much longer.

If we wished to know how much involvement students reported in social action or political groups, the codebook in Figure 13-3 would show us that this information is contained in column 8 of card 5, and that all respondents who have a 1-punch in that column reported "much" participation, those with a 2-punch reported "some" participation, and so forth. Either a counter-sorter or a computer could be used to discover how many students were given each of the punches in question.

If we were interested in the possible relationship between participation in social action and political groups, on the one hand, and attitudes toward the importance of good grades, on the other, the codebook would tell us we must correlate the punches in column 8 of card 5 and column 7 of card 3. How to examine the relationship between two variables such as these will be discussed in Chapter 14.

CODING AND KEYPUNCHING OPTIONS

There are a number of ways in which the coding process may be integrated with the keypunching process so as to provide the desired end product: a set of cards containing the numerically coded data. I'll discuss five different options in this section.

Transfer Sheets

The traditional method of data processing involves the coding of data and the transfer of code assignments to a transfer sheet or code sheet. Such sheets are ruled off in 80 columns corresponding to the data card columns and in rows representing individual cards. Coders write numbers corresponding to the desired punches in the appropriate columns of the sheets.

The code sheets are then given to the keypunchers who punch cards corresponding to the sheets. Once they are punched, the cards are then *verified*. A *verifier* looks very much like a keypunch machine, but instead of punching holes in cards, it reads the punches that have already been punched. The verifier operator loads the deck of punched cards (instead of blank cards) and then simulates the repunching of the code sheets. Whenever the punch attempted for a given column by the verifier operator is the same as the punch already in that column of the card, the card advances to the next column. If the punch attempted by the verifier operator differs from that found in the column, a red light goes on and the machine stops. The verifier operator has two more chances to "punch" the correct number. If an incorrect punch was entered initially, the card is notched over the erroneous column for later correction. After verification and correction, the researcher is provided with a deck of cards that accurately represent the data contained in the questionnaires or other data source-documents. (Incidentally, this method works even when you are the coder, key-puncher, and verifier operator.)

Edge-Coding

Edge-coding is a data-processing method that does away with the need for code sheets. The outside margin of each page of a questionnaire or other data source-document is left blank or is marked with spaces corresponding to data card columns. Rather than transferring code assignments to a separate sheet, the codes are written in the appropriate spaces in the margins. The edge-coded source-documents are then used for keypunching and verification instead of code sheets.

Punching Directly

The earlier discussion of precoding was presented in anticipation of direct punching. This method is especially useful with lengthy questionnaires and other data-collection documents that would present a formidable coding task. If the questionnaires have been adequately designed and precoded, you can *punch directly* from them without the need for separate code sheets or even edge-coding. The precoded questionnaire would contain indications of the columns and the punches to be assigned to questions and responses, and the keypunchers and verifier operators could directly transfer responses to data cards.

When a *punch-direct* method is to be used, it is essential that documents be *edited* before punching. An editor should read through each to insure that every question has been answered (enter a 0 or some other standard code when no answer is given), to insure that there are no multiple answers (change to a single code according to a uniform procedure), and to clarify any unclear responses.

If most of the document is amenable to direct punching (for example, closed-ended questions presented in a clear format), it is also possible to code a few open-ended items and still punch directly. In such a situation, you should enter the code for a given question in a specified location near the question to ease the keypunching job.

The layout of the document is extremely important for effective direct punching. The several question and response categories must be arranged in a logical flow. If most response categories are presented on the right-hand side of the page but one set is presented on the left-hand side, keypunchers frequently miss the deviant set. (*Note*: Many respondents will make the same mistake, so a questionnaire carefully designed for keypunching will be more effective for data collection as well.)

In situations such as content analysis in which coding takes place during data collection, it makes sense to record the data in a form amenable to direct punching. Perhaps a precoded form would be appropriate, or, in some cases, the data might be recorded directly on transfer sheets.

Coding to Optical Scan Sheets

Manual keypunching can be avoided through the use of an *optical scanner*. This machine reads black pencil marks on a special code sheet and punches cards to correspond with those marks. (These sheets are frequently called *mark-sense* sheets.)

It is possible for coders to transfer data to such special sheets in the form of black marks rather than in the form of numbers on a code sheet. The sheets are then fed into an optical scanner and data cards are automatically punched. In some instances, it may be necessary to "translate" the initial punches through the use of a special computer program. In any event, the researcher is ultimately provided with a deck of data cards without the necessity of manual punching. Moreover, it is unnecessary to verify the punching separately.

This use of the optical scanner provides greater accuracy and speed of keypunching. There are several disadvantages, however, which should be mentioned. Some coders find it very difficult to transfer data to the special sheets. Using a conventional code sheet, the coder simply writes the appropriate code number in the next blank space on the sheet. The configuration of op-sense sheets, however, hampers this. Often, it is more difficult to locate the appropriate column, and once the appropriate column is found, the coder must search for the appropriate space to blacken. (The severity of this problem can be appreciated only by attempting to code in both manners.)

Second, the optical scanner has relatively rigid tolerances. Unless the black marks are sufficiently black, the scanner may fail to read and punch. (You will have no way of knowing when this has happened until you begin your analysis.) Moreover, if the op-sense sheets are folded or mutilated, the scanner may refuse to read them at all.

Direct Use of Optical Scan Sheets

It is sometimes possible to use optical scan sheets a little differently and possibly avoid the difficulties they may offer coders. Persons asked to complete questionnaires may be asked to record their responses directly on such sheets. Either standard sheets can be provided with instructions on their use, or special sheets can be prepared for the particular study. Questions can be presented with the several answer categories, and the respondents could be asked to blacken the spaces provided beside the answer they choose. If such sheets are properly laid out, the optical scanner can then read and punch the answers directly. This method may be even more feasible in recording experimental observation or in compiling data in a content analysis.

DATA CLEANING

Whichever data-processing method has been used, you will now have a set of cards that purport to represent the data collected in your study. The next important step is the "cleaning" of those data (eliminating errors).

No matter how, or how carefully, the data have been transferred to cards, some errors are inevitable. Depending on the data-processing method, these errors may result from incorrect coding, incorrect reading of written codes, incorrect sensing of blackened marks, and so forth. Even keypunch verification is not perfect.

Two types of cleaning should be done: *possible-punch* cleaning and *contingency* cleaning. First, for any given variable, there is a specified set of legitimate attributes, translated into a set of possible punches. In the variable *sex*, there will be perhaps three possible punches: 1 for male, 2 for female, and 0 for no answer. If a case is found to contain, say, a 7-punch in the column assigned to sex, it is clear that an error has been made.

Possible-Punch Cleaning

Possible-punch cleaning can be accomplished in two different ways. First, you may have access to computer programs designed for this purpose. You may be able to specify the possible punches associated with each card column, and the computer will then read all the data cards and indicate those cards that have one or more errors. Alternatively, you can examine the distribution of punches in each column (using either the computer or the sorter) and determine whether there are any inappropriate punches. If the column assigned to sex has a 7-punch reported, you might use the sorter to locate the card having this punch. Then you could locate the source-document corresponding to that card (using the ID number), determine what the punch should have been, and make the necessary correction.

Contingency Cleaning

Contingency cleaning is more complicated. The logical structure of the data may place special limits on the responses of certain respondents. For example, a questionnaire may ask for the number of children women have had. All female respondents, then, should have a response punched (or a special code for failure to answer), while no male respondent should have a punch (or should have a special punch indicating the question is inappropriate). If a given male respondent is punched as having borne three children, an error has been made and should be corrected.

Contingency cleaning may be accomplished through computer programs, if available, or through the use of the counter-sorter. In either event, however, the process is more complicated than that for possible-punch cleaning. Computer programs will require a rather complicated set of if-then statements. Manual cleaning will require two or more passes through the counter-sorter to clean each set of items.

Although data cleaning is an essential step in data processing, it should be acknowledged that it may be safely avoided in certain cases. Perhaps you will feel you can safely exclude the very few erroneous punches that appear in a given column —if the exclusion of those cases will not significantly affect your results. Or, some inappropriate contingency responses may be safely ignored. If some men have been given motherhood status, you can limit your analysis of this variable to women. However, you should not use these comments as rationalizations for sloppy research. "Dirty" data will almost always produce misleading research findings.

SUMMARY

Chapter 13 has dealt with the quantification of data: what is often called data processing. The procedures described in this chapter might be applied to data collected in most of the different ways discussed in Part Three. Regardless of how observations initially have been made, the purpose of this phase of research is the same: to transform the records of those observations into standardized, numerical forms suitable for machine processing.

The chapter began with a brief overview of some of the mechanical equipment —hardware—involved in data processing and quantitative data analysis. We discussed keypunch machines, verifiers, sorters, and computers. In that connection, we looked at the manner in which numerical data are stored on data cards: essentially, variables are assigned locations in the form of card columns, and the attributes of those variables are represented by different numerical punches within the appropriate columns.

Following a brief data-processing glossary, the coding process was discussed. We noted that this process is essentially the same as the process of the same name in content analysis. Our discussion focused on the procedures involved in the coding of other types of data, such as experimental or survey data. In this connection, codebooks were discussed and illustrated.

Then, the chapter discussed and described the several different options available to the social researcher in data processing. Some of these options involve manual coding and keypunching, while other options are more mechanized. The relative advantages and disadvantages of each were discussed.

The chapter concluded with a discussion of data cleaning. The purpose of this final stage of data processing is to eliminate any errors that may have been made in coding or keypunching.

MAIN POINTS

1. The quantification of data is necessary in order to permit subsequent statistical manipulations and analyses.

2. The observations describing each unit of analysis must be transformed into standardized, numerical codes for retrieval and manipulation by machine.

3. A given variable is assigned a specific location in the data storage medium: in terms of IBM card columns, for example. That variable is assigned the same location in all the data files containing the data describing the different cases about which observations were made.

4. The attributes of a given variable are represented by different punches in the columns assigned to that variable. (If cards are not being used, other terms apply, but the general idea is the same.)

5. A codebook is the document that describes the locations assigned to different variables and the punches assigned to represent different attributes.

6. A transfer sheet is a special coding sheet upon which numerical codes are recorded. Keypunchers use these transfer sheets to know how to punch the data cards.

7. Edge-coding is an alternative to the use of transfer sheets. The numerical coding is done in the margins of the original documents—such as questionnaires—instead of on transfer sheets.

8. Precoding refers to the assignment of variable locations and appropriate punches for attributes printed on a questionnaire or similar document. Keypunchers are able to punch directly from such original documents if they are properly precoded and edited.

9. Optical scan sheets or mark-sense sheets may be used in some research projects to save time and money in data processing. These are the familiar sheets

used in examinations, on which answers are indicated by black marks in the appropriate spaces. Optical scanners are machines that read the black marks and transfer the same information to data cards by punching them.

10.   Possible-punch cleaning refers to the process of checking punches to see that only those punches assigned to particular attributes—possible punches— appear in given card columns. This process guards against one class of data-processing error.

11.   Contingency cleaning is the process of checking to see that only those cases that *should* have data on a particular variable do in fact have such data. This process guards against another class of data-processing error.

CHAPTER 14
Elementary Analyses

INTRODUCTION

Most social science analysis falls within the general rubric of **multivariate analysis,** and the bulk of Part Four of this book is devoted to the varieties of multivariate analysis. The term simply refers to the examination of several variables simultaneously. The analysis of the simultaneous associations among age, education, and prejudice would be an example of multivariate analysis.

You should realize that multivariate analysis is not a specific form of analysis; specific techniques for conducting a multivariate analysis are factor analysis, smallest-space analysis, multiple correlation, multiple regression, and path analysis, among others. The basic logic of multivariate analysis can best be seen through the use of simple tables, called contingency tables or cross-tabulations. Thus the present chapter is devoted to the construction and understanding of such tables.

Furthermore, multivariate analysis cannot be fully understood without a firm understanding of even more fundamental analytic modes: univariate and bivariate analyses. The chapter, therefore, will begin with these.

UNIVARIATE ANALYSIS

Univariate analysis is the examination of only one variable at a time. We'll begin with the logic and formats for the analysis of univariate data.

The most basic format for presenting univariate data would be the reporting of all individual cases: reporting the attributes describing each case under study in terms of the variable in question. Suppose in a study of corporate executives, you are interested in their ages. (Your data might have been taken from *Who's Who in America*.)

The most direct manner of reporting the ages of corporate executives would be to list them: 63, 57, 49, 62, 80, 72, 55, and so forth. Such a report would provide your reader with the fullest details of the data, but it would be too cumbersome for most purposes.

In the present example, you could report your data in a somewhat more manageable form without losing any of the detail by reporting that 5 executives were 38 years old, 7 were 39, 18 were 40, and so forth. Such a format would avoid duplicate data on this variable.

For an even more manageable format—with a certain loss of detail—you could report executives' ages as a **frequency distribution** of *grouped data*: 256 executives under 45 years of age, 517 between 45 and 50 years of age, and so forth. In this case, your reader would have fewer data to examine and interpret, but he or she would not be able to reproduce fully the original ages of all the executives. Thus, for example, the reader would have no way of knowing how many executives were 41 years of age.

Frequency distributions are often referred to by the term *marginals*, and this term will be used in the following discussions. The above examples have presented marginals in the form of raw numbers. An alternative form would be the use of *percentages*. Thus, for example, you could report that x percent of your corporate executives were under 45, y percent were between 45 and 50, and so forth.

In computing percentages, you frequently must make a decision regarding the *base* from which to compute: that number that represents 100 percent. In the most straightforward case, the base would be the total number of cases under study. A problem arises, however, whenever some cases have missing data. Let's assume, for example, that you have conducted a survey in which respondents were asked to report their ages. If some of the respondents failed to give an answer to the question being reported, however, you have two alternatives. First, you might still base your percentages on the total number of respondents, with those failing to give their ages being reported as a percentage of the total. Second, you could use the number of persons giving an answer as the base from which to compute the percentages. (You should still report the number who did not answer, but they would not figure in the percentages.)

The choice of a base depends wholly on the purposes of the analysis. If, for example, you wish to compare the age distribution of your survey sample with comparable data describing the population from which the sample was drawn, you will probably want to omit the "no answers" from the computation. Your best estimate of the age distribution of all respondents is to be found in the distribution discovered among those answering the question. Since "no answer" is not a meaningful age category, its presence among the base categories would confuse the comparison of sample and population figures. (See Figure 14-1 for an example.)

Moving beyond the reporting of marginals, you may choose to present your data in the form of summary averages or measures of *central tendency*. Your options in this regard include the **mode** (the most frequent attribute, either grouped or ungrouped), the arithmetic **mean**, or the **median** (the *middle* attribute in the ranked distribution of observed attributes). Thus, you might report that most of the corporate executives were between 50 and 55 years of age (mode), that the mean age was 53, or that the median age was 54. Averages have the special advantage to the reader of reducing the raw data to the most manageable form: a single number (or

Figure 14-1   An Illustration of a Univariate Analysis

Ages of Corporate Executives (hypothetical)	
Under 35	9%
36–45	21
46–55	45
56–65	19
66 and older	6
100% =	(433)
No data =	(18)

attribute) can represent all the detailed data collected in regard to the variable. This advantage comes at a cost, of course, since the reader cannot reconstruct the original data from an average. Figure 14-2 illustrates the calculation of these three kinds of averages in detail.

This disadvantage of averages can be somewhat alleviated through the reporting of summaries of the **dispersion** of responses. The simplest measure of dispersion is the range. Thus, in addition to reporting the mean age of 35, you might also indicate that the ages reported ranged from 18 to 69. A somewhat more sophisticated measure of dispersion is the *standard deviation*. This measure was already discussed in Chapter 7 as the standard error of a sampling distribution. As a measure of dispersion in describing data, you might report, for example, that the standard deviation of age among your subjects is 10.5 years, meaning that about 68 percent of the subjects fall within an age range between plus or minus 10.5 years of the mean —between 24.5 and 45.5 years in this example. This measure of dispersion, however, is only appropriate if your data are, in fact, distributed as a *normal curve*—that is, if the distribution of cases both above and below the mean are the same, as in Figure 7-3 in Chapter 7. If, for example, the younger-than-average subjects are bunched together just below the mean and the older-than-average subjects are stretched out more, it wouldn't be appropriate to report the standard deviation.

There are many other measures of dispersion. The *interquartile range* is one example. In reporting intelligence-test scores, for example, you could determine the range of scores of the highest one-fourth of subjects, the second fourth, and so forth. If the highest one-fourth had scores ranging from 120 to 150, and if the lowest one-fourth had scores ranging from 60 to 90, you could report that the interquartile range was 120 to 90, or 30, with a mean score of, let's say, 102.

Throughout the above discussions, we have explored variations in the reporting of a continuous variable, age. If the data being analyzed generated a nominal or limited ordinal variable, then some of the techniques discussed above would not be applicable. If the variable in question were sex, for example, marginals in terms of

Figure 14-2   What Is an Average?

Suppose that an experimenter sets up a situation in which experimental subjects are to complete a particular task within a specified period of time. Some succeed the first time they try it, others succeed the second time, and some take longer. The data below show the number of trials required by different subjects to complete the task. Notice that 7 subjects needed only 1 trial, 12 needed 2 trials, and so forth.

Trials	Number of Subjects
1	7
2	12
3	22
4	18
5	6
6	2

What was the "average" number of trials required for completing the task? This question cannot be answered until we specify which average we mean. Here's how we'd calculate each of the averages discussed in the text.

either raw numbers or percentages would be appropriate and useful. The modal response would be legitimate, but it would convey little useful information to the reader. Reports of mean, median, or dispersion summaries would be inappropriate.

In presenting univariate—and other—data, you will be constrained by two often conflicting goals. On the one hand, you should attempt to provide your reader with the fullest degree of detail regarding those data. On the other hand, the data should be presented in a manageable form. As these two goals often go directly counter to each other, you will find yourself continually seeking the best compromise between them. One useful solution, however, is to report a given set of data in more than one form. In the case of age, for example, you might report both the marginals on ungrouped ages plus the mean age and standard deviation.

, As you can see from this introductory discussion of univariate analysis, this seemingly simple matter can be rather complex. The lessons of this section, in any event, will be important as we move now to a consideration of subgroup descriptions and bivariate analyses.

Mode: 3 trials

The easiest average to calculate is the mode, the most popular value. Since more subjects required 3 trials than any other number of trials, 3 is the mode.

Mean: 3.15 trials

The mean is calculated by totaling the number of trials required by all the subjects:
$(7 \times 1) + (12 \times 2) + (22 \times 3) + (18 \times 4) + (6 \times 5) + (2 \times 6) = 211$ trials. This total is then divided by the number of subjects (67):
$$211 \div 67 = 3.15.$$

Median: 3.18 trials

The median represents the "middle" value. In the case of grouped data, calculating the median is a little tricky. Since there are 67 subjects, subject 34 would be the middle subject if they were arranged in a row according to the number of trials they required in completing the task.

In the imaginary row of subjects, the 7 who only required 1 trial would come first, followed by those requiring 2 trials. The last of those requiring 2 trials would be subject 19. Next come those requiring 3 trials, and the last of these would be subject 41 in the row—meaning that the middle (number 34) subject would have required 3 trials. The median is *not* 3 however.

In calculating the median for grouped data, it matters where *within the group* the middle case appears. In this instance, subject 34 is the fifteenth (of 22) subject in the 3-trial group. To calculate the median, we take the value "3 trials" to represent a range of from 2.5 to 3.5 trials. Then we calculate where subject 34 appears within that range.

The median in this instance, then, is:

$$2.5 + \frac{15}{22} = 3.18.$$

SUBGROUP COMPARISONS

Univariate analyses serve the purpose of *describing* the units of analysis of a study and, if they are a sample drawn from some larger population, of making descriptive inferences about the larger population. Bivariate and multivariate analyses are aimed primarily at *explanation*. Before turning to explanation, however, we should consider the intervening case of subgroup description.

Often you may wish to describe subsets of your subjects. In a straightforward univariate analysis, you might wish to present the distribution of the ages of corporate executives. In exploring this variable in more depth, however, you might want to compare the ages of executives leading new corporations (in terms of the date of incorporation) and old ones. In analyzing a survey of attitudes toward the Ku Klux Klan, you might want to describe the attitudes of whites and blacks separately. In analyzing attitudes toward equal rights for women and men, you might want to analyze the attitudes of men and women separately.

In computing and presenting stratified descriptions, you follow the same steps as outlined in the section on univariate analysis, but the steps are followed independently for each of the relevant subgroups. For example, all men in the sample would be treated as a total sample representing 100 percent, and the distributions of responses or summary averages would be computed for the men. The same would be done for women. Then, you could report that 75 percent of the women approved of sexual equality, and that 63 percent of the men approved. Each group would have been subjected to a simple, univariate analysis. Frequency distributions for subgroups are often referred to as *stratified* marginals.

In some situations, the researcher presents stratified marginals or other subgroup descriptions for purely descriptive purposes. The reporting of census data often has this purpose. The average value of dwelling units on different census blocks may be presented for descriptive purposes. The reader may then note the average house value for any given block.

More often, the purpose of subgroup descriptions is comparative. In the study of sexual equality, you would clearly be interested in determining whether women were *more likely* to approve of the proposition than were men. Moreover, this comparison is not motivated by idle curiosity in most cases. Typically, it is based on an expectation that the stratification variable will have some form of causal effect on the description variable. Whether a subject is a man or a woman should be expected to affect the attitude toward equality of the sexes. Similarly, whether subjects are black or white should be expected to affect their attitudes toward the Ku Klux Klan. When the analysis is motivated by such expectations, we move into the realm of explanation rather than description. At this point, it is appropriate to turn to a discussion of bivariate analysis.

BIVARIATE ANALYSIS

In contrast to univariate analysis, subgroup comparisons constitute a *bivariate analysis* in that two variables are involved. As we noted earlier, the purpose of univariate analysis is purely descriptive. The purpose of subgroup comparisons is also largely descriptive—independently describing the subgroups—but the element of comparison is added. Most bivariate analysis in social research adds another element: relationships among the variables themselves. Thus, whereas univariate analysis and subgroup comparisons focus on describing the *people* (or other units of analysis) under study, bivariate analysis focuses on the *variables*.

Notice, then, that Table 14-1 could be regarded as an instance of subgroup comparisons: independently describing the attitudes of men and women toward sexual equality. We would note—comparatively and descriptively—that the women under study are more supportive of equality than the men.

The same table, seen as an *explanatory* bivariate analysis, tells a somewhat different story. It suggests that the variable *sex* has an effect on the variable *attitudes toward sexual equality*. The attitude is seen as a *dependent variable* that is partially determined by the *independent variable*, sex. Explanatory bivariate analyses, then, involve the "variable language" introduced in Chapter 2. In a subtle shift of focus,

Table 14-1 "Do you approve or
disapprove of the proposition that men and women
should be treated equally in all regards?" (hypothetical data)

	Men	Women
Approve	63%	75%
Disapprove	37	25
	100%	100%
	(400)*	(400)

*The figures shown in parentheses represent the *base* from which the
percentages were computed. In this instance, there are 400 men altogether, 63 percent (252 of the men) of whom approve; 37 percent
(148 of the men) disapprove.

we are no longer talking about men and women as different subgroups but of sex as
a variable: a variable that has an influence on other variables. The logic of interpreting Table 14-1 is as follows:

1. Women generally are accorded an inferior status in American society; thus
they should be more supportive of the proposed equality of the sexes.

2. A respondent's sex should therefore affect (cause) his or her response to the
questionnaire item: women should be more likely to approve than men.

3. If the male and female respondents in the survey are described separately in
terms of their responses, a higher percentage of the women should approve than
of the men.

The data presented in Table 14-1 would confirm this reasoning. Of the women,
75 percent approve of sexual equality as compared to 63 percent of the men.

Adding the logic of causal relationships among variables has an important
implication for the construction and reading of percentage tables. One of the chief
bugaboos for new data analysts is deciding on the appropriate "direction of percentaging" for any given table. In Table 14-1, for example, I have divided the group of
subjects into two subgroups—men and women—and then described each subgroup
in terms of its attitudes. That is the correct method for constructing this table.

Notice, however, that it would have been possible—though inappropriate—to
construct the table differently. We could have first divided the subjects into those
approving of sexual equality and those disapproving of it, and then we could have
described each of those subgroups in terms of the percentage of men and women in
each. This method would make no sense in terms of explanation, however.

Table 14-1 suggests that whether you are a man or a woman will affect how you
feel about sexual equality. Had we used the other method of construction, the table
would suggest that your attitude toward sexual equality affects whether you are a
man or woman—which makes no sense. Your attitude cannot determine your sex.

There is another, related problem that complicates the lives of new data analysts. How do you *read* a percentage table? There is a temptation to read Table
14-1 as follows: "Of the women, 75 percent approved and only 25 percent dis-

approved; therefore being a woman makes you more likely to approve." That is *not* the correct way to read the table, however, though the conclusion seems more or less the same as I gave initially. The conclusion that sex—as a variable—has an effect on attitudes must hinge on a comparison between men and women. Specifically, we note that women are *more likely than men* to approve of sexual equality: comparing the 75 percent with the 63 percent. Suppose, for example, that 100 percent of the men approved. Regardless of the fact that women approved 3 to 1, it wouldn't make sense to say that being a woman increased the likelihood of approval. In fact, the opposite would be true in such a case. The comparison of subgroups, then, is essential in reading an explanatory bivariate table.

In constructing and presenting Table 14-1, I have used a convention called *percentaging down*. This term means that you can add the percentages down each column to total 100 percent. You read this form of table *across* a row. For the row labeled "approve," what percentage of the men approve? what percentage of the women approve?

The direction of percentaging in tables is arbitrary, and some researchers prefer to percentage across. In the present example, they would organize the table so that "men" and "women" were shown on the left side of the table, identifying the two rows, and "approve" and "disapprove" would appear at the top to identify the columns. The actual numbers in the table would be moved around accordingly, and the result would be that each *row* of percentages would total 100 percent. In that case, you would read the table down a column, still asking what percentage of men and of women approved. The logic and the conclusion would be the same in either case; only the form would be different.

In reading a table that someone else has constructed, therefore, you need to find out in which direction it has been percentaged. Usually that will be apparent in the labeling of the table or in the logic of the variables being analyzed. As a last resort, however, you should add the percentages in each column and in each row. If each of the columns totals 100 percent, the table has been percentaged down. If the rows total 100 percent each, it has been percentaged across. Then, the rule of thumb is:

1. If the table is percentaged down, read across.
2. If the table is percentaged across, read down.

Let's take another example. Suppose we are interested in learning something about newspaper editorial policies regarding the legalization of marijuana. Assume we undertake a content analysis of editorials on this subject that have appeared during a given year in a sample of daily newspapers across the nation. Each editorial has been classified as favorable, neutral, or unfavorable toward the legalization of marijuana. Perhaps we might wish to examine the relationship between editorial policies and the types of communities in which the newspapers are published, thinking that rural newspapers might be more conservative in this regard than urban ones. Thus, each newspaper (hence, each editorial) has been classified in terms of the population of the community in which it is published.

Table 14-2 presents some hypothetical data describing the editorial policies of rural and urban newspapers. Note that the unit of analysis in this example is the individual editorial. Table 14-2 tells us that there were 127 editorials regarding marijuana in our sample of newspapers published in communities with populations under 100,000. (*Note*: This cutting point is chosen for simplicity of illustration and does not mean that *rural* refers to a community of less than 100,000 in any absolute sense.) Of these, 11 percent (14 editorials) were favorable toward legalization of marijuana, 29 percent were neutral, and 60 percent were unfavorable. Of the 438 editorials that appeared in our sample of newspapers published in communities of more than 100,000 residents, 32 percent (140 editorials) were favorable toward legalizing marijuana, 40 percent were neutral, and 28 percent were unfavorable. (Remember, this is all hypothetical.)

Table 14-2 Hypothetical Data
Regarding Newspaper Editorials
on the Legalization of Marijuana

Editorial Policy toward Legalizing Marijuana	Community Size	
	Under 100,000	Over 100,000
Favorable	11%	32%
Neutral	29	40
Unfavorable	60	28
100% =	(127)	(438)

When we compare the editorial policies of rural and urban newspapers in our imaginary study, we find—as expected—that rural newspapers are less favorable toward the legalization of marijuana than are urban ones. That is determined by noting that a larger percentage (32 percent) of the urban editorials were favorable than of the rural ones (11 percent). We might note, as well, that rural editorials were more unfavorable (60 percent) than were the urban ones (28 percent). Note that this table shows percentages in such a manner as to assume that the size of a community might affect its newspapers' editorial policies on this issue, rather than that editorial policy might affect the size of communities.

Constructing and Reading Tables

Before turning to an introduction to multivariate analysis, let's review the steps involved in the construction of explanatory bivariate tables. They are as follows:

1. The cases are divided into groups according to their attributes of the independent variable.

2. Each of these subgroups is then described in terms of attributes of the dependent variable.

3. Finally, the table is read by comparing the independent variable subgroups with one another in terms of a given attribute of the dependent variable.

Let's repeat the analysis of sex and attitudes on sexual equality following these steps. For the reasons outlined above, sex is designated as the independent variable; attitudes toward sexual equality constitute the dependent variable. Thus, we proceed as follows:

1. The cases are divided into men and women.

2. Each sex subgrouping is described in terms of approval or disapproval of sexual equality.

3. Men and women are compared in terms of the percentages approving of sexual equality.

In the example of editorial policies regarding the legalization of marijuana, size of community would be the independent variable and a newspaper's editorial policy would be the dependent variable. The table would be constructed as follows:

1. Divide the editorials into subgroups according to the sizes of the communities in which the newspapers are published.

2. Describe each subgroup of editorials in terms of the percentages favorable, neutral, or unfavorable toward the legalization of marijuana.

3. Compare the two subgroups in terms of the percentages favorable toward the legalization of marijuana.

Bivariate analyses typically have an explanatory causal purpose. These two hypothetical examples have hinted at the nature of causation as it is used by social scientists. I hope the rather simplified approach to causation employed in these examples will have a commonsense acceptability for you at this point. This rather superficial, commonsense view of causation will assist you in understanding this chapter and the next. Chapter 16 will take a much closer look at causation. A fundamental understanding of the subjects covered in this chapter and the next one should help you understand more fully the complex nature of causation.

Bivariate Table Formats

The format for presenting contingency table data has never been standardized, with the result that a variety of formats will be found in research literature. As long as a table is easily read and interpreted, there is probably no reason to strive for standardization. However, there are a number of guidelines that should be followed in the presentation of most tabular data.

1. A table should have a heading or a title that succinctly describes what is contained in the table.

2. The original content of the variables should be clearly presented—in the table itself if at all possible—or in the text with a paraphrase in the table. This information is especially critical when a variable is derived from responses to an

attitudinal question, since the meaning of the responses will depend largely on the wording of the question.

3. The attributes of each variable should be clearly indicated. In the case of complex categories, these will have to be abbreviated, but the meaning should be clear in the table and, of course, the full description should be reported in the text.

4. When percentages are presented in the table, the base upon which they are computed should be indicated. Note that it is redundant to present all of the raw numbers for each category, since these could be reconstructed from the percentages and the bases. Moreover, the presentation of both numbers and percentages often confuses a table and makes it more difficult to read.

5. If any cases are omitted from the table because of missing data ("no answer," for example), their numbers should be indicated in the table.

Table 14-3 is an example of a good table.

Table 14-3 "Do you approve or disapprove of the proposition that men and women should be treated equally in all regards?"

	Men	Women
Approve	63%	75%
Disapprove	37	25
	100%	100%
	(400)	(400)
No answer =	(12)	(5)

INTRODUCTION TO MULTIVARIATE ANALYSIS

The logic of multivariate analysis is the topic of later chapters in this book—especially Chapter 17. At this point, however, it will be useful to discuss briefly the construction of multivariate tables: those constructed from several variables.

Multivariate tables may be constructed on the basis of a more complicated subgroup description by following essentially the same steps outlined above for bivariate tables. Instead of one independent variable and one dependent variable, however, we will have more than one independent variable. Instead of explaining the dependent variable on the basis of a single independent variable, we'll seek an explanation through the use of more than one independent variable.

Let's return to the example of attitudes toward sexual equality; suppose that we believed age would also affect such attitudes: that young people would approve of sexual equality more than would older people. As the first step in table construction, we would divide the total sample into subgroups based on the various attributes of *both* independent variables simultaneously: young men, old men, young women, and old women. Then the several subgroups would be described in terms of the dependent variable, and comparisons would be made. Table 14-4 is a hypothetical table that might result.

Table 14-4 "Do you approve or disapprove of the proposition that men and women should be treated equally in all regards?" (multivariate)

| | Under 30 | | 30 and Over | |
	Women	Men	Women	Men
Approve	90%	78%	60%	48%
Disapprove	10	22	40	52
	100%	100%	100%	100%
	(200)	(200)	(200)	(200)
No answer =	(2)	(10)	(3)	(2)

Following the convention of this textbook, this table has also been percentaged down, and it should, therefore, be read across. The interpretation of this table warrants several conclusions:

1. Among both men and women, younger people are more supportive of sexual equality than are older people. Among women, 90 percent and 60 percent, respectively, approve.

2. Within each age group, women are more supportive than are men. Among those respondents under 30 years of age, 90 percent of the women approve, compared with 78 percent of the men. Among those 30 and over, 60 percent of the women and 48 percent of the men approve.

3. As measured in the table, age would appear to have a stronger effect on attitudes than sex. For both men and women, the effect of age may be summarized as a 30 percentage point difference. Within each age group, the percentage point difference between men and women is 12.

4. Both age and sex have independent effects on attitudes. Within a given attribute of one independent variable, different attributes of the second still affect attitudes.

5. Similarly, the two independent variables have a cumulative effect on attitudes. Young women are most supportive, and older men are the least supportive.

Chapter 17 on the *elaboration model* will examine the logic of multivariate analysis in much greater detail. Before we conclude this section, however, it will be useful to note an alternative format for presenting such data.

Several of the tables presented in this chapter are somewhat inefficient. When the dependent variable—attitude toward sexual equality—is dichotomous (two attributes), knowing one attribute permits the reader to easily reconstruct the other. Thus, if we know that 90 percent of the women under 30 years of age approve of sexual equality, then we know automatically that 10 percent disapprove. Reporting the percentages who disapprove, then, is unnecessary. On the basis of this recognition, Table 14-4 could be presented in the alternative format of Table 14-5.

Table 14-5 "Do you approve or disapprove of the proposition that men and women should be treated equally in all regards?" (simplification of Table 14-4)

	Percentage Who Approve	
	Women	Men
Under 30	90	78
	(200)	(200)
30 and Over	60	48
	(200)	(200)

In Table 14-5, the percentages approving of sexual equality are reported in the cells representing the intersections of the two independent variables. The numbers presented in parentheses below each percentage represent the number of cases upon which the percentages are based. Thus, for example, the reader knows that there are 200 women under 30 years of age in the sample, and 90 percent of those approved of sexual equality. This shows, moreover, that 180 of those 200 women approved, and that the other 20 (or 10 percent) disapproved. This new table is easier to read than the former one, and it does not sacrifice any detail.

I want to conclude this discussion with a somewhat more complicated multivariate table, drawn from the literature of social research. This example represents an attempt by sociologist Morris Rosenberg to shed some light on *self-esteem* among adolescent boys.[1] As we see in Table 14-6, Rosenberg has examined the simultaneous impact of three variables on self-esteem:

1. *Sex distribution of siblings*: Do the subjects live in families where girls outnumber boys or where boys either equal or outnumber the girls?

2. *Ordinal position*: Are the subjects older or younger brothers within their families?

3. *Grades*: What kinds of grades do the subjects get in school?

[1]Morris Rosenberg, *Society and the Adolescent Self-Image* (Princeton, N.J.: Princeton University Press, 1965).

Table 14-6   Self-Esteem of Adolescent Boys in Relation
to Sex Distribution of Siblings, Ordinal Position, and Grades

Self-Esteem	Respondent in First Half or Middle of Family			Respondent in Last Half of Family (younger minority)		
	Grades			Grades		
	A–B	C	D–F	A–B	C	D–F
No Brothers or Brothers in the Minority						
High	56%	45%	41%	46%	60%	64%
Medium	20	27	27	19	18	18
Low	24	28	32	35	22	18
Total percent	100%	100%	100%	100%	100%	100%
Number	(79)	(104)	(41)	(26)	(65)	(22)
Brothers in the Majority or Equal						
High	51%	40%	29%	42%	44%	30%
Medium	26	27	18	32	33	20
Low	23	32	53	26	23	50
Total percent	100%	99%	100%	100%	100%	100%
Number	(168)	(240)	(102)	(78)	(86)	(56)

Source: Adapted from *The Logic of Survey Analysis*, by Morris Rosenberg, p. 214, Basic Books, Inc., Publishers.

Note: Study is of families with three or more children.

Let's see what Table 14-6 tells us about self-esteem. To simplify matters, let's focus on the percentages of those who are high in self-esteem in our comparisons. What effect do the three variables listed above have on high self-esteem among adolescent boys?

To determine the impact of the sex distribution of siblings, we compare the top rows of percentages in the two halves of the table: 56 to 51 percent, 45 to 40 percent, 41 to 29 percent, 46 to 42 percent, 60 to 44 percent, and 64 to 30 percent. What pattern do you notice in all those comparisons? In each case, the boys living in families with a sister majority (top half of table) are more likely to have high self-esteem than boys similar to them in every regard except sibling sex distribution. Consistently, living in a sister majority family seems to promote higher self-esteem.

Although consistent, the differences are not uniform, however. Overall, the sex distribution of siblings seems to matter most for those boys who get bad grades in school. There are only small differences among those with good grades.

How about ordinal position? Is self-esteem affected by whether boys are older or younger within their set of brothers and sisters? To find out, we make a different set of comparisons, comparing the right and left halves of the table: 56 to 46 percent, 45 to 60 percent, 41 to 64 percent (in the top half of the table), 51 to 42 percent, 40 to 44 percent, and 29 to 30 percent (in the bottom half). Notice once again, that we are comparing groups of boys who are similar to each other except for their ordinal position.

What pattern do you see in this latest set of comparisons? I don't see much of a pattern. Although the various comparisons reveal differences in self-esteem, we cannot conclude there is a consistent relationship between ordinal position and high self-esteem. Sometimes the older boys have higher self-esteem, sometimes the younger ones do.

Finally, what effect do grades have on self-esteem? Logically, we would probably suspect that good grades would result in high self-esteem and bad grades in low self-esteem. Let's see if that's true. Here the relevant comparisons are among the three grade groupings in each of the four parts of the table: 56 to 45 to 41 percent, 46 to 60 to 64 percent, 51 to 40 to 29 percent, and 42 to 44 to 30 percent. Is our suspicion confirmed by the data?

Grades seem to have the expected effect on self-esteem among those boys who have an older position among their brothers and sisters, but we find a very different pattern among the younger minority brothers. For Rosenberg, the latter set of data pointed to

> . . . the possibility that the younger-minority boy might be characterized by a particular *type* of self-esteem, namely, *unconditional self-acceptance*. While the self-esteem of others appeared to be influenced by their level of academic performance, the self-esteem of the younger-minority boy appeared to be relatively impervious to it. It might thus be that the self-esteem of the younger-minority boy was so firmly established in the family by the interest and affection of his father, mother, and older sisters that it was relatively independent of later extra-familial experiences.[2]

This latest illustration should give you a fuller view of multivariate analysis through the use of percentage tables. At a superficial level, you have now been exposed to the entire process of data analysis.

In this sense, the remaining chapters of this book are a review—at a much deeper level—of materials already covered. Chapter 15 presents the topic of measurement at a more sophisticated level than our earlier discussion as we take up the construction of composite scales and indexes. And although we have looked fleetingly at the topic of causation, Chapter 16 examines it more seriously. Then, Chapters 17 through 19 are a review of and expansion on the basic topic of the present chapter—the logic of data analysis.

It has been essential to cycle and recycle you through the several aspects of data analysis in order to gain a sufficient depth of understanding and ability. For example, you will see in the following chapter that you need a degree of understanding of table construction and of relationships among variables to follow the construction of indexes and scales in fully coming to grips with the problem of measurement. The ability to handle composite measures, in turn, will allow you to get more deeply into the analysis of relationships.

---

[2]Morris Rosenberg, *The Logic of Survey Analysis* (New York: Basic Books, 1968), p. 214.

SUMMARY

Chapter 14 has introduced some of the more elementary methods of quantitative data manipulations. This introduction is based on the belief that you cannot appreciate and understand complex analytical methods unless you fully understand those that seem fairly simple.

The chapter began with univariate analysis: the analysis of a single variable. In short order, we discovered that the social researcher faces a very wide range of options in the analysis and presentation of even a single variable. We looked at different methods of data reduction: ways of summarizing a set of observations, all the while attempting to maintain the greatest amount of detail. We discussed frequency distributions, percentages, grouped data, averages, and measures of dispersion.

Next, the chapter turned to the concept of subgroup comparisons. Here we were concerned with univariate analyses of different subsets of the total population of observations. The univariate descriptions of those subsets were then compared.

Bivariate analysis, examined next, is nothing more than a slightly different interpretation of subgroup comparisons. That slightly different interpretation, however, involves the concepts of causation and explanation. Rather than simply comparing subgroups of a population, the purpose in bivariate analysis is to begin examining the relationships between variables.

Considerable attention was given to the construction and interpretation of bivariate percentage tables, since these are very common in social research, their seeming simplicity is deceptive, and they contain within them the basic logic of explanatory data analysis.

Finally, the chapter turned to an introduction to multivariate analysis. This critical topic will be pursued in considerably more detail in Chapter 17.

MAIN POINTS

1. Univariate analysis is the analysis of a single variable.

2. The full original data collected with regard to a single variable are, in that form, usually impossible to interpret. *Data reduction* is the process of summarizing the original data so as to make them more manageable, all the while maintaining as much of the original detail as possible.

3. A frequency distribution shows the number of cases having each of the attributes of a given variable.

4. Grouped data are created through the combination of attributes of a variable.

5. *Averages* (the mean, median, and mode) reduce data to an easily manageable form, but they do not convey the detail of the original data.

6. Measures of dispersion give a summary indication of the distribution of cases around an average value.

7. To undertake a subgroup comparison: (a) divide cases into the appropriate subgroups, (b) describe each subgroup in terms of a given variable, and (c) compare those descriptions across the subgroups.

8. Bivariate analysis is nothing more than a different interpretation of subgroup comparisons: (a) divide cases into subgroups in terms of their attributes on some *independent variable*, (b) describe each subgroup in terms of some *dependent variable*, (c) compare the *dependent variable* descriptions of the subgroups, and (d) interpret any observed differences as a statistical association between the independent and dependent variables.

9. As a rule of thumb in interpreting bivariate percentage tables: (a) "percentage down" and "read across" in making the subgroup comparisons *or* (b) "percentage across" and "read down" in making subgroup comparisons.

10. Multivariate analysis is a method of analyzing the simultaneous relationships among several variables and may be used in more fully understanding the relationship between two variables.

ANNOTATED BIBLIOGRAPHY

Cole, Stephen, *The Sociological Method* (Chicago: Markham, 1972). A readable introduction to analysis. Cole begins with the general question of what social scientific inquiry is, and then illustrates with easily understood examples. He goes on to an introduction of the elaboration model, and that material is useful also.

Davis, James, *Elementary Survey Analysis* (Englewood Cliffs, N.J.: Prentice-Hall, 1971). An extremely well-written and well-reasoned introduction to analysis. In addition to covering the materials of the present book's Chapter 14, Davis's book is well worth reading in terms of measurement, statistics, and the elaboration model.

Labovitz, Sanford, and Hagedorn, Robert, *Introduction to Social Research* (New York: McGraw-Hill, 1971). Another useful introduction to analysis. Against the background of more general concerns for social scientific inquiry, the authors provide a very readable and useful introduction to elementary analyses in their Chapter 6. Like Cole and Davis, they then go on to a consideration of multivariate analysis and the elaboration model.

Zeisel, Hans, *Say It With Figures* (New York: Harper & Row, 1957). An excellent discussion of table construction and other elementary analyses. Though several years old, this is still perhaps the best available presentation of that specific topic. It is eminently readable and understandable and has many concrete examples.

CHAPTER 15

Index and Scale Construction

INTRODUCTION

Chapter 15, like Chapters 5 and 6, is addressed to the matter of measurement. It is a logical continuation of the earlier discussion of conceptualization and operationalization. The earlier discussions examined some of the ways in which measurement is dealt with in the design of a social research study; the present chapter describes the continuation of that concern during the analysis of data.

This chapter discusses the construction of indexes and scales as composite measures of variables. A short section at the end of the chapter considers typologies. These different types of composite or cumulative measures are very frequently used in social research. Each type involves the combination of several empirical indicators of a variable into a single measure.

There are several reasons for the frequent use of composite measures. First, despite the care taken in designing studies so as to provide valid and reliable measurements of variables, the researcher seldom is able to develop in advance single indicators of complex concepts. That is especially true with regard to attitudes and orientations. The survey researcher, for example, is seldom able to devise single questionnaire items that adequately tap respondents' degrees of prejudice, religiosity, political orientations, alienation, and the like. More likely, you will devise several items, each of which provides *some* indication of the variables. Each of these, however, is likely to prove invalid or unreliable for many respondents.

You should realize that *some* variables are rather easily measured through single indicators. We may determine a survey respondent's sex by asking: Sex: [ ] Male [ ] Female. We may determine a newspaper's circulation by merely looking at the figure the newspaper reports. The number of times an experimental stimulus is administered to an experimental group is clearly defined in the design of the experiment. Nonetheless, social scientists, using a variety of research methods, frequently wish to study variables that have no clear and unambiguous single indicators.

Second, you may wish to employ a rather refined ordinal measure of your variable, arranging cases in several ordinal categories from—for example—very low to very high on a variable. A single data item might not have sufficient categories to provide this range of variations, but an index or scale formed from several items would.

Finally, indexes and scales are *efficient* devices for data analysis. If considering a single data item gives us only a rough indication of a given variable, considering several data items may give us a more comprehensive and more accurate indication. For example, a single newspaper editorial may give us some indication of the political orientations of that newspaper. Examining several editorials, on the other hand, would probably give us a better assessment, but the manipulation of several data items simultaneously could be very complicated. Indexes and scales (especially scales) are efficient *data-reduction devices*: several indicators may be summarized in a single numerical score, while sometimes very nearly maintaining the specific details of all the individual indicators.

INDEXES VERSUS SCALES

The terms *index* and *scale* are typically used imprecisely and interchangeably in social research literature. Before considering the distinctions that this book will make between indexes and scales, let's first see what they have in common.

Both scales and indexes are typically *ordinal* measures of variables. Scales and indexes are constructed in such a way as to rank-order people (or other units of analysis) in terms of specific variables such as religiosity, alienation, socioeconomic status, prejudice, or intellectual sophistication. A person's score on a scale or index of religiosity, for example, gives an indication of his or her relative religiosity vis-à-vis other people.

As the terms will be used in this book, both scales and indexes are *composite measures of variables*: measurements based on more than one data item. Thus, a survey respondent's score on an index or scale of religiosity would be determined by the specific responses given to several questionnaire items, each of which would provide some indication of his or her religiosity. Similarly, a person's IQ score is based on answers to a large number of test questions. The political orientation of a newspaper might be represented by an index or scale score reflecting the newspaper's editorial policy on a number of political issues.

For the purposes of this book, we shall distinguish indexes and scales through the manner in which scores are assigned. An **index** is constructed through the simple accumulation of scores assigned to *individual* attributes. A **scale** is constructed through the assignment of scores to *patterns* of attributes. A scale differs from an index by taking advantage of any *intensity structure* that may exist among those attributes. A simple example should clarify this distinction.

Suppose we wished to measure support of civil liberties for Communists. We might ask in a questionnaire whether a Communist should be allowed to pursue the following occupations: (1) lawyer, (2) doctor, (3) minister, (4) engineer, (5) newspaper reporter. Some people would be willing to allow a Communist to pursue all of the occupations listed; some would be unwilling to permit any. Many, however, would feel that some were permissible while others were not. Each person who gave a mixed set of responses presumably would be indicating that he or she felt some of the occupations to be more important than others. The relative priorities of the different occupations would vary from person to person, however; there is no absolute ranking inherent in the occupations themselves. Given the responses to such a questionnaire, you might construct an index of respondents' relative commitments to civil liberties for Communists on the basis of the *number* of occupations they would hold open to Communists. The respondent who would permit a Communist to hold all the occupations clearly would support a greater degree of civil liberty than one who would close all occupations to a Communist. Moreover, you would assume that the respondent who would permit a Communist to hold three of the occupations would be more supportive of a Communist's civil liberties than the respondent who would hold open only one or two of the occupations, regardless of which one, two, or three occupations are involved. Such an index might provide a useful and accurate ordinal measure of attitudes about civil liberties.

Suppose for a moment, however, that the occupations used in the above example had been: (1) ditch digger, (2) high school teacher, and (3) President of the United States. In this situation, there is every reason to believe that these three items have an *intensity structure*. The person who would permit a Communist to be President would surely permit Communists to be high school teachers and ditch diggers. On the other hand, the respondent who would permit Communists to dig ditches might not permit them in the other two occupations. In all likelihood, in this study, knowing the *number* of occupations approved for Communists would tell us *which* occupations were approved. In such a situation, a composite measure composed of the three items would constitute a *scale* as I have used the term.

It should be apparent that scales are generally superior to indexes, if for no other reason than that scale scores convey more information than do index scores. Still you should be wary of the common misuse of the term *scale*; clearly, calling a given measure a scale rather than an index does not make it better. You should be cautioned against two other misconceptions about scaling. First, whether the combination of several data items results in a scale almost always depends on the particular sample of observations under study. Certain items may form a scale among one sample but not among another, and you should not assume that a given set of items *are* a scale because they have formed a scale among a given sample. Second, the use of certain *scaling techniques* to be discussed does not insure the creation of a scale any more than the use of items that have previously formed scales can offer such insurance.

An examination of the substantive literature based on social science data will show that indexes are used much more frequently than scales. Ironically, however, the methodological literature contains little if any discussion of index construction, while discussions of scale construction abound. There appear to be two reasons for this disparity. First, indexes are more frequently used because scales are often difficult or impossible to construct from the data at hand. Second, methods of index construction are not discussed because they seem obvious and straightforward.

Index construction is not a simple undertaking. Furthermore, I feel that the general failure to develop index construction techniques has resulted in the creation of many bad indexes in social research. With this in mind, I have devoted most of this chapter to the methods of index construction. Once the logic of this activity is fully understood, you will be better equipped to attempt the construction of scales. Indeed, the carefully constructed index may turn out to be a scale anyway.

INDEX CONSTRUCTION

Let's look now at the several steps involved in the creation of an index. I have presented these steps in some detail, since they are not all obvious. You should come away from this section able to create a composite measure that will fully support your subsequent analyses.

Item Selection

A composite index is created for the purpose of measuring some variable. The first criterion for selecting items to be included in the index is *face validity* (or logical validity). If you want to measure political conservatism, for example, each of the items considered should appear on its face to indicate conservatism (or its opposite: liberalism). Political party affiliation would be one such item. If people were asked to approve or disapprove of the views of a well-known conservative public figure, their responses might, logically, provide another indication of their conservatism. If you were interested in constructing an index of religiosity, you might consider church attendance, acceptance of certain religious beliefs, and frequency of prayer; each of these would appear to offer some indication of religiosity.

Typically, the methodological literature on conceptualization and measurement stresses the need for *unidimensionality* in scale and index construction: a composite measure should represent only one dimension. Thus, items reflecting religiosity should not be included in a measure of political conservatism, even though the two variables might be empirically related to one another. In this sense, an index or scale should be unidimensional.

At the same time, you should be constantly aware of the subtle nuances that may exist within the general dimension you are attempting to measure. Thus in the example of religiosity, the indicators mentioned above represent different *types* of religiosity. If you wished to measure ritual participation in religion, you should limit the items included in the measure to those specifically indicating this type of religiosity: church attendance, communion, confession, and the like. If, on the other hand, you wished to measure religiosity in a more general way, you would want to include a balanced set of items, representing each of the different types of religiosity. Ultimately, the nature of the items included will determine how specifically or generally the variable is measured.

In selecting items for inclusion in an index, you must also be concerned with the amount of *variance* provided by those items. If an item provided an indication of political conservatism, for example, you should note what proportion of respondents were identified as conservatives by the item. In the extremes, if a given item identified no one as a conservative or everyone as a conservative, the item would not be very useful in the creation of an index. If nobody indicated approval of a radical right political figure, an item about that person would not be of much use in the construction of an index.

With regard to variance, you have two options. First, you may select several items on which responses divide people about equally in terms of the variable. Thus you might select several items, each of which attains responses that are about half conservative and half liberal. Although none of these items would justify characterization of a person as very conservative, a person who appeared conservative on all of them might be so characterized.

The second option is the selection of items differing in variance. One item might identify about half the subjects as conservative, while another might identify few of the respondents as conservative. (*Note*: This latter option is necessary for scaling, but it is reasonable for the construction of an index as well.)

Bivariate Relationships among Items

The second step in index construction is the examination of the bivariate relationships among the items being considered for inclusion. If each of the items does indeed give an indication of the variable—as suggested on grounds of face validity— then the several items should be related to one another empirically. For example, if several items all reflect conservatism or liberalism, then those who appear conservative in terms of one item should appear conservative in terms of others. Recognize, however, that such items will seldom if ever be perfectly related to one another; persons who appear conservative on one item will appear liberal on another. (This disparity creates the need for constructing composite measures in the first place.) Nevertheless, persons who appear conservative on item A should be more likely to appear conservative on item B than do persons who appear liberal on item A.

You should examine all the possible bivariate relationships among the several items being considered for inclusion in the index to determine the relative strengths of relationships among the several pairs of items. Either percentage tables or correlation coefficients (see Chapter 18), or both, may be used for this purpose. The primary criterion for evaluating these several relationships is the strength of the relationships. The use of this criterion, however, is rather subtle.

Clearly, you should be wary of items that are not related to one another empirically. It is unlikely that they measure the same variable if they are unrelated. More to the point, perhaps, a given item that is unrelated to several of the other items probably should be dropped from consideration.

At the same time a *very* strong relationship between two items presents a different problem. At the extreme, if two items are perfectly related to one another, then only one is necessary for inclusion in the index, since it completely conveys the indications provided by the other. (This problem will become even clearer in the next section.)

To illustrate the steps in index construction, an example from the substantive literature may be useful.[1] A few years ago, I conducted a survey of medical school faculty members to find out about the consequences of a "scientific perspective" on the quality of patient care provided by physicians. The primary intent was to determine whether more scientifically inclined doctors were more impersonal in their treatment of patients than were other doctors.

The survey questionnaire offered several possible indicators of respondents' scientific perspectives. Of those, three items appeared—in terms of face validity—to provide especially clear indications of whether or not the doctors were scientifically oriented. The three items were:

1. "As a medical school faculty member, in what capacity do you feel you can make your greatest *teaching* contribution: as a practicing physician or as a medical researcher?"

2. "As you continue to advance your own medical knowledge, would you say your ultimate medical interests lie primarily in the direction of total patient management or the understanding of basic mechanisms?"

3. "In the field of therapeutic research, are you generally more interested in articles reporting evaluations of the effectiveness of various treatments or articles exploring the basic rationale underlying the treatments?"

In each of the items above, the second answer would indicate a greater scientific orientation than the first answer. Taking the responses to a single item, we might conclude that those respondents who chose the second answer are more scientifically oriented than those who chose the first answer. This *comparative* conclusion is a reasonable one, but we should not be misled into thinking that respondents who chose the second answer to a given item are scientists in any absolute sense. They are simply *more scientific* than those who chose the first answer to the item. This important point will become clearer when we examine the distribution of responses produced by each of the items.

In terms of the first item—best teaching role—only about one-third of the respondents appear scientifically oriented. (Approximately one-third said they could make their greatest teaching contribution as medical researchers.) This does not mean that only one-third of the sample are "scientists," however, for the other two items would suggest quite different conclusions in this regard. In response to the second item—ultimate medical interests—approximately two-thirds chose the scientific answer, saying they were more interested in learning about basic mechanisms than learning about total patient management. In response to the third item—reading preferences—about 80 percent chose the scientific answer.

To repeat, these three questionnaire items cannot tell us how many "scientists" there are in the sample, for none of the items is related to a set of criteria for what constitutes being a scientist in any absolute sense. Using the items for this purpose would present us with the problem of three quite different estimates of how many scientists there were in the sample.

However, these three questionnaire items do provide us with three independent

[1]The example, including tables presented, is taken from Earl R. Babbie, *Science and Morality in Medicine* (Berkeley: University of California Press, 1970).

indicators of respondents' *relative* inclinations toward science in medicine. Each item separates respondents into the *more* scientific and the *less* scientific. In view of the different distribution of responses produced by the three items, it is clear that each of the resulting groupings of more or less scientific respondents will have a somewhat different membership from the others. Respondents who seem scientific in terms of one item will not seem scientific in terms of another. Nevertheless, to the extent that each of the items measures the same general dimension, we should find some correspondence among the several groupings. Respondents who appear scientific in terms of one item should be more likely to appear scientific in their responses to another item than would those who appeared nonscientific in their responses to the first. We should find an association or correlation between the responses given to two items.

Table 15-1 shows the associations among the responses to the three items. Three bivariate tables are presented, showing the conjoint distribution of responses for each pair of items. Although each single item produces a different grouping of "scientific" and "nonscientific" respondents, we see in Table 15-1 that the responses given to each of the items correspond, to a degree, to the responses given to each of the other items.

Table 15-1   Bivariate Relationships of Scientific Orientation Items

			Best Teaching Role	
			Physician	Researcher
Ultimate Medical Interest	Total patient management Basic mechanisms	100% =	49% 51 (285)	13% 87 (196)

			Reading Preferences	
			Effectiveness	Rationale
Ultimate Medical Interest	Total patient management Basic mechanisms	100% =	68% 32 (132)	30% 70 (349)

			Reading Preferences	
			Effectiveness	Rationale
Best Teaching Role	Physician Researcher	100% =	85% 15 (132)	64% 36 (349)

An examination of the three bivariate relationships presented in Table 15-1 supports the belief that the three items all measure the same variable: scientific orientations. Let's begin by looking at the first bivariate relationship in the table. Faculty assessments of their best teaching roles and their expressions of their ultimate medical interests both give indications of scientific orientations. Those who answered "researcher" in the first instance would appear more scientifically inclined than those who answered "physician." Those who answered "basic mechanisms" would appear more scientifically inclined than those who answered "total patient management" in reply to the question concerning ultimate interests. If both these items do indeed measure the same thing, those appearing scientific on one ("researchers") should appear more scientific in answering the second ("basic mechanisms") than those who appeared nonscientific on the first ("physicians"). Looking at the data, we see that 87 percent of the "researchers" are scientific on the second item, as opposed to 51 percent of the "physicians." (*Note*: The fact that the "physicians" are about evenly split in their ultimate medical interests is irrelevant. It is only relevant that they are *less* scientific in their medical interests than are the "researchers.") The strength of this relationship may be summarized as a 36 percentage point difference.

The same general conclusion is to be reached in regard to the other bivariate relationships. The strength of the relationship between reading preferences and ultimate medical interests may be summarized as a 38 percentage point difference; the strength of the relationship between reading preferences and the two teaching roles may be summarized as a 21 percentage point difference.

Initially the three items were selected on the basis of face validity—each appeared to give some indication of faculty members' orientations to science. By examining the bivariate relationship between the pairs of items, we have found support for the expectation that they all measure basically the same thing.

Multivariate Relationships among Items

The discovery of the expected bivariate relationships between pairs of items further suggests their appropriateness for inclusion in a composite index. That is not a sufficient justification, however. The next step in index construction is the examination of the multivariate relationships among the items. We need to examine the simultaneous relationships among the several variables before combining them in a single index.

Recall that the primary purpose of index construction is the development of a method of classifying subjects in terms of some variable such as political conservatism, religiosity, scientific orientations, or whatever. An index of political conservatism should identify those who are very conservative, moderately conservative, not very conservative, and not at all conservative (or moderately liberal and very liberal, respectively, in place of the last two categories). The several gradations in terms of the variable are provided by the combination of responses given to the several items included in the index. Thus, the respondent who appeared conservative on all the items would be considered very conservative overall.

For an index to provide meaningful gradations in this sense, it is essential that each item add something to the evaluation of each respondent. Recall that in the preceding section it was suggested that two items perfectly related to one another would not be appropriate for inclusion in the same index. If one item were included, the other would add nothing to our evaluation of respondents. The examination of multivariate relationships among the items is another way of eliminating deadwood. It also determines the overall power of the particular collection of items in measuring the variable under consideration.

The purposes of this multivariate examination will become clearer if we return to the earlier example of measuring scientific orientations among a sample of medical school faculty members. Table 15-2 presents the trivariate relationship among the three items.

Table 15-2   Trivariate Relationship among Scientific Orientation Items

| | | Percentage Interested in Basic Mechanics | |
| | | Best Teaching Role | |
		Physician	Researcher
Reading Preferences	Effectiveness	27% (66)	58% (12)
	Rationale	58% (219)	89% (130)

Table 15-2 has been presented somewhat differently from Table 15-1. In this instance, the sample respondents have been categorized in four groups according to: (1) their best teaching roles and (2) their reading preferences. The numbers in parentheses indicate the number of respondents in each group. (Thus 66 faculty members said they could best teach as physicians and also said they preferred articles dealing with the effectiveness of treatments.) For each of the four groups, the percentage saying they are ultimately more interested in basic mechanisms has been presented. (Of the 66 faculty mentioned above, 27 percent are primarily interested in basic mechanisms.)

The arrangement of the four groups is based on a previously drawn conclusion regarding scientific orientations. Those in the upper left corner of the table are presumably the least scientifically oriented of the four groups: in terms of their best teaching roles and their reading preferences. Those in the lower right corner of the table are presumably the most scientifically oriented in terms of those items.

Recall that expressing a primary interest in basic mechanisms was also taken as an indication of scientific orientations. As we should expect, then, those in the lower right corner are the most likely to give this response (89 percent) and those in the upper left corner are the least likely (27 percent). The respondents who gave mixed responses in terms of teaching roles and reading preferences have an intermediate rank in their concern for basic mechanisms (58 percent in both cases).

This table tells us many things. First, we may note that the original relationships between pairs of items are not significantly affected by the presence of a third item.

Recall, for example, that the relationship between teaching role and ultimate medical interest was summarized as a 36 percentage point difference. Looking at Table 15-2, we see that among only those respondents who are most interested in articles dealing with the effectiveness of treatments, the relationship between teaching role and ultimate medical interest is 31 percentage points (58 percent minus 27 percent: first row), and the same is true among those most interested in articles dealing with the rationale for treatments (89 percent minus 58 percent: second row). The original relationship between teaching role and ultimate medical interest is essentially the same as in Table 15-1, even among those respondents judged as scientific or non-scientific in terms of reading preferences.

The same conclusion may be drawn as we examine the columns in Table 15-2. Recall that the original relationship between reading preferences and ultimate medical interests was summarized as a 38 percentage point difference. Looking only at the "physicians" in Table 15-2, we see the relationship between the other two items is now 31 percentage points. The same relationship is found among the "researchers" in the second column.

The importance of these observations becomes clearer when we consider what might have happened. Table 15-3 presents hypothetical data to illustrate that.

Table 15-3   Hypothetical Trivariate Relationship among Scientific Orientation Items

		Percentage Interested in Basic Mechanisms	
		Best Teaching Role	
		Physician	Researcher
Reading Preferences	Effectiveness	51%	87%
	Rationale	51%	87%

The hypothetical data in Table 15-3 tell a much different story than did the actual data reported in Table 15-2. In this instance, it is evident that the original relationship between teaching role and ultimate medical interest persists, even when reading preferences are introduced into the picture. In each row of the table the "researchers" are more likely to express an interest in basic mechanisms than are the "physicians." Looking down the columns, however, we note that there is no relationship between reading preferences and ultimate medical interests. If we know whether a respondent feels he or she can best teach as a physician or as a researcher, knowing the respondent's reading preference adds nothing to our evaluation of his or her scientific orientations. If something like Table 15-3 resulted from the actual data, we would conclude that reading preferences should not be included in the same index as teaching roles, since it will contribute nothing to the composite index.

In the present example, only three questionnaire items were involved. If more were being considered, then more complex multivariate tables would be in order. In this instance, we have limited our attention to the trivariate analysis of the three items. The purpose of this step in index construction, again, is to discover the simultaneous interaction of the items to determine whether they are all appropriate for inclusion in the same index.

Index Scoring

When you have arrived at the best items for inclusion in the index, you next assign scores for particular responses, thereby creating a single composite index out of the several items. There are two basic decisions to be made in this step.

First, you must decide the desirable range of the index scores. Certainly one of the primary advantages of an index over a single item is the range of gradations it offers in the measurement of a variable. As noted earlier, political conservatism might be measured from "very conservative" to "not at all conservative" (or "very liberal"). How far to the extremes, then, should the index extend?

In this decision, the question of variance enters once more. Almost always, as the possible extremes of an index are extended, fewer cases are to be found at each end. The researcher who wishes to measure political conservatism to its greatest extreme may find there is almost no one in that category.

The first decision, then, concerns the conflicting desires for (1) a range of measurement in the index and (2) an adequate number of cases at each point in the index. You will be forced to reach some kind of compromise between these conflicting desires.

The second decision concerns the actual assignment of scores for each particular response. Basically you must decide whether to give each item an equal weight in the index or to give them different weights. As we shall see later, scale construction is quite different in this regard, but this is an open issue in index construction. Although there are no firm rules to be followed, I would suggest—and practice tends to support this method—that items should be weighted equally unless there are compelling reasons for differential weighting. That is, the burden of proof should be on differential weighting; equal weighting should be the norm.

Of course, this decision must be related to the earlier issue regarding the balance of items chosen. If the index is to represent the composite of slightly different aspects of a given variable, then you should give each of those aspects the same weight. In some instances, however, you may feel that, say, two items reflect essentially the same aspect, while the third reflects a different aspect. If you wished to have both aspects equally represented by the index, you might decide to give the different item a weight equal to the combination of the two similar ones. In such a situation, you might want to assign a maximum score of 2 to the different item and a maximum score of 1 to each of the similar ones.

Although the rationale for scoring responses should take such concerns as these into account, you will typically experiment with different scoring methods, examining the relative weights given to different aspects but at the same time worrying about the range and distribution of cases provided. Ultimately, the scoring method chosen will represent a compromise among these several demands. (*Note:* In this activity, as in most research activities, the decision is open to revision on the basis of later examinations. Validation of the index, to be discussed shortly, may lead you to recycle your efforts and to construct a completely different index.)

In the example taken from the medical school faculty survey, I decided to weight each of the items equally, since they had been chosen, in part, on the basis of their representing slightly different aspects of the overall variable—scientific orientations. On each of the items, the respondents were given a score of 1 for choosing the "scientific" response to the item and a score of 0 for choosing the "nonscientific" response. Each respondent, then, had a chance of receiving a score of 0, 1, 2, or 3, depending on the number of "scientific" responses he or she chose. This scoring method provided what was considered a useful range of variation—four index categories—and also provided sufficient cases in each category for analysis.

Handling Missing Data

Regardless of the data collection method used, you must frequently face the problem of missing data. In a content analysis of the political orientations of newspapers, for example, you may discover that a particular newspaper has never taken an editorial position on one of the issues being studied—it may never have taken a stand on the United Nations, for example. In an experimental design involving several retests of subjects over time, some subjects may be unable to participate in some of the sessions. In virtually every survey, some respondents fail to answer some questions (or choose a "don't know" response). Although missing data present a problem at all stages of analysis, it is especially troublesome in index construction. (Again, scaling is different in this regard.) There are, however, several methods of dealing with this problem.

First, if there are relatively few cases with missing data, you may decide to exclude them from the construction of the index and the analysis. (In the medical school faculty example discussed above, this was the decision I made regarding missing data.) The primary concerns in this instance are whether the numbers available for analysis will still be sufficient, and whether the exclusion will result in a biased sample whenever the index is used in the analysis. The latter possibility can be examined through a comparison—on other relevant variables—of those who would be included and those excluded from the index.

Second, you may sometimes have grounds for treating missing data the same as one of the available responses. For example, if a questionnaire has asked respondents to indicate their participation in a number of activities by checking "yes" or "no" for each, many respondents may have checked some of the activities "yes" and left the remainder blank. In such a case, you might decide that a failure to answer meant "no," and score missing data in this case as though the respondents had checked the "no" space.

Third, a careful analysis of missing data may yield an interpretation of their meaning. In constructing a measure of political conservatism, for example, you may discover that those respondents who failed to answer a given question were generally as conservative—in terms of other items—as those who gave the conservative answer. As another example, a recent study measuring religious beliefs found that people who answered "don't know" about a given belief were almost identical to the "disbelievers" in their answers regarding other beliefs. (*Note*: You should not take these examples as empirical guides in your own studies, but only as suggestive of ways of analyzing your own data.) Whenever the analysis of missing data yields such interpretations, then, you may decide to score such cases accordingly.

There are a number of other ways for handling this problem. If an item has several possible values, you might assign the middle value to cases with missing data; for example, you could assign a 2 if the values are 0, 1, 2, 3, and 4. In the case of a continuous variable such as age, you could similarly assign the mean to cases with missing data. Or, missing data can be supplied by assigning values at random. All of these are conservative solutions in that they work against any relationships you may expect to find.

If you're creating an index out of several items, it sometimes works to handle missing data by using proportions based on what is observed. Suppose your index is composed of six indicators, and you only have four observations for a particular subject. If the subject has earned 4 points out of a possible 4, you might assign an index score of 6; if the subject has 2 points (half of the possible score on four items), you could assign a score of 3 (half the possible score on six observations).

The choice of a particular method to be used depends so much on the research situation as to preclude the suggestion of a single "best" method or a ranking of the several I have described. Excluding all cases with missing data can bias the representativeness of subsequent findings, but including such cases by assigning scores to missing data can influence the nature of the subsequent findings. The safest and most exemplary method would be to construct the index using alternative methods and see whether the same findings follow from each. Understanding your data is the final goal of analysis anyway.

Index Validation

Up to this point, we have discussed all the steps involved in the selection and scoring of items that result in a composite index purporting to measure some variable. If each of the above discussed steps is carried out carefully, the likelihood of the index actually measuring the variable is enhanced. To prove success, however, there must be *validation* of the index. In the basic logic of validation, we assume that the composite index provides a measure of some variable; that is, the successive scores on the index arrange cases in a rank order in terms of that variable. An index of political conservatism rank-orders people in terms of their relative conservatism. If the index does that successfully, then persons scored as relatively conservative in terms of the index should appear relatively conservative in terms of all *other indications* of political orientations, such as questionnaire items. There are several methods for validating a composite index.

Item Analysis   The first step in index validation is an internal validation called *item analysis*. You should examine the extent to which the composite index is related to (or predicts responses to) the items included in the index itself. If the index has been carefully constructed through the examination of bivariate and multivariate relationships among several items, this step should confirm the validity of that index. In a complex index containing many items, this step provides a more parsimonious test of the independent contribution of each item to the index. If a given item is found to be poorly related to the index, it may be assumed that other items in the index are washing out the contribution of that item. The item in question, then, contributes nothing to the index's power, and it should be excluded.

Although item analysis is an important first test of the index's validity, it is scarcely a sufficient test. If the index adequately measures a given variable, it should successfully predict other indications of that variable. To test that, we must turn to items not included in the index.

External Validation   Persons scored as politically conservative on an index should appear conservative in their responses to other items in the questionnaire. It must be realized, of course, that we are talking about *relative* conservatism, as we are unable to make a final absolute definition of what constitutes conservatism in any ultimate sense. However, those respondents scored as the most conservative in terms of the index should be the most conservative in answering other questions. Those scored as the least conservative on the index should be the least conservative on other items. Indeed, the ranking of groups of respondents on the index should predict the ranking of those groups in answering other questions dealing with political orientations.

In our example of the scientific orientation index, there were several questions in the questionnaire that offered the possibility of further validation. Table 15-4 presents some of those items.

Table 15-4   Validation of Scientific Orientations Index

	Index of Scientific Orientations			
	Low 0	1	2	High 3
Percentage interested in attending scientific lectures at the medical school	34	42	46	65
Percentage who say faculty members should have experience as medical researchers	43	60	65	89
Percentage who would prefer faculty duties involving research activities only	0	8	32	66
Percentage who engaged in research during preceding academic year	61	76	94	99

These items provide several lessons regarding index validation. First, we note that the index strongly predicts the responses to the validating items in the sense that the rank order of scientific responses among the four groups is the same as the rank order provided by the index itself. At the same time, each of the items gives a different *description* of scientific orientations overall. For example, the last validating item indicates that the great majority of *all* faculty were engaged in research during the preceding year. If this were the only indicator of scientific orientation, we would conclude that nearly all faculty were scientific. Nevertheless, those scored as more scientific in terms of the index are more likely to have engaged in research than those who were scored as relatively less scientific. The third validating item provides a different *descriptive* picture: only a minority of the faculty overall say they would prefer duties limited exclusively to research. Nevertheless, the percentages giving this answer correspond to the scores assigned on the index.

Bad Index versus Bad Validators   A dilemma that must be faced by nearly every index constructor is the apparent failure of external items to validate the index. If the internal item analysis shows inconsistent relationships between the items included in the index and the index itself, something is wrong with the index. But if the index fails to predict strongly the external validation items, the conclusion to be drawn is more ambiguous. You must choose between two possibilities: (1) the index does not adequately measure the variable in question, or (2) the validation items do not adequately measure the variable and thereby do not provide a sufficient test of the index.

The researcher who has worked long and conscientiously on the construction of the index will find the second conclusion very compelling. Typically, you will feel you have included the best indicators of the variable in the index; the validating items are, therefore, second-rate indicators. Nevertheless, you should recognize that the index is purportedly a very powerful measure of the variable; thus, it should be somewhat related to any item that taps the variable even poorly.

When external validation fails, you should reexamine the index before deciding that the validating items are insufficient. One method of doing that involves the examination of the relationships between the validating items and the individual items included in the index. If you discover that some of the index items relate to the validators while others do not, that will improve your understanding of the index as it was initially constituted.

There is no cookbook solution to this dilemma; it is an agony the serious researcher must learn to survive. Ultimately, the wisdom of your decision regarding the index will be determined by its utility in your later analyses involving that index. Perhaps you will initially decide that the index is a good one and that the validators are defective, and later find that the variable in question (as measured by the index) is not related to other variables in the ways expected. At that point, you may return again to the composition of the index.

Likert Scaling

Earlier in this chapter, I defined a scale as a composite measure constructed on the basis of an *intensity structure* among items composing the measure. In scale construction, response patterns across several items are scored, whereas in index construction, individual responses are scored and those independent scores are summed. By this definition, the measurement method developed by Rensis Likert, called Likert scaling, represents a more systematic and refined means for constructing indexes from questionnaire data. I'll discuss this method here, therefore, rather than in the sections on scaling to follow.

The term *Likert scale* is associated with a question format that is very frequently used in contemporary survey questionnaires. Basically, the respondent is presented with a *statement* in the questionnaire and is asked to indicate whether he "strongly agrees," "agrees," "disagrees," "strongly disagrees," or is "undecided." Modifications of the wording of the response categories (for example, "approve") may be used, of course.

The particular value of this format is the unambiguous *ordinality* of response categories. If respondents were permitted to volunteer or select such answers as "sort of agree," "pretty much agree," "really agree," and so forth, it would be impossible to judge the relative strength of agreement intended by the various respondents. The Likert format easily resolves this dilemma.

The Likert format also lends itself to a rather straightforward method of index construction. Whereas identical response categories will have been used for several items intended to measure a given variable, each such item might be scored in a uniform manner. With five response categories, scores of 0 to 4 or 1 to 5 might be assigned, taking the direction of the items into account (for example, assign a score of 5 to "strongly agree" for positive items and to "strongly disagree" for negative items). Each respondent would then be assigned an overall score representing the summation of the scores he or she received for responses to the individual items.

The Likert method is based on the assumption that the overall score based on responses to the many items seeming to reflect the variable under consideration provides a reasonably good measure of the variable. These overall scores are not the final product of index construction; rather, they are used for purposes of an *item analysis* resulting in the selection of the *best* items. Essentially, each of the individual items is correlated with the large, composite measure. Items that correlate highest with the composite measure are assumed to provide the best indicators of the variable, and only those items would be included in the index ultimately used for analyses of the variable.

It should be noted that the uniform scoring of Likert-item response categories assumes that each item has about the *same intensity* as the rest. That is the key respect in which the Likert method differs from scaling as the term is used in this book.

You should also realize that Likert-type items can be used in a variety of ways; you are by no means bound to the method described above. Such items can be combined with other types of items in the construction of simple indexes; and, similarly, they can be used in the construction of scales. However, if all the items being considered for inclusion in a composite measure are in the Likert format, then the method described above should be considered.

Semantic Differential

The *semantic differential*, as a question format, has similar advantages to the Likert format. It, too, creates a standardization of answer categories. And like the

Likert format, it creates a balance between positive and negative answers. Here's how it works.

Suppose that you are conducting an experiment to evaluate the effectiveness of a new music appreciation lecture on subjects' appreciation of music. (That makes sense.) Let's say that you have created experimental and control groups as described in Chapter 10. Now, you want to play some musical selections and have the subjects report their feelings about them. A good way to tap those feelings would be through the use of a semantic differential format.

To begin, you must determine the *dimensions* along which each selection should be judged by subjects. Then, you need to find two *opposite* terms, representing the polar extremes along each dimension. Let's suppose one dimension that interests you is simply whether subjects enjoyed the piece or not. Two opposite terms in this case could be "enjoyable" and "unenjoyable." Similarly, you might want to know whether they regarded the individual selections as "complex" or "simple," "harmonic" or "discordant," and so forth.

Once you have determined the relevant dimensions and have found terms to represent the extremes of each, you might prepare a rating sheet to be completed by each subject for each piece of music. Here's an example of what it might look like:

	Very Much	Some-what	Neither	Some-what	Very Much	
Enjoyable	☐	☐	☐	☐	☐	Unenjoyable
Simple	☐	☐	☐	☐	☐	Complex
Discordant	☐	☐	☐	☐	☐	Harmonic
Traditional	☐	☐	☐	☐	☐	Modern
			etc.			

On each line of the rating sheet, the subject would indicate how he or she felt about the piece of music: whether it was enjoyable or unenjoyable, for example, and whether it was "somewhat" that way or "very much" so. To avoid creating a biased pattern of responses to such items, it's a good idea to vary the placement of terms that are likely to be related to each other. Notice, for example, that "discordant" and "traditional" are on the left side of the sheet, with "harmonic" and "modern" on the right side. Very likely, those selections scored as "discordant" would also be scored as "modern" as opposed to "traditional."

Both the Likert and semantic differential formats have a greater rigor and structure than other question formats. Despite common references to Likert scales and semantic differential scales, these formats produce data suitable to both indexing and scaling, as the latter terms are distinguished from one another in this chapter.

Now we'll turn our attention from the creation of cumulative indexes to an examination of scaling techniques. Although many methods of scaling are available, I'm going to limit our discussion to three: Bogardus, Thurstone, and Guttman scales.

SCALE CONSTRUCTION

Good indexes provide an ordinal ranking of cases on a given variable. All indexes are based on the assumption that: a senator who voted for seven conservative bills is considered to be more conservative than one who only voted for four of them. What an index may fail to take into account, however, is that not all indicators of a variable are equally important or equally strong. The first senator might have voted in favor of seven mildly conservative bills, whereas the second senator might have voted in favor of four extremely conservative bills. (The second senator might have considered the other seven bills too liberal and voted against them.)

Scales offer more assurance of ordinality by tapping *structures* among the indicators. The several items going into a composite measure may have different *intensities* in terms of the variable. The three scaling procedures described below will illustrate the variety of techniques available.

Bogardus Social Distance Scale

A good example of a scale is the **Bogardus social distance scale.** Let's suppose that you are interested in the extent to which people are willing to associate with blacks. They might be asked the following questions:

1. Are you willing to permit blacks to live in your country?

2. Are you willing to permit blacks to live in your community?

3. Are you willing to permit blacks to live in your neighborhood?

4. Would you be willing to let a black live next door to you?

5. Would you let your child marry a black?

Note that the several questions increase in the closeness of contact which the respondent may or may not want with black Americans. Beginning with the original concern to measure willingness to associate with blacks, we have developed several questions indicating differing degrees of intensity on this variable.

The clear differences of intensity suggest a structure among the items. Presumably if a person is willing to accept a given kind of association, he or she would be willing to accept all those preceding it in the list—those with lesser intensities. For example, the person who is willing to permit blacks to live in the neighborhood will surely accept them in the community and the nation but may or may not be willing to accept them as next-door neighbors or as relatives. This, then, is the logical structure of intensity inherent among the items.

Empirically, one would expect to find the largest number of people accepting co-citizenship and the fewest accepting intermarriage. In this sense, we speak of "easy items" (co-citizenship) and "hard items" (intermarriage). More people agree to the easy items than to the hard ones. With some inevitable exceptions, logic demands that once a person has refused a relationship presented in the scale, he or she will also refuse all those harder ones that follow it.

The Bogardus social distance scale illustrates the important economy of scaling as a data-reduction device. By knowing *how many* relationships with blacks a given respondent will accept, we know *which* relationships were accepted. Thus, a single number can accurately summarize five or six data items without a loss of information.

Thurstone Scales

Often the inherent structure of the Bogardus social distance scale is not appropriate to the variable being measured. Indeed, such a logical structure among several indicators is seldom apparent. **Thurstone scaling** is an attempt to develop a format for generating groups of indicators of a variable that have at least an *empirical* structure among them. One of the basic formats is that of "equal-appearing intervals."

A group of judges is given perhaps a hundred items felt to be indicators of a given variable. Each judge is then asked to estimate how strong an indicator of the variable each item is—by assigning scores of perhaps 1 to 13. If the variable were prejudice, for example, the judges would be asked to assign the score of 1 to the very weakest indicators of prejudice, the score of 13 to the strongest indicators, and intermediate scores to those felt to be somewhere in between.

Once the judges have completed this task, the researcher examines the scores assigned to each item by all the judges to determine which items produced the greatest agreement among the judges. Those items on which the judges disagreed broadly would be rejected as ambiguous. Among those items producing general agreement in scoring, one or more would be selected to represent each scale score from 1 to 13.

The items selected in this manner might then be included in a survey questionnaire. Respondents who appeared prejudiced on those items representing a strength of 5 would then be expected to appear prejudiced on those having lesser strengths and, if some of those respondents did not appear prejudiced on the items with a strength of 6, it would be expected that they would also not appear prejudiced on those with greater strengths.

If the Thurstone scale items were adequately developed and scored, the economy and effectiveness of data reduction inherent in the Bogardus social distance scale would appear. A single score might be assigned to each respondent (the strength of the hardest item accepted), and that score would adequately represent the responses to several questionnaire items. And as is true of the Bogardus scale, a respondent scored 6 might be regarded as more prejudiced than one scored 5 or less.

Thurstone scaling is not often used in research today, primarily because of the tremendous expenditure of energy required for the judging of items. Several (perhaps 10 to 15) judges would have to spend a considerable amount of time for each of them to score the many initial items. Since the quality of their judgments would depend on their experience with and knowledge of the variable under consideration, the task might require professional researchers. Moreover, the meanings conveyed by the several items indicating a given variable tend to change over time. Thus an item having a given weight at one time might have quite a different weight later on. For a Thurstone scale to be effective, it would have to be periodically updated.

Guttman Scaling

A very popular scaling technique used by researchers today is the one developed by Louis Guttman. Like both Bogardus and Thurstone scaling, **Guttman scaling** is based on the fact that some items under consideration may prove to be harder indicators of the variable than others. If such a structure appears in the data under examination, we may say that the items form a Guttman scale. One example should suffice to illustrate this pattern.

In the earlier example of measuring scientific orientations among medical school faculty members, you'll recall that a simple index was constructed. As we shall see shortly, however, the three items included in the index essentially form a Guttman scale. This possibility first appears when we look for relatively hard and easy indicators of scientific orientations.

The item asking respondents whether they could best serve as practicing physicians or as medical researchers is the hardest of the three: only about one-third would be judged scientific if this were the single indicator of the variable. If the item concerning ultimate medical interests (total patient management versus basic mechanisms) were used as the only indicator, almost two-thirds would be judged scientific. Reading preferences (effectiveness of treatments versus the underlying rationales) is the easiest of the three items: about 80 percent of the respondents would be judged as scientific in terms of this item.

Table 15-5   Scaling Scientific Orientations

	Reading Preference	Ultimate Interests	Teaching Role	Number of Cases
	+	+	+	116
Scale Types:	+	+	−	127
Total = 383	+	−	−	92
	−	−	−	48
	−	+	−	18
Mixed Types:	+	−	+	14
Total = 44	−	−	+	5
	−	+	+	7

To determine whether a scale structure exists among the responses to all three items, we must examine the several possible response patterns given to all three items simultaneously. In Table 15-5, all the possible patterns have been presented in a schematic form. For each of the three items, pluses and minuses have been used to indicate the scientific and nonscientific responses, respectively. (A plus indicates a scientific response, and a minus indicates a nonscientific response.)

The first four response patterns in the table compose what we would call the *scale types*; those patterns that form a scalar structure. Following those respondents who selected all three scientific responses (line 1), we see (line 2) that those with only two scientific responses have chosen the two easier ones; those with only one such response (line 3) chose the easiest of the three. And finally, there are those respondents who selected none of the scientific responses (line 4).

The second part of the table presents those response patterns that violate the scalar structure of the items. The most radical departures from the scalar structure are the last two response patterns: those who accepted only the hardest item, and those who rejected only the easiest one.

The final column in the table indicates the number of survey respondents who gave each of the response patterns. It is immediately apparent that the great majority (90 percent) of the respondents fit into one of the scale types. The presence of mixed types, however, indicates that the items do not form a perfect Guttman scale.

We should recall at this point that one of the chief functions of scaling is efficient data reduction. Scales provide a technique for presenting data in a summary form while maintaining as much of the original information as possible.

When the scientific orientation items were formed into an index in our earlier discussion, respondents were given one point on the index for each scientific response they gave. If these same three items were scored as a Guttman scale, some respondents would receive different scores than were received on the index. Respondents would be assigned those scale scores that would permit the most accurate reproduction of their original responses to all three items.

Respondents fitting into the scale types would receive the same scores as were assigned in the index construction. Persons selecting all three scientific responses would still be scored 3. Note that if we were told a given respondent in this group received a score of 3, we could predict accurately that he or she selected all three scientific responses. For persons in the second row of the table, the assignment of the scale score of 2 would lead us accurately to predict scientific responses to the two easier items and a nonscientific response to the hardest. In each of the four scale types we could predict accurately all the actual responses given by all the respondents.

The mixed types in the table present a problem, however. The first mixed type (− + −) was scored 1 on the index to indicate only one scientific response. If 1 were assigned as a scale score, however, we would predict that all respondents in this group had chosen only the easiest item (+ − −), thereby making two errors for each such respondent. Scale scores are assigned, therefore, with the aim of minimizing the errors that would be made in reconstructing the original responses given. Table 15-6 illustrates the index and scale scores that would be assigned to each of the response patterns in our example.

As mentioned above, the original index scoring for the four scale types would be maintained in the construction of a Guttman scale, and no errors would be made in reproducing the responses given to all three items. The mixed types would be scored differently, however, in an attempt to reduce errors. Note, however, that one error is made for each of the respondents in the mixed types. In the first mixed type we would predict erroneously a scientific response to the easiest item for each of the 18 respondents in this group, making a total of 18 errors.

The extent to which a set of empirical responses form a Guttman scale is determined in terms of the accuracy with which the original responses can be reconstructed from the scale scores. For each of the 427 respondents in this example, we will predict three questionnaire responses, for a total of 1,281 predictions. Table

Table 15-6   Index and Scale Scores

	Response Patterns	Number of Cases	Index Scores	Scale Scores*	Total Scale Errors
Scale Types:	+ + +	116	3	3	0
	+ + −	127	2	2	0
	+ − −	92	1	1	0
	− − −	48	0	0	0
Mixed Types:	− + −	18	1	2	18
	+ − +	14	2	3	14
	− − +	5	1	0	5
	− + +	7	2	3	7

Coefficient of reproducibility $= 1 - \dfrac{\text{number of errors}}{\text{number of cases} \times \text{number of items each} = \text{number of guesses}}$

$$= 1 - \frac{44}{427 \times 3 = 1281}$$

$$= .966$$

$$= 96.6\%.$$

*This table presents one common method for scoring mixed types, but you should be advised that other methods are also used.

15-6 indicates that we will make 44 errors using the scale scores assigned. The percentage of *correct* predictions is called the *coefficient of reproducibility*: the percentage of reproducible responses. In the present example, the coefficient of reproducibility is 1,237/1,281 or 96.6 percent.

Except for the case of perfect (100 percent) reproducibility, there is no way of saying that a set of items does or does not form a Guttman scale in any absolute sense. Virtually all sets of such items *approximate* a scale. As a rule of thumb, however, coefficients of 90 or 95 percent are the commonly used standards in this regard. If the observed reproducibility exceeds the level you've set, you will probably decide to score and use the items as a scale.[2]

One concluding remark should be made with regard to Guttman scaling: it is based on the structure observed among the *actual data under examination*. This is an important point that is often misunderstood. It does not make sense to say that a set of questionnaire items (perhaps developed and used by a previous researcher) constitutes a Guttman scale. Rather, we can say only that they form a scale within a given body of data being analyzed. Scalability, then, is a sample-dependent, empirical question. Although a set of items may form a Guttman scale among one sample

[2]The decision as to criteria in this regard is, of course, arbitrary. Moreover, a high degree of reproducibility does not insure that the scale constructed in fact measures the concept under consideration, although it increases confidence that all the component items measure the same thing. Finally, you should be advised that a high coefficient of reproducibility is more likely when few items are involved.

of survey respondents, for example, there is no guarantee that they will form such a scale among another sample. In this sense, then, a set of questionnaire items in and of themselves never form a scale, but a set of empirical observations may.

TYPOLOGIES

We shall conclude this chapter with a short discussion of typology construction and analysis. Recall that indexes and scales are constructed to provide ordinal measures of given variables. We attempt to assign index or scale scores to cases in such a way as to indicate a rising degree of prejudice, religiosity, conservatism, and so forth. In such cases, we are dealing with single dimensions.

Often, however, the researcher wishes to summarize the intersection of two or more dimensions. You may, for example, wish to examine political orientations separately in terms of domestic issues and foreign policy. The fourfold presentation in Table 15-7 describes such a typology.

Table 15-7   A Political Typology of Newspapers

Domestic Policy	Foreign Policy	
	Conservative	Liberal
Conservative	A	B
Liberal	C	D

Newspapers in cell A of the table are conservative on both foreign policy and domestic policy; those in cell D are liberal in both. Those in cells B and C are conservative on one and liberal on the other. (For purposes of analysis, each of the cell types might be presented by a data card punch [A = 1, B = 2, C = 3, D = 4] and could be easily manipulated in examining the typology's relationship to other variables.)

Frequently, you arrive at a typology in the course of an attempt to construct an index or scale. The items that you felt represented a single variable appear to represent two. In the present example we might have been attempting to construct a single index of political orientations but discovered—empirically—that foreign and domestic politics had to be kept separate.

In any event, you should be warned against a difficulty inherent in typological analysis. Whenever the typology is used as the *independent variable*, there will probably be no problem. In the example above, you might compute and present the percentages of newspapers in each cell that normally endorse Democratic candidates; you could then easily examine the effects of both foreign and domestic policies on political endorsements.

It is extremely difficult, however, to analyze a typology as a *dependent variable*.

If you want to discover why newspapers fall into the different cells of typology, you're in trouble. That becomes apparent when we consider the ways in which you might construct and read your tables. Assume, for example, that you want to examine the effects of community size on political policies. With a single dimension, you could easily determine the percentages of rural and urban newspapers that were scored conservative and liberal on your index or scale. With a typology, however, you would have to present the distribution of the urban newspapers in your sample among types A, B, C, and D. Then you would repeat the procedure for the rural ones in the sample and compare the two distributions. Let us suppose that 80 percent of the rural newspapers are scored as type A (conservative on both dimensions) as compared with 30 percent of the urban ones. Moreover, suppose that only 5 percent of the rural newspapers are scored as type B (conservative only on domestic issues) compared with 40 percent of the urban ones. It would be incorrect to conclude from an examination of type B that urban newspapers are more conservative on domestic issues than rural ones, since 85 percent of the rural newspapers, compared with 70 percent of the urban ones, have this characteristic. The relative sparsity of rural newspapers in type B is due to their concentration in type A. It should be apparent that an interpretation of such data would be very difficult in anything other than description.

In reality, you would probably examine two such dimensions separately, especially if the dependent variable has more categories of responses than did the example given.

Don't think that typologies should always be avoided in social research; often they provide the most appropriate device for understanding the data. You should be warned, however, against the special difficulties involved in using typologies as dependent variables.

SUMMARY

Chapter 15 returns to the issue of measurement, discussed earlier in Chapters 5 and 6. Although the pre-data-collection efforts to conceptualize and operationalize are aimed at effective measurement, we have seen that you can refine your measurements during the analysis phase as well. This chapter has dealt with different types of composite measures: indexes, scales, and typologies.

The chapter began with an acknowledgment that most social science concepts cannot be satisfactorily measured on the basis of single observations. There is no single piece of information that can tell a person's socioeconomic status to the satisfaction of all social scientists. Any single indicator, such as income, would probably misrepresent the status of some people. Composite measures, then, are an answer to this problem. By measuring concepts on the basis of several different indicators, we gain confidence and consensus in the validity of our ultimate characterization of the people or other units of analysis we are studying.

Both indexes and scales are intended as ordinal measures. As we have seen, the manner in which scales are constructed provides us with a greater assurance of ordinality, because scales take advantage of logical or empirical structures that may exist among the individual indicators of a variable. Since relatively less has been written previously about the methods of index construction, the bulk of this chapter was addressed to that theme. Scale construction was given a somewhat briefer treatment.

Index construction begins with the initial selection of individual items or indicators that might be included in the index. That is accomplished on the basis of *face validity*: the extent to which the items *seem* to be valid indicators of the variable under consideration. Next, the bivariate relationships among the items selected are examined. If two items are, in fact, indicators of the same variable, then they should be related empirically to one another.

The examination of bivariate relationships among the items should provide a check on their validity as measures of the variable. Any item that appears unrelated to any of the others probably is not measuring the variable in question. On the other hand, if two items are *very* strongly related to each other, including both in the index would be redundant. The interpretation of bivariate relationships, then, should reduce the number of items considered for inclusion in the index.

The next step in index construction is the examination of multivariate relationships. The nature of this step will depend on the number of items still under consideration for inclusion in the index and the number desired ultimately. All the possible multivariate relationships should be examined. The goal of this step is the discovery of a group of items that demonstrate a cumulative set of interrelationships with one another: each of the items should contribute independently to the interrelationships.

Once the items have been selected, scores should be assigned to the different attributes of the selected items. The discussion of this step presented various scoring methods and several options for handling missing data.

The final step in index construction is *index validation*. If the index is a valid measure of the variable under consideration, it should predict other items in the data files. The discussion of this process illustrated assorted methods of index validation.

The discussion of scale construction began with a brief consideration of the *Bogardus social distance scale*, an excellent illustration of the logical structure that may exist among indicators of a variable. We saw that it is sometimes possible to reduce the answers to several questions to a single number that would be sufficient for us to reproduce all the details of the original data. The Bogardus social distance scale, then, is an efficient data-reduction device.

Next, the chapter considered the *Thurstone scale*. We saw that this technique could yield excellent measures of variables, but a number of practical problems have limited its use in social research.

Guttman scaling is probably the most popular scaling method used by social researchers today. It is based on the discovery of empirical structures among several indicators of a given variable. Some indicators reflect a greater intensity on the variable than others, and cases having the attributes that reflect a great intensity usually also have the attributes that reflect a lesser intensity. Thus, it is often possible to represent a set of attributes by a single scale score that would permit us to reproduce most of the original attributes. The extent to which the original data can be reproduced from a knowledge of the scale scores may be computed as a *coefficient of reproducibility*.

The chapter closed with a brief discussion of typologies in social research. As we saw, typologies are typically a nominal rather than ordinal measure. Thus, they are especially troublesome when used as dependent variables, although they may be effectively used as independent variables.

MAIN POINTS

1. Single indicators of variables seldom have sufficiently clear validity to warrant their use.

2. Composite measures, such as scales and indexes, solve this problem by including several indicators of a variable in one summary measure.

3. Both scales and indexes are intended as ordinal measures of variables, though scales typically satisfy this goal better than indexes.

4. Indexes are based on the simple cumulation of indicators of a variable.

5. Scales take advantage of any logical or empirical intensity structures that exist among the different indicators of a variable.

6. Face validity is the first criterion for the selection of indicators to be included in a composite measure; the term means that an indicator seems, on face value, to provide some measure of the variable.

7. If different items are indeed indicators of the same variable, then they should be related empirically to one another. If, for example, frequency of church attendance and frequency of prayer are both indicators of religiosity, then those people who attend church frequently should be found to pray more than those who attend church less frequently.

8. Once an index or a scale has been constructed, it is essential that it be validated. *Internal validation* refers to the relationship between individual items included in the composite measure and the measure itself. *External validation* refers to the relationships between the composite measure and other indicators of the variable—indicators *not* included in the measure.

9. *Likert scaling* is a measurement technique based on the use of standardized response categories (for example, strongly agree, agree, disagree, strongly disagree) for several questionnaire items. Although Likert scaling is not often used in social research today, the Likert format for questionnaire items is very popular and extremely useful. Likert-format items may be used appropriately in the construction of either indexes or scales.

10. The *Bogardus social distance scale* is a device for measuring the varying degrees to which a person would be willing to associate with a given class of people, such as an ethnic minority. Subjects are asked to indicate whether or not they would be willing to accept different kinds of association. The several responses produced by these questions can be adequately summarized by a single

score, representing the closest association that is acceptable, since those willing to accept a given association also would be willing to accept more distant ones.

11. *Thurstone scaling* is a technique for creating indicators of variables that have a clear intensity structure among them. Judges determine the intensities of different indicators.

12. *Guttman scaling* is probably the most popular scaling technique in social research today. It is a method of discovering and utilizing the empirical intensity structure among several indicators of a given variable.

13. A *coefficient of reproducibility* is a measure of the extent to which all the particular responses given to the individual items included in a scale can be reproduced from the scale score alone.

14. A *typology* is a nominal composite measure often used in social research. Typologies may be used effectively as independent variables, but interpretation is difficult when they are used as dependent variables.

ANNOTATED BIBLIOGRAPHY

Glock, Charles; Ringer, Benjamin; and Babbie, Earl; *To Comfort and to Challenge: A Dilemma of the Contemporary Church* (Berkeley: University of California Press, 1967). An empirical study illustrating composite measures. Since the construction of scales and indexes can be most fully grasped through concrete examples, this might be a useful study to examine. The authors use a variety of composite measures, and they are relatively clear about the methods used in constructing them.

Lazarsfeld, Paul; Pasanella, Ann; and Rosenberg, Morris (eds.); *Continuities in the Language of Social Research* (New York: Free Press, 1972), especially Section 1. An excellent collection of conceptual discussions and concrete illustrations. The construction of composite measures is presented within the more general area of conceptualization and measurement.

Miller, Delbert, *Handbook of Research Design and Social Measurement* (New York: David McKay, 1977). An excellent compilation of frequently used and semi-standardized scales. The many illustrations reported in Part 4 of the Miller book may be directly adaptable to studies or at least suggestive of modified measures. Studying the several different illustrations, moreover, may also give a better understanding of the logic of composite measures in general.

Oppenheim, A. N., *Questionnaire Design and Attitude Measurement* (New York: Basic Books, 1966). An excellent presentation on composite measures, with special reference to questionnaires. Although Oppenheim says little about index construction, he gives an excellent presentation of the logic and the skills of scale construction—the kinds of scales discussed in Chapter 15 of the present book and many not discussed here.

CHAPTER 16

The Logic of Causation

INTRODUCTION

Implicit in much of what has been said in earlier chapters of this book are the notions of *cause* and *effect*, particularly in the Chapter 10 discussion of independent and dependent variables in the context of experiments. One of the chief goals of the scientist, social or other, is to explain why things are the way they are. Typically, we do that by specifying the causes for the way things are: some things are caused by other things.

The general notion of *causation* is at once very simple and very complex. I imagine, on the one hand, that I could have ignored the issue altogether in this book —simply using the terms *cause* and *effect*—and you would have had little difficulty understanding the use of the terms. On the other hand, an adequate discourse on causation would require a whole book in its own right, or a series of books. However, let me attempt a middle-ground treatment of the subject, providing something more than a commonsense perspective on causation without attempting to be definitive.

Chapter 16 will begin with a review and an expansion of the previously mentioned subject of *determinism* in social science. Having done that, we'll return briefly to the topic of deductive and inductive logic. Next we'll consider some appropriate and inappropriate criteria for causality. The chapter will then conclude with a discussion of the links between measurement and association.

DETERMINISM AND SOCIAL SCIENCE

Chapters 1 and 2 of this book touched briefly on the deterministic perspective of science and of social science. Recall that this perspective contrasts with a *freewill* image of human behavior. The fundamental issue is this: Is your behavior the product of your own, personal willpower or the product of forces and factors in the world that you cannot control and may not even recognize? We are going to look at that issue in more depth here. Once we have completed our examination, we'll be in a position to look at the place of causation in social scientific research. We'll start with an example outside the social sciences altogether.

Causation in Physics

Let's do an experiment. Take a pencil or some other small object, hold it up in the air, and let go. What happens? It falls down, right? Why does it do that? If you needed to, you could consult with a high-level physicist, and you'd learn that gravity caused it to fall. I'm being silly, of course, because you already knew that. You wouldn't have to consult a physicist. All of us know that gravity causes the pencil to fall. One of the laws of the universe is that masses attract with a force reflecting their distance from one another and their masses. In practical terms, we see the gravitational force of the earth pulling the pencil to the ground.

To make a point, let me get just a little sillier. What would happen to the pencil if it *didn't want to fall*? Suppose it were afraid of falling and getting bruised. What would happen if you dropped it under that condition? It would fall anyway, of course. Now suppose it really wanted to fall. Maybe the pencil wanted to experience zero gravity or wanted the exhilaration of free fall. What would happen if you dropped it under that condition? It would fall. Finally, suppose the pencil forthrightly denied the existence of gravity. Suppose it could whisper, "I believe that pencils have a willpower that can overcome gravity. I'm going to remain suspended in midair." What would happen, then, when you dropped the pencil? Down it would go.

The point is that we can't imagine the pencil's feelings making the slightest difference to the law of gravity. Even if we were to substitute a human being for the pencil, we simply know that gravity will win out over any feelings that person might have in the matter.

The operation of gravity illustrates our commonsense view of cause-and-effect determinism in the world. We accept the limitation that gravity places on our freedom to do things in the world. Young children learn that they can't walk without surrendering to gravity and that they can't fly no matter how much they may want to. By the time you and I have reached our present stage in life, we have resigned ourselves to the limitations gravity places on us.

Put somewhat differently, our understanding of physics (even though we didn't recognize it as physics at first) has taught us some hard lessons in life: our willpower is limited by certain determinist constraints.

Finding the Causes of Prejudice

Let me shift gears for a minute. Imagine that you have managed to obtain a million-dollar grant from the National Science Foundation to find out the causes of prejudice. That's certainly a laudable aim, and the various government and private foundations are often willing to support such research. Let's suppose you receive the money and spend it doing your research. Now you are ready to send your project report off to the foundation. Here's how the report reads:

> After an exhaustive examination of the subject, we have discovered that some people are prejudiced, and the reason for that is that they *want* to be prejudiced. Other people are not prejudiced, and the reason is that they *don't* want to be prejudiced.

Try to imagine how the foundation would react to that research report.

Obviously, the paragraph would not be a satisfactory conclusion for a research project aimed at finding out what *causes* prejudice. When we look for the causes of prejudice, we look for the reasons: the things that make some people prejudiced and others unprejudiced. Satisfactory reasons would include such things as economic competition, religious ideology, political views, childhood experiences, amount and kind of education, and so forth. We know, for example, that education tends to reduce prejudice. That's the kind of causal explanation that we accept as the end product of social research.

Now let's look at the logic of such an explanation a little more closely. What does it say about the people involved in the research conclusion—the subjects of study? Fundamentally, it says that they turned out prejudiced or unprejudiced as a result of something they did not, themselves, control or choose. It's as though they came to a fork in the road—one turn representing prejudice and the other representing no prejudice—and they were propelled down one or the other road by forces such as their childhood experiences, their inherited religious affiliation, and similar factors they neither controlled nor were even aware of. They turned out prejudiced or unprejudiced for reasons beyond their control.

Reasons Have Reasons

Sometimes people protest this reasoning by arguing that individuals personally choose most of the things that may, in turn, determine how prejudiced they are. For example, let's say that you are quite unprejudiced, and we conclude from research that your lack of prejudice is probably a function of all the education you've received. Didn't *you* choose to go to school? Aren't you, therefore, the source of your being unprejudiced?

The problem with this view is that reasons have reasons. *Why* did you go to school? If you and I were discussing this subject, I know that you'd be able to give me reasons for having continued going to school up to this point. Let's say that your main reason was that you wanted to learn about the world around you, and you thought college would be a good way to do that. That makes sense.

That makes so much sense in fact that we might even say that the desire to learn about the world around you *caused* you to continue going to school. It's as if your desire *forced* you to go to school. Given that you had such a desire, how could you *not* go to school?

"I might not have gone if I hadn't had enough money," you say. That's true. If you hadn't had enough money to go to school, that factor would have *forced* you to stay out of school. But then suppose your desire to learn about the world around you was so powerful that you overcame the lack of money—maybe you got a scholarship or went to work for awhile. In that case, we are back to your powerful desire forcing you to go to school.

Ah, but *why* did you have such a strong desire to go to school? If I could ask you that in person, I know you'd have a reason. Perhaps you grew up in a family where everyone had gone to college generation after generation, and you'd feel you were letting your family down if you didn't go to college. Or perhaps you come from a family where nobody had ever gone to college before, and they were all proud of the fact that you might be the first. In both cases, we can see that those factors *forced* you to have the powerful desire to go to college, and that powerful desire *forced* you to go to college, and going to college *forced* you to be unprejudiced.

Clearly I can't—through a book—deal with all the particular reasons *you* had for doing something like going to college, but I think you'll be able to see that you did it for *reasons*, and that those reasons caused you to go. Moreover, no matter what reason you had at any specific step in the process, your reason would have a reason. The ultimate implication of this discussion is that your being prejudiced or unprejudiced can be traced back through a long and complex chain of reasons that explain why you turned out the way you did.

Recall how silly it seemed to think about whether the pencil wanted to fall when you let go of it. The pencil's feelings had nothing to do with it; gravity caused it to fall. The same thing would have happened to any pencil, so the one we dropped certainly couldn't take any pride in how well it fell. Questions of feeling and pride in accomplishment seem unimportant when we are dealing with a pencil being pulled around by gravity.

However, whether *you* turned out to be prejudiced or unprejudiced seems like a different matter. I know that if you consider yourself to be tolerant or honest or hard-working, you feel that such qualities are a reflection of who *you* are, of the kind of person you are deep down inside. They seem intimately woven into your experience of yourself.

Whenever we undertake explanatory social science research, however—when we set out to discover the causes of prejudice, for example—we adopt a model of human behavior that assumes people have no more individual freedom of choice than the pencil falling at the behest of gravity. We don't say that, of course, but if you look at the implications of asking "Why are people prejudiced?" you'll see that it's so.

The Discomfort of Determinism

The deterministic model of human behavior is an uncomfortable one to consider head-on. It's precisely for that reason that I want to look at it carefully here. (Notice, incidentally, how my reason forced me to do it.) If you are going to undertake explanatory social science, you'll have to come to grips with this model. If you don't come to grips with it, research will never be as much fun as it could be for you.

Every time you are able to explain some aspect of human behavior, a voice deep inside you will ask if that means *you* don't have any personal freedom of choice. If we look at why the deterministic model is so uncomfortable to us, we'll also get a look at the joke imbedded in this model.

I've already suggested one of the uncomfortable aspects of the deterministic model of human behavior. If everything you've done was the product of forces you had no control over, then you can't take any credit for any of your accomplishments. So you're the first person in your family to go to college. So what? Anyone else who had the same set of forces operating on him or her would have done the same thing, just as any pencil you drop will fall to the ground. That realization takes a lot of the joy out of life.

Second, the deterministic model of human behavior makes us feel trapped. Even though we have learned to live with our inability to flap our arms and fly, it's harder to realize that our every action (or inaction) may be totally caused by forces as powerful and relentless as gravity.

So far, we've looked at the way in which forces and factors you can't control caused you to get where you are right now, but the process doesn't end today. Logically, all the forces acting on you right this minute will determine what you do next. You can't turn these forces off. If you were to tear this book into little pieces and burn them, someone would ask you why you did that, and you'd give them a *reason*.

This implication of the model suggests that everything that *will* happen to you has already been determined by the forces acting on you right now. Ultimately, the model suggests that whether you graduate from college or not has already been determined by the vast constellation of forces at work right now. There you are wondering what you can do to insure that you'll graduate, and it's already been determined. According to the deterministic model of human behavior, the time and circumstance of your death are already laid out by forces you can't control.

Let me mention one other aspect of the discomfort we feel in regard to determinism. We tend to worry about how we would act if we accepted the idea of our lack of control as being true. Think about that for a minute. How would *you* change if you totally accepted the view that you have absolutely no control over your behavior? Would you stop caring about things, stop trying to make the world a better place, for example? Would you perhaps drop out of school? Would you simply curl up in a corner and not even move?

Think again. How *could* you change? If the deterministic model of human behavior is really true, and if you accept the view that you have no influence over your actions, how *could* you change anything? Obviously you couldn't, unless you were forced to by all those factors. And here is part of the joke of it all: why should you worry about what you do if you believe you have no control over your actions?

A Rube Goldberg Ecosystem

We'll see another part of the joke in determinism if we ask *what* is causing *what*. Several years ago, an American cartoonist's ingenious creations provided a preview of what is now the modern view of ecosystems in the field of ecology. Rube Goldberg's cartoons presented a simultaneous view of long, related chains of events. Here's an example of what I mean.

A man might accidentally bump into a stepladder, knocking down the can of paint atop the ladder; the paint would pour onto a cat, who would screech in surprise, startling a mother, who would let go of her baby carriage, which would roll into a dining room table and tip over a glass of milk, which would spill on the floor to be slipped on by a man carrying a bowling ball, who'd drop the bowling ball, which would roll into. . . . The chain of events went on and on.

As I've said, Rube Goldberg's drawings portrayed the nature of ecosystems as ecologists now describe them. Biologist Garret Hardin has said the first law of ecology is "You can't do *one* thing." Everything you do has many consequences, and everything that happens in the universe fits into an endless chain of interrelated events, just as the man's bumping the ladder set off a chain of events that went on and on. In ecosystems, everything is related to everything else. Nothing is independent. Ultimately, the rice growing in China and the amount of rain in Spain have some impact on whether you graduate from college; *and* whether you graduate from college has an impact on the rice in China and the rain in Spain.

Figure 16-1 illustrates this idea in terms of the Rube Goldberg example I described a moment ago. Notice in the figure that I have made one adjustment to the description. The figure shows why the man bumped into a stepladder in the first place: he was distracted by the sound of the other man dropping his bowling ball!

Notice how the figure describes a deterministic system of human behavior. Suppose that you are the mother in the drawing. *Why* did you let go of your baby carriage? You were forced to do it by the cat's screeching. The cat's screeching determined your action. But wait a minute. What caused the cat to screech? Look at the figure for a moment, and you'll see that *you* did. Can you see how the mother in the figure was the cause of the whole thing? By letting the baby carriage run into the table, she spilled the milk, which made the man slip, and so forth: the mother caused the cat to screech!

Or suppose for a moment that you were the bowling ball, trying to make your escape before the bowling tournament. By banging on the floor, you distracted the man who bumped into the stepladder, causing the paint to fall on the cat, and so on. The point is that if you take the ecosystem model of determinism *totally* seriously, you have a choice as to what your part in the system is. You can experience yourself as the cause of it all *or* as its effect. Both experiences fit equally well with the facts; each is equally true. If being the helpless victim of the system is an uncomfortable and depressing experience, being the cause of the whole system is more exhilarating than being Superman. That's the heart of the joke that lies behind our unvoiced fears and unhappiness with the deterministic model of human behavior that is so essential to explanatory social research.

A Concluding Comment

I've had a specific purpose in the preceding discussion. The kind of understanding we seek as we analyze social research data inevitably involves a deterministic

Figure 16-1 A Rube Goldberg Ecosystem

model of human behavior. In looking for the reasons why people are and do the things they are and do, we implicitly assume that their characteristics and actions are determined by forces and factors operating on them.

I have observed that when people set out to learn the skills of explanatory social research, that implicit assumption disturbs them. Somewhere, new researchers harbor a concern about whether they are learning to demonstrate that *they* themselves have no free will, no personal freedom in determining the course of their own lives. To the extent that this concern grows and festers, it interferes with the learning of analytic skills and techniques.

My purpose in the first part of this chapter has been to face those concerns head-on at the outset, to look at all the uncomfortable aspects of the issue, and, finally, to see the outrageous joke that often remains hidden under the pile of growing concerns. Once you see that you can't be helplessly trapped in the ecosystem without also and equally being the omnipotent cause of the whole thing, you can set your concerns aside and simply learn how to analyze data and explain how things work in the world. Let's turn to that task now.

IDIOGRAPHIC AND NOMOTHETIC MODELS OF EXPLANATION

Social scientists use two models of explanation in coming to grips with the reasons for human behavior. The preceding discussions, which probed into the multiplicity of reasons that would account for a specific behavior, illustrated the *idiographic model of explanation*. It aims at explanation through the enumeration of the very many, seemingly idiosyncratic, considerations that lie behind a given action. Of course, we never truly exhaust them in practice. Nevertheless, it is important to realize that the idiographic model is employed frequently in many different contexts.

Traditional historians, for example, tend to use the idiographic model, enumerating all the special causes of the French Revolution, or of the United States' decision to enter World War II. Clinical psychologists may tend to employ this model in seeking an explanation for the aberrant behavior of a patient. A criminal court, in response to a plea of extenuating circumstances, may seek to examine all the various considerations that have resulted in the crime in question. And most of us employ the idiographic model in attempting to understand the actions of others around us in everyday life.

Scientists, including social scientists, often employ a different model, which we will call the *nomothetic model of explanation*. This latter model does not involve an exhaustive enumeration of all the considerations that result in a *particular* action or event. Rather, it is a consciously parsimonious model that seeks to discover those considerations that are most important in explaining general classes of actions or events.

Let me illustrate the difference by explaining why people voted the way they did in the 1976 presidential election. For each individual we talked to, we could find out a great many of the numerous reasons why he or she voted for either Carter or Ford. Suppose someone gave us 99 different reasons for voting for Carter. We'd probably feel we had a pretty complete explanation for that person's vote. In fact, if we were to find someone else with those same 99 reasons, we would feel pretty confident in predicting that *that* person also voted for Carter. This approach would represent the idiographic model of explanation.

The nomothetic model of explanation, on the other hand, would involve the isolation of those *relatively few* considerations that would provide a *partial* explanation for the voting behavior of *many* people or of all people. For example, we might well imagine that political orientations—liberal or conservative—would be a consideration of great *general* importance in determining the voting behavior of the electorate as a whole. Most of those sharing the attribute *liberal* probably voted for Carter, while most of those sharing the attribute *conservative* probably voted for Ford. Realize that this single consideration would not provide a complete explanation for all voting behavior. Some liberals voted for Ford; some conservatives voted for Carter. The goal of the nomothetic model of explanation is to provide the greatest amount of explanation with the fewest number of causal variables: to uncover *general* patterns of cause and effect.

The nomothetic model of explanation is inevitably *probabilistic* in its approach to causation. The specification of a few considerations seldom if ever provides complete explanation. (We might discover, of course, that everyone who believed Ford was the best man voted for him, but that would not be a very satisfying explanation.) In the best of all practical worlds, the nomothetic model indicates there is a very high (or very low) probability or likelihood that a given action will occur whenever a limited number of specified considerations are present. Adding more specified considerations to the equation typically increases the degree of explanation, and the inherent parsimony of the model calls for a balancing of a high degree of explanation with a small number of considerations being specified.

The Problem of Dehumanization

As acknowledged earlier in this book, social scientists sometimes are criticized for *dehumanizing* the people they study. This charge is lodged specifically against the nomothetic model of explanation; the severity of the charge is increased when social scientists analyze matters of great human concern. Religious people, for example, are likely to feel robbed of their human individuality when a social scientist reports that their religiosity is largely a function of their sex, age, marital status, and social class. Any religious person will quickly report that there is much more than that to the strength of his or her convictions. And indeed there is, as the use of the idiographic model in the case of any individual person would reveal. Is the idiographic model any less *dehumanizing* than the nomothetic, however?

If everything—including being religious—is a product of prior considerations, is it any more dehumanizing to seek partial but general explanations utilizing only a few of those considerations than to seek total explanation utilizing them all? I suspect the true source of concern, underlying the charges of dehumanization, is based on the more direct confrontation with determinism that the nomothetic model represents. It is important to realize, however, that a careful listing of all the private individual reasons for being religious, or for voting for Candidate X, or any other action, involves the acknowledgment of a deterministic perspective: one that is logically no different from the deterministic perspective that permits us to specify four variables that are the most important in causing religiosity.

CRITERIA FOR CAUSALITY

None of the preceding discussions provides much in the way of practical guidance in the discovery of causal relationships in scientific research. This section will discuss three specific criteria for causality as suggested by Paul Lazarsfeld. The actual use of these criteria in research practice will be illustrated in the following chapter on the *elaboration model*.

The first requirement in a causal relationship between two variables is that the cause precede the effect in time. It makes no sense, in science, to imagine something being caused by something else that happened later on. A bullet leaving the muzzle of a gun does not cause the gunpowder to explode; it works the other way around.

As simple and obvious as this criterion may seem, we will discover endless problems in this regard in the analysis of social science data. Often, the time order connecting two variables is simply unclear. Which comes first: authoritarianism or prejudice? Even when the time order seems essentially clear, exceptions can often be found. For example, we would normally assume that the educational level of parents would be a cause of the educational level of their children. Yet, some parents may return to school as a result of the advanced education of their own children.

The second requirement in a causal relationship is that the two variables be empirically correlated with one another. It would make no sense to say that exploding gunpowder causes bullets to leave muzzles of guns if, in observed reality, the bullets did not come out after the gunpowder exploded.

Again, social science research has difficulties in regard to this seemingly obvious requirement. In the probabilistic world of nomothetic models of explanation at least, there are few perfect correlations. We are forced to ask, therefore, how great the empirical relationship must be for it to be considered causal.

The third requirement is that the observed empirical relationship cannot be explained away as being due to the influence of some third variable that causes both of them. For example, I may observe that my left knee generally aches just before it rains, but this does not mean that my joints affect the weather. A third variable, relative humidity, is the cause of both my aching knee and the rain. (This requirement for causality will be one of the main topics of discussion in Chapter 17. The terms *spuriousness* and *explanation* will be used in that context.)

From the perspective of this textbook, we shall consider two variables to be causally related—that is, one causes the other—if (a) the cause precedes the effect in time, (b) there is an empirical correlation between them, and (c) the relationship is not found to be the result of the effects of some third variable on each of the two initially observed. Any relationship satisfying all these criteria will be regarded as causal, and these are the only criteria.

To emphasize this last point more strongly, it will be useful to examine briefly some other criteria sometimes employed, especially by nonscientists, that will be regarded as inappropriate. In this discussion, I am indebted to Travis Hirschi and Hanan Selvin for an excellent article on this subject and its subsequent expansion in their book on *Delinquency Research*.[1]

[1]Travis Hirschi and Hanan Selvin, *Delinquency Research: An Appraisal of Analytic Methods* (New York: Free Press, 1967). See especially pp. 114–136. The original article appeared in *Social Problems*, Vol. 13 (1966), pp. 254–268.

Necessary and Sufficient Causes

First, to review a point made earlier in the chapter, a *perfect* correlation between variables is *not* a criterion of causality in social science research (or in science generally for that matter). Put another way, exceptions, although they do not prove the rule, do not necessarily deny the rule either. In probabilistic models, there are almost always exceptions to the posited relationship. If a few liberals voted for Ford and a few conservatives voted for Carter, that would not deny the general causal relationship between political orientations and voting in the election.

Within this probabilistic model, it is useful to distinguish two types of causes: *necessary* and *sufficient* causes. A necessary cause represents a condition that must be present for the effect to follow. For example, it is necessary for a person to be a woman in order to become pregnant, even though not all women do become pregnant. A sufficient cause, on the other hand, represents a condition which, if it is present, inevitably results in the effect. Enlisting in the army is a sufficient cause for being given a uniform, even though there are other ways of acquiring uniforms.

The discovery of a *necessary and sufficient cause* is, of course, the most satisfying outcome in research. If cancer were the effect under examination, it would be nice to discover a single condition that (a) had to be present for cancer to develop and (b) always resulted in cancer. In such a case, you would surely feel that you knew precisely what caused cancer. Unfortunately, we seldom discover causes that are both necessary and sufficient, nor, in practice, are the causes perfectly necessary or perfectly sufficient. From the standpoint of this textbook, *either* necessary *or* sufficient causes—even imperfect ones—can be the basis for a causal relationship.

I suspect that you may have greater difficulty accepting the notion of a necessary cause than of a sufficient one. Even in the two examples given at the outset of this discussion, it is no doubt more comfortable to say that enlisting in the army causes you to be given a uniform than to say that being a woman causes you to become pregnant. Everyone who enlists is given a uniform, but not every woman becomes pregnant. The difficulty in accepting necessary causes is usually even greater when a majority of those *caused* to do something do not do it. Let's postulate, for example, that being an anti-Semite is a necessary cause of murdering Jews in the streets. Non-anti-Semites don't do it. This causal relationship is not at all diminished by the fact that the vast majority of anti-Semites do not murder Jews in the streets.

LINKING MEASUREMENT AND ASSOCIATION

As we have seen, one of the key elements in the determination of causation in science is an empirical association between the "cause" and the "effect." All too often, however, the process of *measuring* variables is seen as separate from that of determining the *associations* between variables. This view is, I think, incorrect, or at the very least, misleading.

This section addresses the intimate links between measurement and association within the context of causal interference. To do that, we'll review the traditional, deductive model of science. Then we'll examine some alternative images of science.

In this latter regard, we'll consider the notions of the interchangeability of indexes and fixed-point analysis.

The Traditional Deductive Model

The traditional perspective on the scientific method is based on a set of serial steps, which scientists sometimes follow in their work. These steps may be summarized as follows:

1. Theory construction
2. Derivation of theoretical hypotheses
3. Operationalization of concepts
4. Collection of empirical data
5. Empirical testing of hypotheses

Let's illustrate this view of the scientific research process with an example.

Theory Construction   Faced with an aspect of the natural or social world that interests him or her, the scientist creates an abstract deductive theory to describe it. This is a largely logical exercise. Let's assume for the moment that a social scientist is interested in deviant behavior. He or she constructs—on the basis of existing sociological theory—a theory of deviant behavior. Among other things, this theory includes a variety of concepts relevant to the causes of deviant behavior.

Derivation of Theoretical Hypotheses   On the basis of this total theory of deviant behavior, the scientist derives hypotheses relating to the various concepts composing the theory. That, too, is the logical procedure. Following the above example, let us suppose that the scientist logically derives the hypothesis that juvenile delinquency is a function of supervision: as supervision increases, juvenile delinquency decreases.

Operationalization of Concepts   The next step in the traditional view of the scientific method is the specification of empirical indicators to represent the theoretical concepts. Although theoretical concepts must be somewhat abstract and perhaps vague, the empirical indicators must be precise and specific. Thus, in our example, the scientist might operationalize the concept *juvenile* as anyone under 18 years of age; *delinquency* might be operationalized as being arrested for a criminal act; and *supervision* might be operationalized as the presence of a nonworking adult in the home.

The effect of operationalization is to convert the theoretical hypothesis into an empirical one. In the present case, the empirical hypothesis would be: among persons under 18 years of age, those living in homes with a nonworking adult will be less likely to be arrested for a criminal act than will those without a nonworking adult in the home.

Collection of Empirical Data   Based on the operationalization of theoretical concepts, the scientist collects data relating to the empirical indicators. In the present example, he or she might conduct a survey of persons under 18 years of age. Among other things, the survey questionnaire would ask of each whether the person lived in a home with a nonworking adult and whether the person had ever been arrested for a criminal act.

Empirical Testing of Hypotheses   Once the data have been collected, the final step is the statistical testing of the hypothesis. The scientist determines, empirically, whether those juveniles with nonworking adults in the home are less likely to have been arrested for criminal acts than those lacking nonworking adults. The confirmation or disconfirmation of the empirical hypothesis is then used for purposes of accepting or rejecting the theoretical hypothesis.

Although this traditional image of scientific research can be a useful model for you to have in mind, it tends to conceal some of the practical problems that crop up in most actual research. In particular, there are two basic problems that prevent the easy application of this model in practice.

First, theoretical concepts seldom if ever permit unambiguous operationalization. Because concepts are abstract and general, every specification of empirical indicators must be an approximation. In the previous example, it is unlikely that the general concept of *supervision* is adequately represented by the presence of a nonworking adult in the home. The presence of such an adult does not assure supervision of the juvenile; in some homes lacking such an adult, other arrangements may be made for the juvenile's supervision.

Being arrested for a criminal act cannot be equated with the abstract concept of *delinquency*. Some juveniles may engage in delinquent behavior without being arrested. Others may be arrested falsely. Moreover, the specification of *juvenile* as a person under 18 years of age is an arbitrary one. Other specifications might have been made, and probably none would be unambiguously correct.

Furthermore, it is not sufficient to argue that the scientist should have specified "better" indicators of these concepts. The key point here is that there are almost never perfect indicators of theoretical concepts. Thus, every empirical indicator has some defects; all could be improved upon, and the search for better indicators is an endless one. This difficulty is the fundamental problem of validity that has been discussed several times earlier in the book.

Second, the empirical associations between variables are almost never perfect. In the previous example, if all juveniles with nonworking adults in the home had never been arrested and all those without such adults had been arrested, we might conclude that the hypothesis had been confirmed. Or if both groups had exactly the same records, we might conclude that the hypothesis had been rejected. Neither eventuality is likely in practice, however. Nearly all variables are related empirically to one another to some extent. Specifying the extent that represents acceptance of the hypothesis and the extent that represents rejection, however, is also an arbitrary act. (See Chapter 18 for a discussion of tests of statistical significance.)

Ultimately, then, the scientist uses approximate indicators of theoretical concepts to discover partial associations. And these problems conspire with one another against you. Suppose that you specify an extent of association that will constitute acceptance of the hypothesis, and the empirical analysis falls short. You will quite naturally ask yourself whether different indicators of the concepts might have produced the specified extent of association.

Measurement and association are interrelated concepts. The scientist must handle both simultaneously and logically. Rather than moving through a fixed set of steps, the scientist moves back and forth through them endlessly. Often theoretical constructions are built around the previously observed associations between empirical indicators. Partial theoretical constructions may suggest new empirical data to be examined, and so forth. It is hoped that, after each activity, you understand your subject matter a little better. The "critical experiment" that ultimately determines the fate of an entire theory is a rare thing indeed.

Scientific research, then, is a never-ending enterprise aimed at the understanding of some phenomenon. To that end, you continually measure and examine associations, and you must constantly be aware of their interrelations. The following sections should clarify the nature of the interrelations.

The Interchangeability of Indexes

Paul Lazarsfeld, in his discussions of the interchangeability of indexes, has provided an important conceptual tool for our understanding of the relationship between measurement and association, and as a partial resolution of the two problems discussed in the previous section.[2] His comments grow out of the recognition that there are several possible indicators for any concept.

Let us return for the moment to the notion of a theoretical hypothesis: $Y = f(X)$, first introduced in Figure 1-1 in Chapter 1. It suggests that some dependent variable (Y) can be explained as an effect of the independent variable, X. Lazarsfeld recognizes that there are several possible indicators of a concept like supervision; we might write these as x_1, x_2, x_3, and so forth. Although there may be reasons for believing that some of the possible indicators are better than others, they are essentially interchangeable. Thus, the scientist faces the dilemma of which to use in the testing of the hypothesis: $Y = f(X)$.

The solution to the dilemma lies in the use of *all* indicators. Thus, we test the following empirical hypotheses: $y = f(x_1)$, $y = f(x_2)$, $y = f(x_3)$, and so forth. Rather than having one test of the hypothesis, we have several, as indicated schematically in Figure 16-2.

You already may have anticipated a new dilemma. If following the traditional view of the scientific method created the problem that the single empirical association might not be perfect, now we may be faced with several empirical associations, none of which will be perfect and some of which may conflict with one another. Thus, even if we have specified a particular extent of association that will be

[2]Paul F. Lazarsfeld, "Problems in Methodology," in Robert K. Merton (ed.), *Sociology Today* (New York: Basic Books, 1959), pp. 39–78.

Figure 16-2   The Interchangeability of Indexes

$$Y = f(X)$$

$$y \overset{?}{=} f(x_1)$$

$$y \overset{?}{=} f(x_2)$$

$$y \overset{?}{=} f(x_3)$$

$$y \overset{?}{=} f(x_4)$$

$$y \overset{?}{=} f(x_5)$$

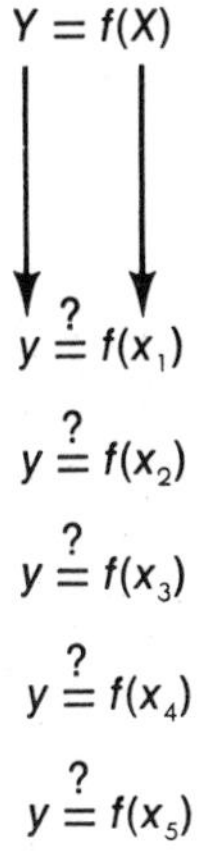

sufficient to confirm the hypothesis, we may discover that the tests involving x_1, x_3, and x_5 meet that specified criterion, but the tests involving x_2 and x_4 do not. Our dilemma is seemingly compounded. In fact, however, the situation really may be clarified.

In terms of the notion of the interchangeability of indexes, the theoretical hypothesis is accepted as a *general* proposition if it is confirmed by all the specified empirical tests. If, for example, juvenile delinquency is a function of supervision in a broadly generalized sense, then juvenile delinquency should be empirically related to every empirical indicator of supervision.

If, however, we discover that only certain indicators of supervision have this property, then we have specified the kinds of supervision for which the proposition holds. In practice, this may help us to reconceptualize *supervision* in more precise terms. Perhaps, for example, juvenile delinquency is a function of structural constraints, and some kinds of supervision are indicators of constraints, but others really are not.

It is very important to realize what we have accomplished through this process. Rather than routinely testing a fixed hypothesis relating to supervision and delinquency, we will have gained a better-defined understanding of the nature of that association. That will make sense, however, only if we view the goal of science as understanding rather than simply as theory construction and hypothesis testing.

There is one additional step required, however, before our understanding of the scientific process is clear. That is to comprehend what I have called *fixed-point analysis*. The notion of interchangeable indexes discussed above focused on the variability of *one* of the concepts, when in fact *all* concepts have this property. That will be the theme of the next section.

Fixed-Point Analysis

In the preceding section, we saw that given a theoretical hypothesis $Y = f(X)$, there are several possible indicators of X, written as x_1, x_2, x_3, and so forth. It may have occurred to you that the discussion of the interchangeability of indexes seemed incomplete. If X can be measured in many ways, isn't the same likely to be true of Y, also? If, for example, we want to find out whether wealth produces conservatism, both wealth and conservatism could be measured variously. Here are some examples:

Wealth (X)	*Conservatism* (Y)
1. Annual income	1. Foreign affairs
2. Savings accounts	2. Domestic issues
3. Property/investments	3. Economic issues
4. Parents' wealth	4. Social issues
5. Life-style	5. Morality

With so many ways to measure wealth and so many ways to measure conservatism, how do we set about discovering if the two variables are related? Clearly, the problem posed here is directly related to the earlier discussions of conceptualization and operationalization. If we had begun with a clear and specific conceptualization of what we mean by *wealth* and *conservatism*, we would have simply created two operational measures appropriate to those concepts. Very often, however, we lack such clarity at the beginning of a research project. Indeed, a common purpose of research is to provide clarity, and it is necessary to create many different measures of variables in order to clarify their relationship to one another. As a result, we often begin our analyses with something that might be represented by a paraphrase of William James as "a buzzing, whirling mess of indicators." This state is illustrated schematically in Part I of Figure 16-3.

In such a situation, there is no safe anchoring point from which to build your analysis. If you knew what *wealth* really meant, you could play with the different measures of conservatism; or if you knew what *conservatism* really meant, you could play around with the various measures of wealth. Given such total uncertainty, however, you may be tempted to give up in despair and wish you had made even arbitrary decisions on conceptualization earlier in your study.

It's possible to extricate yourself from this morass, however, and even experience the thrill of scientific discovery in the process. To do that, you need to drum up some healthy pragmatism and add a large shot of tolerance of ambiguity. I've labeled this approach *fixed-point analysis*.

With all the possible indicators of the two variables floating around with no fixed, anchoring point, you need to begin by "fixing" one. Let's start with wealth. Granting that we don't know the best way of measuring wealth in terms of learning whether it's related to conservatism, let's simply agree to start by measuring it as annual income. With that decision made, we can now begin to examine how wealth relates to the several measures of conservatism. This task is illustrated in Part II of Figure 16-3, where $y_1, \ldots, y_5$ are various indicators of conservatism, and x_1 is annual income.

Figure 16-3   Fixed-Point Analysis

I

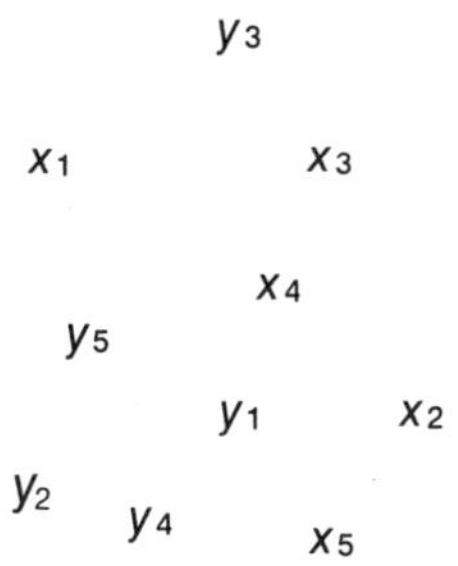

y_3

x_1 x_3

x_4

y_5

y_1 x_2

y_2

y_4

x_5

II

$$Y_1 \overset{?}{=} f(x_1)$$

$$y_2 \overset{?}{=} f(x_1)$$

$$y_3 \overset{?}{=} f(x_1)$$

$$y_4 \overset{?}{=} f(x_1)$$

$$y_5 \overset{?}{=} f(x_1)$$

III

$$y_{134} \overset{?}{=} f(x_1)$$

$$y_{134} \overset{?}{=} f(x_2)$$

$$y_{134} \overset{?}{=} f(x_3)$$

$$y_{134} \overset{?}{=} f(x_4)$$

$$y_{134} \overset{?}{=} f(x_5)$$

IV

$$y_i = x_j$$

Let's suppose that this analysis indicates that wealth (measured as annual income) is strongly related to conservatism in foreign affairs, economic issues, and social issues. Suppose that our measures of conservatism in domestic issues and morality aren't as strongly related to wealth. As a result of this discovery, we might tentatively decide to measure conservatism as some combination (creating a scale or index) of indicators y_1, y_3, and y_4.

With this working measure of conservatism, we could now examine the various indicators of wealth $(x_1, \ldots, x_5)$. This task is illustrated in Part III of Figure 16-3. This latest set of analyses would then give us a better idea of what measure of wealth was the most appropriate in studying its impact on conservatism. Once we decided on the most useful measure of wealth, we could use *it* for purposes of reexamining the various possible measures of conservatism. Ultimately, we would conclude this process with the creation of measures of wealth and conservatism that shed some light on the relationship between the two variables. I've illustrated this in Part IV, using *i* and *j* to indicate the measures arrived at.

In this fashion, then, you can extricate yourself from the confusion of too much variation. Make a decision, see what it tells you, then revise your initial decision.

You should realize that the ultimate outcome of this procedure is quite different from what is suggested by the traditional view of the scientific method and hypothesis testing. It neither asks nor answers the question, "Is *Y* a function of *X*?" Rather, we ask, "*How* is *Y* a function of *X*?" (Under what operationalizations is *Y* a function of *X*?) We do not address the straightforward question of *whether* conservatism increases with wealth; instead the question is "What kinds of conservatism are produced by what kinds of wealth?"

In practice, of course, we might arrive at several answers to this question. That shouldn't be viewed as a problem, however. When you think about it, such questions probably *have* several answers.

The implication of the preceding comments is that measurement and association are importantly intertwined. The measurement of a variable makes little sense outside the empirical and theoretical contexts of the associations to be tested. Asked "How should I measure social class?" the experienced scientist will reply, "What is your purpose for measuring it?" The "proper" way of measuring a given variable depends very heavily on the variables to be associated with it. One further example should make this point clearer.

A controversy has raged recently in the sociology of religion concerning the relationship between religiosity and prejudice. A book by Charles Y. Glock and Rodney Stark entitled *Christian Beliefs and Anti-Semitism*[3] reported empirical data indicating that Christian church members holding orthodox beliefs were more likely to be anti-Semitic than were less orthodox members. The book's findings stirred considerable discussion within the churches, and it resulted in follow-up research on the same topic by other researchers.

One subsequent research project arrived at a conclusion directly opposite that of Glock and Stark. The researchers reported that as orthodoxy increased, prejudice decreased. Upon closer examination, however, it was noted that the measures of orthodoxy in that study were based on acceptance of questionnaire statements of the traditional Christian doctrines of "All men are brothers" and "Love thy neighbor." Not surprisingly, survey respondents who accepted the statements based on these doctrines appeared less prejudiced than those who rejected them. Normally, these research findings would be (and were) challenged on the grounds of "contamination": the two variables being examined (religious orthodoxy and prejudice) actually measured the same or similar qualities. Calling one set of indicators "orthodoxy" and the other "prejudice" does not prove that prejudice decreases with increasing orthodoxy in a general sense. (Of course, the measurement of orthodoxy in terms of brotherly love and equality might be extremely useful in some other context.)

The discussions of this chapter suggest a somewhat different reaction to the two kinds of research findings. Asking *how* orthodoxy and prejudice are associated with each other rather than *whether* they are associated, we would conclude that orthodoxy measured in terms of the Glock-Stark indicators (belief in God, the divinity of Jesus, miracles, and the like) is positively associated with prejudice, while orthodoxy measured as commitment to the norms of brotherly love and equality is negatively associated with prejudice. Both conclusions are empirically correct; neither conclu-

[3]Charles Y. Glock and Rodney Stark, *Christian Beliefs and Anti-Semitism* (New York: Harper & Row, 1967).

sion answers the more general question of *whether* religion and prejudice are related. The final remaining step, of course, is to evaluate the relative utility of the conclusions. The finding that orthodoxy and prejudice are negatively associated would probably be disregarded as either tautological or trivial.

SUMMARY

Chapter 16 has dealt with the knotty subject of causation in social research. Although most people have some idea about what causation is, it is a far more complicated notion than it first appears. The purpose of this chapter has been to get you in touch with the complexities of causation without fully resolving the issue, since it cannot be fully resolved.

The chapter began with a discussion of determinism in relation to social research. We saw that there are two importantly different images of man's ultimate freedom. The *freewill* image suggests that people are the ultimate masters of their own destinies, personally choosing how they will behave in any given situation. The *deterministic* image, on the other hand, suggests that human behavior is a product of socioenvironmental factors—determinants—over which the actors have little or no control, that people are nothing more than stimulus-response machines, albeit complex ones. We looked at how uncomfortable such a notion is, and we saw that the fear of determinism ultimately doesn't make sense.

The general topic of causation was pursued through a discussion of two different explanatory models. The *idiographic* model aims at total explanation of a particular phenomenon through an exhaustive consideration of all relevant factors. This is the model typically employed by historians, for example. The *nomothetic* model of explanation, on the other hand, aims at partial, but generalized, understanding of a *class* of phenomena through the consideration of the relatively few, most relevant factors. This is the model typically employed by social scientists, and it is more parsimonious than the idiographic.

Since social scientific research, especially in regard to its deterministic image of human behavior and its nomothetic model of explanation, is frequently charged with dehumanizing the people under study, this charge was discussed in the chapter. I attempted to show that the seeming dehumanization is more a product of the scientist's explicitness than of a philosophical regard or disregard for people.

Having dealt with these general philosophical issues regarding the notion of causation, the chapter turned to more practical matters. Three basic criteria for causality were discussed: (1) empirical association, (2) time order, and (3) the lack of spuriousness. This discussion was followed by an examination of some common, though inappropriate, criteria for causality. In this latter connection, the notions of *necessary cause* and *sufficient cause* were introduced.

The chapter concluded with a discussion of the link between measurement and association. Having learned earlier in the book that there is no "true" measure for any variable, we discovered in this chapter that the "best" measure of a variable depends—in explanatory research—on the variables with which it is to be associated. Through the discussion of the interchangeability of indexes and fixed-point analysis, the point was made that the question, "Is X related to Y?" is less meaningful than the question, "In what ways is X *related to* Y?"

MAIN POINTS

1. Explanatory scientific research depends implicitly on the notion of cause and effect.

2. Explanatory *social* scientific research depends implicitly on a *deterministic image* of human behavior, at least in part.

3. The *idiographic* model of explanation aims at a complete understanding of a particular phenomenon, utilizing all relevant causal factors.

4. The *nomothetic* model of explanation aims at a general understanding—not necessarily complete—of a *class* of phenomena, utilizing the smallest number of most relevant causal factors. The nomothetic model is more parsimonious than the idiographic model, and it is the one most typically employed in social scientific research.

5. Although social scientists may seem to take a rather dehumanized view of the people they study, that merely reflects their parsimonious point of view. When a social scientist says that political party affiliation is the best predictor of voting behavior, this does not mean that he or she disregards or denies all other influences; the social scientist is simply interested in discovering the most important ones.

6. Most explanatory social research utilizes a *probabilistic* model of causation. X may be said to *cause* Y if it is seen to have *some* influence on Y.

7. There are two important types of causal factors: *necessary* causes and *sufficient* causes. X is a necessary cause of Y if Y cannot happen without X having happened. X is a sufficient cause of Y if Y always happens when X happens. The scientifically most satisfying discovery is a necessary *and* sufficient cause.

8. There are three basic criteria for the determination of causation in scientific research: (1) The independent (cause) and dependent (effect) variables must be empirically related to one another; (2) the independent variable must occur earlier in time than the dependent variable; and (3) the observed relationship cannot be explained away as the artificial product of the effect of another, earlier variable. (This final criterion will be discussed more fully in Chapter 17.)

9. A perfect statistical relationship between two variables is *not* an appropriate criterion for causation in social research. We may say that a causal relationship exists between X and Y, then, even though X is not the *total* cause of Y.

10. The *interchangeability of indexes* suggests that if several specific, though imperfect, indicators of one variable are similarly related to another variable,

then we may assume that the first variable—*in general*—is related to the second. Thus, we may conclude that X is related to Y, even though we cannot satisfactorily define X.

11. *Fixed-point analysis* is a logical model for varying the definitions of variables in such a way as to discover the *different* relationships that exist between variables according to the operational definitions employed. This model suggests that it is more fruitful to ask, "In what ways are X and Y related?" than it is to ask, "Are X and Y related?"

12. *Contamination* of indicators means that the operational measure of one of two variables whose relationship is being examined may be construed as a measure of the other variable as well. For example, it would be an inappropriate test of the relationship between religiosity and prejudice if the measure of religiosity might be seen as a measure of prejudice as well.

ANNOTATED BIBLIOGRAPHY

Hirschi, Travis, and Selvin, Hanan, *Delinquency Research* (New York: Free Press, 1967), especially Part II. Excellent statements on causation within a practical framework. I can think of no better discussions of causation within the context of particular research findings than these. The book is readable, stimulating, and generally just plain excellent.

Kaplan, Abraham, *The Conduct of Inquiry* (San Francisco: Chandler, 1964). A philosopher's perspective on social research. Especially in his discussions of explanation (Part 9), Kaplan lays the logical foundation for an understanding of the nature and analysis of causal relationships in social science.

Lazarsfeld, Paul, Foreword in Hyman, Herbert, *Survey Design and Analysis* (New York: Free Press, 1955). A classic and still valid statement of causation in social science. In the context of the elaboration model, Lazarsfeld provides a clear statement of the criteria for determining causation.

Rosenberg, Morris, *The Logic of Survey Analysis* (New York: Basic Books, 1968). A clear and practical statement of how the social researcher addresses causation. In his opening chapter, Rosenberg discusses the general meaning of causal relationships. In the concluding two chapters, he describes the process through which a researcher may arrive at causal conclusions.

CHAPTER 17

The Elaboration Model

INTRODUCTION

Chapter 17 is devoted to a perspective on social scientific analysis that is referred to variously as the elaboration model, the interpretation method, the Columbia school, or the Lazarsfeld method. This varied nomenclature derives from the fact that the method we'll be discussing aims at the *elaboration* on an empirical relationship among variables in order to *interpret* that relationship in the manner developed by Paul Lazarsfeld while he was at Columbia University.

The elaboration model is used to understand the relationship between two variables through the simultaneous introduction of additional variables. It was developed primarily through the medium of contingency tables, but later chapters of this book will show how it may be used with other statistical techniques.

It is my firm belief that the elaboration model offers the clearest picture of the logic of analysis that is available. Especially through the use of contingency tables, this method portrays the logical processes of scientific analysis. Moreover, if you are able to comprehend fully the use of the elaboration model using contingency tables, you should be in a far better position to use and understand more sophisticated statistical techniques.

HISTORY OF THE ELABORATION MODEL

The historical origins of the elaboration model are especially instructive for a realistic appreciation of scientific research in practice. During World War II, Samuel Stouffer organized and headed a special social research branch within the United States Army. Throughout the war, this group conducted a large number and variety of surveys among American servicemen. Although the objectives of these studies

445

varied somewhat, they generally focused on the factors affecting soldiers' combat effectiveness.

Several of the studies examined the issue of morale in the military. Since morale was believed to affect combat effectiveness, the improvement of morale would increase the effectiveness of the war effort. Stouffer and his research staff, then, sought to uncover some of the variables that affected morale. In part, the group sought to confirm, empirically, some commonly accepted propositions. Among them were the following:

1. Promotions surely affected soldiers' morale, and it was expected that those soldiers serving in units with low promotion rates would have relatively low morale.

2. Given racial segregation and discrimination in the South, it was expected that black soldiers being trained in Northern training camps would have higher morale than those being trained in the South.

3. Those soldiers with more education would be more likely to resent being drafted into the army as enlisted men than would those soldiers with less education.

Each of these propositions made sense logically, and common wisdom held each to be empirically true. Stouffer decided to test each empirically. To his surprise, none of the propositions was confirmed.

First, soldiers serving in the Military Police—where promotions were the slowest in the army—had fewer complaints about the promotion system than did those serving in the Army Air Corps—where promotions were the fastest in the army. This finding was derived from responses to a question asking whether the soldier believed the promotion system to be generally fair.

Second, black soldiers serving in Northern training camps and those serving in Southern training camps seemed to differ little if at all in their general morale.

Third, the less educated soldiers were more likely to resent being drafted into the army than were those with greater amounts of education.

Faced with data such as these, many researchers no doubt would have tried to hide the findings, as a poor reflection on their scientific abilities. Others would have run tests of statistical significance and then tried to publish the results. Stouffer, instead, asked *Why?*

Stouffer found the answer to this question within the concepts of *reference group* and *relative deprivation*. In the simplest overview, Stouffer suggested that soldiers did not evaluate their positions in life in accord with absolute, objective standards, but on the basis of their relative position vis-à-vis others around them. The people they compared themselves with were their reference group, and they felt relative deprivation if they did not compare favorably in that regard.

Within the concepts of reference group and relative deprivation, Stouffer found an answer to each of the anomalies in his empirical data. Regarding promotion, he suggested that soldiers judged the fairness of the promotion system on the basis of their own experiences relative to others around them. In the Military Police, where promotions were few and slow, few soldiers knew of a less qualified buddy who had been promoted faster than they had. In the Army Air Corps, however, the rapid promotion rate meant that many soldiers knew of less qualified buddies who had been promoted faster than seemed appropriate. Thus, ironically, the MPs said the promotion system was generally fair while the air corpsmen said it was not.

A similar explanation seemed appropriate in the case of the black soldiers. Rather than simply comparing conditions in the North with those in the South, they compared their own status—as black soldiers—with the status of the black civilians around them. In the South, where discrimination was at its worst, they found being a soldier somewhat insulated them from adverse cultural norms in the surrounding community. Whereas Southern black civilians were grossly discriminated against and denied self-esteem, good jobs, and so forth, black soldiers had a slightly better status. In the North, however, many of the black civilians they encountered were holding well-paying defense jobs. And with discrimination less severe, being a soldier did not help one's status in the community.

Finally, the concepts of reference group and relative deprivation seemed to explain the anomaly of highly educated draftees accepting their induction more willingly than was true of those with less education. Stouffer reasoned as follows:[1]

1. A person's friends will, on the whole, have about the same educational status as the person himself.

2. Draft-age men with less education would be more likely to engage in semi-skilled production-line occupations and farming than would those with much education.

3. During wartime, many production-line industries and farming were declared vital to the national interest; production-line workers in those industries and farmers would be exempted from the draft.

4. A man with little education would be more likely to have friends who were in draft-exempt occupations than the person with more education.

5. The draftee of little education would be more likely to feel discriminated against than would the draftee with more education, by virtue of each comparing himself with his friends.

These were the explanations that Stouffer suggested to unlock the mystery of the three anomalous findings. Because they were not part of a preplanned study design, he lacked empirical data for testing them, however. Nevertheless, Stouffer's logical exposition provided the basis for the later development of the elaboration model: understanding the relationship between two variables through the controlled introduction of other variables.

The formal development of the elaboration model was the work of Paul Lazarsfeld and his associates at Columbia University. In a methodological review of Stouffer's army studies, Lazarsfeld and Patricia Kendall presented hypothetical tables that would have proved Stouffer's contention regarding education and acceptance of induction had the empirical data been available.[2]

[1]Samuel A. Stouffer *et al.*, *The American Soldier* (Princeton, N.J.: Princeton University Press, 1949), Vol. 1, pp. 122 ff., esp. p. 127.
[2]Patricia L. Kendall and Paul F. Lazarsfeld, "Problems of Survey Analysis," in Robert K. Merton and Paul F. Lazarsfeld (eds.), *Continuities in Social Research: Studies in the Scope and Method of "The American Soldier"* (New York: Free Press, 1950), pp. 133–196.

Table 17-1   Summary of Stouffer's
Data on Education and Acceptance of Induction

	High Ed.	Low Ed.
Should not have been deferred	88%	70%
Should have been deferred	12	30
	100%	100%
	(1761)	(1896)

Source: Tables 17-1, 17-2, 17-3, and 17-4 are modified with permission of the Macmillan Company from *Continuities in Social Research: Studies in the Scope and Method of "The American Soldier"* by Robert K. Merton and Paul F. Lazarsfeld (eds.). Copyright 1950 by The Free Press, a Corporation, renewed 1978 by Robert K. Merton.

Kendall and Lazarsfeld began with Stouffer's data showing the positive association between education and acceptance of induction (see Table 17-1).

Following Stouffer's explanation, Kendall and Lazarsfeld created a hypothetical table, compatible with the empirical data, to show that education was related to whether one had friends who were deferred. In Table 17-2, we note that 19 percent of those with high education reported having friends who were deferred, as compared with 79 percent among those with less education.

Table 17-2   Hypothetical Relationship
between Education and Deferment of Friends

		High Ed.	Low Ed.
	Yes	19%	79%
Friends deferred?	No	81	21
		100%	100%
		(1761)	(1876)

Stouffer's explanation next assumed that soldiers with friends who had been deferred would be more likely to resent their own induction than would those who had no deferred friends. Table 17-3 presents the hypothetical data from Kendall and Lazarsfeld that would have supported that assumption.

The hypothetical data presented in Tables 17-2 and 17-3 confirm the linkages that Stouffer had specified in his explanation. First, soldiers with low education were more likely to have friends who were deferred than those with more education. And, second, having friends who were deferred made a soldier more likely to think he should have been deferred. Stouffer had suggested that these two relationships would clarify the original relationship between education and acceptance of induction. Kendall and Lazarsfeld created the hypothetical table that would confirm that ultimate explanation (see Table 17-4).

Table 17-3 Hypothetical Relationship between
Deferment of Friends and Acceptance of One's Own Induction

	Friends Deferred?	
	Yes	No
Should not have been deferred	63%	94%
Should have been deferred	37	6
	100%	100%
	(1819)	(1818)

Table 17-4 Hypothetical Data Relating Education to Acceptance
of Induction through the Factor of Having Friends Who Were Deferred

	Friends Deferred		No Friends Deferred	
	High Ed.	Low Ed.	High Ed.	Low Ed.
Should not have been deferred	63%	63%	94%	95%
Should have been deferred	37	37	6	5
	100%	100%	100%	100%
	(335)	(1484)	(1426)	(392)

Recall that the original finding was that draftees with high education were more likely to accept their induction into the army as fair than those with less education. In Table 17-4, however, we note that level of education has no effect on the acceptance of induction among those who report having friends deferred: 63 percent among *both* educational groups say they should not have been deferred. Similarly, educational level has no significant effect on acceptance of induction among those who reported having no friends deferred: 94 and 95 percent say they should not have been deferred.

On the other hand, among those with high education the acceptance of induction is strongly related to whether or not one's friends were deferred: 63 percent versus 94 percent. And the same is true among those with less education. The hypothetical data in Table 17-4, then, support Stouffer's contention that education affected acceptance of induction only through the medium of having friends deferred. Highly educated draftees were less likely to have friends deferred and, by virtue of that fact, were more likely to accept their own induction as fair. Those with less education were more likely to have friends deferred and, by virtue of that fact, were less likely to accept their own induction.

It is important to recognize that neither Stouffer's explanation nor the hypothetical data denied the reality of the original relationship. As educational level increased, acceptance of one's own induction also increased. The nature of this empirical relationship, however, was interpreted through the introduction of a third variable. The variable, deferment of friends, did not deny the original relationship; it merely clarified the mechanism through which the original relationship occurred. This, then, is the heart of the elaboration model and of multivariate analysis.

Having observed an empirical relationship between two variables, we seek to understand the nature of that relationship through the effects produced by introducing other variables. Mechanically, we accomplish this by first dividing our sample into subsets on the basis of the *control* or *test* variable. For example, having friends deferred or not is the control variable in our present example, and the sample is divided into those who have deferred friends and those who do not. The relationship between the original two variables is then recomputed separately for each of the subsamples. The tables produced in this manner are called the *partial tables*, and the relationships found in the partial tables are called the *partial relationships*. The partial relationships are then compared with the initial relationship discovered in the total sample.

THE ELABORATION PARADIGM

This section presents guidelines for the reader to follow in the understanding of an elaboration analysis. To begin, we must know whether the test variable is *antecedent* (prior in time) to the other two variables or whether it is *intervening* between them, because these positions suggest different logical relationships in the multivariate model. If the test variable is intervening, as in the case of education, deferment of friends, and acceptance of induction, then the relationships of Figure 17-1 are posited.

Figure 17-1   Intervening Test Variable

The logic of this multivariate relationship is as follows: the independent variable (educational level) affects the intervening test variable (having friends deferred or not), which in turn affects the dependent variable (accepting induction).

If the test variable is antecedent to both the independent and dependent variables, a very different multivariate relationship is posited (see Figure 17-2).

In this second situation, the test variable affects both the "independent" and "dependent" variables.[3] Because of their individual relationships to the test variable, the "independent" and "dependent" variables are empirically related to each

---

[3]Realize, of course, that the terms *independent variable* and *dependent variable* are, strictly speaking, used incorrectly in the diagram. In fact, we have one independent variable (the test variable) and two dependent variables. The incorrect terminology has been used only to provide continuity with the preceding example.

Figure 17-2   Antecedent Test Variable

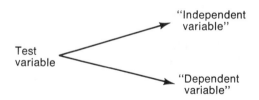

other, but there is no causal link between them. Their empirical relationship is merely a product of their coincidental relationships to the test variable. (Subsequent examples will further clarify this relationship.)

Table 17-5 is a guide to the understanding of an elaboration analysis. The two columns in the table indicate whether the test variable is antecedent or intervening in the sense described above. The left side of the table shows the nature of the partial relationships as compared with the original relationship between the independent and dependent variables. The body of the table gives the technical notations assigned to each case.

Table 17-5   The Elaboration Paradigm

Partial Relationships Compared with Original	Test Variable	
	Antecedent	Intervening
Same relationship	Replication	
Less or none	Explanation	Interpretation
Split*	Specification	

*One partial the same or greater, while the other is less or none.

Replication

Whenever the partial relationships are essentially the same as the original relationship, the term *replication* is assigned to the result, regardless of whether the test variable is antecedent or intervening. The meaning here is essentially the same as common sense would dictate. The original relationship has been replicated under test conditions. If, in our previous example, education still affected acceptance of induction both among those who had friends deferred and those who did not, then we would say the original relationship had been replicated. Note, however, that this finding would not confirm Stouffer's explanation of the original relationship. Having friends deferred or not would not be the mechanism through which education affected the acceptance of induction.

To see what a replication looks like, turn back to Tables 17-3 and 17-4 for a minute. Imagine that our initial discovery was that having friends deferred strongly influenced how soldiers felt about being drafted, as shown in Table 17-3. Had we first discovered this relationship, we might have wanted to see whether it was equally true for soldiers of different educational backgrounds. To find out, we would have made education our control or test variable.

Table 17-4 contains the results of such an examination, though it is constructed somewhat differently from what we would have done had we used education as the control variable. Nevertheless, we see in the table that having friends deferred or not still influences attitudes toward being drafted among those soldiers with high education and those with low education. (Compare columns 1 and 3, then 2 and 4.) This result represents a replication of the relationship between having friends deferred and attitude toward being drafted.

Researchers frequently use the elaboration model rather routinely in the hope of replicating their findings among subsets of the sample. If we discovered a relationship between education and prejudice, for example, we might introduce such test variables as age, region of the country, race, religion, and so forth, to test the stability of that original relationship. If the relationship were replicated among young and old, among persons from different parts of the country, and so forth, that would be grounds for concluding that the original relationship was a genuine and general one.

Explanation

Explanation is the term used to describe a *spurious relationship*; an original relationship that is explained away through the introduction of a test variable. Two conditions are required for that to occur. The test variable must be antecedent to both the independent and dependent variables, and the partial relationships must be zero or significantly less than was found in the original. Three examples will illustrate this situation.

There is an empirical relationship between the number of storks in different areas and the birthrates for those areas. The more storks in an area, the higher the birthrate. This empirical relationship might lead one to assume that the number of storks affects the birthrate. An antecedent test variable explains away this relationship, however. Rural areas have both more storks and higher birthrates than urban areas. Within rural areas, there is no relationship between the number of storks and the birthrate; nor is there a relationship within urban areas.

Figure 17-3 illustrates how the rural/urban variable causes the apparent relationship between storks and birthrates. Part I of the figure shows the original relationship. Notice how all but one of the entries in the box representing towns and cities with lots of storks have high birthrates; all those in the box for towns and cities with few storks have, with one exception, low birthrates. In percentage form, we say that 94 percent of the towns and cities with many storks also had high birthrates, as contrasted with 6 percent of those with few storks. That's a very large percentage point difference and would represent a strong association between the two variables.

Figure 17-3   The Facts of Life about Storks and Babies

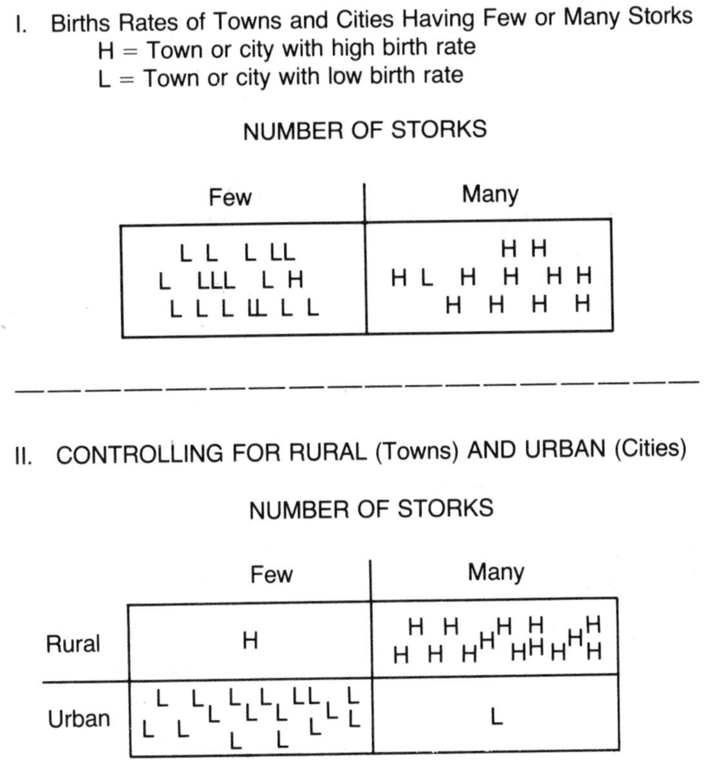

I. Births Rates of Towns and Cities Having Few or Many Storks
    H = Town or city with high birth rate
    L = Town or city with low birth rate

NUMBER OF STORKS

Few	Many
L L L LL L LLL L H L L L L L L L	H H H L H H H H H H H H

- -

II. CONTROLLING FOR RURAL (Towns) AND URBAN (Cities)

NUMBER OF STORKS

	Few	Many
Rural	H	H H H H H H H H H HH H H H
Urban	L L L L LL L L L L L L L L L L	L

Part II of the figure separates the towns from the cities, the rural from urban areas, and examines storks and babies in each type of place separately. Now we can see that all the rural places have high birthrates, and all the urban places have low birthrates. Also notice that only one rural place had few storks and only one urban place had lots of storks.

Here's another similar example. There is a positive relationship between the number of fire trucks responding to a fire and the amount of damage done. If more trucks respond, more damage is done. One might assume from this fact that the fire trucks themselves cause the damage. An antecedent test variable, however, explains away the original relationship: the size of the fire. Large fires do more damage than small ones, and more fire trucks respond to large fires than to small ones. Looking only at large fires, we see that the original relationship would vanish (or perhaps reverse itself); and the same would be true looking only at small fires.

Finally, let's take a real research example. There is an empirical relationship between the region of the country in which medical school faculty members attended medical school, and their attitudes toward Medicare.[4] To simplify matters, only the East and the South will be examined. Of faculty members attending eastern medical schools, 78 percent said they approved of Medicare, compared with 59 percent of those attending southern medical schools. This finding makes sense in view of the fact that the South seems generally more resistant to such programs than the East, and medical school training should presumably affect a doctor's medical attitudes. This relationship is explained away through the introduction of an antecedent test variable: the region of the country in which the faculty member was raised.

Of faculty members raised in the East, 89 percent attended medical school in the East, and 11 percent in the South. Of those raised in the South, 53 percent attended medical school in the East and 47 percent in the South. Moreover, the area in which faculty members were raised is related to attitudes toward Medicare. Of those raised in the East, 84 percent approved of Medicare, as compared with 49 percent of those raised in the South.

Table 17-6 presents the three-variable relationship among region in which raised, region of medical school training, and attitudes toward Medicare.

Table 17-6   Region of Origin, Region of Schooling, and Attitudes toward Medicare

		Percentage Who Approve of Medicare	
		Region in Which Raised	
		East	South
Region of Medical School Training	East	84	50
	South	80	47

Source: Babbie, op. cit., p. 181.

Those faculty members raised in the East are quite likely to approve of Medicare, regardless of where they attended medical school. Those raised in the South are relatively less likely to approve of Medicare, but, again, the region of their medical school training has little or no effect. These data indicate, therefore, that the original relationship between region of medical training and attitudes toward Medicare was spurious; it was due only to the coincidental effect of region of origin on both region of medical training and on attitudes toward Medicare. When region of origin is held constant, as we have done in Table 17-6, the original relationship disappears in the partials.

Interpretation

Interpretation is similar to explanation, except for the time placement of the test variable and the implications that follow from that difference. The earlier example

[4]Earl R. Babbie, *Science and Morality in Medicine* (Berkeley: University of California Press, 1970), see esp. p. 181.

of education, friends deferred, and acceptance of induction is an excellent illustration of interpretation. In the terms of the elaboration model, the effect of education on acceptance of induction is not explained away; it is still a genuine relationship. In a real sense, educational differences *cause* differential acceptance of induction. The intervening variable, deferment of friends, merely helps to interpret the mechanism through which the relationship occurs.

As another example of interpretation, it has been observed by researchers in the past that children from homes with working mothers are more likely to become delinquent than those whose mothers do not work. This relationship may be interpreted, however, through the introduction of supervision as a test variable. Among children who are supervised, delinquency rates are not affected by whether or not their mothers work. The same is true among those who are not supervised. It is the relationship between working mothers and lack of supervision that produced the original relationship.

Specification

Sometimes the elaboration model produces partial relationships that differ significantly from each other. For example, one partial relationship may look very much like the original two-variable relationship, while the second partial relationship is near zero. This situation is referred to as *specification* in the elaboration paradigm. We have specified the conditions under which the original relationship occurs.

In a study of the sources of religious involvement, Glock and his associates discovered that among Episcopal church members, involvement decreased as social class increased.[5] This finding is reported in Table 17-7, which examines mean levels of church involvement among women parishioners at different levels of social class.

Table 17-7   Social Class and Mean
Church Involvement among Episcopal Women

	Social Class Levels				
	Low				High
	0	1	2	3	4
Mean Involvement	.63	.58	.49	.48	.45

Source: Glock *et al.*, *op. cit.*, p. 85. Note that *mean* scores rather than percentages have been used here.

Glock interpreted this finding in the context of others in the analysis and con-

[5]Charles Y. Glock, Benjamin B. Ringer, and Earl R. Babbie, *To Comfort and to Challenge* (Berkeley: University of California Press, 1967), p. 92.

cluded that church involvement provides an alternative form of gratification for those people who are denied gratification in the secular society. This conclusion explained why women were more religious than men, why old people were more religious than young people, and so forth. Glock reasoned that people of lower social class (measured by income and education) had fewer chances to gain self-esteem from the secular society than did people of higher social class. To illustrate this idea, he noted that social class was strongly related to the likelihood that a woman had ever held an office in a secular organization (see Table 17-8).

Table 17-8 Social Class and the
Holding of Office in Secular Organizations

	Social Class Levels				
	Low 0	1	2	3	High 4
Percentage who have held office in a secular organization	46	47	54	60	83

Source: Glock *et al., op. cit.,* p. 92. Note that *percentages* are used in this table.

Glock then reasoned that if social class was related to church involvement only by virtue of the fact that lower-class women would be denied opportunities for gratification in the secular society, the original relationship should *not* hold among women who were getting gratification. As a rough indicator of the receipt of gratification from the secular society, he used as a variable the holding of secular office. In terms of this test, then, social class should be unrelated to church involvement among those who had held such office (see Table 17-9).

Table 17-9 Church Involvement
by Social Class and Holding Secular Office

	Mean Church Involvement for:				
	Social Class Levels				
	Low 0	1	2	3	High 4
Have held office	.46	.53	.46	.46	.46
Have not held office	.62	.55	.47	.46	.40

Source: Glock *et al., op. cit.,* p. 92.

Table 17-9 presents an example of a specification. Among women who have held office in secular organizations, there is essentially no relationship between social class and church involvement. In effect, the table specifies the conditions under which the original relationship holds: among those women lacking gratification in the secular society.

The term *specification* is used in the elaboration paradigm regardless of whether the test variable is antecedent or intervening. In either case, the meaning is the same. We have specified the particular conditions under which the original relationship holds.

Refinements to the Paradigm

The preceding sections have presented the primary logic of the elaboration model as developed by Lazarsfeld and his colleagues. Morris Rosenberg has offered an excellent presentation of the paradigm described above, and he goes beyond it to suggest additional variations.[6]

Rather than reviewing the comments made by Rosenberg, we might find it useful at this point to consider the logically possible variations. Some of these points may be found in Rosenberg's book; others were suggested by it.

First, the basic paradigm assumes an initial relationship between two variables. It might be useful, however, for a more comprehensive model to differentiate between positive and negative relationships. Moreover, Rosenberg suggests the application of the elaboration model to an original relationship of *zero*—with the possibility that relationships will appear in the partials.

Rosenberg cites as an example of such an application a study of union membership and attitudes toward having Jews on the union staff. (See Table 17-10.) The initial analysis indicated that length of union membership did not relate to the attitude: those who had belonged to the union less than four years were as willing to accept Jews on the staff as were those who had belonged to the union for longer than four years. The *age* of union members, however, was found to *suppress* the relationship between length of union membership and attitudes toward Jews. Overall, younger members were more favorable to Jews than were older members. At the same time, of course, younger members were not likely to have been in the union as long as the old members. Within specific age groups, however, those in the union longest were the most supportive of having Jews on the staff. Age, in this case, was a *suppressor variable*, concealing the relationship between length of membership and attitudes toward Jews.

Second, the basic paradigm focuses on partials being the same or weaker than the original relationship, but does not provide guidelines for specifying what constitutes a significant difference between the original and the partials. When you use the elaboration model, you will frequently find yourself making an arbitrary decision as to whether a given partial is significantly weaker than the original. This, then, suggests another dimension to the paradigm.

Third, the limitation of the basic paradigm to partials that are the same as or weaker than the original neglects two other possibilities. A partial relationship might be *stronger* than the original. Or, on the other hand, a partial relationship might be the reverse of the original—negative where the original was positive.

[6]Morris Rosenberg, *The Logic of Survey Analysis* (New York: Basic Books, 1968).

Table 17-10   Example of a Suppressor Variable

I: No Apparent Relationship between
Attitudes toward Jews and Length of Time in the Union

Jews on Union Staff	In Union Less than 4 Years	In Union 4 Years or Longer
Don't care either way	49.2% (126)	50.4% (256)

II.   In Each Age Group, Length of Time in Union
Increases Willingness to Have Jews on Union Staff

Jews on Union Staff	Distribution of Answers by Percentage, According to Age and Longevity					
	29 Years and Under		30–49 Years		50 Years and Older	
	Years in Union					
	Less than 4	4 or More	Less than 4	4 or More	Less than 4	4 or More
Don't care either way	56.4 (78)	62.7 (51)	37.1 (35)	48.3 (116)	38.4 (13)	46.1 (89)

Source: Rosenberg, *op. cit.*, pp. 88–89.

From Arnold M. Rose, *Union Solidarity* (Minneapolis: University of Minnesota Press, 1952), p. 128, Table 42 (abridged and adapted). (Reprinted with permission of the University of Minnesota Press.)

Rosenberg provides a hypothetical example of that by first suggesting that a researcher might find working-class respondents in his study more supportive of the civil rights movement than middle-class respondents. (See Table 17-11.) He further suggests that *race* might be a *distorter variable* in this instance, distorting the true relationship between class and attitudes. Presumably, black respondents would be more supportive of the movement than whites, but blacks would also be overrepresented among working-class respondents and underrepresented among the middle class. Middle-class black respondents might be more supportive of the movement than working-class blacks, however; and the same relationship might be found among whites. *Holding race constant*, then, the researcher would conclude that support for the civil rights movement was greater among the middle class than among the working class.

All these new dimensions further complicate the notion of specification. If one partial is the same as the original, while the other partial is even stronger, how should you react to that situation? You have specified one condition under which the original relationship holds up, but you have also specified another condition under which it holds even more clearly.

Finally, the basic paradigm focuses primarily on dichotomous test variables. In

Table 17-11   Example of a Distorter Variable (Hypothetical)

I: Working-Class Subjects Appear More
Liberal on Civil Rights than Middle-Class Subjects

Civil Rights Score	Middle Class	Working Class
High	37%	45%
Low	73	55
	100%	100%
	(120)	(120)

II: Controlling for Race Shows the
Middle Class to Be More Liberal than the Working Class

	Social Class			
	Blacks		Whites	
Civil Rights Score	Middle Class	Working Class	Middle Class	Working Class
High	70%	50%	30%	20%
Low	30	50	70	80
	100%	100%	100%	100%
	(20)	(100)	(100)	(20)

Source: Rosenberg, *op. cit.*, pp. 94–95.

fact, the elaboration model is not so limited—either in theory or in use—but the basic paradigm becomes more complicated when the test variable divides the sample into three or more subsamples. And the paradigm becomes more complicated yet when more than one test variable is used simultaneously.

These comments are not made with the intention of faulting the basic elaboration paradigm. To the contrary, my intention is to impress upon you that the elaboration model is not a simple algorithm—a set of procedures through which analysis is accomplished. The elaboration model is primarily a logical device for assisting the researcher in the understanding of his or her data. A firm understanding of the elaboration model will facilitate a sophisticated analysis. It does not suggest which variables should be introduced as controls, however, nor does it suggest definitive conclusions as to the nature of elaboration results. For all these things, you must look to your own ingenuity. Such ingenuity, moreover, will come only through extensive experience. By pointing to the oversimplifications in the basic elaboration paradigm, I have sought to bring home the point that the model provides only a logical framework. Sophisticated analysis will be far more complicated than the examples used to illustrate the basic paradigm.

At the same time, the elaboration paradigm is a very powerful logical framework. If you fully understand the basic model, you will be in a far better position for understanding other techniques such as correlations, regressions, factor analyses, and so forth. The next chapter will attempt to place such techniques as partial correlations and partial regressions in the context of the elaboration model.

ELABORATION AND EX POST FACTO HYPOTHESIZING

Before we leave the discussion of the elaboration model, one further word is in order regarding its power in connection with an unfortunate sacred cow in the traditional norms of scientific research. The reader of methodological literature will find countless references to the fallacy of *ex post facto hypothesizing*. The intentions of such injunctions are correct, but the inexperienced researcher is sometimes led astray.

When you observe an empirical relationship between two variables and then simply suggest a reason for that relationship, that is sometimes called ex post facto hypothesizing. You have generated a hypothesis linking two variables after their relationship is already known. We will recall, from an early discussion in this book, that all hypotheses must be subject to disconfirmation. Unless the researcher (or theorist) can specify empirical findings that would disprove his or her hypothesis, it is essentially useless. It is reasoned, therefore, that once you have *observed* a relationship between two variables, any hypothesis regarding that relationship cannot be disproved.

That is a fair assessment in those situations in which you do nothing more than dress up your empirical observations with deceptive hypotheses after the fact. Having observed that women are more religious than men, you should not simply assert that women will be more religious than men because of some general dynamic of social behavior and then rest your case on the initial observation.

The unfortunate spin-off of the injunction against ex post facto hypothesizing is in its inhibition of good, honest hypothesizing after the fact. Inexperienced researchers are often led to believe that they must make all their hypotheses before examining their data—even if that means making a lot of poorly reasoned ones. Furthermore, they are led to ignore any empirically observed relationships that do not confirm some prior hypothesis.

Surely, few researchers would now wish that Sam Stouffer had hushed up his anomalous findings regarding morale among soldiers in the army. Stouffer noted peculiar empirical observations and set about hypothesizing the reasons for those findings. And his reasoning has proved invaluable to subsequent researchers.

There is a further, more sophisticated, point to be made here, however. Anyone can generate hypotheses to explain observed empirical relationships in a body of data, but the elaboration model provides the logical tools for *testing* those hypotheses within the same body of data. A good example of this testing may be found in the earlier discussion of social class and church involvement. Glock explained the original relationship in terms of social deprivation theory. If he had stopped at that point, his comments would have been interesting but hardly persuasive. He went beyond that point, however. He noted that if the hypothesis was correct, then the relationship between social class and church involvement should disappear among those women who were receiving gratification from the secular society—those who had held office in a secular organization. This hypothesis was then subjected to an empirical test. Had the new hypothesis not been confirmed by the data, he would have been forced to reconsider.

These additional comments should further illustrate the point that data analysis is a continuing process, demanding all the ingenuity and perseverance you can muster. The image of a researcher carefully laying out hypotheses and then testing them in a ritualistic fashion results only in ritualistic research.

In case you are concerned that the strength of ex post facto proofs seems to be less than that of the traditional kinds, let me repeat the earlier assertion that "scientific proof" is a contradiction in terms. Nothing is ever proved *scientifically*. Hypotheses, explanations, theories, or hunches can all escape a stream of attempts at disproof, but none can be proved in any absolute sense. The acceptance of a hypothesis, then, is really a function of the extent to which it has been tested and not disconfirmed. No hypothesis, therefore, should be considered sound on the basis of one test—whether the hypothesis was generated before or after the observation of empirical data. With that in mind, you should not deny yourself some of the most fruitful avenues available to you in data analysis. You should always try to reach an honest understanding of your data, develop meaningful theories for more general understanding, and not worry about the manner of reaching that understanding.

SUMMARY

Chapter 17 has discussed the *elaboration model* developed by Paul Lazarsfeld and his colleagues. It provides a logical model for the analysis and interpretation of the relationships among variables. As such, it offers a useful basis for a later understanding of other modes of analysis in social research.

The basic form of the elaboration model is as follows: (a) a relationship between two variables is observed; (b) a third variable—a *control* variable or *test* variable—is then used to subdivide the cases under study; (c) the original relationship between two variables is computed within each of the subgroups; and (d) the comparison of the original *zero-order* relationship with each of the *partial* relationships observed within the subgroups provides the basis for a better understanding of the original relationship itself.

The chapter began with a brief historical overview of the development of the elaboration model. We saw that it arose in connection with the research activities of Samuel Stouffer, working for the United States Army during World War II. Stouffer offered an interesting interpretation of certain anomalous findings, and Lazarsfeld went on to develop the empirical analyses that would have been necessary to confirm Stouffer's interpretation. This effort resulted in a much broader logical model.

Next, the chapter addressed the fundamental paradigm embodied within the elaboration model. We discovered that two important considerations are involved: (1) whether the *control* variable is *antecedent* or *intervening* and (2) the outcome of the comparison between the original relationship and the partial relationships. The possible results are that: (a) the partial relationships are the same as the original one,

(b) the partial relationships all disappear, or (c) one partial relationship disappears while the other is the same as the original relationship. The various outcomes are given the names: *replication*, *interpretation*, *explanation*, and *specification*, and each outcome has a different implication for our understanding of the original relationship.

The chapter concluded with a discussion of the issue of *ex post facto hypothesizing* in connection with the use of the elaboration model in the analysis of social research data.

MAIN POINTS

1. The elaboration model is one method of multivariate analysis appropriate to social research.

2. It was developed by Paul Lazarsfeld in connection with research undertaken by Samuel Stouffer.

3. The elaboration model is primarily a logical model that can illustrate the basic logic of other multivariate methods.

4. The basic steps in elaboration are as follows: (a) a relationship is observed to exist between two variables; (b) a third variable is held constant in the sense that the cases under study are subdivided according to the attributes of that third variable; (c) the original two-variable relationship is recomputed within each of the subgroups; and (d) the comparison of the original relationship with the relationships found within each subgroup provides a fuller understanding of the original relationship itself.

5. An *intervening* control variable is one that occurs in time between the occurrence of the independent variable and the occurrence of the dependent variable.

6. An *antecedent* control variable is one that occurs earlier in time than either the independent or the dependent variables.

7. A *zero-order* relationship is the observed relationship between two variables *without* a third variable being held constant or controlled.

8. A *partial* relationship is the observed relationship between two variables — within a subgroup of cases based on some attribute of the control variable. Thus, the relationship between age and prejudice among men only (that is, controlling for sex) would be a partial relationship.

9. If a set of partial relationships is essentially the same as the corresponding zero-order relationship, this outcome is called a *replication*, regardless of whether the control variable is intervening or antecedent. This means, simply, that the originally observed relationship has been replicated within smaller subgroups, and that the control variable has no influence on that original relationship.

10. If a set of partial relationships is reduced essentially to zero when an *antecedent* variable is held constant, this outcome is called an *explanation*, meaning that the originally observed "relationship" was a *spurious* or ungenuine one. This outcome suggests that the control variable has a causal effect on each of the variables examined in the zero-order relationship, thus resulting in a statistical relationship between those two that does not represent a causal relationship in itself.

11. If a set of partial relationships is reduced essentially to zero when an *intervening* variable is held constant, this outcome is called an *interpretation*, meaning that we have interpreted the manner in which the independent variable has its influence on the dependent variable: the independent variable influences the intervening variable, which, in turn, influences the dependent variable. In this instance, we conclude that the original relationship was a genuine causal relationship; we have shed further light on how that causal process operates.

12. If one partial relationship is reduced essentially to zero while the other remains about the same as the original one, this outcome is called a *specification*, regardless of whether the control variable was intervening or antecedent. This means, simply, that we have specified the conditions under which the originally observed relationship occurs.

13. *Ex post facto hypothesizing* refers to the development of hypotheses "predicting" relationships that have already been observed. This is invalid in science, since it is impossible to disconfirm such hypotheses. Of course, nothing prevents us from suggesting reasons that observed relationships may be the way they are; we simply should not frame those reasons in the form of "hypotheses." More important, one observed relationship and possible reasons for it may suggest hypotheses about other relationships that have not been examined. The elaboration model is an excellent logical device for this kind of unfolding analysis of data.

ANNOTATED BIBLIOGRAPHY

Glock, Charles (ed.), *Survey Research in the Social Sciences* (New York: Russell Sage Foundation, 1967), Chapter 1. An excellent discussion of the logic of elaboration. Glock's own chapter in this book presents the elaboration model, providing concrete illustrations.

Hirschi, Travis, and Selvin, Hanan, *Delinquency Research: An Appraisal of Analytic Methods* (New York: Free Press, 1967). Excellent logical discussions and concrete examples. This book examines the empirical research in the field of delinquency from a rigorously logical perspective. Critiques of specific research examples often set the stage for important and insightful general discussions of elaboration and other aspects of the logic of scientific inquiry.

Hyman, Herbert, *Survey Design and Analysis* (New York: Free Press, 1955). A somewhat dated but milestone statement of the elaboration model. The fundamental paradigm is discussed and illustrated through a number of real surveys. Lazarsfeld's foreword is the most available classic statement of the logic of elaboration. This was and still is an important book. Later sections of the book illustrate the relationship between the logical model and the nitty-gritty details of analyzing data by counter-sorter, an excellent method of developing hand-brain coordination in social research.

Lazarsfeld, Paul; Pasanella, Ann; and Rosenberg, Morris (eds.); *Continuities in the Language of Social Research* (New York: Free Press, 1972). An excellent and classic collection of conceptual discussions and empirical illustrations. Section II is especially relevant, though the logic of elaboration runs throughout most of the volume.

Rosenberg, Morris, *The Logic of Survey Analysis* (New York: Basic Books, 1968). The most comprehensive statement of elaboration available. Rosenberg presents the basic paradigm, and goes on to suggest logical extensions of it. It is difficult to decide what is most important, this aspect of the book or the voluminous illustrations. Both are simply excellent, and this book serves an important instructional purpose.

CHAPTER 18

Social Statistics

INTRODUCTION

Many people are intimidated by empirical research because they feel uncomfortable with mathematics and statistics. And indeed, many research reports are filled with a variety of semispecified computations. The role of statistics in social research is very important, but it is equally important for that role to be seen in its proper perspective.

Empirical research is first and foremost a logical operation rather than a mathematical one. Mathematics is merely a convenient and efficient language for accomplishing the logical operations inherent in good data analysis. Statistics is the applied branch of mathematics especially appropriate to a variety of research analyses.

I want to start this chapter with an informal look at one of the concerns I find people have when they approach statistics. I suspect the beginning exercise will make it easier for you to understand and feel comfortable with the relatively simple statistics that are introduced in the remainder of the chapter. We'll be looking at two types of statistics: **descriptive** and **inferential**. Descriptive statistics is a medium for describing data in manageable forms. Inferential statistics, on the other hand, assists you in drawing conclusions from your actual observations that apply beyond those observations; typically, that involves drawing conclusions about a population from the study of a sample drawn from it.

THE DANGER OF SUCCESS IN MATH

Over the course of teaching research methods involving at least a small amount of statistics, I've been struck by the very large number of students who report that they are "simply no good at math." They generally report this fact as some sort of congenital defect, akin to being born blind or crippled. Not unexpectedly, I have found such people doing pretty badly in statistics, and their more general mastery of quantitative social research has suffered as a result.

To accommodate for this defect, I have increasingly limited the amount and difficulty of statistics to be covered in a course such as the one you're taking. No matter how simple the statistics required has been, however, I've found a large number of students unable to master it—all reporting the *congenital math deficiency syndrome* (CMDS). Just as some people are reported to be inherently tone-deaf and others unable to learn foreign languages, I've found about 90 percent of the college students I've taught to be suffering from CMDS. Some of its common symptoms are frustration, boredom, and drowsiness. I'm delighted to report that I have finally uncovered a major cause of the disease and have brewed up a cure. In the event that you may be a sufferer, I'd like to share it with you before we delve into the statistics of social research.

You may be familiar with the story of Typhoid Mary, whose real name was Mary Mallon. Mary was a typhoid carrier who died in 1938 in New York. Before her death, she worked as a household cook, moving from household to household, and causing 10 outbreaks of typhoid fever. Over fifty people caught the disease from her, and three of them died.

The congenital math deficiency syndrome has a similar cause. After an exhaustive search, I've discovered the culprit, whom I'll call Mathematical Marvin, though he has used countless aliases. If you suffer from CMDS, I suspect you've come in contact with him. Here's how you'll recognize him.

Take a minute to recall your years in high school. In particular, I'd like you to recall that person in your class who was generally regarded by your teachers and your classmates as being a "mathematical genius." Getting A's in all the math classes was only part of it; often the math genius seemed to know math better than the teachers.

If you now have that math genius of your class in mind, let me ask you a few questions. First, what was the person's sex? My guess is that he was probably male. Most of the students I've asked in class report that. But let's consider some other characteristics:

1. How athletic was he?

2. Did he wear glasses?

3. How many parties did he get invited to during high school?

4. If he was invited to parties, did anyone ever talk to him?

5. How often did you find yourself envying the math genius, wishing you could trade places with him?

I've been asking students (including some adult classes) these questions for several years, and the answers I've gotten are amazing. Though the agreement has not been unanimous, a clear profile of Marvin emerges. He is usually unathletic, often either very skinny or overweight. He usually wears glasses, and he seems otherwise rather delicate. During his high school years, he was invited to an average (mean) of 1.2 parties, and nobody talked to him. His complexion was terrible. Finally, I have found almost nobody who ever wanted to change places with him: he was a social misfit, more to be pitied than envied.

If the person you are thinking of squares at all with this description, it seems certain that you've been infected by Mathematical Marvin and rendered mathematically impotent. Beware! Marvin has been known to wear a disguise, and you may have gone to school with him during one of his adventurous periods.

Here's the point of my report on Mathematical Marvin (there *is* a point). As I've discussed Marvin with my students, it has become increasingly clear that most of them have formed a subconscious association between mathematical proficiency and Marvin's unenviable characteristics. Most have formed the conclusion that doing well in math and statistics would turn them into social misfits, and they have regarded that as too high a price to pay.

When I have asked students to raise their hands if they regard themselves as naturally good at math, almost none do. That's not surprising, perhaps. But then I ask, "How would you feel if you overheard me telling another faculty member that I only wish all my students were as good at statistics as you are?" Almost none of the students say they would be pleased with this news, and about half say they would feel uncomfortable if they heard it. Think about it for a minute. Suppose word got around school that *you* were a mathematical genius. There's a good chance that you'd feel uncomfortable with that prospect.

If you are one of those people who is "just no good at math," it's possible that you are carrying around a hidden fear that your face will break out in pimples if you do well in statistics in this course. If so, you're going to be reading the rest of this chapter in a terrible state: wanting to understand it at least until the next exam and, at the same time, worrying that you may understand it too well and lose all your friends.

Before exposing you to any numbers, then, I want to assure you that the level of statistics contained in the rest of this chapter has been proven safe for humans. There has not been a single, documented case of pimples connected to understanding *lambda, gamma, chi square*, or any of the other statistics discussed in the pages to follow. In fact, this level of exposure has been found to be *beneficial* to young social researchers.

By the way, uncovering Marvin can clear up a lot of mysteries. It did for me. (In my high school class, he didn't wear glasses, but he squinted a lot.) At the time, I thought it was caused by the pimples. In the first research methods book I wrote, I presented three statistical computations and got one of them wrong. In the first edition of this book, I got a different one wrong. Most embarrassing of all, however, the first printing of the earlier book had a truly unique feature. I had thought it would be fun to write a computer program to generate my own table of random numbers rather than reprinting one that someone else had created. In doing that, I had the dubious honor of publishing the world's first table of random numbers that *didn't have any nines*! It was not until I tracked Marvin down that I discovered the source of my problems, and statistics has been much more fun (and trouble free) ever since. So enjoy.

DESCRIPTIVE STATISTICS

As I've already suggested, descriptive statistics represents a method for presenting quantitative descriptions in a manageable form. Sometimes we want to describe single variables and sometimes we want to describe the associations that connect one variable with another. Let's look at some of the ways that is done.

Data Reduction

It is useful to begin the discussion of descriptive statistics with a brief look at the raw-data matrix produced by a research project. Table 18-1 presents such a raw-data matrix.

Table 18-1   Typical Raw-Data Matrix

	Variables										
	V_1	V_2	V_3	V_4	V_5	V_6	V_7	V_8	V_9	...	Vn
Case 1	2	5	1	4	3	3	9	2	7	...	6
Case 2	3	2	1	1	8	5	9	1	6	...	1
Case 3	1	3	2	3	2	5	3	7	5	...	2
Case 4	2	1	2	2	5	2	7	4	4	...	3
.	.	.	.	.	.	.	.	.	.		.
.	.	.	.	.	.	.	.	.	.		.
.	.	.	.	.	.	.	.	.	.		.
Case n	1	3	1	2	4	4	6	7	1	...	4

For our purposes, we may think of the variables in Table 18-1 as punch-card columns. Each column represents a coded set of data. Column V_3, for example, might represent sex: 1 for male and 2 for female. The cases in the left column of Table 18-1 would represent the people for whom data were coded.

A raw-data matrix contains all the original coded information that you have collected about your cases. It is worth noting, moreover, that you often see your data in just this form. If the data are coded on transfer sheets for keypunching, those sheets form a raw-data matrix like the one in Table 18-1. And after keypunching the data, you may have the computer list your data file, and the result is a raw-data matrix.

Recalling the earlier discussion of univariate analysis in Chapter 14, we note that the raw-data matrix has the advantage of representing all the available information. If the reader of a research report were provided with the raw-data matrix, he or she would have all the information available to the researcher doing the study.

The prime difficulty of such a data matrix is that it is a very inefficient presentation of the data. Imagine for a moment a matrix containing perhaps 200 variables for each of 2,000 cases. Such a matrix would contain nearly half a million entries. Neither you nor the reader would be able to sift through so many numbers to recognize meaningful patterns in them.

Descriptive statistics provides a method of reducing large data matrices to manageable summaries to permit easy understanding and interpretation. Single variables can be summarized by descriptive statistics, and so can the associations among variables.

Chapter 14 discussed the various methods of summarizing univariate data: frequency distributions in either raw numbers or percentages, either grouping the data into categories or leaving them ungrouped; averages such as the mean, median, or mode; and measures of dispersion such as the range, the standard deviation, and so forth. You should keep in mind the inherent trade-off between summarization and the maintenance of the original data. The prime goal of univariate descriptive statistics is efficiency: the maximum amount of information should be maintained in the simplest summary form. Let's turn now to an extension of those concerns in an examination of the descriptive statistics available for summarizing associations among variables.

Measures of Association

The association between any two variables also may be represented by a data matrix, this time produced by the joint frequency distributions of the two variables. Table 18-2 presents such a matrix.

Table 18-2   Association between Variables as a Data Matrix

	Variable X					
	X_1	X_2	X_3	X_4	X_5	X_6
Y_1	35	27	26	12	15	7
Y_2	38	48	38	22	35	13
Y_3	32	41	75	64	46	22
Y_4	28	45	63	80	79	45
Y_5	20	35	53	90	103	87
Y_6	23	12	76	80	99	165
Y_7	5	8	43	60	73	189

The data matrix presented in Table 18-2 provides all the necessary information for determining the nature and extent of the relationship between variables X and Y. The column headings in the table represent the values of variable X, while the row headings represent the values of variable Y. The numbers in the body of the matrix represent the number of cases having a particular pattern of attributes. For example, 35 cases have the pattern $X_1 Y_1$; 43 cases are $X_3 Y_7$.

Like the raw-data matrix presented in Table 18-1, this one gives you more information than you can easily comprehend. If you study the table carefully, however, you will note that as values of variable X increase from X_1 to X_6, there is a general tendency for values of Y to increase from Y_1 to Y_7, but no more than a general impression is possible. A variety of descriptive statistics permit the summarization of this data matrix, however. Selecting the appropriate measure depends initially on the nature of the two variables.

We'll turn now to some of the options that are available for summarizing the association between two variables. This discussion and those to follow are taken largely from the excellent statistics textbook by Linton C. Freeman.[1]

Each of the measures of association to be discussed in the following sections is based on the same model—*proportionate reduction of error* (PRE). The logic of this model is as follows. First, let's assume that I asked you to guess respondents' attributes on a given variable; for example, whether they answered "yes" or "no" to a given questionnaire item. To assist you, let's assume further that you know the overall distribution of responses in the total sample—say, 60 percent said "yes" and 40 percent said "no." You would make the fewest errors in this process if you always guessed the *modal* (most frequent) response: "yes."

Second, let's assume that you also know the empirical relationship between the first variable and some other variable: say, sex. Now, each time I ask you to guess whether a respondent said "yes" or "no," I'll tell you whether the respondent is a man or a woman. If the two variables are related to each other, you should make fewer errors the second time. It is possible, therefore, to compute the PRE by knowing the relationship between the two variables: the greater the relationship, the greater the reduction of error.

This basic PRE model is modified slightly to take account of different levels of measurement—nominal, ordinal, or interval. The following sections will consider each level of measurement and present one measure of association appropriate to each. You should realize that the three measures discussed are only an arbitrary selection from among many appropriate measures.

Nominal Variables   If the two variables consist of nominal data (for example, sex, religious affiliation, race), lambda (λ) would be one appropriate measure. As discussed above, lambda is based on your ability to guess values on one of the variables: the PRE achieved through knowledge of values on the other variable. A simple hypothetical example will illustrate the logic and method of lambda.

Table 18-3 Hypothetical Data
Relating Sex to Employment Status

	Men	Women	Total
Employed	900	200	1,100
Unemployed	100	800	900
Total	1,000	1,000	2,000

[1]Linton C. Freeman, *Elementary Applied Statistics* (New York: John Wiley, 1968).

Table 18-3 presents hypothetical data relating sex to employment status. Overall, we note that 1,100 people are employed, and 900 are unemployed. If you were to predict whether or not people were employed, knowing only the overall distribution on that variable, you would always predict "employed," since that would result in fewer errors than always predicting "unemployed." Nevertheless, this strategy would result in 900 errors out of 2,000 predictions.

Let's suppose that you had access to the data shown in Table 18-3 and that you were told each person's sex before making your prediction of employment status. Your strategy would change in that case. For every man, you would predict "employed," and for every woman, you would predict "unemployed." In this instance, you would make 300 errors—the 100 unemployed men and the 200 employed women—or 600 fewer errors than would have been made in ignorance of their sexes.

Lambda, then, represents the reduction in errors as a proportion of the errors that would have been made on the basis of the overall distribution. In this hypothetical example, lambda would equal .67: 600 fewer errors divided by 900 errors based on the total distribution of employment status alone. In this fashion, lambda provides a measure of the statistical association between sex and employment status.

If sex and employment status were statistically independent of one another, we would have found the same distribution of employment status for men and women. In this case, knowing sexes would not have affected the number of errors made in predicting employment status, and the resulting lambda would have been zero. If, on the other hand, all men were employed and all women were unemployed, you would have made no errors in predicting employment status, knowing sex. You would have made 900 fewer errors (out of 900) and lambda would have been 1.0—representing a perfect statistical association.

Lambda is only one of several measures of association appropriate to the analysis of two nominal variables. You might want to look at Freeman[2] for a discussion of other appropriate measures.

Ordinal Variables   If the variables being related were ordinal in nature (for example, social class, religiosity, alienation), gamma (γ) would be one appropriate measure of association. Like lambda, gamma is based on your ability to guess values on one variable by knowing values on another. Instead of guessing exact values, however, gamma is based on the ordinal arrangement of values. For any given *pair* of cases, you guess that their ordinal ranking on one variable will correspond (positively or negatively) to their ordinal ranking on the other. Gamma is the proportion of pairs that fit this pattern.

Table 18-4 presents hypothetical data relating social class to prejudice. An inspection of the table will indicate the general nature of the relationship between these two variables: as social class increases, prejudice decreases. There is a negative association between social class and prejudice.

Gamma is computed from two quantities: (1) the number of pairs having the same ranking on the two variables and (2) the number of pairs having the opposite

[2]*Ibid.*

Table 18-4 Hypothetical
Data Relating Social Class to Prejudice

Prejudice	Lower Class	Middle Class	Upper Class
Low	200	400	700
Medium	500	900	400
High	800	300	100

ranking on the two variables. The pairs having the same ranking are computed as follows. The frequency of each cell in the table is multiplied by the sum of all cells appearing below and to the right of it—with all these products being summed. In the present example, the number of pairs with the same ranking would be 200(900 + 300 + 400 + 100) + 500(300 + 100) + 400(400 + 100) + 900(100) or 340,000 + 200,000 + 200,000 + 90,000 = 830,000.

The pairs having the opposite ranking on the two variables are computed as follows: the frequency of each cell in the table is multiplied by the sum of all cells appearing below and to the left of it—with all these products being summed. In this example, the numbers of pairs with opposite rankings would be 700(500 + 800 + 900 + 300) + 400(800 + 300) + 400(500 + 800) + 900(800) or 1,750,000 + 440,000 + 520,000 + 720,000 = 3,430,000.

Gamma is computed from the numbers of same-ranked pairs and opposite-ranked pairs as follows:

$$gamma = (\text{same} - \text{opposite}) \div (\text{same} + \text{opposite}).$$

In the present example, gamma would equal: (830,000 − 3,430,000) divided by (830,000 + 3,430,000) or −.61. The negative sign in this answer indicates the negative association suggested by the initial inspection of the table. Social class and prejudice, in this hypothetical example, are negatively associated with one another. The numerical figure for gamma indicates that 61 percent more of the pairs examined had the opposite ranking than had the same ranking.

Note that while values of lambda vary from 0 to 1, values of gamma vary from −1 to +1, representing the *direction* as well as the magnitude of the association. Since nominal variables have no ordinal structure, it makes no sense to speak of the direction of the relationship. (A negative lambda would indicate that you made more errors in predicting values on one variable while knowing values on the second than you made in ignorance of the second.)

Gamma is only one of several measures of association appropriate to ordinal variables. Again, you are referred to Freeman[3] for a more comprehensive treatment of this subject.

Interval or Ratio Variables   If the variables being associated are interval or ratio in nature (for example, age, income, grade point average, and so forth), one appropriate measure of association would be Pearson's product-moment correlation (r). The derivation and computation of this measure of association is sufficiently

[3] *Ibid.*

complex to lie outside the scope of the present book, so only a few general comments will be made.

Like both gamma and lambda, r is based on guessing the value of one variable on the basis of knowing the other. For continuous interval or ratio variables, however, it is unlikely that you would be able to predict the *precise* value of the variable. But on the other hand, predicting only the ordinal arrangement of values on the two variables would not take advantage of the greater amount of information conveyed by an interval or ratio variable. In a sense, r reflects *how closely* you can guess the value of one variable through your knowledge of the value of the other.

To understand the logic of r, it will be useful to consider the manner in which you might hypothetically guess values that cases have on a given variable. With nominal variables, we have seen that you might always guess the modal value. That is not an appropriate perspective for interval or ratio data, however. Instead, you would minimize your errors by always guessing the mean value of the variable. Although this practice would produce few if any perfect guesses, the extent of your errors would be minimized.

In the computation of lambda, we noted the number of errors produced by always guessing the modal value. In the case of r, errors are measured in terms of the sum of the squared differences between the actual value and the mean. We shall refer to this later as the *total variance*.

To improve your guessing, you construct a *regression line* (see Chapter 19), stated in the form of a regression equation that permits the estimation of values on one variable from values on the other. The general format for this equation is $Y' = a + b(X)$, where a and b are computed values, where X is a given value on one variable, and Y' is the estimated value on the other. The values of a and b are computed in such a way as to minimize the differences between actual values of Y and the corresponding estimates (Y') based on the known value of X. The sum of squared differences between actual and estimated values of Y is called the *unexplained variance*, in that it represents errors that still exist even when estimates are based on known values of X.

The *explained variance* is the difference between the total variance and the unexplained variance. Dividing the explained variance by the total variance produces a measure of the *proportionate reduction of error* corresponding to the similar quantity in the computation of lambda. In the present case, this quantity is the correlation *squared*: r^2. Thus, if $r = .7$, then $r^2 = .49$: meaning that about *half* the variance has been explained.

In practice, we compute r rather than r^2, since the product moment correlation can take either a positive or negative sign, depending on the direction of the relationship between the two variables. (Computing r^2 and taking a square root would always produce a positive quantity.) See Freeman[4] or any other standard statistics textbook for the method of computing r, although I anticipate that most readers using this measure will have access to computer programs designed for this function.[5]

[4]*Ibid.*

[5]Although r is based on a regression model, r is a *symmetrical* measure. (Gamma is also symmetrical, but lambda is not.) We shall see in the next chapter that predicting values of Y from values of X produces a different equation than predicting values of X from values of Y. Thus, although the linear regression model is asymmetrical, the computation of r is such as to produce a symmetrical solution.

Mixed Types of Variables   Often, you will find that your interest lies in the association between two variables that differ in type: one ordinal variable and one nominal variable. A variety of special statistics are appropriate to these different possibilities, and you are encouraged to examine Freeman[6] for the appropriate statistics for his particular situation.

This is an opportune point for a general comment regarding types of variables and the appropriateness of statistical measures. A quick review of social scientific research literature will yield countless examples of statistical measures applied to data that do not meet the logical requirements of the measures. The computation of Pearson's r for ordinal data is perhaps the most typical example. The response to this practice seems to be largely a matter of personal taste. The person who argues against it is correct on statistical grounds: correlation coefficients assume interval data, and ordinal data do not meet that criterion. On the other hand, it is my personal orientation to accept, and even to encourage, the use of whatever statistical techniques help the researcher (and the reader) to understand the body of data under analysis. If the computation of r from ordinal data serves this purpose, then it should be encouraged. However, I strongly object to (and discuss in the next section) the practice of making statistical inferences on the basis of such computations. We are justified in bending the rules if it helps us understand our data, but we must be aware of the implications of bending those rules.

INFERENTIAL STATISTICS

Many, if not most, social scientific research projects involve the examination of data collected from a sample drawn from a larger population. A sample of people may be interviewed in a survey; a sample of divorce records may be coded and analyzed; a sample of newspapers may be examined through content analysis. Samples are seldom if ever studied for the sole purpose of describing the samples per se; in most instances, the ultimate purpose is to make assertions about the larger population from which the sample has been selected. Frequently, then, you will wish to interpret your univariate and multivariate sample findings as the basis for *inferences* about some population.

This section will examine the statistical measures available to the researcher for making such inferences and the logical bases for them. We'll begin with univariate data and move to multivariate.

Univariate Inferences

The opening sections of Chapter 14 dealt with methods of presenting univariate data. Each summary measure was intended as a method of describing the sample studied. Now we have come to the point of using those measures to make broader

[6]Freeman, *op. cit.*

assertions about the population. This section is addressed to two univariate measures: percentages and means.

If 50 percent of a sample of people say they have had colds during the past year, our best estimate of the similar proportion of the total population from which the sample has been drawn is 50 percent. (This estimate assumes a simple random sample, of course.) It is rather unlikely, however, that *precisely* 50 percent of the population have had colds during the year. If a rigorous sampling design for random selection has been followed, however, we will be able to estimate the expected range of error when the sample finding is applied to the population.

Chapter 7 on sampling theory covered the procedures for making such estimates, so they will be only reviewed here. In the case of a percentage, the quantity $\sqrt{pq/n}$, where p is a percentage and q equals $1 - p$, and where n is the sample size, is called the *standard error*. As noted in Chapter 7, this quantity is very important in the estimation of sampling error. We may be 68 percent confident that the population figure falls within plus or minus one standard error of the sample figure, we may be 95 percent confident that it falls within plus or minus two standard errors, and 99.9 percent confident that it falls within plus or minus three standard errors.

Any statement of sampling error, then, must contain two essential components: the *confidence level* (for example, 95 percent) and the *confidence interval* (for example ±2.5 percent). If 50 percent of a sample of 1,600 people say they have had colds during the year, we might say we are 95 percent confident that the population figure is between 47.5 percent and 52.5 percent.

Recognize in this example that we have moved beyond simply describing the sample into the realm of making estimates (inferences) about the larger population. In doing that, we must be wary of several assumptions.

First, the sample must be drawn from the population about which inferences are being made. A sample taken from a telephone directory cannot legitimately be the basis for statistical inferences about the population of a city.

Second, the inferential statistics assume simple random sampling, which is virtually never the case in sample surveys. The statistics assume sampling with replacement, which is almost never done; but that is probably not a serious problem. Although systematic sampling is used more frequently than random sampling, that, too, probably presents no serious problem if done correctly. Stratified sampling, since it improves representativeness, clearly presents no problem. Cluster sampling does present a problem, however, as the estimates of sampling error may be too small. Quite clearly, street corner sampling does not warrant the use of inferential statistics. Also assumed is a 100 percent completion rate. This problem increases in seriousness as the completion rate decreases.

Third, the inferential statistics are addressed to sampling error only; they do not take account of *nonsampling* errors. Thus, it might be quite correct to state that between 47.5 and 52.5 percent of the population (95 percent confidence) would *say* that they had had colds during the previous year, but their reports might be essentially worthless. We could confidently guess the proportion of the population who would *report* colds, but not the proportion who had had them. Whereas nonsampling errors are probably larger than sampling errors in a respectable sample design, we need to be especially cautious in generalizing from our sample findings to the population.

Tests of Statistical Significance

What constitutes a *significant* association between two variables? This question, like many, has no reasonable answer. Nevertheless, it is frequently answered in an unreasonable manner.

There is no scientific answer to the question of whether a given association between two variables is significant, strong, important, interesting, or worth reporting. Perhaps the ultimate test of significance rests with your ability to persuade your audience (present and future) of the association's significance.

At the same time, there is a body of inferential statistics to assist you in this regard: the body of *parametric tests of significance*. As the name suggests, parametric statistics are those that make certain assumptions about the parameters describing the population from which the sample is selected.

Although tests of significance are widely reported in social scientific literature, the logic underlying them is rather subtle and is often misunderstood. Tests of significance are based on the same sampling logic that has been discussed elsewhere in this book. To understand the logic of these tests, let's return for a moment to the concept of sampling error in regard to univariate data.

Recall that a sample statistic normally provides the best single estimate of the corresponding population parameter, but that it is seldom the case that the statistic and the parameter precisely correspond. Thus, we report the probability that the parameter falls within a certain range (confidence interval). The degree of uncertainty within that range is due to normal sampling error. The corollary of such a statement is, of course, that it is *improbable* that the parameter would fall outside the specified range only as a result of sampling error. Thus, if we estimate that a parameter (99.9 percent confidence) lies between 45 percent and 55 percent, we say by implication that it is *extremely improbable* that the parameter is actually, say, 90 percent if our only error of estimation is due to normal sampling. That is the basic logic behind tests of significance.

I think I can illustrate this logic of statistical significance best in a series of diagrams representing the selection of samples from a population. The elements in the logic I'll illustrate are:

1. Assumptions regarding the *independence* of two variables in the population under study.

2. Assumptions regarding the *representativeness* of samples selected through conventional probability sampling procedures.

3. The observed *joint distribution* of sample elements in terms of the two variables.

Figure 18-1 merely represents a hypothetical population of 900 elements. Each dot in the illustration represents an individual member of that population. The lines enclosing the dots represent the *conceptual* boundaries of that population. Notice that the individuals are evenly distributed throughout the *conceptual* space. (The notion of conceptual space will become clearer shortly.)

Figure 18-2 presents an illustration of the distribution of the population elements with regard to two categories of a variable that is designated X. Notice that

Figure 18-1 A Hypothetical Population of 900 Individuals

half the population have the attribute: X_1; the other half have the attribute: X_2. Notice further that the elements are still evenly distributed throughout this *conceptual* space.

Figure 18-3 merely adds another variable (Y) to the conceptual space. Notice that the population is evenly distributed in terms of this second variable: half are Y_1 and half are Y_2. Also notice that the *joint distribution* of individuals in the population indicates that the two variables are *independent* of one another. Whether an individual is X_1 or X_2 has no influence on whether that individual is Y_1 or Y_2. The purpose of Figure 18-3 is to illustrate the notion of statistical independence between two variables in a population.

Figure 18-4 illustrates a probability sample of 400 cases being selected from a population in which two variables are independent of one another. The purpose of this illustration is to introduce the notion of *representativeness*. In this and the following figures, a representative sample will be illustrated as a *square, centered* box inside the population. The graphic shape of the sample corresponds to the graphic shape of the population to the extent that the sample is representative of that

Figure 18-2   Distribution of the Population
in Conceptual Space: An Even Distribution on One Variable

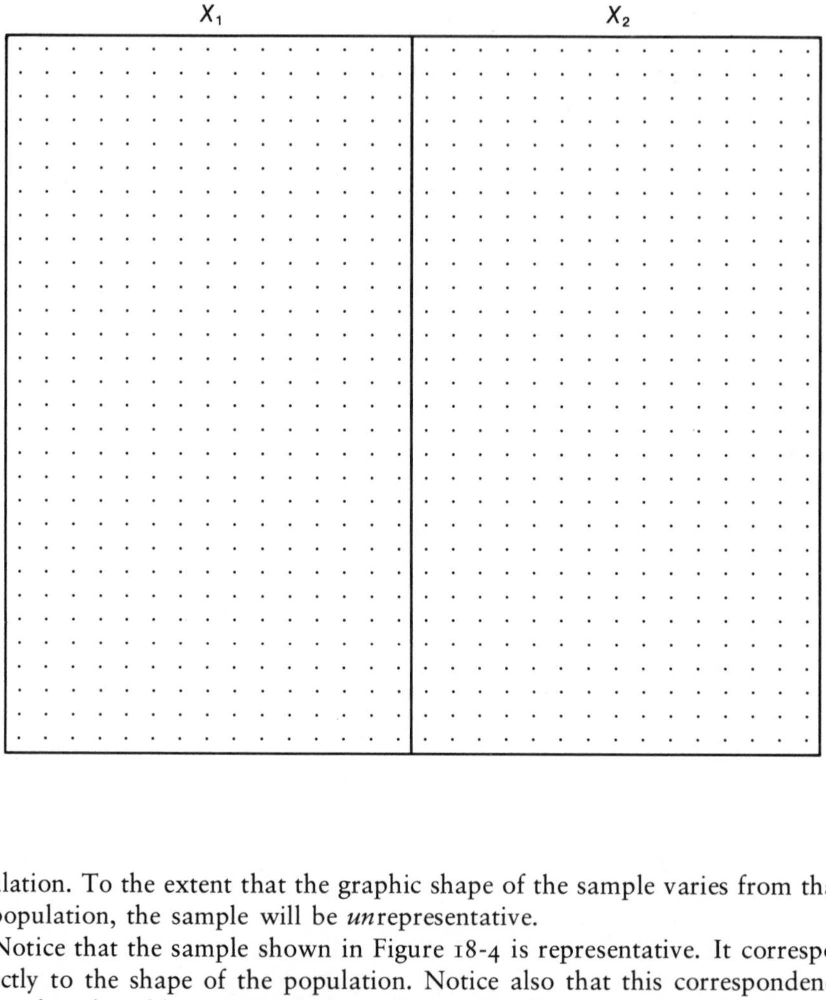

population. To the extent that the graphic shape of the sample varies from that of the population, the sample will be *un*representative.

Notice that the sample shown in Figure 18-4 is representative. It corresponds perfectly to the shape of the population. Notice also that this correspondence is indicated in the tables presented above the graphic illustration. The distribution of cases in the population indicates statistical independence between X and Y, and so does the distribution of cases in the sample.

In practice, we might *assume* statistical independence in the population. (We would not have the data shown in the left table to test that assumption, however.) We might select a probability sample from that population, using methods which support the *assumption* that such a sample would be representative of the larger population. The sample data presented in the right table in Figure 18-4 would confirm *both* of our assumptions: (1) the assumption of statistical independence of the two variables in the population and (2) the assumption of representativeness of our sample.

Figure 18-3   Distribution of the Population
in Conceptual Space: Representing the Total Independence of Two Variables

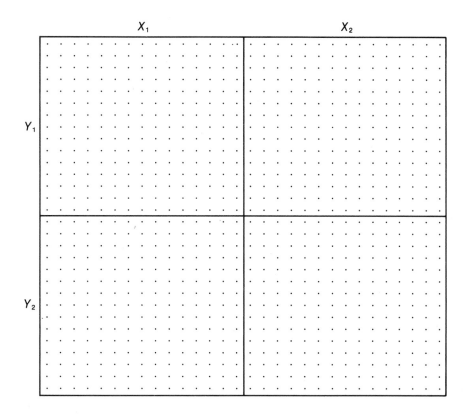

Figure 18-5 is a slightly more realistic illustration of sampling from a population in which two variables are statistically independent of one another. Notice that the sample is *not perfectly* representative of the population. The graphic shape of the sample is not a perfect square, although it closely approximates a square. In the right table above the graphic illustration, notice also that the sample data do not perfectly indicate statistical independence.

The fundamental logic of probability sampling provides for a degree of *sampling error* such as that illustrated in Figure 18-5. We expect that any given sample will be less than perfectly representative. In practice, we might evaluate the sample data shown in the right table of Figure 18-5 as confirming the assumption of statistical independence of the variables in the population and as indicating a slight degree of sampling error.

Turn to Figure 18-6 now and examine the right table, containing the data produced by a sample drawn from the population. Notice that the data grossly contradict the assumption of statistical independence of X and Y. Of the cases having the

Figure 18-4   A Representative Sample Drawn from a
Population Having Two Variables Independent of One Another

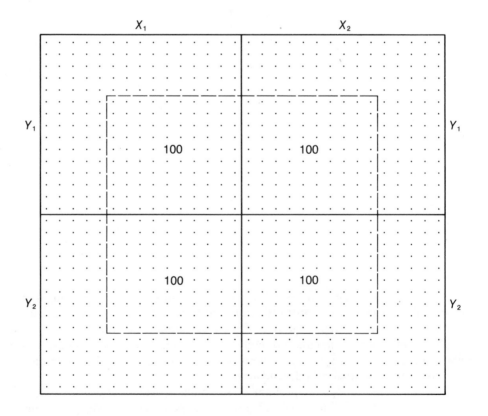

POPULATION			SAMPLE		
	X_1	X_2		X_1	X_2
Y_1	50%	50%	Y_1	50%	50%
Y_2	50	50	Y_2	50	50
T	100%	100%	T	100%	100%

attribute, X_1, 75 percent are Y_1, as compared to only 25 percent of those having the attribute, X_2. These sample data suggest a strong, positive relationship between X and Y, instead of the statistical independence that was assumed.

The graphic portion of Figure 18-6, as well as the left table, offer one explana-

Figure 18-5   A Slightly Unrepresentative Sample Drawn From a Population Having Two Variables Independent of One Another

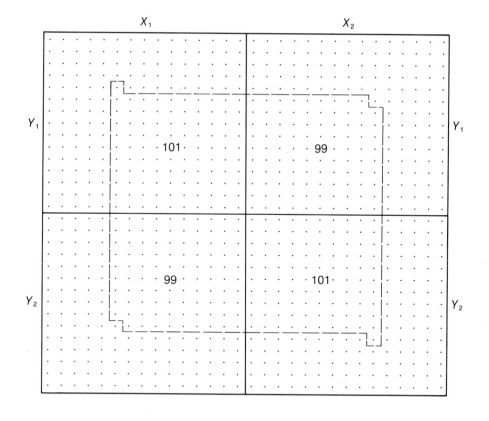

	POPULATION			SAMPLE	
	X_1	X_2		X_1	X_2
Y_1	50%	50%	Y_1	50.5%	49.5%
Y_2	50	50	Y_2	49.5	50.5
T	100%	100%	T	100%	100%

tion for the observed discrepancy between the sample data and the assumed independence of the variables: the sample is grossly *unrepresentative* of the population. This may be seen in the distorted shape of that sample. Notice that the two variables

Figure 18-6   A Grossly Unrepresentative Sample Drawn from a Population Having Two Variables Independent of One Another

POPULATION			SAMPLE		
	X_1	X_2		X_1	X_2
Y_1	50%	50%	Y_1	75%	25%
Y_2	50	50	Y_2	25	75
T	100%	100%	T	100%	100%

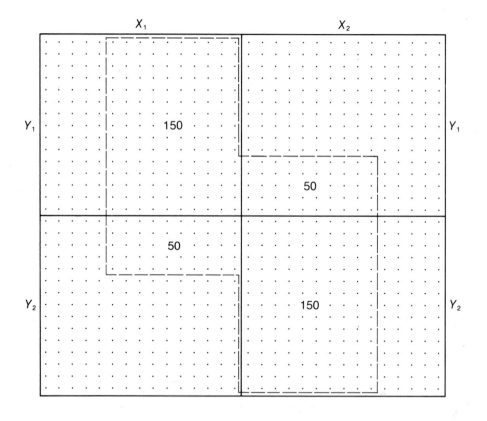

are really independent in the population. The apparent relationship is merely a function of a bad sample.

Given the sample data presented in the right table of Figure 18-6, we are faced with a dilemma. The normal expectations regarding sampling error cannot accommodate a discrepancy of this magnitude. *Some* sampling error is to be expected, but this amount is ridiculous.

To the extent that proper, probability sampling methods have been utilized, we are more likely to assume that the sample is representative of the population. Figure 18-7 illustrates a situation that reconciles the assumption of representativeness and the sample data. It does so by rejecting the assumption of statistical independence between X and Y in the population, assuming instead that the two variables are related to one another in the population approximately as they are related in the sample.

The fundamental logic of tests of statistical significance, then, is this: faced with *any* discrepancy between the assumed independence of variables in a population and the observed distribution of sample elements, we may explain that discrepancy in either of two ways. (1) We may attribute it to an unrepresentative sample. (2) We may reject the assumption of independence. The logic and statistics associated with probability sampling methods offer guidance as to the varying probabilities of varying degrees of unrepresentativeness (expressed as *sampling error*). Most simply put, there is a *high* probability of a *small* degree of unrepresentativeness and a *low* probability of a *large* degree of unrepresentativeness.

The *statistical significance* of a relationship that is observed in a set of sample data, then, is always expressed in terms of probabilities. Significant at the .05 level ($p \leq .05$) simply means that the probability of a relationship as strong as the observed one being attributable to sampling error alone is no more than 5 in 100. Put somewhat differently, *if* two variables are independent of one another in the population, and if 100 probability samples were selected from that population, no more than 5 of those samples should provide a relationship as strong as the one that has been observed.

There is, then, a corollary to confidence intervals in tests of significance, which represents the probability of the measured association being due *only* to *sampling* error. This is called the **level of significance.** Like confidence intervals, levels of significance are derived from a logical model in which several samples are drawn from a given population. In the present case, we assume that there is no association between the variables in the population, and then ask what proportion of the samples drawn from that population would produce associations at least as great as those measured in the empirical data. Three levels of significance are frequently used in research reports: .05, .01, and .001. These mean, respectively, that the chances of obtaining the measured association as a result of sampling error are 5/100, 1/100, and 1/1,000.

Researchers who use tests of significance normally follow one of two patterns in this regard. Some prefer to specify in advance the level of significance that they will regard as sufficient. If any measured association is statistically significant at that level, they will regard it as representing a genuine association between the two variables. In other words, they are willing to discount the possibility of its resulting from sampling error only.

Other researchers prefer to report the specific level of significance for each association, disregarding the conventions of .05, .01, and .001. Rather than reporting that a given association was significant at the .05 level, they would indicate that

Figure 18-7   A Representative Sample Drawn from a
Population Having Two Variables Strongly Related to Each Other

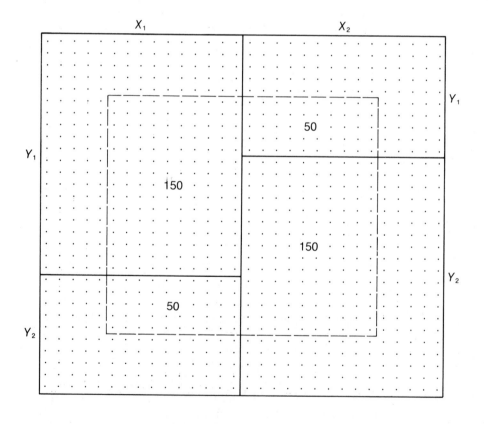

it was significant at the .023 level, indicating the chances of its having resulted from
sampling error as 23 out of 1,000.

Chi square is a frequently used test of significance in social science. It is based
on the **null hypothesis**: the assumption that there is no relationship between the two

variables in the total population. Given the observed distribution of values on the two separate variables, we compute the conjoint distribution that would be expected if there were no relationship between the two variables. The result of this operation is a set of *expected frequencies* for all the cells in the contingency table. We then compare this expected distribution with the distribution of cases actually found in the sample data, and we determine the probability that the discovered discrepancy could have resulted from sampling error alone. An example will illustrate this procedure.

Let's assume that we are interested in the possible relationship between church attendance and gender of the members of a particular church. To test this relationship, we have selected a sample of 100 church members at random. Assume further that we find our sample is made up of 40 men and 60 women. And, finally, assume that 70 percent of our sample report having attended church during the preceding week, while the remaining 30 percent say they did not.

If there were no relationship between sex and church attendance, then we should expect 70 percent of the men in the sample to have attended church during the preceding week and should expect that 30 percent did not. Moreover, we should expect the same proportional results from women. Table 18-5 (Part I) presents the expected frequencies based on this model. Thus, we should expect that 28 men and 42 women would have attended church, and 12 men and 18 women would not have attended church.

Part II of Table 18-5 presents the hypothetically observed cell frequencies discovered among the sample of 100 church members. We note that 20 of the men report having attended church during the preceding week, while the remaining 20 say they did not. Among the women in the sample, 50 attended church and 10 did not. Comparing the expected and observed frequencies (Parts I and II), we note that somewhat fewer men attended church than expected, while somewhat more women than expected attended.

Table 18-5   A Hypothetical Illustration of Chi Square

I. Expected cell frequencies	Men	Women	Total
Attended church	28	42	70
Did not attend church	12	18	30
Total	40	60	100
II. Observed cell frequencies	Men	Women	Total
Attended church	20	50	70
Did not attend church	20	10	30
Total	40	60	100
III. (Observed − expected)^2 ÷ expected	Men	Women	
Attended church	2.29	1.52	$x^2 = 12.70$,
Did not attend church	5.33	3.56	$p = .001$.

Chi square is computed as follows. For each cell in the tables, the researcher (1) subtracts the expected frequency for that cell from the observed frequency, (2) squares this quantity, and (3) divides the squared difference by the expected frequency. This procedure is carried out for each cell in the tables, and the several results are added together. (Part III of Table 18-5 presents the cell-by-cell computations.) The final sum is the value of chi square: 12.70 in the example.

The value that we have now computed is the overall discrepancy between the observed conjoint distribution in the sample and the distribution that we should have expected if the two variables were unrelated to one another. Of course, the mere discovery of a discrepancy does not prove that the two variables are related, since normal sampling error might produce discrepancies even when there was no relationship in the total population. The magnitude of the value of chi square, however, permits us to estimate the probability of that having happened.

To determine the statistical significance of the observed relationship, we must utilize a standard table of chi square values. That will require the computation of the *degrees of freedom*. In the case of chi square, the degrees of freedom are computed as follows: the number of rows in the table, minus one, is multiplied by the number of columns, minus one. This may be written as $(r - 1)(c - 1)$. In the present example, we have two rows and two columns (discounting the *totals*), so there is 1 degree of freedom.

Turning to a table of chi square values (see Appendix D), we find that for one degree of freedom and random sampling from a population in which there is no relationship between two variables, 10 percent of the time we should expect a chi square of at least 2.7. Thus, if we selected 100 samples from such a population, we should expect about 10 of those samples to produce chi squares equal to or greater than 2.7. Moreover, we should expect chi squares of at least 6.6 in 1 percent of the samples. Chi square values of 7.9 should be expected in only .5 percent of the samples. Thus, the lower the computed chi square value, the more probable it is that the value could be attributed to sampling error alone. The higher the chi square value, the less probable it is that it could be due to sampling error alone.

In the present hypothetical example, the computed value of chi square is 12.70. If there were no relationship between sex and church attendance in the whole church member population, and a large number of samples had been selected and studied, then we would expect a chi square of this magnitude in fewer than .1 percent of those samples. Thus, the probability of obtaining a chi square of this magnitude is less than .001, if random sampling has been used and there is no relationship in the population. We report this finding by saying the relationship is statistically significant at the .001 level. Since it is so improbable that the observed relationship could have resulted from sampling error alone, we are likely to reject the null hypothesis and assume that there is a relationship between the two variables in the population of church members.

Most measures of association can be tested for statistical significance in a similar manner. Standard tables of values permit us to determine whether a given association is statistically significant and at what level. Any standard statistics textbook provides instructions on the use of such tables, and we shall not pursue the matter further here.

Tests of significance have the advantage of providing an objective yardstick against which to estimate the significance of associations between variables. They assist us in ruling out associations that may not represent genuine relationships in the population under study. The researcher who uses or reads reports of significance tests should remain wary of several dangers in their interpretation, however.

First, we have been discussing tests of *statistical* significance; there are no objective tests of *substantive* significance. Thus, we may be legitimately convinced that a given association is not due to sampling error, but we may be in the position of asserting without fear of contradiction that two variables are only slightly related to one another. Recall that sampling error is an inverse function of sample size; the larger the sample, the smaller the expected error. Thus, a correlation of, say, .1 might very well be significant (at a given level) if discovered in a large sample, whereas the same correlation between the same two variables would not be significant if found in a smaller sample. Of course, that makes perfectly good sense if one understands the basic logic of tests of significance: in the larger sample, there is less chance that the correlation could be simply the product of sampling error. In both samples, however, it might represent a very weak and essentially zero correlation.

Second, tests of significance are based on the same sampling assumptions as were assumed in the computation of confidence intervals. To the extent that these assumptions are not met by the actual sampling design, the tests of significance are not strictly legitimate.

Third, you should be wary of applying tests of significance to data that represent a total population rather than a sample. If, for example, you have studied *all* the newspapers in the country and discovered a correlation of .3 between two variables, you should not report that the association is significant at the .001 level. Since you have not sampled, there is *no* chance that the association could be due to sampling error. The association between the two variables as measured in the population is *precisely* a correlation of .3—whether that degree of association is a *substantively significant* one, whether it is important, cannot be answered through any objective test. Some researchers feel a test of significance in such a case indicates the probability that the relationship is a general one over time—that it describes newspapers over time and not just at the time of the study.

As is the case for most matter covered by this book, I have a personal prejudice. In this instance, it is against tests of significance. My objection is not the statistical logic of those tests, since the logic is sound. Rather, I am concerned that such tests seem to mislead more than they enlighten. My principal reservations are the following:

1. Tests of significance make sampling assumptions that are virtually never satisfied by actual sampling designs.

2. They assume the absence of nonsampling errors, a questionable assumption in most actual empirical measurements.

3. In practice, they are too often applied to measures of association that have been computed in violation of the assumptions made by those measures (for example, product-moment correlations computed from ordinal data).

4. Statistical significance is too easily misinterpreted as "strength of association," or substantive significance.

At the same time, I feel that tests of significance can be a valuable asset to the researcher—useful tools for the understanding of data. My view in this regard is perhaps paradoxical. Although the above comments suggest an extremely conservative approach to tests of significance—that you should use them only when all assumptions are met—my general perspective is just the reverse. I would encourage you to use any statistical technique — any measure of association or any test of significance — on any set of data if it will help you to understand your data. If the computation of product-moment correlations among nominal variables and the testing of statistical significance in the context of uncontrolled sampling will meet this criterion, then I would encourage such activities. I say this in the spirit of what Hanan Selvin has referred to as data-dredging techniques. Anything goes, if it leads ultimately to the understanding of data and of the social world under study.

The price that must be paid for this radical freedom, however, is the giving up of strict, statistical interpretations. You would not be able to demonstrate the ultimate importance of your finding solely on the basis of your correlation being significant at the .05 level. Whatever the avenue to discovery, empirical data must ultimately be presented in a legitimate manner, and their importance must be argued logically.

SUMMARY

In Chapter 18, I have attempted to provide a brief overview of the different kinds of statistical measures that may be used in quantitative social research. I have made no attempt to be exhaustive in this regard, nor have I attempted to discuss any one statistical measure in full detail. Rather, I have tried to provide a general logical framework within which you might go on to learn statistics.

The chapter began with a discussion of descriptive statistics, those techniques that assist us in summarizing the data being analyzed. In this regard, we returned to the notion of data reduction, this time in terms of summarizing the relationships between variables. The statistical computations that summarize the relationships between variables are called *measures of association*.

Many measures of association are based on the model of the *proportionate reduction of error* (PRE). The logic of this model was discussed, and specific measures of association appropriate to different levels of measurement were described.

Next, the chapter turned to inferential statistics. We noted that few social research projects have the ultimate goal of determining the associations among variables within a particular set of observations. More typically, we wish to generalize our findings to larger, real populations. Inferential statistics, then, provide means whereby the generalizability of observed associations—among a survey sample, for example—to some larger population may be determined. This discussion began with a consideration of univariate inferences, involving a return to the earlier concepts of probability sampling: sampling distribution, standard error, confidence level, and confidence interval.

Next, we examined *tests of statistical significance*. These measures estimate the likelihood that an observed level of association—in a sample—could have been produced solely by sampling error, with there being no association between the variables in the larger population from which the sample was selected. *Chi square* was discussed as an illustration of tests of significance. The chapter concluded with a discussion of the common misuses of tests of statistical significance.

MAIN POINTS

1. Descriptive statistics are used to summarize data under study. Some descriptive statistics summarize the distribution of attributes on a single variable; others summarize the associations between variables.

2. Inferential statistics are used to estimate the generalizability of findings arrived at in the analysis of a sample to the larger population from which the sample has been selected. Some inferential statistics estimate the single-variable characteristics of the population; others—tests of statistical significance—estimate the relationships between variables in the population.

3. Descriptive statistics summarizing the relationships between variables are called *measures of association*.

4. Many measures of association are based on a *proportionate reduction of error* (PRE) model. This model is based on a comparison of (a) the number of errors we would make in attempting to guess the attributes of a given variable for each of the cases under study—if we knew nothing but the distribution of attributes on that variable—and (b) the number of errors we would make if we knew the joint distribution overall and were told for each case the attribute of one variable each time we were asked to guess the attribute of the other.

5. *Lambda* (λ) is an appropriate measure of association to be used in the analysis of two *nominal* variables. It also provides a clear illustration of the PRE model.

6. *Gamma* (γ) is an appropriate measure of association to be used in the analysis of two *ordinal* variables.

7. *Pearson's product-moment correlation* (r) is an appropriate measure of association to be used in the analysis of two *interval* or *ratio* variables.

8. Inferences about some characteristic of a population—such as the percentage of voters favoring Candidate A—must contain an indication of a *confidence interval* (the range within which the value is expected to be: for example, between 45 and 55 percent favor Candidate A) and an indication of the *confidence level* (the likelihood the value does fall within that range; for example, 95 percent confidence). Computations of confidence levels and intervals are based on probability theory and assume that conventional probability sampling techniques have been employed in the study.

9. Inferences about the generalizability to a population of the associations discovered between variables in a sample involve *tests of statistical significance*. Most simply put, these tests estimate the likelihood that an association as large

as the observed one could result from normal sampling error if no such association exists between the variables in the larger population. Tests of statistical significance, then, are also based on probability theory and assume that conventional probability sampling techniques have been employed in the study.

10. Statistical significance must not be confused with *substantive* significance, the latter meaning that an observed association is strong, important, meaningful, or worth writing home to your mother about.

11. The *level of significance* of an observed association is reported in the form of the probability that that association could have been produced merely by sampling error. To say that an association is significant at the .05 level is to say that an association as large as the observed one could not be expected to result from sampling error more than 5 times out of 100.

12. Social researchers tend to utilize a particular set of levels of significance in connection with tests of statistical significance: .05, .01, and .001. That is merely a convention, however.

13. Tests of statistical significance, strictly speaking, make assumptions about data and methods that are almost never satisfied completely by real social research. Despite this, the tests can serve a very useful function in the analysis and interpretation of data. You should be wary of interpreting the "significance" of the test results too precisely, however.

ANNOTATED BIBLIOGRAPHY

Freeman, Linton, *Elementary Applied Statistics* (New York: John Wiley, 1968). An excellent introductory statistics textbook. Everyone has his favorite statistics text, and this is mine. It is clear, well-organized, and understandable. In addition to describing the most frequently used statistical methods in detail, Freeman provides briefer descriptions of many more that might be appropriate in special situations.

Kish, Leslie, *Survey Sampling* (New York: John Wiley, 1965). The definitive reference for sampling statistics. In addition to discussing the logic of statistical inference, Kish provides formulas to cover just about any aspect of sampling that is likely to be encountered.

Morrison, Denton, and Henkel, Ramon (eds.), *The Significance Test Controversy: A Reader* (Chicago: Aldine-Atherton, 1970). A compilation of perspectives—pro and con—on tests of statistical significance. The question of the validity, utility, or significance of tests of statistical significance is one that reappears periodically in social science journals. Each reappearance is marked by an extended exchange between different points of view. This collection of such articles offers an excellent picture of the persistent debate.

CHAPTER 19

Advanced Multivariate Modes of Analysis

INTRODUCTION

For the most part, this book has focused on rather rudimentary forms of data manipulation in social scientific analysis. I have suggested that the logic of data analysis can be most clearly seen through the use of contingency tables and percentages. The elaboration model of analysis was presented in this form.

The preceding chapter has dealt with some other statistical techniques that may be applied to data—especially within the context of contingency tables. Now we shall move one step further and consider briefly a few more complex methods of data analysis and presentation. Each of the techniques examined in this chapter will be presented from the logical perspective of the elaboration model. Four methods of analysis will be discussed: regression analysis, path analysis, factor analysis, and smallest-space analysis. You should realize that these four techniques represent only an arbitrary selection from among the many that are available to the analyst.

Please realize, also, that my intention has been to give you an *introduction* to these techniques. You won't come away from this chapter proficient in the use of the techniques, just familiar with them when you see them in research reports. At the same time, you may find you want to learn more about how to use one or more of these advanced techniques, so I've given you some references for further study.

REGRESSION ANALYSIS

At several points in this text, I have referred to the general formula for describing the association between two variables: $Y = f(X)$. Recall from Chapter 16 that this formula is read "Y is a function of X," meaning that values of Y can be explained in terms of variations in the values of X. Stated more strongly, we might say that X causes Y, so the value of X determines the value of Y. **Regression analysis** is a method of determining the specific function relating Y to X.

The regression model can be seen most clearly in the case of a perfect linear association between two variables. Figure 19-1 is a scattergram presenting in graphic form the conjoint values of X and Y as produced by a hypothetical study.

Figure 19-1   Simple Scattergram of Values of X and Y

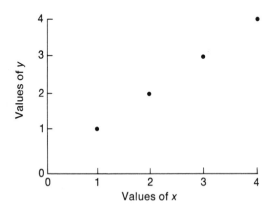

A quick perusal of Figure 19-1 indicates that for the four cases in our study, the values of X and Y are identical in each instance. The case with a value of 1 on X also has a value of 1 on Y, and so forth. The relationship between the two variables in this instance could be described by the equation $Y = X$; this would be the *regression equation*. Since all four points lie on a straight line, we could superimpose that line over the points; this would be the *regression line*.

The regression model has important descriptive uses. The regression line offers a graphic picture of the association between X and Y. And the regression equation is an efficient form for summarizing that association. The regression model has inferential value as well. To the extent that the regression equation correctly describes the *general* association between the two variables, it may be used to predict other sets of values. If, for example, we know that a new case has a value of 3.5 on X, we can predict the value of 3.5 on Y as well.

In practice, of course, studies are seldom limited to four cases, and the associations between variables are seldom as clear as the one presented in Figure 19-1. A somewhat more realistic example is presented in Figure 19-2.

Two observations may be made regarding Figure 19-2. As was the case in our previous example, we note that the values of Y generally correspond to those of X; and as values of X increase, so do values of Y. At the same time, however, the association is not nearly as clear as was the case in Figure 19-1.

Although it is not possible in Figure 19-2 to superimpose a straight line that will

Figure 19-2   Complex Scattergram of Values X and Y

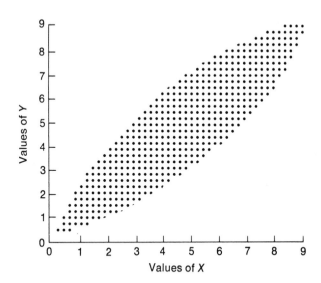

pass through all the points in the scattergram, an approximate line could be constructed. This line would provide the best possible linear representation of the several points.

The statistical procedures for computing the regression line can be found in any standard statistics text, so we'll consider only the *logic* of that procedure here. Assume for the moment that we have drawn through the scattergram a line that seems to represent fairly closely the general pattern of the points. This line would permit us to predict roughly values of Y on the basis of values of X.

For a given value of X, we could locate that value on the approximate regression line and determine the value of Y at that point on the line. Since the several points clearly do not lie directly on the line, however, it is certain that we'll make errors in most predictions of Y on the basis of X. For all those cases with values of X equal to 5 in Figure 19-2, we note that the actual values of Y range between 3 and 7. Given our approximate regression line, then, it is possible to measure the errors in predicting each value of Y from each value of X; these errors can be represented as distances along the Y axis between the points and the line. Figure 19-3 illustrates this pattern with fewer points.

The linear regression line is the straight line that has the property of minimizing the *squared distances* between points and the line—as measured along the Y axis. Thus, the regression line is referred to as the *least-squares line*. The line having this property, then, provides the best summary description of the association between X and Y. Moreover, any straight line can be expressed as an equation, as was the case in Figure 19-1.

Figure 19-3   Measuring Distances between Points and Regression Line

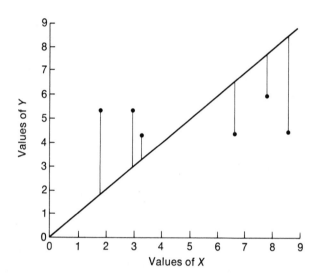

The general form of the regression equation is $Y = a + bX$. In this equation, a indicates the value of Y when $X = 0$. (Note in the equation that for $X = 0$, $Y = a$.) This is referred to as the *Y-intercept*. In the equation, b represents the number of units changed in Y for every increase of *one* unit in the value of X. This is referred to as the *slope*. Note that in the simpler example in Figure 19-1, $a = 0$ and $b = 1$, which reduced the equation to $Y = X$.

Let's assume for the moment that the regression equation for the points in Figure 19-2 is $Y = 2 + 1.3X$. For every given value of X, then, we would be able to estimate the value of Y. If X equals 23, then we would estimate Y as $2 + 1.3(23)$ $= 31.9$.

It is important to note that the regression line that best predicts values of Y on the basis of values of X is different from the regression line that best predicts values of X from values of Y. This will become clear when you experiment with scattergrams and approximate regression lines — comparing errors along the Y axis with errors along the X axis. The regression model, then, assumes a designation of independent and dependent variables.

Before moving to more complex methods of regression analysis, let's detour for the moment to consider the logic of scattergrams in normal research conditions. It is traditional to introduce the notion of regression through the use of a scattergram of points produced by two continuous variables. I have done this in Figure 19-2. In practice, however, social scientific research seldom involves the analysis of continuous variables: typically data is collected in—or reduced to—a limited set of categories. Let's illustrate this with a hypothetical example of an analysis of approval of Medicare on the basis of general political orientations.

Let's assume that you believe attitudes toward Medicare are based on general political orientations. Your data on Medicare attitudes are in the form of the responses: strongly approve (SA), approve (A), disapprove (D), and strongly disapprove (SD). Your data on general political orientations are in the form of subjects' self-characterizations as very conservative (VC), moderately conservative (MC), moderately liberal (ML), and very liberal (VL). The scattergram of points produced by these variables is presented in Figure 19-4.

Figure 19-4   Scattergram for Grouped Data

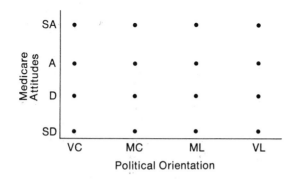

Clearly, Figure 19-4 tells us nothing about the association between political orientations and attitudes toward Medicare, since the points are evenly distributed with no apparent pattern. That is because each point represents more than one case; since the data are grouped, the individual points have been "piled up" on top of each other.

Figure 19-5 is more useful. The several points have been replaced by numbers representing the number of cases giving a particular response pattern. For example, we discover that 100 very conservative subjects said they strongly disapprove of Medicare; 50 moderately conservative subjects approve of Medicare.

Figure 19-5 conveys considerably more information than Figure 19-4. Another interesting observation is in order. Figure 19-5 is nothing more or less than a *contingency table*. A firm understanding of the logic of contingency tables, then, may offer a better base for understanding the logic of the regression model, especially when it is applied to grouped data.

Multiple Regression

Thus far, we have limited our discussion to the linear regression between two variables. The basic regression model, however, is more general than our comments

Figure 19-5   Scattergram of Grouped Data with Frequencies

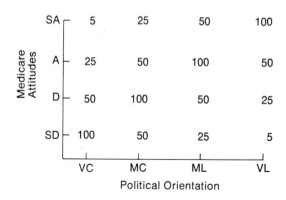

up to now imply. It is possible to extend the model to more than two variables, just as the elaboration model can be so extended.

From the discussion of the elaboration model, we recall that some dependent variables may be affected by more than one independent variable. By constructing more complex contingency tables, you can determine the joint contribution of several independent variables to the prediction of values on the dependent variable.

If, for example, you believe that both age and education affect prejudice, you could construct tables appropriate for testing these relationships. Presumably, if your data confirm your belief, you would find that the oldest subjects having the least education would be the most prejudiced, and the youngest subjects having the most education would be the least prejudiced. That would show the joint effects of age and education on prejudice.

Multiple regression is based on the same logic. Although it is difficult to present a regression line in more than two dimensions, the multiple regression equation can be presented: $P = a + bE + cA$, where P is prejudice, E is education, and A is age. If more independent variables were involved, the equation would simply be extended to take those into account.

Partial Regression

In the discussion of the elaboration model, special attention was paid to the relationship between two variables when a third test variable was held constant. Thus, we might have examined the effect of education on prejudice with age held constant, testing the independent effect of education. To do so, we would have computed the tabular relationship between education and prejudice separately for each age group.

Partial regressions are based on this same logical model. The equation summarizing the relationship between two variables is computed on the basis of the test variables remaining constant. As in the case of the elaboration model, the result may then be compared with the uncontrolled relationship between the two variables to clarify further the nature of the overall relationship.

Curvilinear Regression

Up to now, we have been discussing the association among variables as represented by a straight line—though in more than two dimensions. The regression model is even more general than our discussion thus far implies.

If you have a knowledge of geometry, you will already know that curvilinear functions also can be represented by equations. For example, the equation $X^2 + Y^2 = 25$ describes a circle with a radius of 5. Raising variables to powers greater than 1 has the effect of producing curves rather than straight lines. And from the standpoint of empirical research, there is no reason to assume that the relationship among every set of variables will be linear. In some cases, then, curvilinear regression analysis can provide a better understanding of empirical relationships than can any linear model.

Although curvilinear functions are more difficult to identify and interpret in contingency tables, our previous discussion of scattergrams and tables suggests the possibility of a contingency table similar to the one presented in Figure 19-6.

Figure 19-6   Curvilinear Relationship in a Contingency Table

	X_1	X_2	X_3	X_4	X_5	X_6	X_7
Y_4	0	25	50	100	50	25	0
Y_3	0	50	100	0	100	50	0
Y_2	0	100	25	0	25	100	0
Y_1	100	50	0	0	0	50	100

The data presented in Figure 19-6 roughly describe a curvilinear relationship between X and Y. All cases having the value of X_1 also have the value of Y_4. As we move across the table to X_4, we note the tendency for increasing values of Y; then the values of Y decrease again as we move past X_4 until we discover that all cases with X_7 are also Y_4. Thus the relationship is a curvilinear one, not adequately represented by any straight line.

Curvilinear regression analysis would provide a neater summary of the relationship apparent in Figure 19-6. Moreover, the regression equation would permit one estimate of Y values from X values.

The potential of curvilinear regression analysis is very great, although it has scarcely been approached in practice. Most collections of points representing the coincidence of two variables could be perfectly represented by an equation. With normal social scientific data, however, such an equation would be complex indeed, involving variables raised to very high powers. Such a complex equation might have little practical value, and its theoretical value might be minimal as well.

Recall that a regression line serves two functions. It describes a set of empirical observations, and it provides a general model of the relationship between two variables in the general population that the observations represent. A very complex equation might result in a rather erratic line that would indeed pass through every individual point. In this sense, it would perfectly describe the empirical observations. There would be no guarantee, however, that such a line would adequately predict new observations, or that it in any meaningful way represented the relationship between the two variables in general. Thus, it would have little or no inferential value.

Earlier in this book, we discussed the need for balancing detail and utility in data reduction. Ultimately, you attempt to provide the most faithful, yet also the simplest, representation of your data. This practice also applies when you're using regression analysis. You want to represent your data in the simplest fashion (thus, linear regressions are most frequently used), but in such a way as to best describe the actual data. Curvilinear regression analysis adds a new option to the researcher in this regard, but it does not solve the problems altogether. Nothing does that.

Cautions in Regression Analysis

The use of regression analysis for statistical inferences makes certain assumptions that you should know about. These are the same ones assumed by correlational analysis, concerning simple random sampling, the absence of nonsampling errors, and continuous interval data. Since social scientific research seldom completely satisfies these assumptions, you should use caution in assigning ultimate meaning to the results of regression analyses.

As indicated earlier, however, I would encourage the use of these techniques— even though they may not be statistically justified—in any situation in which their use assists you in understanding your data and, by extension, the world around you.

PATH ANALYSIS

Path analysis offers another graphic presentation of the interrelations among variables. It is based on regression analysis, but it can provide a more useful graphic picture of relationships among several variables than is possible through other means.

Path analysis is a *causal* model for understanding relationships between variables. It assumes that the values on one variable are caused by the values on another, so it is essential that independent and dependent variables be distinguished in path analysis. This requirement is not unique to path analysis, of course, but path analysis provides a unique way of displaying explanatory results for interpretation.

I want to introduce you to the logic of path analysis through the use of something you already know: the elaboration model. If you'll refer back to Table 17-1 in Chapter 17, you'll recall that there was a relationship between soldiers' educational levels and their attitudes about being drafted. The relationship, moreover, was represented by an 18 percentage point difference (called *epsilon*). This finding was presented in the form of a contingency table in Chapter 17; here Figure 19-7 presents the same finding in a different, graphic form.

Figure 19-7   Education Determines Attitude toward Draft

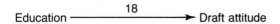

Education $\xrightarrow{\hspace{1.5em} 18 \hspace{1.5em}}$ Draft attitude

Notice that I have connected the two variables—education and draft attitude—by an arrow representing the causal direction of the relationship; educational level causes the attitude toward being drafted. Notice also that I have put the epsilon value on the arrow to indicate the strength of the relationship.

In the same way, Figure 19-8 gives a graphic presentation of the relationship between education and having friends deferred from the draft (presented earlier in Table 17-2). Notice that the epsilon in this case is much higher—60 percentage points—representing a stronger relationship.

Figure 19-8   Education Determines Whether Friends Were Deferred

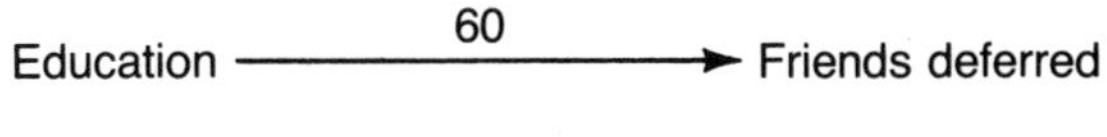

Education $\xrightarrow{\hspace{1.5em} 60 \hspace{1.5em}}$ Friends deferred

Finally, Figure 19-9 presents the last of the bivariate relationships examined earlier in the example. It shows the relationship between having friends deferred and soldiers' attitudes toward the draft, presented earlier in Table 17-3. Here, the epsilon is 31 percentage points.

Figure 19-9   Deferment of Friends Determines Attitude toward Draft

Friends deferred $\xrightarrow{\hspace{3em}}$ Draft attitude

You'll recall from the earlier discussion that Stouffer suggested that the original relationship discovered between education and draft attitudes occurred through the intervening variable: friends deferred. Graphically, that process could be presented as follows:

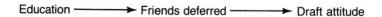

Education ⟶ Friends deferred ⟶ Draft attitude

That model was tested in Table 17-4, and we observed two things: (1) with education controlled, the friends deferred variable still had a strong effect on draft attitudes, with partial epsilons of 31 and 32 percentage points; and (2) with the friends deferred variable controlled, the initial relationship between education and draft attitudes disappeared, producing partial epsilons of 0 and 1.

Figure 19-10 presents this trivariate relationship in the graphic form used for the bivariate relationships. Notice that there are three arrows in the diagram, representing the three causal relationships that could exist, given the time order of the three variables. The epsilons shown for each of the causal relationships linking two variables is the average of the partial epsilons produced by controlling for the third variable. Thus, for example, the 31.5 shown on the arrow connecting the friends deferred variable and draft attitude is simply an average of the 31 and 32 percentage points shown in Table 17-4. This means that whether a soldier's friends were deferred determines attitudes toward being drafted—by an average magnitude of 31.5 percentage points—even when the influence of education is removed.

Figure 19-10   Diagramming the Trivariate Relationship

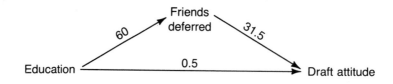

The 60 percentage points, which appeared in the earlier discussion, represent the strength of the relationship between education and the friends deferred variable. Finally, the diagram shows the average relationship—.05 percentage points—between education and draft attitude when the influence of the friends deferred variable is removed: the *direct* impact of education on attitudes.

The diagram presented in Figure 19-10 offers a clear and dramatic answer to the question of whether education affects attitudes toward being drafted (1) directly or (2) through the intervening variable: friends deferred. You might find it useful to think of the diagram as a plumbing system, with water flowing in the direction of the arrows and the pipes having diameters proportionate to the epsilon values. How would most of the water get from education to attitudes toward being drafted? Clearly, most of it goes through the friends deferred variable and very little goes directly.

This illustration demonstrates the basic logic of path analysis. At the same time, it differs from conventional path analyses in several respects. First of all, partial epsilons are seldom if ever used in path analysis. I have done so only as a way of linking this discussion to the earlier one. Conventionally, path analysts represent the strengths of relationships with *standardized regression coefficients*, and they have the same logical meaning as the partial epsilons I have used in the above illustration. The more general term for the values representing the strengths of relationships in a path diagram is *path coefficient*.

In using a regression model in path analysis, we are attempting to account for the *variance* in some dependent variable: draft attitudes in the above illustration. Very seldom, however, is *all* the variance accounted for, even when several independent and intervening variables are used for that purpose. In the Stouffer example examined above, this *unexplained variance* is represented by those soldiers who (1) had friends deferred but did not feel they themselves should have been deferred and (2) did not have friends deferred but nonetheless felt they themselves should have been. Thus, although education and the friends deferred variable partially explained soldiers' attitudes toward being drafted, it is clear that something else had an impact on their attitudes also.

In path analysis, this unexplained variance is represented in the form of a *residual*, symbolized as R and standing for the impact of all those variables not included in the model. In a more complete path diagram, moreover, the unexplained variance in intervening variables is also calculated and presented.

Figure 19-11 illustrates the presentation of residual unexplained variance. Notice that R represents the unexplained variance on Z, and S the unexplained variance on I. Notice one further addition to Figure 19-11. There is a two-headed arrow connecting X and Y. The two-headed arrow indicates that there is no causal order assumed to exist between the two variables.

Figure 19-11   Path Diagram for Four Variables

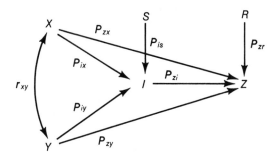

In practice, the form of path diagrams varies according to the nature of the model and the preferences of the researcher. The special strength of path analysis, however, is evident in the various formats used; it lies in the graphic portrayal of relationships among several variables. Figure 19-12 offers an example.

Figure 19-12   Diagramming the Religious Sources of Anti-Semitism
Source: Figure 3 from *Wayward Shepherds—Prejudice & the Protestant Clergy* by Rodney Stark, Bruce D. Foster, Charles Y. Glock, and Harold E. Quinley. Copyright © 1971 by Anti-Defamation League of B'nai Brith. Reprinted by permission of Harper & Row, Publishers, Inc.

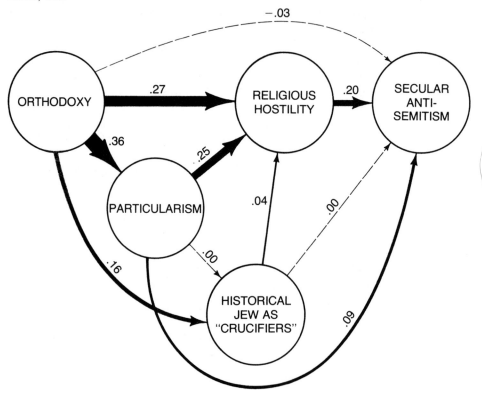

This analysis focuses on the religious causes of anti-Semitism among Christian church members. The variables in the diagram are, from left to right, (1) the extent to which the subjects accept conventional, orthodox beliefs about God, Jesus, the biblical miracles, and so forth; (2) the particularistic belief that one's religion is the "only true faith"; (3) acceptance of the view that Jews were the crucifiers of Jesus; (4) a religious hostility toward contemporary Jews, such as believing that God is punishing them or that they will suffer damnation unless they convert to Christianity; and (5) secular anti-Semitism, such as believing that Jews cheat in business, are disloyal to their country, and so forth.

In preparing for their analysis, the researchers had reasons to believe that secular anti-Semitism was the result of a process moving through the five variables:

orthodoxy caused particularism, which caused the view of the historical Jews as crucifiers, which caused a religious hostility toward contemporary Jews, which resulted, finally, in secular anti-Semitism.

The path diagram tells a different story. The belief in the historical role of Jews as the crucifiers of Jesus, for example, doesn't seem to matter in the process. And, although particularism is a part of one process resulting in secular anti-Semitism, the diagram also shows that anti-Semitism is created more directly by orthodoxy and religious hostility. Orthodoxy produces religious hostility even in the absence of particularism, and religious hostility generates secular hostility in any event.

One last comment on path analysis is in order. Although it is an excellent way of handling complex causal chains and networks of variables, you must realize that path analysis itself does not tell you the causal order of the variables. You do that. Once you do, however, path analysis will provide a clear, graphic picture of the results.

FACTOR ANALYSIS

Factor analysis is a different approach to multivariate analysis. Its statistical basis is sufficiently complex and sufficiently different from the foregoing discussions as to suggest a very general discussion here.

Factor analysis is used to discover patterns among the variations in values of several variables. This is done essentially through the generation of artificial dimensions (factors) that correlate highly with several of the real variables and that are independent of one another. A computer must be used to perform this complex operation.

Let's suppose for the moment that our data file contains several indicators of subjects' prejudice. Each of the items should provide some indication of prejudice, but none of them would give a perfect indication. All of these items, moreover, should be highly intercorrelated empirically. In a factor analysis of the data, it is likely that an artificial dimension would be created that would be highly correlated with each of the items measuring prejudice. Each subject would essentially receive a value on that artificial dimension, and the value assigned would provide a good predictor of the observed attributes on each item.

Suppose now that the same study provided several indicators of subjects' mathematical ability. It is likely that the factor analysis would also generate an artificial dimension highly correlated with each of those items.

The output of a factor analysis program consists of columns representing the several factors (artificial dimensions) generated from the observed relations among variables plus the correlations between each variable and each factor—called the *factor loadings.*

In the above example, it is likely that one factor would more or less represent prejudice, and another would more or less represent mathematical ability. Data items measuring prejudice would have high loadings on (correlations with) the prejudice factor and low loadings on the mathematical ability factor. Data items measuring mathematical ability would have just the opposite pattern.

In practice, however, factor analysis does not proceed in this fashion. Rather, the variables are input to the program, and a series of factors with appropriate factor loadings are the output. You must then determine the meaning of a given factor on the basis of those variables that load highly on it. The generation of factors, however, has no reference to the meaning of variables, only their empirical associations. Two criteria are taken into account: (1) a factor must explain a relatively large portion of the variance found in the study variables; and (2) every factor must be more or less independent of every other factor.[1]

There are a number of advantages in factor analysis. First, it is an efficient method of discovering predominant patterns among a large number of variables. Instead of your being forced to compare countless correlations—simple, partial, and multiple—to discover those patterns, factor analysis can be used for this task. Incidentally, here is a good example of a helpful use of computers.

Second, factor analysis presents data in a form that can be interpreted by the reader or researcher. For a given factor, the reader can easily discover the variables loading highly on it, thus noting clusters of variables. Or, the reader can easily discover which factors a given variable is or is not loaded highly on.

Factor analysis has disadvantages as well. First, as noted above, factors are generated without any regard to substantive meaning. Often you will find factors producing very high loadings for a group of substantively disparate variables. You might find, for example, that prejudice and religiosity have high positive loadings on a given factor with education having an equally high negative loading. Surely the three variables are highly correlated, but what does the factor represent? All too often, inexperienced researchers will be led into naming such factors as "religio-prejudicial lack of education" or something similarly nonsensical.

Second, factor analysis is often criticized on basic philosophical grounds. Recall an earlier statement that to be legitimate, a hypothesis must be disconfirmable. If you are unable to specify the conditions under which your hypothesis would be disproved, your hypothesis is in reality either a tautology or useless. In a sense, factor analysis suffers this defect. No matter what data are input, factor analysis produces a solution in the form of factors. Thus if you were asking, "Are there any patterns among these variables?" the answer always would be "yes." This fact must also be taken into account in evaluating the results of factor analysis. The generation of factors by no means insures meaning.

My personal view of factor analysis is the same as that of other complex modes of analysis. It can be an extremely useful tool for the social science researcher. Its use should be encouraged whenever such activity may assist you in your understanding of a body of data. As in all cases, however, you must maintain an awareness that such tools are only tools and never magical solutions.

SMALLEST-SPACE ANALYSIS

Smallest-space analysis (SSA) is rather different from the previously discussed

[1]This is not true of all factor analytical methods (for example, *oblique* solutions).

methods of multivariate analysis; and, although it is still relatively new, it appears to hold considerable potential for the understanding of data.

Smallest-space analysis is based on the correlations between variables. Any measure of association may be used for this purpose, although we shall use Pearson's r in the examples to follow. Let's begin with a simple correlation matrix describing the associations among variables: A, B, and C (Table 19-1).

Table 19-1 Simple
Correlation Matrix

	A	B	C
A	x	.8	.2
B		x	.5
C			x

Now let's plot these three variables as points on a plane, letting the distance between two points represent the *inverse* of the correlation between the two variables. That is, if two variables are highly correlated, they will be close together; if they are weakly correlated, they will be farther apart. The following diagram would satisfy this design.

$$A \quad B \qquad C$$

Since A and B are the most highly correlated variables, they have been placed relatively close together. The next highest correlation is between B and C, and the distance between these two points is the next shortest. Finally, the correlation between A and C is the weakest of the three correlations, and the distance between A and C is the longest distance in the diagram.

Now let's enlarge our correlation matrix by adding variable D (Table 19-2).

Table 19-2 Correlation
Matrix with Four Variables

	A	B	C	D
A	x	.8	.2	.1
B		x	.5	.3
C			x	.9
D				x

It is still possible to plot these four points in such a fashion that the distance between two points corresponds to the inverse of the correlation between the two variables. It should be noted, however, that the distances do not *equal* the inverse of the correlations. The metric distances are irrelevant; thus SSA is referred to as a *nonmetric* technique. However, the *rank order* of distances between points should be the inverse of the rank order of correlations. The diagram in Figure 19-13 would satisfy the latest correlation matrix.

Figure 19-13   Smallest-Space Analysis: Four Variables

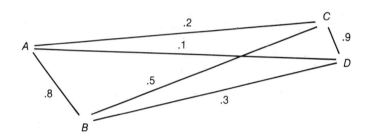

To clarify the new diagram, the points have been connected by lines, which in turn have been labeled with the correlations between the pairs of variables. An examination of the diagram will indicate that the longest distance (*AD*) corresponds to the weakest correlation. The shortest distance (*CD*) corresponds to the strongest correlation. The same is true for all other distances and correlations. (An understanding of plane geometry will help to explain how the diagram was constructed.)

You have probably already realized that there are some correlation matrices that could not be represented in accordance with the rules laid down. That is especially true as more and more variables are added. Given such a situation, SSA permits you to move in two different directions.

First, SSA is not limited to two dimensions (although this textbook essentially is). Like multiple regression, SSA can employ an unlimited number of geometric dimensions. As a general guideline, *n* variables can be plotted perfectly in SSA format within *n* − 1 dimensions. Thus, any two variables can be plotted on a line, any three can be plotted on a plane, any four can be plotted in three dimensions, and so forth. As we have seen in other contexts, however, such liberties can lead into uninterpretable situations.

The second solution to this problem lies in the familiar area of compromise. Perhaps you cannot plot six variables perfectly within two dimensions (a graphic presentation that would be easily read), but you may be able to come close. Thus, it may be possible to plot the points in such a manner that they more or less satisfy the correspondence of rankings between correlations and distances.

At this point, and with the addition of many variables generally, hand tabulations and hand-drawn diagrams become too difficult. But this is the sort of task that the computer handles easily. Computer programs now exist to generate SSA diagrams from an input in the form of a correlation matrix. You must specify the number of dimensions desired in your solution, and the computer works on that basis. In addition to the diagram, moreover, the computer provides a summary statistic called the **coefficient of alienation**. Although the statistic has no common-sensible interpretation, it represents the extent to which the SSA diagram violates the rules of correspondence between distances and correlations. The lower the coefficient, the better the fit of the diagram to the rules.

The computer output from an SSA program will look something like the configuration shown in Figure 19-14.

Figure 19-14   Sample Smallest-Space Analysis Results—Hypothetical

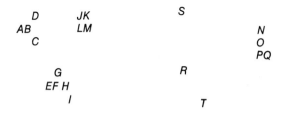

Since each of the letters in this diagram represents a study variable, the diagram would be interpreted in terms of the observed clustering of variables. For example, we note that variables *J*, *K*, *L*, and *M* are closely clustered, and *A-B-C-D* forms another cluster, with both of these clusters being rather distant from the cluster *N-O-P-Q*.

You may have noted from the previous section of this chapter that SSA is quite similar to factor analysis, and it is sometimes referred to as *nonmetric factor analysis*.

SUMMARY

I suspect that my own bias in connection with data analysis has become pretty clear. In case it has not, let me clarify it here: I personally am most inclined toward the use of the elaboration model in the form of simple percentage tables. However, I would not want you to conclude that this is the only "really good" method of multi-variate analysis or even that I hold that belief. In this concluding chapter, therefore, I have provided a series of brief descriptions of other more complex modes of analysis. In each instance, I have sought to indicate how the basic logic of a given mode is essentially the same as that inherent in the elaboration model. That should not be too surprising, of course, if we can assume that social research is scientific.

The chapter began with discussions of the different methods of *regression analysis*. We noted how regressions are related to the notion of product-moment correlations. The end product of a regression analysis is an equation that summarizes the relationship observed between variables. In the simplest case, a dependent variable is shown as equaling some constant value (*a*) plus another value (*b*) that is multiplied by the value of the independent variable. This is a simple *linear regression equation*. Later discussions touched on *multiple* regressions, *partial* regressions, and *curvilinear* regressions.

Next, we looked at *path analysis*, which affords a graphic presentation of the network of causal relationships observed among a large number of variables. Based on regression coefficients, this method provides an excellent vehicle for communicating the nature of extremely complex interrelationships.

Factor analysis was discussed next, very briefly. This analytical technique—feasible by computer only—derives a set of artificial dimensions (*factors*) that appear to best represent the different dimensions reflected by the actual data under study. If the data being analyzed contain indicators of a number of variables representing different political orientations, factor analysis might discover the existence of a general dimension of, say, liberalism-conservatism. None of the actual indicators would provide a perfect measure of this general dimension, but several indicators would be strongly associated with it.

The chapter concluded with a description of *smallest-space analysis* (SSA), which is sometimes called a *nonmetric* factor analysis. Like path analysis, SSA is presented in a graphic form. Variables are represented in SSA as points, and the associations between variables are represented as the distances between points: the greater the distance between two points, the weaker the association; the shorter the distance, the greater the association. SSA is nonmetric in the sense that the final plotting of points aims at maintaining the inverse correspondence of the rank order of distances and the rank order of associations. The actual metric distances do not correspond to the actual metric measures of association. The output of SSA, then, is the plotting of many points, each of which represents a variable. Those points clustered together represent variables that are relatively highly associated with one another. *Clusters* that are far apart from one another represent *clusters* of variables that are very weakly (or negatively) associated with each other.

At the close of Part Three, it was suggested that the "best" research effort would be one that combined different modes of observation; that if different observational methods produced essentially the same conclusions, you might have a greater confidence in those conclusions. A similar point should be made here. The "best" data analysis would be one that examined a given set of data through many different analytical techniques. If each of those analyses pointed to the same conclusions, you might place a greater confidence in them.

MAIN POINTS

1. Regression analysis represents the relationships between variables in the form of equations, which can be used to predict the values of a dependent variable on the basis of values of one or more independent variables.

2. The basic regression equation—for a simple linear regression—is of the form: $Y = a + bX$. Y in this case is the value (estimated) of the dependent variable; a is some constant value; b is another numerical value, which is multiplied by X, the value of the independent variable.

3. Regression equations are computed on the basis of a *regression line*: that geometric line that represents, with the least amount of discrepancy, the actual location of points in a scattergram.

4. A *multiple* regression analysis results in a regression equation, which estimates the values of a dependent variable from the values of several independent variables.

5. A *partial* regression analysis examines the effects of several independent variables, but with each independent variable's effect expressed separately while the effects of all others are held constant.

6. A *curvilinear* regression analysis permits the "best-fitting" regression line to be something other than a straight line. The curvature of the regression line is achieved by permitting the values of the independent variables to be raised to powers greater than 1; for example, squared, cubed, and so forth.

7. *Path analysis* is a method of presenting graphically the networks of causal relationships among several variables. It illustrates graphically the primary "paths" of variables through which independent variables cause dependent ones.

8. *Path coefficients* are standardized regression coefficients, representing the partial relationships between variables.

9. *Factor analysis*, feasible only by computer, is an analytical method of discovering the general dimensions represented by a collection of actual variables. These general dimensions, or *factors*, are calculated hypothetical dimensions that are not perfectly represented by any of the empirical variables under study, but that are highly associated with groups of empirical variables.

10. A *factor loading* indicates the degree of association between a given empirical variable and a given factor.

11. *Smallest-space analysis* (SSA) is a nonmetric method of graphically displaying the associations between a large number of variables.

12. Variables in SSA are presented by points, and the associations between variables are represented by the distances between points, with short distances representing high associations and long distances representing low associations.

13. The primary rule in SSA is that the rank order of the distances between points should be the inverse of the rank order of the associations between the variables those points represent.

14. The *coefficient of alienation* is a measure of the extent to which an actual SSA display fails to follow the rank-order rule exactly.

15. The "best" analysis of data would be one that employed several different analytical modes and resulted in the same set of conclusions from each mode.

ANNOTATED BIBLIOGRAPHY

Regression Analysis

Ezekiel, Mordecai, and Fox, Karl, *Methods of Correlation and Regression Analysis: Linear and Curvilinear* (New York: John Wiley, 1959). A rather comprehensive presentation of correlation and regression methods. This book begins with a very simple introduction to the subject and then moves progressively to more complex aspects. In addition to describing a wide variety of statistical computations, the authors are sensitive to the practical considerations that apply to the use of correlation and regression in social research.

Path Analysis

Borgatta, Edgar (ed.), *Sociological Methodology, 1969* (San Francisco: Jossey-Bass, 1969), especially Chapters 1 and 2. Good discussions of the logic and techniques of path analysis. The chapters by Kenneth Land and David Heise examine a variety of aspects of path analysis and its potential contribution to social research, especially in regard to the discovery of causal relationships. These are both more advanced than would be desired in an introductory presentation, but good introductions to path analysis are hard to find.

Factor Analysis

Harmon, Harry, *Modern Factor Analysis* (Chicago: University of Chicago Press, 1967). A rather comprehensive presentation of factor analytic methods. Harmon discusses both the logic and the specific computational techniques associated with this method of social scientific analysis.

Smallest-Space Analysis

Bloombaum, Milton, "Tribes and Traits," *American Anthropologist* (April 1968) Vol. 70, pp. 328–330. A simple illustration of the use of SSA. This reanalysis of anthropological data describing different societies gives a clear example of SSA results and their meaning.

Katz, Elihu; Gurevitch, Michael; and Haas, Hadassah; "On the Use of the Mass Media for Important Things," *American Sociological Review* (April 1973) Vol. 38, pp. 164–181. A more complex illustration of SSA. In addition to evaluating the relative roles played by the different mass media in Israel, the authors present their data in several analytical formats, further clarifying the interpretation of SSA.

APPENDICES

SOME BASIC CONSIDERATIONS
   Audience
   Form and Length of Report
   Aim of the Report

ORGANIZATION OF THE REPORT
   Purpose and Overview
   Review of the Literature
   Study Design and Execution
   Analysis and Interpretation
   Summary and Conclusions

GUIDELINES FOR REPORTING ANALYSES

Appendix A

The Research Report

This book has considered the variety of activities that compose the *doing* of social research. In this appendix, we'll turn to an often neglected subject: reporting the research to others. Unless the research is properly communicated, all the efforts devoted to previously discussed procedures will go for naught.

Before proceeding further on this topic, I should suggest one absolutely basic guideline. Good social scientific reporting requires good English (unless you are writing in a foreign language). Whenever we ask the "figures to speak for themselves," they tend to remain mute. Whenever we use unduly complex terminology or construction, communication is reduced. Every researcher should read and reread (at approximately three-month intervals) an excellent small book by William Strunk, Jr., and E. B. White, *The Elements of Style*.[1] If you do this faithfully, and if even 10 percent of the contents rub off, you stand a rather good chance of making yourself understood and your findings perhaps appreciated.

Scientific reporting has several functions, and it is a good idea to keep these in mind. First, the report communicates to an audience a body of specific data and ideas. The report should provide those specifics clearly and with sufficient detail to permit an informed evaluation. Second, the scientific report should be viewed as a contribution to the general body of scientific knowledge. While remaining appropriately humble, you should always regard your research report as an addition to what we know about social behavior. Finally, the report should serve the function of stimulating and directing further inquiry.

[1] William Strunk, Jr., and E. B. White, 2d ed. (New York: Macmillan, 1972). The following are other useful references on writing: H. W. Fowler, *A Dictionary of Modern English Usage* (New York: Oxford University Press, 1965); Billy J. Franklin and Harold W. Osborne (eds.), *Research Methods: Issues and Insights* (Belmont, Calif.: Wadsworth, 1971), Part 8.

SOME BASIC CONSIDERATIONS

Despite these general guidelines, different reports serve different purposes. A report appropriate for one purpose might be wholly inappropriate for another. This section of this appendix deals with some of the basic considerations in this regard.

Audience

Before drafting your report, you must ask yourself who you hope will read it. Normally, you should make a distinction between fellow scientists and general readers. If written for the former, you may make certain assumptions as to their existing knowledge and may perhaps summarize certain points rather than explaining them in detail. Similarly, you may appropriately use more technical language than would be appropriate for a general audience.

At the same time, you should remain always aware that any science is composed of factions or cults. Terms and assumptions acceptable to your immediate colleagues may only confuse other scientists. That applies with regard to substance as well as techniques. The sociologist of religion who is writing for a general sociology audience, for example, should explain previous findings in more detail than would be necessary if he or she were addressing an audience of other sociologists of religion.

Form and Length of Report

I should begin this subsection by saying that my comments apply to both written and oral reports. These two forms, however, will affect the nature of the report.

It is useful to think about the variety of reports that might result from a research project. To begin, you may wish to prepare a short *research note* for publication in an academic or technical journal. Such reports should be approximately one to five pages in length (typed, double-spaced) and should be concise and direct. In a short amount of space, you will not be able to present the state of the field in any detail, and your methodological notes must be somewhat abbreviated as well. Basically, you should tell the reader why you feel a brief note is justified by your findings, then tell what those findings are.

Often, researchers must prepare reports for the sponsors of their research. These may vary greatly in length, of course. In preparing such a report, however, you should bear in mind the audience for the report—scientific or lay—and their reasons for sponsoring the project in the first place. It is both bad politics and bad manners to bore the sponsors with research findings that have no interest or value to them. At the same time, it may be useful to summarize the ways in which the research has advanced basic scientific knowledge (if it has).

Working papers or monographs are another form of research reporting. Especially in a large and complex project, it will be useful to obtain comments on your analysis and the interpretation of your data. A working paper constitutes a tentative presentation with an implicit request for comments. Working papers can also vary in length, and they may present all of the research findings of the project or only a portion of them. Since your professional reputation is not at stake in a working paper, you should feel free to present tentative interpretations that you cannot altogether justify—identifying them as such and asking for evaluations.

Many research projects result in papers delivered at professional meetings. Often, these serve the same purpose as working papers. You are able to present findings and ideas of possible interest to your colleagues and ask for their comments. Although the length of professional papers may vary depending on the organization of the meetings, I'd encourage you to say too little rather than too much. Although a working paper may ramble somewhat through a variety of tentative conclusions, conference participants should not be forced to sit through an oral unveiling of the same. Interested listeners can always ask for more details later, and uninterested ones can gratefully escape.

Probably the most popular research report is the article published in an academic journal. Again, lengths vary and you should examine the lengths of articles previously published by the journal in question. As a rough guide, however, 25 typed pages is as good as any. A subsequent section on the organization of the report is primarily based on the structure of a journal article, so I shall say no more at this point, except to indicate that student term papers should be written on this model. As a general rule, a term paper that would make a good journal article would also make a good term paper.

A book, of course, represents the most prestigious form of research report. It has all the advantages of the working paper—length, detail—but it should be a more polished document. Since the publication of research findings as a book gives those findings an appearance of greater substance and worth, you have a special obligation to your audience. Although you will still hope to receive comments from colleagues, possibly leading you to revise your ideas, you must realize that other readers may be led to accept your findings uncritically.

Aim of the Report

Earlier in this book, we considered the different *purposes* of social research projects. In preparing your report, you should keep these same differences in mind.

Some reports may focus primarily on the *exploration* of a topic of interest. Inherent in this aim is the tentativeness and incompleteness of the conclusions. You should clearly indicate to your audience the exploratory aim of the study and point to the shortcomings of the particular project. An important aspect of an exploratory report is to point the way to more refined research on the topic.

Most studies have a *descriptive* purpose, and the research reports from such studies will have a descriptive element. You should carefully distinguish for the reader those descriptions that apply only to the sample and those that are inferred to the population. Whenever inferential descriptions are to be made, you should give your audience some indication of the probable range of error in those descriptions.

Many reports have an *explanatory* aim; you wish to point to causal relationships among variables. Depending on the probable audience for your report, you should carefully delineate the rules of explanation that lie behind your computations and conclusions; and, as in the case of description, you must give your readers some guide to the relative certainty of your conclusions.

Finally, some research reports may have the aim of *proposing action*. For example, the researcher of prejudice may wish to suggest ways in which prejudice may be reduced, on the basis of the research findings. This aim often presents knotty problems, however, because your own values and orientations may interfere with your proposals. Although it is perfectly legitimate for your proposals to be motivated by personal values, you must insure that the specific actions you propose are warranted by your data. Thus, you should be especially careful to spell out the logic by which you move from empirical data to proposed action.

ORGANIZATION OF THE REPORT

Although the organization of reports differs somewhat on the basis of form and purpose, it is possible to suggest a general format for presenting research data. The following comments apply most directly to a journal article, but with some modification they apply to most forms of research reports.

Purpose and Overview

It is always helpful to the reader if you begin with a brief statement of the purpose of the study and the main findings of the analysis. In a journal article, this overview may sometimes be given in the form of an *abstract* or *synopsis*.

Some researchers find this difficult to do. For example, your analysis may have involved considerable detective work, with important findings revealing themselves only as a result of imaginative deduction and data manipulation. You may wish, therefore, to lead the reader through the same exciting process, chronicling the discovery process with a degree of suspense and surprise. To the extent that this form of reporting gives an accurate picture of the research process, I feel it has considerable instructional value. Nevertheless, many readers may not be interested in following your entire research account, and not knowing the purpose and general conclusions in advance may make it difficult for them to understand the significance of the study.

An old forensic dictum says: "Tell them what you're going to tell them; tell them; and tell them what you told them." You would do well to follow this dictum in the preparation of research reports.

Review of the Literature

Since every research report should be placed in the context of the general body of scientific knowledge, it is important to indicate where your report fits in that picture. Having presented the general purpose of your study, you should then bring the reader up to date on the previous research in the area, pointing to general agreements and disagreements among the previous researchers.

In some cases, you may wish to challenge previously accepted ideas. You should carefully review the studies that had led to the acceptance of those ideas, then indicate the factors that have not been previously considered or the logical fallacies present in the previous research.

When you are concerned with resolving a disagreement among previous researchers, you should organize your review of the literature around the opposing points of view. You should summarize the research supporting one view, then summarize the research supporting the other, and finally suggest the reasons for the disagreement.

To an extent, your review of the literature serves a bibliographic function for readers, indexing the previous research on a given topic. This can be overdone, however, and you should avoid an opening paragraph that runs three pages, mentioning every previous study in the field. The comprehensive bibliographic function can best be served by a bibliography at the end of the report, and the review of the literature should focus only on those studies that have direct relevance to the present study.

Study Design and Execution

A research report containing interesting findings and conclusions can be very frustrating when the reader is unable to determine the methodological design and execution of the study. The worth of all scientific findings depends heavily on the manner in which the data were collected and analyzed.

In reporting the design and execution of a survey, for example, you should always include the following: the population, the sampling frame, the sampling method, the sample size, the data collection method, the completion rate, and the methods of data processing and analysis. Comparable details should be given if other methods are used. The experienced researcher is able to report these details in a rather short space, without omitting anything required for the reader's evaluation of the study.

Analysis and Interpretation

Having set the study in the perspective of previous research and having described the design and execution of it, you should then present your data. The following major section will provide further guidelines in this regard. For now, a few general comments are in order.

The presentation of data, the manipulations of those data, and your interpretations should be integrated into a logical whole. It is frustrating to the reader to discover a collection of seemingly unrelated analyses and findings with a promise that all the loose ends will be tied together later on in the report. Every step in the analysis should make sense—at the time it is taken. You should present your rationale for a particular analysis, present the data relevant to it, interpret the results, then indicate where that result leads next.

Summary and Conclusions

Following the forensic dictum mentioned earlier, I believe it is essential to summarize the research report. You should avoid reviewing every specific finding, but you should review all of the significant ones, pointing once more to their general significance.

The report should conclude with a statement of what you have discovered about your subject matter and where future research might be directed. A quick review of recent journal articles will probably indicate a very high frequency of the concluding statement: "It is clear that much more research is needed." This is probably always a true conclusion, but it is of little value unless you can offer pertinent suggestions as to the nature of that future research. You should review the particular shortcomings of your own study and suggest ways in which those shortcomings might be avoided by future researchers.

GUIDELINES FOR REPORTING ANALYSES

The presentation of data analyses should be such as to provide a maximum of detail without being cluttered. You can accomplish that best by continually examining your report to see whether it achieves the following aims.

Quantitative data should be presented in such a way as to permit recomputations by the reader. In the case of percentage tables, for example, the reader should be able to collapse categories and recompute the percentages. Readers should be given sufficient information as to permit them to compute percentages in the table in the opposite direction from your own presentation.

All aspects of the analysis should be described in sufficient detail to permit a secondary analyst to replicate the analysis from the same body of data. This means that he or she should be able to create the same indexes and scales, produce the same tables, arrive at the same regression equations, obtain the same factors and factor loadings, and so forth. That will seldom be done, of course, but if the report is presented in such a manner as to make it possible, the reader will be far better equipped to evaluate the report.

A final guide to the reporting of methodological details is that the reader should be in a position to completely replicate the entire study independently. It should be recalled from an earlier discussion that replicability is an essential norm of science generally. A single study does not prove a point; only a series of studies can begin to do so. Unless studies can be replicated, there can be no meaningful series of studies.

I have previously mentioned the importance of integrating data, analysis, and interpretations in the report. A more specific guideline can be offered in this regard. Tables, charts, and figures, if any, should be integrated into the text of the report— appearing near that portion of the text discussing them. Sometimes students describe their analyses in the body of the report, and place all the tables in an appendix at the end. This procedure greatly impedes the reader. As a general rule, it is best to (1) describe the purpose for presenting the table, (2) present it, and (3) review and interpret it.

Be explicit in drawing conclusions. Although research is typically conducted for the purpose of drawing general conclusions, you should carefully note the specific basis for such conclusions. Otherwise you may lead your reader into accepting unwarranted conclusions.

Point to any qualifications or conditions warranted in the evaluation of conclusions. Typically, you are in the best position to know the shortcomings and tentativeness of your conclusions, and you should give the reader the advantage of that knowledge. Failure to do so can misdirect future research and result in a waste of research funds.

I will conclude with a point made at the outset of this appendix, since it is extremely important. Research reports should be written in the best possible literary style. Writing lucidly is easier for some people than for others, and it is always harder than writing poorly. You are again referred to the Strunk and White volume. Every researcher would do well to follow this procedure: Write. Read Strunk and White. Revise. Reread Strunk and White. Revise again. That will be a difficult and time-consuming endeavor, but so is science.

A perfectly designed, carefully executed, and brilliantly analyzed study will be altogether worthless unless you are able to communicate your findings to others. This appendix has attempted to provide some general and specific guidelines toward that end. The best guides are logic, clarity, and honesty. Ultimately, there is probably no substitute for practice.

Appendix B
Commission on Aging Survey

RESPONDENT'S IDENTIFYING INFORMATION

Name:

Address:

Census Tract Number:

Telephone:

Social Security Number:

Birthdate:

Marital Status: [ ] Single
[ ] Married
[ ] Divorced
[ ] Separated
[ ] Widowed

Interviewer's Name:

Date of Interview:

COMMISSION ON AGING SURVEY

Respondent #: ____

Respondent's Name: ____

Respondent's Address:
Street ____
City/Town ____

Name of Interviewer: ____

Number of Visits

	1	2	3	4	5
Date					
Time Started					
Time Ended					
Time Spent					
Result*					
Appointment Date and Time					

*Codes:
1. Interview completed.
2. Interview partly completed - Appointment made.
3. Appointment made for interview later,
4. Refusal - No interview obtained.
5. No one at home.
6. Eligible respondent not home.
7. Other (SPECIFY) ____

Field Supervisor: ____ Date: ____

Editor: ____ Date: ____

Coder: ____ Date: ____

Keypuncher: ____ Date: ____

Serial Number ____

I. SATISFACTORY HOME AND COMMUNITY ENVIRONMENT

(1) To begin the interview, we would like to learn something about your current living arrangements. First, do you live alone or do you share your quarters with other people?

[ ] Live alone
[ ] Share quarters ⟶

   1a. Who do you live with?

     [ ] Spouse
     [ ] Children: Number ___
     [ ] Grandchildren: Number ___
     [ ] Other relatives: Number ___
     [ ] Unrelated persons: Number ___

   1b. How many people is that altogether?

21/ ___

22-26/ ___

27/ ___

(2) Do you own or rent these living quarters?

[ ] Own ⟶
[ ] Rent

   2a. Do you own it fee-simple, leasehold, or do you have other arrangements?

     [ ] Fee-simple
     [ ] Leasehold
     [ ] Other (specify): ___

28/ ___

(3) How long have you been living in these quarters?

___ (enter number of years)

29/ ___

(4) If you had your choice, do you think you (and your husband/wife) would prefer living alone or living with other people (other than your husband/wife)?

[ ] Prefer living alone
[ ] Prefer living with others

30-31/ ___

(5) How many rooms do you have in these quarters, other than bathrooms, halls, lanais, and so forth?

32/ ___

33/ ___

34/b

I. SATISFACTORY HOME AND COMMUNITY ENVIRONMENT

(6) Do you have a private bathroom or do you share it with other people (other than your husband/wife)?

[ ] Private bathroom
[ ] Shared bathroom

35/ ___

(7) Is there a telephone readily available for your use?

[ ] Yes
[ ] No

36/ ___

(8) Do you have hot and cold running water?

[ ] Yes
[ ] Cold only
[ ] Neither

37/ ___

(9) Do you find the temperature in your home:

[ ] Usually comfortable
[ ] Usually uncomfortable
[ ] About half and half

38/ ___

(10) Do you have enough windows for adequate light on most days?

[ ] Yes
[ ] No

39/ ___

(11) Do you have enough electric lighting in all rooms, in some rooms only, or not enough in any room?

[ ] Enough in all rooms
[ ] Enough in some only
[ ] Not enough in any
[ ] No electrical lighting

40/ ___

(12) Generally speaking, how would you rate the physical condition of your living quarters—such things as plumbing, the roof, the floor, windows, and so forth? Would you describe it as:

[ ] Excellent
[ ] Good
[ ] Fair
[ ] Poor

41/ ___

42/b

I. SATISFACTORY HOME AND COMMUNITY ENVIRONMENT

(13) Would you say that the size of your living quarters is:

[ ] Too large
[ ] Too small
[ ] Just about right

43/_____

(14) How well do you think your present home satisfies your current needs for comfort, convenience, and safety?

[ ] Very well
[ ] Fairly well
[ ] Not too well
[ ] Not at all

44/_____

(15) Would you say that you find such things as home maintenance, keeping up repairs, and general housework:

[ ] Difficult
[ ] Sometimes difficult
[ ] Never a problem

45/_____

(16) Do you have a room where you can usually go and shut the door to be alone if you want to?

[ ] Yes
[ ] No

46/_____

(17) Does noise from either outside or other parts of the building in which you live bother you? (IF YES: Would you say *often* or only *sometimes*?)

[ ] No
[ ] Sometimes
[ ] Often

47/_____

(18) For each of the following, please tell me if it represents a big problem for you, a slight problem, or no problem.

	Big Prob.	Slight Prob.	No. Prob.
a. Pests such as mice, rats, and so forth.	[ ]	[ ]	[ ]
b. Insects	[ ]	[ ]	[ ]
c. Refuse collection	[ ]	[ ]	[ ]
d. Overcrowding in stores, restaurants, and so forth	[ ]	[ ]	[ ]
e. Air pollution	[ ]	[ ]	

48-52/

53/b

I. SATISFACTORY HOME AND COMMUNITY ENVIRONMENT

(19) All things considered, how do you feel about staying in these quarters to moving somewhere else? Would you say you:

[ ] Would definitely prefer to stay here
[ ] Would probably prefer to stay here
[ ] Would probably prefer to move elsewhere
[ ] Would definitely prefer to move elsewhere
[ ] Don't know

54/_____

(20) Since you have lived here, would you say that the neighborhood has changed for the better, for the worse, or stayed about the same?

[ ] For the better
[ ] Stayed about the same
[ ] For the worse

55/_____

(21) How attached are you to your neighborhood? Would you say you:

[ ] Are very attached
[ ] Are fairly attached
[ ] Have no real feeling
[ ] Do not like it and would like to move

56/_____

(22) How good do you think your neighborhood is for the older people to live?

[ ] A good place
[ ] A fair place
[ ] A poor place

57/_____

(23) Generally speaking, are the following places or people a convenient distance from where you live? (If the respondent is not in need of or does not care about being near these things such as a bank, park, etc., then mark "N.A.") (Let the respondent decide convenience.)

	Yes	No	N.A.
a. Friends	[ ]	[ ]	[ ]
b. Relatives	[ ]	[ ]	[ ]
c. Church	[ ]	[ ]	[ ]
d. Stores	[ ]	[ ]	[ ]
e. Medical facilities	[ ]	[ ]	[ ]
f. Bank	[ ]	[ ]	[ ]
g. Park	[ ]	[ ]	[ ]
h. Other recreational facilities	[ ]	[ ]	[ ]
i. Restaurant	[ ]	[ ]	[ ]

58-66/

67-80/b

ID No.: 1-5/

II. PERSONAL HEALTH, SAFETY, AND PHYSICAL WELL-BEING

6/2

(1) Here is a list of health problems that people often have. I'll read them and you tell me if you have any of them. First, a list of conditions which usually continue to require care or treatment or restrict activities:
(Interviewer: check "Yes" or "No" for each item.)

7-14/

	Yes	No
a. Diabetes	[ ]	[ ]
b. High blood pressure	[ ]	[ ]
c. Heart trouble	[ ]	[ ]
d. Stroke	[ ]	[ ]
e. Arthritis	[ ]	[ ]
f. Cancer	[ ]	[ ]
g. Paralysis or Parkinson's disease	[ ]	[ ]
h. Glaucoma (cataracts) or other eye trouble not relieved by glasses	[ ]	[ ]

(2) How many days have you been sick to the point of being unable to carry on your regular activities during the *last four weeks*?

15/

[ ] No days (Interviewer: check "Not sick" on Question 3 and go on to Question 4.)
[ ] 1 to 7 days
[ ] 8 to 14 days
[ ] 15 to 21 days
[ ] 22 days or more

(3) While you were sick during this time, were you mostly:

16/

[ ] (Not sick)
[ ] Just at home
[ ] In bed at home
[ ] In the hospital

(4) For doing each of the following activities please tell me if you have no difficulty, can do it with some difficulty, or if you cannot do it.

17-19/

	No Difficulty	Some Difficulty	Cannot Do It
a. Going up and down stairs	[ ]	[ ]	[ ]
b. Getting about the house	[ ]	[ ]	[ ]
c. Washing and bathing	[ ]	[ ]	[ ]

20/b

II. PERSONAL HEALTH, SAFETY, AND PHYSICAL WELL-BEING

(4) (cont.)

21-24/

	No Difficulty	Some Difficulty	Cannot Do It
d. Dressing and putting on shoes	[ ]	[ ]	[ ]
e. Getting out of the house	[ ]	[ ]	[ ]
f. Watching television	[ ]	[ ]	[ ]
g. Feeding yourself	[ ]	[ ]	[ ]

(5) Please tell me whether you currently need each of the following health aids, and if so, whether you currently have it?

25-33/

	Need?		If YES: do you have it?	
	Yes	No	Yes	No
a. Eyeglasses	[ ]	[ ]	[ ]	[ ]
b. Hearing aid	[ ]	[ ]	[ ]	[ ]
c. False teeth	[ ]	[ ]	[ ]	[ ]
d. Cane or crutch	[ ]	[ ]	[ ]	[ ]
e. Leg brace	[ ]	[ ]	[ ]	[ ]
f. Special shoes	[ ]	[ ]	[ ]	[ ]
g. Truss or abdominal brace	[ ]	[ ]	[ ]	[ ]
h. Wheelchair	[ ]	[ ]	[ ]	[ ]
i. Other health aids	[ ]	[ ]	[ ]	[ ]

34-42/b

II. PERSONAL HEALTH, SAFETY, AND PHYSICAL WELL-BEING

(6) Have you had a medical checkup in the last year?

[ ] Yes
[ ] No ────→ Was there any special reason why you didn't get a checkup?

43/____

(7) Have you had all the immunizations and inoculations you think you should have?

[ ] Yes
[ ] No ────→ Which additional ones do you think you should have?
[ ] Don't know

44/____

45/____

46/____

47/b

II. PERSONAL HEALTH, SAFETY, AND PHYSICAL WELL-BEING

(8) During the past year have you been injured in any of the following kinds of accidents?

	Yes	No
a. An automobile accident	[ ]	[ ]
b. Falling in the home	[ ]	[ ]
c. An injury on the job	[ ]	[ ]
d. Other	[ ]	[ ]

48-51/

(9) Are you currently registered for Medicare?

[ ] Yes
[ ] No

52/

(10) Are you a member of any health care program such as Kaiser, HMSA, Blue Cross, or some program like that?

[ ] Yes
[ ] No

53/

IF YES: Which program do you belong to?

[ ] Kaiser
[ ] HMSA
[ ] Blue Cross
[ ] Other _____

54/

(11) Now I will list to you some groups of food. Would you please tell me how often you eat something from each of the groups. That is, do you eat something from the group almost every day, sometimes, or almost never?

a. Milk, cheese, ice cream, or anything else made out of milk.

[ ] Almost every day
[ ] Sometimes
[ ] Almost never

55/

b. Any kind of meat, including beef, veal, pork, lamb, poultry, or fish, eggs, dry beans, peas, tofu, or nuts.

[ ] Almost every day
[ ] Sometimes
[ ] Almost never

56/

57/b

ID No.: 1-5/

II. PERSONAL HEALTH, SAFETY, AND PHYSICAL WELL-BEING

(11) (cont.)

c. Any fruit or vegetable or juice.
[ ] Almost every day
[ ] Sometimes
[ ] Almost never

58/____

d. Any kind of food made of bread or cereal, or rice.
[ ] Almost every day
[ ] Sometimes
[ ] Almost never

59/____

(12) Do you take vitamin pills every day or almost every day?
[ ] Yes
[ ] No

60/____

(13) In general, would you say your appetite is poor, fair, or good?
[ ] Poor
[ ] Fair
[ ] Good

61/____

(14) Has your appetite been like this only recently, during the past year, or most of your life?
[ ] Recently
[ ] Past year
[ ] Most of life

62/____

(15) Would you say you have been gaining weight, staying the same, or losing weight over the past two years?
[ ] Gaining
[ ] Losing
[ ] Staying the same

63/____

(16) Do you have trouble buying foods that you like?
[ ] Yes
[ ] No
[ ] Sometimes

64/____

6,-80/6

III. ECONOMIC SATISFACTION

Now we would like to learn just a little about your financial situation.

(1) To begin, could you tell me whether you (and your husband/wife) are responsible for managing your day-to-day finances such as buying food and clothing, paying the rent or mortgage payments, and so forth, or are your finances handled by someone else?

[ ] Handled by respondent →
[ ] Handled by someone else →

(1a) Who is responsible for handling your finances?

(1b) Do you receive any financial support from your children or other relatives?
[ ] Yes
[ ] No

6/3

7/____

8/____

(2) During the past year did you (or the person handling your finances) receive any income from the following sources?

Yes   No
[ ] [ ] Wages
[ ] [ ] Income from a business or professional practice
[ ] [ ] Income from farming
[ ] [ ] Social Security
[ ] [ ] Retirement payments or pensions
[ ] [ ] Interest on savings or dividends
[ ] [ ] Others

9/____

10-16/

(3) Could you tell me approximately how much income you (and the person responsible for your finances) had from all sources during the past year?
$

17-21/

(4) How many people were supported by that income?

22-23/

24/6

III. ECONOMIC SATISFACTION

(5) Do you currently have a job?   [ ] Yes   [ ] No   25/___

IF YES

(5a) Do you work full-time or part-time?   26/___

[ ] Full-time
[ ] Part-time

IF NO

(5b) Would you like a job if you could find work you liked and could do?   27/___

[ ] Yes
[ ] No

(6) How well do you think your income and assets satisfy your needs: 28/___

[ ] Very well
[ ] Well
[ ] Adequately
[ ] Barely
[ ] Poorly

IF ANSWER IS "POORLY" OR "BARELY" TO 6 ABOVE:

(6a) How much more money do you and your family need each month to live comfortably?   29/___

[ ] Less than $50
[ ] $50 to $99
[ ] $100 to $149
[ ] $150 or more

30/b

IV. INTELLECTUAL AND SOCIAL SATISFACTION

(1) How often did you visit in person with a member of your family last week?   31/___

[ ] Every day
[ ] A few times
[ ] Once
[ ] Not at all
[ ] No family nearby

(2) How often did you visit in person with friends or neighbors last week?   32/___

[ ] Every day
[ ] A few times
[ ] Once
[ ] Not at all

(3) About how often last week did you talk to friends, relatives, business contacts, or others on the telephone?   33/___

[ ] Every day
[ ] Several times
[ ] Once
[ ] Not at all

(4) Of all your neighbors, about how many do you know well enough to visit with?   34/___

[ ] 5 or more
[ ] 3 or 4
[ ] 1 or 2
[ ] None

(5) Do you have as much contact as you would like with a person you feel close to—somebody that you can trust and confide in?   35/___

[ ] Yes
[ ] No

(6) Do you think that you see enough of your friends, relatives, and neighbors?   36/___

[ ] Yes
[ ] No

37/b

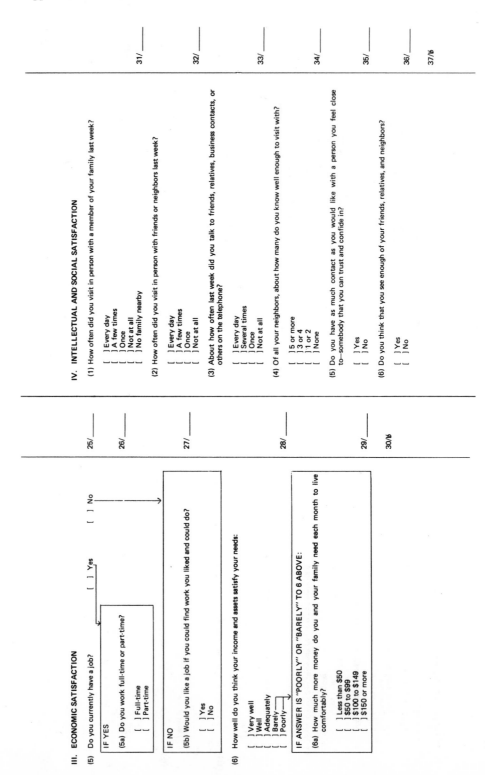

IV. INTELLECTUAL AND SOCIAL SATISFACTION

(7) How often do you find yourself feeling lonely?

[　] Never or hardly
[　] Sometimes
[　] Fairly often
[　] Very often or always

38/____

(8) How often do you get out of doors beyond just outside the door to the mailbox?

[　] Every day
[　] Several times a week
[　] Once a week
[　] Less than weekly

39/____

(9) About how many hours a day on the average do you watch television?

[　] 5 or more hours
[　] 3 or 4
[　] 1 or 2
[　] Less than 1

40/____

(10) About how many hours a day would you say you spend reading newspapers, magazines, or books?

[　] 5 or more hours
[　] 3 or 4
[　] 1 or 2
[　] Less than 1

41/____

(11) How active would you say you are in the following kinds of activities: would you say very active, fairly active, or not very active?

	Very Active	Fairly Active	Not Very Active
a. Religious activities	[　]	[　]	[　]
b. Politics	[　]	[　]	[　]
c. Social clubs	[　]	[　]	[　]
d. Sports as a participant	[　]	[　]	[　]
e. Sports as a spectator	[　]	[　]	[　]

42-46/____

(12) In general, do you usually have enough to do?

[　] Yes
[　] No

47/____

48/b

IV. INTELLECTUAL AND SOCIAL SATISFACTION

(13) How would you describe your general satisfaction with life at the present?

[　] Excellent
[　] Good
[　] Fair
[　] Poor

49/____

(14) Do you feel that the following services and facilities are generally adequate to your needs and desires or are they generally inadequate? (Note: if respondent indicates no need or desire, check "Not appl.")

	Adeq.	Inadeq.	Not Appl.
a. Libraries	[　]	[　]	[　]
b. Museums	[　]	[　]	[　]
c. Cultural events	[　]	[　]	[　]
d. Adult education courses	[　]	[　]	[　]
e. Training programs in skills you might want to learn	[　]	[　]	[　]

50-54/____

(15) Do you usually expect that things will turn out well for you?

[　] Yes
[　] No

55/____

(16) How much would you say you worry about things?

[　] Not at all
[　] Not much
[　] Fairly often
[　] A great deal

56/____

57/b

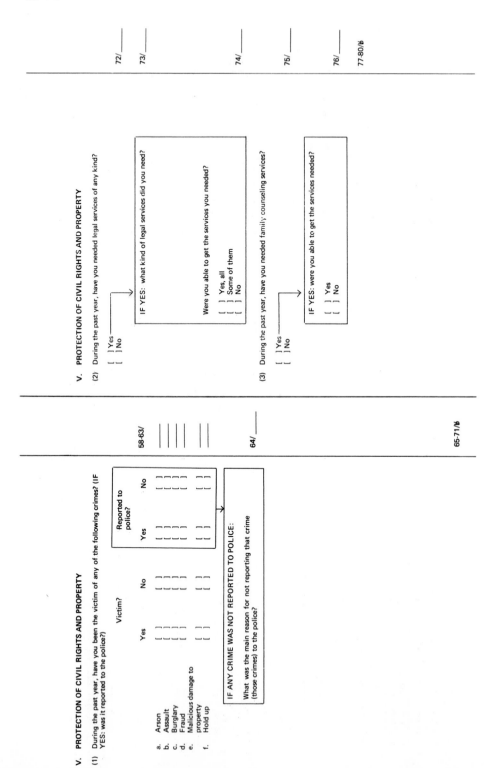

V. PROTECTION OF CIVIL RIGHTS AND PROPERTY

(1) During the past year, have you been the victim of any of the following crimes? (IF YES: was it reported to the police?)

	Victim?		Reported to police?	
	Yes	No	Yes	No
a. Arson	[ ]	[ ]	[ ]	[ ]
b. Assault	[ ]	[ ]	[ ]	[ ]
c. Burglary	[ ]	[ ]	[ ]	[ ]
d. Fraud	[ ]	[ ]	[ ]	[ ]
e. Malicious damage to property	[ ]	[ ]	[ ]	[ ]
f. Hold up	[ ]	[ ]	[ ]	[ ]

58-63/ |||| ||

IF ANY CRIME WAS NOT REPORTED TO POLICE:

What was the main reason for not reporting that crime (those crimes) to the police?

64/ ——

65-71/b

V. PROTECTION OF CIVIL RIGHTS AND PROPERTY

(2) During the past year, have you needed legal services of any kind?

[ ] Yes
[ ] No

72/ ——

IF YES: what kind of legal services did you need?

73/ ——

Were you able to get the services you needed?

[ ] Yes, all
[ ] Some of them
[ ] No

74/ ——

(3) During the past year, have you needed family counseling services?

[ ] Yes
[ ] No

75/ ——

IF YES: were you able to get the services needed?

[ ] Yes
[ ] No

76/ ——

77-80/b

ID No.: 1-5/

V. PROTECTION OF CIVIL RIGHTS AND PROPERTY

(4) During the past year, have you needed financial counseling?

6/4

[ ] Yes
[ ] No

7/___

→ IF YES: were you able to get the counseling needed?

[ ] Yes
[ ] No

8/___

(5) Some older people report that they are often taken advantage of because of their age. Do you feel this has happened to you during the past year?

9/___

[ ] Yes
[ ] No

→ IF YES: please describe what happened.

10/___

(6) Now would you tell me if you think you need or would like to have counseling services available to you on the following matters?

	Yes	No	Not appl.
a. Planning retirement	[ ]	[ ]	[ ]
b. Health protection and care	[ ]	[ ]	[ ]
c. Consumer protection	[ ]	[ ]	[ ]
d. Leisure time activities	[ ]	[ ]	[ ]

11-14/

15/b

PERSONAL CHARACTERISTICS

Finally, we would like to know just a little about you, so that we will be able to understand the answers different kinds of people give in this survey.

(1) INTERVIEWER: CHECK SEX   [ ] Male   [ ] Female

16/___

(2) What is your age please?

17-18/___

(3) Where were you born?

19-20/___

[ ] Oahu
[ ] Neighbor Island (Which: _____
[ ] Mainland U. S. (State: _____
[ ] Foreign Country (Country: _____

(4) Which of the following best describes your racial or ethnic group?

21-22/___

01. [ ] Caucasian, haole
02. [ ] Chinese
03. [ ] Filipino
04. [ ] Hawaiian or part-Hawaiian
05. [ ] Japanese
06. [ ] Korean
07. [ ] Negro, Black
08. [ ] Samoan
09. [ ] Cosmopolitan (without Hawaiian)
10. [ ] Other: _____

23-80/b

Appendix C
Random Numbers

```
10480  15011  01536  02011  81647  91646  69179  14194  62590  36207  20969  99570  91291  90700
22368  46573  25595  85393  30995  89198  27982  53402  93965  34095  52666  19174  39615  99505
24130  48360  22527  97265  76393  64809  15179  24830  49340  32081  30680  19655  63348  58629
42167  93093  06243  61680  07856  16376  39440  53537  71341  57004  00849  74917  97758  16379
37570  39975  81837  16656  06121  91782  60468  81305  49684  60672  14110  06927  01263  54613

77921  06907  11008  42751  27756  53498  18602  70659  90655  15053  21916  81825  44394  42880
99562  72905  56420  69994  98872  31016  71194  18738  44013  48840  63213  21069  10634  12952
96301  91977  05463  07972  18876  20922  94595  56869  69014  60045  18425  84903  42508  32307
89579  14342  63661  10281  17453  18103  57740  84378  25331  12566  58678  44947  05585  56941
85475  36857  53342  53988  53060  59533  38867  62300  08158  17983  16439  11458  18593  64952

28918  69578  88231  33276  70997  79936  56865  05859  90106  31595  01547  85590  91610  78188
63553  40961  48235  03427  49626  69445  18663  72695  52180  20847  12234  90511  33703  90322
09429  93969  52636  92737  88974  33488  36320  17617  30015  08272  84115  27156  30613  74952
10365  61129  87529  85689  48237  52267  67689  93394  01511  26358  85104  20285  29975  89868
07119  97336  71048  08178  77233  13916  47564  81056  97735  85977  29372  74461  28551  90707

51085  12765  51821  51259  77452  16308  60756  92144  49442  53900  70960  63990  75601  40719
02368  21382  52404  60268  89368  19885  55322  44819  01188  65255  64835  44919  05944  55157
01011  54092  33362  94904  31273  04146  18594  29852  71585  85030  51132  01915  92747  64951
52162  53916  46369  58586  23216  14513  83149  98736  23495  64350  94738  17752  35156  35749
07056  97628  33787  09998  42698  06691  76988  13602  51851  46104  88916  19509  25625  58104

48663  91245  85828  14346  09172  30168  90229  04734  59193  22178  30421  61666  99904  32812
54164  58492  22421  74103  47070  25306  76468  26384  58151  06646  21524  15227  96909  44592
32639  32363  05597  24200  13363  38005  94342  28728  35806  06912  17012  64161  18296  22851
29334  27001  87637  87308  58731  00256  45834  15398  46557  41135  10367  07684  36188  18510
02488  33062  28834  07351  19731  92420  60952  61280  50001  67658  32586  86679  50720  94953

81525  72295  04839  96423  24878  82651  66566  14778  76797  14780  13300  87074  79666  95725
29676  20591  68086  26432  46901  20849  89768  81536  86645  12659  92259  57102  80428  25280
00742  57392  39064  66432  84673  40027  32832  61362  98947  96067  64760  64584  96096  98253
05366  04213  25669  26422  44407  44048  37937  63904  45766  66134  75470  66520  34693  90449
91921  26418  64117  94305  26766  25940  39972  22209  71500  64568  91402  42416  07844  69618

00582  04711  87917  77341  42206  35126  74087  99547  81817  42607  43808  76655  62028  76630
00725  69884  62797  56170  86324  88072  76222  36086  84637  93161  76038  65855  77919  88006
69011  65795  95876  55293  18988  27354  26575  08625  40801  59920  29841  80150  12777  48501
25976  57948  29888  88604  67917  48708  18912  82271  65424  69774  33611  54262  85963  03547
09763  83473  73577  12908  30883  18317  28290  35797  05998  41688  34952  37888  38917  88050

91567  42595  27958  30134  04024  86385  29880  99730  55536  84855  29080  09250  79656  73211
17955  56349  90999  49127  20044  59931  06115  20542  18059  02008  73708  83517  36103  42791
46503  18584  18845  49618  02304  51038  20655  58727  28168  15475  56942  53389  20562  87338
92157  89634  94824  78171  84610  82834  09922  25417  44137  48413  25555  21246  35509  20468
14577  62765  35605  81263  39667  47358  56873  56307  61607  49518  89656  20103  77490  18062

98427  07523  33362  64270  01638  92477  66969  98420  04880  45585  46565  04102  46880  45709
34914  63976  88720  82765  34476  17032  87589  40836  32427  70002  70663  88863  77775  69348
70060  28277  39475  46473  23219  53416  94970  25832  69975  94884  19661  72828  00102  66794
53976  54914  06990  67245  68350  82948  11398  42878  80287  88267  47363  46634  06541  97809
76072  29515  40980  07391  58745  25774  22987  80059  39911  96189  41151  14222  60697  59583

90725  52210  83974  33992  65831  38857  50490  83765  55657  14361  31720  57375  56228  41546
64364  67412  33339  31926  14883  24413  59744  92351  97473  89286  35931  04110  23726  51900
08962  00358  31662  25388  61642  34072  81249  35648  56891  69352  48373  45578  78547  81788
95012  68379  93526  70765  10592  04542  76463  54328  02349  17247  28865  14777  62730  92277
15664  10493  20492  38391  91132  21999  59516  81652  27195  48223  46751  22923  32261  85653
```

Abridged from Handbook of Tables for Probability and Statistics, Second Edition, edited by William H. Beyer (Cleveland: The Chemical Rubber Company, 1968.)

16408	81899	04153	53381	79401	21438	83035	92350	36693	31238	59649	91754	72772	02338
18629	81953	05520	91962	04739	13092	97662	24822	94730	06496	35090	04822	86774	98289
73115	35101	47498	87637	99016	71060	88824	71013	18735	20286	72924	72924	35165	43040
57491	16703	23167	49323	45021	33132	12544	41035	80780	45393	44812	12515	98931	91202
30405	83946	23792	14422	15059	45799	22716	19792	09983	74353	68668	30429	70735	25499
16631	35006	85900	98275	32388	52390	16815	69298	82732	38480	95240	32523	41961	44437
96773	20206	42559	78985	05300	22164	24369	54224	35083	19687	68995	91491	60383	19746
38935	64202	14349	82674	66523	44133	00697	35552	35970	19124	88525	29686	03387	59846
31624	76384	17403	53363	44167	64486	64758	75366	76554	31601	93911	33072	60332	92325
78919	19474	23632	27889	47914	02584	37680	20801	72152	39339	89203	08930	85001	87820
03931	33309	57047	74211	63445	17361	62825	39908	05607	91284	68833	25570	38818	46920
74426	33278	43972	10119	89917	15665	52872	73823	73144	88662	88970	74492	51805	99378
09066	00903	20795	95452	92648	45454	09552	88815	16553	51125	79375	97596	16296	66092
42238	12426	87025	14267	20979	04508	64535	31155	86064	29472	47689	05974	52468	16834
16153	08002	26504	41744	81959	65642	74240	56302	00033	67107	77510	70625	28725	34191
21457	40742	29820	96783	29400	21840	15035	34537	33310	06116	41867	14951	16572	06004
21581	57802	02050	89728	17937	37621	47075	42080	97403	48626	34405	56087	33386	21597
55612	78095	83197	33732	05810	24813	86902	60397	16489	03264	57202	94617	05269	92532
44657	66999	99324	51281	84463	60563	79312	93454	68876	25471	94142	25299	12682	73572
91340	84979	46949	81973	37949	61023	43997	15263	80644	43942	02330	74301	99533	50501
91227	21199	31935	27022	84067	05462	35216	14486	29891	68607	84081	66938	91696	85065
50001	38140	66321	19924	72163	09538	12151	06878	91903	18749	81651	50245	82790	70925
65390	05224	72958	28609	81406	39147	25549	48542	42627	45233	66345	81073	23772	07896
27504	96131	83944	41575	10573	08619	64482	73923	36152	05184	54339	58861	84387	34925
37169	94851	39117	89632	00959	16487	65536	49071	39782	17095	80377	35909	00275	48280
11508	70225	51111	38351	19444	66499	71945	05422	13442	78675	41870	52689	93654	59894
37449	30362	06694	54690	04052	53115	62757	95348	78662	11163	59194	52799	34971	52924
46515	70331	85922	38323	57015	15765	97161	17869	45349	61796	12535	12133	49106	79860
30986	81223	42416	58353	21532	30502	32305	86482	05174	07901	95434	98227	74818	46942
63798	64995	46583	09785	44160	78128	83991	42865	92520	83531	18534	03862	81250	54238
82486	84846	99254	67632	43218	50076	21361	64816	51202	88124	08303	09443	51275	83556
21885	32906	92431	09060	64297	51674	64126	62570	26123	05155	85076	56148	28225	85762
60336	98782	07408	53458	13564	59089	26445	29789	85205	41001	34327	11601	14645	23541
43937	46891	24010	25560	86355	33941	25786	54990	71899	15475	35398	88717	21824	19585
97656	63175	89303	16275	07100	92063	21942	18611	47348	20203	17639	93872	78095	50136
03299	01221	05418	38982	55758	92237	26759	36367	21216	98442	88732	76536	82558	75928
79626	06486	03574	17668	07785	76020	79924	25651	83325	88428	88022	18098	34925	50585
85636	68335	47539	03129	65651	11977	02510	26113	99447	68645	37543	95787	35503	93448
18039	14367	61337	06177	12143	46609	32989	74014	64708	00533	76310	04379	37890	47908
08362	15656	60627	36478	65648	16764	53412	09013	07832	41574	79725	51132	28117	75567
79556	29068	04142	16268	15387	12856	66227	38358	22478	73373	80799	09443	82558	05250
92608	82674	27072	32534	17075	27698	98204	63863	11951	34648	53203	56148	34925	57031
23982	25835	40055	67006	12293	02753	14827	23235	35071	99704	06216	11601	35503	85171
09915	96306	05908	97901	28395	14186	00821	80703	70426	75647	97548	88717	37890	40129
59037	33300	26695	62247	69927	76123	50842	43834	86654	70959	19636	93872	28117	19233
42488	78077	69882	61657	34136	79180	97526	43092	04098	73571	80799	76536	71255	64239
46764	86273	63003	93017	31204	36692	40202	35275	57306	55543	53203	18098	47625	88684
03237	45430	55417	63282	90816	17349	88298	36600	90183	78406	06216	95787	42579	90730
86591	81482	52667	61582	14972	90053	89534	49199	43716	43716	97548	04379	46370	28672
38534	01715	94964	87288	65680	43772	39560	86537	62738	62738	19636	51132	25739	56947

Appendix D

Critical Values of Chi Square

d.f.	$\chi^2 0.995$	$\chi^2 0.990$	$\chi^2 0.975$	$\chi^2 0.950$	$\chi^2 0.900$
1	0.0000393	0.0001571	0.0009821	0.0039321	0.0157908
2	0.0100251	0.0201007	0.0506356	0.102587	0.210720
3	0.0717212	0.114832	0.215795	0.351846	0.584375
4	0.206990	0.297110	0.484419	0.710721	1.063623
5	0.411740	0.554300	0.831211	1.145476	1.61031
6	0.675727	0.872085	1.237347	1.63539	2.20413
7	0.989265	1.239043	1.68987	2.16735	2.83311
8	1.344419	1.646482	2.17973	2.73264	3.48954
9	1.734926	2.087912	2.70039	3.32511	4.16816
10	2.15585	2.55821	3.24697	3.94030	4.86518
11	2.60321	3.05347	3.81575	4.57481	5.57779
12	3.07382	3.57056	4.40379	5.22603	6.30380
13	3.56503	4.10691	5.00874	5.89186	7.04150
14	4.07468	4.66043	5.62872	6.57063	7.78953
15	4.60094	5.22935	6.26214	7.26094	8.54675
16	5.14224	5.81221	6.90766	7.96164	9.31223
17	5.69724	6.40776	7.56418	8.67176	10.0852
18	6.26481	7.01491	8.23075	9.39046	10.8649
19	6.84398	7.63273	8.90655	10.1170	11.6509
20	7.43386	8.26040	9.59083	10.8508	12.4426
21	8.03366	8.89720	10.28293	11.5913	13.2396
22	8.64272	9.54249	10.9823	12.3380	14.0415
23	9.26042	10.19567	11.6885	13.0905	14.8479
24	9.88623	10.8564	12.4011	13.8484	15.6587
25	10.5197	11.5240	13.1197	14.6114	16.4734
26	11.1603	12.1981	13.8439	15.3791	17.2919
27	11.8076	12.8786	14.5733	16.1513	18.1138
28	12.4613	13.5648	15.3079	16.9279	18.9392
29	13.1211	14.2565	16.0471	17.7083	19.7677
30	13.7867	14.9535	16.7908	18.4926	20.5992
40	20.7065	22.1643	24.4331	26.5093	29.0505
50	27.9907	29.7067	32.3574	34.7642	37.6886
60	35.5346	37.4848	40.4817	43.1879	46.4589
70	43.2752	45.4418	48.7576	51.7393	55.3290
80	51.1720	53.5400	57.1532	60.3915	64.2778
90	59.1963	61.7541	65.6466	69.1260	73.2912
100	67.3276	70.0648	74.2219	77.9295	82.3581

From "Tables of the Percentage Points of the χ^2-Distribution." *Biometrika*, Vol. 32 (1941), pp. 188–189, by Catherine M. Thompson. Reproduced by permission of Professor E. S. Pearson.

$\chi^2 0.100$	$\chi^2 0.050$	$\chi^2 0.025$	$\chi^2 0.010$	$\chi^2 0.005$	d.f.
2.70554	3.84146	5.02389	6.63490	7.87944	1
4.60517	5.99147	7.37776	9.21034	10.5966	2
6.25139	7.81473	9.34840	11.3449	12.8381	3
7.77944	9.48773	11.1433	13.2767	14.8602	4
9.23635	11.0705	12.8325	15.0863	16.7496	5
10.6446	12.5916	14.4494	16.8119	18.5476	6
12.0170	14.0671	16.0128	18.4753	20.2777	7
13.3616	15.5073	17.5346	20.0902	21.9550	8
14.6837	16.9190	19.0228	21.6660	23.5893	9
15.9871	18.3070	20.4831	23.2093	25.1882	10
17.2750	19.6751	21.9200	24.7250	26.7569	11
18.5494	21.0261	23.3367	26.2170	28.2995	12
19.8119	22.3621	24.7356	27.6883	29.8194	13
21.0642	23.6848	26.1190	29.1413	31.3193	14
22.3072	24.9958	27.4884	30.5779	32.8013	15
23.5418	26.2962	28.8454	31.9999	34.2672	16
24.7690	27.5871	30.1910	33.4087	35.7185	17
25.9894	28.8693	31.5264	34.8053	37.1564	18
27.2036	30.1435	32.8523	36.1908	38.5822	19
28.4120	31.4104	34.1696	37.5662	39.9968	20
29.6151	32.6705	35.4789	38.9321	41.4010	21
30.8133	33.9244	36.7807	40.2894	42.7956	22
32.0069	35.1725	38.0757	41.6384	44.1813	23
33.1963	36.4151	39.3641	42.9798	45.5585	24
34.3816	37.6525	40.6465	44.3141	46.9278	25
35.5631	38.8852	41.9232	45.6417	48.2899	26
36.7412	40.1133	43.1944	46.9630	49.6449	27
37.9159	41.3372	44.4607	48.2782	50.9933	28
39.0875	42.5569	45.7222	49.5879	52.3356	29
40.2560	43.7729	46.9792	50.8922	53.6720	30
51.8050	55.7585	59.3417	63.6907	66.7659	40
63.1671	67.5048	71.4202	76.1539	79.4900	50
74.3970	79.0819	83.2976	88.3794	91.9517	60
85.5271	90.5312	95.0231	100.425	104.215	70
96.5782	101.879	106.629	112.329	116.321	80
107.565	113.145	118.136	124.116	128.299	90
118.498	124.342	129.561	135.807	140.169	100

Appendix E
Normal Curve Areas

z	.00	.01	.02	.03	.04	.05	.06	.07	.08	.09
0.0	.0000	.0040	.0080	.0120	.0160	.0199	.0239	.0279	.0319	.0359
0.1	.0398	.0438	.0478	.0517	.0557	.0596	.0636	.0675	.0714	.0753
0.2	.0793	.0832	.0871	.0910	.0948	.0987	.1026	.1064	.1103	.1141
0.3	.1179	.1217	.1255	.1293	.1331	.1368	.1406	.1443	.1480	.1517
0.4	.1554	.1591	.1628	.1664	.1700	.1736	.1772	.1808	.1844	.1879
0.5	.1915	.1950	.1985	.2019	.2054	.2088	.2123	.2157	.2190	.2224
0.6	.2257	.2291	.2324	.2357	.2389	.2422	.2454	.2486	.2517	.2549
0.7	.2580	.2611	.2642	.2673	.2704	.2734	.2764	.2794	.2823	.2852
0.8	.2881	.2910	.2939	.2967	.2995	.3023	.3051	.3078	.3106	.3133
0.9	.3159	.3186	.3212	.3238	.3264	.3289	.3315	.3340	.3365	.3389
1.0	.3413	.3438	.3461	.3485	.3508	.3531	.3554	.3577	.3599	.3621
1.1	.3643	.3665	.3686	.3708	.3729	.3749	.3770	.3790	.3810	.3830
1.2	.3849	.3869	.3888	.3907	.3925	.3944	.3962	.3980	.3997	.4015
1.3	.4032	.4049	.4066	.4082	.4099	.4115	.4131	.4147	.4162	.4177
1.4	.4192	.4207	.4222	.4236	.4251	.4265	.4279	.4292	.4306	.4319
1.5	.4332	.4345	.4357	.4370	.4382	.4394	.4406	.4418	.4429	.4441
1.6	.4452	.4463	.4474	.4484	.4495	.4505	.4515	.4525	.4535	.4545
1.7	.4554	.4564	.4573	.4582	.4591	.4599	.4608	.4616	.4625	.4633
1.8	.4641	.4649	.4656	.4664	.4671	.4678	.4686	.4693	.4699	.4706
1.9	.4713	.4719	.4726	.4732	.4738	.4744	.4750	.4756	.4761	.4767
2.0	.4772	.4778	.4783	.4788	.4793	.4798	.4803	.4808	.4812	.4817
2.1	.4821	.4826	.4830	.4834	.4838	.4842	.4846	.4850	.4854	.4857
2.2	.4861	.4864	.4868	.4871	.4875	.4878	.4881	.4884	.4887	.4890
2.3	.4893	.4896	.4898	.4901	.4904	.4906	.4909	.4911	.4913	.4916
2.4	.4918	.4920	.4922	.4925	.4927	.4929	.4931	.4932	.4934	.4936
2.5	.4938	.4940	.4941	.4943	.4945	.4946	.4948	.4949	.4951	.4952
2.6	.4953	.4955	.4956	.4957	.4959	.4960	.4961	.4962	.4963	.4964
2.7	.4965	.4966	.4967	.4968	.4969	.4970	.4971	.4972	.4973	.4974
2.8	.4974	.4975	.4976	.4977	.4977	.4978	.4979	.4979	.4980	.4981
2.9	.4981	.4982	.4982	.4983	.4984	.4984	.4985	.4985	.4986	.4986
3.0	.4987	.4987	.4987	.4988	.4988	.4989	.4989	.4989	.4990	.4990

This table is abridged from Table I of *Statistical Tables and Formulas*, by A. Hald (New York: John Wiley & Sons, Inc., 1952). Reproduced by permission of A. Hald and the publishers, John Wiley & Sons, Inc.

Appendix F

Estimated Sampling Error

How to use this table: Find the intersection between the sample size and the approximate percentage distribution of the binomial in the sample. The number appearing at this intersection represents the estimated sampling error, at the 95% confidence level, expressed in percentage points (plus or minus).

Example: In a sample of 400 respondents, 60% answer "Yes" and 40% answer "No." The sampling error is estimated at plus or minus 4.9 percentage points. The confidence interval, then, is between 55.1% and 64.9%. We would estimate (95% confidence) that the proportion of the total population who would say "Yes" is somewhere within that interval.

Sample size	Binomial Percentage Distribution				
	50/50	60/40	70/30	80/20	90/10
100	10	9.8	9.2	8	6
200	7.1	6.9	6.5	5.7	4.2
300	5.8	5.7	5.3	4.6	3.5
400	5	4.9	4.6	4	3
500	4.5	4.4	4.1	3.6	2.7
600	4.1	4	3.7	3.3	2.4
700	3.8	3.7	3.5	3	2.3
800	3.5	3.5	3.2	2.8	2.1
900	3.3	3.3	3.1	2.7	2
1000	3.2	3.1	2.9	2.5	1.9
1100	3	3	2.8	2.4	1.8
1200	2.9	2.8	2.6	2.3	1.7
1300	2.8	2.7	2.5	2.2	1.7
1400	2.7	2.6	2.4	2.1	1.6
1500	2.6	2.5	2.4	2.1	1.5
1600	2.5	2.4	2.3	2	1.5
1700	2.4	2.4	2.2	1.9	1.5
1800	2.4	2.3	2.2	1.9	1.4
1900	2.3	2.2	2.1	1.8	1.4
2000	2.2	2.2	2	1.8	1.3

Appendix G
Square Roots

n	$\sqrt{n}$	n	$\sqrt{n}$
		30	5.477 226
1	1.000 000	31	5.567 764
2	1.414 214	32	5.656 854
3	1.732 051	33	5.744 563
4	2.000 000	34	5.830 952
5	2.236 068	35	5.916 080
6	2.449 490	36	6.000 000
7	2.645 751	37	6.082 763
8	2.828 427	38	6.164 414
9	3.000 000	39	6.244 998
10	3.162 278	40	6.324 555
11	3.316 625	41	6.403 124
12	3.464 102	42	6.480 741
13	3.605 551	43	6.557 439
14	3.741 657	44	6.633 250
15	3.872 983	45	6.708 204
16	4.000 000	46	6.782 330
17	4.123 106	47	6.855 655
18	4.242 641	48	6.928 203
19	4.358 899	49	7.000 000
20	4.472 136	50	7.071 068
21	4.582 576	51	7.141 428
22	4.690 416	52	7.211 103
23	4.795 832	53	7.280 110
24	4.898 979	54	7.348 469
25	5.000 000	55	7.416 198
26	5.099 020	56	7.483 315
27	5.196 152	57	7.549 834
28	5.291 503	58	7.615 773
29	5.385 165	59	7.618 146

n	$\sqrt{n}$	n	$\sqrt{n}$	n	$\sqrt{n}$	n	$\sqrt{n}$	n	$\sqrt{n}$	n	$\sqrt{n}$
60	7.745 967	**100**	10.00000	**140**	11.83216	**180**	13.41641	**220**	14.83240	**260**	16.12452
61	7.810 250	101	10.04998	141	11.87434	181	13.45362	221	14.86607	261	16.15549
62	7.874 008	102	10.09950	142	11.91638	182	13.49074	222	14.89966	262	16.18641
63	7.937 254	103	10.14889	143	11.95826	183	13.52775	223	14.93318	263	16.21727
64	8.000 000	104	10.19804	144	12.00000	184	13.56466	224	14.96663	264	16.24808
65	8.062 258	105	10.24695	145	12.04159	185	13.60147	225	15.00000	265	16.27882
66	8.124 038	106	10.29563	146	12.08305	186	13.63818	226	15.03330	266	16.30951
67	8.185 353	107	10.34408	147	12.12436	187	13.67479	227	15.06652	267	16.34013
68	8.246 211	108	10.39230	148	12.16553	188	13.71131	228	15.09967	268	16.37071
69	8.306 624	109	10.44031	149	12.20656	189	13.74773	229	15.13275	269	16.40122
70	8.366 600	**110**	10.48809	**150**	12.24745	**190**	13.78405	**230**	15.16575	**270**	16.43168
71	8.426 150	111	10.53565	151	12.28821	191	13.82027	231	15.19868	271	16.46208
72	8.485 281	112	10.58301	152	12.32883	192	13.85641	232	15.23155	272	16.49242
73	8.544 004	113	10.63015	153	12.36932	193	13.89244	233	15.26434	273	16.52271
74	8.602 325	114	10.67708	154	12.40967	194	13.92839	234	15.29706	274	16.55295
75	8.660 254	115	10.72381	155	12.44990	195	13.96424	235	15.32971	275	16.58312
76	8.717 798	116	10.77033	156	12.49000	196	14.00000	236	15.36229	276	16.61235
77	8.774 964	117	10.81665	157	12.52996	197	14.03567	237	15.39480	277	16.64332
78	8.831 761	118	10.86278	158	12.56981	198	14.07125	238	15.42725	278	16.67333
79	8.888 194	119	10.90871	159	12.60952	199	14.10674	239	15.45962	279	16.70329
80	8.944 272	**120**	10.95445	**160**	12.64911	**200**	14.14214	**240**	15.49193	**280**	16.73320
81	9.000 000	121	11.00000	161	12.68858	201	14.17745	241	15.52417	281	16.76305
82	9.055 385	122	11.04536	162	12.72792	202	14.21267	242	15.55635	282	16.79286
83	9.110 434	123	11.09054	163	12.76715	203	14.24781	243	15.58846	283	16.82260
84	9.165 151	124	11.13553	164	12.80625	204	14.28286	244	15.62050	284	16.85230
85	9.219 544	125	11.18034	165	12.84523	205	14.31782	245	15.65248	285	16.88194
86	9.273 618	126	11.22497	166	12.88410	206	14.35270	246	15.68439	286	16.91153
87	9.327 379	127	11.26943	167	12.92285	207	14.38749	247	15.71623	287	16.94107
88	9.380 832	128	11.31371	168	12.96148	208	14.42221	248	15.74902	288	16.97056
89	9.433 981	129	11.35782	169	13.00000	209	14.45683	249	15.77973	289	17.00000
90	9.486 833	**130**	11.40175	**170**	13.03840	**210**	14.49138	**250**	15.81139	**290**	17.02939
91	9.539 392	131	11.44552	171	13.07670	211	14.52584	251	15.84298	291	17.05872
92	9.591 663	132	11.48913	172	13.11488	212	14.56022	252	15.87451	292	17.08801
93	9.643 651	133	11.53256	173	13.15295	213	14.59452	253	15.90597	293	17.11724
94	9.695 360	134	11.57584	174	13.19091	214	14.62874	254	15.93738	294	17.14643
95	9.746 794	135	11.61895	175	13.22876	215	14.66288	255	15.96872	295	17.17556
96	9.797 959	136	11.66190	176	13.26650	216	14.69694	256	16.00000	296	17.20465
97	9.848 858	137	11.70470	177	13.30413	217	14.73092	257	16.03122	297	17.23369
98	9.899 495	138	11.74734	178	13.34166	218	14.76482	258	16.06238	298	17.26268
99	9.949 874	139	11.78983	179	13.37909	219	14.79865	259	16.09348	299	17.29162

n	$\sqrt{n}$	n	$\sqrt{n}$	n	$\sqrt{n}$	n	$\sqrt{n}$	n	$\sqrt{n}$	n	$\sqrt{n}$
300	17.32051	340	18.43909	380	19.49359	420	20.49390	460	21.44761	500	22.36068
301	17.34935	341	18.46619	381	19.51922	421	20.51828	461	21.47091	501	22.38303
302	17.37815	342	18.49324	382	19.54482	422	20.54264	462	21.49419	502	22.40536
303	17.40690	343	18.52026	383	19.57039	423	20.56696	463	21.51743	503	22.42766
304	17.43560	344	18.54724	384	19.59592	424	20.59126	464	21.54066	504	22.44994
305	17.46425	345	18.57418	385	19.62142	425	20.61553	465	21.56386	505	22.47221
306	17.49286	346	18.60108	386	19.64688	426	20.63977	466	21.58703	506	22.49444
307	17.52142	347	18.62794	387	19.67232	427	20.66398	467	21.61018	507	22.51666
308	17.54993	348	18.65476	388	19.69772	428	20.68816	468	21.63331	508	22.53886
309	17.57840	349	18.68154	389	19.72308	429	20.71232	469	21.65641	509	22.56103
310	17.60682	350	18.70829	390	19.74842	430	20.73644	470	21.67948	510	22.58318
311	17.63519	351	18.73499	391	19.77372	431	20.76054	471	21.70253	511	22.60531
312	17.66352	352	18.76166	392	19.79899	432	20.78461	472	21.72556	512	22.62742
313	17.69181	353	18.78829	393	19.82423	433	20.80865	473	21.74856	513	22.64950
314	17.72005	354	18.81489	394	19.84943	434	20.83267	474	21.77154	514	22.67157
315	17.74824	355	18.84144	395	19.87461	435	20.85665	475	21.79449	515	22.69361
316	17.77639	356	18.86796	396	19.89975	436	20.88061	476	21.81742	516	22.71563
317	17.80449	357	18.89444	397	19.92486	437	20.90454	477	21.84033	517	22.73763
318	17.83255	358	18.92089	398	19.94994	438	20.92845	478	21.86321	518	22.75961
319	17.86057	359	18.94730	399	19.97498	439	20.95233	479	21.88607	519	22.78157
320	17.88854	360	18.97367	400	20.00000	440	20.97618	480	21.90890	520	22.80351
321	17.91647	361	19.00000	401	20.02498	441	21.00000	481	21.93171	521	22.82542
322	17.94436	362	19.02630	402	20.04994	442	21.02380	482	21.95450	522	22.84732
323	17.97220	363	19.05256	403	20.07486	443	21.04757	483	21.97726	523	22.86919
324	18.00000	364	19.07878	404	20.09975	444	21.07131	484	22.00000	524	22.89105
325	18.02776	365	19.10497	405	20.12461	445	21.09502	485	22.02272	525	22.91288
326	18.05547	366	19.13113	406	20.14944	446	21.11871	486	22.04541	526	22.93469
327	18.08314	367	19.15724	407	20.17424	447	21.14237	487	22.06808	527	22.95648
328	18.11077	368	19.18333	408	20.19901	448	21.16601	488	22.09072	528	22.97825
329	18.13836	369	19.20937	409	20.22375	449	21.18962	489	22.11334	529	23.00000
330	18.16590	370	19.23538	410	20.24864	450	21.21320	490	22.13594	530	23.02173
331	18.19341	371	19.26136	411	20.27313	451	21.23676	491	22.15852	531	23.04344
332	18.22087	372	19.28730	412	20.29778	452	21.26029	492	22.18107	532	23.06513
333	18.24829	373	19.31321	413	20.32240	453	21.28380	493	22.20360	533	23.08679
334	18.27567	374	19.33908	414	20.34699	454	21.30728	494	22.22611	534	23.10844
335	18.30301	375	19.36492	415	20.37155	455	21.33073	495	22.24860	535	23.13007
336	18.33030	376	19.39072	416	20.39608	456	21.35416	496	22.27106	536	23.15167
337	18.35756	377	19.41649	417	20.42058	457	21.37756	497	22.29350	537	23.17326
338	18.38478	378	19.44222	418	20.44505	458	21.40093	498	22.31591	538	23.19483
339	18.41195	379	19.46792	419	20.46949	459	21.42429	499	22.33831	539	23.21637

n	$\sqrt{n}$	n	$\sqrt{n}$	n	$\sqrt{n}$	n	$\sqrt{n}$	n	$\sqrt{n}$	n	$\sqrt{n}$
540	23.23790	580	24.08319	620	24.89980	660	25.69047	700	26.45751	740	27.20294
541	23.25941	581	24.10394	621	24.91987	661	25.70992	701	26.47640	741	27.22132
542	23.28089	582	24.12468	622	24.93993	662	25.72936	702	26.49528	742	27.23968
543	23.30236	583	24.14539	623	24.95997	663	25.74879	703	26.51415	743	27.25803
544	23.32381	584	24.16609	624	24.97999	664	25.76820	704	26.53300	744	27.27636
545	23.34524	585	24.18677	625	25.00000	665	25.78759	705	26.55184	745	27.29469
546	23.36664	586	24.20744	626	25.01999	666	25.80698	706	26.57066	746	27.31300
547	23.38803	587	24.22808	627	25.03997	667	25.82634	707	26.58947	747	27.33130
548	23.40940	588	24.24871	628	25.05993	668	25.84570	708	26.60827	748	27.34959
549	23.43075	589	24.26932	629	25.07987	669	25.86503	709	26.62705	749	27.36786
550	23.45208	590	24.28992	630	25.09980	670	25.88436	710	26.64583	750	27.38613
551	23.47339	591	24.31049	631	25.11971	671	25.90367	711	26.66458	751	27.40438
552	23.49468	592	24.33105	632	25.13961	672	25.92296	712	26.68333	752	27.42262
553	23.51595	593	24.35159	633	25.15949	673	25.94224	713	26.70206	753	27.44085
554	23.53720	594	24.37212	634	25.17936	674	25.96151	714	26.72078	754	27.45906
555	23.55844	595	24.39262	635	25.19921	675	25.98076	715	26.73948	755	27.47726
556	23.57965	596	24.41311	636	25.21904	676	26.00000	716	26.75818	756	27.49545
557	23.60085	597	24.43358	637	25.23886	677	26.01922	717	26.77686	757	27.51363
558	23.62202	598	24.45404	638	25.25866	678	26.03843	718	26.79552	758	27.53180
559	23.64318	599	24.47448	639	25.27845	679	26.05763	719	26.81418	759	27.54995
560	23.66432	600	24.49490	640	25.29822	680	26.07681	720	26.83282	760	27.56810
561	23.68544	601	24.51530	641	25.31798	681	26.09598	721	26.85144	761	27.58623
562	23.70654	602	24.53569	642	25.33772	682	26.11513	722	26.87006	762	27.60435
563	23.72762	603	24.55606	643	25.35744	683	26.13427	723	26.88866	763	27.62245
564	23.74868	604	24.57641	644	25.37716	684	26.15339	724	26.90725	764	27.64055
565	23.76973	605	24.59675	645	25.39685	685	26.17250	725	26.92582	765	27.65863
566	23.79075	606	24.61707	646	25.41653	686	26.19160	726	26.94439	766	27.67671
567	23.81176	607	24.63737	647	25.43619	687	26.21068	727	26.96294	767	27.69476
568	23.83275	608	24.65766	648	25.45584	688	26.22975	728	26.98148	768	27.71281
569	23.85372	609	24.67793	649	25.47548	689	26.24881	729	27.00000	769	27.73085
570	23.87467	610	24.69818	650	25.49510	690	26.26785	730	27.01851	770	27.74887
571	23.89561	611	24.71841	651	25.51470	691	26.28688	731	27.03701	771	27.76689
572	23.91652	612	24.73863	652	25.53429	692	26.30589	732	27.05550	772	27.78489
573	23.93742	613	24.75884	653	25.55386	693	26.32489	733	27.07397	773	27.80288
574	23.95830	614	24.77902	654	25.57342	694	26.34388	734	27.09243	774	27.82086
575	23.97916	615	24.79919	655	25.59297	695	26.36285	735	27.11088	775	27.83882
576	24.00000	616	24.81935	656	25.61250	696	26.38181	736	27.12932	776	27.85678
577	24.02082	617	24.83948	657	25.63201	697	26.40076	737	27.14774	777	27.87472
578	24.04163	618	24.85961	658	25.65151	698	26.41969	738	27.16616	778	27.89265
579	24.06242	619	24.87971	659	25.67100	699	26.43861	739	27.18455	779	27.91057

n	$\sqrt{n}$	n	$\sqrt{n}$	n	$\sqrt{n}$	n	$\sqrt{n}$	n	$\sqrt{n}$	n	$\sqrt{n}$
780	27.92848	**820**	28.63564	**860**	29.32576	**900**	30.00000	**940**	30.65942	**970**	31.14482
781	27.94638	821	28.65310	861	29.34280	901	30.01666	941	30.67572	971	31.16087
782	27.96426	822	28.67054	862	29.35984	902	30.03331	942	30.69202	972	31.17691
783	27.98214	823	28.68798	863	29.37686	903	30.04996	943	30.70831	973	31.19295
784	28.00000	824	28.70540	864	29.39388	904	30.06659	944	30.72458	974	31.20897
785	28.01785	825	28.72281	865	29.41088	905	30.08322	945	30.74085	975	31.22499
786	28.03569	826	28.74022	866	29.42788	906	30.09983	946	30.75711	976	31.24100
787	28.05352	827	28.75761	867	29.44486	907	30.11644	947	30.77337	977	31.25700
788	28.07134	828	28.77499	868	29.46184	908	30.13304	948	30.78961	978	31.27299
789	28.08914	829	28.79236	869	29.47881	909	30.14963	949	30.80584	979	31.28898
790	28.10694	**830**	28.80972	**870**	29.49576	**910**	30.16621	**950**	30.82207	**980**	31.30495
791	28.12472	831	28.82707	871	29.51271	911	30.18278	951	30.83829	981	31.32092
792	28.14249	832	28.84441	872	29.52965	912	30.19934	952	30.85450	982	31.33688
793	28.16026	833	28.86174	873	29.54657	913	30.21589	953	30.87070	983	31.35283
794	28.17801	834	28.87906	874	29.56349	914	30.23243	954	30.88689	984	31.36877
795	28.19574	835	28.89637	875	29.58040	915	30.24897	955	30.90307	985	31.38471
796	28.21347	836	28.91366	876	29.59730	916	30.26549	956	30.91925	986	31.40064
797	28.23119	837	28.93095	877	29.61419	917	30.28201	957	30.93542	987	31.41656
798	28.24889	838	28.94823	878	29.63106	918	30.29851	958	30.95158	988	31.43247
799	28.26659	839	28.96550	879	29.64793	919	30.31501	959	30.96773	989	31.44837
800	28.28472	**840**	28.98275	**880**	29.66479	**920**	30.33150	**960**	30.98387	**990**	31.46427
801	28.30194	841	29.00000	881	29.68164	921	30.34798	961	31.00000	991	31.48015
802	28.31960	842	29.01724	882	29.69848	922	30.36445	962	31.01612	992	31.49603
803	28.33725	843	29.03446	883	29.71532	923	30.38092	963	31.03224	993	31.51190
804	28.35489	844	29.05168	884	29.73214	924	30.39737	964	31.04835	994	31.52777
805	28.37252	845	29.06888	885	29.74895	925	30.41381	965	31.06445	995	31.54362
806	28.39014	846	29.08608	886	29.76575	926	30.43025	966	31.08054	996	31.55947
807	28.40775	847	29.10326	887	29.78255	927	30.44667	967	31.09662	997	31.57531
808	28.42534	848	29.12044	888	29.79933	928	30.46309	968	31.11270	998	31.59114
809	28.44293	849	29.13760	889	29.81610	929	30.47950	969	31.12876	999	31.60696
810	28.46050	**850**	29.15476	**890**	29.83287	**930**	30.49590			**1000**	31.62278
811	28.47806	851	29.17190	891	29.84962	931	30.51229				
812	28.49561	852	29.18904	892	29.86637	932	30.52868				
813	28.51315	853	29.20616	893	29.88311	933	30.54505				
814	28.53069	854	29.22328	894	29.89983	934	30.56141				
815	28.54820	855	29.24038	895	29.91655	935	30.57777				
816	28.56571	856	29.25748	896	29.93326	936	30.59412				
817	28.58321	857	29.27456	897	29.94996	937	30.61046				
818	28.60070	858	29.29164	898	29.96665	938	30.62679				
819	28.61818	859	29.30870	899	29.98333	939	30.64311				

Appendix H

A Student's Guide to SPSS

**Prepared by Gary Kazuo Sakihara
and James E. Dannemiller**

INTRODUCTION

This appendix is designed to be of use in courses that involve the actual processing of survey data along with classroom lectures. It provides a set of instructions and illustrations that assist in translating the textual discussion into a hands-on data processing experience. We have chosen to use the Statistical Package for the Social Sciences (SPSS)[1] to demonstrate how even the novice can use a computer to get analysis done. This package of statistical routines is probably the most widely available data manipulation system on college campuses today. It contains nearly all of the routines necessary to accomplish the research tasks covered in this book and is a suitable package for the beginning researcher as well as the more seasoned veteran.

The appendix has been designed to present the SPSS material in a manner parallel to the text. To facilitate its use even further, we have provided references to textual sections throughout the appendix. In many cases, we also present specific references to the SPSS manual, which covers the techniques in even greater detail. Note that we will present only those SPSS features that are directly relevant to the text. The package contains more extensive and intensive treatment of many useful data processing procedures than will be presented here.

As a source of examples for the appendix, the dataset collected in the survey covered in Chapter 12 (see Figure 12-7) has been used. That will allow for even greater continuity between text and appendix, as well as providing a focus for our presentation. In following the text rather than the technical format of the SPSS manual, we are able to present the computer-use aspect of research in the chronological order in which it would actually occur in a research project.

[1]Norman H. Nie, C. Hadlai Hull, Jean G. Jenkins, Karin Steinbrenner, and Dale H. Bent, *Statistical Package for the Social Sciences*, 2d ed. (New York: McGraw-Hill, 1975).

SETTING UP YOUR DATA

The rationale and schematic for initial data processing is presented in Chapter 13. Having collected the data illustrated in Figure 12-7, edited and coded the survey forms, and completed the keypunching and verification, we now have a set of punched cards that we can use for our data analysis. Specifically, we have 480 cases, and for each one of those cases, we have six punched cards. The card deck is arranged in this order: case 1 card 1; case 1 card 2; case 1 card 3; case 1 card 4; case 1 card 5; case 1 card 6; case 2 card 1; case 2 card 2; and so forth.

Job Control Language

Every computer job begins and ends with a set of cards written in what is known as job control language (JCL).[2] These cards serve to turn the computer on, describe the nature of your job to the machine, do some accounting of time and money, and perform many other functions. The JCL at nearly every computer center is different. Even for installations using the same machine, certain parts of these beginning and ending cards will be different. For this reason, we do not cover JCL in this appendix. Our advice is to seek out someone at your installation who is familiar with JCL and ask him for assistance. The SPSS manual has some information on the topic,[3] and the operator or user consultant at your computer center will also be helpful.

How SPSS Works

The construction of an SPSS computer run is really quite simple. Just list the steps of the job in order and submit the list. Each step is described on one or more cards and is made up of two parts, the *command* and the *argument*. All commands are written in columns 1 through 15 of a punched card, always beginning in column 1. All arguments begin in column 16 and continue for as many columns as necessary. You may use all columns between 16 and 80. If the argument takes more than 64 columns, just start on another card, but be sure to begin in column 16. Do not repeat the command on this second card.

File Descriptors

SPSS has a number of control cards that define the data file and are used with the program. Below is a list of the various control words and a short description of their functions.

[2]Gary Deward Brown, *System 370 Job Control Language* (New York: John Wiley, 1977).
[3]See Nie *et al., op. cit.,* pp. 585–630.

1. *RUN NAME*   This control word provides a header label at the top of each page of printed output.

2. *FILE NAME*   This control word labels the SPSS file. It is necessary when creating a permanent file through the SAVE FILE card and is also necessary if you intend to SAVE FILE.

3. *DATA LIST*   This control word specifies the name and the position of the variables that make up the file and is a necessary part of the file definition.

4. *OF CASES*   This control word specifies the number of cases that make up the data file. The specification field contains the number of cases, or the user may simply specify UNKNOWN as the argument.

5. *INPUT MEDIUM*   This control word specifies the type of device on which your data is stored, such as CARD, TAPE, or DISK.

6. *READ INPUT DATA*   This command has no argument and is placed in the deck after the first procedure. It signals the computer that your file and variables have been defined and it can begin to read in the data. If your INPUT MEDIUM is CARD the data is placed following this command.

7. *FINISH*   This control word specifies that you have finished. It is the last control card in the file.

Specifications for File Definition   The specification for the above control words is quite simple and in most cases quite reasonable. This section will diagram the specifications for these cards.

```
1                16
RUN NAME         RUN LABEL OF UP TO 64 CHARACTERS


1                16
FILE NAME        ALPHANUMBER LABEL OF UP TO 8 CHARACTERS


1                16
                 DISK
INPUT MEDIUM     CARD - MUST BE ONE OF THESE THREE
                 TAPE


1                16
N OF CASES       NUMBER OF CASES OR UNKNOWN


1             16
READ INPUT DATA NO ARGUMENT


1                16
FINISH           NO ARGUMENT
```

The remaining two control words have somewhat more complex specifications and will be dealt with in more detail.

```
1                16
DATA LIST        (DATA TYPE)/(NUMBER OF RECORDS) (RECORD NUMBER) NAME POSITION
                 NAME POSITION/(RECORD NUMBER) NAME POSITION . . .
```

1. Data type—may be either fixed or binary. In social research it will usually be specified as FIXED.

2. No. of records — the number of cards per case in the data file.

3. Record No.—the card on which the variable to be specified resides. Name position—each variable in the file is given avariable name and the columns in which the variable information has been punched are listed.

If we had a hypothetical file with four variables—age, sex, class, and ethnicity— age would be in columns 4 and 5 of the first card; sex in column 65 of the third card; class in column 66 of the third card; and ethnicity in column 6 of the fourth card. The data list specification for these four variables would look like the following:

```
1                16
DATA LIST        FIXED/4 1 AGE 4-5/3 SEX 65 CLASS 66/4 ETHN 6
```

Variable Descriptors

Every variable in the SPSS dataset is described by at least three descriptors: the VARIABLE NAME, the VARIABLE LABEL, and the VALUE LABEL. The VARIABLE NAME has already been defined by our DATA LIST card above. But tables produced with variables named Q1a and having values of 1, 2, 3, . . . , 7 will not be too easy to read. Thus we may want to attach some more information to the SPSS variables to make them easier to handle later on. We do that with the aid of the following cards:

VAR LABELS   The format of the VAR LABELS card is:

```
1                16
VAR LABELS       VAR NAME,VAR LABEL/VAR NAME,VAR LABEL/...
```

And an example taken from our dataset would look like this:

```
VAR LABELS      Q1A, U.N. SHOULD BECOME WORLD GOVERNMENT/
                Q1B, FLAG DEFILERS SHOULD BE JAILED/
                Q1C, U.S. SEES COMMUNIST NATIONS AS A THREAT
```

That's simple enough. The VAR LABELS card is used to attach a variable label up to 40 spaces long to a variable name assigned in the DATA LIST card. You can use all numbers or letters and special characters except the comma, slash, and parentheses.

VALUE LABELS   The format of the VALUE LABELS card looks like this:

```
1               16
VALUE LABELS    VARIABLE NAME  (VALUE) VALUE LABEL (VALUE) VALUE LABEL...
```

And an example from our dataset might look like this:

```
VALUE LABELS    Q1A (1)STRONGLY AGREE (2)AGREE (3)DISAGREE
                (4)STRONGLY DISAGREE (5)DONT KNOW/
```

If we have a lot of variables in a row that have the same value labels, the "TO" convention may be used as follows:

```
        VALUE LABELS  Q1A  TO  Q1J (1)STRONGLY AGREE
  (2)AGREE (3)DISAGREE (4)STRONGLY DISAGREE (5)DONT KNOW/
```

Again, simple enough. The VALUE LABELS command is used to attach a label of up to 20 spaces to a specific value of a variable defined in the DATA LIST card. You can use all characters except the slash and parentheses.

Tasks and Procedures

Once we have our JCL taken care of and have described both our data file and each of our variables in SPSS terms, we need only to instruct the computer to do our work for us. We do that in two ways, by describing TASKS—which tell the computer to manipulate or transform our data in some way—and by describing PROCEDURES—which tell the computer to calculate some statistics for us.

The TASKS that we have selected from the SPSS manual for use in this appendix are RECORD, COMPUTE, and LIST FILEINFO. The PROCEDURES are FREQUENCIES, CROSSTABS, GUTTMAN, CONDESCRIPTIVE, and PEARSON CORR. In general, remember that TASKS must all come before PROCEDURES and that one PROCEDURE and only one must come before the READ INPUT DATA card. The SPSS manual describes some instances in which certain tasks may be starred (*) and thus be usable after PROCEDURES. We will not deal with this case here.

First Run: Simple Frequencies   Now, let's put this information together by using the HEAP dataset as an example. The following figure lists the actual setup for the data that we have used. The specific procedure that we will place before the READ INPUT DATA card is a call for simple frequencies. That should be the first run on any dataset should be run. It serves to check out the setup and take a first look at the data, preparatory to data cleaning.

```
            DATA SETUP FOR THE HEAP DATA

    OPENING JCL CARDS GO HERE

    RUN NAME          SETUP FOR THE HEAP DATA
    FILE NAME         HEAP
    DATA LIST         FIXED(6)/1 Q1A,Q1B,Q1C,Q1D,Q1E,Q1F,Q1G,Q1H,Q1I,
                      Q1J,Q2A,Q2B,Q2C,Q2D,Q2E,Q2F,Q2G,Q2H,Q2I,Q2J 2-25
                      /6 DEMO1 59 DEMO2 60-61 DEMO3 62 DEMO4,DEMO4A
                      DEMO 4B 63-65 DEMO 6 68 DEMO7 69 DEMO8 72 DEMO9A,
                      DEMO 9B 73-74 DEMO10,DEMO11,DEMO12 75-77
    INPUT MEDIUM      TAPE
    N OF CASES        UNKNOWN
    ----------
    VAR LABELS        Q1A,U.N. SHOULD BECOME WORLD GOVERNMENT/
                      Q1B,FLAG DEFILERS SHOULD BE JAILED/
                      Q1C,U.S. SEES COMMUNIST NATIONS AS A THREAT/
                      +
                      +
                      DEMO11,FATHER'S OCCUPATIONAL STATUS/
                      DEMO12,PARENT'S FAMILY INCOME
```

```
VALUE LABELS      Q1A TO Q1J (1)STRONGLY AGREE (2)AGREE
                  (3)DISAGREE (4)STRONGLY DISAGREE (5)DONT KNOW/
                  Q2A TO Q2J (1)AGREE (2)DISAGREE (3)DONT KNOW/
                  +
                  +
                  DEMO12 (1)LESS THAN $3,000 (2)$3,000-$5,000
                  (3)$5,000-$7,500 (4)$7,500-$9,999 (5)$10,000-$14,999
                  (6)$15,000-$19,999 (7)$20,000-$24,999
                  (8)$25,000-$50,000 (9)MORE THAN $50,000
FREQUENCIES       GENERAL=ALL
READ INPUT DATA
FINISH
 FINAL JCL GOES HERE
```

CLEANING DATA (SEE CHAPTER 13)

The computer printout that resulted from the SPSS run described in the previous section provided simple frequency distributions for all the variables in the HEAP dataset. Upon inspection, we found some problems. For instance, the frequency distribution for Q2F, the item on invasion of North Vietnam, contained two 4's. Now 4 is not a legitimate code for Q2F, but the survey forms were not available to us, so we couldn't correct these errors. At the same time, we did not want them cluttering up our analysis, so we made the decision to wipe them out. We did that with the SPSS feature called RECODE.

```
        1               16
        RECODE          Q2F (4=0)
```

If we leave this card in the setup, we won't be bothered by those 4's any more.

In general, the RECODE card can be used to change any value or set of values for some variable equal to any other value. The general format is simply to write the RECODE command, then the ARGUMENTS, which are the names of the variable or variables to be recoded and the changes to be made. Changes are enclosed in parentheses and take the form "old value(s) = new value(s)."

On all of the survey items, there were some blanks in the data. We know that these represent nonresponse, since no legitimate zero codes were used in the survey. Besides, we know that SPSS reads blanks as zeros. That will cause problems for you if on some items you have both legitimate zero codes and blanks for nonresponse. (SPSS does have a solution for this problem.) But in our case, we realized that at a later point in our analysis we'd like to be able to get rid of those zeros. SPSS provides a standard method of handling this situation in its ability to define MISSING VALUES. It's a TASK card and must precede the first procedure. We used it like this:

```
1                    16
MISSING VALUES Q1A TO DEMO10 (0)
```

Now, with these zeros marked, we can choose to either include them or exclude them in any further analysis.

One last item that we included in our data cleaning operation was the SPSS ability to generate an automatic codebook for us. After inserting the Q2F RECODE card and the MISSING VALUES card right before the first procedure, we inserted this card after the READ INPUT DATA card:

```
1                  16
LIST FILEINFO  COMPLETE
```

This command will produce a complete description of the data file that results from SPSS. For each variable, it will list the variable name, variable label, all value labels, missing values, and several other pieces of information. We saved this last run, because the combination of the frequencies and the LIST FILEINFO codebook provides the most complete data description that we could ask for.

ELEMENTARY ANALYSIS (SEE CHAPTER 14)

Univariate Analysis (See section on Univariate Analysis, Chapter 14)

Most of our univariate analysis is actually completed with the FREQUENCIES in the initial run. Thus that printout will support any single-variable analysis that we could do.

Frequency Distribution   About the only thing we would have to do to complete some univariate analysis of this file is to use some of the options attached to the SPSS FREQUENCIES card. Let's say we wanted to do more extensive univariate work with the first set of political items. In particular, we'd like to calculate the mean, median, mode, range, and standard deviation around the mean for each of those items. We could just substitute the following setup for the FREQUENCIES card we used before. (By the way, don't forget to remove the LIST FILEINFO card unless you want another copy of it.

```
1              16
FREQUENCIES    GENERAL=Q1A TO Q1J
OPTIONS        7
STATISTICS     1,3,4,5,9
```

The OPTIONS card above specifies option 7, which causes the actual frequency distributions to be eliminated from the output—we have them in the previous run. This way only the statistics will be printed. The STATISTICS card specifies statistics 1, 3, 4, 5, and 9, which are the mean, median, mode, standard deviation, and range. We could have gotten the minimum value by specifying a 10 and the maximum value by specifying an 11.

Condescriptive   We should add one more thing. Some frequency distributions on interval-level variables may be excessively long. In such cases, the frequency distribution itself is often superfluous. SPSS provides a special procedure for such cases called CONDESCRIPTIVE. To see how it might be used, suppose that we had collected family income in dollar amounts rather than by ranges. Then we might use the following:

```
1                   16
CONDESCRIPTIVE INCOME
```

That would produce, for the data on income, the mean, standard error, standard deviation around the mean, the variance, kurtosis, skewness, range, and minimum and maximum values of the distribution. We advise using it sparingly and only for variables with a very large range.

Bivariate Analysis

The section of Chapter 14 on bivariate analysis introduces the researcher to the core issue in social science research—the relationship between one variable and another. Chapter 17 on the elaboration model carries this form of analysis much further, and other sections on multivariate analysis simply project these principles into the arena of relationships among larger numbers of variables. In the same sense that it is necessary to master the principles of bivariate analysis before proceeding either to the elaboration model or to multivariate analysis, it is also necessary to master the basic SPSS cross-tabulation before proceeding to more complex methods.

Two-Way Cross-tabulation *Basic Mechanics* The basic principles of cross-tabulation are quite simple. We simply invoke the CROSSTABS command, and name our two variables, separated by the word "BY," as the arguments in a TABLES = card:

```
1                16
CROSSTABS        TABLES=VARIABLE BY VARIABLE/
```

Setting Groups and Defining Variables The rules for table construction given on p. 385 specify that you must first define groups of responses in terms of the two variables to be cross-tabulated. In SPSS, we can do this in two ways: by using the RECODE card or by using the VARIABLE= argument card. As an example, let's suppose that we are interested in the relationship between family income and support of the concept of world government. We could produce a simple table like the following:

```
1                16
CROSSTABS        TABLES=Q1A BY DEMO 12/
```

This command would produce the table shown on page 557.

But this command would produce a table that has 7 rows and 11 columns. The 7 rows result from the 5 legitimate answer categories for Q1A, plus a No Data row and a total row. The 11 columns result from the 9 legitimate answer categories for the income question (DEMO12), plus a No Data column and a total column. Such a table may be useful in the early stages of analysis, but it is not the type of table that will be useful throughout the text.

To get a more useful table, let's say that the researcher wishes to dichotomize the item on turning the United Nations into a world government as just those who agree (strongly or not) versus those who disagree (strongly or not). The income item is to be dichotomized at $20,000 of annual parental income. Then we might write the following:

```
1                16
RECODE           Q1A (1,2=1) (3,4=2) (ELSE=3)
VALUE LABELS     Q1A (1)AGREE (2)DISAGREE (3)DK OR ND
RECODE           DEMO12 (1 THRU 6=1) (7,8,9=2) (ELSE=3)
VALUE LABELS     DEMO12 (1)LESS THAN $20,000 (2)$20,000 OR
                 MORE (3)NO DATA
CROSSTABS        TABLES=Q1A BY DEMO12
```

DEMO12

QIA

Cell contents: COUNT / ROW PCT / COL PCT / TOT PCT

QIA		0.	LESS THAN $3,000 (1)	$3,000–$5,000 (2)	$5,000–$7,500 (3)	$7,500–$10,000 (4)	$10,000–$15,000 (5)	$15,000–$20,000 (6)	$20,000–$25,000 (7)	$25,000–$50,000 (8)	MORE THAN $50,000 (9)	ROW TOTAL
0.	COUNT	0	0	1	0	0	1	0	0	0	0	2
	ROW PCT	0.0	0.0	50.0	0.0	0.0	50.0	0.0	0.0	0.0	0.0	0.4
	COL PCT	0.0	0.0	3.0	0.0	0.0	0.7	0.0	0.0	0.0	0.0	
	TOT PCT	0.0	0.0	0.2	0.0	0.0	0.2	0.0	0.0	0.0	0.0	
1. STRONGLY AGREE	COUNT	6	4	4	8	8	23	7	2	2	1	65
	ROW PCT	9.2	6.2	6.2	12.3	12.3	35.4	10.8	3.1	3.1	1.5	13.5
	COL PCT	16.7	23.5	12.1	11.0	8.8	16.7	13.7	8.7	18.2	14.3	
	TOT PCT	1.3	0.8	0.8	1.7	1.7	4.8	1.5	0.4	0.4	0.2	
2. AGREE	COUNT	14	7	8	24	40	48	16	10	6	3	176
	ROW PCT	8.0	4.0	4.5	13.6	22.7	27.3	9.1	5.7	3.4	1.7	36.7
	COL PCT	38.9	41.2	24.2	32.9	44.0	34.8	31.4	43.5	54.5	42.9	
	TOT PCT	2.9	1.5	1.7	5.0	8.3	10.0	3.3	2.1	1.3	0.6	
3. DISAGREE	COUNT	10	5	10	25	28	39	16	8	1	2	144
	ROW PCT	6.9	3.5	6.9	17.4	19.4	27.1	11.1	5.6	0.7	1.4	30.0
	COL PCT	27.8	29.4	30.3	34.2	30.8	28.3	31.4	34.8	9.1	28.6	
	TOT PCT	2.1	1.0	2.1	5.2	5.8	8.1	3.3	1.7	0.2	0.4	
4. STRONGLY DISAGREE	COUNT	3	0	3	14	10	18	6	2	2	1	59
	ROW PCT	5.1	0.0	5.1	23.7	16.9	30.5	10.2	3.4	3.4	1.7	12.3
	COL PCT	8.3	0.0	9.1	19.2	11.0	13.0	11.8	8.7	18.2	14.3	
	TOT PCT	0.6	0.0	0.6	2.9	2.1	3.8	1.3	0.4	0.4	0.2	
5. DON'T KNOW	COUNT	3	1	7	2	5	9	6	1	0	0	34
	ROW PCT	8.8	2.9	20.6	5.9	14.7	26.5	17.6	2.9	0.0	0.0	7.1
	COL PCT	8.3	5.9	21.2	2.7	5.5	6.5	11.8	4.3	0.0	0.0	
	TOT PCT	0.6	0.2	1.5	0.4	1.0	1.9	1.3	0.2	0.0	0.0	
COLUMN TOTAL		36	17	33	73	91	138	51	23	11	7	480
		7.5	3.5	6.9	15.2	19.0	28.8	10.6	4.8	2.3	1.5	100.0

The above cards, placed immediately before the READ INPUT DATA card will produce a table with 4 rows and 4 columns. It will look like this:

```
                        DEMO12
             COUNT  I
             ROW PCT ILESS THA $20,000   NO DATA
             COL PCT IN $20,00 OR MORE              TOTAL
             TOT PCT I        1.I        2.I        3.I
     Q1A     --------I--------I--------I--------I
             1.  I    197  I     24  I     20  I   241
     AGREE       I   81.7  I   10.0  I    8.3  I  50.2
                 I   48.9  I   58.5  I   55.6  I
                 I   41.0  I    5.0  I    4.2  I
             -I--------I--------I--------I--------I
             2.  I    174  I     16  I     13  I   203
     DISAGREE    I   85.7  I    7.9  I    6.4  I  42.3
                 I   43.2  I   39.0  I   36.1  I
                 I   36.3  I    3.3  I    2.7  I
             -I--------I--------I--------I--------I
             3.  I     32  I      1  I      3  I    36
     DK OR ND    I   88.9  I    2.8  I    8.3  I   7.5
                 I    7.9  I    2.4  I    8.3  I
                 I    6.7  I    0.2  I    0.6  I
             -I--------I--------I--------I--------I
             COLUMN      403       41       36      480
             TOTAL      84.0      8.5      7.5    100.0
```

If we wish to use only those cases with complete data for our analysis, then we can screen out the 3's on both questions using the following application of the VARIABLES= card:

```
1                   16
CROSSTABS           VARIABLES=Q1A(1,2),DEMO12(1,2)/
                    TABLES=Q1A BY DEMO12/
OPTIONS             5
```

This command will produce a table that looks like the one on page 559.

Now let's see what we have done here. First, we used a RECODE card to choose the specific operationalization of our measurement of how much people favor world government. That is, on the question "Do you agree that the United Nations should be turned into a form of world government," we decided that agreement (the new 1) would be represented by either strong agreement or agreement on that item, and disagreement (the new 2) would be represented by either strong disagreement or dis-

```
                      DEMO 12
                  COUNT I
                  ROW PCT ILESS THA $20,000       ROW
                  COL PCT IN $20,000 OR MORE      TOTAL
                  TOT PCT I      1  I      2   I
         Q1A      --------I--------I--------I
                     1  I    197  I    24  I    221
         AGREE       I   89.1  I  10.9  I    53.8
                     I   53.1  I  60.0  I
                     I   47.9  I   5.8  I
                    -I--------I--------I
                     2  I    174  I    16  I    190
         DISAGREE    I   91.6  I   8.4  I    46.2
                     I   46.9  I  40.0  I
                     I   42.3  I   3.9  I
                    -I--------I--------I
                  COLUMN      371       40        411
                              90.3      9.7     100.0

      NUMBER OF MISSING OBSERVATIONS =    69
```

agreement. The people who answered that they weren't sure and those who did not answer the question at all were not coded as either agreeing or disagreeing. We then changed the VALUE LABELS on the variable to simple agreement or disagreement. If we hadn't, the value labels on the new table would have been those determined earlier in the run: 1=Strongly Agree and 2=Agree. We then set all the codes for family incomes below $20,000 per year to a 1, and all those codes for family incomes at or above $20,000 per year equal to a 2. People who answered that they did not know their family income and those who did not answer the question at all, were coded as 3. Again, the VALUE LABELS card was used to change the old labels. When we cross-tabulated these variables, we got a 4 by 4 table. If we use the VARIABLES= argument of the CROSSTABS card, we can screen out all the people who weren't sure of their answers or who did not answer at all. That gives us a table of the general type used in this text.

We note that perhaps the elimination of those who do not know their parents' income or those who aren't sure whether the U.N. should be turned into a world government may not be the best solution for some research problems. If that is the case, the RECODE and VARIABLES= cards may be used to accomplish any sort of classification desired.

Logic of Independent and Dependent Variables   The discussion on the logic of dependent and independent variables is a bit more difficult to interpret in SPSS terms (see p. 268). You will note in the tables produced thus far that three sets of percentages have been listed. Thus SPSS allows—in a single table—for the interpretation of either variable as the dependent variable. It also produces percentages by dividing each cell by the total number of cases in the table. If we wish to have our SPSS tables conform to the text format, we will have to learn to manipulate the TABLE card and the percentaging operations available for the CROSSTABS command. In the bivariate CROSSTABS command, you will note that the first variable (the one on the left of the BY feature) is listed down the side of the table. The second variable is listed across the top. We'd like to follow the text's convenient procedure of having the dependent variable printed at the top of tables and the independent variable listed down the side. That simply means that the dependent variable will have to appear *after* the BY feature of the TABLES= card.

In order to follow the rule of thumb of percentaging across the table, we will have to use option 4, which causes the column percentages to be deleted. Option 5 causes the total percentages to be deleted. Thus, to produce a table of the exact type described in Chapter 14 of this text, we would write:

```
1                   16
RECODE              Q1A (1,2=1) (3,4=2) (ELSE=3)
VALUE LABELS        Q1A (1)AGREE (2)DISAGREE (3)DK OR ND/
RECODE              DEMO12 (1 THRU 6=1) (7,8,9=2) (ELSE=3)
VALUE LABELS        DEMO12 (1)LESS THAN $20,000 (2)$20,000 OR MORE
                    (3)NO DATA/
CROSSTABS           VARIABLES=DEMO12(1,2),Q1A(1,2)/
                    TABLES=Q1A BY DEMO12/
OPTIONS             4,5
```

The commands and arguments listed above will produce the final result of our inquiry into the relationship between acceptance of world government and family income. The table will be in the familiar textual format and will look like this:

```
                              DEMO12
                    COUNT  I
                    ROW PCT IAGREE      DISAGREE     ROW
                    COL PCT I                        TOTAL
                    TOT PCT I      1  I      2  I
         Q1A        --------I--------I--------I
                      1  I    197  I    174  I      371
         LESS THAN $20,00 I   53.1  I   46.9  I     90.3
                    -I--------I--------I
                      2  I     24  I     16  I       40
         $20,000 OR MORE  I   60.2  I   40.0  I      9.7
                    -I--------I--------I
                    COLUMN        221        190        411
                                  53.8       46.2      100.0

         NUMBER OF MISSING OBSERVATIONS =     69
```

Multivariate Tables

The extension of the principles of table construction from the bivariate to the trivariate case is a complex task covered in Chapter 17 of this text. As we shall see, however, the extension of the SPSS CROSSTABS command to the trivariate (or greater) case is quite simple. Basically, we do this simply by stringing out our variables connected by the BY feature of the TABLES= card.

N-way Cross-tabulation   As an example, let's say that we have discovered a relationship between the opinion of our sample regarding the proposition that bombing in Vietnam should cease and the sex of the respondent. Specifically, we have found that males tend to disagree with this proposition and females tend to agree with it. Although this relationship is clear, we have the suspicion that family income may be a factor, or we may just want to see if the relationship holds for the wealthy as well as the less fortunate.

Setting Groups and Defining Variables   Looking back at our setup, we find that the bombing cessation item has been named Q2H, that family income is DEMO12, and that the sex of the respondent has been called DEMO1. We know that we should first recode the variables so that they represent the groupings we wish to analyze.

Logic of Independent, Dependent, and Control Variables   Following the logic outline in Chapter 17, we know that our dependent variable is the cessation of bombing item, the independent variable is gender, and the control variable is the family income item.

We have already seen that the first variable on the TABLES= card goes down the side of the table and the second variable is listed across the top of the table. Now note that a third variable in the TABLES= card will cause one table to be printed for each value of that third variable. Thus, if the third variable were sex, then three separate tables would be printed on three separate pages. The first table would include all those respondents coded 0, or no data. The second would include all males (code 1), and the final table would include all females (code 2). No total table would be printed.

To maintain the basic format suggested in the text, the proper order for variables to be entered on the TABLES= card is:

```
1              16
CROSSTABS      TABLES = INDEPENDENT BY DEPENDENT BY CONTROL/
```

As an example, we have found that 28 percent of the students who answered this questionnaire agreed that the United States should invade North Vietnam in order to solve the conflict there. About 19 percent felt that the Viet Cong were actually invaders in South Vietnam, and about 54 percent felt that the power of the United States was the only real force to combat world communism in its attempt to spread. The "invaders" question might indicate a tendency to support the little guy against injustice. The "world communism" questions might be used to measure the tendency to see the world situation—and the Vietnam conflict—in terms of the international struggle between communism and capitalism. It is our objective to identify the combined effect of these two factors in creating student willingness to invade North Vietnam.

Technically, we will consider the invasion of North Vietnam question (Q2E) as the dependent variable, the Viet Cong question (Q1G) as the independent variable, and the world communism item (Q1I) as our control variable. Then our table request would look like this:

```
1                16
RECODE           Q1I,Q1G (1,2=1) (3,4,5=2)
RECODE           Q2E (1=1) (2,3=2)
VALUE LABELS     Q1I,Q1G,Q2E (1)AGREE (2)DISAGREE/
CROSSTABS        VARIABLES=Q1I,Q1G,Q2E(1,2)/
                 TABLES=Q1G BY Q2E BY Q1I/
                 Q1G BY Q2E
OPTIONS          4,5
```

This request will produce a set of three tables that look like these:

```
* * * * * * * * * * * * * * * * *  C R O S S T A B U L A T I O N   O F  * * * * * * * * * * * * *
   Q1G        VIET CONG ARE INVADERS                     BY  Q2E       INVADE NORTH VIETNAM BY U.S.
CONTROLLING FOR..
   Q1I        U.S. POWER STOPS COMMUN.                   VALUE..    1    AGREE
* * * * * * * * * * * * * * * * * * * * * * * * * * * * * * * * * * * * * * * * * * * * * * * *

                        Q2E
              COUNT   I
              ROW PCT IAGREE       DISAGREE     ROW
                      I            )            TOTAL
                      I      1  I      2  I
Q1G           --------I--------I--------I
                  1   I     21  I     67  I      88
    AGREE           I   23.9  I   76.1  I    35.6
                   -I--------I--------I
                  2   I     40  I    119  I     159
  DISAGREE)         I   25.2  I   74.8  I    64.4
                   -I--------I--------I
              COLUMN       61        186        247
              TOTAL      24.7       75.3      100.0
```

```
* * * * * * * * * * * * * * * C R O S S T A B U L A T I O N   O F  * * * * * * * * * * * *
    Q1G      VIET CONG ARE INVADERS          BY  Q2E      INVADE NORTH VIETNAM BY U.S.
CONTROLLING FOR..
    Q1I      U.S. POWER STOPS COMMUN.                  VALUE..    2   DISAGREE)
* * * * * * * * * * * * * * * * * * * * * * * * * * * * * * * * * * * * * * * * * * * * *

                                Q2E
                    COUNT  I
                    ROW PCT IAGREE       DISAGREE     ROW
                           I             )            TOTAL
                           I     1  I       2   I
    Q1G        --------I--------I--------I
                     1 I    12  I      33   I      45
        AGREE          I  26.7  I    73.3   I    21.4
                      -I--------I--------I
                     2 I    22  I     143   I     165
        DISAGREE)      I  13.3  I    86.7   I    78.6
                      -I--------I--------I
                    COLUMN       34        176        210
                    TOTAL      16.2       83.8      100.0

NUMBER OF MISSING OBSERVATIONS =      23
```

```
* * * * * * * * * * * * * * * C R O S S T A B U L A T I O N   O F  * * * * * * * * * * * *
    Q1G      VIET CONG ARE INVADERS          BY  Q2E      INVADE NORTH VIETNAM BY U.S.
* * * * * * * * * * * * * * * * * * * * * * * * * * * * * * * * * * * * * * * * * * * * *

                                Q2E
                    COUNT  I
                    ROW PCT IAGREE       DISAGREE     ROW
                           I             )            TOTAL
                           I     1  I       2   I
    Q1G        --------I--------I--------I
                     1 I    33  I     101   I     134
        AGREE          I  24.6  I    75.4   I    29.2
                      -I--------I--------I
                     2 I    62  I     263   I     325
        DISAGREE)      I  19.1  I    80.9   I    70.8
                      -I--------I--------I
                    COLUMN       95        364        459
                    TOTAL      20.7       79.3      100.0

NUMBER OF MISSING OBSERVATIONS =      21
```

INDEX AND SCALE CONSTRUCTION (SEE CHAPTER 15)

There are many different strategies for the creation of composite measures such as typologies, scales, and indexes. Students with some background in SPSS are encouraged to experiment with the construction of composite variables using the RECODE and the IF cards. The method we will present here largely makes use of the COMPUTE and ASSIGN MISSING cards to produce typologies, indexes, and scales. You will note that our presentation is in a slightly different order than that of the text. It is easier in SPSS to produce typologies first, then move to indexes, then to scales.

The COMPUTE and ASSIGN MISSING Cards

The COMPUTE card is used to create the new composite measure, and the ASSIGN MISSING card solves the problems of missing data within the component variables that make up the measure.

The COMPUTE Card   In the manipulation of data in SPSS the COMPUTE card is one of the most powerful and useful tools. The arguments for this card are quite simple in that you are just computing a new variable using standard arithmetic conventions (for example, / is divide, + is addition, − is subtraction, and * is multiplication). The general form of this card is:

```
1                  16
COMPUTE            COMPUTED VARIABLE = ARITHMETIC EXPRESSION
```

The following are examples of legitimate uses of the COMPUTE card:

```
1                  16
COMPUTE            INDEX = Q1 + Q2 + Q3
COMPUTE            INCOME = DEMO4 / 12
COMPUTE            AGE = BIRTHYR − 1977
COMPUTE            NEWQ1 = Q1 + 10
```

The ASSIGN MISSING Card   A major problem in the creation of typologies (and other types of composite variables) is what to do with particular responses that we do not want included in our new variable. There may be blanks or other missing data, or specific values that we want excluded from our composite indicator. Of course you can eliminate them from the component variables through the use of the RECODE card—setting all the values that you wish to discard equal to some value already defined as missing. But what happens to the specific cases in which some component responses are legitimate and others are not?

The SPSS package handles this problem through the ability to set the value of the new composite variable when any or all components are missing—or defined as missing. We do this through the use of the ASSIGN MISSING card, which has the following format:

```
1                   16
ASSIGN MISSING   NEWVAR(VALUE)
```

The result will be to set the value of a computed variable to the value used in the ASSIGN MISSING card any time one of the component variables has missing data. Component variables are any used in the arithmetic expression part of the compute statement.

Typologies

Armed with the COMPUTE and ASSIGN MISSING card, you can now put them to use in creating your own composite variables.

The first set of 10 items in the questionnaire of Figure 12-7 contains several items that are indicators of how the respondents felt about the power of the state. In particular, we are interested in the items that ask respondents if they agree to the following propositions:

1. Flag defilers should be imprisoned.

2. It is U.S. power that stops world communism.

3. The CIA is too powerful.

4. We should support our country, right or wrong.

All of these items are indicators of whether or not a respondent tends to support the political power of the state. We are interested in developing a composite measure of this tendency.

Our first level of inquiry is to get a nominal measure of the responses. We want to know just how many different ways a person could answer the four questions and how many of our respondents actually used each of those response patterns. We call this type of measure a *typology*.

Our first task is to examine the component variables, making some decisions concerning which values we will use to construct the typology. We have made the decision that we will use only the agree (1, 2) and disagree (3, 4) categories, and discard all nonresponses from our typology. Note that we don't have to make these decisions, but we feel it is appropriate here. Second, we notice that the third item, Q1F, on the CIA, is scored in a reverse order to the other three items. Agreement with the other items indicates agreement that the state should have a lot of power. Agreement with item Q1F indicates the opposite. That will require a reversal of scores. The decisions we make here are reflected in the recodes that precede our COMPUTE card below.

The actual computation of the new variable involves creating a four-digit typology. That is, if a respondent agreed to all four items, then the typology value would be 1111. If disagreement was registered on the second item only, the typology value would be 1211. Any missing values on any component item could result in the value 0000, or simply 0. We accomplish this transformation by multiplying the first item by 1000, the second by 100, the third by 10, and then summing all four. The command set looks like this:

```
1                    16
RECODE               Q1B,Q1I,Q1J (1,2=1) (3,4,5=2)/
                     Q1F (3,4,5=1) (1,2=2)/
VALUE LABELS         Q1B,Q1I,Q1J (1)AGREE (2)DISAGREE/
COMPUTE              TYPO=(Q1B*1000)+(Q1I*100)+(Q1E*10)+Q1J
ASSIGN MISSING       TYPO(0)
FREQUENCIES          GENERAL=TYPO
```

The created composite variable TYPO will have 17 separate values. Of these, 16 will be indicators of specific response patterns to the four component items, and the 17th, 0000, will be used for those cases in which missing data occurred. The resulting categories look like this:

0000	Data missing on one or more components
1111	Agree to all four components (strongly for state power)
1112	Agree to all but the "Our country right or wrong" item
1121	Agree to all but the CIA item
1122	...
.	.
.	.
.	.
2212	...
2221	Disagree with all but the "Our country right or wrong" item
2222	Disagree with all items (strongly against state power)

We should note a few things about the typology we have just constructed before moving on. First, the order of the variables is totally unimportant when constructing a typology. Typologies are a nominal categorization of responses, and all we know about one specific value is that it is not another one. No claim is made for one value having more of some quality (in this case agreement with state power), than another. We will deal with ordinal classifications in a moment.

Second, the number of categories used for each component variable does make a difference. Using 2 values only (agree/disagree), we ended up with 17 typology values. If we had used 3 (agree/not sure/disagree), we would have created 82 separate values. Using all 5 values would have resulted in 3,126 distinct typologies. The formula for calculating the number of typologies is to raise the number of categories used to the nth power (where n = the number of components) and add 1.

Finally, it is often convenient in SPSS to further recode the typology into smaller codes. Thus, we would set oooo to o, IIII to I, III2 to 2, II2I to 3, and so forth. It makes the CROSSTAB command a bit easier to use later on. If we cross-tabulate the typology by other variables, we have to use the VARIABLES= card to declare maximum and minimum values—unless we recode first.

Indexes

An index is a composite variable that has the qualities of ordinal measurement. That is, the value 2 indicates more of the thing being measured than the value 1. Let us now construct an index of the tendency to support the political power of the state.

The first method we could use to do that is simply to RECODE the typology created in the previous section. We would recode all values of the typology in which all component items got agreement as 1, all values in which 3 out of 4 items were agreed to as 2, and so forth. The command set would look like this:

```
1                16
   (THESE CARDS FOLLOW THE COMPUTE FOR THE TYPOLOGY.)
COMPUTE          INDEX=TYPO
RECODE           INDEX (0000=0) (1111=1)(1112,1121,1211,2111=2)
                 (1122,1221,1212,2112,2121,2211=3)
                 (1222,2122,2212,2221=4) (2222=5)
VALUE LABELS     INDEX (1)AGREED TO ALL (2)AGREED TO 3
                 (3)AGREED TO 2 (4)AGREED TO 1 (5)AGREED TO NONE
FREQUENCIES      GENERAL=INDEX
```

A simpler method of constructing the index would be to recode the component items so that they indicated agreement or disagreement and sum them. That will produce the same results as the RECODE system above, but without constructing the typology first. You simply decide whether it is appropriate to look at the typology first. If it is not, use this method to construct your index:

```
RECODE           Q1B,Q1I,Q1J (1,2=1) (3,4,5=0)/
                 Q1F (3,4=1) (1,2,5=0)
COMPUTE          INDEX=Q1B+Q1I+Q1F+Q1J
ASSIGN MISSING   INDEX(5)
VALUE LABELS     INDEX (0)AGREED TO NONE (1)AGREED TO ONE (2)AGREED TO TWO
                 (3)AGREED TO THREE (4)AGREED TO ALL (5)NO DATA/
FREQUENCIES      GENERAL=INDEX
```

Note that the index values in this last example are reversed from those created in the first method. The results are the same in terms of the frequencies produced, but one is an index of agreement and the other an index of disagreement.

Scale Construction

Weighted Indexes as Scales Scales are composite variables that have the properties of interval measurement. That is, the interval between the first and second values is exactly the same as the interval between the second and third (or any other adjacent pair) values. The creation of weighted indexes is an example of a scale that is assumed to have interval properties.

The particular problem we are dealing with here is that of equally weighted items. In the indexes created above, we assumed that agreement with one item was exactly the same as agreement with any other item. Thus it was appropriate to call those examples indexes of agreement/disagreement. Moving a step closer to a rigorous measure of the acceptability of the power of the state, we might appropriately discard that assumption. We could, for instance, make the assumption that agreement with the last item—"Our country right or wrong"—is much more important than the others. Then we would want to weight agreement with that item much more strongly than the others. Let's say we are willing to count it as double. Then we might create a weighted index of agreement or a scale of acceptability of state power. Our method looks like this:

```
1                  16
RECODE             Q1B,Q1I,Q1J (1,2=1) (3,4,5=-1)/
                   Q1F (3,4,5=1) (1,2=-1)/
COMPUTE            SCALE=Q1B+Q1I+Q1E+(2*Q1J)
ASSIGN MISSING     SCALE(99)
VALUE LABELS       SCALE (-5)HIGH DISAGREEMENT (5)HIGH AGREEMENT/
```

This method of creating scales as weighted indexes is quite simple and relatively unsophisticated. It often serves an important function in research, but it has the disadvantage of rather arbitrary rules for construction. It is the basis, however, of a large number of scaling techniques that feature more formal models and more rigorous computational techniques. The reader is referred to the SPSS discussion of forming scales by using factor scores.[4]

Guttman Scaling The method of scale analysis proposed by Guttman is presented in Chapter 15. The SPSS package includes a simple set of commands to carry out this process.

We should note that the Guttman scale analysis routine does *not* produce scales. It is a method of analyzing the scalability of a set of items. It produces information on the extent to which the data at hand are suitable for scale construction. Thus, to

[4]*Ibid.*, pp. 487–489.

construct a scale using the Guttman method, we would first analyze the data for scalability, then construct the scale using the COMPUTE and ASSIGN MISSING cards.

If we assume that the four items we have been using form a scalable set in Guttman's terms, then we can test that assumption through the SPSS GUTTMAN SCALE command. The most important decision in using this procedure is the selection of cutting points for each of our variables. Guttman scale cutting points are specified as a single value for each variable. All values of the variable greater than or equal to the cutting point are considered to indicate the quality that we are attempting to scale.

For this illustration we will develop a scale of antifascism. Therefore, disagreement to items Q1B, Q1I, and Q1J indicate the quality that we are attempting to scale. Agreement with item Q1F would also indicate that quality. A response of "don't know" will not be considered an indication of antifascism. We must therefore recode our items so that indicators of the quality we wish to scale are all above some cutting point. The RECODE cards in the figure below demonstrate one way to accomplish this objective.

After the RECODE cards, we simply invoke the GUTTMAN SCALE command, and string the variables to be included in the scale, followed by their cutting points. The actual setup looks like this:

```
1                      16
RECODE                 Q1B,Q1I,Q1J (5=1)
RECODE                 Q1B (5=1) (4=2) (3=3) (2=4) (1=5)
GUTTMAN SCALE          GSCALE=Q1B(3),Q1I(3),Q1F(4),Q1J(3)
STATISTICS             ALL
```

The resulting output looks like the table on page 570.

The SPSS output tells us that our prospective scaling scheme is a poor one. The coefficient of scalability is .5217, indicating that there is little correspondence between the scaling model and the empirical data. That is not surprising, since one of the requirements of the Guttman scale model is that the items should be cumulative.[5]

If we were satisfied that our scaling scheme was an appropriate one, then we would recode our variables according to the cutting points, compute the Guttman scale value, use an ASSIGN MISSING card to take care of any missing data, and continue with our analysis. The actual computation procedure would be carried out only after the scaling scheme had been validated by the GUTTMAN SCALE command. The command set would look like this:

```
1                      16
RECODE                 Q1B,Q1I,Q1J (3,4=1)(1,2,5=0)
RECODE                 Q1F (1,2=1)(3,4,5=0)
COMPUTE                GUTT=Q1B+Q1I+Q1F+Q1J
ASSIGN MISSING GUTT (9)
```

[5]*Ibid.*, p. 529.

```
* * * * * * *    G U T T M A N   S C A L E   ( G S C A L E    )   U S I
Q1B       FLAG DEFILERS IN PRISON                DIVISION POINT =
Q1I       U.S. POWER STOPS COMMUN.               DIVISION POINT =
Q1F       C.I.A. TOO POWERFUL                    DIVISION POINT =
Q1J       SUPPORT COUNTRY EVEN WHEN WRONG        DIVISION POINT =
* * * * * * * * *   RESP = 1 FOR VALUES EQUAL TO DIVISION POINT AND ABOVE
```

ITEM..	Q1F		Q1I		Q1B		Q1J		
RESP..	0	1 I	0	1 I	0	1 I	0	1 I	TOTAL

```
-----I-ERR-----I-ERR-----I-ERR-----I-ERR-----I
G       I              I              I              I
S   4 I    0    46I    0    46I    0    46I    0    46I    46
C       I------ERRI             I              I              I
A       I              I              I              I              I
L   3 I   54    45I   25    74I   16    83I    4    95I    99
E       I              I------ERRI             I              I
        I              I              I              I              I
    2 I  124    13I   93    44I   45    92I   12   125I   137
        I              I              I------ERRI             I
        I              I              I              I              I
    1 I  142     8I  136    14I  125    25I   47   103I   150
        I              I              I              I------ERRI
        I              I              I              I              I
    0 I   42     0I   42     0I   42     0I   42     0I    42
        I---------I---------I---------I---------I
SUMS     362   112   296   178   228   246   105   369    474
PCTS      76    24    62    38    48    52    22    78
ERRORS     0    66    25    58    61    25    63     0    298
```

```
     ALL CASES WERE PROCESSED
      6 (OR  1.2 PCT) WERE MISSING

STATISTICS..

COEFFICIENT OF REPRODUCIBILITY = 0.8428
MINIMUM MARGINAL REPRODUCIBILITY = 0.6714
PERCENT IMPROVEMENT = 0.1714
COEFFICIENT OF SCALABILITY = 0.5217
```

The new variable GUTT is a scale score for each respondent that was constructed in a manner similar to the simple index. It has the additional property of having been derived from a scalable set of items. That is, it has been scaled according to a particular model rather than some arbitrary computational scheme.

SOCIAL STATISTICS (SEE CHAPTER 18)

Measures of Association through Using CROSSTABS Specific measures of association mentioned in this textbook are quite easily obtained by the simple inclusion of a STATISTICS card along with the CROSSTABS command. Indeed, a total of 13 different measures are obtainable through the STATISTICS card. The ones mentioned in the text have the following numbers:

```
          LAMBDA       4
          GAMMA        8
          CHI SQUARE   1
```

Note that lambda and chi square will produce values for bivariate tables and for each level of multivariate tables. Gamma produces values for bivariate tables, for each level of multivariate tables, and also for the relationships between the component variables of multivariate tables.

As an example of the use of the STATISTICS card, suppose we wished to examine the relationship between the variables Q1C and Q1H and also wanted to calculate the amount of PRE association between them. Noting that the two variables have been measured at the ordinal level, we would choose gamma as the most appropriate measure. Then we'd set up the cards like this:

```
1                  16
CROSSTABS          TABLES=Q1C BY Q1H/
OPTIONS            5
STATISTICS         8
```

We need simply to choose the most appropriate statistic, enter it into our command system, and run the job.

Significance of Measures   For all the measures of association covered in this textbook, SPSS includes an estimate of the precision, or statistical significance, of the measure. It is automatically printed with the measure itself. An example of the table for gamma values discussed above and the resulting output would look like the table at the top of page 572.

Pearson's *r*   One of the measures of association covered in this textbook, the Pearson product-moment correlation coefficient (r), cannot be produced by the STATISTICS card of the CROSSTABS procedure. If both of the variables of interest are measured at the interval level, then you will use the PEARSON CORR procedure, which has the following format:

```
1              16
PEARSON CORR   VARIABLES WITH VARIABLES/VARIABLES....
```

We have no variables measured at the interval level in our example data set. That is often the case with social science data. Our ordinally measured variables indicate that the NONPAR CORR procedure is more appropriate. This procedure, which has the same basic format as the PEARSON CORR procedure, will cause the computation of Spearman's rank-order correlation coefficients. In most cases, however, if both variables are measured at the ordinal level, the Spearman coefficient and the Pearson coefficient are equivalent. For this reason, we present only the PEARSON CORR procedure in this appendix. The set will look like this:

```
1              16
PEARSON CORR   Q1A,Q1B,Q1C WITH Q1D
OPTIONS        2
```

```
* * * * * * * * * * * * * * * *   C R O S S T A B U L A T I O N   O F   * * * * * * * * *
      Q1C     U.S. SEE COMMUNIST THREAT                    BY   Q1H      A-BOMBING JAPAN JUST
* * * * * * * * * * * * * * * * * * * * * * * * * * * * * * * * * * * * * * * * * * * * * *
```

```
                          Q1H
               COUNT   I
               ROW PCT ISTRONGLY AGREE      DISAGREE STRONGLY      ROW
               COL PCT I AGREE                       DISAGRE       TOTAL
                       I      1  I      2  I      3  I      4  I
     Q1C        -------I--------I--------I--------I--------I
                   1   I      8  I     11  I     13  I     15  I     47
     STRONGLY AGREE    I   17.0  I   23.4  I   27.7  I   31.9  I   12.8
                       I   18.6  I    7.0  1   12.1  I   25.4  I
                      -I--------I--------I--------I--------I
                   2   I      9  I     58  I     51  I     27  I    145
                       I    6.2  I   40.0  I   35.2  I   18.6  I   39.5
                       I   20.9  I   36.7  I   47.7  I   45.8  I
                      -I--------I--------I--------I--------I
                   3   I     13  I     75  I     37  I     15  I    140
     DISAGREE          I    9.3  I   53.6  I   26.4  I   10.7  I   38.1
                       I   30.2  I   47.5  I   34.6  I   25.4  I
                      -I--------I--------I--------I--------I
                   4   I     13  I     14  I      6  I      2  I     35
     STRONGLY DISAGRE  I   37.1  I   40.0  I   17.1  I    5.7  I    9.5
                       I   30.2  I    8.9  I    5.6  I    3.4  I
                      -I--------I--------I--------I--------I
               COLUMN        43       158      107       59      367
               TOTAL       11.7      43.1     29.2     16.1    100.0
```

GAMMA = -0.31174

NUMBER OF MISSING OBSERVATIONS = 113

The above procedure set will produce three correlation coefficients. For each one, the output will include the coefficient, the number of cases upon which the coefficient is based, and a significance level on the coefficient. The program deletes all pairs of observations in which any data are missing,[6] so it will be necessary to check the number of cases. The significance tests are the two-tailed t-test specified by OPTION 2. The actual output will look something like this:

```
- - - - - - - - - - - - P E A R S O N   C O R R E L A T I O N   C O E F F I C I E N T S - - - - - - -

          Q1D

Q1A       0.0888
          (  472)
          S=0.027


Q1B      -0.2522
          (  474)
          S=0.001


Q1C       0.3863
          (  473)
          S=0.001

 (COEFFICIENT / (CASES) / SIGNIFICANCE)     (A VALUE OF 99.000 IS PRINTED IF A COEFFICIENT CANNOT BE
```

[6]*Ibid.*, p. 283.

ADVANCED MULTIVARIATE MODES OF ANALYSIS (SEE CHAPTER 19)

The SPSS manual includes simple procedures for carrying out most of the complex forms of analysis covered in this textbook. Algorithms are available for simple and multiple regression analysis, path analysis, and factor analysis. The routines are extremely simple to set up, and the explanations of how to use them are some of the best summaries of these techniques to be found in the literature.

SPSS also has routines for forms of analysis not covered in this textbook. Among them are analysis of variance and covariance and canonical correlation analysis. In addition, a large array of data manipulation techniques that we have not used in this appendix are available.

Only one method of analysis covered in this textbook is not included in the SPSS package, and that is smallest-space analysis. Of course, the author's own elaboration package is also not included in the SPSS manual, but it does provide the means to obtain the necessary N-way cross-tabulations.

We have chosen not to present these complex forms of analysis in any detail in this appendix. You are encouraged to learn them at your own pace, making sure that you understand the methods well before actually attempting to use them.

Glossary

area probability sample   A form of multistage *cluster sample* in which geographical areas such as census blocks or tracts serve as the first-stage sampling unit. Units selected in the first stage of sampling are then listed—all the households on each selected block would be written down after a trip to the block—and such lists would be subsampled.

attributes   Characteristics of persons or things. See *variables* and Chapter 2.

average   An ambiguous term generally suggesting typical or normal. The *mean*, *median*, and *mode* are specific examples of mathematical *averages*.

bias   (1) That quality of a measurement device that tends to result in a misrepresentation of what is being measured in a particular direction. For example, the questionnaire item "Don't you agree that the president is doing a good job?" would be *biased* in that it would generally encourage more favorable responses. See Chapter 6 for more on this topic. (2) The thing inside you that makes other people or groups seem consistently better or worse than they really are. (3) What a nail looks like after you hit it crooked. (If you drink, don't drive.)

binomial   (1) A variable that has only two attributes is binomial. *Sex* would be an example, having the attributes *male* and *female*. (2) The advertising slogan used by the Nomial Widget Co.

bivariate analysis   The analysis of two variables simultaneously, for the purpose of determining the empirical relationship between them. The construction of a simple percentage table or the computation of a simple correlation coefficient would be examples of *bivariate analyses*. See Chapter 14 for more on this topic.

Bogardus social distance scale   A measurement technique for determining the willingness of people to participate in social relations—of varying degrees of closeness—with other kinds of people. It is an especially efficient technique in that several discrete answers may be summarized without losing any of the original details of the data. This technique is described in Chapter 15.

census   An enumeration of the characteristics of some population. A *census* is often similar to a survey, with the difference that the *census* collects data from *all* members of the population while the survey is limited to a sample.

cluster sample   (1) A multistage sample in which natural groups (*clusters*) are sampled initially, with the members of each selected group being subsampled afterward. For example, you might select a sample of United States colleges and universities from a directory, get lists of the students at all the selected schools, then draw samples of students from each. This procedure is discussed in Chapter 7. See also *area probability sample.* (2) Pawing around in a box of macadamia-nut clusters to take all the big ones for yourself.

codebook   (1) The document used in data processing and analysis that tells the location of different data items in a data file. Typically, the codebook identifies the card and column locations of data items and the meaning of the punches used to represent different attributes of variables. See Chapter 13 for more discussion and illustrations. (2) The document that cost you 38 boxtops just to learn that Captain Marvelous wanted you to brush your teeth and always tell the truth. (3) The document that allows CIA agents to learn that Captain Marvelous wants them to brush their teeth.

coding   The process whereby raw data are transformed into standardized form suitable for machine processing and analysis. See Chapters 12 and 13.

coefficient of alienation   (1) A measurement of the extent to which a *smallest-space analysis (SSA)* solution satisfies the rule that the rank order of distances between points must be the inverse of the rank order of the correlations between the variables that the points represent. More accurately, the *coefficient of alienation* is a measure of the extent to which the solution *fails* to satisfy the rule: the smaller, the better. See Chapter 19. (2) The number of times you don't get invited to parties your friends get invited to.

coefficient of reproducibility   (1) A measure of the extent to which a *scale* score allows you to reconstruct accurately the specific data that went into the construction of the scale. See Chapter 15 for a fuller description and an illustration. (2) Fecundity.

cohort study   A study in which some specific group is studied over time although data may be collected from different members in each set of observations. A study of the occupational history of the class of 1970, in which questionnaires were sent every five years, for example, would be a cohort study. See Chapter 4 for more on this topic (if you want more).

conceptualization   The mental process whereby fuzzy and imprecise notions (*concepts*) are made more specific and precise. So you want to study *prejudice*. What do you *mean* by *prejudice*? Are there different kinds of prejudice? What are they? See Chapter 5, which is all about *conceptualization*, and Chapter 6 about its pal, *operationalization.*

confidence interval   (1) The range of values within which a population parameter is estimated to lie. A survey, for example, may show 40 percent of a sample favoring Candidate A (poor devil). Although the best estimate of the support existing among all voters would also be 40 percent, we would not expect it to be exactly that. We might, therefore, compute a *confidence interval* (e.g., from 35 to 45 percent) within which the actual percentage of the population probably lies. Note that it is necessary to specify a *confidence level* in connection with every *confidence interval*. See Chapters 7 and 18. (2) How close you dare to get to an alligator.

confidence level   The estimated probability that a population parameter lies within a given CONFIDENCE INTERVAL. Thus, we might be 95 percent *confident* that between 35 and 45 percent of all voters favor Candidate A. See Chapters 7 and 18.

contingency question   A survey question that is to be asked only of *some* respondents, determined by their responses to some other question. For example, all respondents might be asked whether they belong to the Symbionese Liberation Army, and only those who said "yes" would be asked how often they go to SLA meetings and picnics. The latter would be a *contingency question*. See Chapter 12 for illustrations of this topic.

contingency table   (1) A format for presenting the relationships among variables — in the form of percentage distributions. See Chapter 14 for several illustrations of it and for guides to doing it. (2) The card table you keep around in case your guests bring their seven kids with them to dinner.

control group   In experimentation, a group of subjects to whom *no* experimental stimulus is administered and who should resemble the experimental group in all other respects. The comparison of the *control group* and the experimental group at the end of the experiment points to the effect of the experimental stimulus. See Chapter 10.

control variable   A variable that is held constant in an attempt to further clarify the relationship between two other variables. Having discovered a relationship between education and prejudice, for example, we might hold sex constant by examining the relationship between education and prejudice among men only and then among women only. In this example, sex would be the *control variable*. See Chapter 17 to find out how important the proper use of control variables is in analysis.

cross-sectional study   A study that is based on observations representing a single point in time. Contrasted with a *longitudinal study*.

deduction   (1) The logical model in which specific expectations of *hypotheses* are developed on the basis of general principles. Starting from the general principle that all deans are meanies, you might anticipate that *this* one won't let you change courses. That anticipation would be the result of *deduction*. See also *induction* and Chapters 2 and 16. (2) What the Internal Revenue Service said your good-for-nothing moocher of a brother-in-law technically isn't.

dependent variable   That variable which is assumed to *depend* on or be caused by another (called the *independent variable*). If you find that income is partly a function of amount of formal education, income is being treated as a *dependent variable*.

descriptive statistics   (1) Statistical computations describing either the characteristics of a sample *or* the relationship among variables in a sample. *Descriptive* *statistics* merely summarize a set of sample observations, whereas *inferential statistics* move beyond the description of specific observations to make inferences about the larger population from which the sample observations were drawn. (2) 36-24-36 (A male-chauvinist-pig-of-a-devil made me say that).

dichotomy   A classification having only two categories. See also *binomial*.

dispersion   The distribution of values around some central value, such as an *average*. The *range* is a simple example of a measure of *dispersion*. Thus, we may report that the *mean* age of a group is 37.9, and the range is from 12 to 89.

EPSEM   *Equal probability of selection method*. A sample design in which each member of a population has the same chance of being selected into the sample. See Chapter 7.

external invalidity   Refers to the possibility that conclusions drawn from experimental results may not be generalizable to the "real" world. See Chapter 10 and also *internal invalidity*.

external validation   The process of testing the *validity* of a measure, such as an *index* or *scale*, by examining its relationship to other, presumed indicators of the same variable. If the index really measures *prejudice*, for example, it should correlate with other indicators of prejudice. See Chapter 15 for a fuller discussion of this topic and for illustrations.

face validity   (1) That quality of an indicator that makes it seem a reasonable measure of some variable. That the frequency of church attendance is some indication of a person's religiosity seems to make sense without a lot of explanation. It has *face validity*. (2) Putting the right face on your head when you get up in the morning.

factor analysis   A complex algebraic method for determining the general dimensions or *factors* that exist within a set of concrete observations. See Chapter 19 for more details on this topic.

frequency distribution   A description of the number of times the various attributes of a variable are observed in a sample. The report that 53 percent of a sample was men and 47 percent was women would be a simple example of a *frequency distribution*. Another example would be the report that 15 of the cities studied had populations under 10,000; 23 had populations between 10,000 and 25,000; and so forth.

generalizability   (1) That quality of a research finding that justifies the inference that it represents something more than the specific observations upon which it was based. Sometimes this involves the *generalization* of findings from a sample to a population. Other times, it is a matter of concepts: if you are able to discover why people commit burglaries, can you *generalize* that discovery to other crimes as well? (2) The likelihood that you will ever be a general.

Guttman scale   A type of composite measure used to summarize several discrete observations and to represent some more general variable. See Chapter 15.

hypothesis   (1) An expectation about the nature of things derived from a theory. It is a statement of something that ought to be observed in the real world if the theory is correct. See *deduction* and also Chapters 2 and 4. (2) A graduate student paper explaining why hypopotamuses are the way they are.

hypothesis testing   (1) The determination of whether the expectations that a hypothesis represents are, indeed, found to exist in the real world. See Chapters 2 and 4. (2) An oral examination centering around a graduate student paper explaining why hypopotamuses are the way they are.

independent variable   A variable whose values are *not* problematical in an analysis but are taken as simply given. An *independent variable* is presumed to cause or determine a *dependent variable*. If we discover that religiosity is partly a function of sex—women are more religious than men—*sex* is the *independent variable* and *religiosity* is the dependent variable. Note that any given variable might be treated as *independent* in one part of an analysis and dependent in another part of the analysis. *Religiosity* might become an *independent variable* in the explanation of crime.

index   A type of composite measure that summarizes several specific observations and represents some more general dimension. Contrasted with *scale*. See Chapter 15.

induction   (1) The logical model in which general principles are developed from specific observations. Having noted that Jews and Catholics are more likely to vote Democratic than Protestants are, you might conclude that religious minorities in the United States are more affiliated with the Democratic Party and explain why. That would be an example of *induction*. See also *deduction* and Chapters 2 and 16. (2) The culinary art of stuffing ducks.

inferential statistics   The body of statistical computations relevant to making inferences from findings based on sample observations to some larger population. See also *descriptive statistics* and Chapter 18. Not to be confused with infernal statistics, which have something to do with the population of Hell.

informant   Someone well-versed in the social phenomenon that you wish to study and who is willing to tell you what he or she knows. If you were planning participant observation among the members of a religious sect, you would do well to make friends with someone who already knew about them—possibly a member of the sect—who could give you some background information about them. Not to be confused with a *respondent*.

interchangeability of indexes   A term coined by Paul Lazarsfeld referring to the logical proposition that if some general variable is related to another variable, then all indicators of the variable should have that relationship. See Chapter 16 for a fuller description of this topic and a graphic illustration.

internal invalidity   Refers to the possibility that the conclusions drawn from experimental results may not accurately reflect what went on in the experiment itself. See Chapter 10 and also *external invalidity*.

internal validation   The process whereby the individual items composing a composite measure are correlated with the measure itself. This provides one test of the wisdom of including all the items in the composite measure. See also *external validation* and Chapter 15.

interpretation   A technical term used in connection with the elaboration model. It represents the research outcome in which a *control variable* is discovered to be the mediating factor through which an *independent variable* has its effect on a *dependent variable*. See Chapter 17.

intersubjectivity   That quality of science (and other inquiries) whereby two different researchers, studying the same problem, arrive at the same conclusion. Ultimately, this is the practical criterion for what is called *objectivity*. We agree that something is "objectively true" if independent observers with different subjective orientations conclude that it is "true." See Chapter 2.

interval measure   A level of measurement describing a variable whose attributes are rank-ordered and have equal distances between adjacent attributes. The Fahrenheit temperature scale is an example of this, since the distance between 17° and 18° is the same as that between 89° and 90°. See also *nominal measure, ordinal measure,* and *ratio measure*.

interview   A data-collection encounter in which one person (an interviewer) asks questions of another (a *respondent*). *Interviews* may be conducted face-to-face or by telephone. See Chapter 12 for more information on interviewing as a method of survey research.

judgmental sample   A type of *nonprobability sample* in which you select the units to be observed on the basis of your own *judgment* about which ones will be the most useful or representative. Another name for this is *purposive sample*. See Chapter 7 for more details.

latent content   As used in connection with content analysis, the underlying meaning of communications as distinguished from their *manifest content*. See Chapter 9.

level of significance   In the context of *tests of statistical significance*, the degree of likelihood that an observed, empirical relationship could be attributable to sampling error. A relationship is *significant* at the .05 *level* if the likelihood of its being only a function of sampling error is no greater than 5 out of 100. See Chapter 18.

Likert scale   (1) A type of composite measure developed by Rensis Likert in an attempt to improve the levels of measurement in social research through the use of standardized response categories in survey *questionnaires*. *Likert*-items are those utilizing such response categories as strongly agree, agree, disagree, and strongly disagree. Such items may be used in the construction of true *Likert scales* and may also be used in the construction of other types of composite measures. See Chapter 15. (2) The device that tells how much Ren and Jane Likert weigh.

longitudinal study   A study design involving the collection of data at different points in time, as contrasted with a *cross-sectional study*. See also Chapter 4 and *trend study, cohort study,* and *panel study*.

manifest content   In connection with content analysis, the concrete terms contained in a communication, as distinguished from *latent content*. See Chapter 9.

matching   In connection with experiments, the procedure whereby pairs of subjects are *matched* on the basis of their similarities on one or more variables, and one member of the pair is assigned to the experimental group and the other to the *control group*. See Chapter 10.

mean   (1) An *average*, computed by summing the values of several observations and dividing by the number of observations. If you now have a grade point average of 4.0 based on 10 courses, and you get an F in this course, your new grade point (mean) average will be 3.6. (2) The quality of the thoughts you might have if your instructor did that to you.

median   (1) Another *average*, representing the value of the "middle" case in a rank-ordered set of observations. If the ages of five men are 16, 17, 20, 54, and 88, the *median* would be 20. (The *mean* would be 39.) (2) The dividing line between safe driving and exciting driving.

mode   (1) Still another *average*, representing the most frequently observed value or attribute. If a sample contains 1000 Protestants, 275 Catholics, and 33 Jews, *Protestant* is the *modal* category. See Chapter 14 for more thrilling disclosures about averages. (2) Better than apple pie à la median.

multivariate analysis   The analysis of the simultaneous relationships among several variables. Examining simultaneously the effects of age, sex, and social class on religiosity would be an example of *multivariate analysis*. See Chapters 14, 17, and 19.

nominal measure   A level of measurement describing a variable whose different attributes are *only* different, as distinguished from *ordinal, interval*, or *ratio measures*. Sex would be an example of a nominal measure.

nonprobability sample   A sample selected in some fashion other than those suggested by probability theory. Examples include *judgmental (purposive), quota,* and *snowball samples*. See Chapter 7.

nonsampling error   (1) Those imperfections of data quality that are a result of factors other than sampling error. Examples include misunderstandings of questions by respondents, erroneous recordings by interviewers and coders, keypunch errors, and so forth. (2) The mistake you made in deciding to interview everyone rather than selecting a sample.

null hypothesis   In connection with *hypothesis testing* and *tests of statistical significance*, that *hypothesis* that suggests there is *no* relationship between the variables under study. You may conclude that the two variables *are* related after having statistically rejected the *null hypothesis*.

objectivity   Doesn't exist. See *intersubjectivity*.

operational definitions   The concrete and specific *definition* of something in terms of the *operations* by which observations are to be categorized. The *operational definition* of "earning an A in this course" might be: "correctly answering at least 90 percent of the final exam questions." See Chapter 6.

operationalization   One step beyond *conceptualization*. *Operationalization* is the process of developing *operational definitions*.

ordinal measure   A level of measurement describing a variable whose attributes may be *rank-ordered* along some dimension. An example would be *socioeconomic status* as composed of the attributes, high, medium, low. See also *nominal measure*, *interval measure*, and *ratio measure*.

panel study   A type of *longitudinal study*, in which data are collected from the same sample (the *panel*) at several points in time. See Chapter 4.

path analysis   A form of *multivariate analysis* in which the causal relationships among variables are presented in graphic format. See Chapter 19.

PPS   *Probability proportionate to size.*   (This refers to a type of multistage *cluster sample* in which clusters are selected, not with equal probabilities (see *EPSEM*) but with *probabilities proportionate* to their *sizes*—as measured by the number of units to be subsampled. See Chapter 7.

probability sample   The general term for a sample selected in accord with *probability* theory, typically involving some random-selection mechanism. Specific types of *probability samples* include *area probability sample*, *EPSEM*, *PPS*, *simple random sample*, and *systematic sample*. See Chapter 7.

probe   A technique employed in interviewing to solicit a more complete answer to a question. It is a nondirective phrase or question used to encourage a respondent to elaborate on an answer. Examples include "Anything more?" and "How is that?" See Chapter 12 for a discussion of interviewing.

purposive sample   See *judgmental sample* and Chapter 8.

qualitative analysis   The nonnumerical examination and interpretation of observations, for the purpose of discovering underlying meanings and patterns of relationships. This is most typical of field research and historical research. See Chapter 8.

quantitative analysis   The numerical representation and manipulation of observations for the purpose of describing and explaining the phenomena that those observations reflect. See Chapter 13 especially, and also the remainder of Part Four.

questionnaire   A document containing *questions* and other types of items designed to solicit information appropriate to analysis. *Questionnaires* are used primarily in survey research and also in experiments, field research, and other modes of observation. See Chapters 6 and 12.

quota sample   A type of *nonprobability sample* in which units are selected into the sample on the basis of prespecified characteristics, so that the total sample will have the same distribution of characteristics as are assumed to exist in the population being studied. See Chapter 7.

randomization   A technique for assigning experimental subjects to experimental and *control groups*: randomly. See Chapter 10.

range   A measure of *dispersion*, composed of the highest and lowest values of a variable in some set of observations. In your class, for example, the *range* of ages might be from 17 to 37.

ratio measure   A level of measurement describing a variable whose attributes have all the qualities of *nominal*, *ordinal*, and *interval measures* and in addition are based on a "true zero" point. Age would be an example of a *ratio measure*.

reductionism   A fault of some researchers: a strict limitation (reduction) of the kinds of concepts to be considered relevant to the phenomenon under study.

regression   (1) A method of data analysis in which the relationships among variables are represented in the form of an equation, called a *regression* equation. See Chapter 19 for a discussion of the different forms of *regression* analysis. (2) What seems to happen to your knowledge of social research methods just before an exam.

reliability   That quality of measurement method that suggests that the same data would have been collected each time in repeated observations of the same phenomenon. In the context of a survey, we would expect that the question "Did you attend church last week?" would have higher reliability than the question "About how many times have you attended church in your life?" This is not to be confused with *validity*.

replication   Generally, the duplication of an experiment to expose or reduce error. It is also a technical term used in connection with the elaboration model, referring to the elaboration outcome in which the initially observed relationship between two variables persists when a *control variable* is held constant. See Chapter 17. See Chapter 2 and *intersubjectivity*.

representativeness   (1) That quality of a sample of having the same distribution of characteristics as the population from which it was selected. By implication, descriptions and explanations derived from an analysis of the sample may be assumed to *represent* similar ones in the population. *Representativeness* is enhanced by *probability sampling* and provides for *generalizability* and the use of *inferential statistics*. See Chapter 7. (2) A noticeable quality in the presentation-of-self of some members of the United States Congress.

respondent   A person who provides data for analysis by *responding* to a survey *questionnaire*.

response rate   The number of persons participating in a survey divided by the number selected in the sample, in the form of a percentage. This is also called the completion rate or, in self-administered surveys, the return rate: the percentage of *questionnaires* sent out that are returned. See Chapter 12.

sampling frame   That list or quasi-list of units composing a population from which a sample is selected. If the sample is to be *representative* of the population, it is essential that the *sampling frame* include all (or nearly all) members of the population. See Chapter 7.

sampling interval   The standard distance between elements selected from a population for a sample. See Chapter 7.

sampling ratio   The proportion of elements in the population that are selected to be in a sample. See Chapter 7.

scale   (1) A type of composite measure composed of several items that have a logical or empirical structure among them. Examples of *scales* include Bogardus social distance, Guttman, Likert, and Thurstone scales. Contrasted with index. See also Chapter 15. (2) One of the less appetizing parts of a fish. (3) An early sign of the heartbreak of psoriasis. (4) Except for fish.

secondary analysis   (1) A form of research in which the data collected and processed by one researcher are reanalyzed—often for a different purpose—by another. This is especially appropriate in the case of survey data. Data archives are repositories or libraries for the storage and distribution of data for *secondary analysis*. (2) Estimating the weight and speed of an opposing team's linebackers.

simple random sample   (1) A type of *probability sample* in which the units composing a population are assigned numbers, a set of *random* numbers is then generated, and the units having those numbers are included in the sample. Although probability theory and the calculations it provides assume this basic sampling method, it is seldom used for practical reasons. An equivalent alternative is the *systematic sample* (with a random start). See Chapter 7. (2) A random sample with a low IQ.

smallest-space analysis   A method of *multivariate analysis* in which the correlations among variables are represented graphically in the form of distances separating points. See Chapter 19.

snowball sample   (1) A *nonprobability sampling* method often employed in field research. Each person interviewed may be asked to suggest additional people for interviewing. See Chapter 8. (2) Picking the icy ones to throw at your methods instructor.

specification   Generally, the process through which concepts are made more specific. It is also a technical term used in connection with the elaboration model, representing the elaboration outcome in which an initially observed relationship between two variables is replicated among some subgroups created by the *control variable* and not among others. In such a situation, you will have *specified* the conditions under which the original relationship exists: e.g., among men but not among women. See Chapter 17.

statistical significance   (1) A general term referring to the *un*likeliness that relationships observed in a sample could be attributed to sampling error alone. See *tests of statistical significance* and Chapter 18. (2) How important it would really be if you flunked your statistics exam. I mean, you could always be a poet.

stratification   The grouping of the units composing a population into homogeneous groups (or *strata*) before sampling. This procedure, which may be used in conjunction with *simple random*, *systematic*, or *cluster sampling*, improves the *representativeness* of a sample, at least in terms of the *stratification* variables. See Chapter 7.

systematic sample   (1) A type of *probability sample* in which every *k*th unit in a list is selected for inclusion in the sample: e.g., every 25th student in the college directory of students. *k* is computed by dividing the size of the population by the desired sample size and is called the sampling interval. Within certain constraints, *systematic sampling* is a functional equivalent of *simple random sampling* and usually easier to do. Typically, the first unit is selected at random. See Chapter 7. (2) Picking every third one whether it's icy or not. See *snowball sample* (2).

test of statistical significance (1) A class of statistical computations that indicate the likelihood that the relationship observed between variables in a sample can be attributed to sampling error only. See *inferential statistics* and Chapter 18. (2) A determination of how important statistics have been in improving humankind's lot in life. (3) An examination that can radically affect your grade in this course and your grade point average as well.

Thurstone scale A type of composite measure, constructed in accord with the weights assigned by "judges" to various indicators of some variables. See Chapter 15.

trend study A type of *longitudinal study* in which a given characteristic of some population is monitored over time. An example would be the series of Gallup Polls showing the political-candidate preferences of the electorate over the course of a campaign, even though different samples were interviewed at each point. See Chapter 4.

typology The classification (typically nominal) of observations in terms of their attributes on two or more variables. The classification of newspapers as liberal-urban, liberal-rural, conservative-urban, or conservative-rural would be an example. See Chater 15.

units of analysis The *what* or *whom* being studied. In social science research, the most typical units of analysis are individual people. See Chapter 4.

univariate analysis The analysis of a single variable, for purposes of description. *Frequency distributions, averages,* and measures of *dispersion* would be examples of *univariate analysis,* as distinguished from *bivariate* and *multivariate analysis.* See Chapter 14.

validity A descriptive term used of a measure that accurately reflects the concept that it is intended to measure. For example, your IQ would seem a more *valid* measure of your intelligence than would the number of hours you spend in the library. It is important to realize that the ultimate *validity* of a measure can never be proven. Yet, we may agree to its relative *validity* on the basis of *face validity,* *internal validation,* and *external validation.* This must not be confused with *reliability.*

variables Logical groupings of *attributes.* The variable *sex* is made up of the attributes *male* and *female.*

weighting (1) A procedure employed in connection with sampling whereby units selected with unequal probabilities are assigned weights in such a manner as to make the sample *representative* of the population from which it was selected. See Chapter 7. (2) Olde English for hanging around for somebody who never gets there on time.

INDEX